Police Administration

A Leadership Approach

Police Administration

A Leadership Approach

P. J. Ortmeier
Grossmont College

Joseph J. Davis
Roberts Wesleyan College

POLICE ADMINISTRATION: A LEADERSHIP APPROACH

Published by McGraw-Hill, a business unit of The McGraw-Hill Companies, Inc., 1221 Avenue of the Americas, New York, NY 10020. Copyright © 2012 by The McGraw-Hill Companies, Inc. All rights reserved. No part of this publication may be reproduced or distributed in any form or by any means, or stored in a database or retrieval system, without the prior written consent of The McGraw-Hill Companies, Inc., including, but not limited to, in any network or other electronic storage or transmission, or broadcast for distance learning.

Some ancillaries, including electronic and print components, may not be available to customers outside the United States.

♲ This book is printed on recycled, acid-free paper containing 10% postconsumer waste.

1 2 3 4 5 6 7 8 9 0 QDB/QDB 1 0 9 8 7 6 5 4 3 2 1

ISBN 978-0-07-338000-1
MHID 0-07-338000-8

Vice President & Editor-in-Chief: *Michael Ryan*
Vice President EDP/Central Publishing Services: *Kimberly Meriwether David*
Publisher: *Katie Stevens*
Senior Sponsoring Editor: *William Minick*
Executive Marketing Manager: *Pamela S. Cooper*
Managing Editor: *Meghan Campbell*
Senior Project Manager: *Jane Mohr*
Design Coordinator: *Brenda A. Rolwes*
Cover Designer: *Studio Montage, St. Louis, Missouri*
Senior Photo Research Coordinator: *Natalia Peschiera*
Buyer: *Nicole Baumgartner*
Media Project Manager: *Sridevi Palani*
Compositor: *Glyph International*
Typeface: *10/12 Sabon*
Printer: *Quad/Graphics*

All credits appearing on page or at the end of the book are considered to be an extension of the copyright page.

Library of Congress Cataloging-in-Publication Data

Ortmeier, P. J.
   Police administration: a leadership approach/P.J. Ortmeier, Joseph J. Davis.
      p. cm.
   ISBN 978-0-07-338000-1 (alk. paper)
 1. Police administration.   I. Davis, Joseph J.   II. Title.
   HV7935.O78 2012
   363.2068'4—dc22

2010042719

www.mhhe.com

To Christine and Diane

P. J. Ortmeier holds a bachelor's and a master's degree in criminal justice as well as a PhD in educational leadership with an emphasis in public safety training and development. He is a U.S. Army veteran and a former police officer. Dr. Ortmeier develops and implements courses and degree programs in criminal justice and public safety. As a member of a California Commission on Peace Officer Standards and Training (POST) steering committee, Dr. Ortmeier participated in the integration of leadership, ethics, and community policing concepts and skill development into the basic academy for entry-level California peace officers.

Dr. Ortmeier is the author of *Public Safety and Security Administration, Policing the Community: A Guide for Patrol Operations, Introduction to Law Enforcement and Criminal Justice,* and *Introduction to Security: Operations and Management,* as well as numerous articles appearing in journals such as *The Police Chief, The Law Enforcement Executive Forum, California Security, Police and Security News,* and *Security Management.* With Edwin Meese III, former attorney general of the United States, Dr. Ortmeier coauthored *Leadership, Ethics, and Policing: Challenges for the 21st Century.* He also coauthored *Crime Scene Investigation: The Forensic Technician's Field Manual,* with a colleague, Tina Young. His writing focuses on professional career education, leadership, ethics, management, police field services, forensic technology, and competency development for public safety personnel.

Currently, Dr. Ortmeier is a professor and chair of the 1,500-student Administration of Justice Department at Grossmont College in the San Diego suburb of El Cajon, California. He is a member of the Academy of Criminal Justice Sciences, the American Society of Criminology, the International Association of Chiefs of Police, the International Public Safety Leadership Development Consortium, the California Association of Administration of Justice Educators, and the American Society for Industrial Security. His current interests include homeland defense, forensic science, and development of the leadership skills and career education pathways for law enforcement and other public safety professionals.

Joseph J. Davis is a retired police captain from the Rochester, New York, Police Department where he served for 38 years. He holds a bachelor's degree in mathematics from St. John Fisher College, Rochester, New York, and a master's degree in strategic leadership from Roberts Wesleyan College, Rochester, New York. As a police commanding officer and through extensive work in the Rochester community, Davis gathered extensive experience in supervision, management, and leadership in organizations. His experience includes program operations, professional development (training), problem analysis, program development, budget development, grant management, and capital improvement projects, and significant work with community organizations, not-for-profit organizations, and diverse populations.

Davis developed and managed numerous programs that included a Tri-level Stress Management Program and resultant organizational unit, a language development program and training course in Spanish language, a sign language program, a cultural program for each language studied, and a recruitment and hiring process for new police officers. He managed the conceptualization and building of a new indoor and outdoor police firing range and managed the redevelopment of a police media productions unit that included a video/television production unit.

Davis's experience as a police captain includes the positions of director of training, commanding officer of professional development, patrol section commander, and commanding officer of the Field Investigations Section, Criminal Investigation Division. He is a past president of the Law Enforcement Training Directors Association of New York State.

Davis has also been involved in numerous developmental projects including the New York State Police Supervisor Mandated Training Course for New Police Sergeants; the development of mental health training and confidentiality protocols and policies for police officers; and the conceptualization, development, and implementation of a Police Officer Anger Management Program. In addition, he was a steering committee member for the reorganization of the Rochester Police Department.

Davis is the author or coauthor of numerous presentations for the Academy of Criminal Justice Sciences. He is currently a member of the Academy, the International Association of Chiefs of Police, and the Law Enforcement Training Directors Association of New York State.

Davis serves as an adjunct professor with Roberts Wesleyan College, Rochester, New York, and is a self-employed consultant/trainer for police and government entities, educators, and security personnel.

The authors encourage and solicit comments regarding this book as well as suggestions for future editions. They are also available to provide technical assistance to anyone who adopts this text for a course. The authors may be contacted directly at:

P. J. Ortmeier, PhD
Chair/Professor, Administration of Justice
Grossmont College
8800 Grossmont College Drive
El Cajon, CA 92020

Joseph J. Davis, MS, Retired Police Captain
Roberts Wesleyan College
7320 Fisher Road
Ontario, NY 14519

brief contents

part **III**   *Human Resource Management*   *183*

Police Administration: A Leadership Approach was written to support the need for a text that addresses supervision and management as well as ethics, leadership, and the principles of policing that form the foundation for efficient, effective, and lawful administration of the modern police service. Unlike other texts, this book blends theory with practice. It presents a foundation for the administration and management of a police agency in a logical, flexible, and understandable step-by-step process.

The book sends the clear message that *all* police officers—regardless of rank—must be courageous self-contained leadership agents who think and act ethically to assume control, to influence and motivate others, and to address crime and disorder. Our treatment of ethics and leadership reveals that officers equipped with such skills engage community members and motivate them to partner with police to identify, solve, and prevent problems plaguing a community. Courageous ethical leadership is not based in fear, but rather in ethical action. As Sir Robert Peel is credited with stating, "The police at all times should maintain a relationship with the public that gives reality to the historic tradition that the police are the public and the public are the police." Effective solutions to crime and disorder problems evolve from successful police–community partnerships. This text focuses on the attitudes and strategies essential for police to gain and maintain citizens' trust and participation and to prevent police–citizen conflicts.

Police Administration: A Leadership Approach illustrates how a public safety organization that is consumer focused and based on core values, a vision for a better future, a well-defined mission, and courageous ethical leadership can be successful. As an administrator, the ethical leader maintains open lines of communication, fosters teamwork, is accountable and responsible, and demonstrates an unwavering sense of purpose and commitment to quality service and excellence. The ethical leader respects others, embraces diversity, and pursues the greater good for all.

WHO SHOULD READ THIS BOOK?

The book is intended as a core or primary text for courses in police administration and similar topics at the second-year, upper-division, and graduate levels, a resource for police officers who are preparing for promotion exams and interviews, and a comprehensive reference source for police practitioners.

HOW IS THIS BOOK ORGANIZED?

The book's 15 chapters are organized into 4 parts:

> **Part I: Introduction to Police Administration:** includes perspectives on police administration processes; ethics; leadership; strategies; and challenges.

Part II: Planning, Budgeting, Organization Design, and Assessment: includes separate chapters on these four key aspects of police administration.

Part III: Human Resources Management: includes hiring in the spirit of service; effective communication; training (recruit and in-service), organizational development and development of human resources; leadership and supervision; and personnel challenges facing police agencies.

Part IV: Collateral Functions and Future Trends: addresses the legal aspects of police administration; equipment, facilities, technology, and outsourcing; and the future of police administration.

WHAT MAKES THIS BOOK DIFFERENT?

This book differs from other books on police administration in several key respects:

- It weaves ethics and leadership concepts and practices throughout the chapters. True leadership does not exist without courageous, ethical behavior to accompany it. As courageous, self-contained, ethical leadership agents, all police officers must overcome the fear of being disliked and function as self-starters who persevere and commit to engage in actions that lead to the successful completion of ethical goals.

- It addresses the essential elements of the administrative process in a logical, practical sequence, covering planning and budgeting before other steps in the process to reflect how police administrators actually work.

- It emphasizes critical thinking, creativity, and flexibility with respect to policing principles, philosophies, and strategies. For instance, in Chapter 2, readers gain exposure to a multitude of policing strategies, including traditional policing, community policing, problem-oriented policing, and intelligence-led policing, to name just a few. And they are introduced to the notion that the blend of strategies a particular police agency chooses to adopt depends on local circumstances.

- It discusses the process of change leadership, current models of change management, and ways in which police administrators can formulate and execute change initiatives while taking into account their agency's culture, internal and external politics, and technology.

- It presents information, concepts, best practices, and case studies in a clear and concise manner that enables readers to acquire and retain new knowledge and skills. Characterized by an accessible and engaging writing style, the book presents theories but focuses on their practical application.

- It addresses the numerous challenges, such as political correctness, diversity, and politics, that face today's police.

- It emphasizes strategies and tactics that can help police administrators to:
  - Reduce lawsuits, liability, citizen complaints, and police misconduct.
  - Generate a positive image of the police in the public's mind.
  - Improve the quality of life for all citizens served by a police agency.
  - Increase citizen satisfaction and improve employee morale.

- Improve efficiency and effectiveness.
- Partner with community members to identify and solve crime and disorder problems affecting a community.
- Serve as leaders, teachers, mentors, and partners for citizens.
- Develop ethical leadership competence for all sworn and nonsworn employees to foster civility within the organization. Studies conducted by one of the authors, the International Association of Chiefs of Police (IACP), the Federal Law Enforcement Training Center (FLETC), the Royal Canadian Mounted Police (RCMP), and others reveal that leadership competence is essential for all police officers.

WHAT PEDAGOGICAL FEATURES ARE PROVIDED?

This book offers a wealth of pedagogical features designed to help readers acquire and strengthen their critical thinking, decision-making, and problem-solving skills. Each chapter contains:

- Learning outcomes (objectives)
- Key terms highlighted and defined in the chapter
- *Ethics in Action* and *Leadership on the Job* boxes for critical thinking
- Case studies
- Discussion questions
- Problem-solving exercises, including realistic scenarios that present dilemmas that readers must resolve
- Checklists and step lists for important procedures and processes
- Websites and other sources of information, tools, and guidelines regarding best practices for vital activities such as pre-employment screening, training, and program development

ACKNOWLEDGMENTS

The authors wish to thank the many family members, friends, colleagues, supporters, sources, and acquaintances who helped make this book possible. Gratitude is extended to the editors and staff at McGraw-Hill for their guidance, insights, and helpful suggestions: Katie Stevens, Bill Minick, Kate Scheinman, Jane Mohr, and Amy Mittelman. We also wish to thank our associate project manager Tania Andrabi, our copyeditor Sharon O'Donnell, and our proofreader Virginia Bridges for their keen eyes and diligence.

Special thanks are also extended to our editorial consultants Lauren Keller Johnson and Rodine Dobeck, as well as our assistants Gloria Aldaba, Caitlin Wion, and Deanna Hook for their help with the preparation of the manuscript.

Thank you to the members of the Rochester Police Department and the members of the Law Enforcement Training Directors Association of New York State for your support of courageous leadership. A special thank you to Lt. Michael VanRoo, Rochester Police Department and Chief Charles Koerner, Clyde, New York, Police Department for your helpful suggestions, insights, and observations regarding police agency processes, procedures, and operational practices. Thanks for the contributions provided by the staff and students at Roberts Wesleyan College including Gary Prawel and Leonard Wildman. A special thanks to Dr. Frank Colaprete for his mentorship, scholarship, and continuous support and constant pursuit of excellence.

We are deeply indebted to the following reviewers for their valuable contributions: Rulette Armstead, San Diego State University; Rodney W. Brewer, University of Louisville; John Hill, Salt Lake Community College; Harry Hueston, West Texas A&M University; Stephen F. Kappeler, Eastern Kentucky University; Richard Kuiters, Bergen Community College; Juli Liebler, Michigan State University; Tom O'Connor, Austin Peay State University; Michael D. O'Donovan, Bergen Community College; Jerome Randall, University of Central Florida; and Morag (Scottie) Walls, Delta College.

SUPPLEMENTS PACKAGE

Visit our Online Learning Center website at www.mhhe.com/ortmeier1e for robust student and instructor resources.

For the Student

Our book-specific website features chapter-specific self-tests including multiple-choice, true or false, and essay quizzes that allow students to delve deeper into topics within each chapter.

For the Instructor

The password-protected instructor portion of the website includes the instructor's manual written by the text authors, a comprehensive computerized test bank, and PowerPoint lecture slides. Other dynamic instructor resources include:

CourseSmart is a new way to find and buy eTextbooks. At CourseSmart you can save up to 50 percent off the cost of a print textbook, reduce your impact on the environment, and gain access to powerful Web tools for learning. CourseSmart has the largest selection of eTextbooks available anywhere, offering thousands of the most commonly adopted textbooks from a wide variety of higher education publishers. CourseSmart eTextbooks are available in one standard online reader with full text search, notes and highlighting, and e-mail tools for sharing notes between classmates. For further details contact your sales representative or go to www.coursesmart.com.

McGraw Hill **Tegrity campus**

Tegrity Campus is a service that makes class time available all the time by automatically capturing every lecture in a searchable format for students to review when they study and complete assignments. With a simple one-click start and stop process, you capture all computer screens and corresponding audio. Students replay any part of any class with easy-to-use browser-based viewing on a PC or Mac.

Educators know that the more students can see, hear, and experience class resources, the better they learn. With Tegrity Campus, students quickly recall key moments by using Tegrity Campus's unique search feature. This search helps students efficiently find what they need, when they need it across an entire semester of class recordings. Help turn all your students' study time into learning moments immediately supported by your lecture.

To learn more about Tegrity watch a two-minute Flash demo at http://tegritycampus.mhhe.com.

Course Management Systems   Whether you use WebCT, Blackboard, e-College, or another course management system, McGraw-Hill will provide you with a *Corrections* cartridge that enables you either to conduct your course entirely online or to supplement your lectures with online material.

Design your ideal course materials with McGraw-Hill's *Create* at www.mcgrawhill-create.com! Rearrange or omit chapters, combine material from other sources, or upload your syllabus or any other content you have written to make the perfect resource for your students. Search thousands of leading McGraw-Hill textbooks to find the best content for your students, then arrange it to fit your teaching style. You can even personalize your book's appearance by selecting the cover and adding your name, school, and course information. When you order a *Create* book, you receive a complimentary review copy. Get a printed copy in three to five business days or an electronic copy (eComp) via e-mail in about an hour.

Register today at www.mcgrawhillcreate.com, and craft your course resources to match the way you teach.

Introduction to Police Administration

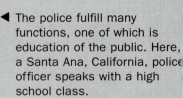

◀ The police fulfill many functions, one of which is education of the public. Here, a Santa Ana, California, police officer speaks with a high school class.

Police Administration: A Perspective

learning outcomes

After completing this chapter, readers should be able to:

- explain the principles of policing attributed to Sir Robert Peel and analyze how they influence policing today.

- discuss how the police motto "To protect and serve" relates to the policing principles attributed to Peel.

- describe the emergence of formal police organizations.

- compare notions of policing strategy as they have evolved since the 1850s.

- define *ethics* and illustrate ethical challenges in policing.

- review examples from the law enforcement codes of ethics and conduct, and relate the codes to the policing principles attributed to Peel.

- define *ethical leadership* and cite examples.
- analyze the characteristics that all professions share, and assess the extent to which policing is a profession.
- distinguish the defining characteristics of management, supervision, and leadership.
- explain how an individual could cultivate leadership abilities.
- describe the activities that constitute police administration, distinguishing among line operations, administrative support activities, and auxiliary services.

Introduction

Congratulations—by opening this book you have taken a crucial first step toward understanding the realities and value of **police administration,** the process, art, and science of the management, supervision, and ethical leadership of a police agency. The concepts, principles, and practices of police administration discussed in this book may be applied in a wide variety of public safety settings (for example, police, courts, corrections, security management, and forensic science).

Without effective administration, no organization—including a police agency—can function and fulfill its mission. Whether you are a criminal justice undergraduate major, a police academy student, an officer working toward a promotion, a mid-level manager, or a chief executive officer, this book will be a valuable companion as you learn what police administration is, why it is important, and how effective administrators and managers operate and how they function as courageous ethical leaders.

In deciding which textbook to assign for the course or training program you are participating in now, your instructor had several choices. Why did the instructor select *Police Administration: A Leadership Approach*? The reason is that this book differs in significant ways from other textbooks on police and criminal justice administration and management. Specifically, unlike other texts, this one presents elements of the police administration process in a logical sequence reflecting how effective agency managers actually work. For instance, real police managers engage in planning and budgeting before making major decisions related to other administrative activities such as assessing agency performance, hiring, leading change, or procuring needed equipment or facilities. To reflect that logical process, this book discusses planning and budgeting before covering other administrative activities. (Many other textbooks give short shrift to planning and budgeting, or cover them late in the book, seemingly as an afterthought.)

Equally important, this book presents ethics and leadership as critical threads running through every step in the administration process. As you will see, leading

Police administration: the process, art, and science of the management, supervision, and ethical leadership of a police agency.

is not the same as supervising or managing. All three activities are important, but they deliver different forms of value for a police agency. The key point we make in this book is that anyone can—and should—be a leader. And when every police administrator and manager shoulders responsibility for leading, the administration process dovetails with all other efforts in the agency to produce stellar public service. Further, true leadership does not exist without ethical behavior to accompany it. As you work through each chapter of this book, you will find a wealth of ideas and practices for strengthening your ethical leadership abilities—no matter what role you eventually occupy in a police organization.

This book also traces the evolution of assumptions regarding what role policing should play in society and what strategies police agencies should use to fulfill their mission. In the past 100 years, definitions of core police responsibilities have bounced between assisting the community and enforcing public safety to fighting crime and back again to helping the community. Of course, in actual police work, most line officers have juggled both—improving quality of life in their community while also battling crime as it arises. As any "real-life" police officer can tell you, during the course of one day, an officer might help a homeless person find shelter and food, rescue a treed cat, and put a drug dealer behind bars. This textbook—unlike others—makes it clear that the two functions of community assistance and crime fighting are not mutually exclusive.

The themes that make this textbook unique—including the principles of policing attributed to Robert Peel, ethics, leadership, and the disciplined application of administration principles—all reflect a viewpoint we hold dear: that any police agency's greatest assets are the human beings who work there. Our intent is to help prepare you to enter the public safety profession equipped with the knowledge, skills, and abilities necessary to survive, to lead, and to serve the public well. As the prestigious United States Army War College explains, there are three pillars of success for anyone seeking to become a leader: formal education, operational experience, and self-development. We believe that this book will help you erect all three pillars as you build your own leadership talents. Another expert maintains that effective leaders know themselves, know their followers, and know their organization (Lutz, 2010). Again, this book will help you master all three of these knowledge areas and become a **self-contained ethical leadership agent** who can motivate others to deliver their best performance and who can garner their trust, respect, and admiration.

Self-contained ethical leadership agent: an individual with the knowledge, skills, and abilities to motivate others to deliver their best performance and who can garner their trust, respect, and admiration.

But before you can develop your leadership ability, you must first gain familiarity with the core elements of police administration. This chapter sets you on that path. We begin by examining principles of policing that have been attributed to the nineteenth-century British home secretary Sir Robert Peel; much of today's policing strategy and procedure derive from these tenets. We then trace the history of police administration, examining how police have organized themselves and how they have viewed themselves over time. We also consider the development of ethics and professionalism in policing and pose the question, "Is policing a profession?"

The chapter next discusses the role of leadership in policing and other public safety arenas, including a preview of how management and supervision differ from leadership. Finally, we introduce common activities making up the police administration process, activities that subsequent chapters will cover in depth. With this broad scope in mind, let's turn now to examining principles of policing attributed to Peel.

PRINCIPLES OF POLICING

Imagine that you have traveled back in time to nineteenth-century London—the birthplace of principles that have profoundly shaped modern police strategy. During the Industrial Revolution of the late eighteenth and early nineteenth centuries, Britain saw major changes in its agricultural, transportation, and manufacturing industries. These changes catalyzed dramatic shifts in the nation's economy and social mores—shifts that spread quickly throughout Europe and North America. In particular, as manufacturing replaced agriculture as the driving force behind economic growth, people began migrating in droves from the countryside to urban centers in search of work. These massive migrations put enormous pressure on all aspects of city life.

London's Metropolitan Police Act

London, in particular, experienced staggering unemployment and poverty. Despite their hopes, unskilled and displaced agrarian workers found only limited job opportunities in the city. The few jobs they did manage to get paid a pittance. Increasing numbers of impoverished, desperate Londoners turned to crime in their attempts to survive, and civil disorder to express their anger. The British Parliament responded in 1829 with the passage of the Act for Improving the Police in and near the Metropolis, commonly referred to as the Metropolitan Police Act. Largely attributed to the efforts of the British home secretary **Sir Robert Peel,** the act established what eventually came to be known as the world's first recognizable local police department.

Peel envisioned a police force comprising citizens who were paid by the community to devote full-time attention

English diplomat, Sir Robert Peel (1788– 1850) circa 1830. The principles of modern public policing are attributed to Peel.

Sir Robert Peel: the nineteenth-century British home secretary influential in passing the Metropolitan Police Act, which established the world's first recognizable local police department.

Principles of policing:

principles regarding the mission and acceptable behavior of police, attributed to Sir Robert Peel.

to preventing crime and disorder. To support this vision—which was unique for nineteenth-century London—Peel reputedly established the following **principles of policing:**

1. The basic mission for which police exist is to prevent crime and disorder as an alternative to repressing crime and disorder by military force and severity of legal punishment.

2. The ability of the police to perform their duties depends on public approval of police existence, actions, and behavior, as well as the ability of the police to secure and maintain public respect.

3. The police must secure the willing cooperation of the public in voluntary observance of the law to be able to secure and maintain public respect.

4. The degree of cooperation that can be secured from the public diminishes, proportionately, with the need to use physical force in achieving police objectives.

5. The police seek and preserve public favor not by catering to public opinion but by constantly demonstrating absolutely impartial service to the law, in complete independence of policy, and without regard to the justice or injustice of the substance of individual laws; by ready offering of individual service and friendship to all members of the society without regard to their race or social standing; by ready exercise of courtesy and friendly good humor; and by ready offering of individual sacrifice in protecting and preserving life.

6. The police should use physical force to the extent necessary to secure observance of the law or to restore order only when the exercise of persuasion, advice, and warning is found to be insufficient to achieve police objectives. Moreover, police should use only the minimum degree of physical force necessary on any particular occasion to achieve a police objective.

7. The police at all times should maintain a relationship with the public that gives reality to the historic tradition that the police are the public and the public are the police. The police are the only members of the public who are paid to give full-time attention to duties that are incumbent on every citizen in the interest of the community's welfare.

8. The police should always direct their actions toward their functions and never appear to usurp the powers of the judiciary by avenging individuals or the state or by authoritatively judging guilt or punishing the guilty.

9. The test of police efficiency is the absence of crime and disorder, not the visible evidence of police actions in dealing with them (Lee, 1901).

Research indicates that no single set of policing principles attributed to Peel can be definitively shown as originating with him. The research findings indicate that "Peel's principles," as they are generally presented today, were actually invented by authors of twentieth-century policing textbooks. However, the fact that the principles cannot be traced directly to Peel does not necessarily make them fiction; nor does it mean they have no relevance for aspiring police administrators and leaders (Lentz & Chaires, 2007).

Protecting and Serving

The vision for policing attributed to Robert Peel, as expressed in these nine principles, emphasized the notion that police are peace officers first, rather than crime fighters. Although responding to crime and disorder is an important police function, the true measure of stellar police performance is the absence of crime and disorder.

Consider the time-honored police motto "To protect and serve." The word *protect* certainly means that police are responsible for securing citizens' safety. It can also mean arresting suspects so they will not victimize citizens, and intervening in public disputes so the combatants and innocent bystanders are not drawn further into violence. The word *serve* has even broader application. Police serve the people every time they answer a call-for-service, give directions, direct traffic, and help a homeless person find shelter for the night. To the average person, the police are all about service to citizens and the communities in which they live. But police are also "serving" when they testify in court, prepare a written incident report, and even when they write a traffic ticket (which may prompt the driver in question to think twice before speeding again).

When you study the policing strategies presented in Chapter 2, keep in mind Peel's vision for the public police service as well as the nine policing principles attributed to him. Policing philosophies, strategies, and operations may change over time, but the basic principles of policing—to protect and serve—remain constant. Thus, the principles we have examined are just as relevant today as they were in Peel's day (Ortmeier & Meese, 2010). But to truly understand the relevance of these principles, we need to go back even earlier in time and trace the history of police administration.

POLICE ADMINISTRATION: A BRIEF HISTORY

Over the centuries, police administration has evolved in several important respects—including how police have been organized and what they considered their core strategy for providing value to the communities they serve. In the sections that follow, we trace these changes.

The Emergence of Formal Police Organizations

Many laws we abide by in the United States today, such as those related to theft and homicide, have their origin in twelfth-century England. In that era, King Henry II established the common law, which included a judiciary that gave each county a king's judge. The county judge, along with 12 local men, meted out justice to the common folk; for example, pitting combatants against each other in physical battle to determine who was in the right. At this time, laws were enforced by appointees of the lords of each county (Delderfield, 1978).

The common law system endured until as late as 1829, when the London Metropolitan Police was founded through the British Parliament's enactment of the Metropolitan Police Act, an event that inspired similar developments in local police organizations within the United States. For example, just seven years later, Boston, Massachusetts, set up a formal local police department. In 1844, New York City followed suit.

Many state- and federal-level police organizations had early origins in the United States as well. For example, the first organization resembling a state police force had come into being in 1823 as the Texas Rangers, originally more of a nonuniformed

The Texas Rangers, founded in 1823, are credited with being the first form of state police in the United States. Here, a group of rangers pose for a photo in Kilgore, Texas.

state militia than a uniformed state-level police force. And the first federal law enforcement agency in America had been created a century earlier, in 1789, when President George Washington appointed eight United States marshals. Much later, in 1908, the development of national-level law enforcement organizations took a large step with the creation of the Bureau of Investigation (subsequently renamed the Federal Bureau of Investigation, or FBI) in the U.S. Department of Justice.

As local, state, and federal law enforcement organizations evolved, so did the notion that police should have the right to collective bargaining. As early as 1893, the National Chiefs of Police Union, forerunner of the International Association of Chiefs of Police (IACP), was established, largely through the efforts of progressive Omaha, Nebraska, police chief Webber Seavey. Each year, the IACP sponsors the Webber Seavey Award, presented to agencies that have made innovative accomplishments.

Evolving Notions of Strategy

Most experts identify periods in U.S. history when people had distinct ideas about what strategies police should use to accomplish their work. Over time, debate has swirled around whether police should focus their strategy on community service, crime fighting, or some other combination of approaches. Below, we take a closer look at these evolving notions of police strategy.

1850–1930: From Community Service to Crime Fighting   From the mid-nineteenth century to about 1930, policing was about community service. Officers were encouraged to live in the same areas they patrolled, so they could get to know and better serve community residents. Citizens felt safe knowing that a police officer lived close by, and everyone was on a first-name basis. Business owners, too, knew that help was close at hand in the event of a robbery or other incident.

However, during this same era, politicians closely directed police activities; thus, corruption ran rampant. Politicians awarded promotions to those officers who supported their elections, and hardly anyone could become a police officer without the approval of a politician.

Between 1929 and 1931, the National Commission on Law Observance and Enforcement (the Wickersham Commission) produced 14 reports for President Herbert Hoover regarding the status of policing and law enforcement in general. According to the reports, many areas needed addressing, especially the matter of police brutality, through which police used mental and physical torture to elicit confessions from suspects. The commissioners' recommendations included centralizing administration in a police jurisdiction, establishing higher personnel standards, and adopting a more professional approach to policing in general (National Commission on Law Observance and Enforcement, 1931).

The commission ushered in a period when police authority derived more from the law than from local politicians. In addition, police activity shifted from community service to crime control and prevention. Most law

A nineteenth-century police officer walks a beat.

Chief August Vollmer of Berkeley, California, was subsequently appointed professor of Police Administration at the University of Chicago. Vollmer's innovations were shared with police agencies around the world.

O. W. Wilson, Vollmer's protégé, is shown while serving as police superintendent in Chicago. Wilson is holding a photo of Richard B. Speck, 25, sought in connection with the deaths of eight student nurses.

enforcement agencies, including the FBI under J. Edgar Hoover, focused on catching criminals.

August Vollmer: chief of police in Berkeley, California, from 1902 to 1932; considered a founder of modern policing.

The person considered one of the founders of modern policing was **August Vollmer**, who served as chief of police in Berkeley, California, from 1902 to 1932. In the early 1920s, Vollmer initiated the use of the police car as a patrol device and the two-way radio as a means for rapidly answering calls-for-service. He also introduced the polygraph as an investigative tool and helped establish college-level courses for police officers. Vollmer also promoted the use of other forensic science technologies, such as fingerprinting, as well as crime laboratories. Moreover, he strongly advocated professionalism in policing.

O. W. Wilson: August Vollmer's protégé; introduced a merit system for promotions and other innovations influential in modern policing.

Vollmer's protégé **O. W. Wilson** worked in Wichita, Kansas, and Chicago, Illinois. Wilson introduced a merit system for promotions, rotated officers' patrol assignments to reduce the chance for corruption, and insisted on higher salaries for officers to help agencies recruit higher-quality candidates.

1930–1980: A Widening Array of Policing Strategies   From the 1930s to about 1980, many police executives and politicians moved to separate policing more completely from politics to create a more professional model of policing. The social function of policing gave way to a war-on-crime model. Police chiefs and sheriffs stepped up pressure on officers to respond to calls-for-service as quickly as possible, and pushed intensive coverage of communities by patrol cars. Unfortunately, crime escalated despite these measures.

This era also saw a widening of the strategies police considered adopting to address the challenges they had been experiencing. During the 1960s, massive social unrest erupting throughout the United States forced police executives to confront the fact that traditional policing (the professional "command and control" model) was not working well. The chasm between citizen and police officer was wider than at almost any other time in history. Several commissions—most notably the President's Commission on Law Enforcement and Administration of Justice (1967), the National Advisory Commission on Civil Disorders (1968), and the National Advisory Commission on Criminal Justice Standards and Goals (1973)— recommended major improvements in policing and the administration of justice (Inciardi, 2005; Kerlikowske, 2004). To be sure, many experts felt certain that the police alone could not control crime and that social unrest stemmed from factors such as social inequality, lack of jobs, and the deterioration of the family. Nevertheless, the stage was set for a change in policing strategies.

Interestingly, the "new" strategies integrated many of the tenets associated with Sir Robert Peel, such as police responsibility for maintaining peace while strengthening connections to the citizens they serve. For example, these newer strategies include community-oriented policing, community-oriented problem-solving policing (COPS), statistics-oriented policing (which includes community mapping and real-time crime analysis approaches such as CompStat), intelligence-led policing, and strategic policing. Many of these are discussed in Chapter 2 as well as in other sections of this book.

1980–Present: Flexibility and Transition   Today, each police agency's executives, in conjunction with citizens and elected political and community leaders, must decide what policing principles and strategies to incorporate into their mission. Most agencies across the country mix traditional policing with community- and problem-oriented policing, some statistical policing, and strategic policing to prepare for the future.

In addition to demonstrating greater flexibility with regard to strategy, the police have also entered a time of transition in terms of how they and others perceive their level of professionalism. If you were to ask police officers whether they view themselves as professionals, most would probably answer "Yes." But many citizens might disagree. This difference in viewpoint stems in part from the fact that police officers regularly see the worst of human behavior and deal with unsavory individuals to keep the rest of us safe. Just as waste management workers bear the stigma of handling human refuse, police officers are expected to manage society's most undesirable elements without receiving any special recognition or reward.

Moreover, for many years, particularly in cities in the Eastern United States, police ranks almost exclusively comprised immigrants, especially Irish. Because many civilian immigrants served people with wealth and power, police officers who were immigrants were seen as having the same low socioeconomic status. It did not help that one needed no special education to become a police officer and that the pay was very low. If a police officer exhibited wealth of any kind, people almost universally assumed that the officer gained that wealth through unethical and corrupt means.

The fact that you are reading a textbook about police administration testifies to how much these circumstances have changed. Today, many police agencies want recruits with some college credits. Police also earn more money now, and they enjoy superior benefits, including generous health insurance coverage and retirement pensions. Many individuals who are drawn to policing as a career have as their goal the desire to help people and to make society a better place. Many are also drawn to public safety careers because of the job security they provide. Later in this chapter, you will find a compelling argument that policing has, in fact, become a profession (Champion & Hooper, 2003; Kelling & Sousa, 2001; Leonard & More, 2000; Ortmeier, 2006).

ETHICS AND PROFESSIONALISM IN POLICING

Ethics:
the philosophical study of conduct that adheres to certain principles of morality.

Ethics is the philosophical study of conduct that adheres to certain principles of morality. People who wish to "do the right thing," "be a good person," and "get along with others" are expressing the desire to behave in an ethical manner. While ethical behavior can certainly include obeying the law, following certain religious tenets, and conforming to societal standards of behavior, ethics itself is not concerned with law, religion, or society.

Instead, ethics centers on demonstrating behavior that reflects specific virtues—examples of moral excellence. Virtues include discretion, integrity, courage, and self-restraint. Religious groups added faith, hope, and love as virtues. Other virtues are honesty, loyalty, generosity, modesty, and responsibility. Demonstrating virtues leads to moral behavior, which in turn forms a foundation for ethics. (See Figure 1-1.) As a general rule, *virtue* refers to who a person is, while *ethics* refers to what a person does (Bennett, 1993; Kleinig, 1996; Pollock, 2007). That is, a person becomes virtuous by behaving ethically.

We all learn to practice ethical behavior, presumably during our early years of growth through maturation as we interact with family and society. Through these interactions, we come to understand the difference between good and bad behavior. Societies everywhere require their members to behave in an ethically acceptable manner (Ortmeier & Meese, 2010).

Ethics, as an aspect of philosophy, originated in ancient Greece. The three philosophical giants who attempted to define and refine ethics were Socrates, Plato, and Aristotle. Socrates argued that with the proper knowledge, a person will always do good. Plato wrote that the highest good comes from loving the truth and doing all things for the sake of the truth. Finally, Aristotle proposed that doing good was a habit that must be inculcated in persons at a very early age, and that once doing good has become habitual, a person could not do other than good (Durant, 1966).

Ethical Challenges in Policing

More than most professions, policing presents its members with ethical dilemmas on a daily basis. Planting drugs on a known drug dealer who has so far escaped justice is unethical and illegal, but some officers may be tempted to do so anyway. An officer might rationalize the action as noble if it boosts the chances that the dealer will be convicted—and thus prevented from selling more drugs and condemning more people to addiction. The officer might further decide to give false testimony about the dealer in court to help secure a conviction and thus serve the "greater good."

figure 1-1 The Relationship among Virtues, Morality, and Ethics

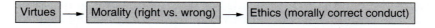

Virtues → Morality (right vs. wrong) → Ethics (morally correct conduct)

Lawyer and judge, with police officer on witness stand. It is essential that officers be truthful and professional.

Deciding not to behave ethically is just as unethical as overtly questionable behavior. For instance, an officer may decide not to arrest a drunk driver because that person is related to an acquaintance or relative of the officer. Like obviously unethical behavior, opting out of doing the right thing also contributes to public perception that police officers are corrupt and untrustworthy. However, this kind of behavior has not commanded the attention of the public in the same way as overt acts have.

Law Enforcement Codes of Ethics and Conduct

A broad-based interest in the idea that police work should be subject to ethical standards emerged with the 1936 publication of August Vollmer's *The Police in Modern Society*, which promoted ethics as an essential ingredient for modern policing. Interest intensified further when the IACP developed a **Law Enforcement Code of Ethics** and **Law Enforcement Code of Conduct** in the association's early years. The codes are accepted as universal standards across the police profession. They include guidelines concerning performance of officer duties, responsibilities, discretion, and use of force, among others. Many police agencies use these codes to define a formal, agency-wide set of standards that they circulate to all agency members and usually post in a prominent location in all facilities. As you review these codes (shown in the box "International Association of Chiefs of Police Codes of Ethics and Conduct"), consider ways in which they reflect the policing principles presented earlier in this chapter, and think about what virtues they emphasize.

Law Enforcement Code of Ethics and **Law Enforcement Code of Conduct:** codes developed by the International Association of Chiefs of Police (IACP) in its early years.

International Association of Chiefs of Police Codes of Ethics and Conduct

Law Enforcement Code of Ethics

As a Law Enforcement Officer, my fundamental duty is to serve mankind; to safeguard lives and property; to protect the innocent against deception, the weak against oppression or intimidation, and the peaceful against violence or disorder; and to respect the Constitutional rights of all men to liberty, equality, and justice.

I will keep my private life unsullied as an example to all; maintain courageous calm in the face of danger, scorn, or ridicule; develop self-restraint; and be constantly mindful of the welfare of others. Honest in thought and deed in both my personal and official life, I will be exemplary in obeying the laws of the land and the regulations of my department.

Whatever I see or hear of a confidential nature or that is confided in me in my official capacity will be kept ever secret unless revelation is necessary in the performance of my duty.

I will never act officiously or permit personal feelings, prejudices, animosities, or friendships to influence my decisions. With no compromise for crime and the relentless prosecution of criminals, I will enforce the law courteously and appropriately without fear of favor, malice, or ill will, never employing unnecessary force or violence and never accepting gratuities.

I recognize the badge of my office as a symbol of public faith, and I accept it as a public trust to be held so long as I am true to the ethics of the police service. I will constantly strive to achieve these objectives and ideals, dedicating myself before God to my chosen profession . . . law enforcement.

Law Enforcement Code of Conduct

All law enforcement officers must be fully aware of the ethical responsibilities of their position and must strive constantly to live up to the highest possible standards of professional policing. The International Association of Chiefs of Police believes it important that police officers have clear advice and counsel available to assist them in performing their duties consistent with these standards, and has adopted the following ethical mandates as guidelines to meet these ends.

Primary Responsibilities of a Police Officer

A police officer acts as an official representative of government who is required and trusted to work within the law. The officer's powers and duties are conferred by statute. The fundamental duties of a police officer include serving the community, safeguarding lives and property, protecting the innocent, keeping the peace, and ensuring the rights of all to liberty, equality, and justice.

Performance of the Duties of a Police Officer

A police officer shall perform all duties impartially, without favor or affection or ill will and without regard to status, sex, race, religion, political belief, or aspiration. All citizens will be treated equally with courtesy, consideration, and dignity. Officers will never allow personal feelings, animosities, or friendships to influence official conduct. Laws will be enforced appropriately and courteously and, in carrying out their responsibilities, officers will strive to obtain maximum cooperation from the public. They will conduct themselves in appearance and department in such a manner as to inspire confidence and respect for the position of the public trust they hold.

Discretion

A police officer will use responsibly the discretion vested in his position and exercise it within the law. The principle of reasonableness will guide the officer's determinations, and the officer will consider all surrounding circumstances in determining whether any legal action shall be taken. Consistent and wise use of discretion, based on professional policing competence, will do much to preserve good relationships and retain the confidence of the public. There can be difficulty in choosing between conflicting courses of action. It is important to remember that a timely word of advice rather than arrest—which may be correct in appropriate circumstances—can be a more effective means of achieving a desired end.

Use of Force

A police officer will never employ unnecessary force or violence and will use only such force in the discharge of duty as is reasonable in all circumstances. The use of force should be used only with the greatest restraint and only after discussion, negotiation, and persuasion have been found to be inappropriate or ineffective. While the use of force is occasionally unavoidable, every police officer will refrain from unnecessary infliction of pain or suffering and will never engage in cruel, degrading, or inhumane treatment of any person.

Confidentiality

Whatever a police officer sees, hears, or learns of that is of a confidential nature will be kept secret unless the performance of duty or legal provision requires otherwise. Members of the public have a right to security and privacy, and information obtained about them must not be improperly divulged.

Integrity

A police officer will not engage in acts of corruption or bribery, nor will an officer condone such acts by other police officers. The public demands that the integrity of police officers be above reproach. Police officers must, therefore, avoid any conduct that might compromise integrity and thus undercut the public confidence in a law enforcement agency. Officers will refuse to accept any gifts, presents, subscriptions, favors, gratuities, or promises that could be interpreted as seeking to cause the officer to refrain from performing official responsibilities honestly and within the law. Police officers must not receive private or special advantage from their official status. Respect from the public cannot be bought; it can only be earned and cultivated.

(continued)

Cooperation with Other Police Officers and Agencies

Police officers will cooperate with all legally authorized agencies and their representatives in the pursuit of justice. An officer or agency may be one among many organizations that may provide law enforcement services to a jurisdiction. It is imperative that a police officer assists colleagues fully and completely with respect and consideration at all times.

Personal-Professional Capabilities

Police officers will be responsible for their own standard of professional performance and will take every reasonable opportunity to enhance and improve their level of knowledge and competence. Through study and experience, a police officer can acquire the high level of knowledge and competence that is essential for the efficient and effective performance of duty. The acquisition of knowledge is a never-ending process of personal and professional development that should be pursued constantly.

Private Life

Police officers will behave in a manner that does not bring discredit to their agencies or themselves. A police officer's character and conduct while off duty must always be exemplary, thus maintaining a position of respect in the community in which he or she lives and serves. The officer's personal behavior must be beyond reproach.

Source: Reprinted with permission of the International Association of Chiefs of Police, 515 North Washington Street, Alexandria, VA 22314 USA, 2010b. Further reproduction without express written permission from IACP is strictly prohibited.

Ethical Leadership by Example

Leadership: the art and science of ethically using communication, activities, and behaviors to influence, motivate (not manipulate), or mobilize others to action.

Ethical leadership: ethical behavior on display.

As you will see throughout this book, all police agency personnel have the power to model ethical behavior—becoming ethical leaders by example. **Leadership** is the art and science of ethically using communication, activities, and behaviors to influence, motivate (not manipulate), or mobilize others to action. **Ethical leadership** is ethical behavior on display. Subordinates model behavior based on what a leader demonstrates. If a perceived leader or supervisor gives "a wink and a nod" when an officer accepts gratuities, followers and subordinates may engage in that same behavior, even if their agency's code of conduct defines it as unethical.

Just as unethical behavior by one individual can trigger it in another, ethical behavior can also spread when individuals model it consistently. In fact, researchers have proven that unethical people who become part of an ethical society or organization soon begin to emulate and embrace ethical behavior (Ritchie, 2007). These findings further underscore the importance of demonstrating ethical behavior—of leading ethically by example.

In time, policing has overcome the negative image it was previously saddled with. Many people see it as a complex job that demands the highest level of communication skills, physical ability, mental acuity, and emotional discipline. Unethical officers tarnish this image and make it difficult for the police to gain and retain citizens' trust, an essential ingredient for effective police work (Allen & Sawhney, 2010; Gaines, Worrall, Southerland, & Angell, 2003). Loss of trust due to unethical behavior on the part of any police agency personnel can also damage hard-won perceptions of policing as a profession.

You may be wondering whether formal training is available to help police personnel at all levels acquire ethical leadership skills. The answer is not encouraging. Police leadership development programs endorsed, certified, and/or presented through state commissions on peace officer standards and training as well as colleges and universities, where such development programs exist, focus primarily on the promotion of police officers to mid- or upper-level management positions. Very few focus on ethical leadership development at all ranks, including police recruits ("Leadership Development around the States," 2009). We strongly suggest that ethical leadership training and development are essential for all police officers, regardless of rank.

Policing as a Profession

A **profession** is an occupation or discipline that requires its members to adhere to prescribed standards of behavior and competence. All professions—including policing—share the following characteristics:

- A recognized body of knowledge specific to the profession
- Common goals and principles
- A code of ethics and standards of conduct
- A public service orientation
- Common language and vocabulary
- A system for licensing or credentialing members
- An association that promotes the profession's standards and interests (in the case of policing, such associations include the International Association of Chiefs of Police, or the IACP, and the Police Executive Research Forum, or PERF).

Profession:
an occupation or discipline that requires its members to adhere to prescribed standards of behavior and competence and that has characteristics including common goals and principles, a common language, a system for licensing or credentialing members, and an association that promotes the profession's standards and interest.

U.S. Attorney General John Ashcroft addressing the 111th International Association of Chiefs of Police (IACP) Annual Conference at the Los Angeles Convention Center.

Graduates of a NYPD
Police Academy
class during their
commencement at
Madison Square
Garden.

To qualify as a member of any profession, including policing, people must gain knowledge and develop skills relevant to that profession. They can do so by attending special schools, colleges, or training centers. They can also accumulate experience and expertise by doing the job. The specialized knowledge police officers acquire through their education, training, and job experience enables them to make decisions and take actions that others without such knowledge are not equipped to make. For instance, the average citizen is not expected to apprehend a suspect during a robbery in progress. However, a police officer is expected to intervene—and to have the skills and knowledge to do so effectively.

Much of the knowledge gained by police officers cannot be absorbed by studying lists of rules but instead must be learned through on-the-job experience. Consider the way aspiring doctors or lawyers must learn the rules and theories of their profession before they practice that profession. Police go through a similar process before they are allowed to work alone on the street.

At various times in the past, experts have characterized police officers as "unprofessional professionals" (Delattre, 1989) or as an "ambivalent force" (Niederhoffer & Blumberg, 1976). Some have used the term "impossible" to describe the directive of police to ensure public safety (Manning & Van Maanen, 1978). These confusing terms reflect the fact that in the United States, the law gives certain powers to police officers while also restricting their actions (Goldstein, 1977) to preserve personal liberty in our democratic society. A good example is the Miranda warning that police are supposed to recite to a suspect in custody before the person can be interrogated. If the suspect confesses before the Miranda warning is delivered, the confession may be inadmissible in court unless the confession falls under one of the judicially recognized exceptions to the Miranda admonition.

Leadership on the job
Police Academies for All

In a large city on the U.S. East Coast, a police captain coordinates an innovative program: a police academy for local senior citizens. Components of the program include a ride-along with patrol officers and the chance to use the computerized firearms simulator that is used in the recruit academy.

"If we gave them a gun and a badge, they would do it," the captain reports. He describes the real purpose of the academy: "Seniors are home during the day, they see a lot, they're the staples in their community. . . . They're the ones who can bring back that 'it takes a village' kind of [mentality]. . . ."

The program underscores a phenomenon that occurs every time police and community residents create a personal connection: police work is demystified for the average citizen, and the police gain supporters in the community. The more people know about how police do their job, the more likely citizens will be to support their efforts.

1. What other community groups might benefit from attending an academy like the one described in this scenario?

2. What other citizen–police activities might increase the bond between the police and the community they serve?

As mentioned earlier, most police officers consider themselves professionals, and certainly the world of policing is closed to those who do not have the appropriate background, training, education, or experience. As police agencies hire more officers who have higher education and demonstrate personal ethical standards, public perceptions of policing as a profession will likely strengthen further.

ETHICS IN ACTION
Technology Exposes Officer's Unethical Behavior

When a 17-year-old male was arrested for a shooting that occurred six days earlier, he was listening to music on his MP3 player. The detective who arrested him questioned the young man for over an hour with neither a lawyer nor his parents present. Unknown to the detective, the young man taped the interrogation using his MP3 player.

During the young man's subsequent trial, the detective denied that an interrogation had taken place. When the defense presented the MP3 tape as evidence, the detective was charged with three felony counts of perjury and terminated by the police department after his conviction. The young man received seven years in prison on a weapons charge, but the charge of attempted murder was dropped after the detective's perjury conviction.

1. What implications does this case have for any other trials at which the detective testified in which the defendant was convicted?

2. What are the implications for public safety when officers manipulate the truth to gain convictions or "not guilty" verdicts?

LEADERSHIP VERSUS MANAGEMENT AND SUPERVISION

Without strong leaders, any organization can fail. Every member of every police agency thus has the opportunity and responsibility to become a leader. Leadership should begin with the chief executive of the agency and spread throughout all levels of the organization, including the line officer level. Line officers have the most direct contact with citizens and possess broad discretionary powers. For these reasons, they must function as leaders whenever they answer a call-for-service—demonstrating skills such as communication, critical thinking, and problem solving. Indeed, every time a patrol officer responds to a call-for-service, a leadership opportunity presents itself. Patrol officers become the stabilizing influence in a crisis situation and have the potential to affect a citizen's life in a positive way, even if the call is nothing more serious than a barking dog.

Choosing to Lead

Police officers at other levels must also demonstrate leadership. Whether working alone or with partners, all officers must identify and solve problems quickly, and communicate effectively with a diverse array of individuals who may differ in terms of age, race, ethnicity, gender, and lifestyle. Whether they wish to be or not, all officers are problem solvers, and problem-solving ability is a leadership skill.

But merely knowing what skills constitute effective leadership is not enough. Police personnel, no matter what rank they hold, must also have the courage

New York State Troopers speak to a reporter outside the house of the family of Linh Voong (L) on April 4, 2009, in Johnson City, New York, a day after Voong killed 13 people and himself at the American Civic Association in nearby Binghamton, New York. Authorities reported that the shooter's name was Linh Voong and that he used Jiverly Wong as an alias to purchase weapons.

(a leadership quality) to put those skills into action—within their agency as well as with community members and partners from other private and public agencies (such as schools, other police agencies, fire departments, and businesses). Without that courage, an officer is just another person in the crowd of badges. Demonstrating courage takes practice. Many police professionals have the knowledge and ability to lead. Yet, they may choose not to exercise their leadership skills—not to do the right thing—because they fear losing the rewards that conformity provides (such as promotion and the preservation of friendships with colleagues). Indeed, a common saying in the field is, "To get along, you have to go along."

Understanding Managers' and Supervisors' Responsibilities

Middle managers and line supervisors have a dual responsibility when it comes to demonstrating leadership: They must be role models and authority figures to both citizens and line officers, as well as communicate executive decisions to the officers reporting to them. Meanwhile, a police agency's chief executive must take responsibility for securing the safety of the community at large as well as be a public role model for exemplary and unblemished police leadership and conduct in general.

Managers and supervisors can, and should, also be leaders. However, management and supervision are not synonymous with leadership. Managers direct their subordinates in the completion of tasks toward the accomplishment of a specific organizational goal. Supervisors oversee the work of their subordinates and are available to answer questions, provide training for certain tasks, and account to superiors for their subordinates' performance.

Leaders may supervise and manage, but they also take responsibility for influencing and motivating others. They empower people by guiding individuals in the process of change, and they account for subordinates' actions. While managers and supervisors focus on directing and maintaining existing operations, leaders guide growth and change in their organization or group with an eye on the future (see Table 1-1).

Therefore, it takes a leader to manage a progressive organization and to plan for the future while also addressing challenges and needs in the present. Throughout

table 1-1 Characteristics of the Manager, Supervisor, and Leader

MANAGER	SUPERVISOR	LEADER
Plans activities	Directs employees	Influences and motivates people
Organizes resources	Inspects work	Displays integrity
Controls costs and quality	Evaluates performance	Models ethical behavior
Directs employees	Rewards good work	Creates mission
	Corrects poor performance	Tenaciously pursues goals
		Builds relationships
		Focuses on strategy

Sources: Davis & Prawel, 2008; Derrick, 2009; Northouse, 2009; Ortmeier, 1997; Townsend, 1970.

this book, you will learn more about leadership, how it applies in the administration of a police organization, and how you can develop and practice leadership skills.

Cultivating Leadership Abilities

A key to becoming a leader is wanting to do so. You can cultivate your own leadership abilities by doing the following:

- Recognize that leaders at different organizational levels will lead differently.
- Recognize that there are leaders at every level of the organization. A person need not possess an official title to be a leader.
- Make sure you know where your organization is headed strategically and where you stand in your development as a leader by performing regular organizational and self-assessments.
- Be certain there is a way for you and other leaders to develop knowledge and skills throughout the organization by regularly interacting with all personnel.
- Tailor your strategic efforts to support your organization's goals and values.
- Regularly communicate your organization's mission, values, and goals to subordinates and others (International Association of Chiefs of Police, 2005).

Supervision and management and how they relate to leadership and administration is covered in greater detail in Chapter 11.

POLICE ADMINISTRATION: COMMON ACTIVITIES

Most large organizations have many complex administrative activities that must be completed on a regular basis. These include (but are not limited to) planning, budgeting, hiring and training employees, and purchasing and maintaining equipment and facilities. Police agencies must carry out these activities, too. Large police agencies have single departments devoted to specific administrative activities, such as a budgeting department or a facilities management team. In smaller agencies, the responsibility for each process may rest on the shoulders of the chief executive, whether that person is a police commissioner, chief, or sheriff.

We can think of a police agency's administrative activities as falling into three broad categories: line operations, administrative support, and auxiliary services.

Line Operations

Activities that serve the public and the goals of the organization directly are usually lumped under a title such as *line operations*. They can include patrolling, traffic management, criminal investigation, communication with the public, organized-crime control, juvenile and community services (such as bicycle inspections and security at sporting events), controlled substance (drug) law enforcement, and school services (for example, drug-abuse prevention programs).

A man is handcuffed and arrested by Aspen, Colorado, police outside the Cannabis Crown 2010 Expo on April 18, 2010. The man was detained by hotel security after carrying a large jar of marijuana out of the marijuana trade show in the basement event space downstairs. Aspen police then found the man had no medical marijuana license and was carrying a set of brass knuckles, which are illegal in Colorado.

Administrative Support

Activities that serve the agency's needs and that have very little direct impact on the community or its residents come under the title *administrative support*. These include hiring and training, budgeting, and internal affairs.

Although these activities are not typically outsourced, smaller jurisdictions have found it cost-effective to outsource some training support by collaborating with other agencies, and may engage outside consultants for such activities. However, outsourcing of other activities may be frowned upon. These include the storage of unclosed case files, property, and evidence. Unclosed case files could contain sensitive and confidential material that, if revealed outside the agency, might compromise the case resolution. The storage of property and evidence must follow certain protocols imposed by the law and the courts. For instance, if a piece of physical evidence found at a crime scene is contaminated or lost, the prosecution and defense in a court case cannot do their jobs effectively.

Auxiliary Services

Activities that support line operations are sometimes known as *auxiliary services*. These typically include records maintenance, property and evidence management, forensic laboratory services, detention, alcohol testing, facilities and equipment maintenance, and coordination of volunteers. Some auxiliary services can be outsourced. For instance, prisoners may be detained at a centralized county facility. And an agency may hire a private company to provide laboratory services or facilities maintenance services.

As you progress through this book, you will learn about these and other activities essential to police administration.

- **Principles of Policing.** Passage of the Metropolitan Police Act in London in 1829 established the world's first recognizable local police department, and came in response to an increase in crime in the city. The British home secretary Sir Robert Peel envisioned a police firm comprising citizens paid by the community to prevent (rather than merely repress) crime and disorder. A set of principles, commonly attributed to Peel, arose to support this vision. These principles emphasize the notion that police are peace officers first, rather than crime fighters. The police motto "To protect and serve" reinforces this notion.

- **Police Administration: A Brief History.** Police administration has evolved in terms of how police have been organized and what they consider their core strategy for providing value to the communities they serve. The founding of the London Metropolitan Police inspired the creation of other local police departments in the United States. Many state and federal-level police organizations (such as the Texas Rangers and the U.S. marshals), as well as police unions, also had early origins. Since the 1850s, notions of policing strategy have also evolved. During 1850–1930, ideas of policing shifted from community service to crime fighting. August Vollmer and his protégé O. W. Wilson laid the foundation for modern policing, by (among other achievements) initiating the use of police cars as patrol devices and rotating patrol assignments to reduce corruption. During 1930–1980, policing strategies proliferated, many of them integrating principles associated with Sir Robert Peel. Since 1980, police agencies have flexibly mixed traditional policing with a range of other strategies, and the question of whether policing constitutes a profession has continued to inspire debate.

- **Ethics and Professionalism in Policing.** Ethics is the philosophical study of conduct that adheres to certain principles of morality, and centers on the demonstration of behavior that reflects specific virtues. More than most professions, policing presents its members with ethical dilemmas on a daily basis. The Law Enforcement Codes of Ethics and Conduct, developed by the International Association of Chiefs of Police, helps establish behavioral standards to combat unethical behavior. Ethical leadership is ethical behavior on display. Policing shares characteristics of all professions, including a recognized body of knowledge specific to the profession, common goals and principles, and a code of ethics and standards of conduct.

- **Leadership versus Management and Supervision.** Every member of a police agency has the opportunity and responsibility to become a leader. Managers and supervisors can and should be leaders, but management and supervision are not synonymous with leadership. Managers direct subordinates in the completion of tasks. Supervisors oversee subordinates' work and provide guidance. Leaders influence and motivate others. Managers and supervisors thus focus on directing and maintaining current operations, while leaders guide growth and change with an eye toward the future. Anyone can take steps to cultivate leadership abilities, including knowing where one's organization is headed strategically and regularly communicating the organization's mission, values, and goals to others.

- **Police Administration: Common Activities.** Police administration activities fall into three categories: (1) line operations (activities that serve the public

directly, such as patrolling, criminal investigation, and juvenile services);
(2) administrative support (activities that serve the agency's needs, such
as training and evidence storage); and (3) auxiliary services (activities that
directly support line operations, such as records maintenance and property
management).

ethical leadership

ethics

Law Enforcement Code of Conduct

Law Enforcement Code of Ethics

leadership

Peel, Sir Robert

police administration

principles of policing

profession

self-contained ethical leadership agent

Vollmer, August

Wilson, O. W.

discussion questions

1. Nine principles of policing commonly attributed to Sir Robert Peel arose in the early 1800s. How did these principles reflect Peel's vision of policing, and how are they relevant in policing today?

2. What contributions to modern policing were made by August Vollmer and O. W. Wilson? In your view, which of these contributions are still relevant and which are not? Why?

3. Why was the decade of the 1960s a critical period for policing and society overall in the United States? In your view, has there been another period just as critical in the last 40 years? If so, what is that period, and why do you consider it as critical as the 1960s?

4. Why did the International Association of Chiefs of Police establish codes of ethics and conduct for police officers? In your opinion, how effective are these codes?

5. Why is ethical leadership important in a police agency?

6. How do management and supervision differ from each other and from leadership? Why are they not synonymous with leadership?

7. Which administrative activities do you consider most critical for a police agency? (Consider examples of line operations, administrative support activities, and auxiliary services.) Explain your rationale.

WHAT WOULD YOU DO?
The People Are the Police

One of the most enduring and frequently quoted policing tenets attributed to Sir Robert Peel is the adage "The police are the people, and the people are the police." The truth of the saying is made real when community members play a hands-on role in making their neighborhoods safe.

In Kansas City, Missouri, a program called Aim4Peace is having some notable success. Reformed criminals spend time in the most troubled spots in the city, working with young people to defuse conflict before it can escalate. Commander Anthony Ell of the Kansas City Police Department's violent crimes division reports, "The work they're doing in that area is having an impact."

About a half-dozen reformed criminals, known as street intervention workers or violence interrupters, resolved 22 conflicts in 2008, and 14 conflicts by the middle of 2009. Kansas City's east side—previously rife with poverty, gangs, drugs, and the city's highest murder rates—is no longer listed as the most dangerous district, according to crime data.

The pilot program for Aim4Peace originated in Chicago, Illinois, and is known as CeaseFire. The program uses a number of means—including violence interrupters and community-mobilization tactics—to reduce shootings and killings in at-risk neighborhoods. The University of Illinois at Chicago, School of Public Health, initiated the Chicago Project for Violence Prevention in 1999, and used public health strategies to develop its own. Recent research confirmed that the program has worked in many targeted neighborhoods, with a 16 to 28 percent reduction in shootings in four out of six sites.

Among the tools CeaseFire uses are major public education campaigns, some of which have emphasized the importance of voting, and essential services like General Equivalency Diploma (GED) programs, substance-abuse treatment, and assistance for citizens seeking paid work or affordable child care. These services, when used, have been shown to improve the lives of all at-risk youths, including gang members.

CeaseFire has inspired contributions from all members of the community. For example, clergy have helped communicate the message of peace to church members, community leaders have done so for neighborhood residents, and citizens have spread the word to gang members and others by means of marches and prayer vigils. The universal message is that the shooting and killing must stop.

When researchers interviewed those at-risk youths who reported benefiting from the program, they found that CeaseFire had become extremely important to these young people. In particular, youths valued the ability to contact their outreach worker. In words reminiscent of a participant in Alcoholics Anonymous, these young people explained that they called or met with their outreach worker "at critical times, when they were tempted to resume taking drugs, were involved in illegal activities, or when they felt that violence was imminent."

The program has also helped the violence interrupters. Their employment with CeaseFire has provided them with meaningful work in their own troubled communities when, as ex-offenders, they might have had trouble finding work at all. They have received a second chance to build productive lives and the opportunity to help their communities, where previously they had been part of the problem (Gross, 2009; Ritter, 2009).

1. Analyze how the Aim4Peace and CeaseFire programs demonstrate the tenet "The police are the people and the people are the police."
2. If reformed violent criminals can successfully counsel at-risk persons to avoid violence, what other criminal behavior might be stemmed by the use of former offenders as counselors?

◄ Police managers and officers, discussing strategy at a weekly meeting.

2

Policing Strategies

After completing this chapter, readers should be able to:

- define what is meant by a policing strategy.
- describe the defining characteristics as well as the advantages and disadvantages of several policing strategies including: traditional policing, community policing, problem-oriented policing, team and neighborhood policing, zero-tolerance policing, intelligence-led policing, and strategic policing.
- explain how and why each strategy evolved.
- articulate how the strategies relate to one another.

Introduction

Many policing strategies have been introduced since the principles of policing attributed to Robert Peel were formulated. A **policing strategy** is an approach to delivering police services based on specific assumptions about matters

learning outcomes

such as how police and community residents should interact, what causes crime to worsen, and how technology might be leveraged. Each strategy has unique advantages and disadvantages. Some strategies are mutually exclusive, while others complement or support one another.

Regardless of which strategies a particular agency uses, most police managers agree that strategies should position an agency to deliver the best possible performance. Yet proving whether a strategy serves this purpose is difficult, in part because some outcomes of effective performance—such as crime prevention as well as quality of life for citizens—are difficult to measure. To complicate matters further, since the September 11, 2001, terrorist attacks, the increased emphasis on homeland defense has redirected police resources away from civilian policing innovations and toward counterterrorism and homeland security initiatives. As a result, many agencies now place less emphasis on policing strategies designed to prevent local crime and disorder.

In this chapter, we examine several strategies in common use today—specifically, traditional policing, community policing, problem-oriented policing, team and neighborhood policing, zero-tolerance policing, intelligence-led policing, and strategic policing. We do not strongly endorse a particular strategy; rather, we maintain that police agencies should select strategies based on their situation and the environment in which they are operating. Modern-day police must demonstrate flexibility—applying the strategies that best address their existing circumstances and being willing to shift strategies as conditions change. That being said, we give special attention to community policing in this chapter, because it appears to be the most comprehensive approach and encompasses some of the other strategies described in the chapter.

We also present the policing strategies in an order designed to demonstrate how policing has evolved—from the traditional twentieth-century, command-and-control model to progressive models including community, problem-oriented, and strategic policing. We lay out the defining characteristics of each strategy, explore how different strategies relate to one another, and consider the strategies' advantages and disadvantages.

TRADITIONAL POLICING

Traditional policing is a highly authoritarian, paramilitary strategy that first took shape in the United States during the 1950s in response to rampant corruption in the police service. To understand how this strategy evolved, we need to look further into the past—as far back as colonial America.

Policing strategy: an approach to delivering police services based on specific assumptions about matters such as how police and community residents should interact, what causes crime to worsen, and how technology might be leveraged.

Traditional policing: an authoritarian, paramilitary strategy developed to mitigate corruption in the police service.

British officer being harassed by colonials in Boston before the Revolutionary War.

THE OFFICER AND THE BARBER'S BOY.

Historical Context

In colonial America, policing was shared among citizens in a community. This approach made sense at the time, because the central British government lay an ocean away, and the colonies were governed by appointed British officials with little or no real authority. Colonial communities relied on male citizens to serve as watchmen who patrolled the streets at night to prevent and respond to criminal activity.

During the nineteenth century, as reforms attributed to Robert Peel reshaped policing in Great Britain, policing in the United States was formalized through the development of public police agencies (Cronkhite, 1995). In the early twentieth century, the focus of American policing shifted from providing service (such as traffic management and assistance) and maintaining order toward controlling crime and viewing police officers as crime fighters. Yet the police were still highly politicized; that is, subject to control by political leaders. As a result, corruption in the police service ran rampant. In response, federal, state, and city governments set out to remove politics from policing as much as possible. They encouraged a paramilitary strategy as a way to eliminate corruption. Beginning in the 1950s, police organizations became highly structured, with strict command-and-control protocols. For instance, decisions about police operations were made at the highest levels of the organization, and line-level supervisors and street officers simply complied with command directives.

Defining Characteristics

As the twentieth century progressed, police strategy in the United States became highly authoritarian. The goal of this strategy was to deliver predictability in police officers' performance. Advocates of traditional policing promote highly supervised field operations as well as prescriptive training for officers; for example, training that tells officers what to do and how to do it rather than fostering individual initiative, leadership, and creative problem solving. To combat possible corruption, they recommend an apolitical philosophy (meaning that officers should not succumb to political influence), centralized administration of police agencies, pinpointed rather than shared responsibility for results, and strong discipline of errant officers. Through these practices, proponents of traditional policing believe that officers' behavior can be made "professional" and "objective" (Goldstein, 2001; Meese & Kurz, 1993; Wilson, 1963).

A police officer places someone under arrest.

In a traditional policing environment, officers patrol an area; take action when they observe illegal activity; and respond rapidly to reported crimes, emergencies, and calls-for-service. They may also conduct follow-up investigations. Evaluations of officer performance are based on visible and quantifiable evidence of police activity, such as increasing numbers of arrests and traffic citations, and reductions in crime rates.

Traditional policing is based on the assumption that an agency can best control crime by improving the procedural and disciplined behavior of police personnel and strengthening the organization overall by creating and sustaining measurable expected performance standards. This strategy discounts the notion that the police can also serve a social function; that is, through their positive interactions with citizens, they can influence and improve the quality of life in both safe and troubled neighborhoods. In agencies using traditional policing, officers do not routinely interact with citizens unless the latter are either victims or offenders.

Advantages and Disadvantages of Traditional Policing

The traditional policing strategy has specific advantages. For example, it is predictable through a calls-for-service orientation. It is measurable through an emphasis on reports written, citations issued, and arrests completed. And it is discipline oriented. It has disadvantages as well. Specifically, it is reactive (police respond to incidents and problems after the fact) rather than proactive (police work to prevent incidents and problems from happening in the first place). Moreover, without regular interaction with community residents, officers cannot develop a sense of crime patterns. Instead, they respond to random calls-for-service, which take them to far-flung locations around the jurisdiction. Under these conditions, officers do not establish collaborative problem-solving relationships with citizens in patrol areas, and citizens do not develop any familiarity with the police personnel who patrol their neighborhoods.

A number of studies have addressed the problems associated with traditional policing. These studies were conducted by several national commissions: the President's Commission on Law Enforcement and Administration of Justice (1967), the National Advisory Commission on Civil Disorders (1968), the National Advisory Commission on the Causes and Prevention of Violence (1969), the President's Commission on Campus Unrest (1970), and the National Advisory Commission on Criminal Justice Standards and Goals (1973) (Goldstein, 1990). The studies revealed that the basic practices used in traditional policing (for example, motorized patrol, rapid response, and follow-up investigations) have little use when it comes to the substantive problems facing neighborhoods, such as drug trafficking and prostitution. In addition, the bureaucratic and autocratic nature of police organizations that emphasize the traditional strategy appears to leave citizens and officers alike unsatisfied. Citizens still fear crime, and officers lack the motivation to address chronic community problems (Couper & Lobitz, 1991; Ortmeier & Meese, 2010; Travis & Langworthy, 2008).

▎ COMMUNITY POLICING ▎

Community policing: an alternative strategy to traditional policing that emphasizes close interaction between police and the neighborhoods they serve.

Community policing reemerged in the 1980s as an alternative to traditional policing, and emphasizes close interaction between police and the neighborhoods they serve. This strategy draws extensively from the principles of policing attributed to Robert Peel.

Connections to Peel's Principles

Dissatisfied with traditional policing's emphasis on separation of police and the public, citizens and police began to collaborate in seeking solutions to chronic community problems. The modern concept of community policing was born. Yet community policing is not new. It is what Robert Peel envisioned. As Dean Esserman, chief of police in Providence, Rhode Island, stated in an interview for *Communities & Banking* in 2005:

> I worked as an intern with the New York City police department. I would have never expected that in my first month, I would be delivering a baby in a tenement with a police officer. Through this experience and others, I came to understand that the police deliver more babies than they shoot bad guys. . . . We help people deal with their landlords. We get them heat when they need it. We find children when they are lost. . . . In many ways, the police are the agency of first and last resort for people, especially people in poverty. (Esserman, 2005)

Defining Characteristics

The community policing strategy is based on the assumption that police and citizens of a specific community share the same values. Thus, community policing may work differently in different communities, depending on what those shared values are.

This diversity makes it difficult to define the strategy in formal terms. However, we can still draw some common conclusions about community policing.

In an agency that uses this strategy, policing efforts are customized to the needs of an individual community. Agency leaders emphasize decentralization of the organization; for example, by allowing line-level officers to make decisions and to help solve problems that directly affect citizens' lives in a particular neighborhood. And they recognize that crime control (law enforcement) is only one function of the police. Officers and citizens work together to articulate the problems unique to that particular community (such as graffiti, abandoned autos, or prostitution). To identify problems, some agencies use citizen surveys, wherein residents of the community define the issues they believe the police should focus on. Demographic and statistical information can also generate important insights, such as which areas in the community contain more elderly or young people, and where income and education disparities are widest. Finally, dialogues with community leaders (elected or unofficial) can produce additional information. The agency and community then develop solutions to the problems, implement them, and evaluate those solutions' effectiveness.

Community policing can take many different forms, but key elements include bonds of trust and collaboration between police and the public. Moreover, agencies that get the most value from this strategy adopt its philosophy and practical application throughout the organization, rather than merely promoting it in just one or two parts of the agency (Ortmeier & Meese, 2010). Finally, community policing occurs every time police officers meet with community members (in groups or one-on-one) to discuss and resolve community-based concerns, and every time solutions are customized to fit the unique needs and circumstances of a community.

A city police officer speaks with young people in an inner-city housing project.

With these characteristics in mind, we may define *community policing* by any or all of the following, drawn from various sources:

- A philosophy, management style, and organizational design that promotes proactive problem solving and police–community partnerships to address the causes of crime, fear of crime, and community issues (California State Department of Justice, Office of the Attorney General, 1996).

- A policing philosophy as well as a strategy that promotes community engagement, participation, and problem solving; action that leads to the discovery and implementation of solutions to community problems (Ortmeier, 1996).

- An approach to policing that focuses on crime and social disorder through the delivery of police services that include aspects of traditional law enforcement as well as prevention, problem solving, community engagement, and partnerships. The community policing model balances reactive responses to calls-for-service with proactive problem solving centered on the causes of crime and disorder. Community policing requires police and citizens to join together as partners in the course of both identifying and effectively addressing these issues (U.S. Department of Justice, Office of Community Oriented Policing Services, 2007).

Praise for Community Policing

In agencies that use the community policing strategy, both police personnel and community residents may accept that the traditional policing strategy is still valuable and appropriate under certain circumstances, such as calls-for-service in times of emergency. But they forge a more intimate relationship than they do under the traditional approach. Everyone involved understands that the police not only enforce the law, they also serve the public. Moreover, unlike traditional policing, community policing is proactive (police and community members work together to prevent problems) rather than reactive.

These characteristics create certain advantages, including meaningful communication between citizens and line officers as well as increased communication between line officers and their immediate superiors—leading to greater confidence in all agency members. People learn that their individual efforts make a significant difference. Cities that have successfully integrated the community policing strategy into their operations have reported increased job satisfaction among all levels of personnel, as well as a sense of empowerment and of being valued (U.S. Department of Justice, Office of Community Oriented Policing Services, 2007).

Criticism and Resistance

Community policing has also encountered some criticism and resistance, particularly from members of the police service itself. For example, some line officers, as well as supervisors and command staff, worry that it erodes effective police practices that took years to develop. In agencies that want to adopt this strategy but in which concerns about it have emerged, managers can emphasize the new role that line officers will play in driving the initiative. This new role includes making suggestions for improving the community. Managers can also point out the community policing makes traditional policing more effective because calls-for-service are received from the same citizens the officers regularly work with.

In some cases, excessive enthusiasm for community policing, coupled with unrealistic expectations of what an agency can accomplish through it, leads to the abandonment of the strategy. If police managers favor traditional gauges of police performance, which value quantitative measurements such as number of arrests, an agency might also decide to steer clear of community policing.

Some officers have suggested that community policing seeks to turn police into social workers who take a "soft" line on crime. On the contrary, proponents of this strategy maintain that individuals who commit crimes must bear the consequences. However, the vast majority of people with whom the police come into contact are not criminals. Even in the most crime-infested areas of a city, most residents are law-abiding citizens. Community policing recognizes that responsible citizens should not be viewed in the same light as chronic criminal offenders. In fact, the practical application of community policing involves citizens and police working together to be tougher on crime.

Another challenge presented by community policing is that it requires knowledge and skills (such as leadership) that differ from those that line officers traditionally have acquired in their training (Gaines & Miller, 2005; "Leadership Development around the States," 2009; Ortmeier & Meese, 2010; Pelfrey, 2004; Spelman & Eck, 1987). To be sure, fostering a sense of community between police representatives and residents is no small feat. The fact that police are highly trained in law enforcement tactics, wear distinctive uniforms, carry weapons, and possess the authority to enforce laws and arrest people creates real distinctions between officers and those they serve. An understandable *us* versus *them* mentality may arise, which often erodes communication between police and citizens and, in some cases, sparks civil unrest.

To combat these problems, police agency members and citizens must strive to cultivate a strong sense of community in which all share responsibility for reducing and preventing crime and disorder. As the most visible and readily available

Spotlight on Surveys

Internal and external surveys can generate insights that can help a police agency strengthen its community policing efforts. Some agencies have circulated internal surveys among their own personnel, asking for their perceptions of community policing and their recommendations for improvements. Agencies can also use external surveys to solicit comments from citizens concerning their experience with officers who respond to calls-for-service. Many such surveys ask citizens to rate responding officers on criteria including professional conduct, level of concern, effort to put the citizen at ease, helpfulness, and subject-matter expertise. Yet managers must use care when evaluating comments and data acquired through external surveys. Citizens may not necessarily respond truthfully. And some line officers might worry that management will use negative comments from the surveys as justification for denying them promotions.

representatives of government, the police can do their part by responding to non-crime concerns (if the response does not unduly restrict crime fighting) and by referring citizens to government agencies capable of addressing their concerns. Likewise, top-level city and county administrators can maintain citizens' confidence in the police by ensuring that their respective agencies respond appropriately when police forward citizen complaints or concerns to them. This kind of collaboration requires effective leadership by the police. Use of tools such as surveys can also help generate information needed to fine-tune an agency's community policing practices. (See the box "Spotlight on Surveys.")

PROBLEM-ORIENTED POLICING

Problem-oriented policing: the tactical implementation of community policing.

The **problem-oriented policing** strategy represents the tactical implementation of community policing. Through this strategy, police and local citizens identify problems facing the community and, together, develop solutions to them.

Defining Characteristics

According to the problem-oriented policing strategy, problems differ from incidents. An *incident* is a single occurrence (such as a shots-fired call) requiring a response from police. A *problem* is the occurrence of two or more incidents of a similar nature (for example, several shots-fired calls coming from the same neighborhood).

Some problems (such as a dog that keeps barking, a group of young people who regularly insult passersby, or a homeless person who frequently sleeps in front of an apartment building) do not necessarily require a police response. However, they may still have great importance for the citizens reporting them. Problem-oriented police officers and managers appreciate the significance of such issues to the community. They prioritize problems according to their importance to the community (top priority), their importance to the police agency (next-level priority), and their frequency of occurrence (next priority). They may also categorize incidents according to crime type, nature, geography (neighborhood), time, or people involved (suspects and victims). Categorizing is useful because it helps an agency identify hot spots (and times) so it can deploy resources appropriately.

Herman Goldstein, the founder of the modern concept of problem-oriented policing, suggests that police agencies interested in adopting this strategy should shift from an inward orientation (using internal evaluation criteria such as number of sworn officers) to an outward orientation (using external criteria such as the agency's impact on chronic problems in the community). Goldstein thus advocates attention to effectiveness over efficiency. Indeed, agencies using the problem-oriented policing strategy place less emphasis on statistics and more emphasis on initiatives designed to eliminate problems (Goldstein, 1990, 2001).

The SARA Problem-Solving Model

One of the most commonly used approaches in problem-oriented policing is the **SARA** (scan, analyze, respond, assess) **problem-solving model**. To use this model, police and community members progress through four steps:

1. *Scan*. Identify crime and disorder problems in the community.
2. *Analyze*. Gather and examine information about the problem (for example, offenders, victims, and time and location of occurrence).
3. *Respond*. Develop and implement solutions to the problem.
4. *Assess*. Evaluate responses' efficiency and effectiveness.

The box titled "SARA in Action" shows an example of how one police agency and community applied this model.

SARA in Action

A city neighborhood struggled with several problems on a particular block. According to community members, the problems included noise, large groups of people obstructing sidewalks, illegal drug activity, and debris discarded in the street. The local police department worked with neighborhood residents to apply the SARA problem-solving model:

1. **Scan.** Through reviewing crime reports, field intelligence reports, and citizen interviews, officers learned that the most visible contributor to all the identified problems was an open-air illegal drug market.

2. **Analyze.** While reviewing information about the drug market, police and community leaders discovered that the illegal drug activity was backed and assisted by people who owned a clothing store located across the street from a high school. Analysis also revealed that the undesirable activities began during the late morning hours and ended around midnight each day.

3. **Respond.** Citizens requested an easily recognizable, visible tool that the drug dealers, their customers, and neighbors would perceive as a proactive community–police response to the problem. To that end, the police allocated a van to the program and affixed a sign to its side panel identifying it as a police–community partnership vehicle. The sign read "ACT One," which stood for Against Crime Together, Precinct One. Neighborhood residents and business representatives refurbished and equipped the van using a community business grant. Corporate grant money was dedicated to outfit the van with video-recording equipment. The city funded insurance for the vehicle. Next, a local bus company trained and certified citizen volunteers to drive the van. The volunteers parked it in front of the drug market each day and videotaped all activity at the store and on the street in front of the store.

4. **Assess.** The illicit drug activity emanating from the clothing store ceased within three months of the ACT One initiative. Subsequently, the building was leased to a legitimate food service operation. The initiative was thus judged a success.

Drug use lends itself to the SARA problem-solving model.

Leadership on the job
Policing Strategies and Social Services

Consider these scenarios:

Scenario 1: A Social Services Approach

In 2007, San Francisco police officers began collaborating with social workers to fight so-called quality-of-life crimes (such as prostitution, loitering, minor drug offenses, and panhandling) that were disturbing the peace in the city. The solution the collaboration generated called for police to apprehend homeless people for infractions such as littering, panhandling, and obstructing sidewalks in tourist areas, and to escort them to facilities that provided shelter and other services.

Scenario 2: A Law Enforcement Approach

At ever-earlier ages, young people in a New York State community were joining gangs. For these often neglected youngsters, gangs provided the structure, sense of belonging, purpose, power, and role models they were hungry for. Social services designed to lure youngsters away from the gang lifestyle (such as after-school programs) had generated little change. The community began adopting law enforcement strategies such as court injunctions for offenders and multijurisdictional task forces that engaged in gang suppression activities over a wide geographic area. These efforts seemed to bear fruit: fewer young people joined gangs.

1. Do you think police officers are also social workers? Why or why not?

2. Is provision of social services an appropriate role for the police? Explain your answer.

3. Can a traditional policing strategy (such as a focus on law enforcement) eliminate gangs by itself? Explain your opinion.

4. Are the two policing strategies represented in the previous scenarios mutually exclusive? Why or why not?

Strengths and Challenges of Problem-Oriented Policing

The problem-oriented policing strategy has been used to resolve a wide variety of specific community problems, including street prostitution (Scott, 2001), graffiti (Lamm Weisel, 2002), shoplifting (Clarke, 2002), and financial crimes against elderly people (Johnson, 2003). It has also been used to address crime and disorder problems affecting broad territories (Skogan, 2005).

But problem-oriented policing also presents some challenges. Like many other progressive strategies, it requires police officers to demonstrate skills that they would not typically acquire through basic and in-service training programs. These skills include engaging citizen groups, thinking critically, analyzing situations, communicating effectively, and assessing the usefulness of responses to problems. Police managers and officers can gain such skills through leadership development programs (Meese & Ortmeier, 2004; Skogan et al., 1999).

TEAM POLICING AND NEIGHBORHOOD POLICING

Team policing and neighborhood policing are examples of community policing in action. Both involve use of police officer teams to address issues and to help residents resolve issues on a small scale. The success of these practices hinges on the quality of the personal encounters between the officers and residents. In fact, in some areas where there is little reduction in actual crime, positive interactions between the police and the public can still markedly decrease residents' *fear* of crime.

Team policing and neighborhood policing: examples of how community policing may be implemented to address problems on a small scale.

Defining Characteristics

In *team policing*, teams usually comprise a supervisor, several patrol officers, a detective, and a subject-matter expert (for instance, an expert on gangs or drugs). The team may be assigned to a specific area with duties based on the problems identified through the SARA model. Through *neighborhood policing*, police work directly with residents of a small geographic area. Officers educate residents on how to reduce opportunities for particular types of crime in their area. *Neighborhood watch programs* are the most visible and widespread example of such policing. Through these programs, residents and police meet regularly to discuss concerns, crime prevention strategies, and the status of crime in the neighborhood. At the same time, police officers acquire information from residents about

Neighborhood Crime Watch sign.

> ## Example of Neighborhood Policing
> An elderly woman lives in a troubled neighborhood in New York State. She maintains that, owing to her continual conversations with the sector police captain and crime prevention officers, she has actively helped address problems with drug dealing and prostitution by asking the police to concentrate on problem properties and landlords. She has provided immediate feedback on the effect of any police actions toward landlords. And during police–community meetings, she has frequently noted that she has the captain's cell phone number and uses it freely.

activities and changes in the neighborhood (Jones-Brown & Terry, 2004; Ortmeier & Meese, 2010).

An Assessment of Team and Neighborhood Policing

The key advantage of team and neighborhood policing is that uniformed officers, detectives, or investigators, along with crime prevention officers, work as partners to solve crime. They actively share information on incidents of crime or crime patterns in specific neighborhoods. Thus the solutions they develop are informed by a detailed base of knowledge. Moreover, police personnel actively engage neighborhood residents and citizens in developing solutions and preventing crime. As a result, community members feel a sense of ownership of those solutions—which increases their commitment to them. (See the box "Example of Neighborhood Policing.")

One disadvantage to team and neighborhood policing is that decentralized police teams may isolate themselves from the larger organization and focus directly on their respective neighborhood policing area. This can result in a lack of communication between decentralized teams with respect to the crime problems, patterns, and initiatives the teams are working on. With lack of communication, teams cannot learn from one another through knowledge sharing.

ZERO-TOLERANCE POLICING

Zero-tolerance policing:
a strategy based on the assumption that full enforcement of the laws will ultimately decrease crime and disorder.

Zero-tolerance policing is based on the assumption that full enforcement of the laws will lead to a decrease in crime and disorder. In some areas, this strategy is referred to as order-maintenance policing.

Defining Characteristics

Zero-tolerance policing diminishes the discretionary authority of police officers (Henry, 2002). That is, advocates of this strategy expect that virtually every crime, infraction, or other violation of the law observed by an officer will result in an arrest or the issuance of a citation. In addition, zero-tolerance policing supposes that underenforcement or nonenforcement of laws related to low-level crimes and

Graffiti, abandoned buildings, and vandalized property contribute to neighborhood deterioration that can lead to increases in crime. The broken windows theory supposes that poor enforcement of minor offenses leads to more serious crime.

violations spawns complacency on the part of offenders and officers and thus establishes an environment in which serious crime can flourish.

Roots in the Broken Windows Theory

Zero tolerance is an outgrowth of the *broken windows theory* developed by James Q. Wilson and George Kelling (1989). According to these theorists, abandoned structures, graffiti, unkempt landscapes, and overall neighborhood deterioration are associated with increases in crime. Wilson and Kelling postulated that in communities where police fail to control such minor criminal offenses as graffiti and vandalism, public disorder reigns—which increases the likelihood that people will commit more serious crimes. Wilson and Kelling suggested that police can restore order by enforcing laws related to minor offenses.

Questions about Zero-Tolerance Policing

Zero-tolerance policing may work as Wilson and Kelling anticipated, though observers have debated this since the strategy was promoted in New York City in the early 1990s. The NYC police used an approach called CompStat (which stands for "computer statistics" or "comparative statistics")—including computer-enabled crime statistics—to identify where and when specific types of crime and disorder problems were happening. Mayor Rudy Giuliani held police commanders accountable for developing and executing effective solutions to problems. And police cracked down on minor violations such as public drunkenness, prostitution, panhandling, and loitering. Crime rates in the city decreased dramatically, though some people question whether these decreases resulted directly from the zero-tolerance practices or from some other forces not related to the strategy. (See the box "Ethics in Action: Zero Tolerance in New York City.")

ETHICS IN ACTION

Zero Tolerance in New York City

Crime statistics suggest that zero-tolerance policing in New York City during the 1990s significantly reduced the crime rate. However, critics of the zero-tolerance policing strategy argue that the decreasing crime rate in New York City simply echoed declines in crime trends that were occurring throughout the nation during the latter part of the twentieth century. Critics also warn that zero-tolerance policing may lead to discrimination. Targets of the strategy often include young people and persons who are mentally ill or homeless, largely individuals who are destitute with few advocates.

1. If evidence suggests that discriminatory law enforcement exists in some cases (for example, the police target homeless persons because of their status), how might such discrimination be prevented?

2. Can homeless persons and other "street people" be motivated to assist in the prevention of crime and disorder? If so, how?

Zero-tolerance policing and saturation patrol were used in New York City in the 1990s.

One major disadvantage of zero-tolerance policing is that it can destroy progress that an agency has made in implementing community policing initiatives. Zero-tolerance strategies can distance police from citizens, who may feel victimized by police intolerance of minor infractions. Residents often complain that they are not familiar with (and thus cannot relate to) the officers patrolling their neighborhoods (Gau & Brunson, 2010; Hosang, 2006; Hunter & Barker, 2011; Pollard, 1998). Research also demonstrates that saturation patrol tactics often associated with zero tolerance do not reduce crime. They merely displace it. Offenders simply relocate to areas where zero tolerance is not employed (Eterno & Silverman, 2010; Marshall, 1999; Silverman, 2001).

INTELLIGENCE-LED POLICING

Intelligence-led policing integrates problem-oriented policing and zero-tolerance policing. Through this strategy, police continuously analyze incidents that occurred in the recent past (typically within the last few weeks) and develop action plans for addressing the problem.

Defining Characteristics

Agencies that emphasize the intelligence-led policing strategy may use CompStat, including Geographic Information Systems, or GIS (such as mapping software) and frequent meetings to analyze the resulting data. (See Chapter 4 for more detailed

Intelligence-led policing: a strategy that integrates problem-oriented policing and zero-tolerance policing through continuous analysis of information about problems and development of action plans to resolve problems.

Geographic Information System (GIS) technology is used by police agencies to identify, analyze, and respond quickly to reported incidents of crime and disorder. GIS management systems are used to pinpoint responsibility and accountability for police efficiency, effectiveness, and overall performance.

Frederick Police Department — SpiresGIS Crime Map — Part I Offenses

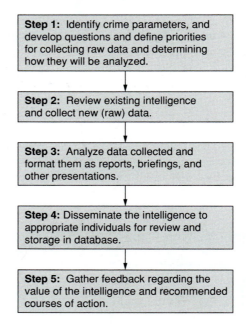

figure 2-1 Five Steps to Intelligence-Led Policing

Step 1: Identify crime parameters, and develop questions and define priorities for collecting raw data and determining how they will be analyzed.

Step 2: Review existing intelligence and collect new (raw) data.

Step 3: Analyze data collected and format them as reports, briefings, and other presentations.

Step 4: Disseminate the intelligence to appropriate individuals for review and storage in database.

Step 5: Gather feedback regarding the value of the intelligence and recommended courses of action.

coverage of CompStat.) CompStat aims to reduce crime through a specific series of actions: gathering of accurate and timely intelligence through direct observation, surveys, and other sources; use of effective tactics such as surveillance, saturation patrol, and community partnerships; rapid deployment of personnel and resources including task forces and teams; and relentless follow-up and assessment of performance outcomes such as citizen satisfaction, police response time, and offender recidivism (Shane, 2007).

Obtaining and processing the information that makes intelligence-led policing a possibility is a cyclical, five-step process. (See Figure 2-1.)

Pros and Cons of Intelligence-Led Policing

One great strength of intelligence-led policing is that it gives agencies an opportunity to intercept troubling trends early. Two or more incidents of a similar nature (for example, several burglaries in a particular part of town) can indicate a trend toward a major problem. This policing strategy can also be implemented simultaneously with other strategies, such as traditional and community policing.

The challenge presented by this strategy is that it demands a high level of technological sophistication to gather and analyze detailed, timely, and accurate information. It also requires daily accountability for demonstrating results, and strong partnerships between the police and the community. Unit commanders must be available on a daily basis to present incident data from the previous 24 hours. In addition, they must know about event trends emerging during the past few weeks. Finally, commanders must have a detailed plan for addressing problems (Burgess, Giblin, & Shafer, 2010; Dabney, 2010; Martin, 2008).

Strategic Policing Example

In one city, prostitutes worked their trade on a busy street in the northwestern corner of the city. For years, police had used a strategy of arresting prostitutes and charging their customers with a violation. But then the police chief, district attorney, and a community-action group developed a new strategy: convict men charged with patronizing prostitutes with a misdemeanor crime rather than just a violation. The more serious charge and conviction were the first to be handed down in 20 years (Veale, 2009). The new strategy stemmed from stakeholders' understanding of the current problem and legal mandates, research into past initiatives' effectiveness, and the decision to tackle the problem of prostitution from a new angle: the "johns" who frequented prostitutes.

STRATEGIC POLICING

Strategic policing is an ingredient of community policing and seeks to integrate proven private- and public-sector organizational management techniques—such as SWOT (strengths, weaknesses, opportunities, threats) analysis and strategic planning—with public policing strategy.

Defining Characteristics

Agencies interested in adopting strategic policing start by establishing goals informed by crime and disorder trends, directives from a chief of police or mayor,

Strategic policing: an approach that seeks to integrate proven private- and public-sector management techniques with public policing strategy.

Detroit, Michigan, Deputy Police Chief Joyce Motley speaks about crime and police issues to residents of Detroit's Morningside neighborhood during the community group's monthly meeting.

or community input. The agency then develops strategies for achieving those goals—strategies that are influenced by the priorities of key stakeholders such as community residents, local government leaders, and area businesses. (See the box "Strategic Policing Example.")

Strategic policing can be an element of community policing—which (as we have seen) allocates police resources in accordance with community priorities. Community policing emphasizes high visibility of police in the neighborhood, rapport with the community, fewer arrests due to the more proactive (preventive) role assumed by the police, and decentralization of the police organizational command structure. Strategic policing calls for visionary incorporation of established police operations into a broader mission focused on peacekeeping and the prevention of crime and disorder (Oliver, 2008; Scheider, 2008).

Requirements for Effective Strategic Policing

To use strategic policing, an agency must develop plans, identify key performance objectives and outcome indicators, and make effective and efficient delivery of services a top priority. It must also establish strong alliances with the community (for instance, through attending neighborhood meetings, establishing police and community interaction committees, and conducting community assessments of police services) to address disorder, prosecute criminals, and prevent crime. All employees should be involved in strategic planning because they are key stakeholders in the organization and create public value for the agency. Employees understand and can articulate the agency's key strengths and weaknesses as well as its formal and informal mandates. Moreover, the agency must shift from a culture of reaction and blind compliance to one of self-motivation, empowerment, and neighborhood ownership of problems and solutions. Everything within the agency—individual and

Los Angeles Mayor Antonio Villaraigosa (L) and LAPD Chief William Bratton discuss a citywide gang suppression strategy with police officers, managers, and the news media in 2007.

Spotlight on SWOT Analysis

SWOT analysis can help a policing agency focus on the right problem and select the right solutions—thus creating value for the community it serves. Through SWOT analysis, agency personnel assess the following:

- **Strengths:** the agency's existing resources and capabilities. In a police agency, strengths may include reputation in the community and highly trained personnel.

- **Weaknesses:** an agency's vulnerabilities. These may include reduced financial resources due to budget cuts or high attrition of personnel.

- **Opportunities:** changes occurring outside the agency that present possibilities for enhancing the agency's efficiency or effectiveness. Examples might include a new software application that makes it easier for the agency to track crime-trend data, or heightened interest among community residents in forging partnerships with police officers.

- **Threats:** developments occurring outside the agency that may impede its smooth operation or its ability to serve the community. For instance, the city council votes to reduce the number of authorized personnel within the agency.

Through SWOT analysis, police managers combine strengths and opportunities to move the agency forward in a productive direction. By recognizing the presence of threats and weaknesses, agency management can take steps to mitigate or eliminate the vulnerabilities (Bryson & Alston, 2005).

team objectives, rewards, training initiatives, communications—must align behind agreed-upon strategies.

Like other progressive policing strategies, strategic policing suggests that police officers are more than first responders and that they should be evaluated on more than just how many arrests they make or how complete their reports are. Though number of arrests and completeness of reports may be important, focusing only on these performance metrics will not encourage officers to seek ownership of a strategic plan.

Strategic policing requires managers and employees to understand strategic plans, their agency's goals, performance measures used, underlying causes of problems, and the timelines for implementation of strategic initiatives. Managers and employees may also need to gain familiarity with some tools commonly used by the private sector, including **SWOT analysis**, whereby they take stock of their agency's internal strengths and weaknesses as well as the external opportunities and threats facing the agency. (See the box "Spotlight on SWOT Analysis.")

Pluses and Minuses of Strategic Policing

Like other policing strategies, strategic policing has its pluses and minuses. On the plus side, it enables an agency to fulfill its mission, realize its mandates, and adapt to ever-changing community concerns—thus improving its effectiveness. This strategy also enhances efficiency by enabling an agency to focus limited resources on key priorities—thus extracting more value from those resources. And by prompting agency leaders to define goals and evaluate progress toward those goals, the strategy fosters learning.

On the minus side, strategic policing agency managers and employees need to master the skills of strategic planning and thinking. Developing these skills takes time and investment—resources that can be in short supply for some agencies.

summary

- **Traditional Policing.** This strategy usually employs an authoritarian style of management. Police officers are controlled and directed to complete tasks. The model assumes that managers know best, that rapid response to events is always necessary and effective, and that objective performance measurements present an unbiased view of police productivity.

- **Community Policing.** Community policing encourages partnerships and suggests a visible interaction between the police and the public to produce desired results. This strategy demands a shift in the police management paradigm from an authoritarian to a participatory model. The shift requires philosophical adjustments within the organization as well as an attitude change on the part of the public.

- **Problem-Oriented Policing.** Problem-oriented policing, the tactical implementation of community policing, is used to address crime and quality-of-life concerns within a community. Problem-solving methods, including the SARA model, require an expansion of police performance measurements as well as police training in leadership, community interaction strategies, and problem solving.

- **Team Policing and Neighborhood Policing.** These strategies are examples of community policing implemented to solve problems on a small scale.

- **Zero-Tolerance Policing.** This strategy is an outgrowth of the *broken windows* theory, which holds that minor criminal offenses such as graffiti and vandalism increase the likelihood that people will commit more serious crimes. According to this strategy, police can restore order by enforcing laws related to minor offenses.

- **Intelligence-Led Policing.** This strategy integrates problem-oriented policing and zero-tolerance policing. Through this strategy, police continuously analyze incidents that occurred in the recent past (typically within the last few weeks) and develop action plans for addressing the problem. Agencies that emphasize this policing strategy may use CompStat.

- **Strategic Policing.** This strategy is an ingredient of community policing and seeks to integrate proven private- and public-sector organizational management techniques (such as SWOT analysis and strategic planning) with public policing strategy.

- **SWOT Analysis.** An extensive analysis of an agencies strengths, weaknesses, opportunities, and threats used to evaluate the organization's inclination and ability to succeed.

key terms

discussion questions

1. What are the basic principles underlying the traditional policing strategy?
2. Describe the basic tenets of community policing. In what respects does this strategy reflect the principles of policing attributed to Robert Peel?
3. How does problem-oriented policing relate to community policing?
4. How do team and neighborhood policing work, and how do these strategies relate to community policing?
5. Describe zero-tolerance and intelligence-led policing and explain how they may complement each other.
6. Describe the defining characteristics of strategic policing. Why is strategy important to policing?
7. Can different policing strategies be applied simultaneously in the same neighborhood? In the same city? Why or why not?

WHAT WOULD YOU DO?
Using Problem-Oriented Policing to Combat Prostitution

A city experienced an increase in incidents of prostitution. In conjunction with community leaders, a local police agency captain developed a plan and led an effort to abate prostitution in a neighborhood that had businesses and residents. The captain's goal was to mitigate prostitution's negative effects on people, property values, and business income. Additional related goals included reducing street-level drug activity, eliminating the unwelcome visible presence of prostitutes and their customers, and improving prostitutes' lives.

The agency selected the problem-oriented policing strategy to implement the plan. It had long used the traditional policing strategy, through which it deployed a large number of personnel to identify problems, saturate areas

(*continued*)

affected by a particular problem, disperse or arrest offenders, and redeploy resources to the next problem needing attention. Agency managers and officers hoped that use of the problem-oriented strategy would produce long-term solutions to the identified problems, as opposed to short-term abatement.

The new plan called for solutions to public health problems related to prostitution (such as sexually transmitted diseases, HIV/AIDS, and drug addiction of prostitutes and their customers); solutions to prostitutes' personal safety problems (such as the risk of assault from clients); and solutions to clients' problems (including the risk of being robbed during encounters with prostitutes).

The neighborhood in question was disintegrating overall. Prostitutes were living in minimally acceptable or abandoned houses, and many were addicted to drugs. Property values were declining, stores and restaurants closing, and building owners and businesses abandoning their properties. Many law-abiding residents had fled to safer neighborhoods. Some simply abandoned their homes, leaving property taxes unpaid and mortgages in default. Slumlords snapped up some of these homes for below-market prices. People moving into the neighborhood openly consumed alcohol on the street, left trash in their yards and on the sidewalks, played radios at top volume at all hours of the day and night, and intimidated local residents.

A leadership team consisting of a police officer and a citizen joined with a neighborhood group to develop solutions to these problems. City court judges agreed that arrested prostitutes and clients would be required to submit to mandatory screening for sexually transmitted diseases. In addition, all drug-related arrestees received an offer of drug court instead of jail time. The prostitutes' clients were also sentenced to participate in weekend community projects and education programs.

Judges agreed to stop allowing unconditional releases for prostitution-related offenders. Meanwhile, citizens agreed to support new legislation designed to increase penalties for prostitution, to monitor arrests for prostitution-related offenses, and to provide social services (such as drug-treatment programs) for prostitutes before and after they were arrested. Local clergy led workshops for prostitutes that addressed their health and spiritual issues, and that encouraged them to obtain high school diplomas.

Did the initiative pay dividends? A reduction in prostitution- and drug-related crimes over one year and evidence that the neighborhood was recovering (including lack of observable prostitution activity and positive feedback from community residents) suggest that the project was a relative success.

1. Do you consider the policing strategy adopted appropriate in this case? Why or why not?

2. Did the strategy used reflect any of the principles of policing attributed to Robert Peel? If so, which ones?

3. Consider all the strategies in addition to problem-oriented policing that you read about in this chapter. Which of these additional strategies would you also consider using to address the issues described in this case? Explain your choice(s).

3

◀ The U.S. population is becoming increasingly diverse.

Challenges Facing Police Organizations

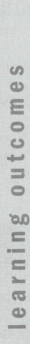

After completing this chapter, readers should be able to:

- explain how the U.S. population's demographic makeup is changing and what challenges these changes pose for police agencies.

- compare the three types of political dynamics police agencies must navigate (intra-agency, interagency, and intergovernment) and describe strategies for navigating each type.

- define *political correctness* and analyze its advantages and disadvantages for a police agency.

- trace the evolution of the police role and explain the multiple aspects of the role today.

- define *bias-based policing, misuse of force,* and *police misconduct,* and examine strategies for combating them.

- appraise the technological advances affecting policing today and explain how police agencies can leverage them.
- assess the forces resulting in resource constraints for police agencies and name ways in which agencies can surmount these constraints.
- explain terrorism's impact on policing and describe systems and processes that the U.S. Department of Homeland Security has put in place to enable police agencies to help combat terrorism.
- describe how the National Incident Management System and the Standardized Emergency Management System work.

Introduction

U.S. society has experienced massive changes over the past several decades—including an increase in ethnic and cultural diversity, rapid advances in information and communication technologies, and intensifying feelings of vulnerability owing to the September 11, 2001, terrorist attacks and a volatile economy. These changes have presented new challenges to police organizations. For example, to communicate with and serve citizens in increasingly diverse communities, officers must familiarize themselves with a broad range of cultural norms and perspectives. To extract value from technology, police personnel need to master new information technology (IT) tools and systems. And to protect the people they serve as well as ease the public's fears, police must coordinate their efforts with an expanding circle of public safety organizations, including the U.S. Department of Homeland Security. All of this takes time, and most of it costs money—in an age when many police organizations are operating under tighter-than-ever budgetary constraints.

Surmounting these and other challenges also requires an agility and openness to change that many police organizations find difficult to achieve. Indeed, as a rule, governmental agencies tend to lag behind private-sector entities when it comes to altering their operations and processes to stay ahead of new developments and deliver high-quality services to their constituents. This inability and unwillingness to change may stem in part from the complex bureaucratic structure and culture of entitlement that characterize many public service organizations: It is difficult to nudge any large, complicated organization in a new direction. It becomes even more daunting when managers and employees in the organization see no need to change, because they feel (understandably) that their jobs are secure and that their organization will continue to exist as it always has.

Yet, in today's increasingly cost-conscious and demanding society, even the most seemingly enduring public service organizations risk going out of existence if they cannot show that they are delivering the best possible service in return for the tax revenues they receive. Police agencies are no exception, and they cannot afford to look the other way when confronted with change. A good first step toward strengthening their ability to change is to understand the challenges confronting today's policing organizations—each of which requires change.

In this chapter, we examine seven such challenges: increased diversity, complex political dynamics, the changing role of police agencies, the need for ethical leadership, technological advances, resource constraints, and terrorism. We consider the ramifications of such challenges for policing organizations and explore ideas for surmounting each challenge.

INCREASED DIVERSITY

The United States has long welcomed people of all faiths, ethnicities, and cultural backgrounds. Such diversity has brought a richness of perspectives, skills, and cultural traditions to American society. Yet diversity can also spark tensions, when people from different religious, ethnic, gender, lifestyle, or cultural backgrounds have difficulty understanding one another. Unfortunately, this lack of understanding can spawn mistrust, stereotyping, prejudice, and even hatred between people. Such problems have been hugely exacerbated by the 9/11 terrorist attacks, which have heightened tensions particularly between non-Muslims and Muslims not only within the United States but also around the globe. (See the box "Jihad or Crusade?")

The in-depth report on diversity and the projected race and ethnic changes in the United States for the years 1995 to 2050 (U.S. Census Bureau, 1999) point to the need for police agencies to learn about other cultural backgrounds and understand the perspectives and possible conflicts between races and ethnic values. Table 3-1

table 3-1 Projected Changes in U.S. Population: 1995–2050
(Millions Resident Population)

YEAR	TOTAL	MINORITY	NONMINORITY (NON-HISPANIC WHITE)	Race				Hispanic Origin	
				WHITE	BLACK	AMERICAN INDIAN ESKIMO AND ALEUT	ASIAN AND PACIFIC ISLANDER	HISPANIC	NON-HISPANIC
1995	262.8	69.3	193.6	218.1	33.1	2.2	9.4	26.9	235.9
2000	274.6	77.6	197.1	225.5	35.5	2.4	11.2	31.4	243.3
2005	286.0	86.2	199.8	232.5	37.7	2.6	13.2	36.1	249.9
2010	297.7	95.3	202.4	239.6	40.1	2.8	15.3	41.1	256.6
2015	310.1	105.1	205.0	247.2	42.6	2.9	17.4	46.7	263.4
2020	322.7	115.3	207.4	254.9	45.1	3.1	19.7	52.7	270.1
2025	335.0	125.9	209.1	262.2	47.5	3.3	22.0	58.9	276.1
2030	346.9	136.9	210.0	269.0	50.0	3.5	24.3	65.6	281.3
2035	358.5	148.4	210.1	275.5	52.5	3.7	26.8	72.0	285.8
2040	370.0	160.4	209.6	281.7	55.1	3.9	29.2	80.2	289.8
2045	381.7	172.9	208.8	288.0	57.8	4.1	31.8	88.1	293.6
2050	393.9	186.0	207.9	294.6	60.6	4.4	34.4	96.5	297.4

Source: U.S. Census Bureau, 1996, *Population Projections of the United States by Age, Sex, Race, and Hispanic Origin: 1995 to 2050,* by Jennifer Cheeseman Day, Current Population Reports, P25-1130. Washington, DC.

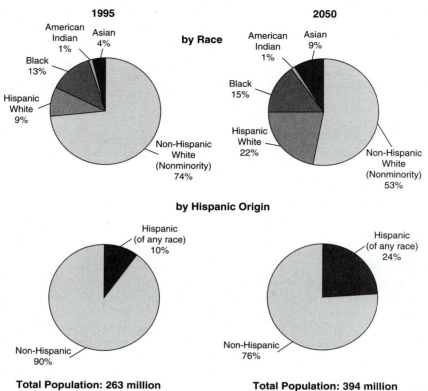

figure 3-1 Projected Shifts in Ratios of Nonminority to Minority Populations

by Race

1995

American Indian 1%
Asian 4%
Black 13%
Hispanic White 9%
Non-Hispanic White (Nonminority) 74%

2050

American Indian 1%
Asian 9%
Black 15%
Hispanic White 22%
Non-Hispanic White (Nonminority) 53%

by Hispanic Origin

Hispanic (of any race) 10%
Non-Hispanic 90%

Total Population: 263 million

Hispanic (of any race) 24%
Non-Hispanic 76%

Total Population: 394 million

Source: U.S. Census Bureau, 1999.

highlights the projections of populations in the United States from the year 1995 to 2050. Particularly important in the table is the growth of the Hispanic population relative to non-Hispanic populations.

Figure 3-1 sheds additional light on demographic changes in the United States. It shows the percent distribution of the U.S. population and highlights projections of population by race. Note that in 1995, the nonminority population represented 74 percent of the nation's total population, and minority populations represented 26 percent of the total population. In 2050, the nonminority population is expected to shrink to 53 percent of the total, while minority populations will constitute 47 percent of the total. What is the implication for police agencies? The demographic makeup of the communities they serve—as well as the personnel they hire and develop—will grow ever more diverse.

Efforts to Foster Tolerance

U.S. lawmakers have tried to encourage tolerance and appreciation of differences through such initiatives as affirmative action and hate-crime legislation. And many schools as well as organizations in the private and public sector offer diversity

Jihad or Crusade?

Since the 9/11 terrorist attacks, the word *jihad* has come to hold a sinister meaning for most people in the United States. But what exactly does the word mean?

Experts agree that from the earliest days of Islam, *jihad* referred to a holy war. According to some interpretations of the Koran, those who fight in holy wars against nonbelievers will be richly rewarded, and those who do not fight will be punished severely in the afterlife. Jihad allows Muslims (those who practice Islam) to command good and combat evil in the name of Allah, or God (Gould, 2005).

Today, most Muslims do not wish to fight in a holy war against Western civilization. However, a few may wish to heed the call to jihad because of the larger implication that Allah requires it and will reward it after death.

Some experts also point out a parallel between Islamic jihad and the early Christian Crusades. In the year 1095, the pope declared that all European Christians must embark on a crusade to liberate Jerusalem, which at that time was under Muslim control. In return, the Christians would receive absolution for all of their sins. More than 60,000 people answered the call and they killed thousands of people. By 1099, they had conquered Jerusalem, only to lose it in 1187 to the legendary Saladin, the warrior sultan of Egypt and Syria. Because of his lenient treatment of his defeated foes, Saladin was a respected Muslim figure throughout Europe and the Middle East (Phillips, 2009).

After the Crusades, various Western leaders attempted to use the idea of a crusade as justification for armed conflict with anyone not of their own religious or political persuasion. Even as late as in 1936, General Francisco Franco of Spain drew on his affiliation with the Catholic Church to legitimize his "crusading" fight against rebels. And during World War I, the U.S. government produced a war film titled *Pershing's Crusaders*, about General John "Black Jack" Pershing.

The al-Qaeda leader Osama bin Laden called on all Muslims to fight against the "Judeo-Crusader alliance" against Islam, and the 9/11 attacks were one result of this call. Former U.S. president George W. Bush said in his response to 9/11: "The United States is presenting a clear choice to every nation: Stand with the civilized world, or stand with the terrorists" (Phillips, 2009).

The lesson? Whether it is called "jihad" or "crusade," conflict among Jews, Christians, and Muslims has a long history. During times such as today, when tensions between these religions has escalated to unprecedented heights, citizens and police alike are finding it increasingly difficult to appreciate even innocuous differences between Judaism, Christianity, and Islam.

education and training to foster cross-cultural understanding. Clearly, Americans are committed to encouraging the acceptance and tolerance of differences among people.

International movements reflect a similar vision. According to the United Nations, all people are entitled to basic human rights, which include freedom from genocide, slavery, and torture, as well as the right to religious tolerance. The UN maintains that people are also entitled to a cultural identity—as long as that culture does not infringe on any basic human rights. For example, suppose a man has grown up in a country where it is common and accepted for men to beat their wives and children. If this man and his family immigrate to a country (such as the United States) where such behavior violates a basic human right, the man cannot express this aspect of his culture without being subject to that host nation's law. Rather, the right to a cultural identity includes engaging in any activities that do not violate human rights—such as enjoying art and food ways notable in one's culture, practicing one's religion, and celebrating holidays meaningful in one's culture (Adler & Proctor, 2011; Ayton-Shenker, 1995).

Challenges for Police

For police, cultural diversity can present numerous challenges. For example, immigrants who come from a country where police are tools used by powerful rulers to control the population may be unwilling to report crimes against them or to be interviewed as witnesses to a crime. This unwillingness makes it difficult for police detectives and investigators to do their work. Officers serving a jurisdiction simmering with racial or ethnic conflict may be called on frequently to intervene in violent clashes between groups. And police personnel who work in the same agency and who come from different cultural backgrounds may harbor prejudicial attitudes toward one another, preventing them from collaborating effectively.

These challenges are daunting, but to protect and serve effectively, police must surmount them. Education and training can help. With cultural diversity training that begins in the academy and continues through in-service training, police can learn about the cultural differences among the citizens living in the jurisdiction they serve. For example, they can gain familiarity with citizens' attitudes toward and expectations of police and with cultural norms governing behaviors, such as

A Tucson, Arizona, police officer questions a woman following a domestic disturbance.

how much eye contact people make with authority figures. They can even acquire a working knowledge of another language, so they can converse with citizens themselves rather than through interpreters.

However, in the area of cultural diversity (as in so many other aspects of police work), there is no substitute for personal contact between citizens and officers. Direct interaction with actual members of the community (for instance, through foot patrols and community policing efforts) are invaluable for assuring citizens that the officers in their neighborhoods know and respect them. Thus assured, citizens are much more open to collaborating with police in making their streets safer (Hunter & Barker, 2011; Ortmeier, 2006; Shusta, Levine, Wong, Olson, & Harris, 2011).

COMPLEX POLITICAL DYNAMICS

In addition to increasing diversity, police agencies face a challenge in the form of complex political dynamics that managers and officers must navigate in their everyday work. These dynamics unfold in three realms: intra-agency (politics within a police agency), interagency (politics between a police agency and other public safety agencies, such as police and fire departments and emergency medical teams), and intergovernment (politics between a police agency and other government entities, e.g., sanitation, public works, and officials).

While police managers and officials may wish that they could do their work unhindered by political maneuvering, they cannot. Politics are a fact of life in all organizations, and knowing how to navigate the political terrain to achieve important goals is an essential skill for everyone—whether in a government agency or a for-profit corporation.

For most police agencies, political considerations in all three realms become most visible during the budgeting process. In this process, constituencies within the agency, neighborhood groups, and competing governmental departments are striving to claim their share of an ever-smaller financial "pie" available to public agencies. Agency executives who have the most political clout and who prove the most persuasive will generally gain the most funding for the coming fiscal year (Ortmeier, 2006). (See Chapter 5 for a more in-depth discussion of the budget process.) Therefore, it is important that police personnel understand the intra-agency, interagency, and intergovernment political dynamics they will need to cope with during budgeting season.

To navigate all three types of politics, leaders must excel at three essential skills:

- **Astuteness.** Leaders must recognize other individuals' attitudes and interpret their body language and speech patterns to determine how best to introduce subjects needing discussion.
- **Networking.** Leaders must have the ability to form mutually beneficial relationships, known as networking, enabling them to create alliances with all types of people, whether colleagues at a police agency, individuals from another agency, or people from large government agencies. It is through alliances that work of any type gets done.
- **Sincerity.** Through sincerity, leaders demonstrate a genuine desire to do what is best for the agency and its personnel as well as the community. While sincerity can be feigned, other astute people will be able to sense a lack of

sincerity on the part of a leader. Ethics demands that leaders be sincere and credible, and be able to deliver on the promises they make (Orrick, 2008).

With these three skills in mind, let's now take a closer look at the three types of political dynamics police personnel must navigate.

Intra-Agency Politics

Intra-agency politics: political dynamics taking place within a police organization.

Intra-agency politics manifest themselves in the working relationships between individuals, units, and sections (such as investigative services, patrol services, and administrative groups) within a police agency. These dynamics are also expressed in the negotiations that take place between those in authority within an agency over issues such as who should be in charge of which activities or responsibilities or what goals the agency should be striving toward (Champoux, 2000; Dabney, 2010).

When it comes to intra-agency politics, many people believe that they should be able to do their job without having to "get political" or "play power games." But as we noted earlier, politics are unavoidable in any organization—especially in a police agency. Why? Police agencies answer to elected officials who represent the people served by the agency. They are also funded primarily by taxes paid by the public. Therefore, politics cannot be separated from policing. Managers and officers alike must learn how to exert political influence within their agency to get work done and deliver the service that citizens expect.

Exerting Political Influence Exerting political influence means using one's strengths, relationships, or personality to effect personal or organizational change (de Janasz, Dowd, & Schneider, 2006). For example:

- **Using one's strengths:** Ricardo, a patrol captain, is often observed driving a radio car, responding to support line-level officers. Most officers refer to Ricardo as a "cop's cop," one who is unafraid to assist officers in the field. Ricardo's participatory leadership and communication style garner tremendous support from front-line officers and police union officials alike.

- **Using one's relationships:** Deborah, a police detective, periodically brings pastries into the office. On those days, she delivers a pastry in person to Charlie, the records administrator working in an isolated and remote office near the rear of the building. Most people at the agency pay attention to Charlie only when they need something from him. But by treating Charlie kindly, Deborah has established a human relationship with him. When she needs him to retrieve specific records for her, he often fulfills her request before turning to requests from others in the agency.

- **Using one's personality:** Akim, a police sergeant, believes that his agency should adopt a new way of scheduling use of fleet vehicles, to better ensure that vehicles are available when needed. Thanks to Akim's long track record of trustworthiness, his demonstrated intelligence, and his engaging sense of humor, the police chief ultimately approves the change that Akim has suggested. Simply put, Akim has a personality that makes people want to embrace his ideas. He therefore can get things done faster and more easily than people who lack this source of influence.

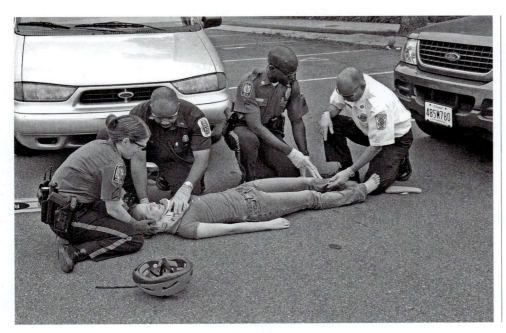

As first responders, police officers, firefighters, and emergency medical personnel treat an accident victim.

Political influence is different from political power and therefore must be wielded differently. See Chapter 11 for a detailed examination of the differences between power and influence and the sources that police personnel draw on to exert each.

Interagency Politics

Interagency politics express themselves as the relationships between a police agency and other public safety organizations—such as fire departments, emergency medical teams, and corrections facilities—serving the schools, residents, and businesses in a particular jurisdiction. All these organizations share a common duty to address crises and emergencies quickly and effectively as first responders. As such, personnel in such organizations are trained to do what most people avoid: run toward danger.

Partnering, Not Posturing   To provide high-quality public safety service, personnel from all these organizations must perform the specialized tasks they are responsible for—without quibbling over questions or concerns such as "Who has the highest status here?" or "How can I be sure my agency will get the credit for a job well done?" For example, at the scene of a vehicle collision, police must respond to the victims, secure the scene, gather evidence, and interview witnesses. Emergency medical technicians (EMTs) must take care of the injured, and firefighters must prevent the vehicles from igniting and extricate any victims who may be trapped inside a vehicle. Given this intimate relationship among public safety agencies and the urgency under which these specialists routinely operate, a sense of partnership and collaboration is essential for the delivery of exceptional service.

To foster cooperation between their agency and other public safety entities, police leaders must train all levels of personnel in critical incident response procedures, encourage frequent interaction between the various public safety service

Interagency politics: political dynamics taking place in the interactions between a police agency and other public safety organizations in the same jurisdiction.

providers, and empower personnel to carry out their unique responsibilities at emergency and critical incident scenes.

Turnover at the Top   Cooperation between and among public safety agencies begins with these organizations' chief executive officers. The individuals in charge of fire safety, emergency medical services, and police services must communicate regularly about incidents, mutual aid, and future needs so they can collaborate and coordinate their efforts. But frequent communication becomes difficult when turnover among these individuals increases; that is, executive officers vacate roles and are replaced. For example, as is true of other public safety agencies, police chiefs are often appointed by the mayor or city manager and must be approved by the city or town council. And as with many corporate chief executives, there is a high turnover rate among police chiefs; average tenure of chiefs is three years. Why the higher rate? Owing to shifts in city or town politics or claims of corruption, a newly appointed police chief may fall out of favor and be replaced by someone else.

High turnover among police chiefs is problematic (Coleman, 2007) because every time a chief departs an agency, the relationships formed with other public safety agency chiefs evaporate, which makes it harder for the agencies to collaborate on public safety calls. For this reason, a few states have enacted civil service policies prohibiting agencies from firing chiefs without clear cause.

Community Collaboration   In jurisdictions where schools, neighborhoods, and businesses are suffering from high rates of crime and other problems, police are stretched ever thinner in an effort to ensure public safety. The problem becomes even worse when police agencies are operating under tighter-than-ever budgetary constraints. In such jurisdictions, police must forge partnerships with community leaders and volunteers to provide the safety that citizens expect. Examples include

North Miami Beach Citizens Patrol volunteers greatly enhance police presence on the streets.

collaborations in which police and volunteers develop safety programs for school-children, elders, business owners, and other stakeholders. (See Chapter 6 for more information on such partnerships.)

Intergovernment Politics

Intergovernment politics are expressed in a police agency's relationships with other governmental agencies that serve or affect the same jurisdiction. These dynamics also include relationships between a police agency's personnel and elected or appointed officials who approve funding for police agency initiatives and who help define an agency's goals. Such government agencies and officials include the mayor's office; city, village, or town councils; county and parish boards; state and federal agencies including offices of emergency services (such as the Federal Emergency Management Agency [FEMA] and grant providers); oversight bodies including state commissions on peace officer standards and training; and significant bureaucrats.

Intergovernment politics: political dynamics taking place in interactions between a police agency and other governmental agencies serving or affecting the same jurisdiction.

Building Bridges   To create a win–win situation for itself and the other governmental agencies serving the same jurisdiction, a police agency may act as a bridge or go-between for funding initiatives that a state agency or funding source awards to a community organization. As an example, a state grant for civilian volunteer and police bicycle patrol was awarded to a community organization that had exhibited questionable fund-accounting practices. State leaders asked the affected police agency precinct leader to control the funds through the government entity's financial department. (A government entity is a town, village, county, or city government that has specific offices that address areas of need in the community. In this case, the government entity was a city.) The police facilitated purchasing of police and volunteer bicycles and supplies, following the government entity's purchasing requirements and processes. All funding had to be approved by the state and police agency in consultation with the community organization. The entire funding appropriation was expended and properly accounted for,

A Cascade, Idaho, police officer on bicycle patrol during a Fourth of July parade.

and the community organization received accolades for implementing a successful police-volunteer bicycle patrol program.

Collaborating toward the Greater Good   Collaboration between and among police agencies and dissimilar government resources helps all parties involved achieve desired goals and establishes working partnerships for future challenges. Consider this example: A county with 13 representative police agencies (including a medium-size city, a county sheriff's agency, and 11 town or village police departments) envisioned a need for recruit officer training that was cost-effective and that met state accreditation and certification requirements. To achieve their personnel goals, agencies with diverse needs joined with a community college to provide an accredited recruit police training program that met the state criteria and specific needs of the attending agencies. Agency leaders, college professionals, and police trainers collaborated to form a police training council that defined curriculum needs and the logistics for recruit training. The agency leader's vision of a greater good for all involved agencies (rather than individual, ego-centered agendas and piecemeal efforts) created a regional training academy at the community college that currently provides police recruit training, in-service training, and administrative management instruction.

Spotlight on Political Correctness

For police leaders, the task of navigating intra-agency and interagency political dynamics as well as intergovernment politics is often complicated by pressure to demonstrate so-called **political correctness**—that is, to avoid saying or doing something that risks offending a particular individual's or group's sensibilities (Atkinson, 2009; *Merriam-Webster's Dictionary and Thesaurus,* 2006). Consider a police manager who is attending a meeting of community volunteers striving to address a problem with street drug activity in their neighborhood. During the meeting, the police manager sums up the work that the various volunteers have been accomplishing. He has noticed that the younger female volunteers have had less success than the older male volunteers with designing wholesome activities for the neighborhood's youth to engage in. But he steers clear of mentioning this fact for fear that the young women will take offense. As a result, no one looks into the reasons behind the two volunteer groups' different experiences. If they had, they might have discovered that since most of the neighborhood's youth were male, the youngsters tended to feel more comfortable around older males than around younger women. They could have used this knowledge to allocate volunteers to youths based on the youngsters' natural affinities.

Going overboard with trying to avoid being political incorrect thus can prevent police managers and officers from developing creative solutions to problems in their community. However, when police managers say things that seem blatantly politically incorrect, they and their agency can pay a steep price. For instance, a police manager attending a neighborhood meeting in a troubled urban area known for drug and gang violence was asked to comment on the police agency's slow response to calls-for-service. She calmly stated that the police department was doing the best it could with available resources and personnel. She further stated that if the citizens were frustrated, they should move to another area or lobby for more police resources. Citizens promptly reported her response to the mayor's office and city council, accusing her of being insensitive and having a negative attitude toward the neighborhood. Neighbors lobbied for more police personnel. The police manager was reprimanded for undermining citizen confidence in the police agency and elected government officials. No one was happy with the end result of the police manager's interaction with the community.

Being politically correct may help police leaders keep the peace by not "ruffling feathers." But as we read earlier, that benefit comes at a cost. Under pressure to avoid giving offense, police hesitate to state their true thoughts about a situation or provide all the relevant facts (Atkinson, 2009).

To offer another illustration, a police precinct captain and the agency's management staff were reluctant to address an urban high school principal regarding the high level of calls-for-service at the school during school hours. Although the school had two assigned school resource officers, those officers and additional police personnel were constantly addressing fights, auto thefts, disruptive student behavior, and trespassing complaints. The police command was gently reminded that openly voicing their frustration to school officials about the school's problems would hurt the high school and school districts' image. Calls-for-service escalated, a stolen vehicle chop-shop operated on the high school campus, arrests of students for assault and weapons charges rose, and additional police personnel had to be assigned to the school for student arrival, student dismissal, and special occasions. Because the agency did not address the problem in a timely manner, the police captain and staff deployed critical staff to the school from other vulnerable geographic areas. The captain and precinct management staff finally discussed the problem with the school principal and respective school staff. Together, they gathered facts about the school's problems, analyzed the data, and implemented solutions that garnered some good results. However, the negative image of the high school remains a significant issue for the school and the school district.

A CHANGING ROLE

Police officers have always been charged with maintaining public safety, but over time, their role has expanded to include additional responsibilities. For example, as crime rates increased during the middle of the twentieth century, the media, the public, and politicians began viewing police officers as primarily crime fighters rather than public safety officers. In later decades, definitions of police officers' role expanded further to include solving community problems.

Solving Community Problems

More recently, with the advent of community policing, experts on policing have maintained that in addition to fighting crime, police should engage citizens and help solve quality-of-life problems such as homelessness and abandoned buildings in the communities they serve. This change spawned some tensions in the policing profession. Specifically, some officers complained that solving community problems should be the responsibility of social workers; police (by contrast) should respond to calls-for-service, solve crimes, and protect people by arresting offenders (Goldstein, 1990; Sherman, 2010).

Police officers mounted on horses are helpful with crowd control and enhancing police–community relations.

But the truth is, no one group can do it all because the problems facing communities today are bigger than any one group. Only by cooperating for the public good can police and other experts—social workers, medical personnel, public defenders, district attorneys—collectively provide the public safety citizens are paying for with their taxes. For example, police can collaborate with social workers to help address issues related to homelessness. Police can also work with city or county building-code departments to condemn and demolish abandoned buildings that function as drug-use houses or otherwise pose a threat to public safety.

Wearing Many "Hats"

Thankfully, in many jurisdictions, police officers have also learned to function in a manner reminiscent of social work while still responding to citizen complaints, solving crime, and keeping the peace. We can think of such officers as wearing many "hats":

- The **public safety provider** comes into play when an officer arrests a drunk driver or reevaluates an elderly citizen's driving ability to prevent innocent citizens from being hurt.

- The **crime fighter** comes to the fore when the same officer apprehends a robbery suspect. (Note, however, that police officers spend most of their time in service-related and order-maintenance functions.)

- The **social worker** emerges when the officer resolves a dispute between two neighbors by listening to their respective concerns and encouraging them to arrive at a compromise that satisfies both citizens.

Police officer leaders are generally comfortable multitasking in this way. In fact, many officers excel at identifying what policing "hat" will be best in any given situation. While today's officers understand that responding quickly to calls-for-service is a significant part of their role, they also want to find solutions to the problems confronting the communities they serve. Enlightened officers see the arrest of an offender as just part of the solution to the problem of crime. They understand that their role must constantly evolve in response to a myriad of new developments (such as increasing crime) and emerging political realities (including lack of fiscal resources) (Stojkovic, Kolinich, & Klofas, 2008).

THE NEED FOR ETHICAL LEADERSHIP

In Chapter 1, we discussed ethics and its role in professional policing. In the pages that follow, we examine the challenges inherent in providing ethical leadership in a police agency—including aligning one's actions with one's words, combating bias-based policing, preventing misuse of force, and eradicating police misconduct.

Aligning Actions with Words

Police administrators should define and encourage ethical behavior and adherence to high moral standards for personnel throughout their agency. But talk, in itself, is not enough. Administrators must also demonstrate ethical behavior and high moral standards—through their actions. As the saying goes, "Actions speak louder than words," and whenever a person's behavior conflicts with that individual's statements, it is the behavior—not the words—that others notice most.

Administrators and managers who function as ethical leaders demonstrate specific actions, behaviors, and personal qualities, including trustworthiness, commitment to their agency's mission, courage, compassion, and accountability for outcomes. By contrast, unethical leaders are secretive and often betray others. They abuse their authority and power and use information for their own benefit.

Ethical leaders also attract followers by virtue of their honesty with appointing authorities, with agency members (sworn and nonsworn), and with members of the community their agency serves. Moreover, they continually model appropriate behavior—explaining their vision through articulate speech, engendering trust by being reliable, and developing their own skills and using them to good effect (Ortmeier & Meese, 2010; Schultz, 2008).

Police leaders must demonstrate all these competencies while also fulfilling the distinct role of public safety officer. In addition, they must always remember that just one instance of unethical behavior can destroy a person's (and a police agency's) trustworthiness and reputation—even if that individual has a long history of ethical behavior. Additional information about ethical leadership is presented in Chapter 11.

Combating Bias-Based Policing

In addition to aligning their actions with their words, ethical leaders must combat **bias-based policing**. According to a 2004 research study performed by Auburn University Montgomery for the state of Virginia, "Bias-based policing includes practices by individual officers, supervisors, managerial practices, and departmental programs,

Bias-based policing: intentional or nonintentional practices that incorporate prejudicial judgments based on gender, race, ethnicity, and other differences that are inappropriately applied.

A Homeland Security Officer and a Border Patrol Agent at a checkpoint searching for weapons and verifying immigration status. Racial profiling is a key concern for police agencies.

both intentional and non-intentional, that incorporate prejudicial judgments based on gender, race, ethnicity, gender, sexual orientation, economic status, religious beliefs, or age that are inappropriately applied" (Charles, Ioimo, Tears, & Becton, 2004).

Racial Profiling   The most blatant example of bias-based policing today is known as racial profiling. Through this type of profiling, law enforcement representatives stop or detain people based on their race as a reason for suspicion that the individuals have, are currently, or will engage in criminal activity (Amnesty International USA, 2009). For example, an officer stops particular drivers or questions certain pedestrians solely because they belong to a specific group (such as African American, Hispanic, Asian, and Middle Eastern), because the officer believes that all members of that group cannot be trusted. Racial profiling is unethical because it is based on prejudice—adverse opinions about members of specific group that are formed without sufficient knowledge of those individuals.

To understand the harm that racial profiling inflicts, imagine driving your car and being pulled over by a police officer for no apparent reason: You have not done anything wrong. Yet the officer clearly suspects you of wrongdoing. You gradually realize that it is the color of your skin that has triggered the stop. How do you feel? Profiling is an assault on people's humanity. If you are like most people, you likely feel anger, perhaps even rage, and you probably lose any trust you once placed in police.

Familiarity: The Antidote to Profiling   Racial profiling has fallen out of favor, and police agencies across the nation have issued formal statements that its practice will not be tolerated. Experts agree that preventing such bias-based policing begins and ends with communication between police and citizens. The more citizens know about how the police do their jobs, the less likely it is that citizens will formulate misconceptions that distance police from those they serve. And the more officers interact with citizens, the more they will come to know and appreciate the similarities and differences among them. We are all people, and familiarity with people—how they live, how they interact with one another, how they feel—fosters harmony not only in neighborhoods but also within and between nations (Graziano, Schuck, & Martin, 2010; Jones-Brown & Terry, 2004; Ortmeier, 2006; Shusta et al., 2011).

Preventing Misuse of Force

In the 1960s and 1970s, the American public turned its attention to the way police officers conducted themselves. Newspapers reported brutality on the part of police when they arrested, detained, and interrogated prisoners—especially if the prisoners were members of minority groups.

Use-of-Force Rules   Today, police agencies have strict rules governing officers' behavior. Aggressive investigations of allegations of abuse, along with severe punishments, have reduced complaints about misuse of force. In the recruit academy and during in-service training, new officers are taught, in no uncertain terms, what they can and cannot do to citizens. For example, during the arrest of a suspected offender, an officer may use whatever force is reasonably necessary to overcome resistance but cannot use excessive force. Use of force, especially deadly force, is strictly governed by laws, policies, and procedures designed to keep officers and suspects safe. In some jurisdictions, the use of deadly physical force has been supplemented by the use of less-than-lethal bean-bag rounds, rubber bullets, or Tasers.

The Use-of-Force Continuum   The best way to ensure that an officer does not "cross the line" regarding use of force is through training from day one. When officers are aware of alternative methods of handling potentially dangerous situations, they are more likely to maintain control of themselves as well as others. Effective tactical communication to reduce conflict is the best alternative. Many police agencies train officers to envision use of force as on a continuum: The type of force an officer may use depends on the level of resistance presented by the other person.

For example, suppose that an officer responding to a domestic violence call encounters one person physically threatening another. The officer commands the person to stop the threatening behavior. The person either complies with the request or continues the threatening behavior. If the person does not comply, the officer may use a physical force hand-to-hand technique to stop the threat or restrain the individual, or deploy a chemical spray agent to gain compliance. Training and consistent and continuous mentoring of recruits and

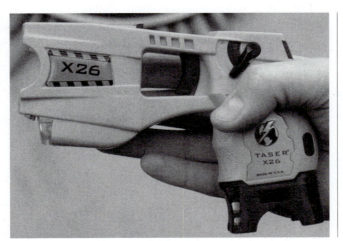

Less-than-lethal weapons, such as a Taser device, should be considered as a viable less-lethal option in subject resistance situations.

less experienced officers have reduced the number of complaints of not only misuse of force but also bias-based policing and other misconduct (Kelling & Sousa, 2001; Michelson, 1999; Peak, 2007; Whisenand & Ferguson, 2005).

Eradicating Police Misconduct

Along with the realization that police conduct had to change in regard to the use of force, the U.S. Congress passed and subsequently amended the Civil Rights Act of 1871, which allows victims of alleged abuse to file lawsuits against the police agencies and individual officers responsible.

Liability Lawsuits According to the law—42 U.S.C. § 1983—if police officers deprive a person of the rights the individual is guaranteed under the U.S. Constitution and other federal law, that person can seek redress through filing a lawsuit, or a "civil action for deprivation of rights" (U.S. House of Representatives, Office of the Law Revision Counsel, 2008). Over time, a segment of law has sprung up that specializes in liability lawsuits—and not just those where police are involved. For instance, since the Constitution states that citizens are entitled to "life," any entity that deprives a citizen of life is liable for that loss. Not surprisingly, lawyers handling wrongful-death suits have proliferated. The fear of lawsuits against police agencies has prompted local government and police leaders to analyze agencies' vulnerabilities with respect to arrest- and nonarrest-related deaths. Agency training, supervision, policies, officer actions, and officer assignments all come into question in wrongful-death lawsuits. During the years 1995 through 2005, the police in the states of California and New York were involved in 66 wrongful-death lawsuits (Fishel, Gabbidon, & Hummer, 2007).

No police agency can afford to neglect assessing its vulnerability to liability lawsuits over arrest-related deaths. As highlighted in the U.S. Bureau of Justice Statistics Special Report, 2007, the number of arrest-related deaths in the United States increased from 622 in 2003 to 703 in 2005. The total number of these deaths from 2003 to 2005, including homicide by law enforcement, is 2,002. As shown in Table 3-2, homicide by law enforcement accounts for 54.7 percent of the total number of deaths for all causes.

table 3-2 Cause of Death: 2003–2005

| CAUSE OF DEATH | NUMBER OF ARREST-RELATED DEATHS | | | | PERCENT |
	2003–2005	2005	2004	2003	2003–2005
All causes	2,002	703	677	622	100
Homicide—					
by law enforcement	1,005	364	365	366	54.7
by other persons	11	4	4	3	0.5
Intoxication	252	90	81	81	12.6
Suicide	234	91	87	56	11.7
Accidental injury	140	47	41	52	7.0
Illness/natural causes	113	38	49	26	5.6
Other/unknown	157	69	50	38	7.8

Note: See *Methodology* for information on missing data by state for each reporting year.

Also notable, in arrest-related homicides, local police agencies account for 74 percent of such homicides, with sheriff's agencies accounting for 19 percent and state and highway patrol 6 percent. Of that amount, arrest-related suicides numbered 234, with 67 percent taking place at the scene of the arrest and the remaining 33 percent at the police station or booking facility. The investigation of these cases of arrest-related deaths was lengthy, involving many levels of government (Mumola, 2007). Police agencies must be ever vigilant to ensure that agency personnel are properly trained and supervised to address the issue of liability, credibility of the agency, and the personal health of agency personnel and the citizens the agency serves.

Table 3-3, which shows arrest-related deaths by most serious offense, emphasizes that violent offenses constitute only about half of the offenses in which arrest-related deaths occur. Property offenses, drug offenses, public-order offenses, and no criminal charges intended account for 33.4 percent of the arrest-related deaths from 2003 to 2005.

Noted in the Bureau of Justice Statistics Special Report (2007), Table 3-4 shows that the increasing number of deaths from 2003 to 2005 is correlated with the use of Tasers and other conducted-energy devices (CEDs). Two issues stand out in this report: first, the number of deaths in which intoxication is a factor and that a violent offense was involved; second, the number of Taser- or CED-involved deaths escalating from 3 in 2003 to 24 in 2005.

Police agencies must be ever cognizant that arrest-related deaths involving law enforcement are on the rise. Liability lawsuits are a grave possibility. Credible and documented training in the use of both armed and unarmed use-of-force techniques is essential for addressing and possibly preventing arrest-related deaths.

The amount of force used to effect an arrest should be that which is reasonably necessary only to overcome resistance from the person being taken into custody.

Police Misconduct Defined

We have been talking about **police misconduct**, but what does the term mean, exactly? Many police officers have asked their agencies to develop a list of behaviors that constitute misconduct. However, most agencies prefer to examine each incident in its context before deciding whether it qualifies as misconduct and how severe the infraction is. Police officers are expected to learn what

Police misconduct: inappropriate behaviors (often including use of excessive force, theft, and other destructive behaviors) and conduct prohibited by a police agency.

table 3-3 Arrest-Related Deaths by Most Serious Offense

MOST SERIOUS OFFENSE	ARREST-RELATED DEATHS 2003–2005	
	NUMBER	PERCENT
All offenses	**2002**	**100**
Violent offenses	**1,119**	**55.9**
Homicide	177	8.8
Murder of a law enforcement officer	8	0.4
Attempted murder of a law enforcement officer	105	5.2
Other murder/manslaughter	64	3.2
Kidnapping	38	1.9
Sexual assault[a]	13	0.6
Robbery	96	4.8
Assault		
Assault on a law enforcement officer	251	12.5
Domestic violence[b]	57	2.8
Other assault	436	21.6
Other violent	51	2.5
Property offenses	**150**	**7.5%**
Burglary	49	2.4
Larceny	14	0.7
Motor vehicle theft	21	1.0
Fraud	11	0.5
Other property[c]	55	2.7
Drug offenses	**154**	**7.7%**
Possession	105	5.2
Trafficking	31	1.5
Other drug	18	0.9
Public-order offenses	**290**	**14.5%**
Weapons	36	1.8
Obstruction of justice	85	4.2
Obstruction of law enforcement activities	55	2.7
Obstruction of court activities	30	1.5
Traffic violations	36	1.8
Driving while intoxicated	29	1.4
Drunkenness, disorderly conduct	74	3.7
Probation/parole violation, escape	21	1.0
Immigration	1	—[d]
Other public-order	8	0.4
No criminal charges intended	**75**	**3.7%**
Mental health transport	44	2.2
Medical transport	9	0.4
Unspecified	22	1.1
Offense not reported	**214**	**10.7%**

[a]Includes rape and other sexual assault.

[b]Some domestic violence causes may be reported as assaults.

[c]Includes arson and stolen property.

[d]Less than 0.05%

table 3-4 Deaths and Conducted-Energy Devices	
CHARACTERISTICS	**NUMBER OF ARREST-RELATED DEATHS INVOLVING THE USE OF CONDUCTED ENERGY DEVICES, 2003–2005**
Total	36
Year	
2003	3
2004	9
2005	24
Cause of death	
Homicide by law enforcement	7
Intoxication	10
Suicide	1
Illness	1
Other/Unknown	9
Most serious offense	
Violent	16
Property	8
Drug	2
Public-order	3
No criminal charges intended	2
Offense not reported	5

constitutes misconduct during their training on federal, state, and local laws; and from their agency's specific policies and procedures known as general orders, special orders, and rules and regulations. Some common examples of misconduct include untruthfulness, discourtesy, use of excessive force, theft, accepting of gratuities, and impaired driving (by alcohol or drugs) (Graziano et al., 2010; Ross, 2006).

The Need for Training and Mentoring Discipline of the previously identified misconduct is covered in Chapter 12, but the best and most proven way to prevent misconduct is through thorough training at the beginning of an officer's career, and through ongoing mentoring and in-service training during an officer's employment with the agency. Senior officers entrusted with mentoring junior officers must exhibit the highest standards of ethical behavior themselves. Agencies should avoid assigning a new officer to any senior or field training officer who has generated complaints of misconduct in the past. Additionally, mentors and trainers should monitor officers throughout their careers to identify and address symptoms of chronic stress or burnout (such as increased absenteeism and difficulty concentrating on work), which may lead to misconduct. By preventing misconduct, an agency avoids embarrassing and costly lawsuits (Crowder, 1998; Morreale, 2002).

Leadership on the job
High-Speed Police Pursuits

High-speed police vehicle pursuits often result in deaths and injuries to participants and innocent bystanders—which can trigger wrongful-death or negligence lawsuits against the officers and agencies involved. Why are such pursuits so dangerous? Generally, the closer an officer gets to a vehicle being pursued, the faster the pursued person will drive, increasing the risk that the chase will end in a collision. For this reason, police agencies develop pursuit policies and procedures. A few agencies have even restricted officers' ability to pursue traffic-law violators, stolen vehicles, and criminal suspects. In such agencies, officers must allow some dangerous people to escape and strive to apprehend them later.

Emerging technologies may provide a long-term solution. For example, the police are experimenting with Global Positioning System (GPS) tracking devices to restrict fuel flow in pursued vehicles equipped by their manufacturer with specific technology that can slow the vehicle to 5 miles per hour or less. As an alternative, there is a laser-guided device capable of launching a magnetized GPS beacon from the grill of a police vehicle at the pursued vehicle. The magnet adheres to the fleeing vehicle, and its GPS beacon transmits a location signal to tracking systems monitored by police.

1. How might police agencies make additional use of technology to improve efficiency and effectiveness with respect to police chases?

2. In your view, could technology eventually make human police officers unnecessary? Why or why not?

3. How might a restrictive police-chase policy enhance or demean officers' role? Consider not only officers' perceptions but also community members' perceptions of the role.

TECHNOLOGICAL ADVANCES

The biggest technology-related challenges facing police agencies today are planning for technological advances, anticipating these advances' effects on the agency, and keeping the agency current with new and proven technology. Agencies can best overcome these challenges by keeping abreast of technological advancements and ensuring appropriate financial planning to acquire new technologies. Performance is mixed on this front: Some agencies have state-of-the-art systems and have automated everything from report writing and record keeping to forensic sciences applied to crime scene investigation. In others agencies, officers still take notes on a lined pad and then use those notes to handwrite their reports back at the office.

The Value of Technology

True, it is not easy for anyone to keep up with the march of technology. Conventional wisdom often suggests that each of us should buy a new computer or the latest version of a software application every six months—or even sooner—to stay current. This is not practical for most individuals, never mind for many public agencies. However, most small police agencies *can* afford to acquire at least a functional and relatively current computer system. And they must acquire it, as such technology is vital to fulfilling their mission.

Moreover, many criminals are using technology for nefarious purposes. For example, child molesters may pose as harmless "friends" on social media sites such as Facebook to attract victims. Police agencies that are not current with such technologies—or that remain unfamiliar with how criminals are using them—cannot hope to provide high-quality policing services.

Essential Information Technology

At the very least, police agencies need access to high-speed connection to the Internet. By searching the Web, officers and detectives can find information that will help them apprehend suspects and other wanted individuals. In addition, computers offer access to such crucial resources as the Automated Fingerprint Identification System (AFIS), the National Crime Information Center (NCIS), and LexusNexus, which provide users with legal and business information. If criminals can access this information, it is even more important for police officers to have the same ability.

An exciting innovation for many police agencies has come with the use of laptop computers in patrol vehicles. Patrol officers can use the laptops to input calls-for-service information directly to the main police agency database, print out reports for complainants to sign, and retrieve information from the Internet about suspects and other people of interest.

Budgets for police agencies may be strained, and resources may be limited. Still, police must be technologically up-to-date, as long as the technology acquired is necessary, to carry out their mission (Ortmeier & Meese, 2010; Young & Ortmeier, 2011).

Police officer using a laptop in a radio patrol car.

ETHICS IN ACTION

How Deep Should They Go?

Many police agencies regularly investigate the online activities of job applicants—including which websites they visit, what they write or read in blogs, what videos they watch, and what images and information they post in any social networking sites they belong to. Like all people, aspiring police personnel are less inhibited online than in face-to-face interactions. Their online personas thus present a potentially rich source of information about their character and personality.

To understand this, think about your own use of, say, Facebook or MySpace. If you use such social media, have you posted photos of yourself drunk at a party, or written a blog entry touting the joys of cocaine? If so, you are making an impression on hiring managers who access your page—an impression you may prefer not to make.

Because a person's online activities reveal so much, police managers justify their investigation into applicants' online life as an important extension of the routine background check conducted during the police hiring process, which includes finding out whether an applicant has used illegal drugs or has been arrested.

At the same time, many police agencies face dwindling applications for employment, so they are considering relaxing their hiring standards by accepting applicants who admit to having used controlled substances in the past. Other standards may be relaxed in the future, including an applicant's admission or online evidence of downloading music without permission or even viewing underage pornographic sites online. An applicant's postings or interactions on questionable websites or blogs may or may not be cause for an applicant character review.

1.   In your opinion, is it ethical and acceptable for police agencies to investigate potential employees' online activities? Why or why not?

2.   Is an applicant's behavior before hiring a valid concern for the agency after a recruit becomes a sworn officer? Why or why not?

RESOURCE CONSTRAINTS

As in many organizations, the hard truth about public agencies' budgets is that one department, one agency, or one program will always get the bulk of the money. Resource constraints for a police agency stem from forces unique to the public agency arena. But police agencies can still take steps to manage such constraints.

Understanding the Forces behind Resource Constraints

Police agencies in many jurisdictions are in the unique position of being downsized or eliminated owing to citizen and government representatives' concern regarding the cost of police services. (In Chapter 14, we discuss the use of outsourcing as one approach to cutting police service costs.) For many jurisdictions, police service is the most costly of all the services on which the government spends taxpayers' money. Police agencies must continually provide statistical data to prove that they are delivering excellent service; for example, by reducing and preventing crime. Citizens may believe that they have to pay twice for police services when they have their own town, village, or city police agency as well as the law enforcement services of the county sheriff's department.

Meanwhile, other institutions in a jurisdiction are also clamoring for financial help from their local governing bodies. School systems are demanding more revenue to pay for teacher salaries; new or renovated facilities; upkeep of buses and computers; and special education services. Business owners at the local city, town, or village level are asking for tax relief so they can build their enterprises and enhance their facilities. Public safety providers including firefighters and emergency medical services teams are demanding updated equipment and facilities. Many suburban and rural public safety providers previously had plenty of volunteers to help out. But volunteerism ebbs during tough economic times because people need to work longer hours to pay their bills and feed their families. Indeed, in many jurisdictions, fire and ambulance services are transforming from all-volunteer services to part-time and full-time paid positions.

Competing for Resources

Police agencies must consider numerous options when competing for scant public dollars within their jurisdiction. One option is to establish a sense of urgency for a specific program or activity an agency wants to initiate. By making a compelling business case for the funding, agency leaders may persuade the city council or city manager or mayor to divert tax revenues from social programs to fund a crime-reduction strategy such as zero-tolerance policing (typically a very expensive program) or to freeze hiring of civilian support personnel to free up money for existing sworn officers to provide for a safer community. The needed revenue will enable the police agency to continue providing current services and implement innovative crime fighting or quality-of-life enhancements.

A second option is to solicit help from the community the agency serves. For instance, some agencies have enlisted citizen volunteers to take telephone reports of incidents that do not require an immediate response. Such volunteers can also perform observation patrols by using neighborhood video systems or riding in specially marked cars and then reporting any suspicious activity to the agency. In addition, some neighborhood residents have participated in citizen police academies in preparation for leading or contributing to Neighborhood Watch programs.

This kind of citizen involvement generates a twofold benefit: First, citizens feel good about helping keep their own streets safe and enabling patrol officers to focus on incidents that demand their immediate attention and specialized skills. Second, citizens and police feel a sense of partnership and collaboration that promotes tolerance and understanding on the part of both groups (Kotter, 1996; Ortmeier, 2006; Sherman, 2010; Stohr & Collins, 2009). (See Chapter 6 for more information on how police can partner with citizen volunteers.)

TERRORISM

A hundred years ago, most police agencies across the United States operated in a vacuum, confined to their own jurisdictions. To deal with cross-jurisdictional crime, they often had to get assistance from private police. (Eventually, the Federal Bureau

New York City's World Trade Center Twin Towers burning after the terrorist attacks on September 11, 2001.

Homeland security: public and private policies, procedures, tactics, strategies, equipment, facilities, and personnel designed or utilized to defend the homeland against domestic- or foreign-initiated threats or hazards (for example, terrorism, natural or human-caused disasters, and pandemics).

of Investigation, or FBI, arose to provide this type of assistance.) Little communication occurred between individual police jurisdictions, so criminals found it relatively easy to move and settle somewhere else without being detected or brought to justice.

All this changed in the twentieth and certainly in the twenty-first century. Owing to the terrorist attacks of 9/11, globalization (manifested as increased flows of people, information, and goods across national borders), and international unrest, police agencies can no longer operate in isolated pockets. Instead, agencies at all levels and in every region and state in the nation must share information and resources to maintain peaceful and safe communities and to achieve **homeland security**. The establishment of the U.S. Department of Homeland Security was a major step toward this goal.

The U.S. Department of Homeland Security (DHS)

The U.S. Department of Homeland Security (DHS), created in response to the 9/11 terrorist attacks, is dedicated to encouraging an interagency approach to policing strategy, especially as it relates to terrorism. Published in July 2002, DHS's *National Strategy for Homeland Security* identifies three major goals: (1) prevent terrorist attacks within the United States, (2) reduce America's vulnerability to terrorism, and (3) minimize damage and recover from any attacks.

DHS's stated vision is to preserve freedom through defense of the homeland. Its goals include increasing awareness of threats to homeland security; preventing terrorism; and defining and executing strategies to protect the nation, its infrastructure, property, and people. Local, county, and state police agencies across the country are required to maintain a heightened state of readiness regarding specific kinds of threats (such as bombs in subways, deliberate depositing of poisons into water supplies, and explosives entering the country in containers on ships coming into ports). In addition, such agencies must provide their personnel with training in how to anticipate and address homeland security–related incidents. And they must take steps to control access to the country and its citizens. Airports, train and bus stations, and ports are extremely vulnerable to terrorist attacks. Those police agencies responsible for protecting transportation systems and critical infrastructure must be particularly vigilant.

Four Phases of Emergency Management   Homeland security emphasizes four phases of emergency management:

1. *Mitigation:* Public safety agencies mitigate emergencies by assessing a wide range of risks, with the goal of identifying vulnerabilities not only to terrorist attacks but also to other catastrophic events such as hurricanes or earthquakes. They then seek to reduce those risks. Examples of risk-reduction practices from a homeland security perspective include passenger screening at airports and the requirement that pilots of private planes report who is on a plane before it lands in the United States.

2. *Preparedness:* This phase involves everything from training first responders to stockpiling supplies. Preparedness facilitates rapid response. It also helps ensure that medical attention will reach people quickly and that criminal perpetrators of emergency events will be identified and apprehended swiftly. With preparation, emergency personnel are regularly trained, tested, and certified to ensure fast and appropriate response to catastrophic events.

3. *Response:* Rapid response is what highly trained personnel provide when an emergency occurs. Personnel respond based on their training and the scope of the emergency—preserving human life first, attending to the dead in a respectful manner, and addressing any property considerations (such as fire suppression). At the scene, responders should function as calm and capable leaders who bring order to chaos and comfort to the confused and injured.

4. *Recovery:* This phase comes in the aftermath of an emergency and entails a return to conditions that prevailed before the event. Public safety agencies analyze statistical measurements of loss of life, injuries sustained, and the values of property lost. Specialists attend to the mental anguish suffered by those affected during and after the emergency.

Homeland security is a comprehensive national public safety strategy designed to prevent major events and foster effective responses to events that do occur. To support this strategy, federal, state, county, and local agencies must communicate and work together (U.S. Department of Homeland Security, Office of Management and Budget, 2007). They have several powerful tools at their disposal for doing so, including the National Incident Management System (NIMS) and the Standardized Emergency Management System (SEMS) established by individual states.

The National Incident Management System (NIMS)

The **National Incident Management System (NIMS)** provides a way for public safety agencies to develop policies and processes for working together to prevent and manage emergencies. Operational protocols, procedures, and standards are developed by the secretary of Homeland Security and administered through agencies at the various levels of government.

NIMS aims to bring together best practices for addressing critical incidents and incorporate those practices into a framework that public and private organizations can use to address emergency situations. NIMS has several key components:

National Incident Management System (NIMS): a nationwide program by which public safety agencies develop policies and processes for collectively preventing and managing emergencies.

Command and Management Structures   Command and management structures include the Incident Command System (ICS), Multi-Agency Coordination Systems, and the Public Information Systems. The *Incident Command System* consists of operating procedures as well as responders from fire departments, police agencies, emergency medical teams, government, and the Red Cross—all organizations involved in the various phases of the incident. In one county in New York State, a central location at a police and fire training facility of a community college serves as the incident command center for a critical situation where NIMS processes would be employed.

The *Multi-Agency Coordination Systems* support incident management by providing organizational structure, operational procedures, and interactive management components for those entities engaged in the incident at the federal, state, local, tribal, and regional levels through written agreements and other arrangements for assistance at critical incidents. These systems define how organizations cooperate and work together to provide comprehensive and productive service delivery.

The *Public Information Systems* refers to those processes, procedures, and systems for communicating timely and accurate information to the public during a crisis or emergency situation. This system provides for a public information officer who communicates directly with the print and electronic media and the operational leadership of the incident command structure.

Preparedness Activities   These activities are instituted before an incident and include deciding how an agency will use personnel, equipment, and other resources during an incident. Training is a particularly crucial preparedness activity. DHS has developed standardized courses on incident command and management, as well as discipline- and agency-specific incident management courses such as the integration and use of supporting technologies. DHS also provides hands-on exercises featuring realistic incident scenarios. For example, participants learn how to operationalize emergency management protocols in their organizations. Public safety agencies can hire facilitators from the organizations that developed these courses, and have them teach the courses to their own personnel or send personnel to locations where the courses are offered.

Individuals who successfully complete training receive a personnel qualification certification. Those who can demonstrate that they have acquired and can operate equipment such as first-responder communication systems, and can demonstrate that the equipment is compatible with other agencies receive an equipment acquisition and operations certification.

As part of preparation, agencies are also expected to forge mutual-aid agreements guaranteeing the sharing of resources, facilities, services, and other support as needed if an incident should occur. Finally, DHS provides standardized forms and documents such as reporting forms and standardized procedures, which agencies can distribute to responders in the case of an incident.

Resource Management   NIMS defines requirements including standardized processes and reporting procedures that establish forms and categorization to describe, inventory, dispatch, track, and recover resources over the life cycle of an incident. For instance, with respect to Hurricane Katrina, responders tried to provide housing for victims at the Superdome, in temporary trailers, and on cruise ships. But these efforts lacked coordination. Responders learned that management of those resources should fall under a specific agency and be responsible to DHS ("Federal Response to Hurricane Katrina: Lessons Learned," 2006).

Communications and Information Management   The Communications and Information Management component of NIMS provides guidelines for agency communications and the use of information during an incident. Effective incident management hinges on having interoperable communication processes, procedures, and systems to support an array of incident management activities across jurisdictions and agencies. Communication between fire and police personnel, as well as between emergency medical services, the Red Cross, transportation services, and housing services, is critical. Communication systems should be compatible and not interfere with one another.

Information management guidelines cover topics including how agencies should collect, analyze, distribute, and share information about the incident (such as number of people injured, property damage, and additional risks). Such information must flow easily and quickly to support the agencies and jurisdictions responsible for managing and directing the incident, the persons or systems affected by the incident, and those trying to help bring resolution to the incident. Effective decision making, direction, and the appropriate implementation of critical resources are driven by vital and timely information management.

Supporting Technologies   The NIMS supporting-technologies component describes the key technologies and technological systems—such as voice and data communication systems, record-keeping and resources tracking systems, and data display systems—needed to support and refine NIMS. For instance, video systems used by emergency response personnel in real-time situations must be interoperable within and across all involved agencies providing the critical response to the incident at hand (U.S. Department of Homeland Security, 2006).

Ongoing Management and Maintenance   The NIMS ongoing management and maintenance component identifies activities for evaluating and continuously improving the system. For example, multiagency practical exercises are assessed to determine which tactics are in need of improvement or modification.

State-Level Standardized Emergency Management System (SEMS)

Individual states comply with NIMS by developing state-level emergency management plans. Most states offer emergency-management guidelines known as the **Standardized Emergency Management System (SEMS)**. These guidelines aim to ensure that state-level agencies' emergency management system complies with NIMS guidelines. To achieve compliance, the state systems should include:

- Information on emergency management for first responders and their constituents
- Training in how NIMS works

Standardized Emergency Management System (SEMS): a set of guidelines that aims to ensure that state-level agencies' emergency management system comply with NIMS guidelines.

- An information management system that supports effective response to critical incidents; for example, through compatible communication systems
- Documented procedures for responding to incidents in the field and as an organization
- Emergency preparedness recommendations for families
- Miscellaneous emergency prevention and preparedness information, including plans for responding to winter rainstorms and landslides, earthquakes, and wildfires (California Emergency Management Agency, 2007; California State Office of Emergency Services, 2007).

NIMS and SEMS are still relatively new. However, they are solidly established while also evolving as the various organizations that use them gain experience by applying them to actual emergencies and homeland security issues. Yet, uniformed local police officers and sheriff's deputies are most often the first responders to *any* emergency. Therefore, it is incumbent on every police agency to prepare these personnel to respond to natural and human-caused disasters. Further, proactive counter-radicalization strategies and activities designed to prevent radicalization of individuals must be employed as well as the typical reactive tactics associated with counterterrorism (Burress, Giblin, & Schafer, 2010; Haberfeld, 2006; Johnson, 2010; Martin, 2008; Oliver, 2007; Ortmeier & Meese, 2010).

summary

- **Increased Diversity.** The demographic and cultural makeup of the U.S. population is becoming increasingly diverse. To better serve diverse communities, police personnel must understand cultural and ethnic differences and foster tolerance for differences within their agencies.
- **Complex Political Dynamics.** Police personnel must navigate three types of political dynamics: intra-agency (political machinations within a particular agency), interagency (politics between a police agency and other public safety agencies serving the same jurisdiction), and intergovernment (politics between a police agency and other government entities and officials serving the same jurisdiction). Astuteness, networking, and sincerity can help personnel navigate all three types of politics. To navigate intra-agency politics, police also need to leverage their personal strengths, relationships, and personality. To manage interagency politics, police should strive to partner with other public safety agencies, control turnover at top management levels in their agency, and foster collaboration with community leaders. To manage intergovernment politics, agency leaders must build bridges to other government entities serving the same jurisdiction and collaborate toward a greater good. Navigating the three types of political dynamics can be complicated by pressure to demonstrate political correctness, which has advantages (such as helping an agency "keep the peace") and disadvantages (specifically, it can prevent police personnel from discussing all aspects of a problem and developing effective solutions).

- **A Changing Role.** Police officers' role has expanded over the years to include not only maintaining public safety but also fighting crime and solving community problems. Today's police officer wears many "hats" and must learn how to function in each type of role.

- **The Need for Ethical Leadership.** In providing ethical leadership, police personnel must grapple with four challenges: aligning one's actions with one's words, combating bias-based policing (including racial profiling), preventing misuse of force by officers, and eradicating police misconduct. Many of these problems can be surmounted through proper training as well as modeling of proper and expected behavior by leaders.

- **Technological Advances.** Improvements in technology have presented police agencies with new opportunities to provide better service. But it can be difficult for some agencies to adopt new technology if personnel are resistant to changing the way they work, or if an agency has serious budget restrictions. Keeping abreast of technology and acquiring and using those technologies most critical to delivering services are two steps agencies must take.

- **Resource Constraints.** Numerous forces (including competition for tax revenues) can subject a police agency to resource constraints. To ensure that they get the funding they need to provide high-quality services, police agencies must demonstrate that they are providing value in return for taxpayers' money and make a compelling business case for the funding they need.

- **Terrorism.** The terrorist attacks of 9/11 made it clear that police agencies could no longer operate in isolation from one another and from other public safety organizations at the local, state, and federal levels. In response to the attacks, the U.S. Department of Homeland Security was created. Its vision is to preserve freedom through defense of the homeland. DHS requires local, county, and state police agencies to maintain a heightened state of readiness regarding security threats through training and emphasizes four phases of emergency management (mitigation, preparedness, response, and recovery). Police agencies have two tools for achieving these goals: the National Incident Management System and the state-level Standardized Emergency Management System.

key terms

bias-based policing
homeland security
interagency politics
intergovernment politics
intra-agency politics
National Incident Management System (NIMS)
police misconduct
political correctness
Standardized Emergency Management System (SEMS)

1. In what ways are the demographic and cultural makeup of the U.S. population changing? What challenges do these changes present for police agencies, and how can police personnel best surmount those challenges?

2. What are the three types of political dynamics managers and officers of a police agency must learn to navigate? Of all the skills you read about in this chapter for navigating such politics, which would you personally want to strengthen most? What steps could you take to strengthen your skills in these areas?

3. Of the many different "hats" today's police officer must wear (including public safety provider, crime fighter, and social worker), which would you find most challenging to wear? Why? What actions could you take to enhance your ability to fill this aspect of your role as a police manager or officer?

4. Cite examples of practices that constitute bias-based policing. Why are such practices unacceptable? How might a police agency discourage such practices among officers?

5. Cite examples of behaviors that constitute misuse of force and police misconduct. In what respects does each of these problems hurt a police agency and the community it serves? What steps can an agency take to prevent misuse of force and police misconduct?

6. What types of technological advances do you consider the most promising for police agencies? Why? If an agency has severe resource constraints, how should it prioritize its investments in technology?

7. Imagine a new service you would like to see your police agency provide. Funding is tight. How would you build a compelling business case to persuade your local or state government to allocate funding to support development of the service you have in mind?

8. Summarize how NIMS and SEMS work and explain why they are both important to helping fulfill DHS's mission.

WHAT WOULD YOU DO?
The Politics of Loyalty

A medium-size police agency in the eastern part of the United States was subjected to internal disciplinary action and external criminal investigations for alleged misuse of administrative and police powers. A police chief of extended tenure who had been previously accused and then absolved of wrongdoing was again the subject of investigation.

The police chief was known as a friendly and politically powerful individual within the department and in the community at large, which happened to be one of the safest cities in the nation. The chief was known to show favoritism to officers loyal to his views and direction, rewarding them with special assignments and promotions. The chief's circle of colleagues included other chiefs who demonstrated similar behavior.

Things took a troubling turn after an off-duty police supervisor loyal to the chief was involved in a hit-and-run motor vehicle accident in which the victims suffered injury. A special counsel to the town supervisor accused the chief of not adequately investigating the accident. Another police supervisor, while on duty, was accused of sexual coercion of a woman who committed a traffic infraction. Both supervisors were arrested, convicted of felonies, and dismissed from the agency. They are currently in prison.

The special counsel to the town supervisor maintained that the chief of police, along with the deputy chief and a police sergeant, had shredded police documents related to the investigations of the two supervisors. The deputy chief resigned, and the chief of police and police sergeant were suspended from their official duties. The community's special counsel was then asked to conduct a more extensive internal inquiry into the department.

The inquiry revealed that the two police supervisors had been disciplined by or fired from a previous police agency. Moreover, both allegedly were friends of the police chief or other politically powerful individuals. The district attorney conducted an investigation into possible criminal activities of the arrested officers and those officers who conducted background investigations for new recruits. Besides the two convicted police supervisors, the chief of police and two additional police sergeants have been criminally charged. An additional police sergeant has been demoted.

1. This police chief's leadership helped make the community one of the safest cities in the United States. Loyalty and belief in the chief's philosophy and practices appeared to support the police agency's mission of public safety. If you had worked in this agency during the time before this saga erupted, would you have strived to demonstrate loyalty to the chief? Why or why not?

2. Do you believe that a community and police agency should allow a police chief to use loyalty as a key management principle if the result is a high level of public safety? Explain your thinking.

3. What steps would you have taken to prevent this situation from happening?

Planning, Budgeting, Organization Design, and Assessment

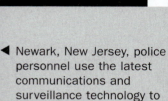

◀ Newark, New Jersey, police personnel use the latest communications and surveillance technology to help plan police activities.

The Nature and Practice of Planning

After completing this chapter, readers should be able to:

- define *planning*.
- explain the importance of balancing short-term and long-term priorities in a police agency.
- define *values*, *vision*, and *mission* and explain how they relate to the planning process.
- describe how a police agency's values, vision, and mission translate into goals and objectives.
- describe common planning pitfalls.
- list types of plans frequently developed by police agencies.
- explain what is meant by strategic planning.
- explain what is meant by Crime Prevention Through Environmental Design.

- describe the three major steps in the planning process.
- explain how police leaders should respond when a plan does not produce the intended results or cannot be implemented as intended.

Introduction

Policing activities alone (patrolling, writing tickets, arresting suspects) are not enough to ensure that a police agency achieves its mission and serves its stakeholders. Like any organization, the agency must also engage in **planning**—a process, formulation, or design used to achieve an intended result. Planning counts among managers', supervisors', and leaders' core responsibilities. And because police agencies also interact closely with the communities they serve, planning is a key responsibility of citizens and community leaders as well.

Planning:
a process, formulation, or design used to achieve an intended result.

Effective planning requires a complex mix of skills. Police managers must take into account available resources, the concerns of agency employees and community members, and any training and development investments needed for personnel to carry out the agency's plans. In addition, planning calls for a balance between short- and long-term views of the agency's objectives and future. Managers must ask questions such as, "How well does the plan we are considering support our values, vision, and mission? Will this plan get us to where we want to be six months from now? A year from now? Five years from now?" (See Figure 4-1.) To develop and execute plans, managers must also avoid common planning pitfalls as well as understand the different types of plans available to choose from—and know when to use each type. They need to take a disciplined approach to carrying out the steps in the planning process. And they must master the art of self-management, which includes demonstrating flexibility and calm when the inevitable happens: things do not go according to plan.

In this chapter, we take a close look at all these aspects of effective planning—starting with the need for a long-term, big-picture view when police managers are developing plans for their agency.

figure 4-1   Steps in the Planning Process

STEP	KEY QUESTIONS	YES	NO
1	Is there a problem or a need to address future changes? If yes, proceed to step 2.		
2	Is the problem or future need adequately defined and understood? If yes, go to step 3.		
3	Has the concern been identified as an immediate issue or based on future demands? If yes, go to step 4.		
4	Is the plan short or long term? If adequately understood, go to step 5.		
5	Does the plan support values, vision, and mission? If yes, proceed to step 6. If no, go back to step 1 and redefine presenting issue.		
6	Have 6-month goals and accomplishments been identified?		
7	Have 1-year goals and accomplishments been identified?		
8	Have 5-year goals and accomplishments been identified?		

ADOPTING A LONG-TERM, BIG-PICTURE VIEW

Unfortunately, in most police agencies, planning centers on small, short-term projects only, such as initiatives designed to reduce auto theft or vandalism in a specific neighborhood. Police and citizens work together to formulate and implement a solution to the identified problem, then declare victory as soon as they begin seeing results. The more victories an agency can achieve, the more successful it appears to stakeholders such as government officials, community members, and agency employees.

Yet limiting planning to this short-term, small-picture approach contains dangers. It makes planning synonymous with validation, an effort merely to prove that an agency is taking steps to solve problems within its jurisdiction. It can spawn the attitude that planning is a clerical function performed by a subunit within the agency—not "real" police work. Most troubling, it does not encourage a thoughtful, deliberate process that will exert a more lasting impact on crime or quality of life in the community an agency serves. Instead, agencies react to whichever citizen complaint or crisis seems most urgent at the time, crafting and executing plans for dealing with the problem. The difficulty eases for a while, but because the agency has not developed plans with the long run in mind, trouble soon returns.

A more effective way to plan is to assume that police and citizens are partners dedicated to solving problems permanently (not just eradicating their immediate symptoms). Aligning plans with agency and community values, vision, and mission can help.

U.S. Capitol Hill police officer listening to a citizen protester's complaint.

ALIGNING PLANS WITH VALUES, VISION, AND MISSION

Many organizations have formally defined values, vision, and mission. For a corporate entity, these might all revolve around how the company intends to treat customers and employees fairly as well as conduct its business ethically. For police organizations, values, vision, and mission usually center on demonstrating integrity, equality, and fairness; making a commitment to safe neighborhoods; being open to community issues; responding quickly and effectively to community needs; and providing a level of service the community expects.

But terms like *values, vision,* and *mission* can sometimes seem abstract and high level. What do they mean, exactly? In the following text we examine possible answers to this question as well as explain how values, vision, and mission can serve as guideposts for a police agency's plans.

Values

Values are fundamental beliefs, principles, or standards that an individual or members of an organization regard as desirable or worthwhile. Examples include honesty, integrity, compassion, respect, and professionalism. Values can be organizational or individual.

In a police agency, *organizational* values are the ideals that the agency incorporates into its basic belief system—those convictions that are reflected in the agency's formally expressed value statement and that all members of the department seek to demonstrate through their daily actions. *Individual* values are personal standards that officers hold based on their own beliefs, preferences, faith, or principles (Hitt, 1988; Johnson, 2004; Meese & Ortmeier, 2004).

Values: fundamental beliefs, principles, or standards that an individual or members of an organization regard as desirable or worthwhile.

A NYPD officer demonstrates compassion on 9/11.

Values are most powerful when their organizational and individual forms align—and when actual behaviors reflect the values. For example, if the agency and the individual officer publicly state that they value honesty and integrity, daily police activities should demonstrate correct behavior and honor for all to see. If the agency has defined honesty as a value but appears manipulative and immoral in its daily interactions with the community, the resulting dissonance may cause citizens to view the agency as untrustworthy.

Vision

Vision:
the image an
organization or
individual has in
mind for a desired
future state.

A **vision** is the image an organization or individual has in mind for a desired future state. A vision is long range and should be so compelling that members of a police agency will strive to make the vision real through their everyday activities (Hitt, 1988). Like other organizations, many police agencies publish a vision statement—a written expression of the future that the agency wants to realize.

An effective vision statement has numerous defining characteristics. It is clear and persuasive—inspiring a yearning for that future within all managers and employees. It expresses an attractive future that members view as achievable, not an out-of-reach picture that everyone knows will never be real. Finally, it is memorable, easy to communicate, and can be explained and understood quickly (Kotter, 1996). (See the box "Sample Vision Statement.")

Mission

Mission:
a short-range task
or assignment an
organization wishes
to achieve.

A **mission** is a short-range task or assignment a police agency wishes to achieve. As with values and vision, a police agency might express its mission in a written statement. The statement may mention values, and it serves as a guide for police managers to develop and implement initiatives that create value for the department's stakeholders. Agency managers can use the mission statement to direct the agency's resources toward its strategic goals (Wood, 2005). An example of a mission statement might be:

> "Through a coordinated police–community effort, public order and safety will be achieved and maintained. We actively encourage community support and participation in a collaborative effort to achieve a safe community."

Translating Values, Vision, and Mission into Goals and Objectives

How do a police agency's values, vision, and mission relate to its planning efforts? Agency managers use them to guide the definition of goals and objectives in their

---

Sample Vision Statement

"Integrity is the foundation of our profession. Therefore, we endeavor to preserve and protect the public trust placed in us by adhering to the highest standards of honesty and ethical practice. We will work in partnership with citizens to establish and maintain peace and enhance the quality of community life."

figure 4-2 The Role of Values, Vision, and Mission in the Planning Process

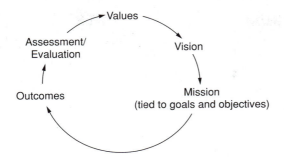

plans. **Goals** are long-range achievements that are desired by the agency and that reflect its values, vision, and mission. An example of a goal might be "Reduce violent crime." **Objectives** are the short-term accomplishments that an agency must reach to achieve a particular goal. For example, to achieve the goal of reducing violent crime, an agency might define objectives involving analyzing violent-crime rates in the community served and launching crime-prevention initiatives (Wood, 2005).

Managers translate statements about the agency's values, vision, and mission into the goals and objectives that (if achieved) would express the agency's values, realize its vision, and fulfill its mission (T. E. Baker, 2006). A plan that lays out clear goals and objectives thus serves as a road map for action for the agency.

Figure 4-2 shows how values, vision, and mission are all parts of an ongoing, iterative process by which a police agency establishes goals, generates outcomes, assesses and evaluates those outcomes, and plans changes as needed to produce better outcomes.

Goals: long-range achievements desired by an organization.

Objectives: short-term accomplishments that lead to achievement of a particular goal.

COMMON PLANNING PITFALLS

Police managers and officers plan all the time: Managers make decisions such as how many new officers to hire, what technology the agency should incorporate, and what crime trends to respond to. Officers plan how they will patrol an area, stop a traffic-law violator, prepare for their next promotion exam, or help train a new recruit. While engaging in planning, however, police personnel can fall prey to some common pitfalls.

For example, some police managers treat planning as merely an intellectual exercise, wherein they think about possible courses of action but never document their thoughts or put their ideas to actual use. Still others participate in *incremental planning*: the plan proceeds one small element at a time, especially when resources are limited. For instance, a police agency's current budget stipulates only two upgraded computers. If the agency needs more than two, managers delay the purchase until funds become available.

Managers may also neglect to assemble a planning task force—which is essential for all but the simplest of plans. Task forces are particularly crucial for plans calling for large-scale changes in a police agency or the community it serves—changes involving numerous objectives and requiring the efforts of many different people. Ideally, when a police agency is planning a major change, managers should put together a task force comprising representatives from all key stakeholder groups: upper- and mid-level commanders, line officers, civilian personnel, citizens, and business owners.

By understanding these common planning pitfalls, police personnel can more easily avoid them. They can further increase their chances of developing effective plans by understanding the types of plans most often used in a police agency.

TYPES OF PLANS

Police agencies use several types of plans that we can think of falling into the major categories of nonstrategic and strategic. Nonstrategic plan types include single-use, repeat-use, tactical, operational, and contingency. (See Table 4-1.) Such plans are intended to handle a police agency's day-to-day responsibilities and are usually developed by and for specific functions within the agency.

Single-use plan: a plan for a one-time event or special circumstance.

Repeat-use plan: a plan that may be replicated for similar events or tactical situations.

Tactical plan: a plan for special events, unique or extraordinary circumstances, or intra-agency or interagency operational needs.

Operational plan: a plan delineating functional activities and agency change processes. Drives an entire agency or units within an agency.

Contingency plan: a plan activated during serious emergencies, critical events, or disasters that affect the agency and demand immediate and/or prolonged response.

table 4-1 Types of Police Agency Plans

PLAN TYPE	PURPOSE(S)	EXAMPLE
Single-use	Provide policing services at unique events, deal with a one-time community problem, or handle a circumstance that may or may not recur.	To provide policing services for a one-time outdoor concert held in town, an agency develops a plan stipulating how officers will control the crowd and provide security for performers.
Repeat-use	Manage recurring events (such as charity drives or holiday celebrations) where large numbers of people will congregate. Develop tactics that can be used in multiple similar settings.	When residents of a specific neighborhood complain about cars speeding on their streets, police create a plan for stopping cars to verify license and registration—discouraging people from speeding through the area. The agency duplicates this same tactic in other neighborhoods within the community.
Tactical	Deal with special crime issues, such as persistent and numerous shots-fired calls, robberies, rapes, and hostage situations.	A police agency develops a plan stipulating when and how to activate a SWAT or other emergency team in a hostage situation so as to contain and end the emergency.
Operational	Drive change in an entire police agency or specific units within the agency.	An agency that decides to set up a canine unit creates a plan for selecting human and canine members of the unit, as well as training, certifying, and deploying them.
Contingency	Activate during emergencies, critical events, or disasters that affect the agency and demand immediate and prolonged response.	An agency develops plans delineating procedures for responding to terrorist attacks and natural disasters (hurricanes, tornadoes, floods) to which the area is particularly vulnerable.

Tactical (SWAT) teams execute tactical plans.

In contrast to nonstrategic plans, **strategic plans** are long-term intended courses of action designed to apply to the entire police organization. Agencies develop such plans to execute police activities directed toward high-level, overarching goals such as enhancing police professionalism, fighting crime, and improving citizen or community satisfaction with quality of life and policing services (Goldstein, 1990; Ortmeier & Meese, 2010).

Strategic plans must not be confused with small, finite series of activities intended to produce a narrowly defined desired result—such as reducing a particular type of crime in a specific part of a city. Instead, strategic plans are the result of a more complex and lengthier process through which police use critical thinking, acquire new knowledge, and execute desired activities to achieve high-level, long-term goals. Like all plans, strategic plans have no value unless they produce action (Bryson, 2004).

Strategic planning is also an ongoing process. To develop strategic plans, police managers progress through a series of steps—including defining where the agency currently is in terms of its operations and performance, establishing what its future state will be, and designing and implementing the activities needed to produce the future state—that are repeated over time. They may use frameworks such as SWOT (strengths, weaknesses, opportunities, threats) analysis (see Chapter 2) to define overarching strategic goals for their agency and then to articulate the initiatives needed to achieve those goals and the resources required to execute the initiatives (Bryson & Alston, 2005). They also take into account the agency's values, vision, and mission, as well as the priorities of stakeholders such as community members and local business leaders.

The U.S. Department of Homeland Security Strategic Plan for fiscal years 2008–2013 is an example. The plan calls for "One Team, One Mission, Securing Our Homeland." Though it is a five-year plan, the department revisits it yearly,

Strategic plans: long-term courses of action intended to apply to the entire police organization.

Leadership on the job
A Neighborhood Block Party?

Residents of a city neighborhood decide to throw a block party. They schedule the event and obtain the appropriate permits, which reveal that approximately 50 local residents and their family members will attend the party. The police department develops a single-use plan for assigning officers to the event to provide security and manage traffic.

On the day of the party, attendance swells to many times the anticipated number. Many of the party-goers turn out to be members of rival street gangs who have a history of reciprocal violence. At nightfall, the officers on detail for the party notice the gang members and become concerned. Their worries have merit: Suddenly, fights erupt among the gangsters. Overwhelmed, the police are unable to prevent injuries and property damage.

1.   Develop a repeat-use plan that could have been implemented at the event just described.

2.   Develop a contingency plan that the police department in this story might have used to prevent or contain the violence and property damage that occurred.

---

assessing core values and guiding principles, defining new goals and objectives, and implementing activities as needed to ensure achievement of the goals and objectives (*One Team, One Mission, Securing Our Homeland*, 2008).

Two especially important planning approaches are Crime Prevention Through Environment Design (CPTED) and CompStat, an approach that has enabled police agencies to reduce crime.

Crime Prevention Through Environmental Design (CPTED)

Crime Prevention Through Environmental Design (CPTED): the process of deciding how to construct or modify the physical environment to deter or discourage criminal activity.

As a type of planning, **Crime Prevention Through Environmental Design (CPTED)** is the process of deciding how to construct or modify the physical environment to deter or discourage criminal activity. By integrating certain elements into physical places, especially during new construction, communities can lower the incidence of crime and increase community cohesion—resulting in higher quality of life for residents (CPTED Watch, 2008). CPTED is an outgrowth of overall thinking about how to keep crime from occurring in the first place—rather than just react to crime after the fact. And it hinges on collaboration among police, community residents, business leaders, and local governing bodies.

Most crime prevention results from the web of security and safety precautions embodied in the institutional settings that characterize daily life. These institutions include families, communities, schools, and workplaces, as well as the legal institutions associated with criminal justice (Sherman et al., 1996). Police agencies and communities can take steps within all these settings to stop crime from taking root.

For example, home-based parenting and counseling combined with programs for preschool children have helped keep children from committing crimes when they grow older. In housing developments, restricting access to the homes and the neighborhood's recreational facilities through gates staffed by private security officers has made it difficult for criminals to enter the area and commit mischief. In areas

Technology, such as surveillance equipment, is being used to enhance police knowledge of potential and actual criminal activity.

troubled by problems such as drug dealing or automobile theft, Neighborhood Watch groups and obvious surveillance by police have helped discourage offenders from committing these sorts of crimes.

Technology has also proved a potent weapon in CPTED. For instance, police agencies have worked with communities to install video cameras on streets to record all activity—innocent and criminal alike—within the lenses' range. When an incident of crime occurs, the videotaped record can help police identify and apprehend the offender. Some evidence also suggests that illuminating areas within a community can lower crime rates by deterring would-be offenders who prefer to operate under the cover of darkness.

If crime can be prevented in places where illegal activity is most prevalent, then overall crime may be reduced. Long-ranging research has shown that most crime occurs in areas with concentrated populations; thus, researchers recommend targeting those places with crime-prevention plans (Braga, 2008).

CPTED Planning Strategies   Four strategies lie at the core of CPTED plans:

- *Natural surveillance* refers to the use of physical features that increase people's visibility in an area. Examples include doors and windows facing streets and parking areas, night-time lighting, and a willingness among residents to keep their window coverings open to observe activity in the area.

- *Territorial reinforcement* emphasizes the use of physical characteristics to differentiate private and public spaces, and to emphasize the ownership of private places while discouraging encroachment. Fences, pavement designs, gates, and landscape architecture can all be used for this purpose.

- *Natural access control* focuses on ensuring that streets and sidewalks are in full view of the community; for example, through removal of tall hedges and solid fences. This openness discourages would-be offenders who prefer to conceal themselves behind opaque barriers. Prominent video cameras on buildings can act as additional deterrents.

- *Target hardening* involves the use of hardware, lighting, and other elements (such as alarm systems and guard or pet dogs) designed to make a home or business less vulnerable to physical intrusion. For example, high-quality window locks and stout deadbolt locks for doors (rather than flimsy door chains) can discourage intrusion. Recessed interior door hinges can make it nearly impossible for burglars to remove hinges and pull a door from its frame.

Pros and Cons of CPTED   One important benefit of CPTED as a type of planning is that it promotes community cohesion. To develop an effective CPTED plan, neighbors must remain alert to what is happening in their community, and everyone needs to shoulder responsibility for residents' overall well-being. But like other forms of planning, CPTED also has its limitations. In particular, executing CPTED plans can be expensive if it requires retrofitting existing buildings and neighborhoods with crime-prevention features (Book & Schneider, 2010).

CompStat

CompStat: a policing approach involving the generation of as much real-time data as possible about crimes and the frequent evaluation of the data to develop strategies to reduce crime as quickly and effectively as possible.

CompStat is a strategic planning approach that has proven useful for reducing crime as well as enhancing the quality of life in neighborhoods, the most dramatic success being demonstrated in New York City during the 1990s (Henry, 2002). (See Chapter 2 for more information on New York City's use of CompStat.) Through the CompStat approach, police agencies can use tools including computer software applications to track crimes and criminal activity and generate real-time data valuable for reducing crime. The data include offender information, details about guns and other weapons involved in crimes, mapping to discover where criminal activity has been clustering, and other important intelligence. Crime-coordination personnel (civilian or sworn) may input data into the system, using preliminary crime reports submitted by reporting officers. Depending on the information technology used by the agency, officers may also input data from crime reports into a database application, which automates sorting of the data into categories useful to agency personnel (such as trends in weapons used or locations of particular types of crimes).

A key element in the CompStat approach is frequent evaluation of the intelligence collected, so police can develop plans for moving quickly and effectively to reduce crime. Before CompStat, statistical crime reports were available at the end of each month instead of in real time. By the time commanders read about and reacted to the statistics, crime trends were days or weeks old. By gathering real-time information, police agencies can deploy personnel and resources rapidly to areas where crimes are occurring. As such, this approach has helped create a sense of urgency for suppressing crime and apprehending suspects, and it has enabled police agencies to focus their resources more sharply on where those resources are needed most.

Relentless follow-up and assessment are additional vital elements of CompStat and help agencies ensure that a crime problem has been solved. For police officers, this can lead to a sense of accomplishment or closure; for citizens, it demonstrates an attention to detail that is often lacking in today's police agencies. Many community residents and business owners feel safer and view the police as more competent, effective, and caring.

CompStat can be a great help when making decisions to deploy police resources to locations where they are most needed.

Although the fundamentals of CompStat methodology appear sound, their implementation and publicized results have also generated some criticism. Certain studies suggest that CompStat has a dark underside, even in New York City, where it was popularized. For example, surveys of retired NYPD police commanders reveal that many felt pressured by their superiors to downgrade major crimes to minor offenses after CompStat was initiated in 1995, to give the appearance that the CompStat approach was effective. If this is true, statistically significant reductions in major crimes in some cases may have resulted from underreporting instead of from any impact from CompStat (Eterno & Silverman, 2010; Gao & Brunson, 2010; Henry, 2002; Silverman, 2001).

KEY STEPS IN THE PLANNING PROCESS

There are several models proposing steps in the planning process. Some of these models are simple (containing a few steps), while others are more complex (containing numerous steps) (Anderson, 2006; Wilson, 1952). Consider this planning-process model a police agency could use:

1. Establish a sense of urgency by stating publicly that the agency needs a plan to move toward its future.
2. Identify a facilitator and group to drive the planning process, and ask everyone to cooperate with them.

3. Define or adjust the agency's vision as needed to clarify where the agency wants to go.

4. Establish or appraise the agency's mission statement to reflect how the agency wants to operate.

5. Conduct a SWOT (strengths, weaknesses, opportunities, threats) analysis. (See Chapter 2.)

6. Articulate the results the agency wants to achieve and pinpoint the steps that will produce that result.

7. Create a step-by-step outline of how to accomplish the plan.

8. Share the plan with key agency managers and request permission to execute it.

9. While executing the plan, regularly examine results and adjust the plan as needed to improve outcomes (Hellriegel, Jackson, & Slocum, 2005; Hitt, 1988; Meese & Ortmeier, 2004).

Regardless of the number of steps a particular planning-process model contains, they can be organized into three steps essential to all planning: assessing needs and risks, developing alternative courses of action, and selecting a course of action. We take a closer look at each of these.

Needs assessment: the process an organization uses to determine whether a need (or problem) exists that could be addressed by a particular course of action.

Step 1: Assessing Needs and Risks

A police agency assesses needs and risks to create awareness that a plan of action is required. These assessments powerfully shape the rest of the planning process.

Needs The agency conducts a **needs assessment** to determine whether a need (or problem) exists that could be addressed by a particular course of action. Children

A needs assessment may reveal that safe places for children to play are not available.

Needs Assessment Tools

- **Community mapping:** Police agencies can use Geographic Information System (GIS) technology to display crime categories, patterns, or trends during a needs assessment. Mapping is often used in conjunction with the various policing strategies (see Chapter 2) and other databases (such as housing patterns and vacant properties) that become part of the assessment process. School, business, and parks locations, as well as census maps, are overlaid to produce a comprehensive view of problems associated with drug markets, petty crime, robberies, burglaries, and stolen autos and correlations with poverty, gangs, and offenders' lack of education or employment (Shane, 2007).

- **Crime analysis:** Agencies may also use various databases and other information to identify crime patterns and trends and decide how best to deploy police officers to prevent or disrupt crime patterns and arrest offenders. Crime analysts are valued specialists who use this tool.

Community mapping: process of visually displaying specific locations, addresses, or areas of noted concern.

Crime analysis: analytical process used to define current and predict future quality-of-life concerns, crime patterns, or trends.

---

playing in the street because recreational facilities and parks are not available is an example of a need.

A needs assessment generates information that guides the actions an agency might take to achieve a stated goal. To illustrate, if an agency has defined a goal of reducing crime, it would likely review crime statistics for the past year as part of its needs assessment. Rising crime rates might suggest the need for a plan to bring down the rates.

Agency leaders might also use a needs assessment to determine whether managers and officers must strengthen particular knowledge, skills, or abilities (KSAs) to meet certain goals—such as satisfying operational and ethical standards, achieving new efficiencies, or improving the agency's effectiveness. Leaders can make this assessment through interviews or casual conversations, or through more formalized information-gathering processes, such as surveys. (The box "Needs Assessment Tools" offers additional information.) This type of needs assessment yields information that can help the agency design or revise training programs to strengthen specific KSAs. It also enables agency leaders to identify trends, clarify priorities, and ensure that the agency is adhering to accreditation standards or legislatively mandated standards.

Risks   A risk is an undesirable circumstance that has not yet occurred but that a police agency should identify and develop plans for mitigating (Hellriegel et al., 2005). An agency conducts a **risk assessment** to determine whether a known or foreseeable threat exists, how likely it is that the threat will materialize, and how severe the consequences would be if the risk did materialize.

Police agencies face numerous types of risks, including the following:

- **Internal organization risks** such as computer network breakdowns or the loss of valued employees to rival agencies

Risk assessment: the process an organization uses to determine whether a known or foreseeable threat exists, how likely it is that the threat will materialize, and how severe the consequences would be if it did materialize.

figure 4-3 Risk-Assessment Matrix

| | SEVERITY OF CONSEQUENCES | | | |
PROBABILITY OF OCCURRENCE	NEGLIGIBLE	MARGINAL	CRITICAL	CATASTROPHIC
Likely	Tripped by uneven terrain			
Possible			Hit by bicycle courier	Killed by car
Unlikely		Mugged		Murdered
Rare			Raped	

- **External risks** such as damage to police vehicles from high-speed pursuits or damage to facilities from natural disasters such as floods or hurricanes
- **Neighborhood risks** such as reductions in quality of life or neighborhood cohesion and increases in crime rates

In assessing risks, the police as leaders consider two criteria: the probability that the undesirable circumstance will occur, and the magnitude of the consequences if it does occur. For risks that are highly probable *and* that would bring the worst consequences, an agency would likely want to develop a plan for mitigating those risks. Police agencies can create a matrix depicting their beliefs about how particular risks stack up in terms of probability and severity. Figure 4-3 shows a simplified example of a matrix that an agency might create to show probability and severity

A risk assessment can be used to determine if a large crowd may require additional police resources.

of different risks related to pedestrians' safety in a particular neighborhood. Risks that cluster near the upper-right-hand area of the matrix are the most probable *and* the most serious—and thus merit a plan for mitigation.

As another illustration, suppose agency leaders believe it is highly probable that conviction of a defendant in a high-profile case will spark riots and that the riots would be violent enough to put citizens' lives or personal safety in danger. In this case, agency administrators and risk managers will likely work with community leaders to develop a plan for preventing the riots. The resulting plan might call for the deployment of officers to control and contain crowds, the enforcement of loitering laws, and the dispersal of large groups before any damage has a chance to occur.

Step 2: Developing Alternative Courses of Action

After agency managers conduct appropriate needs and risks assessments, they develop **alternative courses of action** (possible action plans) for meeting the needs or mitigating the risks they identified. To develop these plans, managers consider the fiscal, physical, and personnel resources available; the activities needed to execute each plan; strategies for managing any resistance to each proposed plan; and ideas for building support for the potential courses of action. For each alternative course of action, managers evaluate probable desirable as well as undesirable consequences (Welsh & Harris, 2004). They also prepare a budget and a cost–benefit analysis for each tentative action plan. (See Chapter 5 for more information on budgeting.)

For example, suppose that a police agency, through its needs and risk assessment, identifies a problem of increasing crime in a particular neighborhood in

Alternative courses of action: possible action plans for meeting identified needs or mitigating identified risks.

Increasing crime can lead to an exodus of people and businesses from the neighborhood.

its jurisdiction. Agency managers decide that failing to address the problem could present several risks—including an exodus of citizens and businesses from the neighborhood. Managers and officers meet to discuss the problem and to generate possible courses of action for solving it.

Through brainstorming, they generate ideas for potential solutions. To ensure that they do not limit themselves to just the first idea that comes to mind or to ideas that seem most familiar, they freely suggest and list ideas without judging any of them. The meeting leader encourages participants to continue offering ideas until the "well" seems to have run dry. The result is a long list of possible courses of action, including the following:

- Increase the number of officers and patrols in the neighborhood.
- Establish a Neighborhood Watch program.
- Implement a comprehensive community policing program, with the goal of reducing crime permanently in the neighborhood.

ETHICS IN ACTION
Community–Police Partnerships

A police agency located in the northeastern part of the United States used interaction committees to open lines of communication between citizens and police officers. Attendees at one of the early interaction meetings concluded that the police department was trying to address too many priorities during each calendar year, with the result that many problems were left unsolved.

The attendees recommended that the citizens define and prioritize three yearly priority problems for a specific patrol area. The agency then trained citizens in the problem-solving process, showed them how to use brainstorming to generate a list of current problems, and helped them reduce their list to the top three problems they wanted the agency to designate as priorities. Surprisingly, while the police identified street crime as a major problem that should go in the top-three list, the citizens did not. Instead, their list included auto theft.

The police and citizens created a committee for each priority problem. Committees were responsible for developing solutions to their assigned problem, putting those solutions into action, and reporting on progress every month. During this time, nonprioritized problems were treated as calls for police service per established police procedures.

1. Should a police agency allow citizens to define and prioritize current agency problems? Discuss how this process might help or hinder police in providing citizens with more effective service.

2. The police agency and citizens differed in their assessment as to the most serious problems facing the affected area. In view of this discrepancy, discuss how a police agency can ethically accept a citizen's evaluation of priority problems to be addressed.

Step 3: Selecting a Course of Action

The final step in the planning process is to select the best possible course of action from the alternatives developed in Step 2. To choose the final plan, police managers consider several criteria—such as which plan best accommodates the agency's available resources, which plays to the agency's strengths, which would garner the most support from various stakeholders (Ortmeier & Meese, 2010), and which would generate the most enduring positive results. For example, managers and officers at the police agency that brainstormed a list of alternative courses of action for reducing crime in a particular neighborhood compared the choices' advantages and disadvantages. Table 4-2 shows their thinking on several of the proposed solutions.

A neighborhood watch effort.

Stakeholders should be invited to contribute to discussions during this step, to help secure their buy-in for the final choice. When people have a say in decisions that will ultimately affect them, they are more likely to develop a sense of ownership over those decisions and therefore support them. Police personnel should also clearly state the goals of each proposed action plan so stakeholders can see how the plan supports the agency's mission.

Selecting a course of action from a set of alternatives requires strong decision-making competence (a leadership skill). Decision making can be more complicated than it might originally appear on the surface because there are many factors to weigh (Bryson & Alston, 2005). For example, will a proposed course of action have enough support from key stakeholders? Does the agency have sufficient resources

table 4-2 Comparing Potential Solutions

SOLUTION	EXPLANATION	ADVANTAGES	DISADVANTAGES
1	Increase the number of officers and patrols	Can be done quickly	Expensive
2	Form Neighborhood Watch program	Least expensive	Takes time
3	Implement a comprehensive community policing program	Most effective in the long term	Takes time; officers must develop leadership skills and citizen–partnership skills

to implement the selected solution? Will those responsible for putting the plan into action approach the task with the required urgency?

In choosing a final action plan, police managers may take a number of different approaches. Several examples include:

- **Accommodating stakeholder priorities.** In police agencies, the loudest or most persistent stakeholder usually captures the most attention, and agency managers often feel pressured to appease that person or group while selecting plans of action. For instance, perhaps an agency chooses a plan that satisfies a politically powerful neighborhood group leader who wants the agency to build a visible citizen–police substation, even though the substation requires additional resources that will be difficult to obtain.

- **Making innovative change.** Agency managers may select a final plan based on its opportunity to effect innovative change. For example, an agency selects an action plan that includes officers' use of a Taser electronic device to subdue agitated or violent subjects without causing injury. A Taser delivers electrical pulses that affect the suspect's motor and sensory functions and can reduce injuries to suspects and officers, which can in turn reduce liability claims against police (Taser International Inc., 2008).

- **Using intuition.** Some managers make decisions by drawing on their past experiences, expertise, knowledge, and intuitive sense for what might constitute the best course of action for solving a particular problem. This "sixth sense" approach hinges on the ability to blend information from both personal and outside sources while arriving at a decision (Angelfire.com, 2009; Casto, 2009; Decision-Making-Confidence.com, 2008; Vaknin, 2006).

- **Clarifying decision roles.** Managers define what role each participant in the decision will play. To illustrate, will everyone involved in selecting a final plan of action provide input and have a say in the ultimate decision? Will the leader of the planning process consult others and solicit their opinions but then make the final choice alone? Will the individuals involved need to arrive at a consensus before the decision is deemed final? Or will they vote on the various alternative plans proposed, and the plan with the most votes will be implemented?

So, what course of action did the police agency seeking to reduce crime in a particular neighborhood select from its list of working alternatives? Ultimately, managers and officers selected Solution 3—implement a comprehensive community policing program—because they believed it would prove most effective in the long run. While other choices were faster or cheaper to implement, those alternatives would not generate the enduring results promised by the community policing alternative.

MASTERING THE ART OF SELF-MANAGEMENT

No matter how carefully a police agency has assessed its needs and risks, developed a full set of alternative plans for addressing those needs and risks, and selected a final course of action to implement, events still may not unfold as expected once the plan is implemented. For example, an unexpected emergency—such as a fire or hurricane or a raft of gang-related shootings—might consume resources that had been set aside for the final action plan the agency selected. Or the agency may put its chosen plan into action, only to learn that the political support managers had counted on has evaporated.

When the inevitable mismatch between results and intentions arises, it is all too easy for planners to grow frustrated and even angry. But that is precisely when they need to summon their powers of **self-management**—the process of monitoring and controlling their emotions and remaining flexible and balanced (Hitt, 1988). Self-management comprises numerous abilities. But the abilities most relevant to police agency planning are as follows:

Regular exercise can help with stress management.

Self-management: the process of monitoring and controlling one's emotions and remaining flexible and balanced in the face of disappointment or frustration.

- **Remaining focused on the agency's goals.** By staying focused on agency goals in the face of frustration or disappointment, police managers and officers can more easily recover from setbacks and determine how to adjust an action plan to produce more desirable results.

- **Knowing one's personal strengths and limitations.** When managers know themselves, they can build on their strengths and manage their limitations. For example, if Barry, a police administrator, knows that he tends to feel stressed when things do not go according to plan, he can take steps to manage his stress, such as practicing relaxation techniques or going for a quick walk.

- **Learning continually from experience** (Buckingham & Clifton, 2001; Hellriegel et al., 2005; Say, 2007). By monitoring the results that a plan produces once it is implemented and comparing those results against the plan's intended outcomes, managers can identify gaps and then look for causes of the gaps. Understanding how and why a plan did not produce the intended results can help managers learn from experience and produce a more effective plan in the future.

- **Assessing the planning process itself.** Just as individual officers receive periodic evaluations, so should the planning process itself. Police managers can periodically assess planning efforts in their agency and identify areas that could benefit from improvement. For example, do planners need to be better at involving stakeholders in developing and evaluating potential courses of action? Should they use a different decision-making approach when selecting a plan from a set of proposed alternatives? By taking an honest look at their planning abilities, police personnel stand a better chance of making needed improvements.

summary

- **Adopting a Long-Term, Big-Picture View.** Police agencies must develop plans for addressing not only small, short-term problems but also major, long-term issues. But in most agencies, planning centers entirely on the former.

- **Aligning Plans with Values, Vision, and Mission.** A police agency's values (fundamental beliefs, principles, or standards), its vision (image of a desired future state), and its mission (a short-range task or assignment it wishes to achieve) guide the definition of the goals (long-range desired achievements) and objectives (short-term accomplishments that lead to achievement of a goal) that the agency's plans contain.

- **Common Planning Pitfalls.** Pitfalls include failing to put proposed ideas into action, moving a plan forward one small step at a time owing to lack of resources, and failure to assemble a task force for plans that call for major change, numerous objectives, and the efforts of many different people.

- **Types of Plans.** Plan types include single-use, repeat-use, tactical, operational, and contingency. Strategic plans are long-term intended courses of action designed to apply to the entire police organization. Crime Prevention Through Environmental Design (CPTED) is a type of planning that entails constructing or modifying the physical environment to discourage criminal activity.

- **Key Steps in the Planning Process.** Steps include assessing needs and risks (using tools including community mapping and crime analysis), developing alternative courses of action for addressing a need or risk (using techniques such as brainstorming), and selecting a final course of action by comparing alternatives' advantages and disadvantages based on criteria such as cost, efficiency, and ability to deliver sustained results. To select a final course of action, agency personnel can use additional approaches, such as accommodating stakeholder priorities, making a selection based on its ability to effect innovative change, using intuition, and clarifying decision roles.

- **Mastering the Art of Self-Management.** If a plan does not deliver its intended result or cannot be implemented as intended (for example, there are fewer resources or less political support than expected), agency personnel must practice self-management—monitoring and controlling their emotions and remaining flexible and balanced. Self-management techniques include remaining focused on the agency's goals, playing to one's strengths while compensating for one's limitations, learning continually from experience, and assessing the planning process itself.

key terms

alternative courses of action
community mapping
CompStat
contingency plans
crime analysis
Crime Prevention Through Environmental Design (CPTED)
goals
mission

needs assessment

objectives

operational plans

planning

repeat-use plans

risk assessment

self-management

single-use plans

strategic plans

tactical plans

values

vision

1. Go to your local police agency and ask what its vision and mission are. Then identify several goals to which the vision and mission might align. For each goal you have identified, what are several objectives that could help lead to achievement of the goal?

2. What event can force a plan to be implemented in an incremental manner? If you had to develop an incremental plan for adding computer laptops to patrol cars, what would your plan consist of?

3. Give an example of a single-use plan, a repeat-use plan, a tactical plan, and an operational plan.

4. What kinds of events would necessitate a contingency plan for a police agency?

5. How do strategic plans differ from other types of plans in a police agency?

6. What is Crime Prevention Through Environmental Design? How might you use this type of planning to improve quality of life in your neighborhood, town, or city? What challenges might using CPTED present?

7. How would you develop a needs assessment process to examine morale in a police agency?

8. Describe a situation that would require a police agency to conduct a risk assessment.

9. Visit your local police agency to learn whether and how it is using needs assessment tools such as community mapping and crime analysis. What do personnel at the agency see as the advantages and disadvantages of these tools?

10. Using the planning process, formulate a solution to address the following problem: A series of residential burglaries have been perpetrated by at least three persons who enter the homeowner's car to obtain and use the garage door opener to gain entry to the residence.

11. How do you typically react when a plan does not produce the intended outcomes or cannot be implemented as you had hoped? What steps might you take to manage any frustration or anger you experience when this happens?

WHAT WOULD YOU DO?

Investigating the Investigators

A medium-size police agency in the northeastern part of the United States reviewed its approach to distributing police investigators and conducting follow-up investigations to felony crimes. In the recent past, the agency had used a specific approach for these tasks. Police supervisors dispersed crime cases for follow-up to those investigators assigned to the hourly platoon that the investigators worked. Crime cases were assigned, deadlines were established, and closed cases were submitted by investigators back to the supervisors for review and acceptance. The supervisors were not trained investigators and generally used a hands-off management style, treating all investigators as experts with respect to their job duties and responsibilities.

When managers reviewed the investigative process and evaluated the efficiency and effectiveness of the follow-up investigation process, they identified several distinct challenges, including difficulties with supervising investigators and case investigations, matching specific cases to investigator strengths, and evaluating investigators on criteria such as timeliness of case closure, number of confessions, and number of cases closed by arrest of perpetrators. The current approach was delivering neither the efficiency nor the effectiveness required to adequately serve the community.

As a result, the agency named a supervisor (police sergeant) with investigator experience as commander of investigators for the affected precinct. The commander assigned all investigations, set deadlines for each investigation, matched investigations to investigator experience and skill level, and evaluated each investigator's case load by type of case closure and methods of investigation. He also conducted numerous in-service investigator training sessions for current investigators. Efficiency and effectiveness improved, as measured by timeliness and case closure status. And the entire agency soon adopted the new model.

1. If you were a police leader who had risen through the ranks of a police agency and investigated numerous crimes, which of the two models of investigator supervision described would you recommend to your agency? Why?

2. What are the strengths and challenges presented by the first model? What are the strengths and challenges presented by the second model?

3. Which model best supports the planning process emphasized in this chapter? Why? Discuss the planning steps reflected in the model you have selected.

5

◀ A Hackettstown, New Jersey, middle school student and a Hackettstown police officer engage in a fund-raising basketball event to benefit the school and the Hackettstown Police Benevolent Association.

Budgeting and Fiscal Management

After completing this chapter, readers should be able to:

- define *budget* and explain its purpose.
- describe public budgeting and its constraints.
- describe the public budgeting process.
- explain the need for flexibility in a police agency's budget.
- identify and compare types of budgets including traditional, line item, program, performance based, zero based, balanced based, activity based, operating, and capital.
- identify the main sections that make up a budget.
- list the basic expenditure categories that appear in a budget.
- identify sources of revenue for government entities.

learning outcomes

- explain how police agencies make resource-allocation decisions through three types of analysis (cost–benefit, return on investment, and value-added contribution).
- explain how police agencies win support for a proposed budget, including dealing with budget cutbacks.
- describe how an agency executes its budget, through activities such as managing projects, calculating maintenance of effort, and auditing.

Introduction

Responsible police managers and line personnel know that public safety is important to the average citizen. Safe communities are also fiscally healthy communities. They stimulate commerce and economic growth, stabilize or grow the population, and increase the community's tax base. To make neighborhoods safe, police agencies need to partner with community teams to create and sustain a civil and livable environment.

Public safety thus requires resources, especially financial ones. Police departments and other law enforcement agencies depend on financial resources—gained primarily through the taxes that citizens pay—to acquire and maintain equipment and facilities, and to hire, train, deploy, and retain the right personnel. Typically, police managers use the budgeting process to determine how much money they need to build and maintain safe neighborhoods. They present the budget to community leaders, who then work those funding requests into their own budgets.

Yet police managers often rush through the budgeting process because it seems to detract from their publicly stated mission of keeping the streets safe. Indeed, many police personnel, no matter what their level in the organization, view budgeting as a task that should be done by "bean counters." However, without a budget, a police agency cannot allocate financial resources appropriately and use them wisely. Just as a family budget enables household members to plan for the future and ensure the family's financial health, a police agency's budget positions the agency to plan for and to safeguard the community's well-being.

In this chapter, we take a close look at the budgeting process—how it works, how it relates to the sound fiscal management and administration of police agencies, and what leadership skills it requires.

WHAT IS A BUDGET?

Budget:
a plan expressed in financial terms.

A **budget** is a plan expressed in financial terms. Budgeting is the thread that weaves through a sound fiscal management strategy. You may maintain a personal budget to compare your income with your expenses on a regular basis (monthly, quarterly, yearly) and to determine when you are spending more than you are earning. A family keeps a household budget to do the same. Companies large and small also use budgets—to identify revenue streams and estimate expenses for specific time periods. (Large organizations' budgets can be highly complex, often containing details that relate specifically to individual business-unit, division, and department levels.) Government entities—such as police agencies—also use budgets to forecast revenue and expenditures for a fiscal period (usually 12 months beginning January 1, July 1, or October 1).

Public Budgeting

Any public organization seeking to develop a budget should take into account its intended strategy, its existing personnel and the services it offers, initiatives in the pipeline (such as projects aimed at developing new services), the resources these efforts will need, and capital investment that will be required to achieve strategic objectives. A budget, in short, shows how the organization plans to make its vision real.

Effective police agencies also use the budgeting process to make and enforce decisions about how community resources will be allocated to meet civic needs. To that end, the public budgeting process must also ensure that projected revenue will cover all authorized expenditures.

Public budgets—such as those used in police agencies—strongly reflect the priorities of the stakeholders served by the organization. For example, a town or city budget reveals citizens' preferences regarding how much taxes will be paid and where the money will be invested. In addition, public budgets reflect the relative power of individuals and groups to influence how an organization or community allocates its resources. Finally, public organizations' budgets can be used as a tool for stakeholders to determine whether the organization is fulfilling its responsibilities. Unlike personal households or private businesses, government entities spend the public's money. Thus, their budgets are subject to public scrutiny, debate, and accountability.

Public finance is used to construct new police facilities.

Constraints in Public Budgeting

Some police agencies budget for a two-year period, or biennium. However, most agencies work on the basis of budgeting for a fiscal year, which is a 12-month period that can cover the calendar year or some other period. For example, the federal government currently uses October 1 to September 30 as its fiscal year (Heniff, 2003; Lectric Law Library, 2009).

Most public budgets are based heavily on the budget for the previous year. Unlike budgets for individuals or corporations, a public budget is constrained by statutory requirements. For example, a state's constitution, a city charter, or a legislative mandate may stipulate that the budget must be balanced (revenues equal expenses), or may limit the amount of taxes available to fund the agency. Public budgets must also reflect citizens' preferences. For instance, citizens are willing to pay for services based on the perceived worth of those services, and they resent paying more than what they see as their fair share.

Public budgeting is also strongly influenced by political dynamics, because it entails negotiations among different parties with different motivations. Conflict often erupts when interest groups' demands clash with the intentions of those who possess the political power. To illustrate, suppose neighborhood residents want foot-patrol officers on a continual basis to provide for a perception of constant police presence. However, the police agency cannot afford foot patrols and wants to use officers in a different way—deploying them as needed to address serious incidents of crime. To resolve such conflicts, the various stakeholders must make compromises. For example, police managers meet with neighborhood residents and agree to develop a citizen foot-patrol initiative that will be supported by agency crime-prevention efforts.

Members of the Chicago Police Department on patrol. While expensive, foot patrol can enhance police–community relations and reduce citizen fear of crime.

The Public Budgeting Process

The public budgeting process typically proceeds in one of two ways: bottom up or top down. For organizations that use the bottom-up approach, unit managers build their budgets, which then get "rolled up" to the chief executive officer (CEO) and then to legislators and other elected officials. For organizations using the top-down approach, high-level managers determine a budget without input from unit managers, and then unit-level budgets are built based on the high-level budget. In this case, unit managers are rarely provided with detailed instructions regarding budget requests, policy choices, and spending controls. A public agency may use either the bottom-up or top-down approach, though top down tends to predominate when money is tight.

Like other public organizations, police agencies typically advance through three steps in building and operationalizing their budget:

1. Prepare the budget documents.
2. Obtain approval of the completed budget.
3. Implement the approved budget.

But these steps do not necessarily unfold in a linear manner. At any time during a fiscal year, a police manager may be involved in executing the current budget, reworking a newly approved budget to plan for unforeseen circumstances, forecasting the upcoming year's budget, and responding to the audit of last year's budget (Rabin, Hildreth, & Miller, 1996; Rubin, 2006).

The size of a police agency can influence how the budgeting process unfolds and who does what during the process. In smaller agencies, the chief of police may assume the entire responsibility for budget preparation. In large agencies, a budget manager or officer may coordinate the process. Individual department managers may

Some police officers face the challenging task of reviewing budget documents.

prepare recommendations for their department's budget, which then becomes part of the larger budget document. The chief of police assumes the role of ultimate decision maker in the final budget approval (Jurkanin, Hoover, Dowling, & Ahmad, 2001).

In large police agencies, bureau chiefs typically get involved in the budgeting process. Many of them want to promote growth in the agency's revenue while maintaining existing services. The agency may also employ an executive-level budget officer to monitor expenditures, prevent waste, and accomplish policy and political goals. Executives most involved in budgeting may be those with the most personal charisma or political "capital." Or they may have the most obvious problems in their departments—an example of "the squeaky wheel gets the grease" principle.

Legislators, meanwhile, may make compromises with other legislators to establish budgets, while seeking to also meet demands from constituents and special-interest groups as well as solve specific problems plaguing their community. Special-interest groups may get involved in the budgeting process in numerous ways as well; for instance, demanding that taxes be earmarked for certain spending priorities. The courts may also enter the picture, usually after an aggrieved party sues a jurisdiction or government entity over a disputed current practice, such as the level of taxes a community levies or a disciplinary fine levied because of inappropriate use of police powers. Honoring these legal priorities often takes precedence over creating a balanced budget. For example, the judgment of a court may require a jail facility to maintain a specified level of healthcare for inmates, even if the funds for doing so are not provided in the budget. The voices of individual citizens are rarely heard while a large police agency is working out its budget.

The Need for Flexibility

As we have seen, a police agency's budget represents a financial plan for the organization for a fiscal year—showing what revenue the agency expects to receive and how it intends to allocate that revenue to serve citizens. However, in preparing a budget, police managers cannot anticipate serious revenue shortfalls or unexpected needs.

Leadership on the job

High Fuel Costs: A Budgeting Challenge

As soaring fuel costs squeezed police agency budgets in 2008, police chiefs and sheriffs sought ways to maintain services while using less gasoline. Some agencies set maximums on per-shift mileage driven. Others modified patrol operations, used alternative fuels, or converted to fuel-efficient vehicles. Still others increased the use of foot and bicycle patrol, field-based reporting, and citizen reporting of minor incidents via telephone.

Some fuel-saving initiatives led to a reduction in police services. For example, several agencies reduced the number of patrol vehicles available for service, thus increasing time required to respond to calls for service.

1. What are some additional methods that would enable police agencies to reduce vehicle fuel consumption while maintaining or even improving police services?

2. Can the strategic and tactical use of community policing and problem-solving methodologies lower an agency's vehicle fuel costs? Explain.

3. How can a police manager anticipate and prepare for high fuel expenses?

Therefore, the budget must be flexible: Once it is implemented, managers must revisit it periodically to determine whether actual revenue and expenditures reflect what they expected while they were preparing the budget. For example, after a budget is approved, a natural disaster (such as a flood) that demands additional police resources will call for some revenue to be redirected away from other activities.

TYPES OF BUDGETS

There are many types of budgets that public organizations can use, including traditional, line item, performance based, zero based, program, balance based, operating, and capital. A single police agency might use several of these types of budgets during a fiscal year, often simultaneously, depending on how well the different types meet the needs of the agency and the community as well as fiscal constraints (Rubin, 2006). In the following text we examine each type and consider when and why an agency might use each.

Traditional Budget

In its most elementary form, a **traditional budget** reflects a simple percentage increase in funding over the most recent budget. A traditional budget for a police agency illustrates detailed costs of items by using item accounts. The budget shows the cost of a class of labor or type of material, along with the organizational unit (for example, the department or division within the agency). Whereas a traditional budget might provide workload information (personnel hours), it does not typically contain efficiency data (production of services per hour worked) or effectiveness data (quality of results). Rather, the overall objective of a traditional budget is

Traditional budget: a budget that reflects a simple percentage increase in funding over the most recent budget.

Police recruits receive a supply of new protective vests.

control of financial resources. Budget decisions are based on item costs per unit of contracted service or products being purchased. For instance, police agencies may purchase a trainer's services by hours of training rendered or purchase firearms based on the cost of each weapon (Sunnyvale, 2008).

A major advantage of traditional budgeting is that it is widely used and easily understood. Moreover, managers can transfer funds among accounts easily and increase or decrease item accounts as the need arises. Indeed, many managers consider it perfectly acceptable to reformulate the budget throughout the fiscal year.

A key disadvantage of traditional budgeting is that it does not account for specific policing activities or the outcomes associated with those activities. It thus does not generate insights about an activity's efficiency or effectiveness.

Line-Item Budget

Line-item budget:
a budget in which each item is described and assigned a place (line), with a corresponding dollar value.

A **line-item budget** (also called an object-of-expenditure budget) counts among the most commonly used of all budget types for most organizations, including police and other public safety agencies. Each item is described and assigned a place (line) in the budget with a corresponding dollar value. Line-item budgeting offers a level of detail and clarity that facilitates planning and cost control (Dossett, 2005).

Line-item budgeting also promotes strict accountability by forcing decision makers to allocate a dollar value to each item on the budget, creating an item-by-item spending schedule. Line-item budgets are easy to audit—another key advantage. The biggest disadvantages of line-item budgeting are its inflexibility (the budget is not updated throughout the fiscal year) and lack of connection to performance objectives. A line-item budget thus does not show whether policing services called for in an agency's strategy have in fact been delivered—or whether they have generated the intended results.

Program Budget

Program budget:
a budget that presents programs and services separately in categories.

A **program budget** is a variation of the line-item budget. Programs such as business crime prevention or drug-abuse resistance education (DARE) are presented separately in categories very similar to those listed in the line-item budget format. A program budget also focuses on the services an organization provides to its customers. For a police agency and the various units within it, "customers" can be external individuals (citizens) or internal entities (agency units) in need of services.

A program budget enables decision makers to compare and analyze the effectiveness of different programs. This analysis minimizes competition for resources among programs and prevents duplication of effort. However, the process of building a program budget may lead unit managers to offer exaggerated explanations for their budget requests to justify how they spend their time and other resources.

Performance-Based Budget

Performance-based budget:
a budget that links measurable activities to established strategic objectives.

A **performance-based budget** focuses on the activities needed to deliver policing services, with the measurable activity as the basic budgeting unit. Measurable activities are linked to established strategic objectives. For example, suppose an objective calls for improving response time to calls for service. Measurable activities associated

Measurable activities for police include traffic citations issued, arrests made, vehicles towed, and vehicle-collision scenes processed.

with that goal might include increasing the number of patrol officers available. Likewise, suppose an objective calls for improving relations with a neighborhood action committee that is concerned about the enforcement of a noise ordinance regarding loud stereos in motor vehicles. Measurable activities associated with that goal might include identifying problem locations, tracking the number of noise ordinance tickets issued, and monitoring the number of vehicles towed owing to violations of the noise ordinance.

Managers can use this type of budget to assess efficiency of these activities, by comparing their cost with their results. To illustrate, consider the noise ordinance example introduced earlier. To enforce the noise ordinance, a police agency must use a noise meter to measure the volume of noise and distance noises can be heard. To accomplish this task, the agency establishes a noise ordinance detail and an area check point. It measures distances, and assigns personnel to various tasks to adequately establish whether violations of the ordinance have occurred. This is all costly, and the costs may outweigh any quantifiable benefits gained. Still, the agency may decide to continue the program because citizens' perceptions that the police care about their concerns creates valuable goodwill in the community.

Performance-based budgets usually place emphasis on planning to achieve specific service objectives rather than basing decisions solely on costs. A major disadvantage of performance-based budgeting is that some types of performance (such as crime prevention) can be difficult to define in quantifiable terms (Dossett, 2004).

Zero-Based Budget

In a **zero-based budget,** all available revenue is allocated to expense categories, resulting in a net zero budget balance. The major advantage to zero-based budgeting

Zero-based budget: a budget in which all available revenue is allocated to expense categories.

is the high degree of control it provides to decision makers. Police managers can use this type of budget to examine current programs and rank them according to how well they support the agency's goals and to develop new programs that directly support important goals. Advocates of zero-based budgeting emphasize its ability to promote innovation, effectiveness, and efficiency.

The disadvantages of zero-based budgeting include its focus on controllable elements of the budget and the subjective decision making often associated with its use. Evaluating the results of budgeted programs is difficult and expensive, and the budget doesn't take into account interrelationships among organizational programs. Also, many people find using the type of budget to be cumbersome.

Balanced-Based Budget

Balanced-based budget: a budget based on an estimate of future revenues.

A **balanced-based budget** is often used when a reduction in revenues forces decreases in expenditures. The budget is based on an estimate of future revenues. Managers allocate funds according to the agency's needs and the community's priorities. Planned programs and activities are clustered together in the budget based on their connection to common organizational objectives.

Managers use three processes to determine expenditure levels for a balanced-based budget: reduction in funding, base level for a balanced budget, and additional funds and explanation of services at each level. This budget method focuses on long-range planning, goals, and outcomes of activities. For example, managers may submit a budget request calling for a 5 percent reduction in funds requested, no change, or a 5 percent increase. They are expected to justify any increases in expenditures they request.

Many jurisdictions use balanced-based budgeting to solicit input from agency personnel regarding which expenditures could be cut, what the costs of maintaining the same level of services might be, what cost-of-living increases they might need, and which new initiatives need to be implemented. Police agencies are especially vulnerable to funding reductions with balanced-based budgets during taxpayer revolts and periods of financial retrenchment. During such times, agencies may be forced to reduce workforce headcount, leave some vacant positions unfilled, or even shut down if elected officials decide to contract with another jurisdiction to provide police services.

Activity-Based Budget

Activity-based budget: a budget that defines and analyzes all the activities consuming an organization's financial resources.

An **activity-based budget** defines and analyzes *all* activities that consume financial resources (such as officers' responding to calls for service in a particular neighborhood, or police vehicles' getting into accidents)—not just those activities directly required to deliver specific policing services. Managers compare the activities to the agency's strategic goals, and allocate funds in the budget for any activities relevant to the goals. Unlike a traditional budget, an activity-based budget is not adjusted to reflect inflation or unexpected increases in revenue.

This type of budget enables decision makers to analyze the potential and actual impact of the agency's services. It thus provides a formula for calculating return on investment. Managers can improve efficiency of activities by consolidating several that support the same strategic goal or by reconfiguring them. Activity-based budgeting thus focuses agency personnel's attention on activities that produce intended results (Garrison, Noreen, & Brewer, 2006).

Operating Budget

An **operating budget** is a short-term (usually 12 months, or fiscal year) budget that accounts for the agency's current operating expenses as distinct from major financial transactions or permanent capital improvements (enhancements of permanent infrastructure). The operating budget includes items such as salaries, education and training, repairs, supplies, lease and rental payments, uniforms, and utilities expenses. It outlines the plan for current noncapital expenditures as well as the proposed means of financing them. An annual operating budget is a primary means through which an agency's authorized revenue and financing acquisitions (income), spending, and service delivery activities are controlled.

The operating budget includes vehicle maintenance. The capital budget reflects the purchase of police vehicles.

Operating budget: a short-term budget that accounts for the agency's current operating expenses as distinct from major financial transactions or permanent capital improvements.

Capital Budget

A **capital budget** is used for projects and expenses that are designed to yield benefits well into the future. Capital budget items therefore tend to include fixed assets such as land, structures, buildings, streets, bridges, and other infrastructure, as well as police vehicles and other equipment—items of major value with life expectancies in excess of one year.

The capital budget usually shows expected expenditures on such assets five to seven years into the future. This type of budgeting ensures that funding for capital expenditures is not diverted to the purchase of other shorter-term items or services. It also helps police agencies replace public safety equipment and structures in an orderly way. The capital budget process usually comprises three steps:

Capital budget: a budget that shows projects and expenses designed to yield benefits well into the future.

1. *Planning.* Managers classify and analyze budget requests, rank the requests according to how well they support the agency's strategic objectives, prepare capital-improvement-plan (CIP) schedules, and forecast necessary and predictable resources.

2. *Budgeting.* Managers evaluate projects under consideration, select some for financing, obtain approval for capital requests from authorizing sources, and appropriate the approved funding.

3. *Implementing.* The agency designs or acquires (through purchase or lease) approved equipment and facilities, or contracts for the construction of such assets (Rabin et al., 1996).

Construction of a firearms range is an example of a capital expenditure. Here recruits use the Worcester County Firearms Training Center in Newark, Maryland.

In proposing a capital expenditure, police agency managers should ask themselves two questions. First, is the project necessary? The answer may depend on a number of criteria. For example, perhaps the project has been mandated by the state legislature. Or maybe it would help the agency achieve new efficiencies, deliver greater value to the community, or avoid a particular hazard. To illustrate, managers may determine that their agency needs a new firearms range because the existing range has been shown to contain a dangerous level of lead particulates or residue from bullets.

Second, will the community support the project? How local politicians and citizens rate the project will determine funding priority. For instance, if the jurisdiction's tax revenue stream is inadequate to support construction of the new firearms range, voters may be asked to approve the sale of municipal bonds to cover the project's costs. In situations like this, police managers need a can-do attitude, a talent for persuasion, and a strong grasp of all the issues and facts regarding the project in question.

BUILDING THE BUDGET

To build a budget, police agencies draft specific sections with an eye toward the expenditures the budget must cover and the revenue needed to fund those expenditures. While deciding how to allocate financial resources across the budget, managers must make tough decisions. Next, we examine the sections that make up a typical budget, the expenditure categories most agencies will show in their budgets, typical sources of revenue for police agencies, and analyses that can help police managers make budget decisions.

Anatomy of a Budget

Most budgets contain four sections: the budget message, the summary schedule, detailed schedules, and supplemental data.

- The *budget message* contains a description of the economic situation of the jurisdiction (municipality, county, state), community priorities, the existence of special circumstances (such as anticipated special events or a wave of personnel retirements), any financial constraints, and key financial and program changes from the previous year's budget.

- The *summary schedule* includes calculations of property and other tax revenues, total revenue and expenses, expenditures assigned to major categories, revenue organized according to source, and possibly expenditures for subunits (such as patrol and support services).

- The *detailed schedules* are organized by the type of service delivered, government entity involved (for example, public works or police), and line items for goods and services to be purchased. In a large agency, exhibits to this section often include detailed budgets of the various units within the agency.

- The *supplemental data* include whatever police officials wish to add, such as an explanation to accompany certain funds, ordinances, capital expenses, debts, trust and agency funds, and grants (Rabin et al., 1996).

Expenditure Categories

A central function of a budget is to show planned expenditures for the fiscal year covered by the budget. A typical budget contains at least five basic **budget categories** related to expenditures:

- **Personnel expenses** include all spending associated with agency employee payroll (such as wages, salaries, benefits, and state and federal payroll taxes). This expenditure category usually represents the largest within any police agency's budget, consuming as much as 85 percent of the budget.

- **Operating expenses** are associated with nontangible expenditures; for example, training and maintenance.

- **Supplies and material expenses** include tangible objects with a life expectancy of a year or less, such as fuel and ammunition.

- **Capital expenses** include tangible depreciable objects with a life expectancy of more than one year, for instance, buildings and computers.

- **Miscellaneous expenses** include any expenditures that are not more appropriately placed in one of the other four basic budget categories, such as travel to professional conferences (Ortmeier & Meese, 2010).

Budget categories: categories in a budget representing types of expenses.

Table 5-1 illustrates expenditure categories, with examples of the items typically included within these budget categories. Figure 5-1 shows how expenditures are allocated in many police agencies.

Sources of Revenue

All police agencies have sources of revenue that are reflected in their budgets. These sources include taxes, fines, and fees; grants; and donations, fund-raisers, IRS reimbursements, and forfeitures. Let's look at each of these.

Taxes, Fines, and Fees   Taxes are a primary source of revenue for most government entities, including police agencies. Not surprisingly, government officials often want to raise taxes to increase money flowing into public entities—while citizens want their taxes reduced. But unless a policy agency can achieve efficiencies that reduce

▎**table 5-1** Categories of Expenditures in Detail

Personnel Expenses	**Supplies and Materials Expenses**
Salaries and wages (hourly)	Fuel
Statutorily-mandated payroll taxes (e.g., Social Security)	Ammunition
Health insurance	Office supplies
Retirement contributions	Computer software
Overtime pay	**Capital Expenses**
Operating Expenses	Firearms
Lease payments (real estate and equipment)	Buildings
Utilities	Vehicle, aircraft, vessels
Insurance	Computers
Legal fees	Communications equipment
Pre-employment screening	**Miscellaneous Expenses**
Training	Depreciation (of capital assets)
Contract services	Travel (e.g., professional conferences)
Maintenance	
Professional fees/memberships	

Source: Ortmeier, 1999.

its expenses, it is virtually impossible to refrain from raising taxes, for several reasons. First, as the cost and standard of living escalate in a community, agencies need more financial resources to maintain policing services. Second, external forces such as the termination of a grant, an economic recession, natural disasters, and war can reduce the revenue flowing into a police agency. Therefore, there's a constant need to increase tax revenue while also recognizing that resistance to raising taxes will persist.

The main sources of tax revenue for a police agency are local sales and property taxes and those collected and shared by the state. In some states, police agencies can generate additional revenue from permit fees (for example, for burning brush), motor-vehicle violation fines, court fines, parking fees and citation payments, and pet licensing fees. However, in several states, fine revenue does not flow to the agency but to the state's general fund.

▎**figure 5-1** Expenditure Categories for a Police Agency

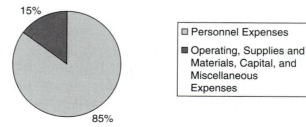

Parking fines can be used as a source of revenue in some jurisdictions. In other jurisdictions, the fine revenue is transferred to the state's general fund. This photo displays a car ticketed in Tampa, Florida.

Some police agencies also charge for services or initiate a special fee structure for traffic control and officer presence at special community events such as baseball and soccer games, bicycle races, and neighborhood block parties. Several agencies charge a fee when they detain an arrestee from another jurisdiction. Other agencies charge fees after a specified number of responses to house and business false alarms. During times of fiscal belt-tightening, agencies use volunteers wherever practicable and reduce overtime expenses by assigning regular on-duty personnel to perform tasks whenever possible (Rabin et al., 1996).

Grants   A grant is an entrustment of funds derived from sources such as individuals, corporations, foundations, family bequests, or government entities. Grants are awarded to help the recipient organization achieve its strategic objectives or develop or enhance its programs. A grant is interest-free and typically nonrefundable.

The grantor—the individual or entity offering the grant—generally designates funds to address a specific service objective or problem experienced by the recipient, or grantee. Thus, to acquire grant funds from any source, a police agency must often define, articulate, or adjust a strategic project or program goal to match the grantor's requirements. To be eligible for funding, the police agency completes a grant application—which calls for strong writing skills. The information provided in the application must meet the grantor's objectives, timelines, and other requirements. If the agency is awarded the grant, it must use the money as directed by the granting authority and report regularly on program expenditures and outcomes.

Grants vary according to type and restrictions. For example, federal grants to a state, county, or municipality typically require the grantee to provide matching resources. The matching resources may include monetary or *in-kind* contributions (for example, personnel or equipment). Grant types include the following:

- **Closed-end grants** limit fund expenditures to narrowly defined products or services and typically include highly detailed compliance requirements.

Closed-end grant: limits fund expenditures to narrowly defined products or services and typically includes highly detailed compliance requirements.

A jurisdiction may receive a closed-end grant for a particular service or equipment such as advanced crime-lab technology, with the jurisdiction matching or paying for any amount exceeding the funds allocated through the grant (Harvey, 2000; Rabin et al., 1996).

During fiscal year 2008, the U.S. Department of Justice, Office of Community Oriented Policing Services, offered approximately $13 million to enhance security in school buildings and on school property. The program provided reimbursement for up to 50 percent of the cost of implementing options such as school safety assessments, placement and use of security technology and equipment, and coordination efforts with policing agencies (U.S. Department of Justice, Office of Community Oriented Policing Services, 2008).

Categorical grant: spending is not as restrictive as for closed-end grant. Expenditures are allowed within a category of programs or services.

- **Categorical grants** typically allow expenditures within a specified category of spending alternatives. Thus they are limited to a set of defined services or programs. In 2005, for example, the municipality of Anchorage, Alaska, applied for and received a federal categorical grant in the amount of $450,000 that included a necessary local match of approximately $170,000. The U.S. Department of Justice, Bureau of Justice Assistance awarded the grant to establish a partnership among local and federal law enforcement agencies, prosecutors, government organizations, and victim service agencies to investigate and prosecute incidents of human trafficking in the area (Municipality of Anchorage, 2005).

Block grant: general-purpose award designed to help meet unfunded services or objectives. Not as expenditure restrictive as closed-end or categorical grants.

- **Block grants** are general-purpose awards designed to help agencies meet specific needs that are otherwise unfunded. The grantor reviews and monitors block grants to ensure that the funds are used for the specified services and not used to fill gaps or deficits in general revenue streams. The Criminal Justice Services Division of the Oregon Office of Homeland Security offered a law enforcement block grant program designed to assist agencies in local government and support programs that help reduce crime and enhance

A forensic latent fingerprint expert examining envelopes at the Nebraska State Crime Laboratory.

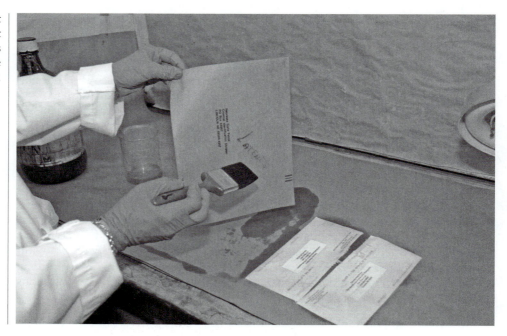

public safety. As another example, the U.S. Department of Justice Juvenile Accountability Block Grant (JABG) program provides states with funding to reduce juvenile delinquency, improve the juvenile justice system, and increase the accountability of juvenile offenders and the systems that serve juvenile offenders. Funded projects include drug and teen courts, and police and probation partnerships. The grants are funded annually, from April 1 through March 31. A small match from the community is required for these grants.

Donations, Fund-Raisers, IRS Reimbursements, and Forfeitures   To generate further revenue, police agencies can solicit donations to be used for a specific need (for example, to purchase protective vests for police dogs). Single-event or continuous fund-raising programs sponsored by private foundations and peace officer associations can provide additional funds.

Internal Revenue Service (IRS) reimbursements can produce revenue as well. State, county, and local police agencies are eligible for IRS rewards and reimbursements for investigations. The IRS pays a 10 percent unpaid tax informer's fee for information on those who fail to report all of their income. Revenue generated through illegal activity, for example, is rarely reported as income by criminal perpetrators. Further, agencies may receive reimbursement from the IRS for expenses associated with investigations into activities such as drug trafficking or money laundering that lead to the recovery of unpaid federal income taxes. Investigative information provided by the police agency must contribute substantially to the recovery of at least $50,000 in unpaid taxes. Reimbursement is limited to 10 percent of the unpaid taxes recovered. However, an agency is not eligible for such reimbursement if it receives compensation under an alternate grant or forfeiture program (U.S. Department of the Treasury, Internal Revenue Service, 2010).

Finally, forfeiture laws in many jurisdictions, including individual states and the federal government, allow police agencies to seize cash and property acquired by criminals through illegal activity (such as drug trafficking, racketeering, gambling, and transportation of contraband). If the criminal's financial gain is proven to result from an illegal enterprise, the seized cash and property is forfeited to the agency's unit of government (the municipality, county, or state). Part or all of the cash and proceeds from the sale of seized property may be returned to the agency that investigated and arrested the perpetrators (*West's Encyclopedia of American Law,* 2010).

Figure 5-2 shows revenue sources for a typical police agency.

figure 5-2 Revenue Sources for a Police Agency

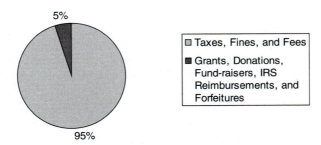

5%

□ Taxes, Fines, and Fees

■ Grants, Donations, Fund-raisers, IRS Reimbursements, and Forfeitures

95%

Contraband seized by investigators. The contraband is forfeited and destroyed.

Making Resource-Allocation Decisions

To build a budget, police managers must make numerous difficult decisions about how to allocate available funds—which can be scarce. There are many expenses to cover, and many new opportunities and programs that may merit investment. How do managers allocate funding? Three types of analysis—cost–benefit analysis, return on investment, and value-added contribution—can help.

Cost–benefit analysis: an analysis through which an organization compares the cost of a program or initiative to the benefit it provides (or may provide) to the organization and/or its constituents.

Cost–Benefit Analysis   Through **cost–benefit analysis**, a police agency compares the cost of a program or initiative to the benefit it provides (or may provide) to the agency and/or community. Ideally, the cost should be equal to or less than the benefit derived (Rabin et al., 1996). Cost–benefit analysis can help agencies create budgets that allocate financial resources wisely, and can help them monitor and control the use of those resources once the budget is implemented.

We can view cost–benefit analysis from two perspectives: cost and process. Using the cost perspective, police managers compare the cost of an activity to the product or service generated. For example, an agency might compare the cost associated with the issuance of traffic citations to the benefits associated with managing traffic and enhancing public safety. Taking a process perspective, the agency would determine whether the cost of providing traffic safety produces what the agency and the community need. In other words, does an increase in the number of traffic tickets written at a location prone to motor-vehicle collisions correlate with a reduction in such collisions? If not, the cost is not producing the anticipated benefit associated with traffic safety. As another example, when police officials measure the outcome of drug enforcement, they typically count the number of arrests made and the quantity of controlled substances seized. A cost–benefit analysis should assess longer-term quality-of-life criteria as well. That is, does drug enforcement actually improve neighborhoods in the long term or does it simply (and temporarily) reduce the availability of drugs or decrease the number of calls for service?

Return on Investment (ROI)   To conduct a **return on investment (ROI)** analysis, police managers calculate the net savings that result from an activity. Consider a major city that is monitoring its downtown area through the use of several uniformed foot-patrol officers. The city's police department decides to install surveillance cameras throughout the area, which are monitored by a single officer or civilian at a central monitoring station. Monitoring personnel dispatch roving patrol officers to problem areas. If the police department saves more money by using the cameras than it cost to buy, install, and use them, then it has earned a return on its investment in the cameras.

Return on investment (ROI): the benefits that result from an activity.

Value-Added Contribution (VAC)   By conducting a **value-added contribution (VAC)** analysis, a police agency determines the additional value (beyond basic service requirements) that an activity contributes to a program or service. In the business world, a VAC may be something added by the seller or manufacturer to increase the value of a product or service to the consumer. (For example, a bottle of shampoo comes with a free sample of conditioner. Or a car dealer offers one year of free oil changes with the purchase of a new or used car.) In policing, a reduction in crime may improve (contribute added value to) citizens' quality of life. The reduction in crime may also increase the property values in a town or city, making it more desirable for residents to remain and invest themselves in the neighborhood.

Value-added contribution (VAC): additional value (beyond basic requirements) that an activity contributes to a program or service.

At first glance, it may be difficult to think of ways that a police agency can offer a VAC to its customers—the citizens who pay the taxes that make police services possible. Because the police deliver services (including peacekeeping, maintenance of order, community education, law enforcement, and public safety), any enhancements of those services add value for citizens. Yet these VAC are often difficult to quantify. After all, how does one measure how much crime has been prevented?

Yet a police organization does make VAC. For one thing, as Sir Robert Peel is often quoted, "The police are the public and the public are the police" (Lee, 1901). Thus the community has a major stake in the services that the police agency provides: excellent service translates into safer communities. For instance, when a police agency exchanges supermarket gift cards for guns, it not only makes the community safer, it also eases citizens' fear—which in turn improves their quality of life even further. Moreover, consumers benefit when police services are effective *and* efficient because such services are at the lowest possible price and still create value for neighborhoods and businesses. Finally, agency employees benefit because progressive, highly regarded police agencies can attract the best possible candidates for vacant positions—people who know that the agency enjoys the respect and admiration of its customers (Brigham & Ehrhardt, 2005).

"SELLING" THE BUDGET

As the next step in the budget process, one or more high-ranking police officials present the completed documents to those responsible for approving the budget. Those who approve the budget may include the mayor, city council members, city manager, county supervisors, legislators, or other government officials. Approvers scrutinize budget categories, and presenters explain the rationale behind each entry in the document.

The process resembles that used by sales representatives making presentations to potential customers. The police officials presenting the budget must be prepared to defend it and to discuss budget balances, expenditures, impact on citizens, program changes, anticipated personnel reductions or additions, and performance indicators (Rabin et al., 1996).

To win support for the budget, presenters should also inform approvers of the budget's ROI and VAC. This information helps approvers see the intended payoff from requested budget increases for personnel, supplies, equipment, or facilities. The agency's customers want to know what they will receive in return for the taxes and user fees they are paying. To secure the revenue requested in the budget, police officials must convince stakeholders that the requested resources are necessary. In effect, they must "sell" the agency's service and even its brand image—perceptions of the agency's worth in the eyes of its customers. For example, a recent research report asserted that DARE programs are more effective when presented by police officers. By pointing out this finding, an agency could enhance citizens' positive perceptions of the local police (Hammond et al., 2008).

Presenting a budget calls for a full range of leadership skills. The police must be knowledgeable about all aspects of their agency's financial situation—as well as skilled in the art of persuasion. Selling the budget successfully calls for persistence and a knack for achieving consensus. Police officials should not come across as risk takers. Rather, they should demonstrate that they plan to dedicate resources to agreed-upon purposes that will create value for citizens now and in the future (Kotter, 1996; Rubin, 2006).

Dealing with Budget Cutbacks

Of course, while seeking to sell the budget (and at any other point in the budgeting process), a police agency may learn of impending budgetary cutbacks. Government agencies of all types face such cutbacks periodically, usually owing to competition, declining tax revenues, or reductions in grants awarded. In many instances, funds are constrained even as the agencies are required to continue providing the same level of service. Providing more service as well as launching new initiatives are all but impossible in agencies hardest hit by budget cutbacks.

Typically, agencies respond to cutbacks by canceling personnel cost-of-living pay increases wherever possible, which is especially difficult when an agency is staffed by a unionized workforce. An agency may also decide to postpone replacement of older equipment or upgrades to computer systems. Some agencies save money by consolidating services. For instance, if adjacent cities maintain canine units, they may combine the units and share the cost. Agencies can make similar arrangements for specialized services such as crime scene investigation.

Many police managers find creative ways to stretch the few dollars they have available for their budgets. For instance, they order equipment from online sources that are less expensive than local providers. They use e-mail instead of paper to disseminate information. They shave training expenses by presenting a single session for attendees from many local jurisdictions. Or they delay hiring and purchasing, cut overtime expenses, and establish an internal review process that monitors and scrutinizes all budget expenditures (Rabin et al., 1996).

EXECUTING THE BUDGET

If a budget wins approval from stakeholders, the police agency moves to the final stage in the budget process: putting the financial plan into action, or executing it. Execution calls for three additional leadership skills: managing the projects proposed in the budget, calculating what is known as maintenance of effort, and auditing. We examine each of these next.

Managing Projects

A *project* is a major undertaking or initiative, stipulated in a police agency's budget, that is intended to create value for the organization and its customers. For an agency, a project may be an innovative program designed to improve service to the public, a new process intended to achieve efficiencies, or an initiative aimed at preparing for future service requirements.

A project may be a new initiative or an expansion of a current program to improve service. A project may also call for replacement of a current resource to increase service capabilities (Brigham & Ehrhardt, 2005). To illustrate, the police may replace computer hardware with new equipment to make it compatible with new software applications.

Every project requires management. Simply stated, **project management** is the process of planning and guiding an initiative from inception to completion. A project might be managed by a single person or a team. In the case of a single accountable project manager, the individual plans the project, organizes the tasks necessary to accomplish the project's goals, develops timelines, obtains support from skilled people who can move the project forward, and reports on the project's progress at predetermined intervals. When more than one person manages a project, the various tasks can be divided among the team members.

Project management: the process of planning and guiding an initiative from inception to completion.

Calculating Maintenance of Effort

Maintenance of effort is the annual cost necessary to maintain a police agency's existing level of service for the fiscal operating year. Usually, police managers calculate maintenance-of-effort expenses by determining the actual cost of each activity in the preceding budget period and adding a cost-of-living adjustment to each for the next budget. The process is similar to the traditional budgeting model. Before submitting a maintenance-of-effort calculation, police officials should analyze the latest approved budget to determine which services are providing value to the organization and the community. They can use this analysis to project which items in the next budget should be eliminated, maintained, or expanded to provide for essential services and public safety.

Maintenance of effort: the annual cost necessary to maintain a police agency's existing level of service for the fiscal operating year.

Auditing

An **audit** is an evaluation of a process, system, or project. A police agency might conduct an audit to determine the reliability and validity of information generated by a process, to assess a system's internal controls, or to examine a project's effectiveness. An audit is intended to provide reasonable assurance that a process, system, or project is free of significant errors or other problems.

Audit: an evaluation of a process, system, or project.

ETHICS IN ACTION

Audit Uncovers Unethical Behavior?

An audit of a major U.S. police agency led to the discovery of several inappropriate bookkeeping activities. One officer appeared to approve his own overtime. Other officers improperly collected fees for coordinating officers' off-duty security-related employment at banks, bars, and major sporting events. The auditor's report could not confirm that the officers involved were guilty of misconduct because the agency's poor recordkeeping made it difficult to determine whether the officers had violated any law or agency policy. Apparently, the auditors could not differentiate between honest mistakes and attempts to defraud because the agency lacked adequate internal controls.

1. Based on the information presented, does it appear that the conduct of the officers involved was illegal? Why or why not? Unethical? Why or why not? Can one be sure of either?

2. What internal controls do you believe this police agency should put in place to ensure compliance and to discourage fraudulent or unethical behavior?

Financial audit: an examination of randomly selected accounting transactions in an organization with the goal of checking for accuracy, completeness, and timeliness.

Fraud examination: an examination of each accounting transaction in an organization in search of any discrepancy.

Traditionally, audits have been conducted on an organization's procedures, policies, operations, financial statements, accounting records, and budget expenditures. In this chapter, we focus on audits of the policing agency's financial and accounting records. Such audits are typically performed by independent third-party accountants or auditors who certify, based on generally accepted standards, that financial and accounting records fairly represent revenues, expenditures, and results. An audit can ensure that a budget is being executed according to plan. It may be a continuous process, or an event that occurs during or after implementation of a budget (U.S. Government Accountability Office, 2007).

Audits associated with accounting systems and fiscal management typically take one of two forms. In a **financial audit,** the examiners look at randomly selected accounting transactions for accuracy, completeness, and timeliness. In a **fraud examination,** they look at each accounting transaction in search of any discrepancy, significant or not. The discovery of a relatively insignificant error could uncover a fraudulent scheme (Cheeseman, 2009).

summary

- **What Is a Budget?** A budget is a plan expressed in financial terms and thus is essential for sound fiscal management. It reflects the resources necessary to accomplish an agency's mission. To build a budget, police agencies anticipate the revenue (income) they will need to cover expenditures for a specified period of time. Police budgets, like budgets for any public organization, have a political component, are accountable to the community, reflect constraints such as taxing limitations, require negotiation and compromise among numerous parties, and require flexibility.

- **Types of Budgets.** Although most agencies gravitate toward a traditional budget model, which is easy to construct and understand, they may use numerous types of budget models simultaneously. These additional types include line-item budgets, program budgets, performance-based budgets, zero-based budgets, balanced-based budgets, activity-based budgets, operating budgets, and capital budgets.

- **Building the Budget.** To build a budget, a police agency develops several main sections (including the budget message, summary schedule, detailed schedules, and supplemental data). They document expenditure categories (specifically, personnel expenses, operating expenses, supplies and material expenses, capital expenses, and miscellaneous expenses). And they identify sources of revenue, which include taxes, fines, and fees; grants; and donations, fund-raisers, and IRS reimbursements. They make resource-allocation decisions in the budget through three types of analysis: cost–benefit, return on investment, and value-added contribution.

- **"Selling" the Budget.** Budget planning, preparation, submission, and approval are interdependent variables in a dynamic process. To sell (win approval for) the budget, police administrators must demonstrate excellent skills in communication, persuasion, and leadership to gain approvers' trust and build consensus toward budget acceptance. They must also grapple with the possibility of budget cutbacks.

- **Executing the Budget.** To ensure proper implementation of the budget, police agencies must manage the projects stipulated in the budget, calculate maintenance of effort, and have examiners conduct audits of the agency's financial and accounting records.

key terms

activity-based budget

audit

balanced-based budget

block grant

budget

budget categories

capital budget

capital expenses

closed-end grant

cost–benefit analysis

categorical grant

financial audit

fraud examination

line-item budget

maintenance of effort

miscellaneous expenses

operating budget

operating expenses

performance-based budget

personnel expenses

program budget

project management

return on investment (ROI)

supplies and materials expenses

traditional budget

value-added contribution (VAC)

zero-based budget

1. The budget process is critical to the viability and economic health of a community. Define the term *budget* and describe what the budget process attempts to achieve. Who may be involved in the creation of an acceptable budget for a police agency?

2. Budgets are generally divided into numerous sections or categories. Describe these sections. What basic expense categories are typically contained in a budget?

3. Numerous types of budgets are used by police agencies. Most agencies gravitate toward the traditional budget model. Why?

4. How does the line-item budget compare to the zero-based budget? The activity-based budget? The performance-based budget? Discuss the strengths and weaknesses of each type.

5. Describe an operating budget, its importance, and duration.

6. Define and explain *capital budgeting process*.

7. Articulate sources of revenue for a police organization.

8. Describe the concepts of cost–benefit analysis, return on investment, and value-added contribution and how they assist with the budget process.

9. Why is selling the budget important to a police agency?

10. How does an auditing procedure help maintain the integrity of a police agency's budgeting process?

WHAT WOULD YOU DO?

Funding a Zero-Tolerance Initiative

The violent-crime rate of a large northeastern city escalated significantly. City residents complained loudly about the situation, and many took steps to protect their children and themselves. For example, they discouraged youngsters from playing outside, and people no longer gathered on the steps of their apartment buildings to visit with friends and family.

The mayor and police chief proposed a zero-tolerance initiative (see Chapter 2) to bring the situation under control. They estimated the cost associated with the initiative at more than $300,000 per week, including expenses associated with police overtime, Neighborhood Watch teams, street outreach groups, and vehicle fuel costs. The city council approved the proposal and voted to fund the initiative by cutting costs in other municipal departments and implementing a hiring freeze.

The zero-tolerance initiative included using saturation patrolling of neighborhoods, targeting previous offenders and curfew violators, and proactively addressing street violence before it escalated to homicide.

1. Where would you cut expenses in this city's budget to fund the zero-tolerance initiative? Why?

2. How long would you pursue the zero-tolerance initiative if it did not achieve its intended results? In other words, if shootings and stabbings continued unabated, what would you do? Would you consider other sources of revenue to further fund the initiative? Change the initiative itself? Design a new initiative? Justify your choice(s).

6

◀ More and more police agencies are engaging in a participatory management style. Here officers of the North Miami Beach, Florida, Police Department engage in a strategy meeting.

Organizational Design

After completing this chapter, readers should be able to:

- describe the vertical, horizontal, and community relationships that make up the structure of a police organization.

- analyze the elements and origins of the command-and-control police culture.

- examine the behavioral standards that police organizations adhere to, and explain how those standards are internalized.

- discuss why the ability to adapt to change is an important behavioral standard for police personnel.

- compare and contrast radical and incremental change as well as directed and nondirected change.

- define *organizational learning* and explain why it is an important behavioral standard for police personnel.

- contrast adaptive learning, proactive learning, and experimentation.

- explain why ethical leadership and the ability to place customers first are additional important behavioral standards for police personnel.

- differentiate the customers whom a police agency serves and explain how police serve customers and discern their changing needs

Introduction

Humans have been organizing themselves for specific purposes for thousands of years. For example, the administrative organizations that Egyptian pharaohs, Alexander the Great, and Julius Caesar used to operate their vast realms still have the power to astound, especially considering the lack of sophisticated technology at the time. Today, most formal organizations are designed to fulfill specific purposes as well: Hospitals are designed to serve patients; corporations, to make money; and police agencies, to protect and serve the jurisdictions they are responsible for.

But what is organizational design, exactly? An organization's design derives from decisions managers make about (1) how relationships are *structured* (for example, who reports to whom), (2) what kind of *culture* the organization will have (for instance, formal command-and-control or informal bottom-up), and (3) what *behavioral standards* (e.g., standards or codes of conduct) are considered acceptable and unacceptable. Structure, culture, and behavioral standards are all tightly interwoven and strongly affect one another. To illustrate, a police agency that has a rigid reporting structure will likely also have a formal culture and behavioral standards that emphasize the importance of obedience to authority figures.

The way police agencies have been designed has changed over time. For example, in the past, they were structured along relatively simple lines, consisting of patrol officers, command personnel, detectives, and civilian (nonsworn) workers such as secretaries. But today's large agencies are multilayered organizations that might contain as many as several thousand full- or part-time male and female sworn officers, with separate divisions for patrol, criminal investigations, drug enforcement, crime scene technology, marine patrol, internal investigations, and budget management.

Many large police agencies are bureaucracies. A *bureaucracy* (as defined by Max Weber, the founder of the modern science of sociology) is a tiered arrangement of management positions and labor devised in such a way as to encourage specialization. Still, there is an increasing movement to design police agencies in the same manner as corporations—including adopting policies designed to enhance employees' job satisfaction, using performance-improvement methodologies such as total quality management (TQM), and making customer service a top priority.

In this chapter, we take a closer look at the key elements of organizational design in a police agency. We begin by examining structure (how the vertical, horizontal, and community relationships are configured in an agency). We then explore culture (defined as the thoughts, speech, actions, values, and beliefs held by everyone who works in the organization). Finally, we consider the behavioral standards established by many police agencies, including the ability to adapt to change, to learn, to demonstrate ethical leadership, and to put the agency's "customers" (citizens and other stakeholders) first.

STRUCTURE: HOW ARE RELATIONSHIPS CONFIGURED?

Organizational structure: refers to the configuration of relationships within an organization.

A police agency's **organizational structure** is reflected in its vertical relationships (who has authority over whom; who reports to whom), its horizontal relationships (who collaborates and communicates with whom), and its community relationships (how agency personnel collaborate with citizens and community leaders to deliver better service). Like most organizations, police agencies often have an *organizational chart* depicting vertical and horizontal relationships. The levels of authority and number of ranks, positions, and functions illustrated in the chart differ depending on the size of the agency as well as the community the agency serves, the scope and nature of the public safety problems the agency must grapple with, and the policing strategies emphasized by the agency. Next, we examine vertical, horizontal, and community relationships more closely. We then consider how the policing strategy that an agency adopts influences its structure.

Chain of command: the notion that authority and decision making should flow down from higher to lower levels in a police agency. Official discussions typically flow up or down through the chain of command.

Vertical Relationships

A police agency's organizational chart depicts those with the highest levels of authority at the top and those with lower levels of authority below them in the chart. Typically, an agency's chart shows the chief of police, sheriff, director, or police commissioner at the top; captains, lieutenants, and sergeants in the middle; and officers as well as civilian personnel (administrative assistants, clerks, secretaries, and budget personnel) near or at the bottom. Individuals report to those above them in the hierarchy. Figure 6-1 shows an example.

These vertical relationships are strongly informed by three concepts: chain of command, unity of command, and span of control:

Unity of command: the concept that each individual working in the agency should report to only one supervisor and that each unit or situation should be under the control of a single individual.

- **Chain of command.** This is the notion that authority and decision making should flow down from higher to lower levels. Official discussions typically flow up or down through the chain of command (*American Heritage Dictionary of the English Language*, 2005a; Barron's Education Services, 2007). Chain of command discourages police personnel from discussing concerns with anyone other than an immediate superior. Indeed, it is considered a breach of conduct, maybe even a betrayal, for personnel to express a complaint or concern to their immediate superior's commanding officer first.

- **Unity of command.** This concept holds that each individual working in the agency should report to only one supervisor and that each unit or situation should be under the control of a single individual. For example, in a crisis situation, an incident commander is designated and must be obeyed—regardless of whether the commander is from the police department, fire department, or some other emergency response organization.

Span of control: the idea that each manager in a police agency should supervise only a reasonable number of individuals or units.

- **Span of control.** This is the idea that each manager in a police agency should supervise only a reasonable number of individuals or units, depending on

figure 6-1 Sample Agency Organizational Chart

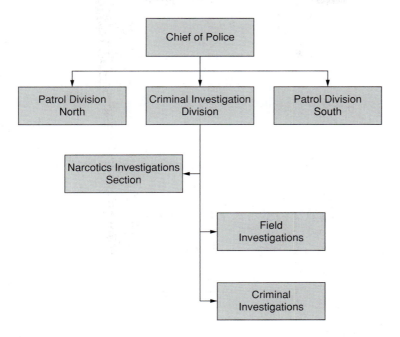

the agency's size. Most experts agree that a wider span of control renders a supervisor or manager less effective. That is because managers have greater difficulty supervising many people, owing to the increased number and complexities of tasks and the demand for high-quality results (Iannone, 1987; Robbins & Judge, 2008).

An incident commander communicating at a crisis situation.

Horizontal Relationships

An agency's structure is also determined by its horizontal relationships—collaborations and communication across its various functions or departments (Hellriegel, Jackson, & Slocum, 2008; Meese & Ortmeier, 2004). For example, Figure 6-2 shows the criminal investigations section from one agency's organizational chart. The section is part of the agency's criminal investigation division and consists of three same-level units: warrants, violent crimes, and missing persons. Each unit is supervised by a sergeant or lieutenant. While these unit supervisors do not have formal authority over one another (rather, each reports to the division head), they communicate regularly across unit lines to achieve the division's goals. To illustrate, the manager of the missing persons unit might meet with the violent-crimes lieutenant to discuss how to determine whether a missing person is a kidnap or murder victim with the suspect still at large.

Community Relationships

Volunteerism: the process by which community members donate their time and effort to a police agency's operations.

In addition to vertical and horizontal relationships, police agencies have community relationships—partnerships forged with citizens and volunteers to solve particular problems. One of the ways police managers form collaborative relationships with community members is through **volunteerism**. If citizens are concerned enough to volunteer for Neighborhood Watch and other civic-minded groups, an effective police organization will involve these community members in its initiatives. Volunteers on the streets in citizen patrols, acting as eyes and ears for the police, can and do make a contribution to the health and safety of their neighborhoods.

Yet many police officers resist the notion of working as partners with citizens. Police officers tend to operate in a culture that has specific formal and informal rules governing entry and inclusion. Police and citizens alike often assume that citizens can never be members of this officer group—for good reason. A police officer becomes acculturated to a certain way of thinking and acting through attendance at the police academy and through job experience. Citizens have no such opportunity.

However, when citizens volunteer, they are reaching out to officers and trying to establish a connection. Officers should make every effort to demonstrate receptivity to these encounters and to seize advantage of the value that can come with having more "eyes and ears on the street." Likewise, citizens who are invited to volunteer will feel they are "taking back" their streets and sharing with police the burden of keeping their neighborhoods safe.

figure 6-2 Section from an Agency's Organizational Chart

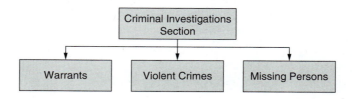

Citizen volunteers with the Prescott, Arizona, Police Department.

To welcome citizens into volunteer work, officers must reduce or eradicate what is known as "occupational arrogance"—the attitude that police are untouchable, have unassailable authority, and are not to be questioned or challenged in any way by citizens. In an agency that chooses to orient itself toward its customers, occupational arrogance will dissipate as officers become flexible and learn how

---

Engaging Volunteers in Baltimore County, Maryland

Officials in Baltimore County, Maryland, conducted a study about how the police could connect with citizens to solve community problems. To that end, they created Citizen Oriented Police Enforcement (COPE) units. The research program proceeded through three phases:

- **Phase 1:** Officers pursued preventive patrol as usual and used crime analysis to help direct those patrols. Citizens had minimal input into how crime was handled. This is the model most often used in police agencies.

- **Phase 2:** Police stepped up encounters with citizens by directing officers to canvas neighborhoods, seek information regarding citizen problems and fears, and use crime-prevention techniques and community meetings to reduce fear and gain citizens' cooperation. Though this phase increased police–citizen communication, it did not reduce crime or significantly decrease citizens' fear, mostly because officers did not use the information they had gathered.

- **Phase 3:** Officers gathered information regarding neighborhood problems and used it to develop and implement new crime-prevention tactics, conduct saturation patrols, and identify law enforcement issues that needed resolution. Citizens' satisfaction increased and crime decreased (Taft, 1986).

valuable volunteer citizens can be (O'Hara, 2005). The box titled "Engaging Volunteers in Baltimore County, Maryland" shows an example.

Use of information provided by citizens has become common practice in such large cities as Fort Worth, Texas, Los Angeles, California, and Rochester, New York. There is even a national organization—Volunteers in Police Service (VIPS)—that helps police departments organize and train volunteers. VIPS provides a broad scope of assistance, including the preparation of agency personnel to conduct volunteer training and what to teach how to pay volunteers' out-of-pocket expenses, and how to manage volunteers once they become active (www.policevolunteers. org, 2008).

To work with volunteers, police managers must make decisions about a wide range of matters:

- **Policy:** What roles will each participant—police and volunteer—play? Who will report to whom? What will the goals of the partnership be?
- **Recruitment:** How will the agency describe the volunteer opportunity to citizens? What will the application and interview process consist of? How will the agency screen applicants and check references and backgrounds to determine potential volunteers' suitability for the work?
- **Training:** What formal training will the agency provide before deploying volunteers? And what remedial training and in-service training will it offer to support ongoing and new activities for volunteers?
- **Support:** How will volunteers be supervised? How will the agency evaluate their effectiveness?
- **Budget:** What materials (uniforms, radios, vehicles, other equipment) will the agency provide to volunteers, and how will those materials be funded?

A police agency that elects to use volunteers should be committed to giving the effort the same commitment it gives to other programs—by clearly establishing the volunteer values, vision, mission, and goals (Citizens Information Board, 1999).

A high-ranking member of a police agency speaks casually (as peers) with a lower-ranking officer.

From Policing Strategy to Organizational Structure

A police agency's structure is strongly determined by the policing strategies adopted by the agency. (Policing strategies are covered extensively in Chapter 2.) For instance, if an agency is oriented toward traditional policing, which emphasizes reducing response time to calls-for-service, management may strive to concentrate authority at the top of the organizational hierarchy and require strict obedience to formalized lines of communication and reporting. There may be little to no attention directed to forging community relationships. If an agency is more oriented toward the problem-solving and community-oriented strategies, management may aim for decentralization—dispersing authority among lower-level employees and allowing communication outside formal, vertical lines of authority (Goldstein, 1990, 2001).

Different divisions, units, and departments within an agency may also emphasize different policing strategies and thus have different relationship configurations that do not necessarily reflect the structure shown in the agency's formal organizational chart. For example, in a division that operates on the principles characterizing the community policing strategy, unit commanders may communicate freely with individuals outside formal lines of authority, such as peers in other units and citizen volunteers.

CULTURE: WHAT DO PERSONNEL THINK, SAY, DO, AND BELIEVE?

How a police agency is structured has close links to what its organizational culture is like. For example, an agency characterized by a relatively informal, open culture may be more likely to have an organizational structure that is less formal and encourages communication across divisions and between individuals who do not have formal authority over one another.

What is **organizational culture**? It is shaped by the thoughts, speech, actions, values, and beliefs held by people who work in the organization (McNamara, 2008). Though police agencies may differ somewhat in their culture, they share some common cultural characteristics that make them collectively distinctive from other types of organizations. In the pages that follow, we explore some of these characteristics.

Organizational culture: shaped by the thoughts, speech, actions, values, and beliefs held by people in the organization.

Command and Control

Many police agencies have a traditional command-and-control culture, in which lines of authority and rules governing communication are rigid. This traditional culture arose for a few reasons: It enables officers to respond swiftly to calls-for-service and to resolve crises. When everyone understands who is in charge of which aspects of a service call or a crisis, people move quickly to fill their roles the instant the need arises. Such clarity about responsibilities reduces the risk of confusion and delay in officers' response time. However, this culture has disadvantages as well. For instance, it restricts communication among peers and limits innovation and creativity, as officers conclude that their ideas are not welcome in the agency's upper ranks. The traditional command-and-control culture is also believed to prevent police corruption because such a culture does not foster police–citizen familiarity and it restricts officer use of discretion.

Elements of the command-and-control culture will always be present in every police agency because calls-for-service and crises will always arise. Therefore, anyone wishing to change an agency's culture—for example, to incorporate

A police chief can set the tone for the organizational culture.

elements of community policing—should build those elements around the command-and-control structures that are already present, rather than trying to replace the traditional culture. To illustrate, all personnel in the agency have the ability to affect those within their sphere of influence, whether or not they are in positions of formal authority. By demonstrating and encouraging elements of community policing among those within their sphere of influence, managers and officers at all levels can slowly alter the culture. Further, the agency's culture may change as managers hire new recruits and instruct them in community policing concepts and applications, and as officers who view community policing with suspicion modify their beliefs and community policing practices are integrated with traditional policing strategy.

Researchers have identified six forces that give rise to the traditional police culture: law; bureaucracy; safety, competence, and morality; and demonstrated individual courage (Herbert, 1998).

- **Law.** The police are responsible for enforcing the law. Because the law is constant and immutable, there can be no compromise when it comes to enforcing it. Theoretically, the police must be impervious to pleas of innocence, tears, or bribes. Furthermore, those who violate the law tend to want to avoid being arrested, and they will do whatever it takes to do so, including using violence. Given these facts, police must maintain an attitude of command and control toward citizens who violate the law.

- **Bureaucracy.** The bureaucratic structure exists in public organizations, as in many private organizations, to ensure adherence to established, critical policies and procedures. In combination with the law, bureaucracy fosters the formal aspects of traditional police culture.

- **Safety, competence, and morality.** These forces are all directly related to police personnel interactions with the citizens the agency serves. To ensure citizen and officer safety, officers must make it a priority. They can do so by (for example) avoiding police vehicle chases on crowded streets and helping people to safety away from the scene of a fire or other disaster before

Citizen safety is a police officer's number one priority.

performing any other duty. *Competence* means using training to solve whatever problems present themselves during the course of an officer's designated shift. *Morality* in this context means that officers will deal fairly and impartially with all citizens. Various cultures may define *morality* differently, and officers must acknowledge such differences. But most cultures still uphold universal moral standards common to virtually any society; for instance, the standard associated with the moral and legal wrong of murder. (*Note:* A street gang member who kills a member of a rival gang may not consider the killing morally or ethically wrong.)

- **Individual courage.** While all officers should demonstrate individual courage, some possess more than others, and this quality appears to determine an officer's reputation (Herbert, 1998). Those officers who demonstrate consistent and visible bravery are often more revered than those who solve problems through negotiation or who occupy desk jobs that give little opportunity to demonstrate courage. The command-and-control culture rewards courage. Although it does not disparage other forms of problem solving such as negotiation, the officer who garners headlines with reckless, albeit courageous behavior offers the image of hero that many citizens want to associate with their police agency.

Officer Unity

As a consequence of the command-and-control culture characterizing most police agencies, many police officers feel isolated from those who do not work in law enforcement. In addition, they tend to distrust their superiors within the department, and they often feel comfortable only in the company of other officers who are closely associated in rank. Moreover, most of them believe that any person who is not a police officer cannot understand the pressures and unwritten rules inherent in police work.

For instance, there is an almost universal understanding among many police officers that one does not inform police administrators if a fellow officer's actions may be considered unethical or immoral or possibly even illegal. To illustrate, an officer who assaults an unruly subject after a brief chase and traffic stop expects that the backup officer or partner will support the individual and not advise a superior officer of the "street justice" occurrence. Officers who violate this unwritten rule about not informing on one another may end up being ostracized by their peers. This can place the reporting officers in real danger if peers refuse to "watch their backs" in perilous situations on the job.

Leader Officer or Street Officer?

Individual officers can help soften the hard edges of traditional command-and-control police culture by shifting fluidly between command-and-control tactics and community policing as dictated by the situation. Officers demonstrating this flexibility—we can think of them as *leader officers*—are highly effective on the street and elsewhere because they can adapt their behavior as needed to manage different types of situations.

For example, leader officers are more likely to negotiate with suspects than approach them with firearm drawn. They do not shy away from confrontation, but they employ verbal skills first, rather than physical force, to gain control of a situation and an offender. By diffusing a situation through words rather than a show of weapons, officers reduce the risk that the situation may turn violent.

By contrast, *street officers* most commonly exhibit aggressive behavior. They enjoy arresting persons who may become violent so they can subdue and control them. These officers participate enthusiastically in situations fraught with danger, such as high-speed vehicle pursuits or foot chases. Unfortunately, many of them view leader officers as weak or ineffective. Yet street officers tend to be less effective than leader officers in most situations. Although stern command-and-control tactics may be required in some situations, most police encounters do not necessitate strong verbal commands or the use of force. Owing to their relative lack of communication skills and their exclusionary attitude, street officers may be unable to deliver the calm, reasoned, and respectful direction (e.g., tactical communication) essential for deescalation of conflict and successful resolution of an incident.

Through training, street officers can strengthen the

Police officers, as leaders, can take control of emergency situations and deescalate the conflict by using a Long-Range Acoustic Device to broadcast warnings and instructions.

"soft" skills—such as communication, negotiation, and tolerance—essential to being a leader officer. Yet sometimes command and control is the best approach. Thus, leader officers can and should further enhance their ability to respond with command-and-control tactics as needed in situations where they, partners, or citizens may be in imminent physical danger.

BEHAVIORAL STANDARDS: WHAT IS CONSIDERED ACCEPTABLE?

Like structure and culture, **behavioral standards (standards of conduct)** constitute a key component of a police agency's organizational design. Indeed, behavioral standards are strongly interlinked with culture, as these standards influence what people say, think, and do in the organization. New members of police agencies go through a process to internalize the agency's behavioral standards. Behaviors that are particularly valuable and advantageous in a police agency include adapting to change, learning, demonstrating ethical leadership, and placing "customers" first.

Behavioral standards (standards of conduct): standards of conduct as defined by the police agency. The standards are particularly valuable and advantageous to the agency's culture and structure.

Internalizing Behavioral Standards

Almost all organizations—police agencies included—establish standards for acceptable behavior and ensure compliance with these standards through employee preservice and in-service training and documented and published policies and procedures. The "Law Enforcement Code of Conduct" you read in Chapter 1 is an

Police supervisors and field training officers provide training for new recruits. Here Broward County, Florida, Sheriff's Department Police Explorers engage in a training exercise.

Leadership on the job
Held to a Higher Standard?

Many citizens believe that police officers should be held to a higher standard of behavior than the average person, owing to the authority they possess to enforce law and the fact that they carry weapons. The sheriff of one California city is now hoping that officers will demonstrate commitment to this higher standard by leaving their guns behind when they plan to consume alcoholic beverages. The reason? In several jurisdictions, armed and intoxicated police officers, while off duty, used poor judgment and fired their weapons.

The sheriff noticed that in a one-year period, there were 65 alcohol-related arrests of off-duty deputies, a marked increase over previous years. Despite protests from leaders of the local Police Officer Association and the Association for Deputy Sheriffs,

the sheriff is standing his ground and hoping his deputies will follow his lead in insisting on the leave-your-gun-behind rule. As he put it, "Everyone comes back to this basic, commonsense truth: Alcohol and guns don't mix. Putting [this] truth to policy makes for a better, safer city."

1.   In many jurisdictions, police officers are expected to react to disturbances even when they are off duty. How does the policy just described hamper this expectation? If officers are still expected to react, how can they do so without a firearm?

2.   How might this policy affect the way citizens view off-duty police officers?

example of documentation of such behavioral standards. Those who deviate from accepted behavioral norms are encouraged to change their behavior and, if needed, to take part in remedial training programs. If a person continues to violate codes of behavior, the agency will likely initiate a disciplinary process that may start with a formal reprimand and could move to suspension, resignation, or termination if the problematic behavior continues. (See Chapter 12 for more information on discipline.)

In a police organization, new members are first acculturated to the organization's behavioral standards through the academy experience, field training, and the probationary period. (See Chapter 10.) During this time of acculturation, newcomers learn what behaviors are considered acceptable as well as unacceptable. More seasoned members of the organization observe and judge new members on how well they demonstrate acceptable behavior. Police work is unique in that behavior both on and off duty may strongly influence a police officer's personal life, relationships, career opportunities, longevity with the agency, and professional reputation.

Adapting to Change

Like other organizations, police agencies are constantly subjected to change—in the form of new challenges, new theories and practices about how to better serve communities, new technologies, and so forth. Change can be triggered by both internal and external events. For instance, when a new police chief is appointed, this internal change may lead to other management personnel changes as well as modifications in the agency's strategies and the day-to-day activities carried out by line officers. An example of an external change is the election of a new governor or mayor who then seeks to fulfill campaign promises by (for instance) mandating new safety initiatives that police agencies will be required to implement (Swanson, Territo, & Taylor, 2008).

A police agency must be willing and able to adapt to change. Change may imply that the police must be ready to adjust and/or reorder priorities especially when political leadership changes.

The most effective agencies adapt fluidly to new developments; for example, updating their IT platform to better track and respond to crime, or modifying their hiring practices to bring in recruits with stronger leadership qualities. Police managers and officers who can adapt to change help their agency achieve the flexibility needed to keep pace with new developments and deliver increasingly better service to the community.

Change is a large and widely debated subject, and definitions of the term abound. Here is one way to define it: "to make different, either in a small or large way, a modification, a shift from one to another, or a transition, transformation, or substitution" (*Merriam-Webster's*, 2006). Change can also take numerous forms. Within a police agency, change may be radical or incremental, as well as directed or nondirected. Moreover, it presents both challenges and opportunities.

Radical and Incremental Change   Through **radical change**, a specific innovation transforms the way a police agency delivers customer service. The introduction of the Managing Criminal Investigations (MCI) concept is one example. Officers who subscribe to MCI determine whether a follow-up investigation needs to be implemented for a specific incident. A major goal of MCI is to empower patrol officers to conduct a thorough initial investigation of a crime and then determine whether a follow-up investigation by a detective or police investigator has merit. In making this determination, officers consider questions such as whether a case

Radical change: new ways of operation stemming from a specific innovation that transforms the way a police agency delivers customer service.

can be solved in a reasonable amount of time if a follow-up is implemented (Hastings & Rickard, 1976; Young & Ortmeier, 2011). MCI thus aims to create a criminal investigation process that makes more effective and efficient use of police investigators' time and other agency resources. (See the box "Spotlight on MCI" for additional information.)

Two police officers interrogate David Westerfield (R) on February 5, 2002, in San Diego, California. Westerfield was questioned in the disappearance of Danielle Van Dam, one of his neighbor's children. Van Dam was later found murdered and Westerfield was charged, convicted, and sentenced to death for Danielle's kidnapping and murder.

> ## Spotlight on MCI
> MCI has helped introduce three valuable innovations in processes for police agencies:
>
> - **Improved use of resources.** Patrol officers consider several "solvability factors" while deciding whether to recommend that a case they have investigated should be closed or referred for follow-up investigation. Solvability factors might include known witnesses, fingerprints, video depicting criminal intent, serial numbers on stolen property, and known suspects. If solvability factors are numerous and significant, and agency follow-up investigative policy allows, the patrol officers may recommend that they solve the case themselves. Otherwise, they might suggest that police detectives or investigators conduct a follow-up investigation. Additionally, the case may be continued for follow-up investigation if officers believe that the case would cause considerable concern in the community or is part of a current crime pattern.
> - **Better collaboration.** Police officers and investigators collaborate with prosecutors by seeking legal guidance on cases being presented. Officers ensure that written documentation offered to prosecutors is meticulous and provides comprehensive information on events and investigative resources. Prosecutors may assist police investigators by monitoring ongoing investigative efforts and suggesting additional investigative initiative to anticipate successful case prosecution (Rochester Police Department, G.O. 409, 1996).
> - **More effective training.** Agencies train all patrol officers in the primary investigation process with the intent that they will become responsible for this process rather than merely taking reports. Eventually, patrol supervisors could become investigation supervisors with the knowledge and skills necessary to assign cases for closure or follow-up (Greenwood, 1979).

Incremental change: a police agency's gradual adoption of new ways of operating designed to improve community service over time.

By contrast, through **incremental change**, a police agency adapts slowly, over time, to new or tested approaches. An example might be an agency that agrees to begin participating in emergency communications (9-1-1) arrangements or drug enforcement task forces with other agencies to serve communities more efficiently (Hellriegel et al., 2008).

Directed change: a carefully planned, strategic process designed to improve every area of a police agency.

Directed and Nondirected Change In addition to taking radical or incremental form, change in a police agency can be directed or nondirected. **Directed change** is a carefully planned, strategic process designed to improve every area of the agency, with progress formally evaluated during and after the change is implemented. Directed change is agency-wide, comprehensive, and formal.

A good example of directed change is a police agency's installation of a new computer system. This type of change must not be implemented in a disjointed, random manner but must be planned for and executed carefully, step by step. Ideally,

Information technology has dramatically changed the way police gather, store, analyze, and retrieve information.

one person will take charge of the overall implementation, delegating various stages (such as selecting the system, installing it, troubleshooting, and training personnel to use it) to subordinates. Without careful planning, the installation of a new computer system or software may simply speed up the mess, leading to confusion as well as expensive downtime and repairs.

Nondirected change is a less formal process and affects only those individuals who implement it. For example, in an area suffering from high crime rates and drug-related problems, command officers might direct their crime-prevention personnel to make early-morning stops of all pedestrians to ascertain the identity and purpose of the individuals' presence. The goal of this change is to stop violence related to the drug culture.

Nondirected change: an informal process of altering the way tasks are accomplished, affecting only those individuals who will implement the change.

Opportunities and Challenges Presented by Change   For a police agency, change presents both opportunities and challenges. For example, during the 1980s and in response to changes in society at large, police experts introduced new leadership concepts and reexamined the policing principles attributed to Sir Robert Peel. These developments inspired some police agencies to experiment with new ways of operating. Many agencies began emphasizing the importance of strengthening relationships with the communities they served. This transformation was further fueled by several pivotal developments—namely, the advent of community policing, technology advances such as CompStat (computer or comparative statistics) and communities' demand for new standards of professionalism and accountability from police. These developments demand a new style of police leadership that promises to extend from the top level of agency management down to line officers on the street (Meese & Ortmeier, 2004).

However, police officers are notoriously resistant to change. As evidence of this, consider the massive changes that U.S. society experienced from 1950 through the

Despite the flood of women entering the workforce in the latter half of the twentieth century, significant numbers of women in policing is still not a reality.

1970s—including a flood of women into the workplace and an increase in ethnic diversity in the population. Despite these changes, it still took many years before significant numbers of women and members of minority groups were allowed or encouraged to become police officers. In addition, long after corporations had embraced advances in information technology, police reports in many agencies are still being written by hand, typed, and kept in paper manila folders in metal file cabinets.

Leading Change Despite the Challenges   A lack of willingness or an inability to adapt to change can sabotage a transformation effort in any organization, not just a police agency. Indeed, owing to such resistance, many change initiatives deliver minimal results or less than the expected benefits to the organization (Hellriegel et al., 2008; Peak, Gaines, & Glensor, 2010).

How can police leaders wishing to effect organizational change boost their chances of succeeding? The following guidelines may help:

- Introduce a change initiative slowly and methodically, and make it transparent to every member of their agency by issuing regular progress reports and notices of upcoming changes to the entire agency.

- Establish a sense of urgency—a feeling that change must happen for the agency to survive and thrive. For example, point out that unless the agency makes a required change, it will lose funding or may be required to implement a reduction in force (lay off personnel).

- Build a committed coalition of stakeholders including key internal stakeholders such as supervisors, managers, and union representatives and key external stakeholders such as business owners, community leaders, and residents who embrace the vision of the better future promised by the change. These stakeholders can help drive change by convincing skeptics of its value and reassuring resistors that the change will generate important benefits.

- Develop a plan for implementing the change. To illustrate, define when the new IT system will be installed and how and when people will receive training on how to use it (Kotter, 1996).
- Continually communicate the change effort's status to everyone in the agency (Bryson, 2004; Kotter, 1996).

Learning

An openness and ability to learn is another highly desirable behavior in a police agency—in part because learning enables people to adapt to change. In the past, leaders often drove change by having subordinates engage in training. Taking part in training is no longer sufficient, given the complexity of changes facing police agencies today. To position agency personnel to adapt to change, leaders must now create an environment that fosters what is known as organizational learning. In such an environment, individuals throughout a police agency—from top to bottom, and across all functions and units—are constantly strengthening their knowledge, skills, and abilities to adapt to change (Greer & Plunkett, 2007; Meese & Ortmeier, 2004).

Organizational learning is a social process in which individuals interact with one another to exchange information that enables them to make well-informed decisions. An organization in which people can learn and adapt as part of standard operating procedure is remarkably effective. Individuals excel at absorbing ideas they encounter in one field of endeavor and using those ideas to excel in another field.

Organizational learning: a social process in which individuals interact with one another to exchange information that enables them to make well-informed decisions.

The police can use community meetings to learn about citizen concerns firsthand.

For instance, town meetings have traditionally been used to enable residents to express their opinions about such matters as how tax money is to be allotted for town improvements or whether a traffic light would be beneficial at an intersection where many car accidents have occurred. However, at some point, an enterprising person may decide to use this venue to also discover how town or city residents view the quality of life in their community, as well as the performance of their police department.

Learning Processes   In mastering the ability to change, people use several types of learning processes: adaptive learning, proactive learning, and experimentation.

- Through *adaptive learning*, people make changes in reaction to alterations in their environment. To illustrate, if people drive over an unexpected pothole that jars their vehicles, the next time they drive down that street they will swerve to avoid the pothole.

- Through *proactive learning*, they modify their behavior and work processes more deliberately, by anticipating what *might* change in their environment and then deciding how to prepare. An example might be the appointment of a new police chief. Those who wish to be ready for the new chief might review information about the other agencies where the chief worked, what changes were made there, and what changes were promised and not made. Because learning proactively goes beyond simply reacting to an environmental change (Robbins & Judge, 2008), it positions people to prepare for the future.

    Both adaptive and proactive learning have their place, as there are situations in which people cannot prepare for a change (such as the September 11, 2001, terrorist attacks) and other situations in which people can prepare (for example, a job offer that necessitates relocation to another state).

- Through *experimentation*, people try something new and then use the information and insights gained from the effort to effect change. For instance, one police agency conducted an experiment that involved establishing a Community Volunteer Response Team (CVRT), a police-trained staff of volunteers who responded to calls from neighborhoods when homicides occurred. The team's job was to debrief residents after a homicide, to help citizens process the event emotionally, and to demonstrate the police's concern for the community. But the debriefing process had another important benefit as well: it generated information that the police, the district attorney's office, and homicide investigators could all use in their efforts to solve the crimes. The experiment with creating a new kind of team thus generated valuable lessons that enabled the agency to operate more effectively.

Leading for Organizational Learning   Organizational learning cannot occur unless leaders create conditions that foster it (such as systems for generating and exchanging information) and encourage abilities essential to learning (such as a willingness and ability to draw lessons from experiences and apply those lessons in new situations). This long-term process and commitment begins at the top level of the organization and is directed to subordinate leaders. Thus, a police agency cannot become a learning organization until it develops leaders at all levels who will drive the effort.

However, most police agencies do not possess managers, supervisors, or line officers with the leadership talent necessary to spearhead a transition from a command-and-control culture to one of organizational learning. Therefore, these

Organizational learning cannot occur unless leaders create conditions that foster the learning such as systems for generating and exchanging information. Here is a view of the Real Time Crime Center at police headquarters in New York City.

agencies must groom personnel for this role through an organized leadership program (Wuestewald, 2006). The best leadership programs:

- Acknowledge the challenges of transforming an organization's culture into one of learning.
- Familiarize aspiring leaders with the change process.
- Explain how continual learning supports an agency's mission and objectives.
- Provide support for learning in the form of learning teams and executive coaching (Goleman, Boyatzis, & McKee, 2002).

Still, most police agencies only scratch the surface of organizational learning by providing in-service training programs that merely refresh topics recruits have already encountered in school or through other training experiences. To support organizational learning, leadership programs must go beyond these topics and cover areas such as organizational change processes and proactive learning, including the value of conducting research. These programs also need to teach aspiring leaders how to make continual learning a core value in their agency; for example, by rewarding personnel for sharing information, viewing and using mistakes as opportunities for improvement, and experimenting with promising ideas.

Demonstrating Ethical Leadership

Like adapting to change and learning, demonstrating ethical leadership should (and has) become a vital behavioral standard in police agencies—in part in response to the wave of scandals that has marred the reputation of business and government in recent years. When police administrators and officers behave ethically, they generate important benefits for their agency. For example, they earn stakeholders' trust and respect. And they help their agency avoid the expenses (such as lawsuits) and criticism that accompany police misconduct.

Ethical leadership is a willingness and an ability to do what "ought" to be done in any given situation and to encourage, motivate, and influence others to behave ethically. A leader who is struggling to determine whether a particular behavior is ethical or unethical can ask three questions:

• Does the behavior in question adhere to laws and government codes?

• Does the behavior adhere to standards of ethical behavior defined by my agency?

• Does the behavior adhere to stated professional standards of what is considered ethical behavior (Mathis & Jackson, 2005; Ortmeier, 2006; Souryal, 2003)?

If a leader can answer "yes" to all three of these questions, then the behavior in question is likely ethical.

Of course, it is relatively easy to consult laws, organizational codes of conduct, and professional standards of ethics to determine which kinds of behaviors are allowed and which are not. However, these reference sources may not cover situations where there are many acceptable courses of action but choosing one means making a trade-off. For example, suppose that Paul, a police supervisor, discovers that Tonya, one of his best officers, lied about her education credentials. Should he fire her—and lose the skills and value she brings to the agency? Should he ignore the lie and keep Tonya on staff—and risk sending a message to other officers that the agency does not value education credentials as much as it says it does? Paul

ETHICS IN ACTION
How Long before Reporting a Problem?

Newly promoted Sergeant Gina Harris has been assigned to the midnight shift. She loves the work. The officers under her command are informal and experienced, and they appear to accept her without reservation. In the eight weeks since she assumed her new position, she has encountered only one real problem: Officer Walter Johnson has appeared at times to be under the influence of alcohol or drugs. He has called in sick on two occasions and, once, he asked a fellow officer to drive him home after he "fell ill."

Gina is not eager to make waves, especially since she has no concrete proof that Walter is abusing alcohol or drugs. Then, one night when Walter is off duty, the agency receives a call about a hit-and-run accident. Gina drives to the scene, where she finds an abandoned car that she recognizes as Walter's. In the other car involved in the accident, a pregnant woman is writhing and bleeding in the driver's seat. She has gone into labor following the collision. A subsequent investigation reveals that Walter was driving his car when the collision occurred.

1. At what point should Gina have confronted Walter and then (if necessary) reported his alleged misconduct to a superior officer?

2. What sort of discipline (if any) should she receive for not addressing Walter's alleged drinking or drug use sooner?

could make a reasonable case for either course of action, but each would come with a price (a true ethical dilemma). To resolve such dilemmas, police personnel cannot rely solely on documented codes of conduct. They must augment those resources by learning how to weigh the complex ramifications of each proposed course of action and make informed judgment calls.

Putting Customers First

Thanks to the concept of the customer-oriented cop (Ortmeier & Meese, 2010), many police agencies are searching for new ways to engage the public they serve. Putting customers first by understanding and exceeding their expectations and requirements has become an important behavioral standard. Police agencies represent their local and state governments as visible and recognizable providers of service to customers. But who exactly is the customer, and what does the customer want? What is customer service? And how can police deepen their understanding of customers? In the pages that follow, we delve into these questions more deeply.

Who Is the Customer?   A "customer" is defined any individual, group, or organization that receives a product or service and that is directly served by an individual or organization (*Business Dictionary*, 2007). Police agencies have several types of customers:

- **Citizens:** These are individuals (victims, witnesses, violators of public law), neighborhoods, community groups, and businesses in the jurisdiction a police agency serves.

- **Other public agencies served by the police.** For instance, a police agency provides services to code enforcement officers and emergency medical services by offering assistance for inspections and helping with the evaluation and provision of services to hostile patients or victims.

Medical examiners work with the police, such as these King County, Washington, sheriff's deputies, at crime scenes.

- **Internal customers.** These are groups or individuals within the police agency that are served by other groups. To illustrate, a team provides in-service training to sworn officers, and the medical examiner's office works closely with the agency's crime-investigation unit.

How Do Police Agencies Serve Their Customers? Police agencies offer a variety of services to their customers. Of course, these services comprise the primary activities police perform, such as patrolling neighborhoods, explaining how residents can make their homes burglar-resistant, apprehending offenders, and solving crimes. But an agency's services also include providing information to customers, such as:

- Crime statistics or motor vehicle-accident reports.
- Written overviews of public safety initiatives launched by the agency.
- Driving directions to individual citizens who request them.

With any of these services, customers generally expect timely, complete, responsive, and empathetic service that is of a higher quality than they may provide for themselves.

A police organization may also want to offer services that differ from what its customers are saying they need. For example, the agency may wish to place patrol cars at strategic locations around schools during the hours that students are arriving at and departing from school to control potential rowdy behavior and provide for safe passage.

How Can Police Know Customers' Changing Needs? Like managers in other occupations, many police managers have a tendency to focus more on completing tasks (such as writing reports and responding to calls for service) than on knowing and meeting customers' changing needs (Bossidy & Charan, 2002). Like all customers, those served by a police agency have constantly evolving needs. To deliver consistently high-quality service, agency personnel must know how those needs are shifting. They can do this by gathering information and then using it to modify the services they provide. For example, an agency may use data to identify seasonal patterns in convenience store robberies, then design a patrol strategy to ensure that police are positioned near the most vulnerable stores during times when robberies are most likely to occur. By knowing how customers' needs change, police managers can more effectively allocate their agency's resources to efforts that will produce the best possible service for the community.

In monitoring customers' changing needs, police administrators must determine not only what each customer wants but also when the service will be provided, why the particular service is needed, how long it will last, and what other services may be attached to the request. To illustrate, suppose a town's citizens ask the police department to help discourage high school seniors from drinking and driving on a special event (e.g., a sports event or a dance) night. To serve this need, the department might design some public awareness communication campaigns (such as "Don't drink and drive!" ads in the local paper). It might also assemble a team of experts and volunteers to put on a staged "accident" depicting the tragic realities that can come with drunk driving. Some agencies have even placed a crushed vehicle on the front lawn of high schools to demonstrate how a car looks after a drunk driver has been involved in a collision.

To further determine and fulfill customers' service needs, police managers can segment customers into groups based on similar needs, expectations, conduct, and other variables that affect how a police agency delivers its services and what kinds of resources will need to be deployed (Wood, 2005). An example of a customer segment might be residents who schedule neighborhood gatherings. Police routinely provide traffic-regulation services such as road-closure assistance and traffic direction to neighborhood events. But if neighborhood events expand from simple block parties (requiring limited police resources) to larger events featuring outside entertainment, the police may have to provide additional services, such as parking, traffic and crowd control, and security. To anticipate escalations in these and other needs, police should maintain ongoing contact with neighborhood customers.

Satisfied customers are crucial to any police agency's success, if not its very survival. By working to anticipate and satisfy customers' needs, "customer-oriented cops" can help ensure that their agency receives the resources it needs to serve the communities in its jurisdiction well (Hellriegel et al., 2008). (See Chapter 7 for more on customer service and satisfaction.)

summary

- **Structure: How Are Relationships Configured?** A police agency's structure is reflected in its vertical relationships (who has authority over whom; who reports to whom), its horizontal relationships (who collaborates and communicates with whom), and its community relationships (how agency personnel work with citizens and community leaders to deliver better service). An organizational chart depicts an agency's vertical and horizontal relationships. The policing strategy that an agency adopts strongly influences the agency's structure.

- **Culture: What Do Personnel Think, Say, Do, and Believe?** A police agency's culture is shaped by the thoughts, speech, actions, values, and beliefs held by everyone who works in the organization. Many police agencies have a command-and-control culture, characterized by rigid lines of authority and rules governing communication and officer unity. This culture enables officers to respond quickly to calls-for-service and to resolve crises. Thus elements of this culture will always exist in every agency. The command-and-control culture has been shaped by several factors: law, bureaucracy, safety, competence, morality, and an emphasis on individual courage.

- **Behavioral Standards: What Is Considered Acceptable?** Police agencies establish standards of acceptable behavior and ensure compliance with these standards through training and written polices and procedures (including codes of conduct). Failure to meet these standards triggers a disciplinary process. Four behavioral standards especially important for police personnel are the ability to adapt to change (whether radical or incremental, or directed or nondirected), the ability to learn continually (whether through adaptive learning, proactive learning, or experimentation), the ability to demonstrate ethical leadership, and the willingness and ability to put customers first (including understanding who a police agency's customers are, seeking to improve services delivered to them, and striving to understand their changing needs).

key terms

behavioral standard (standard of conduct)

chain of command

directed change

incremental change

nondirected change

organizational culture

organizational learning

organizational structure

radical change

span of control

unity of command

volunteerism

discussion questions

1. What are the three types of relationships that make up a police agency's structure? Provide an example of each type of relationship that is different from those provided in the chapter. Which of these relationship types are depicted on a police agency's organizational chart?

2. What are chain of command, unity of command, and span of control? How do they affect communication and authority relationships in a police agency? What challenges do they present?

3. Provide an example of how a policing strategy that an agency adopts affects its organizational structure.

4. What characterizes a command-and-control culture? How did such a culture arise? What are its advantages and disadvantages? What factors have shaped the command-and-control culture?

5. What is officer unity? How did it arise, and what challenges does it present?

6. What are *leader officers* and how do they differ from *street officers*? Can one be a leader officer as well as a street officer?

7. Cite examples of common behavioral standards established by police agencies. How do police organizations ensure compliance with the behavioral standards they have established?

8. Why is the ability to adapt to change an important behavioral standard for police personnel? Give an example of radical change, incremental change, directed change, and nondirected change.

9. What are some practices that can help police leaders successfully drive a change initiative in their agency?

10. What is organizational learning? How does it benefit a police agency? What are some processes police personnel can use to foster a culture of continual learning in their agency?

11. Why is demonstrating ethical leadership an important behavioral standard for police personnel? If you were facing a situation where the correct and ethical course of action was not clear, what steps would you take to determine a course of action?

12. Why is the ability to put customers first by knowing and exceeding their expectations and requirements an important behavioral standard for police personnel?

13. Which types of customers does a typical police agency serve? Provide an example of how to serve each type.

14. What techniques would you use to identify changes in the needs of customers served by a police agency?

WHAT WOULD YOU DO?
The Value of Volunteering

Before 1999, the Eugene, Oregon, police volunteer program was disjointed and ineffective. One police manager after another was assigned to head the program, but the managers already had more than enough work to do and never made the program a priority. Of the eight volunteers participating in the program, five were college students and three were retirees. Those citizens who called to offer their volunteer services were typically transferred from one person to another, none of whom seemed to know how to handle the calls. Volunteer activities usually took the form of clerical duties.

In 1999, the city council approved the hiring of a full-time coordinator for the volunteer program, in an effort to bolster the council's community policing efforts. The following year, the Eugene police department launched its new volunteer program. The program focused on developing volunteer opportunities that would promote the agency's goals, such as strengthening ties between the agency and its citizens, as well as attract people of all ages and backgrounds.

Once the department had defined the scope of the program and outlined an implementation plan, police began disseminating information about the program and organized a call for volunteers. The effort paid off: as many as 10 to 20 calls came in each month. The volunteers were required to fill out an application as well as go through and interview and a background check. Most of these first applicants were students, but eventually retirees began applying as well.

One thing that became crystal clear from the beginning was that not all potential volunteers were interested in clerical duties such as filing, data entry, or document copying. Retirees in particular expressed the desire to take a more active role in helping ensure community safety. The police department responded by establishing the Seniors on Patrol project. Patrol volunteers

(continued)

participated in a weeklong academy, and today the Seniors on Patrol unit serves as an auxiliary unit, with their own specially marked police cars. Members primarily observe and report suspicious activity while providing a visible police presence in the community.

Over the years, other volunteer opportunities have emerged. These include Certified Child Passenger Safety Technician, Graffiti Tracking, and various duties in the Financial Crimes Unit, Forensic Evidence Unit, and Operations Analysis Unit. The volunteer program is still a strong and viable part of Eugene's police agency and its community. It continues to strengthen connections between agency members and citizens as they work together to make their city's streets safer and to deliver important services to the community.

1. In what ways did the Eugene police department's organizational structure and behavioral standards hamper the initial efforts to build an effective volunteer program?

2. What structural changes enabled this police agency to improve the effectiveness of its volunteer program?

3. Imagine that you are tasked with developing a volunteer police program for a police agency that does not yet have one. Assume that grant money is available to finance the effort. What organizational structures would you put in place to ensure the program's success? What cultural norms would you emphasize? What behavioral standards would you stipulate as most crucial for the program's effectiveness?

◀ Police recruit knowledge, skills, and abilities are measured against performance standards.

Organizational Performance Assessment and Evaluation

After completing this chapter, readers should be able to:

- compare and contrast performance assessment and evaluation.

- describe the benefits of assessment and evaluation for a police agency.

- explain how assessment and evaluation relate to community policing.

- differentiate efficiency and effectiveness as measures of organizational performance.

- compare and contrast the balanced scorecard and total quality management (TQM) as performance-management frameworks.

- describe how a police agency can create and use a balanced scorecard.

- describe how a police agency can implement total quality management (TQM).

- discuss the costs to a police agency if it provides poor service.
- illustrate how a police agency can use segmentation to improve the quality of its services.
- analyze the role that accreditation plays in a police agency's assessment and evaluation of its performance.
- explain how accreditation benefits a police agency.
- list the steps in the accreditation process.

Introduction

If you are like most people, you regularly assess your performance in many dimensions of your life—work, school, sports, and so forth. For instance, suppose you train for and run road races. You probably keep track of your pace (minutes per mile) during every training run to spot patterns, such as whether your pace is increasing or decreasing overall, whether you run better or worse under certain weather conditions, and how the terrain affects your performance. Your assessment then leads to an evaluation—a summary of what you have observed and a statement about the quality of your performance. For instance, your evaluation might be: "I'm having a lot more trouble with hilly terrain than I thought. It looks like I need to do more endurance training." You assess and evaluate your performance because you want to identify problems, address them, and improve.

Like individuals, all organizations, including police agencies, can benefit from regularly assessing and evaluating their performance. These processes enable them to determine how well they are fulfilling their missions and achieving their goals. For example, a police agency should periodically take stock of how effectively it is serving its customers and how efficiently it is allocating key resources such as personnel, revenue, supplies, and equipment to achieve important objectives. By assessing and evaluating these and other aspects of its performance, the agency can identify and address problems—which could range anywhere from inefficient use of resources to lack of understanding of customers' needs to errors in core processes such as gathering evidence or interviewing witnesses to a crime. Assessment and evaluation are thus critical tools for any police agency seeking to continually improve its performance.

In this chapter, we examine key aspects of organizational performance assessment and evaluation. We begin by looking more closely at why it is important to assess and evaluate performance. We then examine two particularly crucial performance measures: efficiency and effectiveness. Next we consider two performance management frameworks that many organizations use to assess, evaluate, and improve their performance. We take a closer look at customer service, since it constitutes such a prominent theme in any assessment, evaluation, and improvement effort. Finally, we consider the role of accreditation in police agencies' performance-improvement efforts.

WHY ASSESS AND EVALUATE?

Assessment and evaluation are powerful tools that can help police agencies continually enhance their performance and adapt to the inevitable changes that make their work more challenging. Yet assessing and evaluating are different in important respects. In the following text we examine their differences, discuss how these processes support continuous performance improvement, and examine how police agencies use these tools.

Defining *Assessment* and *Evaluation*

Assessment is the completion of an appraisal with respect to an object (for example, the condition of a police vehicle) or an activity (such as the way a police officer conducts a traffic stop of a speeding driver). Through assessment, police agencies observe the object or activity in question and offer a value-neutral description of it; for instance, "Two-thirds of the vehicles in our fleet have signs of rust."

Evaluation is an examination or deliberation to decide the quality, value, criticalness, scope, or necessity of a service or activity (Ortmeier, 2006). For example, "Our fleet is in poor condition overall, and we need to improve maintenance of our vehicles." An evaluation thus summarizes the assessment's findings and assigns a value to the performance assessed.

Supporting Continuous Improvement

To meet and exceed the demands of their internal and external customers, police agencies must be committed to **continuous improvement**—a process through which

Assessment:
the completion of an appraisal with respect to an object or an activity.

Evaluation:
an examination or deliberation to decide the quality, value, criticalness, scope, or necessity of a service or activity; a summary of an assessment's findings and assignment of a value to the performance assessed.

Continuous improvement:
a process through which an organization repeatedly assesses the effectiveness of the policies and procedures it has established for achieving key objectives.

Police agencies may share resources during times of special need, such as a funeral of a slain police officer.

the organization repeatedly assesses the effectiveness of the policies and procedures it has established for satisfying customers. Because police agencies exist to serve customers, customer satisfaction ought to be a key agency objective and should be the driving force behind the agency's goals and objectives (Toolingu, 2008) as well as its performance-improvement efforts.

Continuous evaluation:
the process by which an organization, on an ongoing basis, measures actual performance outcomes against intended outcomes to identify and close gaps.

Continuous evaluation complements continuous improvement by enabling agency leaders to identify gaps between desired and actual performance—with an eye toward changing behaviors, policies, or procedures as needed to close those gaps. Through continuous evaluation, a police agency, on an ongoing basis (such as monthly, quarterly, or annually), measures actual outcomes (for instance, percentage reduction in violent crime in the agency's jurisdiction) against intended outcomes. If actual outcomes fall short of intended outcomes ("Violent crime decreased by only 2 percent, and our goal was to decrease it by 5 percent"), agency personnel launch change initiatives to close the gap.

Effecting Needed Change

Continuous improvement through assessment, along with continuous evaluation, positions a police agency to make the changes needed to improve its performance. Through assessment and evaluation, managers identify operations that must be implemented, altered, or discarded to enhance performance.

But agency managers must always keep in mind that improving performance means delivering better service to customers—the residents, business owners, and other individuals who rely on the police for service. It does not mean making changes just to produce outcomes that satisfy internal notions of good performance or that alleviate political pressures on the police. For instance, skipping steps in the crime-investigation process so officers can close crime cases faster may make an agency's "numbers" look better and may please a jurisdiction's political leaders. But it does not make the community safer if it leads to mistakes such as those that result in dismissal of criminal cases in court or arresting the wrong individuals.

When Police and Customer Expectations Conflict

Police agency personnel have a responsibility to identify operations within their organization that need to be changed. However, the agency's customers may have concerns that bear little relation to change initiatives developed by the agency staff. When this happens, police and customer expectations can come into conflict. For instance, citizens in a neighborhood served by the agency may believe that good police work means to prevent the congregation of groups of young people on street corners. The citizens feel safer under those conditions. The police, however, may believe that good police work is more accurately defined as responding to service calls quickly or reducing violent crime in the community. They may see the prevention of gatherings on street corners as a relatively low priority.

While it is true that agency personnel must keep the big picture in mind when defining goals and providing service, they must also understand that most citizens have a narrower focus. Any change initiative considered by police must address both perspectives, not just one or the other. The only way to strike this balance is to foster open communication between police and members of the community they serve. A community policing strategy (see Chapter 2) can help.

Police can gather a wealth of information by communicating with citizens and business owners.

Assessment, Evaluation, and Community Policing

In agencies that have adopted a community policing strategy, police assess performance, identify needed change initiatives, and manage those initiatives using input not only from managers and line officers but also from customers (e.g., citizens).

ETHICS IN ACTION
To Tell the Truth

Jose, a police lieutenant, has been given the task of spearheading the accreditation process for the department. Carla, the chief of police, tells him that accreditation is essential to obtaining additional funding from the city council for important initiatives. "We need to do everything possible," Carla says, "to ensure accreditation, even if that means 'fudging' a few statistics."

Jose starts reviewing his agency's current procedures and policies and recognizes that the department does not meet all the standards necessary for accreditation. Additionally, it looks as if the department has not made any effort toward continuous improvement and is not working toward meeting the required standards of effectiveness that accreditation mandates.

1. Jose decides to approach Carla and express his concerns about what he is seeing. What issues should he raise in the meeting?

2. As the leader of this effort, and knowing that the agency is not capable of meeting the accreditation standards, what recommendations can Jose make to Carla that would help the agency meet the accreditation standards without "fudging" any statistics?

Agency personnel demonstrate that they value citizens' input, and no person's opinion is discounted, dismissed, or derided.

How do police gather information about citizens' opinions and suggestions for change? The process does not necessarily have to be complex or formal. Foot- or beat-patrol officers can simply converse with business owners and residents during the course of a shift. Other methods may be more formal, such as surveys as well as meetings at which citizens and officers discuss the community's problems and develop solutions (Haberfeld, 2002; Michelson & Maher, 1993; Ortmeier & Meese, 2010).

EFFICIENCY VERSUS EFFECTIVENESS: STRIKING A BALANCE

There are many ways to evaluate a police agency's performance. However, managers must identify desirable outcomes before they can begin. Two outcomes considered desirable by many police organizations are efficiency and effectiveness. These are very different manifestations of performance, and agency managers must determine whether they want to strive for both, or whether one or the other is more important at a particular time or under certain conditions.

Efficiency

Efficiency is a comparison of what is actually produced or performed with what can be achieved with the same consumption of resources (such as money, time, and labor). It is thus an important factor in determination of productivity. In a police agency, efficiency is often measured in terms of response time, number of callbacks (returns by a police officer to a location or incident), number of service minutes allotted per call, and crime statistics. As in many organizations, efficiency in a police agency may also manifest itself as "doing more with less"; for example, speeding up response time even after reductions in staff or other resources. Efficiency is almost always about numbers and easily measurable results, such as number of citations issued or number of cases solved.

Effectiveness

Effectiveness is the degree to which objectives are achieved and the extent to which targeted problems are resolved. Because effectiveness is often subjective, it is more difficult to measure than efficiency. In for-profit companies, effectiveness is often gauged by levels of customer satisfaction. One

Efficiency: a comparison of what is actually produced or performed with what can be achieved with the same consumption of resources (money, time, and labor). Efficiency is an important factor in determination of productivity.

Effectiveness: the degree to which objectives are achieved and the extent to which targeted problems are resolved.

Efficiency is measured against the consumption of labor, money, and time.

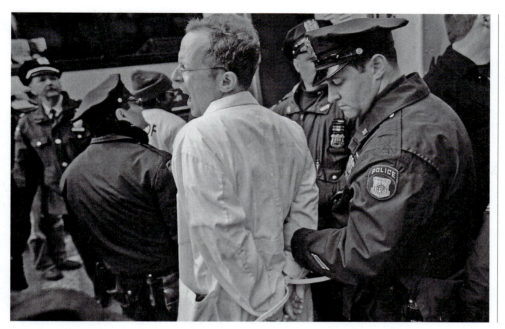

Police performance should be measured by several criteria, not just the number of arrests.

can measure customer satisfaction by asking customers how satisfied they are. But different customers may rate their satisfaction in different ways, using different criteria. By contrast, the time it takes to respond to a call for service (a measure of efficiency) can be easily and objectively measured. Unlike efficiency, effectiveness is determined without reference to costs. Whereas efficiency means "doing the thing right," effectiveness means "doing the right thing."

Another reason that effectiveness in policing is more difficult to assess than efficiency is the existence of conflicting desires among stakeholders. For instance, people walking on the street may view the police as effective if officers restrain a highly agitated emotionally disturbed person and take the individual into custody and transport them to a detention facility to prevent the possibility of violence. But the family of the mentally ill individual may judge the officers as ineffective because they believe that the person should have been taken to a mental health facility instead.

Achieving a Balance

Efficiency *and* effectiveness are important measures of performance for any police agency. To create a formula for achieving both, police agencies and their customers must work together to measure agency outcomes according to three criteria: outstanding performance, unique impact, and persistent durability (Collins, 2005).

Outstanding Performance Outstanding performance means completing assignments in such a way that stakeholders' needs are met and officers need not make a return call (Hellriegel et al., 2008). The results are applauded by onlookers and colleagues alike. Outstanding performance does not necessarily mean heroism, but it may include acts of bravery. An officer who helps a homeless person find a shelter and food demonstrates the same kind of outstanding performance as an officer who performs CPR on a heart-attack victim before emergency medical personnel arrive.

As a first responder, a police officer may perform CPR on a heart attack victim before emergency medical personnel arrive.

Unique Impact A unique impact (best practice) is evidenced by pride in the agency on the part of officers and customers, and by the desire in other police organizations to emulate the agency's programs or initiatives. Police managers constantly seek the next innovation in the day-to-day performance of police work. When successful new programs are highly publicized, decision makers across the nation may recommend that their own agencies adopt them. A good example is the CompStat program initiated in New York City in the mid-1990s (Dabney, 2010; Eterno & Silverman, 2010; Silverman, 2001). CompStat was replicated in many jurisdictions.

Persistent Durability With persistent durability, a police agency sustains its efficiency and effectiveness even after its management changes or new developments and challenges emerge in the communities it serves. Agency administrators foster persistent durability by creating structures, processes, and systems for transferring knowledge between seasoned and new personnel. They also put in place a succession plan to ensure that all sworn officers have the opportunity to rise in the ranks and assume administrative roles. When such officers are promoted in these ways, they share their knowledge with lower-level officers—further preserving the approaches that previously enabled the agency to succeed.

PERFORMANCE-MANAGEMENT FRAMEWORKS

Assessing and evaluating performance with an eye toward improving efficiency and effectiveness is no small feat. For that reason, frameworks have been developed that can help a police agency manage these processes. Two of these frameworks are the balanced scorecard (BSC) and total quality management (TQM).

With persistent durability, a police agency sustains its efficiency and effectiveness even after management changes. Here a senior officer discusses a report with a junior officer in Dubuque, Iowa.

The Balanced Scorecard

The **balanced scorecard** is a performance-management framework based on the assumption that to improve performance, organizations must execute the strategy they have defined for generating desired results. BSC encourages organizations to translate their strategy into day-to-day operations needed to carry out the strategy, ensure that all employees understand the strategy and how their own work supports it, make strategy execution a continuous process, and drive strategic change through effective leadership (Kaplan & Norton, 2001). The framework also holds that financial results are only one aspect of an organization's performance. Additional important aspects include the efficiency and effectiveness of the organization's processes, the well-being of its customers, and the growth and learning of its workforce. (This attention to a comprehensive range of results, not just financial, explains the use of the word *balanced* in the framework's name.)

Balanced scorecard: a performance-management framework based on the assumption that to improve performance, organizations must execute the strategy they have defined for generating desired results.

Building a Scorecard   Many policing, public safety, and public utility organizations (along with corporations and educational and health care institutions) have used the balanced scorecard to improve their performance. To use the scorecard, a police agency follows this process:

1. **Articulate the strategy:** For example, an agency might define its strategy as "Leveraging leading-edge technology to collaborate with partnering organizations and deliver outstanding service to our community."

2. **Define strategic objectives:** Managers work together to define strategic objectives that must be met in order to carry out the strategy. They define objectives for all dimensions of performance: financial, customer, processes, and workforce. For example, objectives for the strategy described in Step 1 might include "Update IT system" (the process dimension of performance),

"Enhance leadership skills throughout our organization" (the workforce dimension), "Forge closer partnerships with citizens" (the customer dimension), and "Increase funding from taxes" (the financial dimension).

3. **Select performance measures:** For each strategic objective, agency managers select measures for assessing and evaluating performance on that objective. For instance, the measure for the objective "Enhance leadership skills throughout our organization" could be "Percentage of agency personnel who have completed our leadership training program and earned a passing grade."

4. **Set targets:** Managers set targets for each measure. Take the measure "Percentage of agency personnel who have completed the leadership training program and earned a passing grade." The target for this measure could be something like "80 percent by end of this year."

5. **Define strategic initiatives:** Managers identify strategic initiatives needed to meet the targets they have set for each strategic objective. These initiatives could be relatively focused change projects as well as large-scale transformation programs. For instance, to ensure that 80 percent of police personnel have completed the leadership training program and earned a passing grade, the agency could launch an initiative that entails revising shift schedules so officers who have not yet attended the training can do so.

Table 7-1 shows an excerpt from the balanced scorecard created by one police agency that uses the problem-oriented policing strategy. (See Chapter 2.) The agency is seeking to improve its ability to reduce homicides and violent attacks in its community. Sample strategic objectives are depicted for each performance dimension.

table 7-1 Urban Police Department Sample Scorecard

CUSTOMER OBJECTIVES

- Reduce shots-fired calls
- Reduce homicides
- Reduce vacant houses
- Reduce calls for service

FINANCIAL OBJECTIVES

- Secure operational funds
- Secure special overtime funds
- Create special housing capital

INTERNAL PROCESS OBJECTIVES

- Establish partnerships between educational, police, community, and business leaders
- Create an agreement between government and community resources as to strategic objectives
- Align police resources toward objectives

WORKFORCE OBJECTIVES

- Train and improve police officers' knowledge and skills regarding problem-oriented policing
- Teach the concept of teamwork and how to communicate persuasively with police, government, business, and community participants
- Establish an environment of enthusiasm

Using the Scorecard   Once a police agency has created its balanced scorecard, it tracks actual performance on each strategic objective and compares that to the performance targets it set. Any gaps between actual and targeted performance (for example, "Only 60 percent of our personnel have completed the course and earned a passing grade, and we targeted 80 percent") should trigger a discussion about what is causing the shortfall and how the gap can be closed. For instance, perhaps a particular strategic initiative is not being managed well, and the agency assigns a new project leader to guide the initiative. Or managers launch an entirely different initiative to ensure that the performance targets are met during the next evaluation period.

The agency should set a target for performance and compare it with actual performance.

Total Quality Management (TQM)

Many police agencies also use the **total quality management (TQM)** performance-management framework to take a disciplined approach to quality control and assurance. Sometimes used in combination with the balanced scorecard, TQM enables an organization to further assess, evaluate, and improve its performance.

To understand how the TQM framework operates, we need first to define what quality means in the context of policing and then consider several processes (quality control and quality assurance) an agency might use to manage its performance.

Defining *Quality*   In the realms of public service and policing, *quality* means specific things:

- Excellent service that satisfies customers
- Efficient *and* effective results that support the agency's mission and that extract the most value from its available resources
- Outstanding group and individual performance that is applauded by citizens, makes an obvious impact on neighborhoods, and produces long-term positive results, not simply news-media headlines (Collins, 2005)
- Performance that is sustained through successive command changes

Using Quality Control   Through **quality control**, police managers verify that an activity is completed correctly (efficiently and effectively) the first time (American Society for Quality, 2008; Wideman, 2001). For example, suppose a police officer responds to a call for service from a citizen who says that someone has broken into her home. The officer resolves the incident by quickly confirming that the home has been burglarized, making sure the burglar is not on the premises, helping the woman secure

Total quality management (TQM): a performance-management framework that can help a police agency take a disciplined approach to quality control and assurance.

Quality control: verifying that an activity is completed correctly (efficiently and effectively) the first time.

her property so it is no longer vulnerable, and properly documenting (reporting) the incident. There is no need for a return call to the same incident. This activity was completed correctly the first time, evidence of a high level of quality control. To exercise quality control related to activities such as responding to calls for service, police academies and agencies carefully train officers on how to handle such calls.

Quality assurance: ensuring that service actions comply with agency directives and that they support the agency's mission.

Achieving Quality Assurance   Quality control helps a police agency achieve **quality assurance**—the confidence that service actions comply with agency directives and that they support the agency's mission (American Society for Quality, 2008). Whereas quality control is about taking measurements during delivery of a service, quality assurance is the outcome gained through "QC."

In an agency that has achieved quality assurance, initiatives are focused on providing excellent services that solve customers' problems and that deliver long-term, positive impacts. Agency personnel assess not just the quantity of services delivered but also their quality. Quality assurance indicates that the agency has continuously improved its performance (Ortmeier & Meese, 2010).

Quality assurance was first used in manufacturing companies to ensure the quality of products—measured by criteria such as minimum number of product defects. "QA" was designed to instill confidence in the products consumers purchased. Through attention to internal processes and operations, coupled with input from customers themselves (such as data on defective products), managers tailored their organization's operations to provide the best product. But recently, not-for-profit organizations and service organizations such as police agencies have begun using quality assurance to enhance the efficiency and effectiveness of the services they deliver.

Quality assurance through observation is used to enhance efficiency and effectiveness.

Implementing TQM   To implement TQM, agency managers must:

- Know who the agency's customers are (internal and external)
- Know what performance outcomes will satisfy each customer group
- Define the mission, goals, and processes for producing those outcomes
- Secure the resources needed to deliver the outcomes
- Establish workforce–management practices to encourage attention to quality, such as recognition of goals achieved, training, and encouragement

Demonstrating Total Quality Leadership   To implement a TQM program in a police agency (including focusing everyone's attention on improving service quality), managers must demonstrate **total quality leadership**—the commitment and behavior needed to carry out and ultimately integrate TQM practices throughout their agency. Total quality leaders take the following steps:

1. Commit to the notion that service quality is a viable and desirable goal.
2. Conduct an internal assessment to determine the agency's current level of service quality.
3. Actively lead the TQM implementation in the agency; for example, by explaining the importance of improving service quality and helping people make the changes needed to focus more sharply on quality.
4. Integrate the model of quality throughout the agency by replicating processes that accomplish goals well (T. E. Baker, 2006; George & Weimerskirch, 1998).

Total quality leaders know that to integrate TQM throughout their agency, they must convince managers and line officers to reach goals that are community or neighborhood focused. Such leaders ensure that these goals are clearly stated and that they express desired outcomes important to customers (not just the agency). As leaders, agency personnel also establish processes for identifying and collecting data that agency personnel can analyze to assess progress toward the goals. Analysis should readily show whether the agency has had a positive, negative, or neutral impact on the community problems it seeks to address.

For example, suppose an agency has identified an increase in vehicle theft as a problem. To align managers, supervisors, and officers behind an effort to reduce vehicle thefts, agency administrators must explain the importance of solving the problem for the community and identify the customers affected. In addition, they must describe data the agency is collecting and measurements it is using to assess progress (such as number of vehicle thefts reported in the coming six months). Finally, they must define the anticipated results of the quality improvement effort (for instance, a 10 percent reduction in thefts by the end of the evaluation period).

When an agency has total quality leaders, discussions about agency activities will no longer center only on questions of efficiency, such as how many weapons were removed from the street or how many bands of youths were dispersed. Instead, police managers, front-line officers, and community members will spend more time talking about how much these efficiency gains have improved the effectiveness of the agency's services and the value extracted from the resources used. For example, they will ask, "Do citizens feel safer now than they did before?" "Are there fewer injuries and deaths now than before?" and "Are more young people staying in school longer?"

Total quality leadership: the commitment and behavior needed to carry out and integrate TQM practices throughout a police agency.

A gun buy-back program can increase safety in a neighborhood and improve its quality of life.

A CLOSER LOOK AT CUSTOMER SERVICE

The theme of customer service runs through the examination of assessment, evaluation, efficiency versus effectiveness, and performance-management methodologies we have just completed. For this reason, it is valuable to take a closer look at customer service in the context of policing.

As we have seen, in a police agency, serving customers means meeting public needs. Police agencies provide services for the public benefit while ensuring peaceful and safe communities (Jurkanin et al., 2001; Stillman, 2005). Failing to provide good service can carry a high price.

Understanding the Costs of Providing Poor Service

Customers of any organization who are dissatisfied with the quality of a product or service may find other sources for that product or service (Hellriegel et al., 2008). The primary service provided by a police agency is the public safety that citizens and business owners in the agency's jurisdiction expect. If any of these customers consider police services inadequate, they may relocate to actual or perceived safer neighborhoods or communities, stop reporting crime or suspicious circumstances to the police, or seek public safety services from other resources, such as vendors of private security services. Dissatisfied business owners may move their businesses

Those with financial resources may supplement public police services with private security.

elsewhere. And people who shop at those companies may start buying from enterprises located in areas perceived as safer.

Such migrations out of an unsafe area carry high costs for everyone. For the jurisdiction, it can mean a shrunken tax base and thus fewer funds allocated to police. In addition, if people abandon buildings to move to safer places, the abandoned structures become eyesores as well as neighborhood hazards when unsupervised children play in them or drug users and dealers congregate in them.

Delivering Service Ethically

For police, delivering high-quality customer service includes paying attention to ethics while interacting with all customers—whether they are private citizens, business owners or employees, or suspects and arrestees who (not surprisingly) will likely have an antagonistic relationship with the police. Ethical service delivery means treating *all* customers (no matter who they are) with respect, fairness, courtesy, and civility.

It also includes using every means at the police agency's disposal to provide service. For example, after interviewing a robbery victim, a police officer may quickly enlist agency forensic technicians for evidence collection and seek the cooperation of the district attorney's office in prosecuting suspects.

Segmenting Services

Segmenting police services—putting them into groups based on specific criteria—can help police agencies improve the quality of those services. An agency can group its services according to the following criteria:

- **Customer type served:** Customer types include private homeowners, business owners, citizen volunteers, neighborhood organizations, and schools.

The police perform many services including the storage of evidence. This photo depicts an evidence storage facility at the Los Angeles Police Department.

- **Service delivery method:** Methods of delivering services include direct interaction with citizens, preventive patrol, traffic management, follow-up crime investigation, and specialized operations related to illegal drugs, gangs, and intelligence gathering.

- **Service delivery location:** Locations include the agency's building, specific offices within the buildings, and places outside the agency's facility, such as neighborhood streets, schools, and business offices.

- **Service deployment hours:** The hours during which a service is deployed depend on variables such as an agency's hours of operation, shift schedules, and customers' needs.

- **Service process type:** Within a police agency, there are many different processes essential for delivery of services, and each may be handled by a different department (if a large agency). Such processes might range from developing communications for the news media and the community the agency serves to safeguarding and storing crime-scene evidence to performing a background check on citizens applying for handgun permits (Hodge & Anthony, 1979; Lawrence & Lorsch, 1967; Robbins & Judge, 2008).

Once the agency has segmented its services, managers and officers can analyze the segments they have defined and determine which changes (if any) in procedures and policies are needed to enhance customers' satisfaction while still supporting the agency's mission.

For example, managers at one agency discussed with customers the agency's current service delivery locations, service deployment hours, and service delivery methods used. They learned that citizens, volunteers, and business owners

Leadership on the job

Unhappy Citizens

Community meetings are not always comfortable for police officers to attend, given the unresolved neighborhood issues that can stir up unrest among residents. Though meetings can be emotionally charged, they are an important part of policing in today's world. Suppose that you, a police manager, have been invited to take part in a neighborhood meeting where citizens are complaining about a recent rash of vehicle thefts. You cannot make the meeting and decide to delegate this activity to the evening sergeant in the precinct. You are advised through neighborhood gossip that the meeting may be volatile, and

that the citizens want something done now about the thefts.

1. As a leader, how would you decide which officers are best equipped to accompany the sergeant and participate in this community meeting?

2. How would you prepare the officers to attend the meeting?

3. What kind of feedback would you expect the officers to return from the meeting with?

4. How would you use the information gathered at the meeting?

---

wanted visual police presence in neighborhoods during evening hours. This contrasted sharply with the calls-for-service model the agency had been using, through which police had been reacting to calls and avoiding interaction with bystanders.

To provide more of the visible interaction with police that this agency's customers wanted, managers worked with community leaders to establish a small police–volunteer substation in the neighborhood. The substation became the locus for police–volunteer interaction, meetings, police report writing and review, and personal breaks for area officers and volunteers.

THE ROLE OF ACCREDITATION IN ASSESSMENT AND EVALUATION

Accreditation plays an important role in a police agency's assessment, evaluation, and performance-improvement efforts. Be it national or state, accreditation ensures that a police agency meets minimum standards regarding policies, operating procedures, employee knowledge, documentation, and community interaction. Standards also cover law enforcement responsibilities, relationships with other agencies, quality of management and administration, agency personnel structure and human resource processes, traffic operations, prisoner and court activities, communications, and property and evidence control.

Through accreditation, outside evaluators knowledgeable about police agency operations and procedures assess an agency's performance against the standards. The accreditation process serves as an assurance that the agency being assessed meets or exceeds accreditation criteria.

Accreditation can play an important role in a police agency's assessment, evaluation, and performance improvement efforts.

Accrediting Bodies

The concept of police agency accreditation dates back to the mid-twentieth century when many policing experts and organizations (along with some citizens) concluded that setting minimum standards for police agency policies, procedures, activities, and service delivery could help ensure reliable performance and establish agencies' credibility in the eyes of stakeholders. Since then, to be accredited means that an agency has received a certification confirming that it adheres to standards that meet or exceed specified minimum requirements. The Commission on Accreditation for Law Enforcement Agencies (CALEA) is an accrediting body that determines those standards and awards the accreditation to those agencies in compliance. CALEA includes such distinguished organizations as the International Association of Chiefs of Police (IACP), the National Organization of Black Law Enforcement Executives (NOBLE), the National Sheriffs Association (NSA), and the Police Executive Research Forum (PERF).

Many states have also elected to create their own accreditation programs based on the expectation that, statewide, a police agency will adhere to or exceed specified standards. For example, New York State has an accreditation program that was established in 1989. The program comprises 130 standards and contains four tenets:

- To increase effectiveness and efficiency
- To encourage cooperation among agencies within the community
- To guarantee training standards
- To solicit and retain the confidence of the public

The Benefits of Accreditation

The purpose of accreditation is to create and maintain excellent public safety service delivery. The advantages of accreditation include recognition of an agency's professional excellence by government officials and citizens who gain increased confidence in the agency. Accreditation is one way to ensure that police agencies across the country are performing in a consistent and professional manner. Because there are documented standards, any agency that performs at a higher level than those standards can rightfully call itself exceptional.

For some agencies, the most important benefit of accreditation is that it strengthens the agency's defense against lawsuits and complaints, one of the most prevalent difficulties faced by police agencies today. Accredited agencies have proven to be better able to defend themselves against allegations of misconduct as well as lawsuits. Accreditation thus represents a reduction in agency risk and liability exposure. This can help reduce an agency's liability insurance premiums.

Disadvantages include the possibility that some officers will view accreditation as a threat. For example, an agency requires line officers to upgrade their skills through training so that the agency can meet a minimum standard. Officers must complete the new training but do not receive additional compensation for their time or upgraded skills. Another disadvantage is the cost of the accreditation process which may strain an agency's budget.

The Accreditation Process

The accreditation process comprises several steps:

1. The agency submits an application for accreditation.
2. It conducts a self-assessment of its performance against the accrediting body's standards.
3. Outside evaluators conduct an on-site assessment, by reviewing policies, procedures, and outcomes.
4. The accrediting organization reviews the application and the findings from all assessments and decides whether to approve accreditation.
5. If approved, the agency is awarded accredited status (Commission on Accreditation for Law Enforcement Agencies, 2008; Crowder, 1998).

summary

- **Why Assess and Evaluate?** Through assessment, police agencies describe in neutral terms an activity or object important to its performance. Through evaluation, agencies summarize an assessment's findings and assign a value to the performance assessed. Assessment and evaluation help agencies identify and address problems, and thus continually improve performance by making needed changes. In agencies using the community policing strategy, customers provide input into the assessment and evaluation processes.

- **Efficiency versus Effectiveness: Striking a Balance.** Efficiency is a comparison of what an activity actually produces or how a person performs with what can be achieved with the same consumption of resources. Effectiveness is the degree to which an agency achieves its objectives and resolves targeted problems. Efficiency and effectiveness are important measures of performance for a police agency. Police leaders know that their agency has achieved both when the outcomes generated by the agency meet three criteria: outstanding performance, unique impact, and persistent durability.

- **Performance-Management Frameworks.** The balanced scorecard framework is based on the assumption that to improve performance, a police agency must execute the strategy it has defined for generating desired results. To build a balanced scorecard, an agency articulates its strategy, defines objectives that must be met to execute the strategy, selects performance measures for each strategic objective, sets targets for each measure, and defines strategic initiatives needed to reach the targets. The agency reports and tracks actual performance on each measure against targeted performance, identifies gaps, and selects actions to close the gaps.

The total quality management (TQM) framework is sometimes integrated with the balanced scorecard. TQM uses quality control techniques (verifying that an activity is completed correctly the first time) to achieve quality assurance (the confidence that service actions comply with agency directors and support the agency's mission). To implement TQM, agency managers must demonstrate specific knowledge and behaviors, including knowing who the agency's customers are and securing the resources needed to deliver desired outcomes. Anyone leading a TQM effort must also possess certain traits and exhibit specific actions, including explaining the importance of improving service quality and helping people make the changes needed to focus on quality.

- **A Closer Look at Customer Service.** Police agencies are service providers. Thus, their assessment and evaluation efforts, as well as their use of performance-management frameworks, typically have customer service improvement as their central goal. By understanding the costs of providing poor service, agency personnel can become more motivated to improve service. The criteria for high-quality service include ethical delivery of service—treating all customers with respect, fairness, courtesy, and civility. Agencies can generate ideas for improving customer service by segmenting their services by various criteria, such as customer type, delivery method, delivery location, deployment hours, and service process type.

- **The Role of Accreditation in Assessment and Evaluation.** Accreditation ensures that a police agency meets minimum standards regarding policies, operating procedures, employee knowledge, documentation, and community interaction. Standards are determined by organizations such as the Commission on Accreditation for Law Enforcement Agencies (CALEA). Agencies that receive accreditation gain recognition from stakeholders, demonstrate that they are performing with excellence, and can better defend themselves against allegations of misconduct and lawsuits, thus reducing their risk and liability exposure. The accreditation process starts with an agency submitting an application for accreditation and includes internal reviews of its performance as well as reviews conducted by outside evaluators.

key terms

assessment

balanced scorecard

continuous evaluation

continuous improvement

effectiveness

efficiency

evaluation

quality assurance

quality control

total quality leadership

total quality management (TQM)

1. What is the difference between organizational performance assessment and evaluation? What benefits does a police agency gain by assessing and evaluating its performance continually?

2. How do assessment and evaluation differ in a police agency that uses the community policing strategy, as compared with agencies that use the traditional policing strategy?

3. What is the difference between efficiency and effectiveness? Give an example of each.

4. Why is it important that a police agency demonstrate both efficiency and effectiveness in its performance? What three criteria are essential for balancing efficiency with effectiveness?

5. What is the balanced scorecard? How does it help a police agency improve performance? If you wished to introduce the balanced scorecard in a police agency, what steps would you advise agency personnel to follow?

6. What is total quality management (TQM)? How does it relate to quality control and quality assurance? If you were tasked with implementing TQM in a police agency, what knowledge would you need to possess, and what behaviors would you have to demonstrate? If you were tasked with leading a TQM effort in an agency, what personal qualities would you need to exhibit, and what actions would you need to take?

7. What are some costs of providing poor service to a police agency's customers?

8. What does "delivering service ethically" mean? Cite an example not provided in this chapter.

9. What are some criteria by which a police agency can segment its services? Propose an example (not the one provided in this chapter) of how segmentation of services can help a police agency improve the quality of its services.

10. What is accreditation? How can it benefit a police agency? If you wished to initiate the accreditation process in a police agency, what is the first step you would take?

WHAT WOULD YOU DO?
Determining Service Quality

Ben, a small-town police agency's newly appointed police chief, wants to assess and improve the agency's response to citizen complaints. Because of limited resources, major crime (such as murder and robbery) in the area is managed by the county sheriff or the state police. Ben's agency addresses lower-level crime (including vandalism and vehicle theft) and quality-of-life complaints from citizens.

The agency concerns itself with three types of customer service issues: (1) quality-of-life concerns such as street-drug sales, trash, noise, parking, and loitering; (2) school-related issues such as crimes committed by or against students, safe passages of students to and from school, and general maintenance of order; and (3) business or commercial concerns, such as customers who have parking complaints and companies needing nightly building checks.

Ben believes that analysis of crime rates, complaints regarding police performance, and the number of calls-for-service do not offer a complete picture of the quality of service his agency provides. Through informal communication with private citizens, community groups, and business owners, he has learned that the community does not report complaints of problems and that police officers do not have high visibility in the community. Further review revealed that citizens do not call the police because they do not want to bother or annoy the emergency communication dispatcher (9-1-1) with petty concerns. This lack of willingness to call in public safety concerns stems in part from poor police response in the past.

Ben decides to establish a plan for developing a more accurate assessment of his agency's customer service. After thoroughly discussing the issue with the agency's officers, they decide that Ben and the officers will periodically meet with citizens by attending meetings with senior citizen groups, the Veterans of Foreign Wars (VFW), the Lions Club, and other community groups. Ben institutes a monthly, well-advertised, Speak to the Chief Night featuring topics such as the role of the police in the community, approachability of police officers, and the importance of calling 9-1-1.

Ben's agency also sets up a 24-hour citizen-service phone line. When citizens use the line to express complaints about police service, the complaints will be addressed by the chief himself within 24 hours. In addition, the agency develops a Neighborhood Watch crime-prevention program and monthly business-leader meetings. Finally, Ben institutes a crime follow-up procedure whereby all crime incidents and reports are reviewed and evaluated by an objective senior officer.

1. In distinguishing service quality, Ben employed informal methods of assessment. What methods did he use? Do you think these methods will produce a more accurate assessment of the agency's service? If so, why might these methods be particularly effective in a smaller agency?

2. Ben's agency, like others, has formal records of service. What are the agency's current formal processes? Do you consider them adequate for service-quality assessment? Why or why not?

3. What additional techniques would you advise Ben to use to accurately assess and evaluate the quality of police service to the community, and to improve performance where needed?

Human Resource Management

8

Hiring in the Spirit of Service

After completing this chapter, readers should be able to:

- describe the hiring challenges facing police agencies.

- explain how police agencies can lay the groundwork for effective recruiting.

- distinguish effective recruitment strategies.

- explain how police agencies conduct pre-employment screening.

- identify a variety of compensation and benefits programs used to attract desirable candidates.

- define *civil work environment* and articulate why it is important to the hiring process.

Introduction

If you are considering a career in policing, what has drawn you to this line of work? A study released by the U.S. Department of Justice in 2008 suggests that your goals in building such a career may affect your effectiveness on the job—and your satisfaction with the work. The study revealed that individuals who are attracted to a police career because it gives them the opportunity to support and serve communities are better suited for police work than people who are drawn to the profession in pursuit of adventurous activities often associated with criminal law enforcement.

These findings support the contention that people with a predisposition toward service to the community are better prepared to face the challenges and meet the demands placed on today's police officers. Further, the quality of police services correlates directly with the behavior of individual officers (U.S. Department of Justice, Office of Community Oriented Policing Services, 2008). The study lends credibility to the notion that police officers should possess and demonstrate strong ethical leadership and interpersonal skills—which are essential for community service.

Staffing an agency with such officers begins with recruiting and selecting the right people to wear a badge—people who demonstrate the skills and attitudes required to fulfill policing's increasingly complex mandate. Like any organization that provides services, a police agency is only as good as its people. A well-trained, respectful police officer is a credit to the community served, while an officer with poor training and a cynical attitude can inflict enormous damage on the community, the reputation of the agency, and the officer.

In this chapter, we focus on how police agencies can hire in the spirit of service. We begin by examining the challenges characterizing hiring today and then consider how police agencies can set the stage for smart recruiting, formulate effective recruiting strategies, and select the best new hires from candidate pools. We close the chapter by taking a close look at two additional keys to hiring for service: designing the right compensation and benefits packages, and fostering a culture of civility.

UNDERSTANDING TODAY'S HIRING CHALLENGES

Effective agencies develop hiring strategies with an eye toward ensuring that the organization has the right people doing the right things at the right time to achieve stated goals and objectives. To make sure all this happens, an agency's human resource function must manage several vital activities: recruiting and selecting people with the best capabilities; training; assessing recruits' learning and skill development; offering ongoing recognition, reward, and retention programs; establishing a process to develop employees' cognitive, affective (ethical leadership), and technical abilities; and helping new employees identify a career pathway (Kearns, 2005). None of this is easy, given the challenges facing agencies seeking to hire today. These challenges include an increasingly complex mandate for police service, and the need to build a diverse workforce in police agencies to reflect the composition of the communities served.

Fulfilling a Complex Mandate

Policing has always been far more than just law enforcement. It encompasses peacekeeping, order maintenance, traffic management, education of the public, homeland security, and public safety. Most of all, policing is about serving people in the community—residents, business owners, schoolchildren, and others. To fulfill all these demands, police officers must do more than just enforce the law. They must also keep order in a society that is increasingly diverse. Policing thus demands exceptional mental and emotional skills as well as excellent competencies in human relations, communication, and ethical leadership. Simply put, today's police officers must possess *people skills*.

Yet too many police agencies seek merely to fill the basic (preservice) academy with bodies. As long as minimum entrance requirements are satisfied (for example, passing a test; meeting minimal educational, physical, and psychological standards; and having a satisfactory background check), a person is accepted into the academy. Once there, many students experience little difficulty completing a probationary

Police officers must be and remain physically fit.

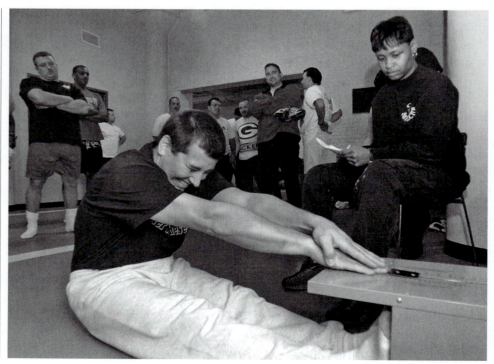

period. Recruits are evaluated at the end of the probationary period to determine whether they meet the minimum performance standards. They are seldom evaluated on their commitment to helping and serving others in their capacity as police officers. Lacking these and other people skills, they may ultimately deliver mediocre performance and find little satisfaction in police work.

Building a Diverse Workforce

The complex mandate police agencies must fulfill includes the need to recruit and retain a diverse workforce that reflects the community served. Achieving this diversity is difficult for several reasons. To illustrate, what motivates an individual to enter public service as a police officer varies greatly across cultures. If an agency cannot tap into the particular motives influencing some individuals' career choices, it will be unable to attract those individuals to police work. In addition, men and women alike increasingly want to have satisfying family and personal lives in addition to a career. Agencies may experience difficulty recruiting people who view police work as not conducive to a balanced lifestyle. Finally, the number of qualified entry-level candidates can fluctuate dramatically, depending on economic conditions and the attractiveness of other occupations to candidates. For example, if many Asians or Latinos in a particular community are entering careers other than police work, an agency may find it impossible to hire members of these groups.

Demographic changes have added to the challenge of building a diverse workforce. For example, many new police officers are members of Generation Y (those born after 1980). Their expectations, motivations, values, and priorities differ from those of the baby boomer generation. "Gen Y" recruits want a package that includes a decent salary, benefits (medical coverage, retirement, and paid time off), the opportunity for specialization and promotion, job security and fulfillment, and pride and excitement in what they do. Police agencies that do not offer this package will have difficulty recruiting members of this generation.

SETTING THE STAGE FOR SMART RECRUITING

Despite the challenges, an agency can still hire a diverse workforce if qualified men and women—from a variety of backgrounds, cultures, and life experiences—view employment with the agency as a worthwhile and rewarding endeavor. To foster that view and attract qualified candidates, an agency can take steps that set the stage for smart recruiting. These include conducting a human resource needs assessment and looking beyond minimum hiring standards.

Conducting a Human Resource Needs Assessment

In addition to considering potential recruits' needs while developing recruitment strategies, an agency must also assess its own needs. For instance, managers must know how many officers are necessary to deliver the services a community requires and supports, as well as what type of officers are needed and which specific duties they will be expected to perform (T. E. Baker, 2006; Ortmeier, 1999). Toward this end, they must conduct a job task analysis to identify actual police tasks the agency

Leadership on the job
Drug Use as a Disqualifier

A police agency in a major city experienced difficulty locating qualified candidates to fill new recruit classes. The mandate from city officials was to hire as many officers as possible in an effort to increase police presence on the streets. Police managers decided to relax hiring standards and to consider applicants who had used marijuana, cocaine, heroin, or other illegal substances in the past. Thus, previous drug use no longer automatically disqualified candidates.

Agency administrators justified this decision by citing the fact that the FBI, which many people consider one of the most professional law enforcement agencies in the country, had begun considering applicants with drug use histories. The administrators also claimed that societal standards had changed and that a history of drug use is no longer viewed in the same manner as it was years ago. Each candidate, they added, should be evaluated according to the circumstances and frequency of the drug use.

Dissenters maintained that the agency was lowering its hiring standards to an unacceptable level. Some of them argued that many excellent candidates who had never used drugs were available—why not select them? Others argued that drug use indicated a lack of character and that officers with a record of drug use would be more likely to ignore the same behavior in others.

1. Under what conditions, if any, may a history of drug use be waived by an employing agency? If you are not sure, where might you find this information?

2. In your view, does drug use diminish a person's character? Why or why not?

must carry out. A well-prepared job task analysis also defines the physical, emotional, and character elements of the job: the "who, what, why, where, when, and how" associated with a task to be successfully accomplished. (See the "Deployment: Putting Human Resources to the Best Use" section in Chapter 10 for additional information on conducting a human resource needs assessment.)

Looking beyond Minimum Hiring Standards

Few businesses in the private sector tolerate minimal hiring standards. Managers know that it is unrealistic and impractical to advertise for workers who meet minimum standards, take time to train the new hires, and then expect them to deliver top-notch performance. For police officers—who operate in environments requiring the highest ethical standard, effective judgment, and emotional stability in life or death situations—anything less than outstanding performance is unacceptable. To employ people who can deliver this level of performance, the agency must look beyond minimal hiring standards—with an eye toward attracting the best people to the job in the first place (Jurkanin et al., 2001).

Yet as we have seen, many police agencies recruit merely by identifying how many people are needed to fill the next academy class. To fill the class, an agency makes the community aware of its intentions and, if applicants meet the minimum standards and are available within the acceptable pool of candidates, they are selected for the academy. Agency managers assume that the majority of the recruits will graduate from the academy and obtain a permanent job at the organization.

A police officer candidate engaged in an interview in Santa Ana, California.

Many managers make little effort to determine whether the recruits have a philosophy and passion for service to people. They also neglect to assess whether candidates have an inclination toward policing as a profession and the ethical values that law enforcement professionals must demonstrate.

Agencies must look beyond minimum hiring standards and seek candidates who not only meet those standards but also demonstrate the personal qualities (such as integrity, collegiality, and a desire to learn and to serve) and the skills (including communication, leadership, strategic thinking, and self-control) that lie at the core of an excellent (not merely good) police officer. Agencies must measure every candidate against these qualities (T. E. Baker, 2006). Those that do so will stand a far better chance of hiring individuals interested in community service than agencies that use only minimal hiring standards as criteria for evaluating candidates.

FORMULATING RECRUITMENT STRATEGIES

Recruitment for a police agency is no different than recruiting for any position of authority in an organization. The agency defines desired qualities and skills in candidates and uses these as benchmarks of applicants' suitability. A candidate who embodies and rates high in the majority of the desired attributes, qualities, and skills should have a reasonable expectation of being hired. However, developing effective recruitment strategies is more complex than it might appear on the surface. To craft strategies that bring in the new hires an agency needs, managers must use the right channels to reach candidates, develop a positive brand image that will attract qualified candidates, recruit for diversity, and consider the education levels the ideal candidate will bring to the table.

Using the Right Channels

To attract the best people, a police agency should use the right channels to explicitly seek passionate, enthusiastic, and service-oriented people who are committed to making a positive difference in others' lives. An agency can use a number of different channels to recruit candidates to fill vacancies. It can recruit internally through promotion, transfer, or an upgrade in the vacant position. And it can do so externally, by advertising vacancies and inviting applications through these channels:

- The news media
- Professional journals
- The Internet (for example, job websites)
- Labor organizations
- Employment agencies
- Job (career) fairs (Ortmeier, 1999)

Figure 8-1 illustrates a job posting similar to one that was published in a midwestern newspaper. This advertisement is particularly effective because it provides comprehensive information—including an overview of the department that is recruiting, salary and benefits, basic requirements, the department's hiring process, and contact information. Additional points reveal the department's interest in hiring women and minorities, and in supporting officers' acquisition of higher education.

figure 8-1 A Sample Job Posting

Police Officer
Anytown, USA

Anytown Police Department
Personnel/Recruiting Section
10 Police Avenue
Anytown, State, 12345-0000
Phone: 000-000-0000
Website: www.city.state,us/police

Application Deadline: **Open until filled**

The City of Anytown is seeking men and women from all backgrounds and cultures to join the Anytown Police Department and help maintain a police department that is responsive to the needs of the community.

Overview of the Anytown Police Department

The Anytown Police Department operates with the goal of providing the highest level of professional public service to the residents of Anytown, the largest city in the state of Mind. The city of Anytown is unique in that it is home to a wide range of ethnic and diverse groups. The police department actively pursues interaction and involvement with the community to provide better services to the community and to enhance the working environment of members of the department.

Anytown covers 139 square miles and is divided into 12 police districts. These areas are patrolled by both uniformed and plainclothes officers.

Besides patrol duty, the police department has numerous specialized units that offer the career-minded professional unparalleled opportunities to grow with one of the most progressive police departments in the country. A few of the specialized units available are the Mounted Equestrian Section, Bomb Squad, Aviation Section, Harbormaster Section, and Canine (K-9).

Officers with specialized skills are encouraged by the department to use and develop their abilities by instituting new programs and units within the department.

The Anytown Police Department is one of the best trained and most progressive departments in the country. You are invited to join this outstanding department and begin your career in law enforcement.

Salary and Benefits

Competitive medical, dental, and optical plans

College tuition reimbursement

Twenty vacation days per year

Eight paid holidays per year

Twelve sick days per year

Pension plan/deferred compensation plan

Department-issued uniforms and equipment

Longevity pay/off-duty court appearances

Shift differential pay (afternoon/midnight shifts)

Uniform cleaning allowance

Required Qualifications (Basic Requirements)

1. Applicant must be at least 18 years old and a U.S. citizen.
2. Applicant's vision must be 20/20, or corrected to 20/20, in each eye. Depth and color perception must be normal.
3. Applicant must be a high school graduate or have earned a GED.
4. Applicant must possess a valid driver's license (at time of application).
5. Applicant must not have been convicted of a felony or misdemeanor involving domestic violence. Other misdemeanor arrests or convictions are subject to review on an individual basis.
6. Applicant must be capable of performing the essential functions of a police officer with or without accommodation as determined by the hiring criteria.

Women and minorities are encouraged to apply!

Hiring Process

Applicants must successfully complete the Anytown Police Department's selection process, as outlined below. No applicants are guaranteed processing at any stage.

1. Complete an application and meet the basic requirements, including a check of the applicant's driving record and a criminal history check.
2. Pass a written examination.
3. Pass a physical agility examination.
4. Pass an initial preinvestigation interview.
5. Complete a background investigation.
6. Pass a final oral interview.
7. Pass a psychological examination and psychological interview.
8. Pass a medical examination.

Contact Information

See the top of this posting.

Among other mechanisms, the police use job fairs to recruit new officers.

Police organizations considering using an employment agency to locate candidates should take steps to ensure that they select the right agency. For example, managers should:

- Find out how the agency's costs work. For example, are "finder's fees" based on a percentage of the compensation paid to new hires delivered by the agency?

- Provide as much specific and precise information as possible about what qualities and skills the police organization is looking for in candidates presented by the employment agency.

- Ask to interview other police organizations' personnel that have used the employment agency, to learn their impressions of the agency's effectiveness.

In addition, agency managers can review applications already on file. Perhaps a qualified applicant who could not be hired earlier because of budget cuts or some other constraint could now be offered a position. Word of mouth is another effective recruiting tactic; indeed, 95 percent of police agencies use it. To activate word of mouth, managers can ask current and former employees and agency retirees, as well as employees' friends and relatives, to suggest candidates. Other useful recruitment methods include targeting military veterans and graduates of college criminal justice programs. These can be rich sources of candidates, especially if the agency can offer internships that enable graduates to explore a career in the profession before making a long-term commitment.

Developing a Positive Brand Image

Candidates should not enter the policing profession with unrealistic expectations of what the work will be like. Literature can help provide a comprehensive picture, but nothing is more effective than a sworn officer who speaks with potential candidates about the positive and negative realities of policing.

Managers should also stress the positive aspects of policing—by developing a positive **brand image**. Brand image is an instinctive response from individuals toward an agency or a service (Neumeier, 2006). Although the concept is normally applied to for-profit businesses, it is also appropriate for public organizations, especially police agencies. Because police officers interact with the public on a daily basis, brand image is extremely important. When citizens of the jurisdiction have a positive brand image of the local police, they are much more likely to trust and engage with officers on levels deeper than just calls-for-service.

A poster, sign, or badge can illustrate a police agency's brand. The Tulsa Police Department's brand image is "Justice for All."

A police agency's brand must express, through every means possible, how the agency differs from other departments (Neumeier, 2006). For example, the brand could be depicted through posters showing a police officer helping a child, with an accompanying motto declaring an emotional connection to citizens. Brands can also be expressed through taglines such as "To protect and serve" (the Toronto Police Service) and "Serving with pride" (the Rochester, New York, Police Department). Whatever the brand, the agency's hiring practices should all reinforce the brand rather than conflict with or contradict it. For example, if an agency identifies its brand as superior customer service, hiring managers should emphasize such service in the language used in job postings. They would also look for candidates who demonstrate excellent interpersonal communication skills and other talents essential for delivering exceptional service to the community.

Brand image: an instinctive response from individuals toward an agency or a service.

Recruiting for Diversity

Societies throughout the world are becoming more diverse. The word **diversity** refers to differences among people with respect to wealth, age, gender, culture, lifestyle, race, ethnicity, and sexual orientation. Diversity creates pluralistic communities the police must serve without bias or prejudice. In some jurisdictions, the police workforce itself is becoming more diverse. Yet women, minorities, and other groups are still underrepresented in many police and other public safety agencies.

Diversity: differences among people with respect to wealth, age, gender, culture, lifestyle, race, ethnicity, and sexual orientation.

A police force is an integral part of the community it serves; thus, police personnel should reflect the composition of that community. An agency should make every effort to recruit (as well as promote and retain) qualified members of diverse groups. Yet latent, and sometimes overt, discrimination against women and minorities still occurs in some jurisdictions. Although career opportunities have improved for underrepresented groups, agencies should still pursue legitimate and innovative recruitment (and retention) programs to build the most diverse workforce possible. For example, if an agency has been having difficulty recruiting Latinos, it can place job ads in newspapers and on TV and radio stations that are most popular among Latinos in the community. Or it can sponsor cultural activities, such as games or musical events, attended primarily by Latinos.

The diversity of a police department should reflect the diversity of the community it serves.

But managers must also take care to avoid common missteps in recruiting for diversity: Recruiting minorities solely in an effort to ameliorate special interests in the jurisdiction may lead to another kind of discrimination. For instance, consider an agency that hires African American officers specifically to assign them to prominently black neighborhoods. This can result in these officers' being denied regular promotions or reassignments. Why? They are so effective at dealing with their own ethnic group that the agency wants to keep them in that role. Instead of pigeonholing officers in this way, police managers must strive to make every officer—regardless of race, gender, or ethnic origin—capable of dealing with every person living in the communities the agency serves. Only then can an agency build a truly diverse workforce (Cordner & Scarborough, 2007; Lord & Peak, 2005).

Recruiting for Educational Level

A great debate surrounds the idea of whether police agencies should strive to hire people with a college education or maintain the more traditional standard of hiring those who possess a high school diploma or its equivalent. Over the years, much has happened on this front. In 1929, the University of Southern California became one of the first postsecondary institutions to offer a degree in public administration with a specialization in law enforcement. The need of a four-year college degree as an entrance requirement for police was reinforced by the Wickersham Commission in 1931. In the 1960s, the International Association of Police Professors and the International Association of Chiefs of Police issued proclamations stating that police personnel should pursue higher education.

Recruiting candidates who have a college degree offers numerous advantages. A college education based in the liberal arts can help students develop problem-solving skills and expose them to ideas and concepts that make it easier to accept and work within a diverse population. Those with higher education generally possess the ability to apply their knowledge in a multitude of situations with a minimum of conflict. In addition, studies indicate that officers with a college education are more adept at dealing with people and are less likely to use excessive force. They demonstrate a greater appreciation for diversity, and are better communicators. They also experience a much lower risk of disciplinary action than their high-school-educated counterparts (Bohm & Haley, 2005; Vodicka, 1994).

However, at a time when our society has more college graduates than ever before in our history, the police profession still lags behind in employing people with higher education degrees. One reason may be that requiring a two- or four-year degree can limit the pool of available candidates. When some police agencies encounter difficulty recruiting enough college-educated people to fill vacant positions, they drop the educational requirements so they can attract a full complement of officers. Another reason may be that many college-educated individuals believe that they will earn more compensation in fields of endeavor other than police work. Thus they gravitate toward those other career paths.

The debate continues, with each police agency making its own decision about recruits' education requirements. However, as officers without higher education retire and are replaced by college-educated officers, the value of higher education may become more evident (Meese & Kurz, 1993; Ortmeier & Meese, 2010; "Pressed for Applicants," 2000). When agencies begin to see that value, they may step up efforts to seek recruits with college degrees.

SELECTING NEW HIRES

Once a police agency has executed its recruitment strategies and attracted applicants, it must determine which candidates to select for hiring. Like recruitment, selection is challenging, and the stakes are high. Selecting the wrong people can result in mistreatment of citizens and do long-term damage to the community and the agency. Ultimately, all police actions are visible to the public. And in a high-tech age, inappropriate police actions can be captured on video and broadcast around the world within seconds. Once published, these images cannot be suppressed, no matter how talented the police agency's public relations people might be. The videotaped image of the 1991 Rodney King incident in California illustrates how police officers' actions can attract international attention and accusations of police violations of the public trust.

Other more recent cases provide additional evidence that a police agency must be ever vigilant in protecting the public's perception of the agency's ethical standards and worthiness of public confidence. Selecting the wrong hires can lead to disaster. For example, a medium-size agency in the northeastern part of the United States has suffered significant damage to its image by the arrest and conviction of two police sergeants in unrelated incidents. Both officers were hired as lateral transfer officers from other police agencies and were subsequently promoted to police sergeant. One sergeant was convicted of leaving the scene of an injury-causing motor-vehicle collision. The other sergeant was convicted of coercing two women to have sex with him. Both men are currently imprisoned for their actions. The chief of police, the deputy chief of police, and other command personnel have been suspended from their official duties because of these criminal cases. The department is under investigation locally by the district attorney (prosecutor). And public confidence in the agency is at stake even though the town where the crimes occurred is rated as one of the safest places to live in the United States (McDermott, 2009).

To improve the odds of selecting the right people, an agency can take the following steps: conduct a pre-employment screening, use the assessment center process, and swiftly correct any selection mistakes.

Conducting a Pre-Employment Screening

Most police officer candidates undergo a pre-employment screening process to determine whether they possess the requisite physical, intellectual, and emotional abilities to become an officer. Minimum qualification for employment as a police officer within the United States generally requires applicants to be an 18- to 21-year-old U.S. citizen who possesses a valid driver's license and who has achieved a specific level of formal education. In addition, the applicant must be free of any felony convictions or any misdemeanor convictions involving domestic violence.

However, as we discussed previously, it is important for a police agency to look beyond these minimum qualifications in recruiting and selecting officers. A

Pre-employment screening process: a sequence of steps designed to help a police agency compare job applicants and select the most promising candidates. Elements of the process include an employment application/questionnaire, aptitude test, physical abilities test, and other assessments.

The pre-employment screening process typically begins with the completion of an employment application/questionnaire.

pre-employment screening process can help generate the additional information needed to compare candidates' potential and determine which individuals have the traits and skills required for community service. The pre-employment screening process typically includes many or all of the following elements:

- Employment application/questionnaire
- Aptitude test
- Physical abilities test
- Interview
- Background investigation
- Integrity testing
- Psychological evaluation
- Medical evaluation

Taken together, these elements generate a wide range of information and data that an agency can use to evaluate a candidate's potential and determine whether to offer the individual a position.

Employment Application/Questionnaire   Interested individuals complete an application and a questionnaire that ask them to provide personal information and write responses to questions about their personal history. The process sheds light on candidates' basic skills (such as writing ability and reading comprehension). If both documents are required, pre-employment screeners can search for inconsistencies in the applicants' statements. Candidates can complete these documents at home and mail them to the agency, or email them if the documents are provided electronically (online).

The Abington Township Police Department of Abington, Pennsylvania, has an innovative application process resembling a civil service process for the Montgomery County Consortium of Communities. Fifteen police agencies use this examination process (*Examination Announcement,* 2009).

The online application denotes which police agency an applicant is applying to, the cost to apply for the examination, and specific questions an applicant must answer to complete the application. The application consists of 13 questions, including "Are you a U.S. citizen?" and "Do you hold 60 college credits or have two years' police experience?"

Aptitude Test   An aptitude test, which usually consists of multiple-choice and essay questions, further assesses candidates' basic skills, including reading comprehension, vocabulary, writing acumen, and math abilities. Typically this is a general-knowledge test designed to measure a candidate's ability to succeed in the basic academy. It is administered to a group of applicants by agency or other government employees at a predetermined location (such as the agency, a local college or school, or a civic center). The test may include a situational judgment component used to determine the applicant's ability to analyze and respond to events or circumstances.

Physical Abilities Test   The physical abilities test measures a candidate's endurance, physical agility, and strength for tasks that are associated with the job. The test consists of specific job-related physical routines: for instance, running, climbing, and the ability to move an object with the weight and mass equivalent to an adult person.

The physical abilities test has generated some debate. For example, because of strength differences, particularly in the upper body, between men and women, some agencies modify the test to reflect these differences. Modification enables them to admit more females to the academy and thus increase the diversity of their workforce. At times, observers have decried this practice as providing special treatment to female candidates. Agencies also complain that police officers who passed the test as recruits have not remained physically fit. These officers would be unable to pass the physical abilities test later in their careers. However, some experts maintain that these officers are still effective in their jobs—raising doubts about whether the initial physical abilities test is really effective or necessary. Whatever the physical abilities test or fitness requirements, they should relate to the actual physical tasks performed by police officers on the job. Further, officers should be encouraged to maintain their fitness throughout their careers. Fitness for duty is discussed extensively in Chapter 12.

Interview   An oral interview generally follows successful completion of the physical abilities test. During the interview, the applicant is evaluated on oral communication and interpersonal skills, as well as judgment. To gauge these criteria, the interviewer may present hypothetical problems (situational judgment scenarios) to test the candidate's critical thinking and analytical abilities. In some agencies, the oral interview is the last phase of the selection process.

Background Investigation (BI)   We recommend that an agency obtain a personal history from the candidate, ideally provided in the employment application or questionnaire. The completed personal history statement provides information such as jobs held, previous residences, drug use, and encounters with the police. But managers must take care in the questions they include in the history. According to U.S. law, an agency cannot ask questions in written or oral form about the candidate's race, religion, national origin, age, sexual orientation, gender, physical capabilities, or marital status. The only questions permitted are those that are relevant to the position the candidate seeks and the requirements of that position (Cheeseman, 2009).

The agency uses the personal history to conduct a **background investigation (BI)** on the individual. This investigation is a critical part of the pre-employment screening process. Although time-consuming and expensive, a thorough BI may help avoid tremendous grief and liability later. The BI inquiry is conducted through accessing of databases as well as questionnaires and telephone and in-person interviews. It should assess the following:

Background investigation (BI): a step in the pre-employment screening process in which a police agency verifies a candidate's qualifications including criminal and credit histories, educational and employment histories, and claims about matters such as moral character, work habits, and stress tolerance.

- *Leadership ability*: demonstrated leadership competence or the ability to develop leadership skills.

- *Interpersonal skills*: tolerance, sensitivity to diversity (of race, gender, lifestyle, age, and opinion), social interest, persuasiveness.

- *Moral character*: integrity, honesty, impartiality, trustworthiness, ethical behavior, confidentiality, free of substance abuse.

- *Intellectual abilities*: problem-solving, decision-making, judgment, learning abilities.

- *Criminal, motor-vehicle, and credit histories*: poor credit history, which may indicate irresponsible behavior or susceptibility to bribes.

- *Educational and employment histories*: verified educational credentials and previous employment.

Police recruiters access databases to conduct background investigations on applicants.

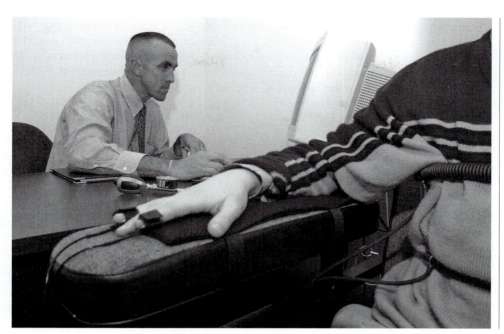

In some agencies, applicants are required to take a polygraph test as part of the pre-employment screening process.

- *Work habits*: reliable, dependable, responsible, accountable, conscientious.
- *Stress tolerance*: ability to maintain a positive attitude; maintain an even temper; ability to confront, overcome, and recover well from stressful situations and adversity.

Integrity Test An agency should also administer an integrity test to verify information provided by the candidate in the employment application and the personal history statement, and to check for additional concerns. Integrity testing can be accomplished through a written exam, a polygraph or voice stress analysis, and a drug test. Agency managers can also phone references to confirm the information (such as employment history and job performance) provided by the applicant.

Psychological Evaluation Finally, before an agency decides to extend a job offer to a candidate, it may require the person to participate in a psychological evaluation to determine whether the applicant's mental state and personality characteristics are suitable for policing. Psychological evaluations can take numerous forms, including the Minnesota Multiphasic Personality Inventory (MMPI), the Myers-Briggs Type Indicator, the Strong Interest Inventory, the California Psychological Inventory, or the Watson-Glaser Critical Thinking Appraisal. An incompatible personality profile may indicate that the applicant might develop anger management problems or could instigate negative confrontations with citizens or fellow officers.

Medical Evaluation A police agency's offer of employment is also conditional on the applicant's ability to pass a medical evaluation. This evaluation is conducted to ensure that the applicant does not have any medical condition that would restrict the person's ability to safely perform tasks required for police work.

Every step in the pre-employment screening process should produce information that helps the agency determine whether a candidate possesses—or has the potential to develop—the character traits and skills needed to deliver excellent service to the community. As we have seen, these criteria include communicative, judgmental, and problem-solving abilities, integrity, an ethical orientation, a positive attitude, intelligence, impulse control (for example, politely rejecting sexual advances from a motorist stopped for a traffic violation), self-motivation, empathy, social competence, compassion, leadership potential, and self-restraint (such as refraining from using excessive force) (T. E. Baker, 2006; Ortmeier, 2006).

Using the Assessment Center Process

In addition to conducting a pre-employment screening, agencies can also use what is called the assessment center process to determine which candidates to select for hire. Assessment centers were used by the Germans during World War I to select people with traits well suited for special intelligence assignments. In World War II, the centers were resurrected by the Germans and used by the British to select military officer candidates. In the United States, the federal government used such centers to determine who would make the best intelligence agents.

Assessment center process: a series of activities designed to measure an applicant's or officer's knowledge, skills, and abilities (KSAs) as well as personal attributes and behavioral characteristics related to work-specific scenarios.

How the Process Works   An assessment center is not a physical place but rather a means to determine a person's suitability for employment, promotion, or special assignment. The **assessment center process** includes activities designed to measure an applicant's or officer's knowledge, skills, and abilities (KSAs) as well as personal attributes and behavioral characteristics related to work-specific scenarios (All About Performance, 2005). Behavioral characteristics may include judgment, decision making, problem solving, initiative, oral and written communication, and creativity.

Through a series of interviews, psychological tests, and job-related simulations, an assessment center can further help an agency detect problems a police recruit may experience with activities such as responding to domestic violence incidents or interviewing suspects. During assessment center simulations, the candidate participates in activities that simulate the critical tasks associated with the position for which the

Police officer skills may be assessed using simulators such as this driving simulator in San Diego, California.

candidate is being assessed. An example is the high-speed pursuit simulation (which can be conducted on a computer or in a simulator). Before an officer engages in a pursuit, the individual must assess the situation and determine its potential danger to the officer(s) involved, to those pursued, and to innocent citizens. If the officer decides to engage in a pursuit, the person should discontinue the pursuit if it puts citizens in peril. Generally, pursuits should also be terminated when environmental conditions (such as rain, ice, and traffic congestion) dictate. High-speed pursuit simulations demand split-second decision making based on training and agency policy.

During all simulations, trained assessors observe and rate the candidate's responses based on the critical behaviors required to complete the job tasks successfully. All measured behaviors are rated against criticality to job performance for the position. For instance, if decisiveness is being tested, assessors evaluate the candidate's ability to make a timely decision. If the simulation demands an immediate decision and the candidate hesitates too long or cannot make a decision at all, the person receives a low rating on this behavioral characteristic.

Assessment centers are usually one or two days in length. To shield the process from claims of bias, an agency may have outside contractors or civil service personnel conduct the centers. The assessment centers are often used in conjunction with standardized testing models, such as a formal written test instrument designed to determine whether a candidate qualifies for the center.

Advantages and Disadvantages of the Assessment Center Process Many experts view the assessment center process as a progressive and acceptable method of determining a candidate's KSAs. Yet critics of the process express concerns that it is too lengthy—involving protracted task analyses, assessor training and monitoring, exercise development, and personnel reassignments. Some critics fear that assessors make errors, have mental biases that distort their interpretation of a candidate's performance, or pay insufficient attention during simulations. Assessment centers can also be expensive to operate, owing to the time needed to reassign personnel to simulations, the use of contracted facilities and personnel for the exercises and administrative processes, and outside consulting and testing procedures, all of which need funding (Inn, 2000). Because of the high cost, many police agencies do not use assessment centers during recruitment and selection phases of hiring. Instead, they use them for sworn officers who seek a promotion.

Avoiding and Correcting Selection Mistakes

As part of the selection process, a police agency strives to ensure that an employment candidate has an unblemished history and that nothing in the applicant's background points to foreseeable problems on the job. Police agencies are often subject to accusations of and liability for negligent hiring and retention if anyone can trace officer misconduct to pre-employment behavior that an agency overlooked, discounted, or dismissed during the screening process. If agency personnel are aware (or should know) that a candidate is not suitable for employment as a police officer, the candidate's application should be rejected.

A *thorough* background investigation, including a psychological evaluation of potential candidates during the pre-employment screening process, can help agencies avoid selecting the unsuitable new hire. With current technology, managers can perform computerized database searches on virtually every individual who is alive today, including searches of a candidate's criminal and credit history. Further, psychological tests contain key indicators of personality traits indicative of positive police officer performance; serious psychological problems; and potential positive, marginal, or negative behaviors. The findings from these tests can help alert professional evaluators to desirable and undesirable traits in candidates.

Unfortunately, a candidate may successfully pass all phases of the pre-employment screening process, including the background investigation, and still prove to be a problem employee. Although an agency may not be liable for negligent hiring, it could be liable for negligent retention if it does not take swift, decisive action after learning that the officer has behaved inappropriately. Action might consist of remedial training, supervised work assignments, and coaching and counseling sessions. An agency might also put an officer on administrative duty while the person is under investigation, to prevent further incidents.

Police management may also be held liable for failing to take definitive action against an officer who injures or otherwise abuses others before or after exhausting all possible remedies to correct the officer's actions and behaviors. The jurisdiction and its management may be held liable if administrators and supervisors fail to properly supervise problem officers.

The lesson? Agencies must avoid making selection mistakes in the first place. If a mistake is made, managers should correct it immediately and effectively.

ETHICS IN ACTION
Due Diligence in Hiring

Frank, a police officer from a small jurisdiction, transferred to another jurisdiction in the same state. Jan, the chief of police of the new jurisdiction, hired Frank without performing a background check or calling his former supervisor.

One day when he was off duty, Frank observed a young woman driving on a country road. Frank was in his personal vehicle, a pickup truck that he had outfitted with blue and red flashing lights on the dashboard. He turned on the lights and pulled the woman over.

The woman was clearly confused by the stop because she was obeying all traffic laws. When Frank asked questions about her marital and relationship status, she became suspicious and telephoned 9-1-1. Frank was arrested and later fined and jailed for acting outside a police officer's scope of authority.

1. Do you think that laterally transferring police officers should be subject to the same background check and psychological reviews as new recruits? Why or why not?

2. Is the agency that employed Frank subject to a negligent hiring or retention civil lawsuit by the offended party? Why or why not? If you do not know, where might you look for information to answer this question?

DESIGNING COMPENSATION AND BENEFITS PROGRAMS

As another key to hiring police officers who are committed to service, agencies must design compensation and benefits programs that will attract them and keep them committed to the agency and the work. Compensation for police officers must be fair, reasonable, equitable, and tied to what the organization wishes to accomplish—but also competitive enough to attract and retain valued employees.

Compensation in a police organization includes items such as salary and benefits (specifically, medical, dental, life, and disability insurance; vacation and sick leave; pensions; and uniform allowances) and many other personnel-related expenses (Collins, 2002). Compensation can take numerous forms:

- **Direct compensation** includes base pay (hourly wages or salaried) plus overtime pay for hourly employees.
- **Variable compensation** is tied to personal, team, or organizational performance and may include bonuses and incentives for special assignments as well as shift differentials.
- **Rewards-based compensation** (merit pay) enhances the earnings of top performers and places value on people rather than job categories (Hitt, 1988).
- **Indirect compensation** includes items such as medical and life insurance, paid time off, pensions, flexible schedules, and education incentives (such as higher pay for officers who obtain a college degree) (Mathis & Jackson, 2005). Indirect benefits may also include a take-home police vehicle. (See the box "A Closer Look at Incentives" for additional information.)

In most agencies, compensation packages are powerfully influenced by forces such as market trends (including changes in labor supply and demand), union contracts, and structured civil service salary schedules. Moreover, agencies may have different compensation philosophies and practices. **Entitlement-oriented compensation** denotes automatic pay increases for employees, along with increases in benefits. This philosophy and practice helps reduce personnel complaints, is easy to implement, and

---

Direct compensation: compensation that includes base pay (hourly wages or salaried) plus overtime pay for hourly employees.

Variable compensation: compensation that is tied to personal, team, or organizational performance and that may include bonuses and incentives for special assignments as well as shift differential.

Rewards-based compensation: also known as merit pay; compensation that enhances the earnings of top performers and places value on people rather than job categories.

Indirect compensation: compensation that includes items such as medical and life insurance, paid time off, pensions, flexible schedules, education incentives, and a take-home police vehicle.

Entitlement-oriented compensation: automatic pay increases for employees, along with increases in benefits.

A Closer Look at Incentives

An "incentive" may be defined as that which motivates an individual to action or encourages effort (*American Heritage Dictionary*, 2005b). Incentives are not generally included as part of a police officer's base salary. Formal incentives include hiring bonuses and bilingual pay, as well as pay incentives linked to special assignments, housing, utility bills, child care, flexible work schedules, maintenance of uniforms, and paid time off based on length of service.

Indirect incentives may take the form of items in or characteristics of the physical working environment as well. Police facilities that are modern, well lit, free of particulates, and a comfortable temperature will be far more motivating than facilities that lack these qualities. Police vehicles, which serve as police officers' mobile offices, should also be in good condition and contain the latest technology (*Police Officer Incentives*, 2009; *U.S. Police Officer Compensation Survey*, 2004).

Exemplary performance can be recognized through mediums other than financial rewards.

is viewed as fair by the poor-to-average performers in the organization (Hitt, 1988; Mathis & Jackson, 2005). **Competency-based compensation** refers to payment for competencies acquired and exhibited by members of the organization. As members develop and demonstrate increasing levels of skills, their earning potential increases. This type of compensation is often received by officers in airborne, motorcycle, or canine units.

Competency-based compensation: payment for competencies acquired and exhibited by members of the organization.

The driving force shaping compensation and benefits in many police organizations is a police union. Managers of unionized agencies have little control over the compensation package for individual officers. Rather, salaries, wages, benefits, premium pay for specialized assignments, and pension plans are prescribed by negotiated union contracts. Most unionized agencies do not offer merit pay.

Within police organizations, compensation is often equitable within job classifications requiring comparable knowledge, skills, and abilities, although specific duties may differ. In addition, compensation may be contingent on the region of the country in which the police agency is located, the jurisdiction within the region, or the budgetary constraints imposed. The high cost of living in certain locales often dictates the level of compensation available to officers. Low salaries in high-cost-of-living areas can severely restrict an agency's ability to attract well-qualified candidates.

For agencies that have little control over their monetary compensation policies, nonmonetary compensation can provide a way to attract and retain talent. Nonmonetary compensation includes intrinsic social and psychological rewards (such as recognition and appreciation) that are central to employees' job satisfaction. An agency can publicly recognize exemplary police officers not only to keep them engaged but also to garner community residents' respect and appreciation for these high performers. For example, press coverage of officers who have taken dangerous individuals off the streets can further burnish the officers' and the agency's reputations in the community. As another powerful form of nonmonetary compensation, an agency can give officers opportunities to develop themselves personally and professionally; for example, through special training programs or assignments (Hellriegel et al., 2005). Still, debate swirls around some public safety (e.g., police, fire, corrections) compensation packages and benefits, particularly retirement benefits, as cash-strapped jurisdictions seek mechanisms to lower long-term personnel costs associated with retiree pensions and health care.

CREATING A CIVIL WORK ENVIRONMENT

To hire in the spirit of service, a police agency must demonstrate civility during every phase of the hiring process and while new hires are being acculturated. The goal is to create a civil work environment, which further encourages excellent service to the community. Civility does not mean tolerance of unethical or criminal conduct demonstrated by police officers. Unethical behavior should be confronted, and criminal offenders must receive treatment according to established laws, policies, and procedures. Rather, a **civil work environment** is characterized by positive interactions, optimism, and the dismissal of cynicism and pessimistic beliefs (Souryal, 2003).

Until recently, civility in the workplace received little attention. However, the emergence of casual or undisciplined work environments in many industries over the last few decades has spawned a culture of incivility in too many organizations. This culture's defining characteristics include discourtesy, constant unapologetic interruptions, and vulgar language and gossip, as well as rude and distracting emails. In any business or service environment, such an atmosphere will negatively impact individual, unit, section, or agency performance (Tytel, 2007) as well as customer satisfaction and loyalty.

Civility matters because it powerfully shapes the culture of a police agency, its employees, and the community it serves. Civility determines how people interact, perform, solve problems, and interact within a common work environment. In policing, life and death situations abound. When people treat each other civilly in these situations, they are more likely to survive.

Throughout a new officer's training and probationary period, supervisors, instructors, counselors, and field training officers must teach civility by demonstrating civil behavior themselves and by mentoring those who are just starting out in their police career. Trainers can model civil behavior by showing respect for others and projecting a positive, can-do attitude; by demonstrating genuine concern for and acceptance of others; by acknowledging kindnesses and potential; and by actively listening to others' concerns rather than talking incessantly. Finally, trainers and mentors can demonstrate anger management (Gulf Coast Community Foundation, 2007a).

A culture of civility during pre-employment screening, basic police academy, and probationary periods creates productive, service-focused, and satisfied employees. Officers who are content with and positive about their careers and their agency deliver excellent service, which in turn produces satisfied citizens. In a civil work environment, police officers also have more emotional energy available to tend to their personal lives as well as their careers (an uncivil environment saps their energy and morale). High morale, open communication, and productivity are positive byproducts of a civil work environment (Gulf Coast Community Foundation, 2007b).

Despite the benefits of civility, some trainers and supervisors subject new recruits in the academy, field training period, or final stages of probation to verbal abuse. This behavior often

Civil work environment: a workplace characterized by positive interactions, optimism, and the dismissal of cynicism and pessimistic beliefs.

Civil work environments improve morale and productivity.

stems from an antiquated belief that the person in charge must demonstrate aggressive and dominating behavior. Such individuals often view empathy, respectfulness, and kindness as weaknesses, and dominance as a sign of strength (Hartt, 1999).

Although officers should learn to be assertive, the aggressive and dominating behavior associated with obedience-oriented, military-style police training can be dangerous. Militaristic training and attitudes produce arrogant officers who may disregard laws and policies designed to protect citizens as well as the officers themselves (City of Los Angeles, 2003; Goldstein, 2001; Kelling, 1999; Ortmeier & Meese, 2010).

summary

- **Understanding Today's Hiring Challenges.** Today's police agencies face several hiring challenges, including fulfilling a complex mandate that encompasses numerous responsibilities, as well as building a workforce that reflects the diversity of the community an agency serves.

- **Setting the Stage for Smart Recruiting.** To establish the right conditions for effective recruiting, police agencies must conduct a human resource needs assessment and look beyond minimum hiring standards.

- **Formulating Recruitment Strategies.** To develop effective recruitment strategies, police agencies must select the right channels for seeking applicants, develop a positive brand image through every aspect of the hiring process, and recruit with an eye toward diversity and educational level.

- **Selecting New Hires.** To improve the odds of selecting the right people from a pool of applicants, police agencies must conduct a pre-employment screening (which includes components such as an employment application, aptitude test, physical abilities test, interview, background investigation, integrity testing, psychological evaluation, and medical evaluation), consider using the assessment center process (which comprises activities designed to measure a candidate's knowledge, skills, abilities, and personal attributes), and avoid selection mistakes (while correcting any mistakes made).

- **Designing Compensation and Benefits Programs.** The right compensation and benefits programs can further help a police agency hire in the spirit of service. Compensation may take numerous forms—including direct, variable, rewards-based, and indirect. Compensation philosophies include an entitlement orientation and a competency orientation.

- **Creating a Civil Work Environment.** To hire in the spirit of service, a police agency must demonstrate civility—expressed as positive interactions, optimism, and the dismissal of cynicism and pessimistic beliefs—at every stage in the hiring process and while new hires are being acculturated. A civil work environment encourages excellent service to the community.

key terms

assessment center process

background investigation (BI)

brand image

civil work environment

competency-based compensation

direct compensation

diversity

entitlement-oriented compensation

indirect compensation

negligent hiring and retention

pre-employment screening process

rewards-based compensation

variable compensation

discussion questions

1. What are minimum hiring standards a police agency might consider when reviewing job candidates? Why is it important for an agency to look beyond these minimum standards while evaluating applicants?

2. When hiring officers, police agencies must identify the qualities and skills they desire in candidates. Identify five qualities or skills that a police officer candidate should demonstrate. Why is each important to a police agency and the community it serves?

3. Select two recruiting channels a police agency might use to seek the right job applicants. Decide how you would use those channels most effectively.

4. Police agencies use the pre-employment screening process to identify highly qualified candidates. What are the elements of this screening process, and why is each element important?

5. The background investigation (BI) is a crucial part of pre-employment screening. What are the most important dimensions of the BI? Why are these dimensions critical to a police agency? How can a thorough BI help the agency defend itself against a claim of negligent hiring or retention?

6. The question of whether police agencies should emphasize a college education in their recruitment efforts has stimulated debate. Where do you stand on the issue? Do you think agencies should step up recruitment of officers with a college education? Why or why not?

7. Civility is critical for hiring in the spirit of service. Describe the elements of a civil work environment. How can the lack of civility negatively impact the service a police agency delivers to a community?

WHAT WOULD YOU DO?
Stopping the Exodus

A police agency in a major city struggled to reach its goal of 2,000 full-time sworn police officers on the job. Many of the agency's junior officers were transferring to other jurisdictions. The city's management was unable to provide a reason for the exodus. Over the course of one year, 9 percent of the force departed after obtaining employment with other agencies.

A city council member exclaimed, "We have as many people coming as going because of the competition from other police agencies around the country!" The agency's management launched an inquiry and conducted exit interviews of departing officers to identify the causes of the exodus. According to exit interviews, 50 percent of the departing officers took lateral transfers or lower-paying jobs.

The city could not reach its goal of 2,000 officers. For a time, each of the city's zones had one beat unstaffed during each shift. Compounding the problem, police managers included recruits in the total staffing statistics, although recruits could not be deployed to work the streets for at least nine months.

The agency's budget was a major concern for city officials. The city's general fund reflected a deficit of more than $50 million for the previous fiscal year. The current budget for the agency was almost $150 million—more than any other city department. Concerned about funding, the mayor refused to fill 50 vacant positions in the police department. He also enacted budget cuts and hoped to avoid raising property taxes.

1. If you were a high-level manager in this agency, what recruitment issue would you strive to overcome to hire new officers and retain tenured officers?

2. What problems are vacant positions creating for this agency? What would you do to attract candidates who will remain with the agency?

9

◀ The police must communicate in a vast array of settings and through numerous mediums, including public speaking.

The Power and Practice of Effective Communication

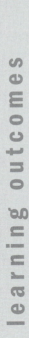

After completing this chapter, readers should be able to:

- define *communication*.
- distinguish the purposes that communication serves.
- describe the nature of communication in a police agency.
- analyze common barriers to effective communication.
- compare and contrast verbal, nonverbal, and written channels of communication.
- explain how to prepare for and conduct an effective meeting.
- explain how to use newsletters and the grapevine as communication tools.
- demonstrate how to communicate effectively with people from different cultures and genders, and with members of special populations.

- assess the quality of a police agency's relationships with the news media and other agencies, and explain how to improve those relationships.
- use four important communication skills: facilitation, persuasion, feedback, and conflict management.

Introduction

Police personnel must demonstrate many different technical skills to do their job—including knowing how to use a police vehicle mobile data terminal (MDT) and various speed-measurement radar and laser devices. But technical skills are just part of the picture; police managers and officers also need to master a set of nontechnical skills to serve their community and agency. In fact, in a relatively recent study (Ortmeier, 1996) experts on policing cited effective communication as the *most* important nontechnical skill required of officers. The study's respondents agreed on several additional points as well: Effective communication skills are critical to success in policing. And police personnel spend more time communicating with others than they do in any other activity.

Communication is a powerful human activity with wide-ranging impact. For example, it not only enables us to exchange ideas, it also fulfills a deep social need to connect with others. (Indeed, studies have shown that people who are prevented from communicating with others are at greater risk of experiencing mental and physical illness.) Finally, communication is irreversible: Once you convey a message to someone else—through the spoken or written word, or through some other medium—you cannot take it back.

Communication also has strong links to leadership. Excellent police leaders are effective communicators. They use communication to build and sustain trust, to promote understanding of the agency's mission, and to empower others to deliver their best performance on the job. They listen attentively, facilitate interaction between agency members and between police and community residents, and maintain cohesion among all stakeholders—despite the diversity of views and priorities that stakeholders often have.

The benefits accrue even further: In police work, exceptional communicators reduce victim distress and gain compliance from others without having to resort to force. Moreover, they de-escalate conflict and emotion, and inspire citizens to participate in solving their community's problems. In short, they improve quality of life in the communities they serve and motivate all stakeholders to work toward realizing a compelling vision of a better future (Ortmeier, 1996).

In this chapter, we examine the art and science of communication. We look at what communication is and how it functions in a police agency. We consider barriers to effective communication as well as the wide variety of channels through which communication occurs. We take a closer look at three channels: meetings, newsletters, and the organizational "grapevine." And we analyze several types of special communication challenges police personnel typically encounter—namely, communicating across cultures and genders, and communicating with special populations. We then consider how police personnel can communicate most effectively with two important constituencies: the news media as well as other agencies. Finally, we explore four particularly essential communication skills: facilitation, persuasion, feedback, and conflict management.

WHAT IS COMMUNICATION?

Communication among human beings is a distinctive process that fulfills specific purposes. Within a police agency, it demonstrates unique patterns in terms of the directions in which information flows and the formality or informality of communication. In the pages that follow, we look at these aspects of communication.

A Distinctive Process

Communication is a process, not an event. The process involves an exchange of information between a sender and a receiver and includes the transmittal, receipt, and sharing of problems, ideas, facts, beliefs, feelings, and values. Communication is also a reciprocal interchange between the parties involved: Through encoding (the translation of information into a communication medium), the sender transmits symbols (characters, letters, words, images) through a channel (such as an e-mail or a comment made at a meeting) to a receiver. The receiver then decodes (interprets) the message. How the receiver *responds* to the message is strongly determined by how the person *interpreted* the message (de Janasz, Dowd, & Schneider, 2006; Hellriegel, & Slocum, 2009).

Communication: a process involving the exchange of information between a sender and a receiver.

For example, suppose that Daniel, a police supervisor, sends an e-mailed request for information to Paula, an officer. The e-mail goes unacknowledged. Daniel interprets the lack of acknowledgment as evidence that Paula has not taken the request seriously. Offended, he shows annoyance during his next encounter with her. Now suppose that Daniel had interpreted the lack of acknowledgment differently—for instance, as a signal that the agency's server may have crashed, and that Paula simply did not receive the message. With this interpretation, his response would likely have been entirely different, and probably not as negative.

Complex Purposes

Communication serves complex purposes for human beings. Every time we communicate with others, we may have several goals in addition to merely exchanging information. For example, we might seek to fulfill the following goals:

- **Be understood.** Terry, a police officer, explains to Meredith, his supervisor, why he handled a shots-fired call as he did.

Communication is a
process rather than
an event.

- **Understand others.** Meredith listens to Terry and then asks questions to gain additional information about how Terry handled the call and why he handled it as he did.
- **Persuade others to take a particular action or embrace a particular idea.** Meredith suggests to Terry how he might handle the next shots-fired call more effectively.

Communication in a Police Agency

In a police agency (as in any organization), communication can flow in several different directions. (See Table 9-1.)

table 9-1 Communication Directions

DIRECTION	EXPLANATION	EXAMPLES
Vertical	Between people who are at different levels in the reporting hierarchy but who work in the same function	A field training officer sends an e-mail to a new recruit whose training he is overseeing, laying out possible goals for the next training session. The recruit asks the FTO several questions about the proposed goals.
Horizontal	Between people who are at the same levels in the reporting hierarchy but who may work in different functions	The head of IT and the facilities manager in a police agency meet to discuss how the agency's computer network should be changed to accommodate facilities that are being constructed for the agency.
Diagonal	Between people who are at different levels in the organizational hierarchy but who work in different functions	A member of a police agency's special weapons and tactics (SWAT) team talks with the leader of the hazardous-materials team to share best practices (such as specific safety procedures) that could benefit both teams.

Communication can flow through informal or formal channels, such as an "all-hands" meeting requested by the chief of police.

In addition to flowing in a number of different directions, communication in a police agency can flow through several types of channels—formal and informal:

- **Formal channels** are often vertical and represent protocols established by the agency. They might include all-hands meetings called by the chief of police, performance evaluations conducted by a supervisor for a subordinate, or complaints filed by an officer with the agency's ombudsperson.

- **Informal channels** tend to be more horizontal. Examples include hallway chats or e-mail exchanges between fellow officers or members of a task force.

Within police agencies, supervisors and officers tend to prefer a more formal system of communication. The language and format characterizing police reports provide a good example. A police report serves as a written record of an incident, describing what happened, who was involved, and how the situation was resolved. Managers and officers can access police reports to clarify procedures or policies or to determine whether police misconduct has occurred. Police reports are thus important repositories of information. Figure 9-1 shows a police report form used in New York State.

However, as in any other organization, members of a police agency also engage in informal communication. These exchanges might be about work or other topics, and usually take place between people who feel comfortable with one another (regardless of whether the individuals have a formal reporting relationship). Employees seeking to communicate informally look for others who make them feel comfortable and who can help them reach their goals (Hunter & Barker, 2011; Lewis, 1975).

Informal communication often occurs between officers of equal rank or position, but it can also take place between new recruits and veterans or mentor officers. To illustrate, Terry, a new recruit, develops a positive and productive working relationship with Mark, her field training officer. Some months after completing field training, Terry stops by Mark's desk and asks for his advice about some possible career paths she is considering.

figure 9-1 Sample Police Incident Report

1 Location		3 M	D	Y	R	4 CR #

5 Context of FIF

					Context #
1. Drugs 2. Intelligence 3. Burglary	4. Robbery 5. Sex offense 6. Gang activity 7. Forgery	8. Weapons 9. Officer safety 10. Arson 11. Murder	12. Public order 13. Gambling 14. Organized crime 15. Alcohol offense	16. Known offender 17. Suspicious person 18. Suspicious vehicle 19. Other	

6 Source

1. Informant 2. Relative	3. First hand 2. Hearsay	5. Police officer 6. Other agency	7. Phone 8. Other	Source #

7 Evaluation of information

1. Confirmed   2. Probable   3. Doubtful   4. Improbable   5. Unknown

8 Status of information

1. Founded   2. Unfounded   3. Undetermined

9 Evaluation of source (if any)

1. Reliable   2. Usually reliable   3. Unreliable   4. Unknown

10 • Name	Address	DOB

Sex	Race	Height	Weight	Hair color	Hair length	Eye color	Facial hair	Ethnicity	Record #

Clothing, distinguishing jewelry	Physical oddities

Monicker/Alias	Place of employment	Phone #	☐ On parole ☐ On probation	Alien	☐ Driver ☐ Passenger

• Name	Address	DOB

Sex	Race	Height	Weight	Hair color	Hair length	Eye color	Facial hair	Ethnicity	Record #

Clothing, distinguishing jewelry	Physical oddities

Monicker/Alias	Place of employment	Phone #	☐ On parole ☐ On probation	Alien	☐ Driver ☐ Passenger

11 V E H	Year	Make	Model	Type	Color	Plate #	State	Interior color

Exterior 1. Custom wheels 3. Vinyl top 2. Custom paint 4. Sunroof	Windows front 1. Dark tint 3. Damage 2. Reflective	Left Right Rear	Other identifying marks/Characteristics

12. Narrative

	XC to:

Reporting officer ID #	CAR #	Section	Supervisor's review/Approval ID #	

Source: Chief Charles Koerner, Clyde New York Police Department.
Reproduced with permission from Chief Charles Koerner.

BARRIERS TO EFFECTIVE COMMUNICATION

When communication is working as senders and receivers intend, everyone involved arrives at a shared understanding of how to use the information exchanged. But communication does not always produce the results participants want. Experts have identified a number of **barriers to effective communication** that can derail even the best-intended exchanges between police or between agency personnel and community members. Such barriers frequently take the form of mind-sets or cultural orientations that stand between a communication receiver and giver, preventing one from understanding the other. For instance, a person for whom Spanish is the primary language may misinterpret an English speaker's actual words and intent of the communication (de Janasz et al., 2006). Next, we discuss several common barriers.

Barriers to effective communication: mind-sets or cultural orientations that stand between a communication receiver and giver, preventing one from understanding the other.

Poor Communication Skills

In an exchange characterized by poor communication skills, one or more participants lack the personal traits, experience, training, education, or intelligence to communicate effectively. For instance, a newly hired officer lacks self-confidence and has difficulty hearing criticism of his job performance. When his supervisor offers him constructive feedback on how to improve his performance, the officer becomes defensive and cannot learn from the feedback.

Poor communication skills can be frustrating. However, all individuals can improve their skills through training, role playing, and coaching.

One should work to overcome barriers to effective communication, including barriers that may be based on gender or cultural differences.

Background Differences

For each of us, our experiences, biases, prejudices, lack of understanding of cultural differences, and personal beliefs influence how we receive and interpret a message coming from someone else. When people from different backgrounds try to communicate, misunderstandings can result.

Consider this exchange between two new recruits, David and Antonio, at a police agency. David grew up in a neighborhood with little ethnic diversity, and was the only child in a household headed by parents of English extraction. Antonio was raised in a large, expressive, and boisterous family of Italian immigrants who had settled in an ethically diverse community.

Antonio (striding up to David's desk first thing on a Monday morning): Davey! How was your weekend, bro? (He slaps David on the shoulder.)

David (wincing): Fine…. How was yours?

Antonio: What's the matter? You trying to hide something? (He pulls up a chair and settles into it.) Wait'll you hear about *my* weekend.

David (sighing and turning back to the report he is working on): Look, Antonio, I've got a lot of work to do. I don't really have time to chat.

Antonio: What a grouch! (He gets up and strides off, looking for someone else to talk with.)

In this exchange, background differences could lead both David and Antonio to misunderstand one another. David could interpret Antonio's outgoing style, his physicality, and his questions about David's personal life as rudeness. Antonio could interpret David's apparent coolness and lack of responsiveness as unfriendliness or disapproval. Such misunderstandings could cause the two recruits to begin avoiding each other, unnecessarily preventing them from forging a strong working partnership.

Fortunately, we can take steps to overcome the effect of background differences on our communication. Ongoing contact with people who are different from us can help, along with cultural diversity training.

Noncredible Source

In some communication situations, the sender lacks credibility because the person delivered false or inaccurate information in the past. Even if the most recent information is accurate, the receiver may still discount it and react to it inappropriately.

For instance, Hank, a reclusive elderly man living alone in a small town, has phoned the police department many times complaining about a "suspicious" person he sees walking by his house. Each time the police have sent a patrol car out to investigate, there was

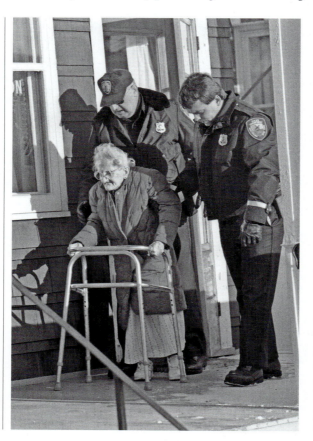

Amsterdam, New York, police officers evacuate a senior citizen from her home as a fire consumes the property next door.

either no one walking down the street, or the person Hank had seen turned out to be a neighbor out for a stroll or visitors of neighbors exploring the area. One night, Hank phones the police yet again about a suspicious person. The police, distracted by a shots-fired call and assuming that (as in the past) Hank has nothing to worry about, take longer than usual to send a car out to Hank's street. Before the patrol car arrives, a burglar has broken into Hank's truck, hot-wired it, and driven off.

As part of ongoing training, police officers should be encouraged to exhibit sensitivity to people who are vulnerable like older persons, many of whom are fearful of strangers or may misinterpret what they are observing. Although calls-for-service are prioritized as to urgency (shots-fired calls are higher on the list than suspicious person calls), no call should be devalued because it comes from someone with a history of calls that yield no or limited results.

Complex Communication Channels

When senders use complex communication channels, their message can become distorted. To illustrate, suppose the chief of police in a large agency describes an important new initiative verbally to his immediate subordinates, then expects them to convey the message to their own reports, who will then do the same with their employees. With such a complicated series of messages, it is likely that by the time the message makes it to the bottom of the reporting hierarchy, it will be distorted. A message that started out as "Tell everyone that I want to improve the way we use CompStat" ends up being interpreted as "We need a new computer network in here."

The best way police personnel can remove this barrier to effective communication is to be as clear and specific as possible in their communication and to ask receivers to confirm their understanding of the message. For example, the chief of police in the example we just discussed could have said to his direct reports, "Tell everyone that I want to improve the way we use CompStat. I think the IT platform we're using now is fine, but I want to see us analyzing the data more frequently than we're doing now—like once a week instead of every 10 days. Does anyone have any questions about what I'm talking about? If not, I'd like you to present this idea to your people during your next staff meeting."

Denial

Messages that conflict with information that a receiver has already accepted as fact may cause the person to reject them. For instance, suppose that Lewis, the recruitment director at a large police agency, believes that new recruits who have a college degree will eventually get bored with police work and leave—costing the agency heavily in terms of time and money invested in training. Beth, a supervisor, believes that new officers with a college education would bring more value to the agency. She suggests to Lewis that he expand his criteria for hiring to include a college degree. He ignores her recommendation.

To counteract Lewis's denial, Beth could cite studies about the value of college-educated police officers. However, she would likely get better results by encouraging Lewis to talk with those officers who have college experience or a degree. Getting to know such officers firsthand would probably help Lewis understand that many police officers enter the profession for more than just exciting car chases and opportunities to arrest perpetrators.

Officers should use simple, ordinary language when speaking with citizens, not police jargon or legalistic vocabulary.

Unfamiliar Language

The language a sender uses to convey a message may contain jargon—terminology specific to a profession. To a receiver who is unfamiliar with the language, the message may be confusing or irritating. Police work is characterized by extensive use of jargon because officers are taught by academy trainers, field training officers, or supervisors to speak and write in a legalistic, investigative, and precise way. The resulting language can confuse citizens who are not familiar with it. For example, an officer interviewing witnesses to a vehicle collision that injured the occupants may ask a question using technical language, such as "Did you observe massive hematoma?"

To bridge this barrier, officers can learn to use simpler, more ordinary language when speaking with citizens. In the previous example, the officer could instead ask, "Was the person bleeding a lot?"

Lack of Motivation

Lack of motivation on the part of the sender or receiver can act as another barrier to effective communication. For instance, a police supervisor who must deliver critical feedback during a performance review for a new recruit may worry about upsetting the recruit, and so is not motivated to present the feedback in clear, candid terms. A receiver may also lack the motivation necessary to listen to the message. For example, the new recruit in the prior example might truly believe she is delivering adequate performance. She therefore discounts her supervisor's critical feedback.

The remedy for this barrier when you are a sender is to deliver concise, to-the-point messages. By using livelier language and pointing out how listening to your message can benefit your listener, you stir up enthusiasm for your message in the other person. When you are a receiver, practice paying attention to the content of messages communicated to you, even if doing so is difficult. By actively attending to messages, you increase the chances of absorbing them and interpreting them in the way the sender intended.

Organizational Culture

As in any organization, the culture in a police agency can have characteristics that constitute barriers to good communication. For example, in an agency where distractions and disruptions occur frequently throughout the workday, people may have difficulty communicating. Consider two officers who have started talking about how to provide security for an upcoming fund-raising activity in their community. Their colleagues and supervisors freely stop by and interrupt them with questions or comments about various topics. The officers will likely find it difficult to stay focused on their conversation and arrive at agreed-upon strategies.

To reduce distractions and disruptions in their agency, police managers can provide a separate place for officers to meet to discuss matters such as security for upcoming events. There are usually conference rooms available. If none happens to be available, personnel can use an interrogation room that is not needed at the moment.

The culture at a police agency might also discourage open communication, if the agency takes a command-and-control approach to policing. When people lower down in the chain of command learn that their input is not welcome during decision making, they stop offering it. Communication dries up and morale erodes. Altering such a culture requires establishing new rules promoting sharing of opinions and ideas as well as opening lines of communication (Stojkovic, Kalinich, & Klofas, 2008).

COMMUNICATION CHANNELS

Personnel in a police agency may use a blend of communication channels, depending on the situation, the relationship and motivation of the parties involved, and participants' communication skills. Primary channels used are verbal, nonverbal, and written.

Verbal Channels

Verbal channels include face-to-face talking, telephone conversations, and transmissions over a radio—any channel through which people use the spoken word. Communication through verbal channels can occur in numerous settings, such as during one-on-one conversations, team or task force meetings, interviews, interrogations, news conferences, and public-speaking events.

To communicate effectively through verbal channels, police personnel—through their words—must demonstrate respect, cooperativeness, and a willingness and ability to understand another person's position (empathy). They should also strive to minimize differences in social status, authority, or power; to accept others' viewpoints; and to candidly express their own beliefs. By contrast, words that convey a desire to control, manipulate, or judge; insincerity; aggression; or an air of superiority will only spark defensiveness within listeners (Hellriegel & Slocum, 2009).

Much of police work involves communicating face-to-face during an interview or interrogation.

Consider these examples of effective and ineffective verbal communication by a police officer who has pulled over a motorist for speeding:

- **Effective:** "Good afternoon, sir. Could I see your license, registration, and proof of insurance please? Thank you. I've stopped you because you were going 20 miles per hour over the speed limit in a school zone."

- **Ineffective:** "Do you have *any* clue how fast you were going! You don't seem give a hoot about the safety of the kids in this neighborhood."

On some occasions (for example, when a criminal suspect verbally threatens an officer), strong, forceful language may be necessary to prevent an outbreak of violence. However, during most encounters, such language will be neither necessary nor appropriate. In sum, effective verbal communication is an essential ingredient in the recipe for deescalating conflict and keeping the peace (Ortmeier & Meese, 2010).

For anyone participating in verbal communication, *listening* can play a major role in the success of the exchange. Failure to listen can lead to misunderstandings that result in costly or fatal mistakes (Cook, 2003). For example, a police officer who fails to detect the panic in a 9-1-1 phone caller's voice or who neglects to listen carefully to the details the caller is conveying may incorrectly conclude that the caller is not in imminent danger—and might not respond swiftly enough.

Unlike talking, listening does not necessarily come naturally to individuals. Some people must learn how to listen. The following tips can help:

- Focus on the speaker, giving full attention and concentration to what the person is saying.

- Do not interrupt the speaker until a natural pause occurs. During the pause, ask questions if needed to clarify the message.

- Strive to be objective about what the speaker is saying, rather than judging what you are hearing.
- Paraphrase or ask for confirmation ("So, what you're saying is ..." "Do I understand you correctly?") to ensure that you are hearing what the speaker intends to say.

Nonverbal Channels

Nonverbal channels of communication—such as body language, facial expression, and tone of voice—have just as much impact as words during any exchange between a sender and receiver. In fact, there is an entire science—known as *kinesics*—devoted to how people interpret nonverbal cues such as facial expressions, eye movement, posture, stance, gestures, and other human physiological behaviors and presentations while communicating (Ottenheimer, 2007). Not surprisingly, police have long strived to read others' body language during interviews and interrogations.

Nonverbal communication involves the use of body movements as well as (in some cases) clothing, hairstyle, physical attractiveness, and speaking style to communicate a message. Nonverbal cues can be expressed consciously or unconsciously, depending on the sender's intentions and interests. For example, a criminal who is being interrogated at a police station and who wants to convince the police that he is innocent might *consciously* strive to sit up straight and maintain a calm tone of voice—behaviors that suggest honesty and credibility. However, the criminal might also *unconsciously* demonstrate some nonverbal behaviors (such as an inability to maintain eye contact or an occasional nervous tapping of fingers on the desk) that reveal his guilt.

Nonverbal communication is often subtle. The meaning of a specific form of nonverbal communication can also be ambiguous, depending on the culture, relationship, and gender of the participants. For instance, in some cultures, people show respect by

Nonverbal communication: the use of voluntary and involuntary body movements and, in some cases, clothing, hairstyle, physical attractiveness, and speaking style, to communicate a message.

Nonverbal communication includes the use of body language, facial expressions, tone of voice, and gestures.

making eye contact with a person they are communicating with. In other cultures, making direct eye contact with an authority figure is considered disrespectful. A police officer who is not aware of such differences might incorrectly interpret a witness's unwillingness to make eye contact as a sign of disrespect or dishonesty. The misunderstanding could lead the officer to express anger or frustration—causing tensions to escalate.

Oftentimes, receivers pay more attention to a sender's nonverbal communication than to the sender's words. If the two types of communication send conflicting messages, the receiver will likely consider the nonverbal message more credible than the verbal one. For example, suppose a police manager says he values officers' input in decisions but acts distracted when officers present their ideas. In this case, the officers will likely conclude that the manager in fact does *not* want to hear their ideas.

Written Channels

Written channels of communication include everything from interoffice memos, incident reports, performance evaluations, and motivational posters tacked to a police agency's wall to e-mails, text messages, and job postings published in a newspaper. All officers and civilian employees of a police agency, regardless of rank or position, must demonstrate the ability to communicate effectively in writing. For instance, line-level officers must document facts surrounding an incident, an interview, or an interrogation as well as criminal activity occurring in the community. Many police reports are scrutinized by the judiciary and by journalists, so these

ETHICS IN ACTION
Special Treatment for Business Owners?

Many people believe that police officers often give special consideration to certain constituents—such as business owners in the community—by providing additional patrols or "turning a blind eye" to unethical or even illegal practices in return for free coffee, meals, or other gratuities. Consider the following communication situations in the light of ethical policing, then decide how you would respond:

1. Your brother-in-law, who runs a restaurant that has been robbed several times in the past year, asks you to encourage patrol officers to patronize his restaurant. He states that it will be "well worth their while." How do you reply?

2. Inadvertently, you overhear a veteran officer telling a new officer, "You can get a free sandwich at the corner diner, the dry-cleaning place next door will give you a discount on your uniform cleaning, and the deli down the street gives free coffee to any cop who walks in and stays for a while." What would you say?

3. There have been a series of rapes in your jurisdiction. Your supervisor instructs you to file future rape complaints as nonsexual assaults unless you believe a legitimate rape can be proven. You suspect that your supervisor has issued this instruction because it will help lower the overall crime numbers or create the impression that the neighborhood is safer than it really is. How would you respond to this directive?

documents must be clear, accurate, and language appropriate. Police administrators, for their part, must write policies and directives; document human resource activities such as training programs; and transmit information about the agency's work to politicians, the news media, and citizens.

Although a detailed discussion of written communication techniques is beyond the scope of this book, a few basic principles can help police managers and officers communicate effectively through such channels. Acceptable writing:

- Communicates ideas clearly
- Demonstrates the writer's understanding of the intended reader's needs and goals
- Shows a sufficient command of the language
- Is free of typographical errors as well as grammar, spelling, and punctuation mistakes
- Has a clear organization so that ideas flow smoothly
- Follows established protocol for the type of written document at hand (such as incident reports or e-mail messages) (Guffey, 2005; Parr, 1999; Wallace & Roberson, 2009).

A CLOSER LOOK AT MEETINGS, NEWSLETTERS, AND THE GRAPEVINE

As we have seen, there are numerous verbal, nonverbal, and written channels through which police personnel communicate. Communication can be formal or informal. In the pages that follow, we look closely at three commonly used types of communication: meetings (verbal, formal), newsletters (written, formal) and "the grapevine" (verbal, informal).

Meetings

A *meeting* is a formal gathering to exchange information. In part due to the implementation of CompStat (see Chapter 2), many police agencies organize meetings on a regular basis to review crime statistics, discuss new initiatives, and communicate changes to policies or procedures. However, to generate useful information and outcomes (and to make effective use of time), meetings must be properly planned and executed. For example, a meeting with a clear agenda and dedicated facilitator can result in increased agreement among participants on what problems need to be addressed and how the agency can best solve them.

Before the Meeting   The agenda for a meeting should be prepared and distributed in advance by the person who will facilitate the meeting. An agenda can be as simple as a list of topics to be covered, or as complicated as a formal multilevel outline that will be distributed ahead of time to participants. Following are some tips for developing an effective meeting agenda:

- **Time frame:** Indicate precisely when the meeting will start and end. When determining an ending time, consider selecting a time that is difficult to extend, such as the end of a work shift. A time limit for discussion of each agenda item may be indicated as well.

- **Order:** Position the most important items to be covered in the meeting at the top of the agenda and the remaining items in descending order of importance. That way, participants will be able to deal with the most demanding items early in the meeting—when they are freshest.

- **Announcements:** If appropriate and if time will allow, list announcements such as promotions or transfers at the end of the meeting agenda.

During the Meeting   If you facilitate a meeting, do everything possible to ensure that the meeting begins and ends on time. If you get into the habit of starting meetings late, participants will likely begin arriving late as well because they will have learned that there is no penalty for tardiness. If participants arrive chronically late to your meetings even though the meetings start on time, consider locking the door to the meeting room immediately after the start time, to encourage promptness.

Make it clear at the outset of the meeting whether breaks will be given and whether interruptions (such as participants talking to each other during the meeting, responding to cell phones, or reading text message alerts) will be tolerated. During the meeting, also allow participants to offer suggestions regarding the agenda; for example, "Can we table this issue for now and focus on the next one?" You may or may not accept each suggestion, but it is valuable to let participants know they are welcome to contribute ideas. If suggestions are off-topic, create a separate and temporary list of such topics and display it so all participants understand that these issues are also important and may be agenda items at a future meeting.

Ensure that discussion centers on the agenda topics and that disagreements do not take a personal turn. Consider this example from a fictional meeting called to address an increase in house break-ins in the jurisdiction served by this agency:

Harry: I think we should step up patrols of the area.

Jane (rolling her eyes): Harry, apparently you weren't paying attention the last time we tried that. Otherwise, you would have known it doesn't work.

You (the facilitator): Okay, Harry has offered an idea, and Jane disagrees. Jane, we can dispense with the sarcasm. To use our time most productively, let's discuss the legitimate pros and cons of the various solutions we've explored for this problem.

After the Meeting   End the meeting with a summary of the key points covered and a review of tasks that were assigned during the meeting and their deadlines. Prepare minutes of the meeting (notes about what happened and what was decided) as soon as possible afterward, and distribute them promptly to all interested parties. Keep a copy of the minutes in a file so people can refer to them readily if needed.

Newsletters

Newsletters can be brief (1 or 2 pages) or relatively long (10 or 12 pages), depending on the subject matter they cover, the goals of the entity publishing them, and the publication schedule. (For instance, a newsletter that is published monthly may be shorter than one that is published only twice a year.) Newsletters may also be published in print or digital form. Online newsletters (often called e-newsletters or e-zines) are cheaper and faster to publish than their printed versions, and can be distributed more widely through e-mail or through access of websites where each issue

Clark County, Ohio, Sheriff Gene Kelly displays a "Fight Crime: Invest in Kids" newsletter. Kelly spoke on behalf of police officials throughout Ohio in February 2005 to urge that federal funding for foster care not be capped.

may be posted. Electronic newsletters may also contain video attachments or links to other sources of information, advantages that print-only newsletters cannot offer.

Most newsletters published by police agencies are directed to agency personnel, both sworn and civilian. Topics covered may include acknowledgment of newly hired employees; advertisements for community activities; and notices of weddings, births, deaths, and other events of interest to agency personnel. Each issue of the newsletter can also be used as an educational tool, offering regular columns about topics such as police ethics or practical skills (for example, report writing or vehicular safety).

The Grapevine

Some people call it gossip. In the Navy, it is known as *scuttlebutt*. But in most police agencies, the channel through which people exchange information verbally and informally is referred to as the *grapevine*. Through the grapevine, peers as well as supervisors and direct subordinates may share accurate information as well as rumors and other unsubstantiated information in an effort to determine what is happening.

The wise police manager pays as much attention to the grapevine as to formal communication channels (Moore, 2004), because the content of the grapevine can strongly affect morale—especially if the content is inaccurate. For instance, if unfounded rumors that an agency will be shutting down its mounted division are racing through the grapevine, people worried about losing their jobs may panic and take unnecessary and disruptive action (such as launching a job search). Or they may obsessively discuss the rumor instead of doing their jobs, eroding productivity.

Yet the grapevine is so deeply embedded in most organizations' culture that managers and supervisors should not try to forbid it or discount the information circulating through it. When a police manager admonishes subordinates not to talk about something, it is akin to a parent telling a small child not to touch something—few people can resist doing precisely what has been forbidden to them.

The wise police manager is attentive to the *grapevine* and other informal communications among officers.

Instead, effective leaders take a productive approach to the grapevine, using tactics like these:

- **Encourage open communication at all levels in the agency.** This strategy causes the grapevine to lose much of its strength. When people are regularly made aware of the current status of police initiatives, key players, and future changes, they will feel less compelled to gossip about these matters in secret.

- **Use the grapevine as a communication tool.** Learn what information is being circulated through the grapevine to discover how subordinates really feel about changes or conditions in the agency. Further, allow people to communicate through the grapevine; you will enable them to experience the emotional release that comes when people speak freely with peers about concerns. Likewise, disseminate positive and truthful information (such as purchasing of new police vehicles and dates for promotions) through the grapevine, which may be viewed as more credible than information released through a more formal means, such as a memo from the chief of police.

Grapevines are here to stay. Rather than trying to eradicate them, savvy police managers build on the strengths of their agency's grapevine, manage the grapevine's negative consequences (such as escalation of unfounded rumors), and use the grapevine as a communication tool.

SPECIAL COMMUNICATION CHALLENGES

No matter which communication channel is being used, participants can expect to encounter several challenges. In the pages that follow, we explore three such challenges: communicating across cultures, communicating across genders, and communicating with special populations.

Communicating across Cultures

Culture is the pattern of a group's behavior. It stems from the customs, moral systems, language, behaviors, and mind-set that give a group a specific identity. People from the same ethnic background, those identifying as a particular nationality, and those in a similar socioeconomic class may all have a cultural identity. But organizations, including police agencies, also develop cultures. Within an agency, "microcultures" may exist; for example, members of a SWAT team might have different behavioral norms than members of the management team. People working in a police agency may be communicating cross-culturally with their own supervisors and colleagues—as well as with people in the community the agency serves.

Cross-cultural communication occurs anytime a person of one culture sends a message to, or receives a message from, a person of another culture. Misunderstanding can occur easily during this process because individuals from different cultures often perceive and evaluate each other differently. For example, if a police officer is called to an incident in a Hispanic neighborhood, the officer should address the male participant if both a man and a woman are present. Not doing so would be considered disrespectful, and could cause the participants to refuse to cooperate with the police.

Police personnel who are aware of cultural differences and who strive to understand cultural norms, forms of address, and nonverbal cues are more effective and experience less stress than those who lack these attitudes. They are more resourceful, healthier, and more satisfied with their work, and they generate fewer citizen complaints.

To communicate effectively in a multicultural environment, police personnel must gain familiarity with cultural differences, respect them, and be willing to adapt to them. All this requires patience. Talking with people from other cultures can also help police personnel adapt to these differences (Adler & Proctor, 2011; Coffey, 1990; Ortmeier, 2006). Following are tips for strengthening your ability to communicate across cultures:

- Take every opportunity to interact with people of a cultural orientation different from yours. If you are on foot patrol, talk with business owners or other citizens who live and work in culturally diverse sections of the area. If you patrol by car, ask respectful questions during a call-for-service.

- Learn another language. Just as there are nuances in the English language, other languages possess them as well and will give you a window into the way people from other cultures view the world.

- If you are invited to attend a community event or religious service centered on a culture other than yours, do so willingly and with an openness to adapt to that culture's customs. For instance, if you attend a mosque, be willing to follow the protocol of removing your shoes.

Cross-cultural communication: a process that occurs anytime a person of one culture sends a message to, or receives a message from, a person of another culture.

Learn more about cross-cultural communication and strategies for managing communication conflict through the University of Colorado's Conflict Research Consortium at www.colorado. edu/conflict/peace/ treatment.

Communicating across Genders

Consider the following exchange: Maria, a newly recruited police officer, runs into Tim, a fellow officer, in the hallway and says, "Do you want to get some coffee?" Tim has just downed a cup of coffee on his way to work and replies, "No thanks." Maria, who was hoping that getting coffee with Tim would enable her to talk with him about her new job and gain some insights, feels disappointed and rejected. She starts wondering whether Tim has something against her.

Cross-gender communication: a process that occurs anytime a person of one gender sends a message to, or receives a message from, a person of another gender.

This scenario illustrates the difficulties that can arise during **cross-gender communication**. Differences in how women and men communicate and what their goals are during communication can lead to misunderstanding and conflict in personal as well as professional relationships. For example, some linguists maintain that women use communication to build relationships, while men use it to accomplish tasks and to determine where individuals fit in a hierarchy of relationships (de Janasz et al., 2006; Githens, 1991; Tannen, 1990). In the previous scenario, Maria used an invitation to coffee to begin building a working relationship with Tim. He declined her invitation simply because he had already had coffee and saw no need to have more. Because both parties had different purposes in mind during the exchange and used different styles, the exchange failed to generate a positive outcome.

One way to accommodate cross-gender communication differences is to treat them the same way you would treat cross-cultural communication differences: Acknowledge the differences, gain familiarity with gender communication styles that differ from your own, and practice speaking the other gender's language when you can. For instance, Maria could try accepting the idea that someone declining her invitation for coffee might simply not want any coffee—and is not rejecting her personally. And Tim could consider the possibility that an invitation for coffee might really be a suggestion for a meeting to discuss career issues. Role playing during cross-gender communication sensitivity training can also help people master these skills.

Communicating with Special Populations

Special populations: populations that include people with hearing or visual impairments, developmental disabilities, mental illnesses or substance-abuse problems, and those who present an immediate danger to themselves or others.

In their everyday work with colleagues and community members, police personnel often communicate with members of **special populations**. These populations may include people with hearing or visual impairments, developmental disabilities, mental illnesses or substance-abuse problems, and those who present an immediate danger to themselves or others. In the pages that follow, we focus on how to communicate effectively during an incident in which a person with mental illness is experiencing a crisis. Skills crucial for handling such incidents include gauging the situation, communicating effectively with the persons involved, and concluding the incident productively.

Gauging the Situation   Individuals with mental illness respond differently than mentally healthy people do to ordinary stressors—such as being fatigued, experiencing extensive sensory stimulation, or forgetting to take a prescribed medication. Under these and other conditions, a person with mental illness might become frightened, suspicious, or aggressive. Alcohol or drug consumption may exacerbate the symptoms of any mental illness and cause these persons to become dangerous to themselves (for example, wandering into traffic or attempting suicide) or to others (such as attacking strangers or family members).

If police line officers receive a call about a person with mental illness, they should gauge the situation as soon as they arrive. Before attempting to communicate with the individual, they must accept that the person's behavior could be unpredictable. Officers must also protect the public by isolating the afflicted person and making dispatchers and response personnel aware of the nature of the situation. In addition, officers should identify the exits and entrances to the environment, as well as exercise extreme caution in case the person has a weapon.

Officers should be patient with the person and gauge the level of danger that the individual presents to self or others. Officers must establish a safe distance between the person and others. If possible, only one (primary) officer should interact with the subject.

Many situations provide special communications challenges for the police, especially when a subject is mentally ill or suicidal.

Communicating with the Person   After gauging the situation, the primary officer can engage the person verbally. The officer should initiate conversation with an introduction and, in a respectful manner, state the reason for the police presence. Officers should present a calm, confident demeanor demonstrating that the police are in control of the situation. While engaging the person in conversation, they should attempt to remove any dangerous objects from the individual's reach while maneuvering the person into a safe area. Officers should seek to avoid a physical confrontation. If the person refuses to communicate, the primary officer should encourage a response by using simple language; for example, "You must be very upset that someone stole your car" or "You look as if you need to speak with someone." If the person begins to speak, the officer can maintain a dialog by using leading statements such as "Go on" or "And, then?"

The officer should acknowledge the individual's emotions yet avoid expressing agreement with any delusions or hallucinations that the person is experiencing. The officer should never whisper, laugh, or joke with the individual; minimize the person's concerns; or unnecessarily touch the person. Introducing additional stimuli to the situation may only confuse or upset the individual and escalate any agitation the person may be experiencing (Wildman & Morschauser, 2007).

Concluding the Incident   Hopefully, the person will be taken into custody in a calm, respectful, and nonviolent manner. A successful conclusion may include a criminal arrest or a mental hygiene detention, physical transport to and a medical examination at a local hospital, or an intervention with professionals at a local mental health facility.

Communicating effectively with special populations requires knowledge, patience, and maturity—all of which officers can develop through experience and appropriate training. Each encounter and follow-up debriefing with command staff and colleagues can further help officers strengthen these important skills.

Leadership on the job

The Newsgroup

Police agencies offer citizens several methods of communication with the agency: face-to-face discussion, 9-1-1 calls for emergency service, 3-1-1 calls for less urgent matters, and written communications (such as letters and e-mail). One police lieutenant in a California city, however, brought the agency in that city into the twenty-first century by establishing a website to foster communication between the agency and the citizens it serves. The site featured a live newsgroup that was made available to citizens 24 hours a day and was monitored by police personnel.

Through the newsgroup, citizens began communicating in real time with police officers who responded to citizen nonemergency concerns. For instance, one woman sent a message to the agency that vehicles were speeding out of control on the street where she lived. She was reluctant to let her child play in the front yard. Within hours an officer responded to her, stating that several citations for speeding on that street had been issued that day. The officer thanked the woman for notifying the police and assured her that the area would remain a target of future patrols.

Citizens of this city report that the newsgroup has given them a better idea of what is happening in their neighborhoods. They receive information in a more timely and personal way than before. Patrol officers and sergeants who originally feared that the newsgroup would merely become another means for citizens to complain about police behavior report that the newsgroup was not a complaint vehicle. A councilwoman for the city says that the newsgroup has taken the mystery out of police work for most residents.

The lieutenant's idea spurred a high-ranking official in the agency to note, "This is real community policing, citizens and police in real-time, constant contact about real problems and solutions. Now we really belong to the same team; some of us wear uniforms and some do not."

1. You are a police supervisor in a small agency. Your chief approaches you with a journal article describing the electronic messaging system just described. The chief wishes to implement a similar newsgroup. How would you respond to the chief's request?

2. What are some of the communication challenges that could arise in a newsgroup system like the one described? For example, could messages between citizens and police be misunderstood because of cultural or gender differences? What steps would you suggest the agency take to prevent or surmount any such challenges?

Spotlight on Communication Technology

Advancements in electronic communication technology—cell phones, fax machines, e-mail, voice mail, text messaging, blogs, wireless access—have made it easier than ever for police personnel to communicate instantaneously with various constituencies. The ease and immediacy of electronic communication has also led to a laxness in professionalism and decorum. People have become all too willing to send e-mails or text or cell phone messages without checking for errors. The inappropriate inclusion of confidential information, or the use of improper language is unacceptable. These forms of communication are easily monitored by outsiders. A lack of professionalism in such messages can cause a police manager or officer—even the entire agency—to lose credibility.

Electronic forms of communication demand the same level of professionalism as traditional interpersonal and written communication methods. Before sending a message through any electronic communication channel, ask yourself:

- "Does my message contain any information that I would not reveal in a face-to-face meeting?" If so, consider omitting the information.

- "Have I made any errors in spelling, grammar, and sentence structure?"

- "Is my message clear and concise?" Rambling, overly lengthy, and confusing voice or e-mail messages will likely be ignored by your intended recipient.

- "Have I expressed what I want from the recipient?" For example, if you would like the recipient of an e-mail you are sending to phone or visit you to discuss the e-mail's content, have you articulated this wish in your message?

- "Does my message contain any inappropriate language?" Avoid use of obscene or sexually explicit language or images, off-color jokes, and language that expresses aggression or a condescending attitude. Also, if someone sends you an e-mail that contains inappropriate language (such as a racist or obscene joke), do not forward it to others.

COMMUNICATING WITH THE NEWS MEDIA

Police communicate not only with one another and with members of the communities they serve, but also with the news media. Because of their central role in community life, police personnel—especially those in managerial and supervisory roles—are often interviewed by the press. Of course, like anyone else, police prefer to receive favorable treatment from the news media. They would much rather see newspapers and television news programs report stories about officers' courage and low crime rates than stories revealing problems or scandals associated with the police.

Yet favorable news coverage of the police is rare. Instead, news stories tend to focus on the negative—because that is what "sells." For instance, if an officer is cited for use of excessive force or other misconduct, the story usually makes the front page of local and even national newspapers. Stories of horrific crimes, officer-involved shootings, and high-speed vehicle pursuits also attract the attention of print and broadcast news media. The adage "If it bleeds, it leads" reflects the media's awareness of the public's hunger for drama and gore.

The police often criticize the media for publishing more unfavorable than favorable stories about police behavior and operations. Meanwhile, many broadcast and print journalists—immersed in mostly sensational stories—accuse the police of being insensitive to citizens' concerns and rights and even downright brutal to those they suspect of having committed a crime. Such criticisms, from both sides, erode trust between police and the media. Moreover, a preponderance of negative news stories about the police causes citizens to conclude that life is more dangerous than it actually is—instilling unnecessary fear. It also jeopardizes police agencies' chances of receiving

Communications with the news media should be truthful and viewed as opportunities to develop positive relationships with the press.

funding because it gives the impression that police are not doing their job effectively. Finally, police operations should be transparent, visible, and accessible to the common citizen, and the news media provide the best avenue for creating those conditions. For all these reasons, police agencies should strive to cultivate positive relationships with the media. Indeed, the quality of an agency's relationship with the press can strongly determine how positive or negative news accounts of police activities will be.

Improving Communication with the Media

How might a police agency improve the quality and effectiveness of communication with the media? The following steps can help:

- **Appoint a public information officer (PIO) or clearly designate who is authorized to speak to the press.** This position should be voluntary (not assigned). Also, the individual who fills this role must be comfortable with and skilled at speaking to groups and must have a genuine desire to do the job (Rosenthal, 2005). PIOs should also have a clear understanding of which information is acceptable to share with the public and which is not (such as details about a crime that could sabotage the investigation if they were made public).

- **Make press releases brief and to the point.** Be sure the latest and most important information appears at the beginning of a press release. Print a brief headline at the top of the release (Rosenthal, 2003). Provide enough information to satisfy the media while not jeopardizing investigations or police operations.

- **Manage media conferences strategically.** Police agencies usually conduct media conferences after a high-profile incident has generated intense media and community interest. Often, police will discuss major cases and ask for the public's help, or they will use the conference to inform the public of an ongoing dangerous situation—such as an escaped felon in their area. As with press releases, the opening statement of a media conference should be brief and to the point, and answers to journalists' questions should be equally short and pointed (Garner, 2005).

- **Control information leaks.** Information can leak from a police agency out to the public, if officers or civilian workers inadvertently mention details about an investigation to someone during a conversation. Such leaks can jeopardize an investigation. To control them, police managers and supervisors should strive to be the first to provide truthful and factual information to the media. That way, journalists will not be tempted to rely solely on leaks (Gary, 2003; Parrish, 2003).

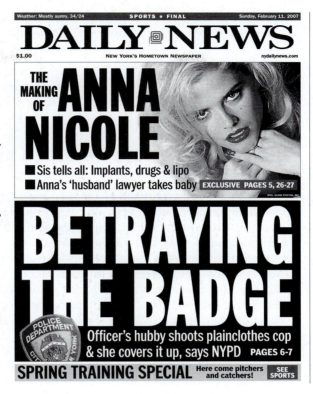

Media headlines about the police are not always positive.

Building a Positive Relationship with the Media

Police officers should remember that a news reporter's job is to locate and publicize a story. Reporters search for stories that will catch the public's interest. The more "eyeballs" a news outlet attracts, the more advertising dollars flow to that outlet from companies seeking to sell their products or services to readers and viewers. And sensational stories attract the public. Thus the news media's very business model means that journalists will tend to focus on the negative, the violent, and the frightening aspects of police work.

Still, this does not mean that police managers should try to control the media or refuse to provide information: That would threaten the free and open press that is vital to our democracy. Instead, the police should build a positive relationship with the media, through actions such as the following:

- **Provide information.** A "No comment" statement to the press is like a red flag to a bull. It makes journalists suspect that the police are concealing information.

- **Include media representatives in some police briefings.** During these briefings, share information about how the agency defines and meets goals, and how it helps the community achieve its vision of a better future.

- **Demonstrate professionalism.** Avoid getting into confrontations and shouting matches with the media. Admit mistakes you have made. Avoid using police jargon and officious speech. And do not make off-the-record statements.

By building a positive relationship with the media, the police may increase the odds that journalists will publish balanced and accurate accounts of the work that a police agency is doing (Ortmeier & Meese, 2010).

COMMUNICATING WITH OTHER AGENCIES

In addition to communicating with the news media, police communicate with people from other agencies, such as the local corrections department, the prosecuting attorney's office, fire safety agencies, emergency medical services, social services, security organizations, hospitals, and nursing homes. But they tend to do so only when it is necessary, such as when a suspect crosses jurisdictional lines and officers in adjacent jurisdictions must be informed. However, regular communication among agencies can increase the effectiveness of each agency involved, because such communication facilitates the exchange of valuable information and the cooperation agencies need to make decisions (Estey, 2005).

Technology advances have made interagency communication easier than ever. One example of a program that uses technology to improve interagency communication is SAFECOM, instituted in 2004 by the U.S. Department of Homeland Security's Office of Interoperability and Compatibility (OIC). According to program managers, "SAFECOM . . . provides research, development, testing and evaluation, guidance, tools and templates on interoperable communication-related issues to state, local, tribal, and federal emergency response agencies" (U.S. Department of Homeland Security, SAFECOM Program, 2004).

The primary purpose of SAFECOM is to enhance "communication interoperability" among more than 50,000 public safety agencies (for example, police, fire, and medical emergency services) across the United States. In general, "interoperability" refers to the ability of emergency responders to work seamlessly with other systems or products without any special effort. Wireless communications interoperability specifically refers to the ability of emergency response officials to share information via voice and data signals on demand, in real time, when needed, and as authorized. For example, when communications systems are interoperable:

- Police and firefighters responding to an incident can speak with one another to coordinate efforts.
- Emergency response agencies can respond to catastrophic accidents or disasters to work effectively together.
- Emergency response personnel can maximize resources in planning for major predictable events such as the Super Bowl or an inauguration, or for disaster relief and recovery efforts.

Fostering good working relationships with people from other agencies is essential to providing optimum service to citizens. Communication can help build such relationships. For example, police officers should converse with these professionals to gain familiarity with how personnel work in each of these settings, what

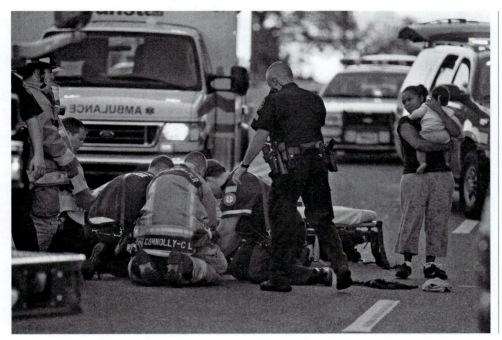

Various types of public safety personnel (police, fire, emergency medical, corrections) must communicate well among one another, especially in emergency situations. Here, Clearwater, Florida, rescuers work to save a small child.

resources the various entities offer, and the limitations of each entity. Informed by this knowledge, officers can direct a citizen in need of assistance to the agency that can best satisfy the need.

FOUR ESSENTIAL COMMUNICATION SKILLS

In any communication situation, with any audience, there are several essential skills that can help police personnel enhance their effectiveness—whether they are seeking to solve a problem, arrive at a decision, or improve their agency's performance. These skills include facilitation, persuasion, feedback, and conflict management.

Facilitation

People use **facilitation** to effectively and agreeably develop solutions to problems. Facilitation comprises a range of specialized functions that help a group deliberate (Bostrom, Anson, & Clawson, 1993). Although difficult to accomplish in a traditional command and control environment, facilitation can motivate others to develop and implement new ideas and initiatives by promoting transparency and synergistic efforts (Eastman Kodak Company, 1995).

> **Facilitation:** a communication skill through which police personnel develop solutions to problems.

Police leaders incorporate facilitation into their daily encounters, whether at a staff meeting or during spontaneous conversations or encounters with colleagues, subordinates, or citizens. Hallmarks of facilitation include the following:

- Creating a safe, receptive, and nonthreatening environment in which people can share ideas and challenge one another's thinking

- Encouraging subordinates and others to express themselves openly and freely
- Keeping an open mind; that is, listening without judging
- Seeking to understand what is being said
- Avoiding side conversations and personal agendas
- Respecting others' opinions
- Making salient points in a calm manner
- Offering and receiving relevant information (Brassard & Ritter, 1995)

Persuasion

Persuasion: the ability to influence outcomes, using methods other than the issuance of direct orders.

The ability to persuade is another essential communication skill. **Persuasion** is the ability to influence outcomes, using methods other than the issuance of direct orders. In a police agency, everyone can benefit from mastering the art of persuasion. For example:

- Paul, an officer, is called to the scene of a domestic dispute and finds a man holding a woman at gunpoint. By demonstrating calm and helping the man see how his behavior could lead to devastating consequences for himself and the woman, Paul persuades the man to drop the gun and give himself up.

- Karla, a new police recruit, is convinced that the agency where she works could deliver even better service to the community if it updated its computer systems. She presents the relevant facts to her chief, including information on the costs of the upgrade and the potential gains, and persuades him to approve funding for the project.

In the private as well as the public sectors, persuasion has emerged as the preferred method for fostering change and achieving valued results. That is because enabling change and achieving results often require collaboration among people who do not have formal authority over one another. Whenever possible, police officers should seek to persuade others to take action, rather than dictate outcomes. Using persuasion more than command and control helps create a more participatory work environment—which in turn enhances productivity and job satisfaction.

Effective persuaders exhibit distinctive personal characteristics, including empathy, credibility (by being knowledgeable about the subject matter at hand), reliability, humility, confidence, and calmness. They also demonstrate the following behaviors:

- Readily soliciting and providing feedback
- Thinking creatively about what might be the best solution for all parties
- Presenting information in a manner that facilitates comprehension by others
- Presenting a positive impression through good grooming and dress, enthusiasm, and impeccable personal credentials
- Connecting with diverse audiences and building consensus
- Inviting alternative approaches to resolving problems
- Articulating and promoting a compelling vision of a desirable future
- Using relevant facts and evidence to make their points

Communication is a process that may involve several goals, including persuading others to take action or embrace an idea.

- Exhibiting passion when presenting their ideas
- Resonating with others' feelings, fears, values, dreams, frustrations, egos, needs, and desires (de Janasz et al., 2006)

Feedback

Feedback is a special kind of communication through which a sender gives specific information (a response) to a receiver. Feedback can be given in all types of communication channels—verbal, nonverbal, and written. It can result from a question; for example, a firearms-safety trainer asks learners to rate the training's value to them. Feedback can also be personal; for instance, after a subordinate completes a project, the supervisor gives an impression of the person's performance.

Within a police agency, supervisors and managers offer feedback to subordinates—such as giving praise or offering instruction—on a daily, informal basis, over and above what may be given during performance reviews. In all types of work (including police work), giving immediate feedback can be far more effective than waiting for a less frequent occasion (such as a quarterly or annual performance review). Why? When people receive feedback while their action or performance is fresh in their minds, they learn more from that information.

In some police agencies, supervisors can also ask subordinates to provide feedback on management's performance and policies. However, this is not the norm in such settings. Many supervisors may be reluctant to ask for feedback from anyone, because it could turn attention to areas where they are lacking while ignoring their strengths (Cordner & Scarborough, 2007). Moreover, subordinates may be reluctant to give their superiors honest feedback because they

Feedback: a special kind of communication through which a sender gives specific information (a response) to a receiver.

fear it will spark retaliation (in forms such as demotions or withholding of valued professional opportunities).

Feedback can flow not only between personnel in a police agency but also between the agency and the communities it serves. For instance, an agency might distribute a written or online survey to citizens asking them to assess the quality of police services provided. The responses to such surveys can help police managers modify procedures (for example, providing more frequent patrols of a neighborhood plagued by increasing crime rates) and design needed new initiatives (such as establishing a mounted equestrian unit to provide better crowd control).

Conflict Management

Conflict is inevitable—part of human nature. It arises when people believe they have incompatible goals, compete over scarce resources, or interfere with each other's efforts. Knowing how to manage conflict through effective communication is a core skill for all police personnel.

The first step is to understand the difference between productive and destructive conflict. In a *productive* conflict, participants balance cooperation with competition, resulting in a gain for all parties. They also keep the discussion centered on the issues at hand, rather than allowing it to devolve into personal and character attacks. In a *destructive* conflict, disputants often seek to win for themselves rather than achieve a collective gain, and they resort to personal attacks instead of resolving the issues at hand.

For example, after learning about an impending budget cut, managers at a police agency discuss ways to deliver the same services with less funding for the forthcoming fiscal year. Tension escalates initially, as people lobby to get a significant share of the available funding for their own departments and teams. Yet the participants are then able to move from destructive to productive conflict by keeping the bigger picture in mind: sustaining high quality in the agency's services. By looking beyond their individual interests to the larger goal, they arrive at a solution for allocating funds that benefits the agency overall.

When it comes to managing conflict, effective police managers and front-line officers seek to de-escalate destructive conflict by watching for and correcting symptoms of unproductive conflict. These symptoms include participants ridiculing or threatening one another, impugning each other's character, refusing to express their thoughts, and harboring resentments (Adler & Proctor, 2011). For instance, if a police manager leading a meeting notices that one person is uncharacteristically silent, the manager might call on that person and encourage sharing of thoughts, concerns, and ideas. Or if the manager observes several participants making character attacks ("You really don't seem to care about this department!" "Can you actually be that ignorant?"), the manager refocuses the conversation away from personalities and back onto the issues ("Let's set aside the personal attacks and return to the decision facing us.")

Adroit communicators also adapt their communication style to the situation. For instance, when arresting a suspect, an officer may use an assertive, task-oriented, and decisive communication style ("Put your hands on your head and face the wall"). That same officer may use a collaborative communication style when facilitating a meeting in which task force members will generate ideas for reducing speeding in a neighborhood (Ortmeier & Meese, 2010; Wallace & Roberson, 2009). ("Viktor, we haven't heard from you yet. What are your thoughts about the strategy currently on the table?")

- **What Is Communication?** Communication is a process involving an exchange of information between a sender and a receiver. It serves several purposes including being understood, understanding others, and persuading others. Communication in a police agency can flow in vertical, horizontal, and diagonal directions, and through formal and informal channels.

- **Barriers to Effective Communication.** Barriers include poor communication skills, background differences, lack of credibility in a message source, complex communication channels, denial in a message receiver, unfamiliar language, lack of motivation in senders or receivers, and an organizational culture that stifles communication.

- **Communication Channels.** Channels may be verbal, nonverbal, or written.

- **A Closer Look at Meetings, Newsletters, and the Grapevine.** Before a meeting, the meeting leader should prepare and distribute a clear agenda. During the meeting, the leader must clarify rules about interruptions, invite and manage input from participants, and ensure that the discussion stays focused on agenda topics and that disagreements do not take a personal turn. After the meeting, the leader should distribute minutes and keep a copy of minutes in a file. Police agencies can also use newsletters as a tool for communication with internal and external constituencies. Police managers can take a productive approach to the grapevine (the informal verbal communication channel among agency personnel) by encouraging open communication at all levels and tap into the grapevine to learn employees' opinions and feelings about changes or conditions in the agency.

- **Special Communication Challenges.** Communicating with people from different cultures, different genders, and special populations (such as persons who are mentally or physically disabled) presents unique challenges for police officers. Police can surmount these challenges by, for example, learning as much as possible about cultures different from their own; acknowledging and accommodating differences in communication styles between men and women; and learning how to gauge an incident in which a member of a special population is involved, engage the person, and conclude the incident effectively.

- **Communicating with the News Media.** News media and police often have an antagonistic relationship. This erodes trust between both sides, instills fear in citizens when news media publish a preponderance of negative stories about police, and prevents police agencies from making their activities transparent and accessible to the public. To address this problem, police must improve their communication with the news media (including controlling information leaks and managing media conferences strategically) and strengthen their relationship with the media (for example, by including media representatives in police briefings and demonstrating professionalism while interacting with journalists).

- **Communicating with Other Agencies.** Police can improve collaboration with other agencies by communicating frequently with them and taking advantage of technological advances such as SAFECOM.

- **Four Essential Communication Skills.** Four skills that can further help police enhance their effectiveness are facilitation of problem solving, persuasion to influence people over whom they have no formal authority, giving feedback to guide subordinates' performance-improvement efforts and gathering feedback from community members, and conflict management.

key terms

barriers to effective communication
communication
cross-cultural communication
cross-gender communication
facilitation

feedback
nonverbal communication
persuasion
special populations

discussion questions

1. Why is communication a process rather than an event?
2. What purposes does communication serve for human beings?
3. What are some examples of vertical, horizontal, and diagonal communication flow within an agency (other than the examples provided in this chapter)?
4. What are some examples of formal and informal communication channels in a police agency?
5. Select three barriers to effective communication described in this chapter. What steps would you take to overcome each of the barriers you selected?
6. Identify ways in which police officers can effectively use verbal channels of communication.
7. Identify strategies that can help police officers effectively use nonverbal channels of communication.
8. What are some basic guidelines for communicating effectively through written channels?
9. How would you prepare to facilitate a meeting for a task force you are leading? What challenges would you expect to encounter while conducting the meeting? How would you address those challenges? What tasks would you perform after the meeting?
10. How would you use newsletters to enhance communication among a police agency's personnel and between the agency and the community it serves?
11. Should police managers try to suppress the grapevine (the gossip or rumor mill) in their agency? Why or why not? If not, how can managers extract value from the grapevine?
12. What steps would you take to learn about a culture that is different from yours?
13. What challenges have you experienced in communicating with people of a gender different from yours? How might you improve your cross-gender communication?
14. What communication processes should a police officer use when encountering a person with mental illness who is in crisis?
15. Why is effective communication with the news media important in policing? How might police agencies improve their communication and their relationships with the media?
16. Why is effective communication with other agencies important in policing? How might police agencies improve their communication and their relationship with other agencies?
17. For each of the following skills, cite three hallmarks of effectiveness: facilitation, persuasion, feedback, and conflict management.
18. Some experts on policing suggest that effective communications skill may be the most important nontechnical skill a police officer can possess and demonstrate. Why?

WHAT WOULD YOU DO?
De-escalating Conflict at a Rock Concert

At a rock concert in a midsize city, a police agency assigns a detail to provide crowd control, manage traffic, ensure the personal safety of attendees, and prevent illegal activity (such as the use of controlled substances). During the concert, the officers on duty notice that a young Hispanic man seems to be suffering from negative side effects of substance abuse. He is yelling, slurring his words, staggering through the crowd, sweating profusely, and gesticulating wildly. The officers approach the man, and one of them snaps, "Hey buddy, let's calm down, okay?" The young man ignores the request and hurls a few insults at the officer—who promptly arrests him and calls for a transport van.

While waiting for the van, the young man continues to harangue the officers with belligerent comments. His friends gather and shout additional insults at the police, calling them names and demanding that they leave him alone. Most of the concert-goers are young Hispanics and African Americans. The officers in charge are primarily white and in their middle years.

The confrontation escalates as harsh words are exchanged between the concert-goers and officers. Some of the concert-goers march up to the officers and yell, "Listen, you pig! Don't hurt him!" A few of the officers, driven to the end of their patience, let loose with some choice words of their own, including a few racial slurs.

A command officer arrives to find the situation deteriorating rapidly. The commander approaches the officers. In a calm voice, he says, "It's okay, guys. Let's dial it down a bit, all right?" The commander then addresses the young man. Again using a calm tone of voice, the command officer says, "Sir, I know you're confused and afraid. But we're worried about the drugs in your system, and we want to be sure you're okay. Let's head for the station, so we can be sure you get the help you need." The officer diverts the young man's attention long enough for the police transport van to arrive. The man's friends, listening to the exchange, realize that the police have no intention of harming the man. Their friend remains calm and is escorted to the van without further incident. No one is injured, the crowd disperses, and the concert environment returns to normal.

1. What communication techniques were used by the officers who initially responded to the scene of the disturbance? If you had been on the scene as an officer, what (if anything) would you have done differently? Why?

2. What barriers to communication may have led to the confrontation between the officers and the young man's friends?

3. In what respect could cultural differences have played a role in the escalation of this conflict? If you had been on the scene, what would you have done to communicate more effectively across cultures?

4. What techniques did the command officer use to gain control of the situation?

■ From the beginning of a police officer's career to the end, training is an essential part of the officer's job.

10

Training, Development, and Deployment of Human Resources

After completing this chapter, readers should be able to:

- define *training* and compare three types of training used by police agencies (basic preservice training, on-the-job or field training, and in-service or continuous professional training).

- examine how training can be augmented by higher education.

- define *development* and appraise the forms it can take; specifically, career planning, leadership development programs, and succession planning.

- define *deployment* and assess the processes police agencies use for deployment; namely, strategic or task assignments, workforce scheduling, and assembly and use of working groups.

Introduction

A police agency is made up of human beings who uniquely influence citizens' everyday lives. Officers and citizens interact with one another frequently, so the ways in which an agency trains, develops, and deploys its human resources can make or break the quality of those interactions. Compelling evidence suggests that these three personnel practices—when applied effectively—greatly reduce the probability that officers will be involved in misconduct (Hughes & Andre, 2007).

But effective training, development, and deployment require an agency culture that emphasizes learning and growth. Unfortunately, many police agencies exhibit a culture that promotes a sense of entitlement instead. Entitlement culture derives from certain civil service rules (such as nonprobationary status and disciplinary procedures); guarantees of retirement benefits based on years of service and percentages of annual income; and contractual union requirements such as guarantee of union legal representation, mandated disciplinary processes, and assignment preference based on seniority.

There is good news, however: Many police agencies are seeking to foster a culture of learning and growth rather than entitlement (Tichy, 1997). Agencies striving toward this new direction define staff training, development, and deployment as top priorities while continuing to provide the swift and effective responses to crises and calls-for-service that the public expects.

In this chapter, we explore these three crucial personnel practices in detail. We begin with *training*, the imparting or enhancing of specific knowledge or skills to police personnel—including types of training, the role of licensing boards and commissions in training, and the question of how higher education can augment training. We then move to the subject of *development*, or the enhancing of police personnel's knowledge, skills, and abilities (KSAs) through ongoing career experiences. We examine three core forms of development: career planning, leadership development programs, and succession planning. Finally, we take a close look at *deployment*—how a police agency puts its human resources to use through strategic project or job assignment, scheduling, and the assembly of working groups.

TRAINING: DEVELOPING SKILLS AND PREPARING FOR POLICE WORK

Some people argue that the terms *training* and *education* are synonymous, but those who train and educate may disagree. As a rule, **training** encompasses knowledge and skill development and the kind of on-the-job preparation found in policing. **Education** involves learning and comprehending concepts as well as developing problem-solving and critical thinking skills through a school, college, or university experience.

Training: knowledge and skill development and on-the-job preparation.

Education: the learning of concepts and development of problem-solving and critical thinking skills through a school, college, or university experience.

Firearms training is a regular part of an officer's in-service training regimen.

Most police academies strive to blend training with education, since police officers use job-related as well as critical thinking skills during the course of their employment. For instance, training in firearms usage and safety is skill based, conducted at a location (a firing range) specifically designed for this purpose. But officers can gain an education in firearms usage and safety (as well as other knowledge areas crucial to their jobs) through college-level courses, seminars, and other educational opportunities.

Much of a police officer's training is skill and abilities oriented.

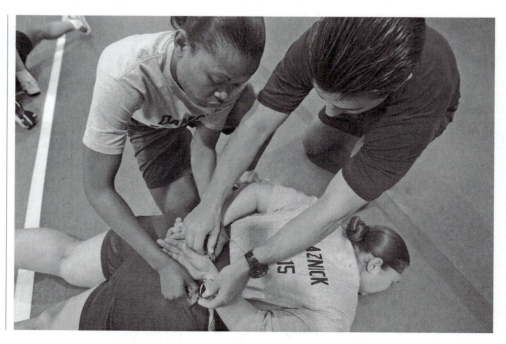

Teaching adult learners—including police officers—is vastly different from teaching high school and traditional college-age students. Adult learners have more life experience and are generally better informed than younger students. Mature learners expect to apply what they learn, and they may have different learning styles. For example, one person may learn more effectively by watching others carry out tasks, while another learns best by reading instructions. By providing different types of training activities, an agency can deliver experiences that accommodate many different learning styles.

Types of Training

Police officers undergo extensive training before they become tenured officers and they continue their training while they are on the job. Training can take numerous forms. In the following pages, we examine the most common and important types of training, including basic preservice training, on-the-job (field) training, and in-service (continuous professional) training.

Basic Preservice Training   Recruits who are assessed and hired (see Chapter 8) begin **basic preservice training.** This training, usually provided at a police academy, introduces recruits to police work and provides an overview of the justice system, including the roles of the police, courts, and corrections agencies. The curriculum also includes physical fitness, report writing, criminal and motor vehicle laws and procedures, rules of evidence, search and seizure, communications, patrol strategies, arrest procedures, firearms training, and basic investigations. (See Table 10-1.)

Some police jurisdictions provide basic preservice training through an academy serving that one jurisdiction. Others have a different academy structure. For instance, many states and rural areas have centralized academy facilities that serve

Basic preservice training: academy-based training that introduces recruits to police work, provides an overview of the justice system, and includes classes on specific skills and knowledge areas related to police work.

Recruits at the San Diego County Sheriff's Training Academy engaged in physical fitness training.

table 10-1 Sample Academy Curriculum

Although the length and subject areas of preservice training programs may vary, all such programs address the basic knowledge, skills, and abilities (KSAs) a police officer should possess and demonstrate. As an example of preservice training, the state-established minimum requirements for California police academy content (learning domains) and hourly requirements are presented below. Most California police academies exceed the minimum content and hourly requirements.

DOMAIN NUMBER	DOMAIN DESCRIPTION	MINIMUM HOURS	DOMAIN NUMBER	DOMAIN DESCRIPTION	MINIMUM HOURS
01	Leadership, Professionalism, & Ethics	8 hours	27	Missing Persons	4 hours
02	Criminal Justice System	2 hours	28	Traffic Enforcement	16 hours
03	Policing in the Community	18 hours	29	Traffic Collision Investigations	12 hours
04	Victimology/Crisis Intervention	6 hours	30	Crime Scenes, Evidence, and Forensics	12 hours
05	Introduction to Criminal Law	4 hours	31	Custody	2 hours
06	Property Crimes	6 hours	32	Lifetime Fitness	44 hours
07	Crimes against Persons/Death Investigation	6 hours	33	Arrest Methods/Defensive Tactics	60 hours
08	General Criminal Statutes	2 hours	34	First Aid and CPR	21 hours
09	Crimes against Children	4 hours	35	Firearms/Chemical Agents	72 hours
10	Sex Crimes	4 hours	36	Information Systems	2 hours
11	Juvenile Law and Procedure	3 hours	37	People with Disabilities	6 hours
12	Controlled Substances	12 hours	38	Gang Awareness	2 hours
13	ABC Law	2 hours	39	Crimes against the Justice System	4 hours
15	Laws of Arrest	12 hours	40	Weapons Violations	4 hours
16	Search and Seizure	12 hours	41	Hazardous Materials Awareness	4 hours
17	Presentation of Evidence	6 hours	42	Cultural Diversity/Discrimination	16 hours
18	Investigative Report Writing	52 hours	43	Emergency Management	16 hours
19	Vehicle Operations	24 hours		Minimum Instructional Hours	560 hours
20	Use of Force	12 hours		The minimum number of hours allocated to testing are shown below	
21	Patrol Techniques	12 hours			
22	Vehicle Pullovers	14 hours		Scenario Tests (40 hours test administration; 18 hours Scenario Demonstration)	58 hours
23	Crimes in Progress	20 hours			
24	Handling Disputes/Crowd Control	8 hours		Written Tests (25 hours test administration; 15 hours examination review)	40 hours
25	Domestic Violence	10 hours			
26	Unusual Occurrences	4 hours		Exercise Tests (Physical Skills Pilot Tests)	6 hours
				Total Minimum Required Hours	664 hours

Source: California Commission on Peace Officer Standards and Training, 2009.

numerous agencies in the region. Small jurisdictions send their recruits to one of these centralized academy facilities.

The curriculum of most police academies falls into two categories: conceptual and practical. Conceptual courses may cover topics such as leadership, ethics, the writings of Sir Robert Peel, and the use of force. Courses focused on practical application may concentrate on skill areas such as firearms use, defensive tactics, vehicle operations, and conflict management. (See Table 10-2.)

table 10-2   Police Academy Statistics

In 2006, the U.S. Bureau of Justice Statistics (BJS) conducted a census of state and local law enforcement training academies. The *2006 BJS Census of Law Enforcement Training Academies* findings included the following:

- Basic training programs averaged 19 weeks in length.
- Topics with the most instruction time included firearms (median of 60 hours), self-defense (51 hours), health and fitness (46 hours), patrol procedures (40 hours), investigations (40 hours), emergency vehicle operations (40 hours), criminal law (36 hours), and basic first aid (24 hours).
- Of an estimated 57,000 recruits who entered basic training programs during 2005, 86 percent successfully completed the program and graduated from the academy.
- Academies with a predominately nonstress (academic) orientation (89 percent) experienced a higher completion rate than academies with a predominately stress (paramilitary) orientation (80 percent) (U.S. Bureau of Justice Statistics, 2009).

To reflect changes in regulations, American culture, and politics, today's police officer should be required to master several topics in addition to the traditional subjects covered in basic preservice training. These include the following:

- **Leadership:** Leadership development should begin in the police academy, where recruits are first introduced to the policing profession; the role of personal and organizational leadership; and the concepts of power, authority, and legitimate influence of others. At the academy, instructors must emphasize motivational leadership—the ability to influence others to do what the leader wants because it is also what the people want.
- **Civil liability law:** Gone are the days when line and command officers viewed the use of force as standard procedure. Today, any officer who uses force may come under intensive scrutiny by command officers and legal representatives to determine whether the situation justified the degree of force used. And if a police officer uses physical force—especially deadly force—the victim or victim's family will likely file a civil lawsuit against the officer as well as the agency. (See Chapter 13 for more information on legal issues in policing.)
- **Agency relations:** During basic preservice training, police recruits must also learn which agencies are responsible for which services offered to the community. For instance, when a fire breaks out in an apartment building, police, fire service, and emergency medical services (EMS) personnel will be dispatched to the scene. Everyone involved must know who is in charge of which activities, such as administering CPR, interviewing witnesses, and suppressing the fire.
- **Terrorism:** Since September 11, 2001, the federal government has mandated that police academies provide training in how to handle mass casualties and what to do during and after a terrorist attack. The U.S. Department of Homeland Security also offers similar training and other support to state and local police agencies to accomplish its objective of preparing first responders.
- **Cultural diversity:** The United States has always been home to diverse populations. Thus many police agencies serve communities in which residents

vary widely in ethnic background, religious belief, economic circumstances, and other characteristics. A police officer's primary mission is to protect and serve *all* people, regardless of such differences. Cultural diversity training can help officers learn to recognize and respect these and other differences. For instance, many recent immigrants hail from countries where citizens fear and mistrust the police. When they witness or become victims of a crime, they may be too frightened to talk with officers about the incident. By understanding this particular cultural legacy, officers can use verbal and nonverbal communication to reassure witnesses or victims that the police are there to help, and thereby overcome their fears. Cultural diversity training cannot entirely eliminate any biases an individual officer may have toward members of specific groups; however, it can help the officer appreciate differences and understand why people from different cultures, ethnic backgrounds, or socioeconomic standing behave as they do. The bottom line is that police officers must strive to treat all citizens with respect and civility (Police Executive Research Forum, 2004), and cultural diversity training can help them fulfill this responsibility.

Finally, some police academies emphasize *military-style stress programs*. Although instructors must evaluate a recruit's ability to handle stressful situations, obedience-oriented, military-style basic training may be detrimental to the learning process and inconsistent with actual civilian police work. Military-style marching and over-emphasis of uncritical obedience has little value in the performance of modern-day police tasks. Stress-related training in police academies should simulate the actual occupational environment of police officers (City of Los Angeles, 2003; Goldstein, 2001; Meese & Ortmeier, 2004), thus it should be used only to assess a recruit's ability to respond and exercise effective judgment in stressful situations encountered on the job.

On-the-Job (Field) Training   After successfully completing the basic preservice academy program, a recruit typically enters on-the-job (field) training under the direct supervision of a senior officer or designated **field training officer (FTO)**. The FTO uses a field training guide (a manual) to instruct the recruit and document the person's progress. The **field training program** focuses on the KSAs required of a police officer on the job. FTOs must assess how recruits apply what they learned in the academy to real-world contexts, placing special emphasis on recruits' ability to relate to victims, suspects, citizens, groups, and persons within the agency, including fellow officers and command staff. The relationship between a recruit and the FTO can be quite close, with the FTO serving as a mentor and role model for the recruit.

Field training officer (FTO): a knowledgeable, seasoned, and competent officer trained in adult education and evaluation procedures, who supervises recruits' on-the-job (field) training.

Field training program: training that focuses on the knowledge, skills, and abilities (KSAs) required of a police officer on the job.

FTOs should be knowledgeable, competent, and seasoned officers trained in adult education and evaluation procedures. During field training, the FTO sets the pace and takes the lead, allowing the new officer to slowly assume more duties of a full-time seasoned officer. By the end of the field training program, the new officer should be performing 100 percent of a police officer's duties and responsibilities. The FTO writes a formal report that highlights the probationary officer's strengths, weaknesses, and level of competence in subject-matter areas and performance, and submits it to a command officer.

The probationary officer's training continues for several months, during which the individual works alone but is guided by a first-line supervisor who monitors performance, provides remedial training for performance shortfalls or knowledge gaps, and prepares and submits monthly evaluations. Upon successful completion of the probationary period, the individual becomes a tenured full-time sworn officer.

Unlike basic preservice training methodology, field training methodology varies considerably. Many police agencies (as well as academies and continuous professional training efforts) use *progressive training programs*, which emphasize scenario- and problem-based learning. An example of such programs is California's basic academy and field training format. The goal is to help probationary officers develop critical thinking, problem-solving, and ethical leadership abilities.

On-the-job training with a certified field training officer (FTO) or supervisor is part of a recruit's training protocol.

In-Service (Continuous Professional) Training Like lawyers and doctors, police practitioners must not only maintain but also periodically update their skills. They can do so through **in-service continuous professional training (CPT)**. State commissions on peace officer standards and training, as well as police agencies, prescribe in-service training subject areas and specify hourly requirements. Mandatory in-service training typically focuses on legal updates, technological advances, and refresher training related to perishable skills such as CPR, use of force, firearms, defensive tactics, tactical communications, report writing, and vehicle operations.

CPT can also be optional. Such training may address counterterrorism, fraudulent document recognition, or the role of the FTO, or may help officers prepare for promotion. For instance, many police agencies as well as licensing authorities provide officer training programs in supervision, leadership, and promotion exam preparation. (See the box "The Role of Licensing Boards and Commissions in Officer Training.")

Additional optional CPT examples include training specifically associated with traffic safety management. Such training may cover commercial vehicle code enforcement as well as driving under the influence (DUI) or driving while intoxicated (DWI) detection, field sobriety testing, and breath analyzer operations. Training specific to youth services may include juvenile delinquency and drug abuse resistance education (DARE) for schoolchildren and their parents.

In-service training is usually conducted by certified or proficient instructors who are experts in the subject matter being taught. It may be offered on a semiannual or annual basis, and may be provided for individuals, teams, or entire departments. For instance, an officer who wants or needs to know more about cultural diversity may receive customized training. Or members of a police agency's K9 team (officers and their dogs) may participate in workshops on canine handling and task performance.

In-service continuous professional training (CPT): training designed to enable police practitioners to maintain and periodically update their skills.

ETHICS IN ACTION

Is Ethics Training Necessary?

One autumn morning, Sergeant Philip Ross placed his 9mm handgun into his waist band and walked into the woods behind his home. Ross thought of his wife, his daughter, and a close family of fellow officers he was leaving behind. A note in his pocket read, "I'm sorry, please forgive me." A New Jersey grand jury indictment bearing his name was attached to the note.

Ross had been indicted for lying to strengthen a criminal case against a major drug dealer. He lied by claiming in an investigative report that drugs found in the dealer's home were the fruit of a search warrant. In fact, the drugs were uncovered during a protective sweep before the search warrant was issued, rendering the search illegal and the drugs inadmissible as evidence.

Ross's wife discovered that her husband had left the house. She ran into the woods and found Ross in time to stop him from committing suicide. The two returned home and drove to the courthouse so Ross could face his criminal charge. Later, Ross said, "For years I trained . . . firearms, tactics, officer safety, and in the end I destroyed my own career and almost my life with one stupid decision" (Sutton, 2006). Sergeant Ross's statement implies that he received training to prepare him for the physical dangers of police work, but not the dangers that come with ethical dilemmas.

1. Why might ethics training in police work be as important as skills training?

2. Using what you have learned about ethics in previous chapters, design an ethics curriculum for police recruits.

Officers engaged in a refresher in-service training course in the use of force and defensive tactics.

The Role of Licensing Boards and Commissions in Officer Training

State-based licensing boards and peace officer standards and training (POST) commissions set minimum selection and training standards for officers. Participating agencies agree to operate according to the standards established by POST. The licensing authorities provide technical assistance, services, and benefits such as job task assessment tools, research to improve officer selection standards, management consulting services, reimbursement for training, and supervisory or leadership development programs.

In conjunction with subject-matter experts (SMEs), who determine what subject matter will be taught, licensing boards and commissions modify basic preservice and in-service training curricula and develop new courses as the need arises. POST commissions certify trainers, issue professional certificates in recognition of officer achievement and proficiency, and maintain a centralized database of individual officers' training records. Because most states mandate in-service as well as basic preservice training of officers, the state-based licensing authorities also monitor officers' in-service training requirements and participation.

Augmenting Training with Higher Education

As you read in Chapter 8, study results indicate that police officers who possess a college education bring numerous forms of value to the job. For example, they exercise better judgment and understanding of government and its processes than officers without a college degree, and they are more creative and less rigid when facing difficult (especially stressful) situations. College-educated officers demonstrate greater empathy toward others, are more communicative, are less authoritarian and ego-centered, and are more participative and engaging (Bostrom, 2005; Friedmann, 2006).

Convinced by such studies, many police agencies have begun offering incentives to officers for advancing their formal education after beginning their careers. These incentives may take the form of tuition reimbursement, promotion points, or higher salaries. Numerous agencies also require undergraduate and graduate degrees for advancement to the highest administrative positions. Officers must achieve a certain educational level to be eligible to take the requisite test before being considered for promotion.

To develop a culture in which everyone in a police agency values higher learning, agency leaders must send a clear message that higher education defines the professional police officer. They must explain how higher education benefits officers, the agency, and the community. Finally, they must reinforce the message by promoting such officers as well as involving them in the agency's plans and decisions.

DEVELOPMENT: ENHANCING OFFICERS' KNOWLEDGE, SKILLS, AND ABILITIES (KSAs)

Development of personal and professional KSAs is as important as training for every police officer because it contributes to officers' lifelong learning and growth. Development can take several forms, including career planning, leadership development programs, and succession planning.

Career Planning for an Aspiring Police Sergeant

Patrick, a 10-year veteran police officer, would like to become a police supervisor but has not earned scores high enough on the sergeant's exam oral boards to be considered for the promotion. He requests help from his agency's training department. Training personnel inform him that the next sergeant's exam is in 10 months. They advise him to prepare for the exam by attending training sessions on leadership as well as communication and presentation skills, and by reviewing articles, books, and research papers on these topics. They also suggest that he join a local public-speaking club to further strengthen his skills. A sergeant from the training department promises to contact Patrick in a week to follow up and to establish a master plan for reaching Patrick's goal.

Career Planning

Career plan: a document describing a police officer's personal career vision; a timetable for action; and detailed descriptions of any training, education, and career steps necessary to complete the plan.

The career plan for every police officer begins when the candidate completes an employment application and ends with each individual's retirement from the law profession. A police officer's **career plan** may result from a formal department protocol or an informal process through which the officer creates the plan with or without assistance. (See the box "Career Planning for an Aspiring Police Sergeant.") Regardless of how it comes about, the plan should include a personal career vision; a timetable for action; and detailed descriptions of any training, education, and career steps necessary to carry out the plan.

In-service training is a useful place to begin planning for an officer's career because it focuses the officer's and supervisors' attention on the KSAs the individual must develop to handle critical job areas such as firearms, defensive tactics, ethics, leadership, and legal updates. To strengthen particular KSAs through in-service

Many police officers enhance their career opportunities by continuing their formal college education.

Miami, Florida, officers take part in a certification program graduation ceremony of the Canine (K9) Academy in 2007.

training, officers might take advantage of seminars on particular topics, computer-based training, and formal training experiences. Self-directed learning can also prove valuable. This type of learning might take several forms, including reading police journals, training bulletins, legal updates, study guides for promotions, and police websites. Officers can also complete formal coursework or audit college courses.

To further develop their careers, officers can also take advantage of training and certification programs that focus on special areas of police work—such as evidence collection procedures, special weapons and tactics, canine or scuba operations, or equestrian (mounted) or motorcycle patrol. Subject-matter certifications are also available for collision investigation, explosive devices, and hazardous materials.

Certification in any of these special topics may require a part-time or full-time commitment from the officer. For example, background investigator and FTO training prepares officers for part-time department commitments during the hiring process. A full-time commitment may be necessary for other positions, such as evidence technician or equestrian officer.

A career plan should include informal enrichment opportunities in addition to formal ones. For instance, officers can seize advantage of opportunities to learn on the job—by observing crime-scene procedures, interrogation practices, or the trial process. Or they may obtain instructor status with the agency or fill an adjunct faculty position at a local educational institution. Officers can also develop their careers through formal advancement through the agency's ranks or by securing a special assignment such as public relations officer, aid to the chief, or crime analyst. Lateral transfers to another municipal, county, state, or federal agency can provide additional career-development experiences.

Regardless of the specifics laid out in an officer's career plan, the plan should contain a feedback process through which a mentor or supervisor provides timely information on the officer's progress, as well as a follow-up component through which the officer can expect a review and update to the plan (Gravenkemper, 2008). However, no officer should leave a career plan to fate. Officers must take ownership of their plans and shoulder the responsibility for creating and regularly updating their plans.

Leadership Development Programs

All officers in a police agency can benefit from learning how to lead—that is, how to influence, motivate, guide, and direct. This includes *front-line personnel*—the line-level officers who patrol the jurisdiction, whether on bicycles, horses, or foot, or in a vehicle, boat, or aircraft. But until recently, leadership training for front-line officers was not a major concern in most agencies, because line officers were viewed as call takers, report writers, and crime fighters. Promotions were based on civil service or other tests that focused on the officer's potential to move into a supervisory position. There were virtually no leadership development strategies for line-level police personnel (Jurkanin et al., 2001; Ortmeier, 1995; Polisar, 2004).

Fortunately, this situation has begun to change, as police officers and agencies are called on to be more accountable for their actions within the department and the community. More agencies value leadership at all ranks and have begun providing leadership development programs at all levels, including front-line personnel. The best agencies treat leadership development as an ongoing effort for all police officers—supporting that effort through their communications to the organization and the community, and through their resource-allocation decisions. By making it clear that top management values leadership competencies in personnel throughout the agency, managers encourage officers at every level to embrace this priority.

At first glance, it may appear that leadership development for front-line officers is not as important as training in other subject matter. But consider these two scenarios:

- **Scenario 1: Responding to a possible domestic violence incident.** Robert, a patrol officer, responds to a frantic phone call from a woman who says that her husband has threatened to kill her. When Robert arrives, no other officers are present. The woman opens the door, and Robert can see an agitated man pacing back and forth behind her in the kitchen. Robert is the only voice of authority for the incident. He must function as a leader—for example, by embodying calm in a situation where emotions are running high, and by accurately and swiftly taking stock of the situation. (For instance, does the man have a weapon? Is there a history of domestic abuse in this household? How likely is it that the man will follow through on his threat?) If Robert cannot or will not step into the role of leader, the conflict may escalate quickly, compromising the safety of everyone present. Or if Robert misreads the situation (for example, by concluding that the man is not likely to follow through on his threat), things may take a violent turn after he leaves the premises.

- **Scenario 2: Stopping a motorist for a traffic violation.** Pauline, an on-duty officer, is driving along a busy roadway and sees a motorist speed through a red light. She decides to pull the motorist over, investigate the situation, and determine how to respond. To do all this, Pauline must exercise an array of leadership skills to ensure everyone's safety during this event. For example, she needs to select a safe place, out of the way of other traffic, for her and the motorist to pull over. She must approach the driver's side door from a safe angle, request his license and registration, and inform him of the violation. She should determine what caused the behavior. (For instance, did the motorist simply not see the red light? Is there an emergency that caused the person to ignore the light?) She will also need to radio in his license and registration information to see whether he has a record of criminal activity or whether the vehicle he is driving has been stolen. While she is doing all this, Pauline will be gathering additional information, such as whether the vehicle's inspection sticker is up-to-date. At each point during this process, Pauline will need to exercise judgment, communicate effectively, and make decisions based on the information she is collecting—all activities that require strong leadership skills.

Leadership development in a police environment may take the form of classes or seminars that help people identify leadership attributes based on personalities or master leadership behaviors through role plays and other exercises. Supervisors can also coach employees in the improvement of traits and skills that characterize excellent leadership—such as the ability to attract followers, to provide focus and direction, and to strengthen their organization through their efforts (Monteith, 2007). (See Chapter 11 for a focused analysis of leadership.)

Line-level officers who develop their leadership competencies will begin demonstrating specific new behaviors and attitudes. They will earn citizens' respect and loyalty, so people *want* to follow them. They will communicate effectively, persuasively, and with empathy to colleagues and community members. They will know what the agency's mission is and how officers' everyday activities can support fulfillment of that mission. If the police agency is committed to community partnering and problem solving, police officer-leaders will understand what these concepts mean, how they inform their interactions with community residents, and how to motivate citizens to participate in addressing the problems affecting them.

Leadership on the job

Training versus Action

On September 3, 2006, a 23-year-old off-duty rookie police officer shot and wounded a professional football player after an early-morning vehicle chase. The officer, out of uniform and driving his own car, followed the player, suspecting that he was driving under the influence of alcohol or drugs. During the pursuit, the officer notified on-duty colleagues while flashing his headlights in an attempt to stop the other driver. When the pursuit ended in a residential cul-de-sac, the athlete left his vehicle and approached the off-duty officer—who shot him twice, wounding him in the back of the left knee and hip. In July 2008, the city that employed the officer agreed to pay $5.5 million to settle a lawsuit initiated by the player. During the civil trial leading to the "no-fault" settlement, the officer conceded that his actions (pursuing a suspect while off duty in his own vehicle) during the incident were inconsistent with the training he had received in the police academy.

1. How can agency leaders ensure that police actions will be consistent with the training that recruits receive?

2. Describe how the off-duty officer did or did not use leadership skills effectively. What would you have done differently in this situation?

Succession Planning

In addition to providing career planning and leadership development programs, police agencies must engage in succession planning to further develop employees' competencies and ensure that the right talent can be deployed when it is needed. **Succession planning** ensures that adequate qualified personnel are available to replace those who vacate positions through promotion, transfer, retirement, termination, or agency expansion.

Through succession planning, an agency identifies and grooms people to fill vacant positions within the organization, taking into account how well a prospect's personality, knowledge, skill level, and attitudes render the individual suitable for the position (Human Capital Advisor, 2005). Agencies skilled at succession planning hire, promote, and transfer employees to new assignments or temporary positions in a manner consistent with the agency's vision, mission, and goals. Almost continuously, they fill positions from inside the organization through promotion or reassignment or externally through hiring. For example, an agency might fill vacant positions through promotional testing or appointment by the hiring authority, often the chief, commissioner, or sheriff. It may also staff special assignments and short-term projects by using an internal selection process. For example, managers might know that an officer has experience with or education in public relations and thus might function well as the agency's public information officer.

For key positions and assignments, an agency should develop a three- to five-year succession plan. Thus, this kind of planning requires patience and care. To ensure successful staffing of critical positions, agencies must select and retain the right people for these positions; identify and promote the best performers; motivate and train employees; help them acquire or strengthen the skills needed to achieve desirable results; and prepare employees to move into new, more challenging positions (Succession Planning 101, 2007).

To do all this, agency managers assess the behaviors and attitudes required of potential candidates for specific positions and then determine which candidates fulfill or have the potential to meet those requirements. An effective succession plan paves the way for the agency to promote people with the KSAs needed for particular roles (LaPla & Gravenkemper, 2007) and to groom promising individuals to take on new roles.

To groom individuals to assume specialty, supervisory, and command assignments, an agency provides developmental opportunities, educational incentives, and leadership skills training. For example, officers take on increasingly challenging responsibilities through job rotation, community service, and special project assignments (AME Info, 2007). By developing their personal and professional skills through these experiences, officers ready themselves to move into roles where they will provide the most value for the community the agency serves.

DEPLOYMENT: PUTTING HUMAN RESOURCES TO THE BEST USE

Deployment of human resources is the process of placing the right person in the right job or on the right tasks or projects, according to a candidate's strengths, weaknesses, and KSAs—as well as interests. A police agency can determine how best to deploy its human resources by using three processes: strategic project or task assignments,

Succession planning: activities intended to ensure that adequate qualified personnel are available to replace those who vacate positions through promotion, transfer, retirement, termination, or agency expansion.

Deployment of human resources: the process of placing the right person in the right job or on the right tasks or projects, according to a candidate's strengths, weaknesses, knowledge, skills, and abilities (KSAs)—as well as interests.

workforce scheduling, and assembly and use of working groups.

Strategic Project or Task Assignments

Through strategic *project or task assignments*, a police agency determines its needs and matches the right personnel—based on KSAs as well as interests—to projects and job assignments so needs are met. For example, agency leaders determine who is most suitable for the SWAT team and who is best suited for a project that involves extensive collaboration with community leaders. Or they identify officers who excel at and enjoy interacting

Emergency services (SWAT) team members in action.

with members of the community, and assign them to efforts that require relationship building. Meanwhile, they assign officers with a strong desire to combat crime to initiatives emphasizing law enforcement.

When an agency makes a good match between a person's KSAs and interests and a job or project, employees are more motivated and productive, and they derive greater satisfaction from their work. All this translates into better performance and stronger loyalty to the agency. These benefits in turn lead to more satisfied community residents and lower costs for the agency, as managers do not have to recruit and train new hires to replace defectors.

Yet proper placement of a deserving individual is not always easy. Seniority rules and union contracts often prescribe who is eligible for special assignments or promotions. Agency leaders must work within those constraints in seeking to match the right people to the right types of work. For example, progressive agencies generally negotiate with their police representative bodies to agree that seniority will be the deciding factor if all other requirements for a position are equal between employees interested in the job. Those requirements may include physical fitness standards and a positive disciplinary record for entrance to (for instance) a SWAT or K9 handler position. Requirements for a firearms police instructor position may include an above-average score on past qualifying firearms tests, demonstrations of necessary standards of physical fitness, a firearms instructor certification, and a history of assisting or instructing classes or individuals in various topics (such as training volunteers for organizations like the Red Cross).

Workforce Scheduling

In addition to knowing whom to assign to which projects and tasks, agency managers must also engage in smart workforce scheduling. Through *workforce scheduling*,

table 10-3 Sample 8-Hour Shift Schedule		
Shift A	2230 hours to 0730 hours	(10:30 p.m. to 7:30 a.m.)
Shift B	0630 hours to 1530 hours	(6:30 a.m. to 3:30 p.m.)
Shift C	1430 hours to 2330 hours	(2:30 p.m. to 11:30 p.m.)
Shift D*	1830 hours to 0330 hours	(6:30 p.m. to 3:30 a.m.)

*Optional D shift for peak activity period.

the agency determines how many people are required for particular assignments and how much time they should devote to the work. A needs assessment can help managers develop a workforce schedule. For instance, if an assignment (area or post) requires continuous patrol or staffing (24 hours per day, 7 days per week), about 4.5 full-time equivalent (FTE) officers will be required to cover that assignment. This estimate accounts for vacations, holidays, and sick leave, but not overtime.

A needs assessment should also reveal an assignment's estimated workload. For example, information on the number of calls for police service, types of calls, time requirement per call, and backup officer requirement frequency can help the agency determine how many officers are needed to adequately staff a service area (such as a beat or a district). The most effective workforce scheduling maximizes coverage and service quality while minimizing resources required.

Agencies typically schedule three 8-hour shifts to ensure 24-hour coverage. Managers may add a fourth shift to cover daily peak activity periods. The resulting schedule will take into account meal breaks and roll calls. (See Table 10-3.)

To improve morale and reduce overtime and sick-leave abuse, some agencies schedule three 10-hour shifts designed to overlap during peak periods. Fewer officers are required for each shift, yet a greater number are available during peak periods. Officers work four 10-hour shifts, with three days off. (See Table 10-4.)

A few agencies schedule 12.5-hour shifts. With this arrangement, officers work three or four days each week, alternating every seven-day period. The 12.5-hour shift arrangement necessitates only two shift changes every 24 hours. Decreasing the number of shift changes typically reduces personnel costs. However, some might also argue that long shifts introduce inefficiency because officers tire and therefore become less productive toward the end of the shift. Further, tired officers can become careless, and with carelessness comes the risk of poor judgment and mistakes, which can lead to use of excessive force, mistreatment of citizens, and even officer injuries or fatalities (Ortmeier, 1999, 2009; Payton & Amaral, 2004).

Scheduling personnel in policing and other public safety environments can be extremely complex and labor intensive. Collective bargaining rules, seniority systems,

table 10-4 Sample 10-Hour Shift Schedule		
Shift A	2400 hours to 1000 hours	(midnight to 10:00 a.m.)
Shift B	0800 hours to 1800 hours	(8:00 a.m. to 6:00 p.m.)
Shift C	1600 hours to 0200 hours	(4:00 p.m. to 2:00 a.m.)
Shift D*	1700 hours to 0300 hours	(5:00 p.m. to 3:00 a.m.)

*Shift D optional.

A typical shift change at a police agency.

assignment variations, unforeseen emergencies, and around-the-clock operations complicate the process. However, technological advancements—such as commercially available software programs—can make scheduling easier. Moreover, police managers must keep in mind that scheduling should not be based solely on the number and nature of calls-for-service. They also need to take into account the agency's mission, goals, and budgetary constraints when establishing a workforce schedule. For example, an agency that is prevention oriented may opt to assign police personnel to a neighborhood even though residents issue only infrequent calls-for-service. This strategy would not only maintain the neighborhood's safety, it would also enable the police to respond quickly to any calls-for-service that do arise.

Working Groups

A third valuable deployment practice is the assembly and use of working groups. Such groups are assigned to meet specific needs and can be permanent or temporary (existing for a specified number of days, weeks, or months.) Working groups can take three forms: teams, task forces, and police–community partnerships.

Teams   A **team** consists of a group of people who receive specialized training and use that training to address a specific incident. Teams are relatively permanent. For instance, an agency summons its SWAT team to respond to a situation in which an armed suspect has seized several hostages and is barricaded in a building. The agency charges the scuba team with recovering a body or a vehicle submerged in water. It calls on the bomb squad or hazardous-materials disposal team to investigate and dispose of a suspicious package or toxic substance. It deploys the emotionally disturbed person response team (EDPRT) to help a citizen who is threatening suicide. Or it calls on the gang unit to investigate and address the escalation of gang-related violence in a particular neighborhood.

Team:
a group of people who receive specialized training and use that training to address a specific incident.

A police scuba team preparing to dive to retrieve a body.

Task force: a temporary working group assembled to address a specific problem or manage a particular event requiring specialized expertise.

Police–community partnerships: collaborations between officers and community citizens to address citizens' concerns.

Task Forces   A task force is a temporary working group assembled to address a specific problem or manage an event requiring specialized expertise. The group may include an array of specialists from different agencies who pool their diverse knowledge and skills to address a specific need. For instance, a task force might be assembled to provide security in a city that is expecting a visit from the U.S. president, or to determine how to reduce prostitution or drug dealing in a particular neighborhood.

Most people are familiar with task forces through high-profile serial-murder cases. Washington State's Green River Killer is one example. In this case, the King County Sheriff's Office assembled a task force in the early 1980s comprising several detectives, a criminal profiling expert, and the sheriff himself to pursue leads and to apprehend what seemed to be a serial killer. The task force's work led to identification of Gary Ridgeway as a suspect in 1983. It took many years to compile enough evidence to arrest Ridgeway, which police did in 2001. Ridgeway pleaded guilty to 48 charges of aggravated first-degree murder as part of a plea bargain that would spare him execution in return for his cooperation in providing information about his remaining victims. He was sentenced to life in prison.

Police–Community Partnerships   Police–community partnerships often stem from an agency's decision to use a community policing strategy. (See Chapter 2.) In fact, engagement with citizens to form collaborative partnerships is essential to any worthwhile community policing and problem-solving effort. How do such partnerships work? Here is an example: Leaders of a community become concerned about the lack of a safe play area for children. They alert the police, who join forces with community members to develop and implement a solution. The police and community ultimately decide to have neighborhood volunteers supervise the children at play.

Many police–community partnerships focus on noncriminal quality-of-life problems experienced by the community the agency serves. For instance, police might bring together members of diverse populations in the community to brainstorm and implement ideas for making the streets safer in the community overall, especially if recreational facilities, playgrounds, parks, and similar venues are not available, leaving the streets the only place where children may congregate and play.

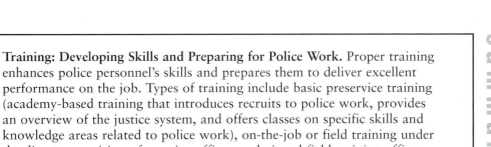

A Washington State Green River Task Force member ponders investigative strategy.

- **Training: Developing Skills and Preparing for Police Work.** Proper training enhances police personnel's skills and prepares them to deliver excellent performance on the job. Types of training include basic preservice training (academy-based training that introduces recruits to police work, provides an overview of the justice system, and offers classes on specific skills and knowledge areas related to police work), on-the-job or field training under the direct supervision of a senior officer or designed field training officer (FTO), and in-service or continuous professional training, which enables police practitioners to maintain and periodically update their skills. Many police agencies are augmenting training with higher education; for example, by offering incentives to officers for advancing their formal education after beginning their careers.

- **Development: Enhancing Officers' Knowledge, Skills, and Abilities (KSAs).** Development contributes to officers' lifelong learning and growth. It can take several forms, including career planning (articulating an officer's career vision, developing a timetable for action, and describing any training, education, and career steps needed to complete the plan); leadership development programs (which teach officers how to influence, motivate, guide, direct, and make decisions; and succession planning (which comprises activities intended to ensure that adequate qualified personnel are available to replace those who vacate positions through promotion, transfer, retirement, termination, or agency expansion).

- **Deployment: Putting Human Resources to the Best Use.** Deployment is the process of placing the right person in the right job or on the right tasks or projects, according to an individual's strengths, weaknesses, KSAs, as well as interests and the needs of the police agency. An agency deploys personnel using several processes. These include strategic project or task assignment (determining the agency's needs and matching the right personnel to projects and job assignments so those needs are met), workforce scheduling (determining how many people are required for particular assignments and how much time they should devote to the work), and assembly and use of working groups such as teams, task forces, and police–community partnerships.

key terms

basic preservice training
career plan
police–community partnerships
deployment of human resources
education
field training officer (FTO)
field training program

in-service continuous professional training (CPT)
succession planning
task force
team
training

discussion questions

1. The training process for new police officers consists of more than classroom lectures and tests. How do the three types of training described in this chapter (basic pre-service, on-the-job or field, and in-service or continuous professional) differ in their focus and purpose?

2. Basic preservice training is a crucial part of a new police officer's learning. What are some examples of the subject areas traditionally covered in police academy curricula? What are some special topics now covered during basic preservice training because of changes in regulations, American culture, and politics?

3. How does development differ from training? Select one of the three forms of development described in this chapter (career planning, leadership development programs, and success planning). What are the key defining elements of the development form you selected? How does the form differ in its purpose from the other two forms?

4. Why is it important for line officers to develop leadership skills? Think of a scenario (not one of the scenarios presented in this chapter) in which an officer would need to demonstrate leadership. What skills would the officer need to exercise in the scenario you have chosen? What risks would arise if the officer failed to lead? In what ways would strong leadership by the officer in this scenario help produce desirable outcomes?

5. What is meant by deployment in a police agency? How does deployment differ from development and training in its processes and purpose?

6. What considerations do police agencies weigh while seeking to match personnel to project or task assignments?

7. What decisions must a police agency make while developing a workforce schedule? In addition to trying to maximize coverage and service quality through effective workforce scheduling, what else does an agency seek to do regarding resources?

8. The assembly and use of working groups are key processes in deployment of human resources at a police agency. What are the three types of working groups described in this chapter, and how do they compare and contrast in terms of their purpose, composition, and length of duration?

WHAT WOULD YOU DO?

Evaluating Evan

You are a sergeant in a medium-size police agency. Evan, a probationary police officer, has been assigned to you as a direct report. Your agency is currently understaffed and is experiencing severe budget constraints. For these reasons, it is not planning to hire any officers for at least one year. Evan has completed basic preservice and field training, and is finishing the probationary officer phase of training in two weeks. Your commanding officer has asked you to review Evan's performance and submit a report including your recommendation as to whether the agency should retain Evan.

Evan passed the academy with minimal grades and, in your view, has demonstrated average to below-average performance. He finally completed field training only after being allowed to extend the training several times and after receiving numerous hours of remedial help. He needs constant supervision, takes longer than his peers to complete assignments, and continually asks for remedial training from you. Other officers in your platoon have said that Evan often asks for advice regarding how he should handle calls-for-service.

On the other hand, Evan is never out sick, always arrives at work on time, and has a positive attitude. He is also well liked by his fellow officers and appears to get along with other commanders and with members of the community. Indeed, several community residents have commented on Evan's helpfulness and his sensitivity to cultural differences in their neighborhood.

1. After weighing Evan's positive and negative qualities and performance, would you recommend that your agency retain Evan? Why or why not?

2. If you would recommend retaining Evan, would you offer him any training and/or developmental opportunities to help improve his performance? If so, what types of training or development would you want to provide? How might you take your agency's budgetary constraints into account during this decision?

3. Given Evan's strengths and weaknesses, along with your agency's fiscal constraints, how could Evan best be deployed if the agency retains him? What types of assignments would make the best use of his skills and strengths? What types of assignments would be least appropriate for him?

11

◀ Ethical leadership and supervisory skills are essential for all police officers, regardless of rank.

Leadership and Supervision

After completing this chapter, readers should be able to:

- compare leadership theories.
- identify major categories of leadership skills.
- distinguish leadership from supervision.
- distinguish authority from power and explain how leaders use both.
- compare leadership styles.
- explain how leadership differs from toxic management.
- demonstrate leadership skills.

Introduction

When citizens contact the police, they expect responding officers to lead them from a state of chaos, confusion, or danger to a place of order and safety. This expectation casts each responding police officer into the role of leader; consequently all officers must develop and demonstrate leadership skills. Leaders motivate or influence others to action, thus leadership differs from supervision, through which managers direct others toward the accomplishment of specific tasks and organizational objectives.

In this chapter, we take a close look at the nature and practice of leadership and consider how police personnel can serve as effective leaders in their agencies and communities. We start by summarizing major leadership theories—researchers' conclusions about the defining principles of leadership. We then describe leadership skills (the abilities required to lead). Although we treat leadership as different from supervision, we also show how leadership is an ingredient of effective supervision. We examine the nature of authority and power, considering how leaders use these tools. Finally, we examine a range of leadership styles, which constitute the practices and application of leadership theories. We also contrast effective leadership with toxic, or dysfunctional, supervision.

LEADERSHIP THEORIES

Theories about leadership have evolved over the past century. For example, researchers in the early twentieth century suggested that leaders had inherent traits that differentiated them from followers. Later in the twentieth century, researchers theorized that characteristics of the situations (not a person's inborn traits) most strongly determined whether leadership occurred. Still later, researchers began considering not only how specific situations affected leaders' and followers' behavior but also how such behavior affected situations. Today, many scholars emphasize leaders' ability to motivate, influence, and persuade over their ability to control and direct others. And they argue that with the right training and experience, anyone can learn to become a leader (Ortmeier, 1995; Ortmeier & Meese, 2010). This i' the stance we take in this book.

Examining the major leadership theories that have evolved over time can p' vide you with a foundation of knowledge useful for developing leadership sl in yourself and others in your agency. It can also help you construct and in ment a leadership style appropriate to your circumstances. To that end, we b describe several types of theories that are categorized based on whether they on leaders, followers or situational context, or leader–follower interactio Table 11-1.) We do not endorse a single leadership theory or approach. Ra encourage you to evaluate them all and to consider how they might best in your own circumstances.

> **table 11-1** Leadership Theory Categories

THEORIES CENTERING ON . . .	INCLUDE . . .
The leader	• Trait theory • Behavior theory • Personal–situational theory • Interaction–expectation theory
Followers and situational context	• Motivation–hygiene theory • Situational theory • Contingency theory • Path–goal leadership theory • Meta-leadership theory
Leader–follower interactions	• Leader–follower exchange theory • Transactional and transformational theories • Psychodynamic approach

Sources: Northouse, 2007; Ortmeier & Meese, 2010.

Theories Centering on the Leader

Trait theory: theory that seeks to identify the individual traits distinguishing leaders from followers.

Trait Theory   Trait theory represents one of the first attempts to define leadership. In the early 1900s, theorists studied great leaders to identify the individual traits that distinguished them and that enabled them to inspire others to follow them. These traits included popularity, self-confidence, judgment, humor, aggressiveness, desire, adaptability, assertiveness, courage, decisiveness, intelligence, initiative, persistence, and the ability to cooperate (Bass, 1990).

However, in the mid-1900s, research questioning the universality of leadership traits arose to challenge trait theory (Northouse, 2007). According to these theorists, since settings that require leadership are complex, trait theories cannot fully explain the nature of leadership (Vinzant & Crothers, 1998).

Behavior theory: theory that identifies the behaviors distinguishing leaders who achieve desired results.

Behavior Theory   Behavior theory differs markedly from trait theory. While trait theorists focus on inborn qualities as well as what leaders do and how they act, behavior theorists suggest that circumstances can cause an individual to take a leadership role. Effective leaders, these scholars add, are those who engage in behaviors that are likely to achieve desired results.

Those who study the behavior approach to leadership focus on two general types of behaviors:

- *Task* behaviors facilitate goal accomplishment. For instance, a command officer directs (orders) a line officer to secure (protect) a crime scene.
- *Relationship* behaviors help others develop comfortable feelings about themselves, other people, and the situation. For example, the command officer consults with the line officer about the best way to secure the crime scene.

Effective leaders combine task and relationship behaviors to influence others to achieve an objective.

Behavior theory broadens the scope of leadership research beyond the limitations of trait theory, and it has been validated by a wide range of studies (Blake & Mouton, 1965). However, it still has its shortcomings. Specifically, researchers have not established a link between leadership behaviors and outcomes, and they have not identified a universal leadership style that could be effective in most situations (Northouse, 2007).

A command officer directs a line officer to carry out a specific task.

Personal–Situational Theory

The **personal–situational theory** was the first to address leadership's full complexity. The theory supposes that a mix of personal characteristics (an individual's thoughts, emotions, and actions) interact with specific conditions in the person's environment to create successful leadership. Effectiveness depends on the leader's ability to understand followers and the environment in which the followers function, and to react appropriately as followers and the situation change (Bennis, 1961).

Personal–situational theory: theory proposing that a mix of personal characteristics interact with specific conditions in an individual's environment to produce leadership.

Interaction–Expectation Theory Interaction–expectation theory proposes that leadership is the act of initiating a structure (such as a process for accomplishing a particular task, or an approach to resolving a specific type of problem) that group members support. Members support a structure if it helps solve their problems and it conforms to group norms, and if they believe that success will result if they follow the leader. Thus, leadership involves initiating as well as fulfilling others' expectations (Adler, 2007; Stogdill, 1959).

Interaction–expectation theory: theory proposing that leadership is the act of initiating a structure that group members support.

Theories Centering on Followers and Situational Context

Motivation–Hygiene Theory Motivation–hygiene theory was developed by Frederick Herzberg in the 1950s. Herzberg conducted studies to determine which factors in an employee's work environment caused satisfaction or dissatisfaction. According to Herzberg, job satisfaction, and presumably motivation, and job dissatisfaction acted independently of each other. He referred to satisfiers (such as achievement, recognition, and advancement) as "motivators" and dissatisfiers (including supervision, working conditions, and salary) as "hygiene factors."

Motivation–hygiene theory: theory proposing which factors increase satisfaction and dissatisfaction among employees in an organization.

Herzberg maintained that motivators provide satisfaction arising from the intrinsic conditions of the job, such as recognition and personal growth. Hygiene factors do not provide satisfaction, although dissatisfaction results from their absence. These factors are all extrinsic to the work itself. Basically, positive hygiene factors (such as good working conditions and an attractive salary) are needed to ensure that employees do not become dissatisfied (Herzberg, Mausner, & Snyderman, 1959).

Today, most researchers do not view satisfaction and dissatisfaction factors as existing separately. Further, the theory does not allow for individual differences (for example, personality traits) that might affect a person's unique response to a motivating or a hygiene factor.

Situational theory: theory proposing that different situations demand different styles of leadership.

Situational Theory Situational theory—developed, refined, and revised between the late 1960s and 1990s by Paul Hersey and Ken Blanchard (1982)—counts among the most widely recognized theories of leadership. According to situational theory, different situations demand different styles of leadership. To be effective, leaders must adapt their leadership style to specific characteristics of a situation, such as a follower's skill level or degree of motivation for completing a particular task or working toward a goal.

Situational leadership theory is practical, easily understood, and prescriptive (it tells one what to do) rather than descriptive. It emphasizes leaders' flexibility, and underscores the importance of adapting to followers' unique needs. However, as with other theories, critics have pointed out shortcomings. Specifically, few studies have been conducted that justify the assumptions underlying the theory. Moreover, situational leadership questionnaires force respondents to choose predetermined responses that favor situational theory rather than other leadership behaviors not described in the theory.

Contingency theory: theory that attempts to match leaders to specific types of situations.

Contingency Theory Similar to situational theory, **contingency theory**, developed in the 1960s, reinforces the notion that effective leaders demonstrate styles that fit the situation. Rather than focusing on a person's ability to adopt a style that fits a situation, contingency theory attempts to match leaders to specific types of situations.

Research suggests that contingency theory is a valid and reliable approach to explaining effective leadership. Moreover, this theory recognizes that leaders cannot be effective in all situations. However, its critics maintain that contingency theory does not fully explain why certain leadership styles may be effective in some situations but not in others. Critics also point out that the theory fails to support the notion that leaders can be taught adaptive skills necessary in changing situations (Fiedler, 1967; Northouse, 2007).

Path–goal theory: theory suggesting that a leader's role is to enhance followers' performance by motivating them and by rewarding achievement of goals.

Path–Goal Theory Path–goal theory, proposed in the early 1970s, suggests that a leader's role is to enhance followers' performance by motivating them and by rewarding achievement of goals. Unlike situational theory, which suggests that leaders must adapt to followers' developmental level, and contingency theory, which supposes a match between a leader's style and situational variables, the path–goal approach suggests that leaders should use a style that eliminates barriers to achievement of goals and meets followers' motivational needs (House, 1971; Ortmeier & Meese, 2010).

Meta-leadership: overarching leadership framework designed to link organizational units or organizations; attempts to transcend usual organizational confines.

Meta-Leadership Theory Meta-leadership theory, a recent development, incorporates findings from the research of such theorists as Warren Bennis and Ronald Heifetz. Meta-leadership is an overarching framework designed to link the efforts of different organizational units or different organizations. Meta-leaders wish to transcend usual organizational confines and influence, motivate, and activate change above and beyond the established lines of their dominion and control. According to the theory, meta-leaders are driven and motivated by purposes broader than those prescribed by their formal roles (Marcus, Dorn, & Henderson, 2006). However, meta-leadership theorists tend to define *leadership* in terms of a recognized span of authority a person holds in a formal role, rather than in informal as well as formal roles.

Theories Centering on Leader–Follower Interactions

Leader–Follower Exchange Theory Leader–follower exchange theory, which emerged in the 1970s, departs from theories that focus on leaders (such as trait and styles approaches) or on context (for example, situational or contingency approaches). Rather than concentrating on what leaders do toward followers or how leaders and followers behave within specific situations, leader–follower exchange theory examines the relationships between leaders and followers. Researchers discovered two types of relationships:

Leader–follower exchange theory: theory that examines the nature and quality of the relationships between leaders and followers.

- *In-group* relationships arise from expanded and negotiated role responsibilities. Followers whose performance goes beyond the expected and who expand their roles with the leader become members of the in-group.

- *Out-group* relationships result from defined roles such as those found in employment contracts. Followers who achieve only what is expected are members of the out-group.

Later research into this theory suggested that the quality of the exchange between leaders and followers is related to positive outcomes for leaders, followers, groups, and organizations. Specifically, high-quality leader–follower relationships reduce follower attrition (such as employee turnover) and result in more positive performance evaluations, greater commitment to goal achievement, better attitudes, and more attention and support from the leader (Graen & Uhl-Bien, 1995; Northouse, 2007).

Transactional theory: process in which the leader and follower make simple exchanges or transactions (e.g., money for work completed).

Transactional and Transformational Theories Transformational theory was first introduced by J. V. Downton (1973), but James MacGregor Burns popularized the theory. According to Burns, most leadership models propose a **transactional theory** (or process), in which leaders and followers make exchanges (Burns, 1978). For example, a police officer exchanges a verbal warning for a traffic citation if a motorist behaves civilly when stopped for a motor-vehicle code violation.

Transformational theory proposes a process through which leaders engage others and create a connection that enhances motivation and morality in themselves as well as followers. With transactional leadership, both leaders and followers raise each other to higher levels on consciousness and satisfaction. In other words, they are transformed to a higher level. Transformational leaders possess strong internal values and motivate others to put aside self-interest (Burns, 1978).

Transformational theory: theory that proposes a process through which leaders engage others and create a connection that enhances motivation and morality in themselves as well as followers.

Transformational leadership theory has weaknesses also. It makes vague references to motivation, vision, trust, and nurturing. The theory also tends to treat leadership as a personality trait rather than as a behavior that individuals can learn. In practice, transformational leadership can also lead to abuse, if leaders change followers' values in a destructive way. When a transformational leader influences followers to adopt inappropriate values, followers may be steered in the wrong direction (Northouse, 2007).

Psychodynamic approach: an approach suggesting that leaders are more effective if they have insight into the psychological makeup of themselves and their followers.

The Psychodynamic Approach   The **psychodynamic approach** can trace its origin to the work of Sigmund Freud in his development of psychoanalysis in the 1930s. It represents an approach to leadership rather than a coherent theory, because it adapts ideas from several behavioral theorists, scholars, and practitioners.

According to this approach, leaders are more effective if they have insight into the psychological makeup of themselves and their followers. This approach makes none of the assumptions that underlie trait, behavioral, and situational leadership theories. It does not presume that a particular personality type is best suited for leadership, nor does it attempt to match leadership styles to followers or to particular situations. Instead, it emphasizes the importance of leaders' and followers' awareness of their own personality characteristics, and of their understanding of why and how they respond to each other as they do. According to this approach, effective leaders work to gain insights into their own tendencies and needs, and they help followers do the same.

Critics of this approach are uncomfortable with the subjective nature of insight development. They also point out that research on the approach relies primarily on the clinical observations of psychologists and psychiatrists, whose opinions may be biased in favor of the approach because it focuses on individuals. Finally, the approach does not account for organizational variables (such as a company's culture, power structure, challenges, tasks) that might influence leaders' and followers' behavior (Meese & Ortmeier, 2004; Northouse, 2007; Stech, 2001).

ETHICS IN ACTION
Demotion without Honor

One skill essential to leaders in a police agency is the ability to decide how to handle potential ethics violations. A police chief in a midwestern municipality faced just this situation. With the approval of the mayor and the city council, the chief demoted a long-time friend and police captain to a nonsupervisory sergeant's position. The demotion which came after a lengthy investigation conducted by the city's department of civil rights concluded that the captain gave preferential treatment to officers with whom he socialized. The captain denied the allegations. Yet city officials approved the demotion (rather than termination) to avoid further costly legal action. The city had already spent nearly $500,000 on investigations, out-of-court settlements, and the suspended captain's compensation.

Hailed as a trailblazer with innovative ideas when he was initially promoted, the captain had a troubled tenure. Four officers sued him and the agency, alleging various acts of discrimination. The civil rights department investigation revealed that the captain was involved in three intimate relationships with subordinate employees. On several occasions, officers observed the captain embracing another officer while on duty.

1. In what respects were the captain's actions unethical?

2. Was the captain's demotion justified? Explain your reasoning.

3. Based on the facts presented, should the captain be terminated instead of demoted? Why or why not?

Training of Federal Air Marshals at the Federal Law Enforcement Training Center.

LEADERSHIP SKILLS

A leader is someone others wish to follow, rather than someone who simply issues commands or coerces others into action (Ortmeier, 2006). As an unknown, ancient Chinese philosopher is credited with stating, "When the best leader's work is done, the people will say 'We did it ourselves.'" Anyone in a police agency can be a leader, regardless of rank, position, or title. But leadership requires mastery of specific skills, rather than possession of particular qualities (such as inborn personal traits).

A **leadership skill** is an ability that can be measured objectively; that is, there are clear metrics for assessing its results and for determining whether a person has exhibited the skill. Leadership skills can be learned and developed through experience, training, and education (see the box

Leadership skill: an ability that can be measured objectively.

An officer of the Royal Canadian Mounted Police.

Training for Ethical Leadership

As we saw in Chapter 1, key leadership skills include demonstrating ethical behavior. Unfortunately, few police leadership development programs endorsed, certified, and/or presented through state commissions on peace officer standards and training as well as colleges and universities focus on ethical leadership development at all ranks, including police recruits ("Leadership Development around the States," 2009). We strongly suggest that ethical leadership training and development are essential for all police officers, regardless of rank.

"Training for Ethical Leadership"). But while anyone can become a leader, most studies on leadership skills focus on supervisory-level leadership. For example, in 1996, Anderson and King conducted studies to identify leadership skills necessary for police supervisors and managers in British Columbia (Anderson & King, 1996a, 1996b). A few studies address leadership skills required of front-line officers. Ortmeier (1996) is one such study—and is believed to be the first. Another such study was completed in 1997, when the Federal Law Enforcement Training Center (FLETC), in conjunction with the Royal Canadian Mounted Police (RCMP), developed a list of leadership skills for police officers.

A Closer Look at the Ortmeier Study

The study conducted by P. J. Ortmeier in 1995 focused on the leadership skills essential for police officers in an environment that emphasizes community participation, engagement, and problem solving—all of which are important ingredients for effective policing. Ortmeier defined leadership as the ability to influence or mobilize individual citizens, groups, businesses, and public and private agencies to collaborate and participate in activities designed to discover and implement solutions to community problems. The participants in the study included Herman Goldstein, who pioneered in the development of problem-oriented policing; former U.S. Attorney General Edwin Meese III; police executives and line officers from throughout the United States; and law enforcement scholars from Harvard and Stanford Universities and the John Jay College of Criminal Justice.

Ortmeier grouped the skills his study identified into five major categories. (See Table 11-2.)

Spotlight on Communication

Modern policing requires skills beyond those traditionally taught in police academies and college classrooms (Meese & Ortmeier, 2004). Communication, for example, must be nurtured and encouraged with

Former U. S. Attorney General, Edwin Meese III.

table 11-2 Five Skill Categories

CATEGORY	SKILLS
Communications and related interpersonal skills	• Communicating verbally and in writing • Listening • Counseling • Possessing knowledge of different ethnic and racial cultures and demonstrating empathy • Facilitating interaction • Maintaining group cohesiveness and member satisfaction • Speaking in public
Motivation	• Encouraging creativity and innovation • Catalyzing proactive behavior in others • Building teams and cooperative relationships • Demonstrating persistence and consistency • Showing enthusiasm • Committing to assignments • Recognizing and encouraging other responsible leaders • Demonstrating intellectual curiosity
Problem solving	• Analyzing situations • Identifying and evaluating constituents' needs • Identifying and analyzing problems • Adapting strategies to situations • Mediating and negotiating • Enabling others to attain goals • Prescribing prioritized actions to solve a problem
Planning and organizing	• Promoting needed change • Creating and maintaining a vision • Defining objectives and maintaining progress toward them • Prioritizing and assigning tasks • Organizing resources • Creating and maintaining an environment that encourages open communication • Providing for and maintaining group processes • Delegating
Actuation and implementation	• Translating a vision into action • Completing multiple projects on schedule • Evaluating individual and group goals • Representing others' interests and concerns • Understanding and articulating the police agency's impact • Learning from mistakes

Source: Ortmeier, 1996.

staff, other people in the organization, and the community at large. Residents in the community served by a police organization may express concern about issues plaguing their community, such as crime or poverty. All police officers must listen, understand the issues from residents' perspective, and reassure residents that action will be taken. By acknowledging the presence of a concern or problem, officers forge a connection with community members. And once citizens realize police want to join with them, change can occur (Davis, Givens, Perez, Bialaszewski, & Wiliams, 2004).

It is thus essential for officers to keep lines of communication open. Effective police-officer leaders interact daily with other officers, with administrative personnel, and with elected or appointed officials. They also regularly encounter people in the community—citizens as well as residents who are perceived as unofficial leaders—and ask for their opinions regarding the agency's performance. Finally, they encourage fellow officers to follow up with concerned community members.

The best police leaders also take a participatory rather than an authoritative approach to establishing and managing interpersonal relationships. They are empathetic—able to appreciate other people's feelings and needs. And they excel at persuasion and negotiation (de Janasz et al., 2006). All of these abilities hinge on a talent for communication.

Spotlight on Motivation

Like communication, motivation is a critical skill category for all officers seeking to strengthen their leadership skills. But motivation is a subjective phenomenon. What

Police executive speaking with public officials.

motivates one person to work toward a goal or to effect needed change may not motivate another. To lead, police officers must understand what motivates others—their subordinates, their superiors, politicians, and community members. And they must avoid trying to motivate through fear and control. Great leaders embrace the notion that people are motivated by different needs, whether for social connection, achievement, monetary reward, or some other form of value important to them (Hellriegel et al., 2005). For example, overtime pay may be one officer's primary motivation, while another's may be the opportunity to work on a special project and enjoy the resulting job satisfaction and pride in improving the way the agency operates.

How can aspiring leaders learn to identify what most motivates another person? They must become students of human nature—taking time to get to know others and appreciating others for who they are. At the same time, leaders must recognize that motivators change: What inspires one person to action today may not motivate that same person tomorrow. For example, a new police officer may initially be motivated primarily by the opportunity to learn new skills on the job. If the officer later becomes a parent, monetary rewards or a more manageable work schedule may become more motivating.

LEADERSHIP VERSUS SUPERVISION

As we have noted, leadership is not the same as supervision (also called management). Although the two are interrelated, they represent very different ways of operating. A leader may also be a supervisor—but not every supervisor is a leader. Leadership is thus broader than supervision, and it occurs anytime a person motivates another person or a group to produce change. In contrast, supervision occurs when someone directs others toward organizational goals (Hersey & Blanchard, 1982). Leadership is thus about creating a better future, while supervision is about maintaining order and consistency (Kotter, 1990). (Table 11-3 shows how one expert distinguishes between these two ways of operating.)

table 11-3 Comparing Leadership and Management

A leader . . .	A manager . . .
Innovates	Administers
Is an original	Is a copy
Develops	Maintains
Focuses on people	Focuses on systems and structures
Inspires trust	Relies on control
Takes a long-range view	Takes a short-range view
Asks what and why	Asks how and when
Keeps an eye on the horizon	Keeps an eye on the bottom line
Challenges the status quo	Accepts the status quo
Is unique	Is the classic good soldier
Does the right thing	Does things right

Source: Bennis, 1993, p. 214.

The Police Leader-Supervisor

Some police personnel are both leaders and supervisors. They not only exhibit the leadership skills we have been examining, but they also demonstrate solid supervisory skills. Their valuable blend of talents includes mentoring and role modeling, crisis management, resource management, and personnel development.

Mentoring and Role Modeling   Police leader-supervisors directly oversee the individuals who report to them and may act in a supervisory capacity for anyone who needs guidance. They teach subordinates to complete practical tasks associated with the job, give directives that others acknowledge and follow, and serve as mentors and role models, so that subordinates seek development opportunities from them rather than from others.

Role model:
a person who exhibits values, attitudes, and behaviors considered desirable in a particular organization.

A **role model** is a person who exhibits values, attitudes, and behaviors considered desirable in a particular organization. Through their everyday actions on the job, role models demonstrate which behaviors, values, and attitudes are positive and appropriate and which should be avoided. They thus constitute vital human resources in any organization (Clark & Clark, 1996; *Concepts of Leadership,* 2010; Lad, 2010; National Institute of Standards and Technology, 2001).

Role models demonstrate behaviors (such as taking responsibility for tasks and respecting others) that inspire subordinates and other constituents to grow and to contribute to the organization in a meaningful way. By acting ethically, they influence other personnel to behave ethically (Hitt, 1988). Role models also offset the cynicism and "putting out fires" crisis management style that pervades many police organizations. All too many police managers merely try to get through each day instead of working to move their organization forward. They fear change, and do little more than cope with situations that arise. Subordinates learn inappropriate behaviors from these poor managers, which lead directly to inadequate protection for citizens. Modeling correct behaviors is one of the most powerful ways to prevent the disasters that can stem from ineffective leadership and pervasive cynicism.

Crisis Management   Police leader-supervisors also deftly handle crises. They may make swift decisions on the street or intervene in conflicts between peers, subordinates, or citizens. They always consider the moral, ethical, and legal implications of any decision, and they function as advisors to others in the agency—whether direct reports, peers, or superiors.

Resource Management   Police leader-supervisors know how to summon the resources needed to complete the job. For example, they may write or facilitate search warrant affidavits (sworn applications), thus providing a link to the prosecuting attorney's office. Or they help a citizen who is mentally disturbed find and take advantage of community resources available for such problems.

Personnel Development   The best leader-supervisors develop their subordinates, including helping them acquire leadership skills themselves. They challenge those who report to them to learn new tasks and processes, to reach beyond their job description, and to find new ways for the agency to accomplish its mission (Davis, 2006; Rosser, 2010). They also take responsibility for organizing the departmental staff, allocating police vehicles to shifts, creating career development plans for

Cardinal Sean Patrick O'Malley serves Christmas Eve lunch at the Pine Street Inn, New England's largest homeless shelter in Boston, on December 24, 2009.

subordinates, and implementing succession plans designed to position subordinates to become supervisors in the future.

Clearly, leadership is essential to the success of any policing organization and its personnel. Yet many officers and police supervisors disregard the art and skill of leadership as it relates to supervision. They should instead make this valuable combination of skills a high priority and consider it a crucial part of a police supervisor's role.

LEADERSHIP TOOLS: AUTHORITY AND POWER

In any police agency, effective use of two tools—authority and power—constitutes a crucial aspect of leadership. **Authority** is a legitimate *right* bestowed by an organization on an individual to direct activities or persons. It is thus a function of the organization. **Power** is the *ability* of an individual to influence other persons or groups, to shape an organization's direction and priorities, and to influence situations and a variety of affairs and objects. It is therefore a capacity of the person. In the pages that follow, we take a closer look at how leaders use these tools.

Authority

Leaders derive authority from the formal mandates of laws, rules, and organizational directives (Bryson, 2004). This authority gives them the right to enforce laws and to take decisive action with respect to a variety of public safety activities. But authority alone is not sufficient to manage an organization (Hellriegel et al., 2005). It must also come with responsibility (obligation to do what is ethically correct) and accountability (being answerable or liable for one's actions or inaction).

Authority:
a legitimate right bestowed by an organization on an individual to direct activities or persons.

Power:
the ability of an individual to influence others; shape an organization's direction and priorities; and influence situations, affairs, and objects.

Authority can also be the formal acknowledgment of power granted by the organization to a command or supervisory officer. Yet this does not automatically mean that a person with authority will be followed. Some followers might still subvert, reject, or refuse to comply with written or verbal directives. Leaders in a police agency can use formal disciplinary options (including verbal counseling and other protocols) to correct such behavior. However, the use of formal or coercive power may spawn resentment and resistance, which can erode morale, performance, and the agency's ability to achieve its mission and objectives (T. E. Baker, 2006; Iannone, 1987).

Clearly, formal authority—even when symbolized by a person's title or rank—is not enough to ensure that an individual will be considered a leader. Indeed, in addition to those granted formal authority, unofficial or informal leaders may emerge in an agency and ultimately exert more influence and power than those with a high rank, an executive-level position, or an impressive title. Often, such unofficial leaders derive their authority from charisma and from social norms. (For instance, in some organizations, someone who is highly regarded and respected attracts followers.) Wise police managers leverage informal leaders, acknowledging them and enlisting their support in promoting the agency's vision, mission, and goals.

Power

Power and authority may go hand in hand—or they may not. A person may exercise power yet have no authority. An armed robber, for example, exercises power over a victim but does not have authority (formal or informal legitimacy) to enforce the victim's compliance. In a police agency, power and authority often overlap. Moreover, there are several sources of power. Next, we examine five sources.

Rank   Some power derives from a person's rank in the organization. For example, police chiefs have both the formal authority (the right) and the power (the ability) to hire, discipline, and transfer personnel, and to define goals for the organization. Police officers have the authority and power to enforce laws, make arrests, and direct others' actions.

Fear   Some people acquire power by evoking fear in others—by coercing or compelling others through the threat of punishment or negative sanction (T. E. Baker, 2006). People whose power comes from this source may have high rank; a special affiliation with a higher, more influential person or group; or a personal attribute such as the ability to play on people's fears or an imposing physical size. An example of what this type of power looks like in action is a police union president who pressures union members to protest a change initiative being advocated by a police agency by playing on union members' fears that the initiative will cost jobs or result in wage cuts.

Rewards   Some people have power because they have the capacity to distribute valued rewards (such as recognition, promotions, and special assignments) within an organization. These rewards may be used to recognize an individual's or a group's accomplishment. Rewards-based power is valuable because timely and personal recognition engenders a sense of loyalty in others and a willingness to follow. However, rewards-based power is also subject to abuse if the person with the power discriminates against a person or group.

A forensic technician at work.

Expertise   Other individuals are powerful because they have special skills or expertise valued and needed by the police agency. Examples include crime scene technicians, auto collision reconstruction specialists, homicide investigators, and detectives.

Charisma   Some people have power because they are charismatic. Their communication style, personal philosophy, ethical standards, physical attributes, likeability, personality, or reputation make others want to follow them (*Charisma*, n.d.; Cordner & Scarborough, 2007). Charismatic leaders may appear as saviors to an organization, especially during times of uncertainty and confusion.

Charisma does not necessarily translate into successful leadership. For example, Adolf Hitler was a charismatic person who accumulated immense power. Yet he also became one of the most destructive dictators in human history. He had so much charisma that his followers accepted his directives unquestioningly and embraced the horrific values and goals he promoted. True leaders use their power to inspire followers to new heights of performance on appropriate goals, are humble rather than highly charismatic, and have a strong will (Collins, 2005).

The Optimal Blend of Authority and Power

In a police agency, leaders are particularly effective when they have sanctioned (legitimate) authority *and* power (when they use their power appropriately). Officers who have unsanctioned authority and who abuse their power may engage in activities that support their own personal interests at the expense of their agency's priorities. An officer with sanctioned authority but a limited degree of power may fail to discipline, reward, or adequately direct subordinates—wanting to be regarded as a friend rather than a superior. Finally, an individual who lacks sufficient degrees of authority and power may try to command authority that the agency has not granted to the person's current position. The individual cannot influence others owing to the lack of position or special circumstance, and will likely disappear within the organizational structure.

▍LEADERSHIP STYLES ▍

Leadership styles derive from the practice of leadership skills and may reflect several leadership theories. There are numerous styles that a police leader-supervisor can choose to adopt and demonstrate. A particular style derives from how a leader communicates and acts to influence followers to give their best on the job. Indeed, effective leaders adapt their style as needed to get optimal results from their followers.

In the pages that follow, we examine several of these styles (some drawn from theories discussed earlier in the chapter) and consider when a leader might choose to adopt them. Again, we do not suggest that one style is better than others. In a real-world situation, the style (or integration of several styles) a person selects will depend on the circumstances surrounding the situation.

Meeting Followers' Hierarchy of Needs

Hierarchy of needs model: Abraham Maslow's framework proposing five needs that human beings attempt to meet in a specific sequence.

Some leaders adopt a style that emphasizes meeting a hierarchy of needs in their followers. This style derives from American psychologist Abraham Maslow's work on human needs. Maslow's **hierarchy of needs** model depicts five needs: physiological, security, affiliation, esteem, and self-actualization. (See Figure 11-1.) Physiological needs are the most basic and are those necessary for human survival: food, water, shelter, and clothing. Only when physiological needs are met will people turn to

▍**figure 11-1** Maslow's Hierarchy of Needs

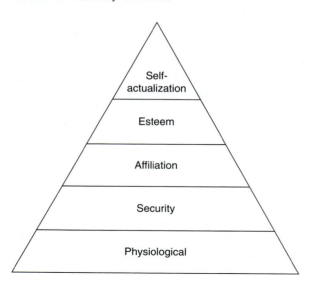

satisfying their security needs—for stability, safety, good health, and the absence of threats or pain. Likewise, when people feel secure, they next attend to their affiliation needs, for friendship, belonging, and love. If affiliation needs are met, people take care of their esteem needs, for self-respect, personal achievement, and recognition from others. Finally, only after all lower-level needs are met, people strive to fulfill their self-actualization needs, for personal growth, self-fulfillment, and the realization of their full potential (Hellriegel, Jackson, & Slocum, 2005; Maslow, 1970).

How might police personnel demonstrate a leadership style based on Maslow's framework? They cannot assume that subordinates' basic needs (such as for physical survival and security) are met simply because the employees receive a paycheck. Effective leaders attempt to determine whether a subordinate is struggling economically and arrive at solutions if the answer is yes. For example, they may take steps to reassure a subordinate who is worried about job security during periods of budgetary constraints and rumors of impending layoffs.

For subordinates who require recognition and personal achievement, leader-supervisors can assign projects that will present new challenges and offer recognition and other rewards for completion of goals. For subordinates who are at the highest level of need (self-actualization), police leader-supervisors can offer assistance with promotion or transfer to a more challenging position that will provide opportunity for personal and professional growth.

Line-level officers can practice this style of leadership as well. For example, they can appreciate that community members who live at or below the poverty level often feel hopeless as they struggle to keep themselves and their children safe. Police officers who know that such residents are at the most basic level of need can help connect people with vital resources such as food banks and organizations that provide housing assistance. In neighborhoods where residents' basic needs are satisfied, police officers can help satisfy the next level of need—for friendship and self-respect—by communicating respectfully to residents, learning their names, and listening when they speak. Officers who demonstrate respectful behavior enrich the community, become role models for young people and others, help ensure their own safety, and encourage citizen cooperation with the police.

Addressing Followers' Frustrations

Another leadership style draws its inspiration from Clay Alderfer's model of needs, which proposes three categories of need: existence, relatedness, and growth. In what's known as Alderfer's **ERG theory**, existence needs are for elements (water, food, shelter) contributing to physical well-being. Relatedness refers to desires to establish and maintain good interpersonal bonds. And growth needs include the desire for creativity, productivity, and personal development. (See Figure 11-2.)

Alderfer's model contains a dimension called the frustration-regression hypothesis, which suggests that when people encounter real or imagined obstacles while seeking to meet higher-level needs, they refocus on lower-level needs. This is a problem because the obstacles restrict a person's productivity and growth. To support followers' productivity and growth, leaders should strive to identify and remove obstacles to achieving higher-level needs (Alderfer, 1972).

For example, suppose that Philip, a police officer reporting to Michelle, is seeking a promotion (reflecting a need for growth). To adopt a leadership style drawn from Alderfer's model, Michelle might speak with Philip to identify and

ERG theory:
Clay Alderfer's framework proposing that human beings need elements for physical survival, relatedness, and personal growth.

figure 11-2 Alderfer's ERG Theory

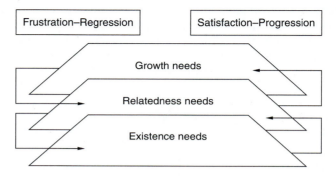

acknowledge any obstacles he perceives to achieving the promotion he wants. If Philip mentions that he's worried about passing an exam necessary for the promotion, Michelle may offer encouragement and perhaps arrange for tutoring from another officer who has achieved a similar promotion.

Addressing Conflicting Needs

Learned needs theory: David McClelland's framework suggesting that human beings have three key needs: affiliation, achievement, and power.

Another police leadership style draws from David McClelland's **learned needs theory.** According to this model, people have three key needs: affiliation (satisfying interpersonal relationships), achievement (success), and power (ability to control and influence others and one's surroundings).

If more than one motive dominates an individual's personality, conflict between the motives can occur. For example, a person's desire for friendships (affiliation) at work may conflict with an equally strong desire to produce and to seek promotion (achievement). When motives conflict, frustration results, leading to poor self-esteem and low productivity. To avoid such scenarios, police leader-supervisors should strive to recognize and balance followers' conflicting motives (McClelland, 1971).

For instance, Jorge, a police manager, knows that Pat, a subordinate, craves affiliation but that her intense focus on achieving professional goals has been preventing her from spending as much time with others as she needs to forge human connections. So, he assigns tasks to her that not only support her desired career path (by helping her develop new skills) but also require interaction with others in the agency or the community; for example, as the head of a community task force.

Satisfying Expectations about Performance and Outcomes

Expectancy theory: Victor Vroom's framework holding that people will be motivated to deliver their best on the job if they believe that a specific level of performance will lead to an outcome that they value highly.

Another leadership style is based on **expectancy theory,** formulated by Victor Vroom in the early 1970s. Vroom's theory holds that people will be motivated to deliver their best on the job if they believe that a specific level of performance will lead to an outcome that they value highly. (See Figure 11-3.) Police leaders who

figure 11-3 Expectancy Theory

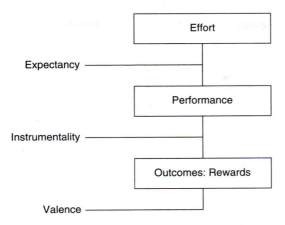

Source: Used by permission of Victor Vroom.

demonstrate this style identify outcomes that followers and community residents truly value (such as safe streets) and encourage the delivery of job performance that will produce those outcomes. For example, police officers who place a high value on safe streets will partner with community residents to encourage and assist with neighborhood watches. They might also explain to city council members why such initiatives might generate more value than merely racking up more arrests.

Aligning Followers and Agency Goals while Cultivating Trust

Some police personnel demonstrate a leadership style informed by the work of theorists Douglas McGregor in the 1950s and William Ouchi in the 1980s. McGregor proposed two theories of leadership and supervision. The first was **Theory X,** which is manifested as a command-and-control management style common in police environments. Supervisors who subscribe to Theory X make the following assumptions about their subordinates:

- The average human being has an inherent dislike of work and will avoid work if possible.
- Because people inherently dislike work, most of them must be coerced, controlled, directed, or threatened with punishment before they will put forth adequate effort toward achievement of objectives.
- People are self-centered, prefer to be directed, wish to avoid responsibility, have relatively little ambition, and want security above all.

McGregor suggested that Theory X supervisors fail to recognize critical factors associated with motivation and thus are not the most effective leaders. For example, human beings are "wanting" animals. As soon as we satisfy one need, we move on to satisfy another. Moreover, human needs are organized in a hierarchy of importance. McGregor proposed an alternative—**Theory Y**—which he maintained could help

Theory X:
Douglas McGregor's model describing command-and-control management style in an organization.

Theory Y:
Douglas McGregor's description of a motivational management style in organizations.

supervisors lead more skillfully. Leaders (supervisors) who subscribe to Theory Y make the following assumptions about their followers (which differ markedly from assumptions made by Theory X supervisors):

- The expenditure of physical and mental effort in work comes as naturally to people as play or rest.
- External control and the threat of punishment are not the only means to elicit the effort necessary to reach objectives. People will exercise self-direction and self-control in the service of objectives to which they are committed.
- The right rewards can motivate people to work toward a particular achievement.
- Under proper conditions, people learn to accept as well as seek responsibility.
- Most people have the capacity to exercise a relatively high degree of imagination, ingenuity, and creativity in the search for solutions to problems.
- Under the conditions of modern industrial life, the intellectual potential of the average human being are only partially realized (McGregor, 1960).

Theory Z:
William Ouchi's adaptation of Theory Y emphasizing a leadership style that advocates trusting followers and enabling them to feel they are part of the organization.

In the 1980s, William Ouchi proposed an adaptation of Theory Y. Ouchi's **Theory Z** is a leadership style that advocates trusting followers and creating an environment in which followers consider themselves as an integral part of the group or organization. According to this theory, trust promotes increased productivity and goal achievement (Ouchi, 1981).

Even if they work in an agency characterized by Theory X leadership overall, police personnel can adopt a Theory Y or Theory Z leadership style within their sphere of influence. For example, to demonstrate Theory Y leadership, they can encourage peers and subordinates to pursue goals that enrich the operational unit or agency. Managers demonstrating Theory Y leadership can make the transition to Theory Z by showing that they trust followers to have good intentions and the skills needed to solve problems. For instance, if a particular unit is experiencing a problem of increasing auto theft within its area of responsibility, leaders can encourage problem-solving sessions with unit and community members, establish goals, create steps to reach the goals, implement the steps, and evaluate the results.

Blending Concern for People with Concern for Production

Managerial grid:
Robert Blake and Jane Mouton's model identifying five leadership styles that vary in concern for people and concern for productivity.

Another leadership style is drawn from what's called the **managerial grid** (later renamed the leadership grid) developed by Robert Blake and Jane Mouton (1965). This theoretical framework identifies five leadership styles that show varying degrees of concern for people and for production (such as number of arrests made or calls answered, or degree of crime-rate reduction). (See Figure 11-4.)

Each axis on the managerial grid has a scale of 1 to 10, with 1 being the lowest and 10 the highest. Each style is positioned on the grid according to where it rates on the scales. For example:

- The *impoverished* managerial style demonstrates low concern for people and production. Managers utilizing this style exert minimal effort and seek to maintain the status quo. They place a high priority on their own personal security within the organization.
- Through the *country club style,* managers demonstrate high concern for people but low concern for production. They try to create an atmosphere of

figure 11-4 The Managerial Grid

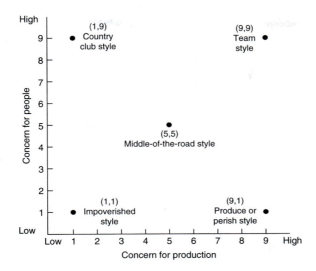

Source: The Managerial Grid used by permission of Grid International, Inc.

high morale and loyalty and hope that their subordinates will perform at a high level without further involvement from them.

- Low concern for people and high concern for production characterize the *produce-or-perish* management style. Managers practicing this style use coercion and rule enforcement to achieve high production. (If this style sounds familiar, that's because it strongly resembles Theory X behavior as defined by McGregor.)

- Through the *middle-of-the-road* style, managers strive to balance follower needs with a concern for production. They try to maintain employee morale at a level just high enough to ensure that minimal performance goals are met.

- Through the *team* style, managers demonstrate high concern for people as well as production by fostering inclusion, agreed-upon goals, and commitment among members of the organization. Blake and Mouton saw this as the optimal management style. It is consistent with McGregor's Theory Y.

Adapting to Followers' Readiness

Some leaders adapt their style based on followers' readiness—that is, their level of skill, experience, and motivation. This approach echoes the work of Paul Hersey and Ken Blanchard, who created the **situational leadership model** suggesting four styles: delegating, supportive, selling, and telling. (See Figure 11-5.)

With followers who are mature, competent, and motivated (in other words, very ready), leaders might elect to use the *delegating* style, giving followers responsibility for taking on tasks. With followers who are less ready (for instance, they lack confidence in their abilities or experience?), leaders might use the *supportive* style to encourage, assist, and maintain communication with these followers. With followers

Situational leadership model:
Paul Hersey and Ken Blanchard's model suggesting four leadership styles: delegating, supportive, selling, and telling.

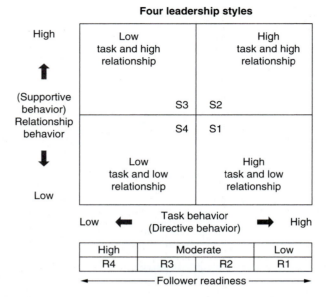

figure 11-5 Hersey's Situational Leadership Model

Four leadership styles

Low task and high relationship	High task and high relationship
Low task and low relationship	High task and low relationship

High ↑ (Supportive behavior) Relationship behavior ↓ Low

S3 S2
S4 S1

Low ← Task behavior (Directive behavior) → High

High	Moderate		Low
R4	R3	R2	R1

←———— Follower readiness ————→

Source: Adapted and printed with permission from Dr. Paul Hersey, *Management of Organizational Behavior: Leading Human Resources,* 9th ed. (Upper Saddle River, New Jersey: Pearson Education, Inc., 2008), p. 134.

who are even less ready (perhaps they are confused about their role, unmotivated, or skeptical about what they are being asked to do), leaders might adopt the *selling* style—providing some direction, encouraging communication, building confidence, and motivating these followers. Finally, with followers who are not at all ready (they have no experience with or knowledge of the tasks they are being asked to do), leaders might select the *telling* style, supplying clear and specific instructions (Hersey & Blanchard, 1982).

A leader can (and often must) blend all four styles at once, especially in complex situations. To illustrate, when a community expressed concern about rising auto theft, police managers assembled a team comprising officers and members of the community as well as an outside consultant. Together, they developed a plan that called for police managers to use the *selling* style to enlist subordinate's commitment to solving the problem. Managers used the *supportive* style with community residents who favored the project and were motivated to get involved. They *delegated* tasks to police-team members with experience and an interest in confronting the auto-theft problem. And they used the *telling* style to train citizens on auto-theft prevention who were not familiar with the strategies. The effort paid off: Within one year, auto thefts had decreased by 48 percent.

Vroom–Jago Time–Drive Leadership Model: Victor Vroom's model postulating that time constraints drive a leader's decision-making process.

Weighing Contingencies

Police leader-supervisors can also decide on a leadership style using the **Vroom–Jago time–drive leadership model.** (See Figure 11-6.) This model postulates that time

A Long Beach, California, police officer explaining a situation to a group of citizens.

constraints drive a leader's decision-making process. The model also identifies contingency variables (including team support and goal sharing, likelihood of follower commitment, and significance of a decision) that a leader should consider when selecting a leadership style. Victor Vroom created a Windows-based computer program that enables supervisors to record the strength of presence of each contingency variable in a given situation.

The model also identifies five leadership styles leaders can select from, depending on how strongly present the contingency variables are:

- *Decide:* The leader decides on the best course of action and then directs followers.
- *Consult individually:* The leader makes a decision after consulting with followers individually.
- *Consult team:* The leader makes a decision after holding an open meeting with all followers.
- *Facilitate:* The leader facilitates problem solving and decision making by building consensus for a potential course of action within the team.
- *Delegate:* The leader allows followers to arrive at a decision within limits prescribed by the leader (Vroom, 1964, 2000).

Owing to the complexity of the Vroom–Jago model, it works best when a police organization is trying to drive massive change or is experiencing a problem the resolution of which requires extensive analysis and teamwork. For instance, if an agency is committed to moving from a traditional (professional) model of policing to a more community-oriented style, managers must solicit opinions from all levels of the organization and enlist the commitment of every person—from line officers

figure 11-6 The Vroom–Jago Time–Drive Leadership Model

Problem	Decision significance	Importance of commitment	Leader expertise	Likelihood of commitment	Team support	Team expertise	Team competence	Suggested style
H	H	H	H	H	.....	.....	.....	Decide
				L	H	H	H	Delegate
							L	Consult team
						L	.....	Consult team
					L	.....	.....	Consult team
			L	H	H	H	H	Facilitate
							L	Consult individually
						L	.....	Consult individually
					L	.....	.....	Consult individually
			L	L	H	H	H	Facilitate
							L	Consult team
						L	.....	Consult team
					L	.....	.....	Consult team
		L	H	.....	.....	.....	.....	Decide
			H	.....	H	H	H	Facilitate
							L	Consult individually
						L	.....	Consult individually
					L	.....	.....	Consult individually
L	H	.....	H	.....	.....	.....	.....	Decide
			L	.....	.....	.....	H	Delegate
							L	Facilitate
	L	.....	.....	.....	.....	.....	.....	Decide

Note: An "H" indicates a high level of importance with that contingency variable, an "L" indicates a low level of importance, and a dashed line (.....) indicates "not a factor."

Source: Used by permission of Victor Vroom.

to the chief. In this scenario, change leaders conduct meetings, define goals and communicate them to all parties, and establish a detailed timeline. Because a major organizational transformation can take years, constant open communication and complete dedication to the goal is critical.

Tapping into Followers' Motivation

Path–goal motivational leadership model: R. J. House's framework suggesting that followers will be motivated to give their best if they believe that they are capable of performing the tasks assigned, that their efforts will produce certain results, and that the rewards for completing tasks are worthwhile.

Another model—R. J. House's **path–goal motivational leadership model**—calls for tapping into followers' level of motivation in determining a leadership style. (See Figure 11-7.) The assumption underlying this model is that followers will be motivated to give their best if they believe that they are capable of performing the tasks assigned, that their efforts will produce certain results, and that the rewards for completing tasks are worthwhile. The leader-manager's challenge is to demonstrate the behaviors that best motivate a particular follower to accomplish a specific goal.

The model identifies eight possible behaviors: directive, supportive, participative, achievement-oriented, work facilitation (helping followers achieve tasks), group-oriented decision processes, work-group representation of stakeholders and networking, and leadership behaviors based on organizational values (House, 1996). The model reminds leaders/managers that their central purpose is to motivate and assist followers with goal achievement in the most efficient manner possible (Meese & Ortmeier, 2004; Northouse, 2007).

figure 11-7 The Path–Goal Motivational Leadership Model

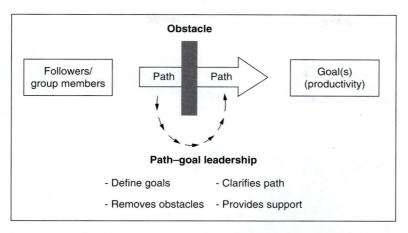

Source: "Path-goal theory of leadership: Lessons, legacy and a reformulated theory" by Robert J. House from *THE LEADERSHIP QUARTERLY,* Autumn, 1996, Vol. 7, No 3, p. 30. Reprinted by permission of Elsevier Ltd.

Serving Followers

Some leaders adopt a style that emphasizes sensitivity, awareness, and empathy, per Robert K. Greenleaf's **servant leadership** concept, which he introduced in a 1970 essay titled *The Servant as Leader.* This essay made a lasting impression on leaders, educators, and others around the world. More than a theory, the concept of the leader-as-servant is a way of life that encourages those in management positions to discover how they can best serve the people they lead (Greenleaf, 1991).

Since the Industrial Revolution, many managers have viewed subordinates as tools to be used or as parts in a well-oiled machine. If one of these "tools" or "parts" wears out, managers simply replace "it" with no loss of productivity. Servant leadership returns humanity to the workplace by assuming a symbiotic relationship (one of mutual dependence) between worker and supervisor. The concept thus blurs the line between leader and follower, and requires both to hold themselves and one another to a higher standard of behavior and understanding.

Here is an example of servant leadership in action: In a particular community, reducing auto theft is a high priority for community members but not for the police. Nevertheless, police servant-leaders demonstrate appreciation for the community's concern and commit to reducing auto theft. Police and community leaders then work together to develop solutions, implement those solutions, and evaluate the results.

> **Servant leadership:** Robert K. Greenleaf's approach to leadership emphasizing sensitivity, awareness, and empathy toward followers.

Building the Best Possible Organization

Police leaders who adopt a style that emphasizes the organization's interests over their own interests are drawing from management expert Jim Collins's concept of **Level 5 leadership,** which he described in his book *Good to Great and the Social Sectors.* Simply stated, Level 5 leaders channel their ambition toward building a better organization rather than promoting themselves and their personal agendas.

> **Level 5 leadership:** Jim Collins's concept proposing that leaders channel their ambition toward building a better organization rather than promoting themselves and their personal agendas.

A police officer using sign language with a deaf man.

Level 5 leaders are humble; they credit their organization's success to factors other than themselves, but they take responsibility for poor results. Though modest, they are driven to produce long-lasting change. They groom peers and subordinates for leadership, ensuring the organization's future success. Although Level 5 leaders may not occupy the spotlight, they exist in almost every organization (Collins, 2001).

One Level 5 leader was a police chief who took the job knowing that the agency was mediocre. He set out to improve the situation. The chief gathered the right staff and designed various projects and activities based on ideas from all. He allocated funds to complete the projects and activities, asking only to be kept informed on progress. The chief communicated a compelling vision of a better future for the agency and guided staff to take the steps needed to make that vision real. As a result of this leader's style, the agency established successful canine patrols; family crisis-intervention teams; criminal-investigation management strategies; indoor and outdoor firearms training ranges; and programs supporting police-citizen partnership, stress management and field training for officers, victims' assistance, and officers' use of Spanish and sign language.

TOXIC MANAGEMENT

Within many police organizations, certain barriers can prevent individuals from practicing leadership and effective supervision—no matter how many theories and styles are available to draw from. Understanding these barriers and the problems they present can bring the contrast between good and poor supervision into sharper relief for aspiring police leader-supervisors. In the following text we examine several barriers:

- *Nepotism.* Nepotism is the promotion and preferential treatment of a manager's close friends or relatives whether they deserve it or not. Nepotism in an organization breeds mediocrity in the favored employees and cynicism in workers who witness it (Collins, 2001).

- *Paramilitary culture.* Many police organizations are characterized by a paramilitary culture. In such agencies, upper management does not tolerate differences of opinions among employees and lower-level managers (Davis & Colaprete, 2005). Sensing the intolerance, people stop contributing their ideas, depriving the agency of the fresh and diverse thinking needed to provide excellent service to the community.

- *Misguided assumptions.* One of the most insidious barriers to effective leadership consists of misguided assumptions among leaders or supervisors themselves. Unfortunately, many police managers literally point at subordinates and tell them what to do, assuming that employees are unwilling or unable to carry out needed tasks. Others threaten employees with punishment, believing that people consistently do whatever it takes to avoid unpleasantness or pain (Beauchamp, Bowie, & Arnold, 2009).

- *Fadishness.* In some policing organizations, supervisors and commanders promote whichever management fad is currently occupying the headlines, without considering whether the advocated approach is right for their organization. They may try to force people to adopt the latest fad, only to activate intense resistance that blocks progress. Ultimately, they waste significant time, effort, and even financial resources.

- *Hypocrisy.* In other policing organizations, managers pay lip service to well-regarded leadership theories that emphasize eliciting ideas and opinions from subordinates. But when employees offer their input, managers do not value or use them. As a result, employees feel disfranchised. They also grow cynical, realizing (correctly) that their managers do not trust employees' ideas or respect their opinions.

These and other barriers can create organizations characterized by **toxic management** (Davis & Colaprete, 2005). Toxic managers exhibit poor judgment and negative behaviors, have no skill at building rapport and positive relationships, and cannot cultivate an environment of mutual respect. Such supervisors and managers will damage the human resources of any organization, especially in a police agency (Reed, 2004). They alienate staff and project an image of weakness. They also spawn an atmosphere in which people refuse direction and contradict management. Simply put, toxic managers create a poisonous environment.

In some organizations, if a toxic manager cannot be removed, an effective leader (toxic handler) may emerge to minimize the manager's destructive impact on people. Sometimes this takes the form of serving as a buffer between the manager and the workforce. For example, the *toxic handler* may translate the ineffective manager's harsh language or autocratic dictates into more palatable terms for employees. Or the toxic handler might urge people not to take the manager's tirades personally. The danger with relying too much on toxic handlers is that they can eventually burn out (Frost, 2003; *Toxic Bosses and Toxic Handlers,* 2004).

Toxic management: a situation in which a manager exhibits poor judgment and negative behaviors, has no skill at building rapport and positive relationships, and cannot cultivate an environment of mutual respect.

Leadership on the job

A Lesson Learned Early

Over 20 years ago, young police officer Ricardo Alvarez was wrestling with a belligerent drunk on a dark street corner. Alvarez radioed for backup just in case. Within moments, as Alvarez handcuffed the drunk, a police car arrived. The driver yelled: "Ricardo, you need my help?" Officer Alvarez looked up in amazement, recognizing the driver as his captain. "No sir," Alvarez replied. "I'm OK, but thank you."

Over two decades later, Alvarez is a police captain himself, having risen through the ranks of his 2,000-officer agency. He recalls the backup and personal presence provided by his captain years earlier. "I can't tell you how great that felt, knowing my captain knew my name and was there to help if I needed it." The experience helped shape Captain Alvarez' management style.

Today, Alvarez manages 160 police officers and 40 civilian employees. He spends a lot of time in the field, often responding to radio calls himself. He listens to his officers and does not micromanage. Captain Alvarez is quick to exclaim: "It's not about me. It's about the team."

1. What leadership style did Captain Alvarez (and his captain before him) demonstrate?

2. Should high-ranking officers in large police agencies engage in line-level (operational) police activities, as Alvarez and his former captain have done? Why or why not?

summary

- **Leadership Theories.** Theories about what distinguishes leadership and what its defining principles are have evolved over time. Major theories focus on leaders' inborn traits, their behaviors (such as facilitating task accomplishment or relationship building), the interaction of a leader's personal characteristics with situational characteristics, the impact of followers' expectations, the importance of adapting leadership style to situations and to followers' motivational needs, ramifications of the quality of relationships between leaders and followers, distinctions between merely transactional interactions between leaders and followers and transformational interactions, and the importance of leaders' understanding their own and their followers' psychological makeup.

- **Leadership Skills.** Whereas theories attempt to identify leadership's defining principles, skills are the abilities needed to exercise leadership. These skills can be acquired through education, experience, and training. Five categories of skills are suggested as indispensable for police officer effectiveness: communications and related interpersonal skills, motivational skills, problem-solving skills, planning and organizing skills, and actuation and implementation skills.

- **Leadership versus Supervision.** Leadership differs from supervision in numerous ways. Leadership is broader than supervision: While a leader may also be a supervisor, not all supervisors are leaders. Police leader-supervisors exhibit a valuable blend of talents, including mentoring and role modeling, crisis management, resource management, and personnel development.

- **Leadership Tools: Authority and Power.** Authority is the legitimate right bestowed by an organization on an individual to direct activities or persons. Power is the ability of an individual to influence others, to shape an organization's direction and priorities, and to influence situations and a variety of affairs and objects. Leaders exhibit a blend of authority and power. They derive their authority from sources such as formal mandates, personal charisma, and social norms. They derive power from sources such as rank, fear, rewards, expertise, and personal charisma.

- **Leadership Styles.** Leadership styles derive from how leaders communicate and act to influence others. Styles consist of practices and the application of leadership skills. They may be influenced by a combination of different leadership theories. Styles include meeting followers' hierarchy of needs, addressing followers' frustrations and conflicting needs, satisfying followers' expectations about performance and outcomes, aligning followers' and agency goals while cultivating trust, blending concern for people with concern for production, adapting to followers' level of readiness, weighing contingencies, tapping into followers' changing motivations, serving followers, and building the best possible organization. Exceptional leaders can demonstrate a blend of styles and change styles to meet the needs of their own unique, changing circumstances.

- **Toxic Management.** Barriers that can prevent individuals from demonstrating leadership and effective supervision include nepotism, a paramilitary culture in an organization, misguided assumptions, faddishness, and hypocrisy. Toxic managers damage the human resources of any organization. If they cannot be removed, sometimes leaders known as toxic handlers will emerge to mitigate a toxic manager's destructive impact. But overreliance on toxic handlers can cause them to suffer burnout.

key terms

authority
behavior theory
contingency theory
ERG theory
expectancy theory
hierarchy of needs model
interaction-expectation theory
leader–follower exchange theory
leadership skill
learned needs theory
Level 5 leadership
meta-leadership theory
managerial grid
motivation-hygiene theory
path-goal motivational leadership model

path–goal theory

personal-situational theory

power

psychodynamic approach

role model

servant leadership

situational leadership model

situational theory

Theory X

Theory Y

Theory Z

toxic management

trait theory

transactional theory

transformational theory

Vroom–Jago time-drive leadership model

discussion questions

1. Define *leadership*. Is leadership an inborn capacity, or can anyone become a leader?

2. Select and review three leadership theories from this chapter. Can each theory be applied in a police organization?

3. Review the major categories of leadership skills presented in this chapter. How might front-line officers, supervisors, and commanders in a police organization exercise these skills?

4. How are supervisors/managers and leaders different? How are they similar?

5. How do the concepts of leadership and supervision complement one another in a police organization?

6. How does authority differ from power? Where do leaders derive their authority and power? Does a leader need both of these tools to be effective?

7. Select and review three leadership styles described in this chapter. What would cause you to adopt each style you selected? What are the advantages and disadvantages of each style?

8. Have you ever worked in an organization that had a toxic manager? If so, what behaviors characterized the person? What impact did this individual have on the organization? Have you ever served in the toxic handler role? If so, in what ways did you mitigate the damage created by the toxic manager in question?

WHAT WOULD YOU DO?

Leadership on a Bike

The bicycle patrol in a midsize northeastern city was highly successful at apprehending suspects in places inaccessible to police patrol cars. By 2003, however, the agency had significantly reduced the number of officers assigned to bicycle patrol, owing to budget cuts and a shift in priorities. Moreover, only half of the remaining officers had serviceable bicycles.

Mark, a former bicycle patrol lieutenant, decided that the bike patrol should be revitalized, to enhance public relations and because officers had been experiencing difficulty apprehending suspects in places inaccessible to patrol cars. Mark's captain, Cheryl, advised him to develop a plan that would make use of existing equipment, since no funds were available to purchase new bikes. Cheryl placed Mark in charge of the project, and supported the brief action plan that he developed and presented.

With his plan approved, Mark salvaged parts from unusable bicycles to repair those that were less damaged. The strategy resulted in 10 complete and functional bicycles. Additional officers were trained for bicycle duty, and many previously trained bike officers returned to the reactivated bike patrol. Impressed by the bike unit's results, including enhanced public relations and an increase in the number of drug suspects arrested, agency management budgeted $10,000 for the purchase of new bikes. The bike patrol became a model patrol methodology in urban neighborhoods, won praise from residents, and was sought after as a prestigious assignment by police officers. The patrol's success was attributed to the leadership skills of a motivated lieutenant and a supportive police captain.

1. What leadership style did Cheryl exhibit with Mark?

2. What leadership theories are reflected in this story?

3. What leadership skills did Mark use to plan and implement the bicycle patrol project?

4. If you had been in charge of the project, would the leadership style that Cheryl exhibited have come naturally to you? If not, what might you have done to develop your ability to use that style?

◀ The police are subject to periodic individual performance appraisals.

Human Relations Challenges in a Police Agency

After completing this chapter, readers should be able to:

- describe how a police agency develops and uses general orders.
- explain how an agency uses policies, procedures, and job descriptions and specifications to evaluate individual officers' performance.
- discuss how performance appraisals help police agencies foster excellence.
- identify two purposes that individual performance appraisals can serve.
- define *succession management* and assess its importance in policing.
- identify protocols a police agency might use to make promotion decisions.
- recognize practices that police agencies use to develop promising candidates for specific roles.

learning outcomes

- assess the negative impact high workforce attrition (turnover) can have on a police agency.

- illustrate the use of clear communication of agency values and policies to improve talent retention.

- explain how collaboration among individuals with fresh perspectives and skills can improve employee retention.

- explain how a police agency can motivate officers to give their best on the job, and how high motivation leads to lower turnover.

- examine the rise of citizen review boards and explain their role in responding to complaints about possible police misconduct.

- compare differing perspectives on citizen review boards' value for police agencies and the communities they serve.

- trace the process that police agencies use to discipline officers accused of misconduct.

- discuss how police agencies can establish early warning systems to identify and address problematic police conduct before it escalates.

- identify symptoms of stress in police agency personnel and describe practices for mitigating dangerous levels of stress.

- explain how police agencies can help officers mitigate the impact of stress on their private lives.

- differentiate training that prepares police officers to survive on the street while they are on and off duty from training that can prepare them to navigate political dynamics within their agency.

- distinguish between moral and immoral political power.

Introduction

In the world of policing, many challenges that arise have less to do with actual policing and more to do with human relations. For example, how can a police agency develop and communicate clear policies and procedures, so officers and other personnel know what behaviors and attitudes are expected of them? How might police managers and supervisors appraise individual officers' job perfor-mance to strengthen their knowledge, skills, and abilities as well as help them develop their careers? Speaking of career development, through what means should an agency manage the succession of officers and other individual contribu-tors into managerial and supervisory roles—or lateral roles for those who are not interested in or are not ready for management?

Once an agency has deployed talented individuals into key roles throughout the organization, how can it keep them there to avoid the high costs of replacing departing employees and training newcomers? Moreover, if officers and other personnel break the rules laid out by the agency in its policies, procedures, and other behavioral mandates, how should agency leaders respond? What recourse do the civilians served by the agency have?

Of course, even under the best conditions, police officers have one of the toughest jobs around, and many of them suffer from job-related stress. How can agencies design stress-management programs to protect officers' health and enable them to consistently deliver top-notch performance on the job? Finally, while officers know all about how to survive the physical perils of police work, most know much less about how to survive the political machinations swirling within the organization that employs them. How can an agency help them understand and navigate the political terrain so they master the art of exercising power and influence appropriately—a defining competency of ethical leadership?

In this chapter, we address each of these questions in turn. We closely examine the human relations challenges at hand and offer suggestions for how police organizations can surmount them. Tackling the complexities of human relations will never be easy, but by putting the right systems and practices in place, agency leaders stand a better chance of ensuring that officers and other personnel are motivated to excel, loyal, effective, and physically and mentally healthy.

POLICIES AND PROCEDURES

Policies (how a police agency intends to operate) and procedures (the steps needed to put policies into action) form the backbone for employees' behavior. In most policing organizations, documented policies and procedures are known as **general orders,** modeled on those found in the U.S. military services (Delattre & Behan, 2003).

General orders: a police agency's documented policies and procedures.

Developing General Orders

Policies: the basic principles directing and limiting a police agency's actions in pursuit of long-term goals.

Procedures: the sequence of activities or courses of action that must be followed in a police agency to correctly perform tasks.

Ideally, a police agency develops its **policies**—its basic principles directing and limiting its actions in pursuit of long-term goals—first and then defines the corresponding **procedures,** or the sequence of activities or courses of action that must be followed to correctly perform tasks. The agency's chief executive officer (for example, the chief of police, sheriff, or commissioner) typically writes the policies or directs their creation. Policies might relate to a broad range of topics—including the agency's general goals and objectives, press relations, public relations, employee conduct, administrative matters, and community relations, among others. Once an agency establishes its policies, it can develop procedures, which help embed the policies into the agency's culture and into officers' everyday behavior (National Advisory Commission on Criminal Justice Standards and Goals, 1973; Stohr & Collins, 2009). National and state accreditation standards may provide additional guidance for agencies seeking to develop or modify their general orders.

A police agency's general orders usually begin with a description of how the agency is structured; that is, who reports to whom, and how the organization's departments and units are configured. The document may then describe the duties of specific groups of officers, such as sergeants and patrol officers, or provide a broad overview of personnel duties. All general orders also document policies governing the agency's daily operations (such as patrol assignments and traffic management), investigations, training, and the legal process. The format of the general orders may range from very formal (with an identifying numerical tag for every paragraph) to relatively informal (paragraphs with numbered lists of directives as appropriate). However, almost every general order will begin with a statement of the policy to which the procedures apply.

A woman whose LAPD father was killed in the line of duty is comforted by another LAPD officer.

General orders for a police agency commonly state the agency's policies for specific areas and then provide procedural guidelines for fulfilling those policies. For example, a police agency in the northeastern United States has a policy for notification of agency personnel's immediate family in the event an officer is injured in the line of duty. The policy states that the agency assumes the responsibility of notifying an officer's family in such an event. The procedures associated with that policy spell out actions to be taken by the injured officer's immediate supervisor, the Office of the Chief of Police, and any agency personnel who notify the news media of the event. Procedures direct how information will be gathered before the family is notified and stipulate that the notification will be made in person by police command (Rochester Police Department, 2001).

The most effective written policies and procedures use active rather than passive voice, for easier understanding by everyone in the agency. For example, instead of reading "A supervisor's signature should be obtained on the form," the document should read, "Take the completed form to your supervisor for signature."

Using General Orders

The most important thing about general orders is that they guide police officers' behavior in a myriad of common and uncommon situations that officers might encounter. Behind the general orders is the understanding that police are expected to act within the law at all times, even while officers know that they have an enormous amount of discretion in performing their duties.

Leadership on the job
Work-Prep Overtime Policies

Several police officers filed a lawsuit against the city that employed them, contending that certain tasks they performed as preparation for duty constituted uncompensated "work" as defined by federal law. The officers claimed that they were owed back pay and overtime pay because city policy required them to load equipment into their police vehicles and review e-mail before their shifts officially began at roll call.

The city's attorney contended that the tasks for which the officers claimed extra compensation could be performed after the work shift officially began. During the trial, a few officers testified that they decided to carry out routine tasks (such as loading equipment into patrol cars) before their work shift for specific reasons (for instance, so they could lay claim to their favorite vehicles) (Bernstein, 2009).

1. In your view, did the officers have a legitimate case regarding their back pay and overtime claim? Why or why not?

2. Do you see this lawsuit as frivolous or as important regarding employment conditions and the provision of public safety services? Explain your reasoning.

Police officers do not need to know every detail of their agency's general orders. Nevertheless, they should familiarize themselves with those policies and procedures that apply most closely to their job responsibilities, whether their responsibilities center on firearms usage, arrest and detention practices, or crime scene investigations.

OFFICER PERFORMANCE APPRAISALS

Performance appraisal: assessment of an individual's job performance in an organization.

In Chapter 7, you learned how a police agency assesses and evaluates its overall performance as an organization. But a **performance appraisal**—an assessment of an individual's job performance—is also important for each employee working within a police agency. In traditional police agencies, performance evaluations for officers typically center on quantifiable outcomes, such as number of arrests made or number of citations issued. However, in agencies that have adopted the community policing strategy (see Chapter 2), appraisals also consider more qualitative results, such as citizens' perceptions of their safety and the quality of life in their neighborhood. The ideal performance evaluation addresses an officer's quantitative *and* qualitative impact on the community the agency serves (Michelson & Maher, 1993; Ortmeier & Meese, 2010).

Linking Performance to Policies, Procedures, and Job Descriptions and Specifications

Most police agencies have used traditional performance evaluations to measure officers' knowledge, skills, and abilities, as well as their ability to adhere to the agency's policies and procedures. When an officer's performance is good or excellent, that evaluation suggests that the supervisor and other superiors responsible for that officer have effectively guided and developed the individual (Whisenand & Rush, 2007).

Performance evaluations are also typically structured on the job description and specifications for the positions in question. Of course, police officers must thoroughly understand the details of their job to fulfill its requirements. During performance appraisals, supervisors evaluate officers according to how well they have met their job responsibilities, how much effort they have extended, how knowledgeable and skillful they are in carrying out their duties, and how appropriate their conduct has been. A positive evaluation in these areas indicates that the officer's level of performance is acceptable (Crowder, 1998; Haberfeld, 2002).

Fostering Excellence in the Agency

However, performance appraisals are not just a means to evaluate how a police officer is performing on the job. They can—and should—also help an agency create and sustain a culture of growth, service excellence, professionalism, and continuous individual and organizational improvement. An agency that is dedicated to the development of its employees uses evaluations to analyze past problems as well as anticipate and address future ones. Through performance appraisals, supervisors provide valuable feedback to employees at each stage in their careers. These appraisals commence in the recruit academy and continue through field training, probationary periods, regular assessments held annually or semiannually, and during times of promotion. With every evaluation, employees receive feedback on their strengths and on the areas where they need to improve.

Distinguishing between Appraisal's Dual Purposes

Performance appraisals serve dual purposes. A police agency may use them as an administrative tool; for example, to determine whether an employee "fits" in the organization in terms of its culture and values, to decide which assignments an officer would best fill, and to gauge an officer's qualification for promotion and other rewards. The agency may also use appraisal as a career development tool. For instance, during an officer's performance appraisal, a police supervisor may ask "Where would you like to go in your career?" or "What abilities would you like to strengthen to take the next step in your career?" The supervisor might then share information about training, job assignments, and other developmental opportunities that would help the officer achieve career goals.

This dual-purpose nature of performance appraisals can present challenges for a police agency. Specifically, officers may be reluctant to talk about their career goals—including discussing knowledge areas, skills, or abilities they would like to improve—if they think that acknowledging the need for improvement in specific areas would disqualify them for promotion or earn them criticism from their supervisor (Mathis & Jackson, 2005; Morreale, 2002). For this reason, some management experts suggest conducting performance evaluation discussions separately from career development discussions. For supervisors who adopt this approach, it is vital to explain during a career development discussion that information shared during the meeting will not affect the officer's performance rating or compensation.

Moreover, whether a performance appraisal is used for administrative or career-development purposes, the person conducting the appraisal should apply the following practices:

- **Be candid about the employee's strengths and areas for improvement or growth.** As difficult as it might be to deliver negative feedback to an officer, such feedback is essential if the officer hopes to deliver improved performance.

- **Provide specific examples.** While evaluating an officer's performance, appraisers should provide specific examples to back up their assessments, rather than general or vague comments. For example, instead of saying, "You're doing a great job with public relations," the appraiser could say something like, "The driver safety event you organized was a huge success. Eighty percent of the town's high school students attended it. That was a major increase over last year's attendance."

- **Connect performance to agency goals.** Appraisers should consistently connect the person's knowledge, skills, and abilities to the agency's operations and strategic plans. For example, "To execute our community policing strategy, we need more officers to learn at least one other language in addition to their first language. The more we can speak the languages used by the citizens we are serving, the better we can help them. So, might you be interested in signing up for one of the language classes we are offering this year?"

- **Conclude with an action plan.** The supervisor and employee should conclude the appraisal by developing an agreed-upon plan for meeting performance or career objectives. The development of a plan for the employee's improvement and growth within the agency is the best way to ensure that topics discussed and decisions made during the appraisal are translated into actions that deliver the desired outcomes (Bossidy & Charan, 2002).

SUCCESSION MANAGEMENT

Succession management: preparation of individuals in a police agency who are interested in leadership for higher-level management and supervisory positions as well as specialized assignments.

Succession planning: the identification of high-potential employees in a police agency and the provision of training, coaching, and developmental opportunities needed to enable them to move into influential or specialized positions.

If a police agency expects to survive and thrive, it must excel at **succession management.** Through this crucial process, agency managers prepare those who are interested in leadership for higher-level management and supervisory positions. Of course, not everyone in an organization necessarily wants to become a manager. Nor is every person suited for a managerial or supervisory role. Succession management thus may also include developing the knowledge, skills, and abilities of employees who wish to make lateral career moves; for instance, from a patrol position to one involving crime scene investigation and analysis.

Understanding the Importance of Succession Management

Why is succession management so important? Through effective **succession planning,** an agency establishes continuity of service and execution of its strategic plan by identifying high-potential employees and providing them with the training, coaching, and developmental opportunities they need to move into influential or specialized positions (Mathis & Jackson, 2005).

Succession management also helps agencies ensure that they have enough talent in the right roles. In any organization, if a key position remains vacant for too long, the organization will have difficulty operating as it should. Imagine trying to manage a police agency that has no one to head the crime investigation unit or the information technology (IT) department. In police agencies that successfully orchestrate succession management, leaders anticipate vacancies in key positions long before they occur; identify employees who have the skills, ability, interest, and potential to fill the vacancies; and recruit, prepare, or promote promising talent to move into those positions. By staying ahead of anticipated vacancies, leaders help create a pool of talent they can tap to ensure that the right people move into the right roles when needed.

Applying Promotion Protocols

Most police agencies have a limited number of management and supervisory positions, a condition that constrains individual officers' ability to gain promotion into such roles. Given this constraint, agencies must ensure that the process of promoting officers to these positions is fair and above reproach. As in other professions, not every officer is a good prospect for a management or supervisory position. To identify those who are, agencies should look for officers who demonstrate leadership ability, excellent communication skills, and consistent positive performance—and consider them first for promotion into management. For employees who are interested in making lateral moves into key positions that are not at the management level, agencies can help those individuals develop the knowledge, skills, and abilities needed to excel in their new roles.

Most police agencies use written tests to determine which officers to select for first-line supervisory positions (such as corporal or sergeant) and mid-level positions (including lieutenant or captain). The written promotional exam may include questions testing officers' knowledge of the agency's current policies and procedures, effective supervisory and management practices, ethics, leadership, current criminal law and procedure, and vehicle and traffic statutes and laws. The exams may also

Officers use agency policy manuals, textbooks, and other resources to prepare for promotion exams.

An assessment panel is typically used to decide whether to promote an officer.

assess officers' comprehension of written material. Most police jurisdictions advise promotional applicants to review and become familiar with certain approved police textbooks, agency policy manuals, and the current state and federal laws affecting police competence and performance.

In addition to the written test, agencies may also use an oral interview, situational assessment exercises, and past performance appraisals to make promotion decisions. In larger agencies, the decision process may be led by a promotion or assessment panel and may include a review by the commissioner, chief of police, or sheriff. Evaluators consider candidates' education and any specialized training candidates may have received, along with their specific skills, productivity levels, personal appearance, commitment to community service, and loyalty to the agency's vision, mission, goals, and leadership.

Although officers aspiring to advance into management will likely be familiar with their agency's promotion protocols, the succession management process is organized and directed at the supervisory level. For instance, a sergeant who expects to retire soon may single out a first-line officer who exhibits the correct attitude and behaviors for a supervisory position, then coach that officer in how to attain the sergeant's rank. There is no guarantee that the retiring sergeant's job will be filled by that officer, but the officer receives the benefit of the sergeant's years of experience. And the retiring sergeant helps identify and groom a possible replacement—saving the agency the time and expense.

Developing Promising Candidates

Succession planning should be an ongoing, proactive process rather than a one-time event that a police agency initiates only after a key position has been vacated. The goal of this process is to widen the agency's pool of talent so employees can be promoted or moved laterally into roles as needed. That way, the agency avoids the risk of having positions remain vacant indefinitely.

A young police officer "job shadowing" a senior colleague.

The succession management process should also be simple and transparent, so prospective candidates and leaders can focus on candidates' talents and skills. For instance, when an agency develops clear and concise job descriptions and specifications, everyone involved in the succession management process knows what is expected of those who may fill a vacant position. Moreover, even if the agency's human relations department spearheads the definition of promotion protocols, managers must take ownership of the process of identifying and developing promising employees (deKoning, 2005; Hunter & Barker, 2011).

When a manager or supervisor identifies a successful candidate for promotion or lateral movement in the agency, on-the-job development should begin. For instance, suppose that Carol, a patrol officer, is interested in eventually working in the area of crime investigation. Paul, her supervisor, should encourage her to talk with police detectives and perhaps even spend some time "job shadowing" to learn more about how they do their work. Paul might also "sculpt" Carol's job—giving her assignments that present her with new challenges related to the work she is interested in. To illustrate, he might advise her to survey neighborhood residents to discover their perceptions of how well the agency prevents crime in their community and to suggest potential solutions to problems identified in the survey responses. Paul should then coach and support Carol as needed while she carries out the assignment. For instance, perhaps she needs suggestions for how to design the survey questions or how to interpret community residents' responses to the questions.

Last, all managers should encourage and help promising candidates to forge mutually beneficial connections with peers, superiors, and others within and outside the agency. These connections will help candidates learn how to collaborate and interact effectively with subordinates, superiors, and customers. Members of an aspiring manager's support network can teach the person a lot about the core responsibilities of management—including how to achieve important goals through other people, develop direct reports' talents, and inspire exceptional performance. According to some estimates, roughly 40 percent of newly promoted managers and supervisors fail within 18 months of promotion because they do not know how to cultivate strong relationships with colleagues and subordinates. It is much better to set the stage for success early rather than wait until a promotion has occurred—and then hope that the person can handle the job (deKoning, 2005; Stevens, 2011).

TALENT RETENTION

Police officers who resign or retire early from an agency may cause high attrition (turnover) among remaining personnel. Turnover raises daunting challenges for the agency. Specifically:

Morale: the state of the spirits of a person or group as exhibited by confidence, cheerfulness, discipline, and willingness to perform assigned tasks.

- High turnover levels can erode **morale**—defined as the state of the spirit of a person or group as exhibited by confidence, cheerfulness, discipline, and willingness to perform assigned tasks—in those who remain at the agency. Employees begin wondering why so many of their colleagues are leaving, and their own commitment to the agency may waver.

- If the next class of recruits is unable to assume their positions for several months, the agency risks being unable to provide the public safety so crucial to its mission.

- Screening, hiring, and training new officers are expensive.

- It often takes time for inexperienced officers to begin performing at acceptable levels (Haarr, 2005). If an agency loses experienced officers on a regular basis, its overall effectiveness will diminish.

In all these respects, high turnover is costly for an agency.

Despite turnover's high price tag, police and other public safety agencies often devote enormous resources to recruiting and selecting employees—and then neglect to retain their best performers. To keep valued employees onboard, an agency can take several powerful steps—including communicating values and policies clearly, bringing in new people with fresh perspectives, and sustaining talented professionals' motivation to excel on the job.

Communicating Values and Policies

When an agency clearly communicates its values and policies to applicants as well as existing employees, newcomers and old-timers alike know what to expect from their employment there. And when realities match their expectations, they are much less likely to experience disappointment with the job and seek to work elsewhere.

Agency administrators have numerous channels at their disposal for this communication. For example, during pre-employment and promotion interviews, they should describe negative as well as positive aspects of the job, along with how the agency operates and what its core values are. During orientation of recruits and

Cleveland, Ohio, police recruits during their first week on the job in October 2006.

those who have earned a promotion, they can further explain values and policies as well as the behaviors and results expected in the new position. Finally, by providing proper training, including remediation of skill deficiencies, agencies can reinforce messages about values and policies. Training also helps officers improve their performance—which often strengthens loyalty to the agency.

Bringing in Fresh Perspectives and Skills

While costly, turnover also presents a vital opportunity for an agency: to bring in new employees with fresh perspectives and skills, such as an openness and ability to effect change or a commitment to ethical behavior. Some officers who are leaving the agency might have opposed earlier changes, become ineffective in their jobs, or developed unethical behaviors (Orrick, 2008). Their attitudes and actions can corrode morale and loyalty in their colleagues: No one likes to work with incompetent fellow employees or colleagues who harbor negative attitudes. And no one wants to work for an organization that seems to accept or even reward mediocrity.

Whenever a problematic officer leaves an agency, leaders should take an honest look at not only any knowledge or skills the person had but also the shortcomings embodied in that individual. The agency can then work to replace any assets that are being lost as well as bring in someone new who possesses the talents, attitudes, and values lacking in the person who left predecessors. When agencies bring in new individuals with fresh perspectives and skills, morale and loyalty in the remaining staff often improve. That boosts the agency's chances of keeping its best performers.

Sustaining Officer Motivation

Often, high turnover in a police agency stems in part from lack of motivation. To keep officers motivated to give their best on the job, managers must recognize achievement and offer incentives that people see as attainable and worth the effort. Leaders also motivate sub-ordinates by empowering them to make decisions central to their jobs. In turn, empowerment breeds self-confidence and well-being, essential ingredients for accomplishing goals. And when people accomplish goals, they feel motivated to achieve even more.

Another way to motivate officers is to offer stimulating experiences, such as job rotations, new and challenging responsibilities, and assignments that stretch people beyond their comfort zone. Job rotation can be as simple as changing an officer's shift; every shift offers unique problems and challenges. When an officer makes a more significant change, such as moving from gang intelligence investigations and surveillance to drug enforcement, the challenge can prove equally motivating.

Increasing officers' responsibilities within their current job posting is also a potent motivational tool. For example, an officer can participate in a special community project or prepare a statistical report. Such experiences can constitute a refreshing change from "business as usual." To help officers embrace new responsibilities, supervisors can explain that such projects generate important results for the agency and the community, as well as supporting the officer's own career development.

Job challenges related to community policing and problem solving are particularly useful for enhancing morale and officers' job satisfaction. After tackling such challenges successfully, officers feel they are making a real difference in the communities they serve (Orrick, 2008). Such experiences—for instance, working with citizens to make their homes and businesses more resistant to burglars or strengthening relationships between citizens and the police—also help develop officers' critical thinking skills. And they give officers opportunities to learn new ways of analyzing problems and crafting solutions.

Executing challenging assignments helps make officers feel empowered to generate results for the agency and shape their own careers. Supervisors and managers who fail to provide such empowerment risk seeing their direct reports develop a negative attitude toward the job and an unwillingness to do anything beyond the minimum requirements for the patrol officer role. Minimum job performance or job effort becomes the new standard. If one officer develops this attitude, it can spread throughout the agency, leading to poor morale in others. In the worst cases, officers may even fear taking any initiative, because they believe that the agency will not support them in their efforts to grow (T. E. Baker, 2006; Shusta et al., 2011).

Police officers must be sensitive to the racial and ethnic backgrounds of others.

ETHICS IN ACTION

ICE 287(g): Controversial Crime-Prevention Program

The U.S. Immigration and Customs Enforcement (ICE) agency, a part of the U.S. Department of Homeland Security, has a program known as 287(g). This program allows the agency to empower state, county, and local police officers to enforce immigration law. Through 287(g), local police officials can question individuals about their immigration status. If that status appears uncertain, law enforcement personnel can refer the individuals for possible deportation. Until the inception of this program, immigration monitoring was solely the purview of federal authorities.

Opponents of 287(g) point out that detaining an individual because that person might someday commit a crime goes directly against one of the United States' oldest tenets: a person is innocent until proven guilty. Opponents further say that making line police officers responsible for enforcing immigration law will seriously hamper police efforts in areas characterized by a high concentration of immigrants. In particular, questioning people about their immigration status makes it harder than ever for police to build trust between themselves and the citizens in the communities their agency serves.

To further complicate the situation, some immigrants who could be deported have lived in the United States long enough to give birth to children, who are U.S. citizens by law. Thus, deportation may separate family members, parents, and children.

For these reasons, many police jurisdictions have refused to join the ICE 287(g) program. Others that have joined are facing mounting complaints about the program and have been forced to modify their participation; for example, by refraining from inquiring about immigration status unless the person in question is suspected of a felony (Shahani & Greene, 2009; U.S. House of Representatives Committee on the Judiciary, the Republicans, 2009; U.S. Immigration and Customs Enforcement, 2009).

1. If police take on the task of enforcing immigration laws in addition to their usual crime fighting and community policing responsibilities, what impacts—positive and negative—could this added responsibility have on their ability to do their job? Discuss.

2. To question individuals on their immigration status, local police should develop unrelated criteria for determining who to stop and question. For example, if a motorist is stopped and detained for a motor-vehicle infraction, the police can inquire about the detainee's immigration status. Stopping someone simply because of skin color could be classified as racial profiling, a practice deemed illegal in many areas.

Currently, the law is unsettled with respect to stopping someone and inquiring of their immigration status. In your opinion, is this practice legal? Why or why not? Is it ethical? Why or why not?

MANAGEMENT OF POLICE MISCONDUCT

We discussed police misconduct in Chapter 3, but in the pages that follow, we look at several particular aspects of misconduct: the role of citizen review boards in drawing attention to misconduct, use of discipline in response to misconduct, and use of early warning systems to detect problem officers before they act inappropriately.

Working with Citizen Review Boards

Citizen review board: an independent group comprising local citizens appointed by the mayor or other politicians that investigates complaints, decides whether a complaint is justified based on the evidence at hand, and offers recommendations.

Almost every police agency across the United States has a formal process in place for citizens to file complaints against individual officers. Some complaints focus on the use of force or discourtesy; others on possible unethical or illegal behavior. Usually, a **citizen review board**—an independent group comprising local citizens appointed by the mayor or other politicians—investigates complaints, decides whether a complaint is justified based on the evidence at hand, and offers recommendations. The recommendations may include officer discipline, new training initiatives, refresher training, or notification to the complainant that the police actions taken were proper and justified.

A Controversial Concept   The concept of the citizen review board has sparked contention between police and citizens since the mid-1960s, when disfranchised groups in almost every major city began demanding protection of their civil rights and liberties. Today, some police still resist such boards because of what they view as civilians' lack of understanding about the complex realities of police work

In many jurisdictions, citizen review boards are used to review complaints made against police officers.

and the indignity (according to police) of being reviewed by someone outside the agency (Peak et al., 2010). Police who resist civilian oversight assert that such oversight is politicized and destroys the credibility of the police as a group and that police misconduct is not as pervasive as citizen review boards would have the public believe.

Those who support such boards maintain that police officers cannot be objective about one another's behavior and that police subculture pressures officers to support each other even if a fellow officer commits illegal behavior. Supporters further contend that a greater number of officers are found guilty and disciplined through civilian oversight than through their agency's internal processes or the formal justice system, that the punishment serves as a powerful deterrent, and that civilian oversight improves an agency's image by demonstrating its willingness to work with the community to prevent abuse of police power.

A Variety of Complaint Processes   Because no ideal system of civilian review exists as yet, police jurisdictions have developed methods for processing complaints that suit their unique characteristics, their citizen population, and their police force (Farrow, 2003).

For example, in some jurisdictions, citizens file complaints initially with the command officers where the incident occurred or with the agency's internal affairs/ professional responsibility section. Those who file a complaint through such channels and who feel that the complaint has not received sufficient attention have the option of presenting the complaint to the citizen review board. The board then assesses the investigation's thoroughness, analyzes the findings, and makes recommendations for changes in agency policy, procedure, or training. In other jurisdictions, community residents present complaints directly to a citizen review board, which then initiates an investigation by addressing the appropriate department within the police agency.

Words versus Deeds   Numerous police agencies say they are committed to the complaint procedure and to taking action against officers found guilty of misconduct. However, police agencies in many jurisdictions have managed to stall or even halt the complaint process by responding slowly to complaints. In some instances, agencies have even "lost" a complaint altogether. But even if an agency processes a complaint appropriately, there is no consistent form of discipline.

For instance, in San Francisco, 70 percent of officers who were accused of using excessive force between 1996 and 2004 received only a reprimand or perfunctory intervention (such as verbal counseling or a written memorandum of record). Even though voters established the Office of Citizen Complaints to remedy the situation, the office was understaffed, lacked effective leaders, and met with fierce opposition from the police agency itself and its union, the Police Officers Association (Sward, Wallace, & Fernandez, 2006).

The Importance and Limits of Civilian Review   No police agency can afford to ignore citizen complaints about police conduct, agency policy and procedure, and service quality. Such complaints may signify serious problems with an agency's management of personnel or its ability to fulfill its mission. Complaints also shed light on where citizens may lack understanding of current laws, enforcement practices, police procedures, and service priorities. For these reasons, agencies

Many jurisdictions are installing dashboard video cameras in police vehicles to substantiate that officers act properly, and to protect officers from unfounded complaints by citizens.

must handle all citizen inquiries and grievances swiftly and thoroughly. The right response can help the agency build trust and strengthen its credibility with its customers.

Of course, the possibility exists that some citizens will make false allegations against the police. In most states, it is a criminal offense to file a false allegation of police misconduct. In some situations, video cameras mounted on police-vehicle dashboards and on light poles at city intersections have helped police agencies prove that an officer has acted properly—thus exposing a false allegation. In other cases, analysis of a complainant's medical condition has proved that the person's injuries could not have been caused by police behavior cited in the complaint.

Two Models of Citizen Review   Some police jurisdictions use an agency-focused citizen review model; others use a customer-focused model. Those with the agency-focused model use citizen review to address problems with employee competence, policy and procedure compliance, and personnel behaviors and attitudes. This model drives strict adherence to or possible minor adjustment of the agency's current systems.

In jurisdictions with the customer-focused model, agencies use citizen review to improve service quality. This model encourages agency management to solve problems, anticipate the community's future needs, and devise ways to meet those needs. It thus fosters proactivity and a spirit of innovation (Walker, 2001).

Regardless of which model an agency uses, leaders must be able to clearly define the model for personnel throughout the organization. Through such clarity, everyone in the agency knows how they are expected to behave and what the agency's priorities are.

Disciplining Officers Accused of Misconduct

If clear and verifiable evidence of police misconduct exists, experts recommend swift and fair **discipline**—actions taken to correct problematic behavior—to satisfy the complainant as well as the general public and to discourage further misconduct. In most police environments, discipline is progressive: It starts with remedial training, then (if misconduct recurs) moves to oral reprimand, written reprimand, and eventually the loss of vacation or compensatory time off. The most serious infractions, incompetence, or continual progressive disciplinary cases may lead to retraining or transfer of the offender to a less challenging assignment, suspension (with or without pay), demotion, or even termination.

Criminal prosecution of police personnel accused of misconduct generally suspends the administrative disciplinary process until the case is resolved. Agencies may also offer an employee the opportunity to resign from the organization in lieu of the possibility of demotion or termination.

Leading by example and delivering a reprimand in brief, pointed increments is preferable to a public or even private "dressing down" of an officer. When a reprimand is necessary, the following process is recommended:

1. Reprimand the officer as soon as possible after the problem behavior has occurred.

2. Be specific about what is wrong with the behavior; that is, why it creates problems for the officer, the agency and the community the agency serves. For example, "You arrived late for your shift twice this week. When you do that, we risk not having the coverage we need to respond to calls for service. And someone else has to cover for you."

3. Express specific feelings about the behavior. For instance, "I'm upset and disappointed."

4. Pause to let silence emphasis those feelings.

5. Assure the officer that the person's contribution to the department is valued and that the agency thinks well of the individual. However, the problem behavior in this instance is unacceptable (T. E. Baker, 2006; Bennett & Hess 2007; Blanchard & Johnson, 1982).

Discipline: actions taken to correct problematic behavior.

Establishing Early Warning Systems

Many police agencies have established an **early warning system** to identify and address problematic behaviors before they can reach disastrous levels. For specific individuals, the agency documents behaviors that have the potential to escalate into more frequent and serious problems, using indicators to monitor trends. Indicators include the number of citizen complaints filed against an officer within a specified time period, use of excessive force incidents, number of police-vehicle accidents, and excessive firearm discharge reports.

Early warning systems enable an agency to intervene promptly when managers see negative behaviors emerging. Counseling, remedial training, and stricter supervision can help to change an officer's problem behavior. The first-line supervisor or sergeant plays a crucial role in this effort, as this individual should know the problem officer quite well. In fact, problem officers tend to be known by others in

Early warning system: a set of practices enabling a police agency to identify and address problematic behaviors before they can reach disastrous levels.

the agency as having chronic performance problems. Such problems may manifest themselves as work that is below or at minimum performance standards, questionable arrest practices, lack of performance documentation, and high-risk behaviors such as substance abuse or dangerous leisure-time activities (Ortmeier & Meese, 2010; Walker, Alpert, & Kenney, 2001).

STRESS MANAGEMENT

The second most stressful job in the United States is police officer (the first is inner-city high school teacher) (Centers for Disease Control and Prevention, 2006). Officers are the first people exposed to situations in which human beings have behaved badly toward one another. Death scenes, domestic abuse injuries, drug overdoses, fatal car collisions, child molestation, and other incidents are regular parts of a police officer's life. The average citizen may see no more than one or two dead bodies or seriously injured people in a lifetime; an officer who works in a large city may see one or two dead bodies weekly and often encounter people who have suffered horrific injuries.

While officers may become conditioned to viewing horrible sights and may not be shocked by these tragedies after a few years' experience, the scenes can still leave their mark on their psyche. Officers learn that life is fragile, and many feel frustrated by the limitations of the help they can give. Given these harsh realities, it is easy to understand how the effects of stress can build within a person. As physi-

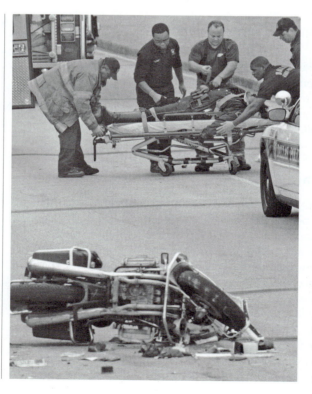

Police officers witness disturbing scenes such as this scene of a fatally injured Dallas Police Department motorcycle officer resulting from a collision while escorting Hillary Clinton's motorcade.

cal, emotional, and spiritual damage from stress accumulates, the officer may become cynical, depressed, and angry. Stress can also shorten life spans. In the United States, average life expectancy for men is a little over 74 years; a little over 80 years for women. For police officers with 10 to 19 years on the job, life expectancy is just 53 to 66 years (Aveni, 1999; Lindsey & Kelly, 2004; Violanti, 2002).

What is cutting so many officers' lives short? More than one hundred police officers die in the line of duty each year. Stress-related diseases associated with cancer and heart ailments also take their toll. In addition, active-duty and retired police officers commit suicide at a rate nearly three times the national average. Evidence suggests that police officers are eight times more likely to take their own lives than they are to be killed by a criminal while on duty (National Law Enforcement Officers Memorial Fund, 2010; National P.O.L.I.C.E. Suicide Foundation, 2010).

Recognizing the Symptoms of Stress

Symptoms of psychological stress can include boredom, depression, hostility, paranoia, and sudden mood changes. An officer's colleagues and family members who witness such behaviors can ask questions, express concern, and empathize with the officer. Superiors can take affected officers aside and strongly recommend that they seek help independently or through the agency-sponsored employee assistance program without a report being filed in the officers' personnel file. However, most observers, be they family, friends, colleagues, or supervisors, hesitate to address stress-related concerns because they fear violating the officer's super-hero persona—the sense that the individual is in charge and can deal with any situation.

The worst manifestation of psychological stress is posttraumatic stress disorder (PTSD). After experiencing a traumatic event (for example, combat, rape, or a car crash), an individual who then suffers from PTSD can exhibit symptoms including nightmares, emotional numbness, and difficulty controlling thoughts of the event. Whereas these symptoms may diminish or disappear, others may arise, such as anger, a sense of detachment from others, increased startle response, difficulty sleeping or concentrating, headaches, stomach problems, and chest pain. Some PTSD sufferers even feel suicidal.

To address PTSD promptly, police officers and managers must understand how the disorder manifests itself. To that end, some police agencies have instituted training in PTSD to inoculate officers before they experience a traumatic event. Agencies may also provide immediate psychological debriefing and follow-up counseling services to police officers affected by the traumatic incident.

Mitigating Dangerous Stress

To mitigate dangerous levels of stress for officers, police agencies must excel at **stress management** by putting in place a blend of prevention, training, and intervention programs for all employees. Many agencies have developed their own stress-management programs. Agencies unable to do so because of budgetary or other constraints can join a community-based employee assistance program or encourage officers to take advantage of a program offered through the agency's health care provider. Although most programs include professional counseling and addiction treatment options, many agencies have additional prevention options available. The box titled "A Tri-Level Stress-Prevention Program" shows one example from a police agency in the northeastern United States.

The tri-level program succeeded because it delivered stress-management and anger-management training to all in-service and new police officers. Every agency employee—from police recruit officer to police chief—had access to the training. Data collected from agency personnel who attended the training revealed that attendees had gained a basic awareness of stress and its effects. Students expressed awareness of how to manage the negative effects of stress, including anger, and how to access needed counseling services. Students qualitatively stated that the training

Stress management: a blend of prevention, training, and intervention programs that a police agency puts in place to mitigate dangerous levels of stress among officers.

A Tri-Level Stress-Prevention Program

A police agency in the northeastern region of the United States instituted a tri-level program to prevent negative impacts of stress on individual personnel and the organization overall.

PRIMARY LEVEL	SECONDARY LEVEL	TERTIARY LEVEL
• Basic stress management training for recruits, supervisors, mid-level managers, and executives • Significant-other training • Traumatic incident training • Women in policing training • Anger-management training	• Peer counseling training and intervention • Traumatic incident debriefing for groups and individuals	• Individual counseling and referral services • Inpatient services • Substance-abuse treatment programs • Gambling treatment program • Psychiatric treatment and care

Sources: Davis, 1994; Quick, Quick, Nelson, & Hurrell, 2003.

had a positive effect on the way they handled on-the-job and personal/relationship concerns.

In this program, *primary level* referred to training-based offerings intended to support personal growth and professional development. This training included group presentations as well as practice exercises on stress awareness and stress-management techniques (such as relaxation exercises, breath control, and muscle relaxation). *Secondary level* provided for early intervention for those officers experiencing stress-related problems. Traumatic incident debriefing was mandatory for all officers involved in deadly physical force occurrences such as police shootings—whether an officer was the one who used deadly physical force, was the victim of a gunshot, or witnessed a police shooting incident. Through the peer counseling intervention part of this level, trained officers diplomatically approach and address officers who appear to be experiencing negative stress in their lives or for whom stress seems to be affecting job performance. Finally, the *tertiary level* provided agency-paid confidential psychiatric visits, in-hospital care, and alcohol or drug abuse inpatient or outpatient treatment for agency personnel in need. All three levels in the program emphasized positive health and personal well-being for officers, not discipline. All treatment remained confidential and was not documented in officers' personnel records.

The best stress-management programs cover the topic of how to recognize the behaviors, emotions, and verbal statements suggesting that a person is suicidal. Through peer counseling programs, officers can learn when and how to approach and offer assistance to a fellow officer who may be at risk of suicide. Stress-management programs should also include a written policy on confidentiality for training sessions, peer counseling, traumatic incident debriefing, and tertiary care services. Without confidentiality, officers may be reluctant to take advantage of these much needed services, for fear that their problems will be made public.

Police officers may attend classes that focus on stress-management techniques.

Easing Stress's Impact on Officers' Private Lives

Policing is not a job that someone can easily "leave at the office" at the end of a workday. When officers are suffering from dangerous levels of stress, their loved ones often do, too. Many officers who have families worry intensely about their spouse's and children's safety because they see every kind of appalling and frightening behavior every day on the job. They may refrain from discussing work at home to avoid alarming their loved ones. This decision is understandable, but it can make officers feel isolated from their families. And isolation, in turn, causes them to suppress stress and other corrosive emotions, which can then spawn physical and mental health problems.

Difficulty Transitioning Out of the Workday   During academy training, police agencies invest enormous time and money to train officers for the profession of policing. As we read in Chapter 10, officers learn to keep the peace, take command and be assertive, observe safety measures while enforcing the law, and solve problems. However, few academies have trained police officers on how to transition out of their stressful role at the end of their shift. Many spouses and life partners of officers have noted that when their loved one returns from a day of policing the streets, the individual continues exhibiting police behaviors, such as barking orders at others, acting suspiciously, and practicing officer safety techniques when in public places. For example, off-duty officers enjoying a meal with family members or friends may keep their back to the wall and consistently scan the room and patrons, looking for suspicious or dangerous activity.

Left unaddressed, this inability to navigate the transition from police officer to ordinary family member can have serious consequences, including alcoholism, infidelity, emotional indifference, and drug abuse. It can also lead to mental and

One of the best stress relievers for a police officer is to relax at home with family and friends.

physical health problems, as well as officer suicide or domestic abuse of significant others.

Strategies for Easing the Transition   Stress cannot be totally eliminated from police work. However, fortunately, many police academies and agencies have begun offering educational programs that teach officers not only how to cope with the demands of the job but also how to disconnect from the job after hours so their home lives are not negatively affected. Techniques for disconnecting from the job at the end of a shift include "leaving the job behind" by making personal responsibilities and commitments a priority. Many officers also learn to manage stress effectively themselves; for instance, by following a vigorous exercise regime, eating a healthy diet, and developing interests that have nothing to do with policing. These practices require a firm commitment and a conscious effort to separate professional from private life (Haberfeld, 2002; Ortmeier, 2006; *Stress and the Police,* 2007).

Many police academies' curricula also now include training for family members as well. Known variously as "family programs," "significant-other training," or "police-spouse seminars," these programs aim to educate police officers' families about the nature of police work: how shifts work, what police jargon means, what salaries and benefits their loved ones have, and what types of incidents, individuals, and equipment officers deal with. Some offer ride-along programs, which enable family members to observe police officers in action. Developers of such programs hope that by demystifying the police profession, the programs help families understand what officers face on a daily basis. Informed by this understanding, spouses and significant others may work with their officer life partners to overcome

Many agencies have ride-along programs in which family members and others (such as the media) are allowed to ride with and observe police officers in action.

stress-related challenges that might interfere with healthy personal relationships. For example, they can commit to having dinner together as a family at least a few nights a week, or agree to spend time each week discussing the stresses they are experiencing and exchanging emotional support.

SURVIVAL ON THE STREET AND IN THE AGENCY

Police officers face two survival challenges: how to stay alive on the street while they are on and off duty (with or without family members), and how to navigate the political and ethical terrain within the agency that employs them. Many officers are more comfortable with the former challenge, because much of their training focuses on strengthening their on-the-street survival skills. Through such training, officers learn how to rely on verbal adeptness, unarmed defense tactics, and (if necessary) deadly physical force to stay alive in the face of peril, whether they are on duty or off duty. But training says little about how to survive **agency politics**—the political machinations, ambitions, and personal agendas that shape interpersonal dynamics within a police agency, and that can "kill" an officer's career.

Navigating the Political Landscape

Although officers may personally loathe internal politics and agency managers may insist that "politics has no place in policing," agencies are organizations made up of human beings. Thus, politics is a fact of life in all police agencies—like it or not. Navigating the political terrain can be difficult for some people, but officers can still learn how to survive and even thrive politically in their agency.

Agency politics: political machinations, ambitions, and personal agendas that shape interpersonal dynamics within a police agency.

Moral versus Immoral Political Power Politics can be defined as a competition over power and position in an organization. (See Chapter 11 for more discussion of power and authority.) Contestants can compete for these two things using moral or immoral tactics. Individuals who practice **moral political power** seek to influence and motivate others with an eye toward achieving agency goals rather than satisfying their own interests. They take time to learn what subordinates do and what suggestions they might have for improving the services the agency provides. They promote their most promising direct reports and forge mutually beneficial relationships with other departments (Dwyer, 2008).

Individuals who manipulate others only for personal gain are exercising **immoral political power.** They do not communicate effectively; in fact, they rarely give credit for work well done, and they frequently and publicly criticize subordinates and peers. Moreover, they are unaware of or disregard the permanent damage they inflict on other employees' morale and the agency's performance (Quimby, 2009).

Tactics for Exerting Moral Political Power Politics is a reality in policing because the authority granted to the police and control over the police ultimately rest with elected representatives of the people. The police are thus responsible for and accountable to the electorate, yet police officers often find themselves caught between politics and the realities of policing. They themselves may become political targets when they are unable to contain or control a crime or disorder problem. Agency personnel are often blamed for situations (such as crime spawned by poverty or lack of effective social institutions) that lie beyond their control. Police officers may also be confronted by political leaders who wish to pacify voters even though voters' desires are not consistent with the law.

Successfully balancing politics with the police mission requires agency personnel to serve all citizens well while also respecting the values and wishes of each political leader's constituency. No single strategy works well in all communities. However, unbiased professional behavior on the part of the police will operate as a defense to charges of police discrimination (Coffey, 1990; Goldstein, 2001).

One of the best ways for police officers, supervisors, and managers to navigate among the various political players within their agency is to identify, observe, learn from, and support leaders who exercise moral political power. By aligning with such leaders in these ways, aspiring leader deepen their own understanding of what moral political power is, why it is important, and how people acquire and use it (Quimby, 2009). Additional strategies for mastering the art of moral politics include the following:

- Identify your agency's goals and suggest ideas for achieving them.
- Clarify your career goals and formulate a plan for reaching them that does not involve taking advantage of others or preventing others from reaching their own career aspirations.
- Cultivate mutually beneficial relationships with leaders, peers, and others in your agency who demonstrate ethical behavior and integrity.
- Learn to listen carefully to what people are saying, and offer help when it seems appropriate.
- Ask questions to start conversations. Invite others to join in the discussion and explain what they know about the subject.

Moral political power: attempts to influence and motivate others with an eye toward achieving organizational goals rather than satisfying one's own interests.

Immoral political power: manipulation of others for personal gain.

- Avoid people who insist on gossiping or spreading hurtful rumors; excuse yourself from the conversation as soon as possible. If the gossip involves the harassment of one employee by another, inform a superior as soon as possible (Dwyer, 2008).

An agency's vision and mission, shared and supported by all officers, can help sustain an environment that minimizes the impact of political interference.

Avoiding Ethical Pitfalls

According to Randy Sutton, a 29-year police veteran one of your authors interviewed, ethical pitfalls are at least as prevalent as physical perils for police officers—and officers are better protected against the latter type of danger (Sutton, 2006). As Sutton explains, "In my department alone, for every officer lost in the line of duty in the last five years, 70 were fired for ethical misconduct. And unlike those who died honorably, these officers are alive but disgraced."

Sadly, ethical misconduct does not always manifest itself as flagrant breaking of rules. It can consist of behavior that is not covered by a rule—such as accepting discounted refreshments at local eateries or discounts on dry-cleaning of uniforms. Without rules laying out the dos and don'ts of ethical behavior, officers may mistakenly assume that a behavior is ethically sound.

While training can prepare officers to avoid such ethical pitfalls, Sutton notes that self-definition—knowing who you are and respecting yourself and others—is equally important. Some experts have defined ethical behavior as the conduct one displays even when no one else is looking. If that is true, then such behavior must become so ingrained in officers' psyche that there will be no question about what to do in questionable circumstances. Ethical behavior will have become second nature.

summary

- **Policies and Procedures.** In most policing organizations, documented policies and procedures are known as general orders. Agencies develop policies first and then procedures, and use the resulting general orders to guide officers' behavior.
- **Officer Performance Appraisals.** Police agencies can use policies, procedures, and job descriptions and specifications to evaluate individual officers' performance. The resulting performance appraisals can help an agency foster a culture of excellence. Agencies can use performance appraisals to make decisions such as which rewards an officer is qualified to receive as well as to help police personnel develop their careers. The most effective performance appraisals candidly cite the employee's strengths and areas needing improvement, provide specific examples of each, connect performance to agency goals, and conclude with an action plan for building on strengths and addressing improvement areas.
- **Succession Management.** Through succession management, a police agency prepares those who are interested in leadership for higher-level management and supervisory positions. Success management is essential for ensuring that police agencies have enough talent available for the right roles when the need

arises. Agencies use several means to make promotion decisions, including written tests and interviews. They strive to make succession planning an ongoing, proactive process rather than a one-time event initiated only after a key position becomes vacant. Agencies can use several means to groom an individual for another position, such as job shadowing and redesign of current responsibilities.

- **Talent Retention.** High turnover among police agency personnel raises daunting challenges, including erosion of morale and costs to train replacements for the vacated positions. To combat high turnover, agencies can communicate their values and policies clearly to job candidates so they understand what is expected of them and can determine if a job with a particular agency would be a good match for them. Agencies can also strive to bring in new hires with fresh pespectives and skills, which often improve morale and loyalty among remaining staff and persuades high performers to stay. Sustaining officer motivation (for example, by giving them challenging stretch assignments) is another powerful weapon for reducing turnover: motivated individuals often achieve more goals, which inspires them to strive for even more success. And success makes people want to stay with their current organization.

- **Management of Police Misconduct.** Many police jurisdictions have citizen review boards that investigate complaints of possible police misconduct and offer recommendations for action. Opinions differ on the value and role of citizen review boards for police agencies, and methods for processing complaints differ across agencies. If police misconduct is proved, an agency should apply a swift and fair process for disciplining the officer(s) involved. They should also establish early warning systems to spot and address problematic behaviors before they can escalate. Such systems can be used to track indicators such as citizen complaints filed against an officer, use-of-excessive-force incidents, and number of police-vehicle collisions.

- **Stress Management.** The second most stressful job in the United States (behind inner-city high school teacher) is police officer. Symptoms of dangerous stress include mood swings, depression, and hostility (among others). Posttraumatic stress disorder is the worst manifestation of stress. To mitigate dangerous stress, police agencies must establish prevention, training, and intervention programs. Such programs can help officers manage stress on the job as well as make the difficult transition from their workday to their private lives. Many police agencies also have programs that help family members of police officers learn more about the sources of stress officers must face and about ways to help manage stress.

- **Survival on the Street and in the Agency.** Officers receive extensive training in how to survive the perils of the job, but many receive far less guidance on how to navigate the political landscape in their agency and how to exert moral political power. One effective way to survive agency politics is to identify, observe, learn from, and support leaders who exercise moral political power. To avoid ethical pitfalls in exercising power, officers can also strive for self-definition—knowing who they are and respecting themselves and others, and displaying ethical behavior even when no one else is watching them. These practices can help ensure that ethical behavior becomes ingrained in officers' psyches.

key terms

agency politics
citizen review board
discipline
early warning system
general orders
immoral political power
morale
moral political power
performance appraisal
policies
procedures
stress management
succession management
succession planning

discussion questions

1. Why should an agency's chief of police or sheriff be inherently involved in the development of the agency's policies and procedures? Should police personnel also provide input? Why or why not?

2. If performance appraisals are used for the development of the employee, what areas should the supervisor document to ensure that each appraisal produces meaningful insights?

3. Most police agencies have not established a formalized approach to succession management. What challenges might this raise for an agency?

4. How might poor morale affect the performance and retention of quality police officers?

5. In what respects are citizen review boards valuable to police agencies? In what ways have they generated controversy?

6. Why is discipline necessary in a police agency, and what are the benefits of a progressive disciplinary model?

7. Police officers are affected by stress in numerous ways. Outline an effective stress-management program for an agency in your geographical area. What components do you believe would be absolutely necessary for your program?

8. Being a police officer is like being a doctor, in that officers are never really off duty. Discuss how this situation may have a negative effect on police officers' professional and private lives.

9. How would you advise police officers to navigate the complex political environment characterizing police agencies?

WHAT WOULD YOU DO?
Failure to Follow Procedures Ends in Officer Deaths

When faced with several bound volumes of general orders, new police officers might groan in frustration. How can anyone hope to learn so many rules, much less abide by them? Unfortunately, *not* following the rules can have grave consequences, as they did in Pittsburgh, Pennsylvania.

A call came in on 9-1-1 that a woman was fighting with her son, and two officers were assigned to the call with a third assigned as backup. The operator who answered the call was aware that the son had guns in his possession, but she did not tell police dispatchers because, reportedly, she did not think the guns were a factor. Her conversation with the man's mother was casual, and the woman mentioned nothing about feeling threatened. The operator did not elicit any additional information from the caller, which is against 9-1-1 procedure. Because dispatchers did not know about the guns, they could not warn the responding officers.

Unaware of the weapons, the responding officers approached the house expecting to face a simple domestic dispute. When the man's mother opened the door, she allegedly did not know that her son was standing behind her with a gun. He shot and killed two of the officers, then went outside and killed the third (Staff, Associated Press, 2009).

1. In this case study, the 9-1-1 operator failed to give complete information to the dispatcher, who could not know there were guns involved and therefore could not inform the responding officers. This may have been a faulty judgment call on the part of the original operator or a flaw in her training. If you were tasked with developing a method for training all those involved in the reporting of and response to 9-1-1 calls, what type of training would you propose?

2. Is there anything the responding officers could have done differently, even with their lack of knowledge? If so, what? If not, should police take responsibility for asking for more information before proceeding with any call?

Collateral Functions and Future Trends

13

◀ Courtroom trial in session.

Legal Aspects of Police Administration

After completing this chapter, readers should be able to:

- recall federal employment laws and explain how they are intended to foster fairness in the workplace.

- discuss the implications of affirmative action for police agencies.

- describe the challenges of hiring for diversity in police agencies.

- analyze the development of unions, including police unions and other representative groups.

- examine the implications for police officers of the Boston Police Strike of 1919.

- describe labor laws affecting unions and unfair labor practices.

- compare nonnegotiable and negotiable management rights.

learning outcomes

- discuss the reasons individuals decide to join unions.
- assess the complexities of the relationships between police union leaders, union members, and police agency managers.
- explain trends in union influence over time.
- explore the process of labor negotiation, including collective bargaining, binding arbitration, and meet-and-confer.
- describe the information that is included in a labor contract.
- explain how the grievance process works and why it is important in the realm of labor-contract law.
- compare expressed and implied contracts as well as valid and breached contracts.
- describe the basic concepts related to administrative law, property law, tort law, and privacy law, and explain why police administrators should gain familiarity with such law.
- contrast three types of liability and propose ways in which police administrators can help their agencies and the officers employed there avoid liability.

Introduction

All organizations with employees—including police agencies—are subject to laws concerning whom they employ, what they can ask during the hiring process, the minimum wages they must pay employees, and additional human resource and management concerns. While police officers must obey laws governing how police provide services to the public, police agency managers and supervisors must also adhere to laws concerning the employment of police officers. These laws include how police management and government entities work and negotiate with labor unions or other representative groups.

This chapter addresses employment law that applies to police administration, as well as general labor laws in the United States. The chapter also discusses laws regarding managers' interaction with labor unions. In addition to federal hiring laws, police administrators must also be knowledgeable regarding state employment laws mandating what public safety employees can and cannot do. For instance, almost all police officers are prohibited by law from going on strike. Because the states vary so widely in their employment laws, it is not possible to explore state laws in detail in this book. If you are interested in learning more about a particular state's laws, you can locate this information at your nearest physical or online library.

After examining national employment law, this chapter discusses police unionization, including the emergence of unions, labor laws affecting unions, unfair labor practices, management rights, reasons for joining a union, the labor negotiation and grievances processes, and other relevant topics. We then examine five areas of law with which police administrators should be familiar: contract law, administrative law, property law, tort law, and privacy law. We conclude the chapter with a section on how police agencies can mitigate their legal liability.

NATIONAL EMPLOYMENT LAWS

Over the years, the U.S. government has enacted numerous employment laws intended to foster fairness in the workplace. All organizations are subject to such laws in some fashion. These federal mandates have a common theme: protecting employees against discrimination based on characteristics such as gender, age, sexual orientation, race, ethnicity, religion, and ability. Theoretically, if an individual has the skills, education, and physical and mental abilities required to perform the activities and tasks entailed by a particular job, that individual should be seriously considered and possibly hired for the position.

If a police recruit applicant can adequately pass the written and physical agility tests, as well as the medical screening, psychological tests, psychiatric interview, and any other criteria developed by a police agency (including the background investigation), the applicant should be considered for employment. If the person is not hired but believes that all the required testing was satisfactorily completed, then the applicant may individually or upon consultation with an attorney appeal the decision. The person may also initiate a lawsuit against the department citing hiring practices that do not conform to labor laws. See the box "Federal Employment Laws" for a sampling of laws enacted in the United States since the 1960s.

Legislative efforts to ensure fair employment in the workplace have inspired public dialogue about how organizations might achieve diversity in their workforces. In the United States, a concept known as affirmative action arose in the public discourse as a path to workforce diversity. For police agencies, efforts to build a diverse workforce have faced unique challenges. We discuss affirmative action and diversity in police agency workforces in more detail in the following pages.

Federal Employment Laws
Equal Pay Act of 1963
Employers are not allowed to pay different wages based on gender. For instance, if a man and a woman are performing the same job, they should receive equal compensation.

Civil Rights Act of 1964, amended in 1972 as the Equal Employment Opportunity Act
Private employers, unions, and employment agencies of 15 or more persons are not allowed to discriminate against persons with respect to race, color, gender, religion, or national origin. This law extends protection to individuals

(*continued on page 330*)

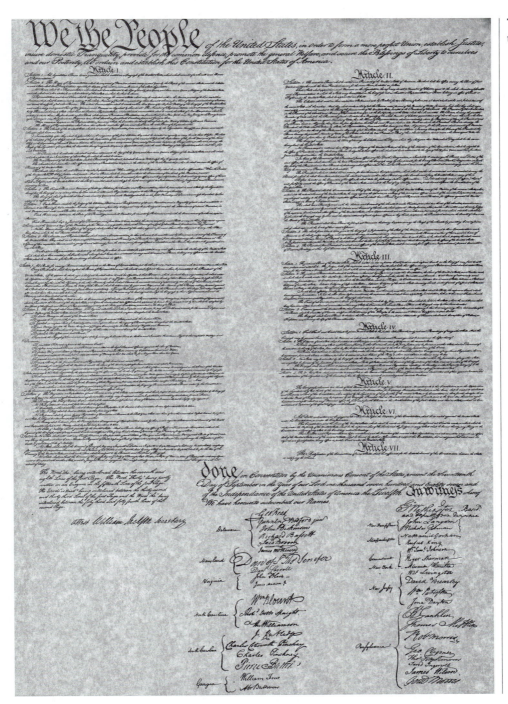

The Constitution of
the United States.

regarding employment, promotion, professional advancement, training, and compensation. The U.S. Equal Employment Opportunity Commission (EEOC) has enforcement powers with respect to the Equal Opportunity Employment Act.

Age Discrimination in Employment Act (ADEA) of 1967 (amended in 1975)
Employers are not allowed to discriminate against applicants and employees based on age for individuals 40 years of age and older with respect to hiring; promotion; discharge; compensation; or terms, conditions, or privileges of employment. The ADEA is enforced by the EEOC.

Occupational Safety and Health Act of 1970
Employers must furnish a place of employment that is free of recognizable hazards that are causing or are likely to cause death or serious physical harm. All employers and employees must comply with all the rules, occupational safety and health standards, regulations, and orders pursuant to the act. The act is administered by the Occupational Health and Safety Administration (OSHA).

Title IX of 1972, Education Amendments
All people are entitled to education benefits if provided (such as tuition reimbursement and adequate participation opportunities for female students in athletics) regardless of their race, religion, gender, color, or national origin.

Rehabilitation Act of 1973
Individuals who are disabled may not be discriminated against by the federal government and/or those who have contracted to provide services or products to the federal government.

Pregnancy Discrimination Act of 1978
Employers who have 15 or more employees, as well as government entities, unions, and employment agencies, may not discriminate against individuals because they are pregnant or have given birth.

Civil Service Reform Act of 1978
The Civil Service Reform Act of 1978 replaced the Civil Service Law of 1883. The act established the federal Office of Personnel Management (OPM), the Merit Systems Protection Board (MSPB), and the Federal Labor Relations Authority (FLRA). The act calls for greater accountability of federal employees for their performance and establishes protection for "whistle blowers," employees who report government abuses. This act also requires the federal government to ensure that its workforce reflects the diversity of the nation's population. Many police agencies have embraced the spirit of the act by hiring a diverse employee base to reflect the population of the communities the agencies serve.

Immigration Reform and Control Act of 1986
Qualified noncitizens may not be discriminated against on the basis of their national origin.

Worker Adjustment and Retraining Notification Act (WARN) of 1988
WARN protects workers, their families, and communities by requiring most employers with 100 or more employees to provide a 60-day notice of plant

closings and mass layoffs. Workers covered under this act include hourly workers, salaried employees, managers, and supervisors.

Employee Polygraph Protection Act (EPPA) of 1988

The EPPA generally prevents private-sector employers from using a truth verification or similar test for pre-employment screening or during an employee's tenure with an organization. The act reads that an employer may not require or request any employee or applicant to take the test and cannot discipline or discharge an employee or applicant for refusing to take a polygraph test. There are exemptions for certain private organizations (such as drug and security companies) and public safety agencies (for example, police organizations). Some police agencies administer a polygraph test during the pre-employment screening process to verify information provided by the applicant but rarely use the polygraph with current employees.

Americans with Disabilities Act (ADA) of 1990

Employers who have 15 or more employees may not discriminate against individuals who have a physical, medical, or emotional disability. The ADA forbids discrimination against persons who are disabled with respect to employment and forbids testing or questioning applicants for physical or medical disability until after a conditional offer of employment is made. The job offer may be conditional on the successful completion of a medical

A U.S. Army soldier.

(continued)

examination. The act also directs employers to make accommodations for employees who are disabled.

The Family and Medical Leave Act of 1993

Employers who have 50 or more employees must give employees 12 weeks of unpaid leave of absence during any 12-month period for the birth and/or care of their child, a spouse, or a parent who has a serious health problem, or for a serious health problem that makes it impossible for an employee to perform the necessary tasks associated with the job.

The Uniformed Services Employment and Reemployment Rights Act (USERRA) of 1994

This law was enacted to ensure that no person called to serve on active military duty suffers loss of seniority, status, or wages for a cumulative period of five years unless a noted exception (such as initial enlistment of more than five years) exists. USERRA protects the rights of military veterans and members of military reserve and national guard components. It also protects veterans with disabilities by requiring employers to make reasonable efforts to accommodate the disability.

Sources: T. E. Baker, 2006; Cheeseman, 2009; Kearney, 2009; Ortmeier, 2006; U.S. Department of Labor, 2010b, 2010c, 2010d, 2010e, 2010f; U.S. Office of Personnel Management, 2010; Vaughn, 2003; Vikesland, 1998.

Understanding Affirmative Action

Affirmative action: the means by which employers ensure that applicants and persons seeking advancement in their respective agencies or companies are not discriminated against or denied employment or promotion based on race, creed, color, or national origin.

Affirmative action, a term originating in the United States, is the means by which employers ensure that applicants and persons seeking advancement in their respective agencies or companies are not discriminated against or denied employment or promotion based on race, creed, color, or national origin. Similar procedures are known by different names in other countries; for example, *reservation* in India, *positive discrimination* in the United Kingdom, and employment *equity* in Canada. Through affirmative action, businesses, public organizations, and educational institutions seek to use recruitment, hiring/admissions and promotion practices, and other initiatives (including training and outreach efforts) to build a workforce or student population that represents the percentage of minorities in the community or society at large (Cahn, 1995; U.S. Department of Labor, 2010).

For example, employers and educational institutions that support affirmative action maintain that if 25 percent of the general population consists of Hispanics, then at least 25 percent of a company's workforce or a university's student body should consist of Hispanics. Groups that have been statistically underrepresented in the workforce and in academic enrollments (where such requirements exist) include (but are not limited to) African Americans, Asians, Hispanics, Native Americans, individuals with disabilities, members of certain religious groups, people with alternative lifestyles, those with substance-abuse problems, veterans, women, and young people (Walker, Spohn, & Delone, 2004).

Affirmative action is not in itself a law, and employers and educational institutions vary in their policies regarding it. For example, there are no affirmative action requirements in California state employment or state-funded colleges or universities. The laws listed in the previous box support affirmative action by specifying nondiscriminatory practices in hiring, promotions, and educational admissions.

However, confusion and controversy have surrounded affirmative action. For example, some state laws (such as in California and Michigan) restrict the use of affirmative action procedures in state-tax-supported employment. Yet the Civil Rights Act of 1964 guarantees that public agencies must conform to affirmative action guarantees if the government entity the agency represents receives federal financial assistance (Cahn, 1995; Robbins & Judge, 2008). Meanwhile, the U.S. Supreme Court has ruled that the use of mandatory quotas for such populations is actually unconstitutional, owing to the unintended consequences that have come from reverse discrimination (Scuro, 2004). For example, an employer who hires a member of a minority population to meet a diversity quota, even if that person is not as qualified for the job as an applicant who is a member of the majority, is engaging in reverse discrimination.

Clearly, affirmative action is a complex concept that will continue to evolve as lawmakers and the public consider its implications.

Hiring for Diversity in Police Agencies

The notion of affirmative action has inspired many police agencies to make a concerted effort to recruit and hire members of populations that have long been underrepresented in the police workforce, especially African Americans, Hispanics, and Native Americans (Ho, 2005). After all, an agency that purports to serve all should be represented by all who live in the community. But hiring for such diversity in police work can be challenging. Many minorities are not interested in public safety occupations, or they obtain gainful employment in other career streams. In addition, they may be discouraged from entering police work by family and friends.

To surmount this challenge, many police agencies seek to laterally transfer officers who represent special populations from other agencies that already have an adequately diverse workforce. An agency may use additional strategies as well, such as initiating outreach programs targeting underrepresented populations, hosting career days to attract potential new hires from different groups, developing mentoring programs, and helping applicants prepare for written and physical-agility exams.

If any employer—including a police agency—violates or is perceived to violate equal opportunity standards regarding hiring or promotion decisions, the affected person or group may take legal action. For example, some individuals

The police officers of an agency should reflect the diversity of the community they serve.

Leadership on the job
The Struggle for Diversity

Most police agencies across the United States are committed to providing a diverse police force to the citizens they serve. However, fulfilling this commitment has proved more difficult than many thought. In Montgomery County, Maryland, 13 percent of the county's population is Latino, but only 5 percent of the police force is Latino. Asians comprise 13 percent of the population, but just 3 percent of the police agency is Asian. Only the African American population comes close: 14 percent of the police agency is black, nearly matching the 15 percent in the general population. Mauricio Veiga, one of the agency's recruiting officers, says that it is always a struggle to find qualified minority candidates. Many who pass the written and physical agility exams are eventually disqualified because of an undesirable background or drug use uncovered during the candidate's background investigation (Londoño, 2006).

In Reading, Pennsylvania, the population is 51 percent Hispanic, while the police force of 206 sworn officers has only 14 Hispanics, a mere 7 percent of the force (Montgomery, 2008). In Rochester, New York, where the population is 52 percent nonwhite, only 9 percent of the police force is African American, 10 percent is Hispanic, and 2 percent is Asian. Reverend Marlowe Washington, speaking at city high schools shortly before a graduation, implied that nonwhite students today want to *get* the police, not *be* the police. Rochester's Mayor Robert Duffy blamed the 50 percent school dropout rate for the dearth of qualified candidates for police work (Sharp, 2009).

In 2003, the state of Delaware was compelled to pay $1,425,000 to qualified African American police recruits who were denied employment because of a particular test they were required to complete but which was later deemed unfair. In addition to the monetary settlement, the state was required to provide priority job offers with retroactive seniority and pension relief (*Justice Dept. Settles Lawsuit regarding Delaware Police Hiring Practices,* n.d.). In Chicago, the police department is giving serious thought to discontinuing the police entrance exam to widen its selection of qualified minority candidates (Bryant, 2010).

The New York City Police Department (NYPD) appears to be progressing toward true diversity. Of the 5,593 officers hired between 2006 and 2010, 1,042 were foreign born, representing 88 different countries. The NYPD has over 35,000 officers, of which 263 come from the Dominican Republic, 78 from Haiti, 59 from Jamaica, 29 from Pakistan, and 18 from Russia. The latest graduates of the NYPD police academy include individuals who represent speakers of 28 languages, including Bengali, Punjabi, Yoruba, and Creole (*NYPD Working to Improve Its Diversity,* 2010). To facilitate its diversity employment efforts, the NYPD employed Wilbur Chapman, who had served as commander of the department's Recruiting and Applicant Processing Division in 1992. Chapman was instrumental in bringing onboard NYPD's most diverse group of recruits and oversaw the department's training efforts (Faherty, 2007).

1. What steps would you advise your local police agency to take to evaluate the diversity of its workforce and to set and achieve diversity goals?

2. In your view, is workforce diversity a legitimate objective for a police agency? Why or why not?

3. If an agency has difficulty hiring and/or retaining a diverse workforce, what consequences may it face?

have filed petitions to the federal courts for legal remedy or have filed liability lawsuits against employers for such violations. Police agencies perceived as violating equal opportunity standards for hiring may be subjected to a judicially mandated decree dictating the ratio of minorities and underrepresented genders to majorities for an academy class. One police agency in the northeastern part of the United States is currently under a decree reading that it must employ one minority candidate for every three majority candidates it hires.

UNIONIZATION

Just as police administrators must be familiar with national employment laws to ensure that their agency is obeying federal law, administrators must also understand how unionization affects their agency. Unionization is not unique to police agencies, nor is it unique to modern workplaces. However, police unions differ in some ways from other types of unions, and administrators must understand such differences in order to manage their agency's workforce effectively. But before we explore police unions in particular, it can be helpful to consider unionization from a more general perspective, including how unions emerged and what laws the U.S. government has defined regarding unions.

The Emergence of Unions

People with specialized knowledge and skills have been joining together in groups since ancient times. For example, physicians in ancient Greece would not share their medical treatment secrets with anyone except other physicians. By the Middle Ages in Europe, tradespeople such as glass workers, shoemakers, and stonecutters were banding into guilds, often seen as the precursors to unions. Many guilds had a common fund to which members contributed, and some of the money was used to sponsor apprenticeships for young workers. Guild members were self-employed and owned the materials and tools of their trade. They powerfully influenced commerce by maintaining trade secrets, protecting proprietary information and work processes, and controlling membership numbers and wages.

Today, unions are a more common mechanism through which workers join together to gain influence over their working conditions including hours and compensation. They do so through a process known as collective bargaining (discussed in more detail later in this chapter). Experts debate when the first union took shape in America. Some sources maintain that shoemakers in Philadelphia formed the first recognizable union in 1792. Others assert that Boston shoemakers created the first union earlier, in 1648 (Kearney, 2009).

Regardless of who is correct, unions have traveled a rocky road in their evolution. For many years, business owners fought to keep collective bargaining out of industrial plants, but unions persisted. They gained ground by stopping work until their employers met their demands, despite business owners' efforts to constrain them with court injunctions and *yellow dog contracts* that forbade new employees from joining unions. Since the 1930s, unions have benefited from the passage of labor laws protecting employees' right to bargain collectively. The box titled "Labor Laws Affecting Unions" describes such legislation.

While industrial workers labored to set up the first unions, police officers made fledgling efforts to unionize

Medieval guild members engaging in their trades.

by receiving charters from the established traditional trade unions. Many of these efforts faltered because states passed laws forbidding public employees (such as police, fire, and corrections) from going on strike. As a result, police officers forged their own worker-support groups in the form of fraternal organizations. An example is the Fraternal Order of Police (FOP), a national organization founded in 1915. The FOP works to advance the health and welfare of police officers, including providing death benefits for the families of officers who have lost their lives in the line of duty. At the state level, similar organizations were formed, such as the Police Officers Research Association of California (PORAC) and local *police associations*.

The Boston Police Strike of 1919

In 1919, Boston police officers went on strike to protest harsh working conditions, including wages that could not keep up with inflation, 70- to 90-hour workweeks, the requirement that officers purchase their own uniforms, and work assignments based on favoritism. During several September evenings that year, the lack of adequate police coverage resulted in widespread hooliganism in the city, in which the National Guard struggled to suppress the disorder. Gunfire and rioting left seven dead, resulted in hundreds of injuries, and wrought vast property damage.

The officers who went on strike were fired. However, their replacements reaped the benefits of their actions. The new officers received higher salaries, the city

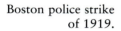

Boston police strike of 1919.

created a pension system for the police, and the agency provided officers with uniforms instead of insisting that they buy their own. Police officers began demanding that they be treated as professionals and that they have a voice in their working conditions (Allen & Sawhney, 2010; Peak et al., 2010).

Still, the strike had some negative consequences as well for police. Boston had suffered much damage while the police were striking. Bowing to political pressure, the American Federation of Labor (AFL) revoked the charters it had granted to the police. This action ended efforts for police unionism, until after World War II. Thus, it was mandated that police officers could not legally go on strike.

Police Unions Today

Today, unions for police agency members typically fall into one of three categories: benevolent associations (created to function as fraternities for the betterment of the police and their families); agency, regional, or state-affiliated independent unions; or affiliations with national unions like the American Federation of Labor-Congress of Industrial Organizations (AFL-CIO).

Unlike many other groups, police officers have numerous organizations in addition to unions that represent them and protect their rights under the contract. The oldest is the FOP. Such national-scale organizations also include the International Brotherhood of Police Officers, the American Federation of Police, and the National Association of Police Organizations. This last entity is actually a collection of federal-, state-, and municipal-level police unions and associations. These groups monitor organized-labor organizations for collective bargaining purposes and lobby for various constituencies; for example, active-duty and retired law enforcement officers and their families. Some states' laws also provide for a police officer bill of rights, which stipulates (for example) that officers are entitled to due process while under investigation and that they cannot be prevented from engaging in political activity (such as seeking election to a local school board) (Adams, 2007).

Unfair Labor Practices

To fully understand police unionization, a brief review of **unfair labor practices** is necessary. The term refers to actions taken by unions or employers that violate the U.S. National Labor Relations Act (NLRA). The actions are investigated by the National Labor Relations Board (NLRB). This subject is addressed in great detail in the U.S. Code, Title 5, Government Organization and Employees, which sets forth statutes regarding what is permissible by government agencies, employers, and labor organizations regarding unions (U.S. Government Printing Office, 2008). As stated in Title 5, a *government agency* (including a police agency) may *not* do the following:

Unfair labor practices: actions taken by unions or employers that violate the U.S. National Labor Relations Act (NLRA).

- Interfere with any employee who exercises any right under this code
- Encourage or discourage union membership by discriminating in hiring, tenure, or promotion
- Assist any labor organization except to furnish, upon request, services and facilities (such as a meeting hall and time) if these are also furnished to other labor organizations on an impartial basis
- Discipline an employee for filing a complaint, affidavit, or petition under this code

Labor Laws Affecting Unions

The Norris-LaGuardia Act of 1932

This law controls how employers can use court injunctions to prevent unions from initiating work stoppages. The law also makes *yellow dog contracts* (through which employees pledge not to join a union) illegal. The act defines the term *labor dispute* and stipulates that a federal court can issue an injunction against a work stoppage only after an appropriate court hearing

The National Labor Relations Act of 1935

This law, also known as the Wagner Act, made collective bargaining legal by guaranteeing employees the right to organize, create, join, or help labor organizations bargain through representatives. It required employers to engage in fair bargaining efforts with their employees' representatives or union delegates, and forbade unfair labor practices (such as refusing to bargain collectively) by employers. The act created the NLRB to arbitrate deadlocked labor–management disagreements and to assist, where necessary, with democratic union elections.

The Fair Labor Standards Act (FLSA) of 1938

This act established standards for a minimum wage and for overtime pay of one and one-half times the regular rate of pay. It also established standards for the employment of children under the age of 16. For example, minimum ages of employment and hours of work for children are regulated by federal law. In addition, it set standards for children under the age of 18 regarding their employment in dangerous jobs such as mining.

The Taft-Hartley Act of 1947

This act banned several unfair labor practices to balance power between unions and management. For example, it declared that the practice of closed shops, which prohibited management from hiring nonunion workers, was illegal. It permitted union shops only when the majority of employees voted for them. The act addressed the issue of strikes, determined that certain labor activities (such as prohibiting nonunion workers from crossing pocket lines) were unfair, and forbade unions from donating money directly to local, state, or national political campaigns. The act has since been modified to allow labor unions, along with other restricted entities like corporations and special-interest groups, to create *political action committees* for the sole purpose of supporting political campaigns (*Columbia Electronic Encyclopedia,* 2007b).

The Landrum-Griffin Act of 1959

This act, officially known as the Labor-Management Reporting and Disclosure Act, required regular elections of union officers using a secret-ballot system and regulated the handling of union funds. The act included a bill of rights protecting freedom of speech for union members. It also addressed the issue of union corruption by regulating unions' internal affairs and their officials' relationships with employers

Sources: Bernstein, 2010; Cheeseman, 2009; *Columbia Electronic Encyclopedia,* 2007a; eNotes, 2010; "Our Documents," 2010.

- Refuse to consult or negotiate in good faith with a labor organization
- Fail or refuse to cooperate in impasse procedures and decisions
- Enforce any rule that conflicts with a collective bargaining agreement that was in effect before the date of the rule

Title 5 also spells out restrictions on *labor organizations* (that is, unions). Specifically, it reads that labor organizations may *not* do the following:

- Influence any employee in the exercise of an employee's right under this code (such as refusing to bargain with the employer of the employees it represents)
- Cause an agency to discriminate against any employee who exercises any right under this code
- Hinder or impede a union member's work performance or the discharge of the member's duties as an employee
- Discriminate against a union applicant with regard to the terms or conditions of membership in the labor organization on the basis of race, color, creed, national origin, sex, age, preferential or nonpreferential civil service status, political affiliation, marital status, or disabling condition
- Refuse to negotiate in good faith with a government agency
- Refuse to cooperate in impasse procedures and decisions
- Participate in a work stoppage or slowdown or picketing of an agency in a labor–management dispute if it interferes with an agency's operations
- Refuse employees who desire union membership if they meet reasonable occupational standards uniformly required for admission and/or pay dues required as a condition of membership

Management Rights

Title 5 also spells out nonnegotiable and negotiable management rights. **Nonnegotiable management rights** describe what the management of a government agency may do without having to negotiate with a labor organization. For example, according to Title 5, management has the nonnegotiable right to:

- Determine the mission, budget, organization, number of employees, and internal security practices of the agency
- Hire, assign, direct, lay off, and retain employees in the agency, or suspend, remove, reduce in grade or pay, or take other disciplinary action against such employees
- Assign work, make determinations with respect to contracting out work, and determine the personnel needed to conduct agency operations
- Make selections for appointments from among properly ranked and certified candidates for promotion or from any other appropriate source
- Take whatever actions may be necessary to carry out the agency's mission during emergencies

Negotiable management rights describe those areas wherein nothing in Title 5 precludes an agency or a labor organization from negotiating the numbers, types, and grades (ranks) of employees or positions assigned to any organizational

Nonnegotiable management rights: what the management of a government agency may do without having to negotiate with a labor organization.

Negotiable management rights: areas wherein nothing in Title 5 precludes an agency or a labor organization from negotiating the numbers, types, and grades (ranks) of employees or positions assigned to any organizational subdivision, work project, or tour of duty; the technology, methods, and means of performing work; or the procedures an agency uses to exercise authority.

subdivision, work project, or tour of duty; or the technology, methods, and means of performing work. For instance, police management and a police union may negotiate how many officers are assigned to a particular patrol area. This includes the number of police lieutenants, police sergeants, and patrol officers assigned to each eight-hour shift within that patrol area, as well as the types of patrols (such as foot, vehicle, and bike).

Negotiable management rights in Title 5 also include the procedures that agency managers will observe in exercising any authority and the appropriate redress for employees adversely affected by the exercise of authority. To illustrate, police managers and police employee organizations may negotiate how discipline will be exercised in the agency. A police sergeant may commence the agreed-upon discipline process by giving oral instructions and remedial training to an officer who has violated agency rules and regulations. Additionally, the police sergeant may be obliged to document the disciplinary actions by issuing a counseling memorandum. Police officers who believe that they were adversely affected by the supervisory action or were directed to take an action that violates the contractual agreement have the right to exercise the provisions of the grievance procedure mutually agreed on by management and labor.

Reasons for Joining a Union

Employees, including police officers, enroll in a union for many reasons. A fundamental reason is to have a representative group negotiate the next labor contract through the collective bargaining process (Etheridge, 2008). A union has the responsibility to negotiate numerous contractual issues, including working conditions, pay, and benefits (for example, health insurance, retirement options, and seniority rights) (Ivers, 2008).

Unionized workers in the early twentieth century lobbying for shorter workdays.

A Police Agency Negotiates an Agreed-upon Workweek

Police agencies have had difficulty accommodating a 40-hour workweek. For example, an agency in the northeastern United States currently has a workweek of 41.25 hours. The additional 1.25 hours represents the daily 15-minute roll call required for each shift. The roll call has been deemed so important that the union and management have agreed that only in an emergency may an officer respond to a call for service during roll call.

In the same agency, union leaders and managers have agreed that training is mandatory and that it counts as a full 8.25-hour workday. In special cases such as half-day firearms qualification, trainees are assigned to the academy for about half of the 8.25-hour workday. During regular patrol duties and agency training periods, this agency continues conducting its usual roll calls.

Another primary reason for joining a union may be dissatisfaction with job conditions. However, workers must also believe that their demands will be met, in full or in part if they join a union, and that their union representatives have the will and power to effect change. For example, unionized workers lobbied for years from the 1800s to the early mid-1900s to have their workdays shortened to eight hours, with overtime wages paid for any hours worked over the maximum eight hours (Kearney, 2009). Their efforts produced results: Today, the eight-hour day is still the norm for most hourly employees. (See the box "A Police Agency Negotiates an Agreed-upon Workweek.")

Some individuals join a union because they feel there is a lack of communication between management and line officers, and that management is generally unconcerned about employees' needs. Others join under peer pressure or because they believe that management is unfairly favoring some employees over others. Groups of employees may opt to join because they feel powerless against management. They know that unions, owing to their strength in numbers, have a greater chance of negotiating for change than an individual employee has.

Union Leaders, Union Members, and Management: A Complex Relationship

In any organization, relationships among union leaders, union members, and management can be complex and even adversarial. In a police agency, these complexities can present unique challenges. For instance, if a police chief severely punishes an officer for misconduct, the union may accuse the chief of pandering to the media and community activists. But if the chief shows leniency toward the officer, the media and those same activists may charge the chief with pandering to the union (DeLord & Sanders 2006).

Thankfully, most police union leaders and agency managers have a more constructive, albeit still complex, relationship. At the very least, elected union officials must balance the needs of those they represent with the expressed desires of the agency's management. For instance, union demands for salary and benefits must be balanced against the government entity's ability to pay. Police managers (especially an agency's chief executive) must also strike a balance—addressing the needs of not only union members but also other government officials as well as community constituents. To illustrate, unions may demand salary increases, forcing management to lay off workers.

In a police agency (just as in any organization), tensions can also arise between union leaders and the employees they represent. For example, union leaders must take care not to give the impression that they are collaborating with or siding with the agency's management. Perceptions of such collaboration may spawn distrust of union leaders among members, which can lead to discontent and an inability to trust leaders' recommendations.

Police agency managers and union leaders can also end up on different sides of political campaigns—a situation that can spark tensions within the agency. For instance, police unions have been known to involve themselves in elections, by supporting one candidate or another who seems most willing and able to serve their needs. If the union supports a candidate who ultimately loses the election, tensions can arise between union members and the winning candidate—as well as between members and police agency managers who supported the winning candidate.

A further difficulty for police managers is that union participation can differ radically among jurisdictions. For example, one city's police agency may have a large, active union, while an adjacent city's agency has a small union. As a result, the agencies may have difficulty knowing how to work together on challenges of mutual interest. The best thing a police executive can do in such a situation is to strive to maintain positive relationships with everyone in the department, with the union leadership, and with politicians in the controlling government entity. By staying in touch with day-to-day operations, police executives will never be blindsided by unionized line officers' demands. Instead, they will constantly be aware of what line officers most desire—and that awareness will foster more fluid communication about those desires and how to meet them.

Union Power

Despite national and state laws prohibiting public agencies (including police) from going on strike, many police unions have considerable power in their jurisdictions. In some cities, the union has succeeded in preventing the establishment of a citizen review board. (See Chapter 12 for a full discussion of citizen review boards.) In other cities, they have constrained the funding of the citizen review board so tightly that the board is understaffed and cannot investigate complaints properly (Sward et al., 2006). A strong police union can finance political advertising and thus influence the outcome of elections to key positions (such as mayor and judge), as well as influence how officers are disciplined for misconduct.

Union membership in government organizations has been expanding beyond such membership in the private sector. In 2009, for the first time in American history, union membership for public agencies stood at 7.9 million employees, while 7.4 million private-sector workers belonged to unions. Within the public sector, police officers, teachers, and firefighters are highly unionized. That is, larger percentages of their workforces belong to unions, or their unions are more powerful, or their unions deliver more benefits to members. The decline of private-sector union membership has been especially apparent in the manufacturing and construction industries, and has stemmed from the recession. Unionized employees who go on strike are replaced with lower-paid nonunion workers. And as companies go bankrupt, they are replaced with companies that are not unionized.

Union membership strength in the public sector also varies across states. For example, New York has the highest union membership rate at 25.2 percent, while North Carolina has the lowest rate at 3.1 percent (Greenhouse, 2010; U.S. Department of Labor, Bureau of Labor Statistics, 2010). These differences reflect the differences in local culture and the history of unions in each area.

As another manifestation of their power, some police union members have found ways to get around laws prohibiting officers from going on strike. For instance, officers can slow their agency's production when officers feign illness, becoming afflicted with the so-called *blue flu,* calling in "sick" simply to make it more difficult for managers to deploy officers effectively. If they do report for duty, they may decline to write the usual number of traffic or parking citations or to respond quickly to calls-for-service.

While police unions have been powerful in the past, many unions across the nation have been weakened by economic downturns. For instance, some communities seeking to save money and balance their budgets have outsourced their entire police department to county sheriffs' offices or to the state police. Many cities have initiated hiring and pay freezes for municipal employees. In some states, pension benefits are also being reduced for new police recruits. In the face of such severe lack of funding for law enforcement services, unions have far less power to bargain for the interests of their members. Only time will reveal what these realities imply for unions in this country.

Labor Negotiation

Labor negotiation is the process through which union leaders and managers create or modify a labor contract. This process is also known as **collective bargaining,** which, according to the U.S. Department of Labor's Employment Relations Service (2009a), is a series of steps through which certified unions and employers arrive at collective agreements. A **collective agreement** is a labor contract that covers two or more employees who are union members.

Collective bargaining: a series of steps through which certified unions and employers arrive at collective agreements.

Collective agreement: a labor contract that covers two or more employees who are union members.

Large police agencies may have a union that represents line officers, another union for sergeants, a union for lieutenants, and yet another union for civilian employees. In such agencies, labor contracts for each union must be negotiated individually. The collective bargaining process can thus become confusing for members and management alike.

Collective bargaining is a time-consuming and complicated procedure even under the best of conditions. According to the Employment Relations Act of 2000, such bargaining must be exercised in good faith.

People sitting at a bargaining table and negotiating.

Good faith: bargaining behaviors required by the Employee Relations Act of 2000.

Good faith, as highlighted by the U.S. Department of Labor's Employment Relations Service (2009b), mandates that opposing parties:

- Use their best endeavors to agree to an effective bargaining process.
- Meet to consider and respond to proposals made by either side.
- Continue to bargain about any matters on which they have not reached agreement, even if they have come to a standstill or deadlock.
- Respect the role of the other's representative by not seeking to bargain directly with those for whom the representative acts.
- Do nothing to undermine the bargaining process or the authority of the other's representative.
- Not undermine collective bargaining or collective agreements by automatically passing on collectively bargained terms and conditions to employees not covered by that collective bargaining or agreement.
- Conclude a labor negotiation, unless there is a genuine reason based on reasonable grounds not to do so. A genuine reason does not include a party's opposition or objection to the principle of collective bargaining or being covered by a collective agreement. It also does not include a dispute over whether the collective agreement should include a bargaining fee clause.

The Collective Bargaining Process Where unions exist, the state determines what method of collective bargaining the two sides can use. The steps generally include gathering information on items to be negotiated, bargaining in good faith, calling in a mediator if the parties reach an impasse, conducting binding arbitration, finding facts on matters such as finances, and arriving at a final decision by a governing body such as a city council. The goal of the collective bargaining process is to complete labor–management contract negotiations (Guild, 1998).

The process begins with each side developing a detailed list of what it wants. For example, unionized police officers may cite wants such as a 5 percent pay increase, full medical coverage, and additional compensatory time off in the form of vacation days. The police agency's management team might identify wants such as a wage freeze, employees' paying a higher percentage of health care costs, and elimination of the seniority system. In most police agencies, the union and management can come to agreement on many items on the list without dissension and therefore do not need to negotiate these items. For example, perhaps a reserved parking space may be designated for the person who receives the *officer of the month* award. Some items are nonnegotiable, such as (as we have seen) agency management's right to determine how many officers to employ (Nowicki, 2003; U.S. Government Printing Office, 2008).

Other items (such as the amount that the government entity contributes to employees' retirement system) require more time and effort before labor and management arrive at agreement, with each side making a concession where possible. Finally, the two sides may become mired in hotly contested issues that require the intervention of an arbitrator, depending on the laws of the state. In police agencies, these tough-to-resolve issues often center on salary and working conditions.

Police services are very difficult to negotiate, because (depending on an agency's size), these services may be impossible to provide through other means if officers stop work to bargain for some desired gain. While an agency that employs one to five officers may be supplemented by a sheriff's department or state police agency, a large

A police officer receiving an award at an assembly in Landover, Maryland.

agency that employs hundreds or thousands of police officers cannot be replaced. As we have seen, taking into account the issue of community public safety and the complexity of a government response to a labor strike by police, federal and state laws prohibit police strikes (Kearney, 2009; U.S. Government Printing Office, 2008).

Negotiation through Binding Arbitration   Binding arbitration is a common negotiation method. Through **binding arbitration**, the involved parties agree to adhere to an arbitrator's decision and award (*West's Encyclopedia of American Law,* 2008a). The arbitrator makes a decision according to state law and labor standards, and bases the decision on the arguments made by management and union representatives. Decisions can be made on an issue-by-issue basis, by which each issue is decided separately and is not subject to the position of management or the union. A *final decision* can also be made on an issue-by-issue basis, through which each issue is decided according to the position of either management or the union. Last, in a *total package* decision, the arbitrator chooses the entire set of positions of management or the union (Aitchison, 2004).

Binding arbitration: a negotiation process through which the involved parties agree to adhere to an arbitrator's decision and award.

Negotiation through Meet-and-Confer   In some states, the law stipulates that unionized police officers and agency managers use a *meet-and-confer* process. Through this process, the police union may prepare demands and negotiate directly with management representatives, who are not obligated to do anything other than meet and confer in good faith with union representatives. This method offers several advantages for management and labor. For example, it forces both parties to continue the conversation and discussions. Management need not adjust its offer, and labor may continue to stress its positions. However, it does not provide for any means of resolving a dispute on any of the issues under negotiation. Management can simply present its offer to the employees, and the union must accept that offer.

In this instance, wise leaders will try to satisfy employee requests for the sake of morale and agency efficiency while still pushing forward agency-wide goals and objectives (Burke, 2009; Texas Municipal League, 2009).

When Bargainers Lack a Negotiation Mechanism   In states that have no formal labor negotiation mechanism in place, communication can decay between a police agency's management and rank-and-file officers, spawning poor morale and high turn-over. To avoid this scenario, managers must develop some method for learning what line officers want and for satisfying requests that appear reasonable. For example, they can work toward flexible scheduling that helps accommodate officers' lifestyles.

The Content of a Labor Contract   Most labor contracts forged through the labor negotiation process begin by specifying who is covered by the contract and

---

ETHICS IN ACTION

To Rehire or Not

A deputy of a large midwestern sheriff's agency was driving drunk one night while off duty. He telephoned the county dispatcher to learn whether one of his close friends was one of the deputies on patrol, so he could avoid being arrested for driving under the influence. In a separate and much earlier incident, the deputy had hampered an investigation by giving a friend a ride after a domestic dispute. He then denied doing so. As a result of these incidents and others, many for which he was disciplined, the deputy was fired.

The terminated deputy was a member of his agency's police union. He filed a grievance that led to arbitration, and the arbitrator ruled that the deputy should get his job back. The sheriff appealed this decision because the deputy provided no evidence that he had addressed his serious drinking problem. The sheriff fought back by accusing the arbitrator of showing favoritism to the deputy and the union, and of ignoring the deputy's long history of alcohol-related behavior problems on and off duty.

The arbitrator countered with the accusation that the sheriff's office had issued less harsh penalties to employees who committed similar indiscretions. (Later, it was discovered that these employees were not sworn officers.) The sheriff maintained that deputies must be held to a higher standard, both on and off duty. At the time of this writing, the disciplined deputy was on unpaid leave for over a year.

1. In your view, should an arbitrator have the authority to force a police agency's chief executive to rehire an employee who has exhibited unethical and illegal behavior consistently? Why or why not?

2. What is the effect on the public's perception of a police agency and union when the union supports questionable behavior in police officers? What is the effect on other members of the police agency?

who is not. The contract also states the responsibility of union members and their representatives, as well as the responsibilities of nonunionized managers. Important provisions of the contract include wages, work hours, disposition of uniforms and equipment, vacations, holidays, sick, bereavement, and personal leave time, and other employment conditions.

Because the contract is a binding legal instrument, the language used to write it must be precise and resistant to misinterpretation. Ambiguities in the language can result in future grievances filed or the need for arbitration. For instance, if the contract states that the agency will provide uniforms for officers, it should provide details specifying exactly what the uniforms will consist of, such as "two pairs of pants, two short-sleeve shirts, and two long-sleeve shirts." The more explicit the language, the less likely controversy or misunderstandings will arise.

After all concerned parties have ratified the labor contract, the parties are bound to operate according to its terms. Therefore, union members and agency managers should have a thorough knowledge of those terms. All parties will receive a copy of the final contract.

While the average person might have difficulty wading through the legal language in the contract, most police agencies augment contracts with *explanatory charts* or summaries written in more ordinary language. Short excerpts of these charts or summaries may be included in a contract; for example, a chart reflecting different pay grades for different police officer ranks with expected pay increases over a two- or three-year period. However, owing to the increased complexity of labor negotiations, explanatory charts may soon be a thing of the past. For example, a village in upstate New York is facing possible dissolution. The police agency labor organization agreed to a 2 percent reduction in wages to help reduce government spending in the village. In addition to the wage decrease, management and labor also discussed an increase in educational benefits for employees, changes in police pensions, and an increase in health expenses for different categories of police officers. It is possible that the complexity of the terms in the resulting labor contract could not be adequately captured in explanatory charts (Morrell, 2010).

Grievances

A **grievance** is an employee claim that a policy or contract provision has been misapplied, interpreted incorrectly, or violated, thereby causing injury, loss, or inconvenience to the employee. Examples of grievances include the following:

- A police agency does not compensate employees appropriately.
- Managers inflict unfair discipline on an employee.
- An agency does not promote an employee.

In all kinds of organizations, grievances can be filed by any employee—unionized or not—though individuals filing grievances may have more success if they have the support of a union behind them. In a police agency, only employees covered by a union contract can bring grievances. For employees who are not unionized, grievances proceed through whatever formal or informal process the organization has established. If an agency is not unionized, it should establish a mechanism for handling grievances.

Grievance: an employee claim that a policy or contract provision has been misapplied, interpreted incorrectly, or violated, thereby causing injury, loss, or inconvenience to the employee.

The Grievance Process   Most police agencies' grievance processes specify a series of steps the employee must take to obtain redress of the grievance. For instance, the employee usually has to document the grievance in writing and submit it to the individual's immediate supervisor. The supervisor has a certain time period to respond to the grievance. If the employee is not satisfied with the supervisor's resolution, the grievance may proceed to the next supervisory level, the chief of police or, subsequently, the city manager or mayor.

There is always a time constraint placed on responding to grievances, because failure to respond in a timely manner may constitute a grievance in itself. In unionized police agencies, an unresolved grievance may result in arbitration by a third party to obtain a resolution.

If grievances are not contract based and do not concern salaries, benefits, or conditions of employment that were negotiated during labor negotiations, they can usually be resolved by the employee's immediate supervisor. The individual (or individuals) bringing the grievance meets with the supervisor to discuss the situation, explore alternative solutions, and arrive at an agreement for resolving the grievance. In most cases, it is best if grievances can be addressed and resolved informally, with all involved parties arriving at a mutually agreeable consensus.

Mediation and Arbitration of Grievances   If the grievance is contract based and/or cannot be resolved at any of the usual steps in the process, the parties may decide to bring in a third party to mediate or arbitrate. Through *mediation*, the neutral third party hears both sides of the grievance argument and recommends a resolution based on the available information. Neither party to the mediation is bound by this resolution.

Arbitration is a more formal process than mediation. An arbitrator listens to both sides, just as the mediator does. However, the recommended solution to the grievance made by the arbitrator will often be binding on both opposing parties, a fact that the parties know when they choose arbitration.

A grievance meeting between two parties may be held with a third-party arbitrator.

Depending on the level of communication and willingness of management and union representatives to work together, grievances could be frequent or rare in a particular police agency. Studies suggest that open, honest communication and cooperation between labor and management can minimize grievances by giving concerned parties a balanced and fair outcome (Kearney, 2009; *Section 11.45. Contract Grievance Procedure*, 2008; United University Professions, 2006) and by fostering trust.

CONTRACT LAW

In addition to labor contracts, a police agency may forge a number of additional types of contracts. For instance, it may contract with a service vendor to handle certain business processes, such as police-vehicle maintenance or 9-1-1 emergency communications. Or perhaps the agency arrives at a contract with an office-building owner to lease or purchase a facility. Or the agency contracts with a weapons or radar systems manufacturer to purchase equipment required for law enforcement.

A **contract** is any legally binding, voluntary promise between two or more people that contains the following:

Contract: legally binding, voluntary promise between two or more people.

- An agreement (offer and acceptance)
- A consideration (something of value that is being exchanged)
- Legal subject matter (service or purposes)
- Contractual capacity (assurance that each party is of an age or mental capability permissible to enter into a contract)

Expressed and Implied Contracts

An *expressed contract* is written or verbal, with all terms explicitly stated. Expressed contracts are most often used in labor agreements as well as purchasing or leasing of buildings, equipment, or services. Written expressed contracts do not necessarily have to be in hard-copy form. For example, electronic mail (e-mail) contracts are valid if they contain all required elements of a contract. Indeed, the federal Electronic Signature in Global and National Commerce Act of 2000 provides that an electronic signature in an e-mailed contract is as enforceable as a handwritten signature on a piece of paper.

A contract.

An *implied contract* is unwritten and unspoken but results from the actions of the parties to the contract. For instance, a custom that permits senior officers to park closer to the entrance to police headquarters may be construed as an implied contract.

Valid and Breached Contracts

Contracts are *valid* if an offer and an acceptance are arrived at through good-faith negotiation (Cheeseman, 2009; Mann & Roberts, 2006; Ortmeier, 2009). Such negotiation can include *counteroffers*—instances when an individual considering an offer proposes modifying the conditions of the original offer. For example, the owner of an office building offers to rent space to a police agency for a specific amount. The agency's facilities manager expresses interest in inking a deal but suggests an amount lower than what the building owner has proposed.

Breach of contract: failure of any party to a contract to comply with the terms and conditions spelled out in the contract.

A **breach of contract** may occur if any party to the contract fails to comply with the terms and conditions spelled out in the contract. Examples of such breaches include the following:

- A police agency that has agreed to rent office space for a specified monthly amount fails to pay the rent on time.

- The building owner who has rented space to the agency neglects to make repairs stipulated in the rental agreement.

- A service provider with whom an agency has contracted to analyze crime scene evidence does not complete evidence analyses within the time frame specified in the contract.

- The police agency that has contracted with the evidence-analysis service provider fails to preserve the evidence in ways it agreed to while forging the contract.

A breach of contract may be resolved through negotiation, mediation, arbitration, legal action, or termination, depending on the breach-of-contract language that should be expressed in the contract. Most breaches are resolved through negotiation and mutual agreement between the parties.

ADMINISTRATIVE LAW

Administrative law: public law promulgated by administrative agencies at the federal, state, and local levels.

Administrative law is public law (rules and regulations) promulgated by administrative agencies at the federal, state, and local levels—such as the U.S. Department of Homeland Security, the Internal Revenue Service, the OSHA, state-level departments of motor vehicles (DMVs), and municipal entities. The public law coming from such agencies affects police agencies in specific ways. To illustrate, federal law specifies that anyone convicted of a felony or a misdemeanor involving domestic violence cannot possess a concealable firearm. Further, with few exceptions, one cannot board a commercial airline flight without being screened by U.S. Transportation Security Administration personnel. The privilege to drive a motor vehicle is issued through a state's DMV.

Administrative agencies are created through passage of federal and state laws. Because the legislative process is time consuming, state legislatures and the

A Transportation Security Administration (TSA) screening checkpoint at an airport.

U.S. Congress allow these administrative agencies to respond quickly to immediate or ever-changing conditions by formulating and implementing rules and regulations that carry the impact of law. Examples of such rules and regulations affecting police agencies include homeland defense, health and welfare, and traffic safety.

Administrative agencies usually have the authority to investigate and prosecute violators of their rules and regulations. However, their powers (for example, to search for evidence of the rule or regulation violated) are subject to the same U.S. constitutional restrictions as those of other government law enforcement personnel who are searching for evidence of a crime (Cheeseman, 2009; Mann & Roberts, 2006; Ortmeier, 2009).

Learn more about U.S. federal, state, and territorial laws through the Law Library of Congress' *Guide to Law Online* at www.loc.gov/law/public/law-guide.html.

PROPERTY LAW

In addition to contract and administrative law, property law directly affects police agencies. The concept of property holds an eminent place in free societies. In a democracy, property includes almost every right protected under law except the right to personal liberty. Property can be *tangible* (physical), such as a vehicle or building to which one holds a possessory title or right. Property can also be *intangible* (nonphysical); for example, a possessory right contained in a copyright, corporate stock, or proprietary information.

Personal property includes almost any form of tangible or intangible property, excluding land and its permanent or semipermanent fixtures (for instance, buildings). *Real property* (real estate) includes a building or landscaping (trees,

A vehicle is personal property.

plants, minerals) that is affixed to land. If a building is separated or plantings or minerals are removed from land, the building or plantings and minerals are transformed into personal property.

Property rights are also distinguished by ownership and possession. One who owns property holds title to it. One who leases property holds a possessory right to the property, not title to it. Whether owned or leased, tangible or intangible, property can be insured against damage or loss, tort liability/negligence, or criminal activity (Cheeseman, 2009; Mann & Roberts, 2006; Ortmeier, 2009).

Property rights are relevant to police agencies in several respects. Specifically, a local police agency's responsibilities include protecting community members' property; for instance, by patrolling neighborhoods to prevent break-ins. To protect citizens' and business owners' property, officers must be familiar with property laws, such as rules stipulating when it is legally permissible to enter a private residence. In addition, the agency itself may own or lease tangible or intangible forms of property. Police administrators must understand the laws regarding (for example) how the agency may use a facility it is leasing or how it may protect intellectual property such as police criminal intelligence reports and criminal history information.

TORT LAW

Tort: a private wrong committed against a person or a person's property.

A **tort** is a private wrong committed against a person or a person's property. Examples of torts include the following:

- Negligence (improper performance of an act)
- False imprisonment (an unlawful violation of a person's liberty)
- Wrongful death (the causing of another person's death through negligent conduct)

Land and buildings are real estate (real property).

Torts can be unintentional or intentional, and each type has specific implications for the individual or organization involved.

Unintentional Torts

An *unintentional (accidental) tort* may be committed when an individual fails to act with ordinary, reasonable, and prudent care, and another person is injured as a result. For example, a police officer improperly handcuffs a suspect, and the act leads to injury. In such cases, the injured party can sue for damages. The accused can be held civilly liable if the individual owes a duty of care to the plaintiff, was derelict (breached) in the duty, the dereliction was the direct cause of the injury, and there is legally recognizable injury (damages) to the plaintiff.

In such cases, the person who is civilly liable is deemed negligent for the wrongful act or failure to act. Individuals as well as an entire organization may be held civilly liable for negligence. For instance, if a police agency hires an officer who has a tendency toward violence, and the officer uses excessive force on a crime suspect, the agency is liable and may have to pay compensatory and punitive damages. Invasion of privacy, false arrest, use of excessive force, and failure to protect confidential personal information are other situations that can constitute unintentional torts for which a police agency can be held liable.

Intentional Torts

An *intentional tort* (civil wrong) is a willful act that culminates in an injury such as an assault, battery, wrongful death, or false imprisonment. Intentional torts may also form the foundation for criminal liability. Torts are not limited to acts that result in physical damage to someone; they also include defamation of character in the form of libel or slander, as well as invasion of privacy.

Libel   *Libel* includes writings, photos, or signs that an individual or organization creates to injure the reputation of another individual or organization. In many legal systems, such materials are libelous only if they express false statements. Examples of libel include the following:

- A town resident seeking to support her friend's candidacy for the school committee publishes an opinion piece in the local newspaper falsely stating that the candidate's opponent embezzled funds from the town.
- A stockbroker who wants to discredit a colleague competing for the same promotion in their company photographs the colleague holding a drink at a party. He then circulates the photo to others in the organization and to customers, with the caption "Would you trust *your* retirement account to this man?"

Police managers and officers must be familiar with libel law because people may call the police if they feel their character has been defamed through libel. However, police officers cannot arrest for libel because it is a civil wrong (tort), not a crime. The injured party must hire a lawyer and file a lawsuit against the person who is alleged to have made the libelous statement.

Slander   *Slander,* like libel, is defamation of a person's or organization's character, but it is done through the spoken word, not through the written word or graphic images. Examples include public disclosure of an individual's private facts, often resulting from unauthorized intrusion into someone's private affairs. Supervisors and organizations may be held civilly liable for defamation if they communicate derogatory information about a current or former employee; for example, by telling a potential employer who calls for a reference that the former worker who is the subject of the inquiry used drugs on the job. If the statement communicated is true, the person or organization it described may not have a cause of action for slander. The truth of the statement is typically a defense to a civil suit for slander. Still, the expenses associated with litigation, even if one wins the case, can be considerable.

Public officials (including police officers and celebrities) are not typically protected from derogatory statements because of their public status. However, police officers and managers can be held civilly liable for disclosure of private or derogatory information that is not classified as public information. (Example: public information typically includes conviction records but not arrest records.)

PRIVACY LAW

Confidential information: anything written or spoken that is intended only for the eyes and/or ears of the receiver.

Privacy law involves **confidential information**—anything written or spoken that is intended only for the eyes and/or ears of the receiver. Confidential implies secret, intended to be heard by a select few (*Merriam-Webster's*, 2006b). According to privacy law, confidential communication privileges exist between an attorney and client, between members of the clergy when speaking to individuals under their spiritual care, and between physicians and patients.

Confidential communications between a husband and wife, who are legally married, are usually private unless disclosure relies on the consent of one of the parties. The issue of testifying against a spouse differs from state to state. If a person who is an independent witness has information relevant to a case, that individual may choose not to testify. However, a judge may issue a subpoena directing a witness to testify if the information is necessary or meaningful to the case, the testimony involves injury to the witness-spouse or one of the couple's children by the suspect spouse, or the respondent/defendant waives the spousal privilege. The spousal privilege terminates upon dissolution (divorce) of the marriage because a relationship that requires legal protection no longer exists.

What does all this mean for police officers? In some states, officers may not be required to disclose the identity of confidential informants (CIs). However, confidential informants may be identified and be required to testify in a court proceeding to ensure a fair trial for the defendant. For example, if the CI is the only eyewitness to the incident and, therefore, a material witness, the CI may be compelled to testify.

Journalists in a few states are not compelled to provide the source of their information and may refuse to disclose unpublished information. Finally, while some people may choose to assist the police with an investigation, others may choose not to give support or aid to the police if they fear that doing so would put them in danger. Such individuals generally cannot be forced to help police with an investigation (Lawyers.com, 2010; Zalman, 2011).

Police agencies have policies or rules regarding the disclosure of information that is considered confidential. Generally, an agency will publish a rule or regulation stipulating that no member of the agency can discuss evidence or police information with the media, the general public, or those who have no right to know unless provisions for publication are permitted by established authority or mandated by law (Rochester, New York, Police Department, 1981).

The Privacy Act of 1974

The Privacy Act of 1974 (Public Law 93-579) was created by Congress in 1974 and became effective in 1975. According to the Freedom of Information Act/Privacy Act Team (2010), the act guarantees American citizens and lawfully admitted immigrants that the following will apply to information gathered about them:

- There is no federal system of personal records whose existence is secret.

- Any personal information files held by the federal government are limited to those that are clearly necessary.

- People have the right to see what information about them the federal government is keeping and to challenge its accuracy.

- Personal information collected for one purpose cannot be used for another purpose without the individual's consent.

- If disclosures are made, a person may learn to whom the disclosures were made, for what purpose, and on what date.

Under the privacy act and laws enacted by many states, employees also have the right to privacy. The laws allow employees access to their personnel records to address unfavorable information, to correct misinformation, and to learn when and if an employer has given information about them to others; for example, personal history details (Mathis & Jackson, 2005). Police managers, supervisors, and employment services personnel should be aware of these rights.

The Perils of Violating Privacy

Knowledge of privacy law is vital for police administrators managing internal operations and for police officers as they interact with the public. Officers should respect the privacy of community members they encounter during their daily business; for instance, by avoiding situations in which intended persons may overhear conversations and by sharing information only on a legal need-to-know basis.

However, it is not uncommon for officers, both on and off duty, to openly discuss investigations and encounters with members of the public. Many officers openly discuss calls-for-service at coffee shops or restaurants. Domestic violence calls, neighbors complaining about each other, drug-house locations, or nuisance calls often become topics of conversation in the presence of curious bystanders. Officers must remember that information travels fast in neighborhoods and communities. Revealing facts and names related to particular investigations could result in retaliation or other conflicts between neighbors. Further, disclosure could expose the officer to civil liability.

Confidentiality with respect to investigations is paramount when it comes to the issues of drug and violent crime investigations. Police should carefully guard the techniques, tactics, and strategies they use to solve these complicated cases. Otherwise, investigations may be compromised, and anyone involved—officers, victims, suspects, witnesses—can be placed in danger. As an example, one of the authors of this book recently overheard a police officer discuss a buy-bust (buy-arrest) procedure regarding a drug investigation over a cell phone while boarding a

When discussing police business, officers must be careful that their conversations are not overheard by curious bystanders.

commercial airplane. If an accomplice of the drug suspect had overheard the same conversation, the identity of the cell phone operator as an undercover police investigator could have placed that officer in jeopardy. The investigation would have been compromised as well.

To avoid such situations, officers should treat all police communications and investigations as confidential—not to be discussed and analyzed in public.

LIABILITY MANAGEMENT

All police officers, especially those in management or supervisory positions, should be knowledgeable about laws related to the topics discussed so far in this chapter—including federal employment and unionization, as well as contracts; rules and regulations coming from federal, state, and local levels; property; tort; and privacy. Why? Society has grown increasingly litigious, and lawsuits are expensive. For example, by 2005, Los Angeles paid an estimated $70 million to settle lawsuits arising from the Rampart Division corruption scandal that severely damaged the reputation of the LAPD in 1999 (Ross, 2006; Stohr & Collins, 2009).

Civil Lawsuits

In a *civil lawsuit,* a complaint is filed by a plaintiff who alleges a civil wrong committed by the respondent (defendant). The respondent answers the complainant's allegation. Procedurally, a civil lawsuit is similar to but does not replicate a criminal prosecution. Restrictions against the admission of hearsay evidence, testimonial privileges, the burden of proof, and the rules of evidence are more relaxed in civil proceedings. Further, unlike criminal cases that require unanimous verdicts for conviction, civil court juries can rule for or against a plaintiff through a majority and a finding of civil liability through a preponderance of the evidence (over 50 percent certainty) rather than the more strict degree (or standard) proof of guilt beyond a reasonable doubt required in criminal prosecutions (Mann & Roberts, 2006; Ross, 2006; Rutledge, 2000).

In recent years, it is not uncommon for aggrieved parties to bring a civil lawsuit against a jurisdiction, the police agency located in that jurisdiction, police management, and individual police officers for events such as police motor-vehicle and high-speed pursuit collisions or wrongful death or injury that occurs during an

A judge presiding in a courtroom.

encounter with the police. Besides naming the individual officer in the lawsuit, many people filing lawsuits also name as many other individuals and parties as possible— including supervisors, lieutenants, the chief, and the government entity involved. Their strategy in naming all these defendants is to increase their chances of receiving a larger settlement if they win the case. Such individuals subscribe to the *deep pockets* theory: In an attempt to secure maximum remuneration or compensation for an alleged wrongdoing, they target all in an attempt to secure a judgment against the entity that is best able to pay because it has the most assets or capital. In the world of policing, that entity is most likely the agency or jurisdiction.

To mitigate their agency's vulnerability to such lawsuits, police personnel should familiarize themselves with several legal concepts in addition to what has been discussed so far in this chapter. These concepts include types of liability, negligence, sexual harassment, and proximate cause. We examine each of these in more detail next.

Types of Liability

There are several kinds of liability—direct, strict, and vicarious (indirect)—all common terms in lawsuits.

Direct liability: liability that is embodied in the person who commits the act in question.

Direct Liability   Direct liability is embodied in the person who commits the act in question. For example, an officer who uses excessive force while arresting a suspect and injures the person as a result is directly liable.

Strict liability: liability for damages, injury, or loss regardless of the person's culpability (blame or fault).

Strict Liability   Strict liability (liability without fault) makes a person responsible for damages, injury, or loss regardless of the person's culpability (blame or fault). Strict liability is often imposed on those engaged in hazardous or inherently dangerous activities. A police officer making an arrest, for example, is engaged in an inherently dangerous activity. The officer or agency *may be* held liable if injury occurs to the suspect after arrest and while the person is in custody. Claims that the officer acted in good faith or took all reasonable precautions in conducting the arrest and putting the person in custody may not be valid defenses against a lawsuit.

Vicarious (indirect) liability: legal responsibility for the actions or damages that have resulted from someone else's negligence.

Vicarious (Indirect) Liability   Vicarious (indirect) liability refers to the legal responsibility for the actions or damages that have resulted from someone else's negligence. For instance, a police supervisor, manager, chief, or government entity is indirectly liable if the individual or entity is held responsible for a subordinate's actions. (A supervisor cannot be held *directly* liable for a subordinate's actions unless the supervisor participates in the act itself.)

Vicarious liability is a form of strict secondary liability that arises from the common law doctrine of *respondent superior*. This doctrine states that the superior (supervisor) is responsible (liable) for actions that resulted in injury, wrongful death, and so forth (such as use of excessive force) that were committed by a subordinate within the scope of employment (*American Heritage Dictionary—Dictionary of Business Terms*, 2009; Cheeseman, 2009; del Carmen, 1989; Michaels, 1999).

Negligence: failure to exercise the degree of care that an ordinary, reasonable, and prudent person would demonstrate under the same circumstances.

Negligence

One of the broadest areas of liability is negligence, a subject we touched on earlier in this chapter. **Negligence** may be defined as a failure to exercise the degree of care that an ordinary, reasonable, and prudent person would demonstrate under the same circumstances. As we have seen, the consequence of the negligent action or lack of action may be unintended injury, death, or loss of property. When a person fails to exercise proper care according to the demands of a particular situation (for example, driving while talking on a cell phone and being inattentive to traffic), the failure is classified as *simple negligence*. *Gross negligence* is the deliberate lack of care for life or property (for instance, driving while intoxicated).

Courts are more interested in holding supervisors liable in cases of gross negligence rather than simple negligence (Peak et al., 2010; *West's Encyclopedia of American Law,* 2008b). The concern regarding the negligence of police managers regarding subordinates' actions centers on whether the managers allowed, instigated, or turned a "blind eye" to (condoned) subordinates' conduct. Police managers must be mindful that negligence can also occur through the performance of everyday administrative duties, if such performance leads to injury, wrongful death, and so forth. For example:

- *Hiring:* A manager hires an officer who has psychological or behavioral problems or a background of incompetence, and those problems result in the officers' injuring someone else.

- *Retention:* An agency continues to employ an officer even after the person has demonstrated violent tendencies, and the officer hurts someone else.

- *Training:* The agency fails to adequately train officers to carry out their duties properly, and the resulting incompetence leads to injury or death of a community member.

- *Supervision:* A police supervisor fails to offer guidance, training, remediation, and evaluation in a timely manner to subordinates. Consequently, one of the supervisor's direct reports mishandles investigation of a crime, and an innocent person is sent to jail.

- *Assignment:* A police supervisor assigns an officer known for intolerance of diverse opinions to a diverse neighborhood. The officer engages in uncivil conduct or uses excessive force against a minority group member.

Sexual Harassment

Sexual harassment constitutes another area of concern for police managers seeking to mitigate their agency's vulnerability to lawsuits. The term applies to touching, intimidation, lewd remarks, and other conduct or communication of a sexual nature that is offensive to a prudent and reasonable person. It involves actions or communications motivated by hostility toward another's gender or a desire to control the other person, even someone of the same gender. For example:

- A male officer resentful of a female colleague's promotion tells obscene jokes to her as a way to make her uncomfortable.

- A female supervisor sexually interested in a subordinate makes it clear that the subordinate will receive a promotion only if he sleeps with her.

Laws and court decisions generally read or hold that an employer is liable for sexual harassment if the communication or conduct is unreasonably condoned, improperly investigated, or left uncorrected. To avoid sexual harassment lawsuits,

Sexual harassment: touching, intimidation, lewd remarks, and other conduct or communication of a sexual nature that is offensive to a prudent and reasonable person.

Learn more about sexual harassment policies from the U.S. Equal Employment Opportunity Commission (EEOC) at www.eeoc.gov.

all organizations should have a clear, written antisexual harassment policy that is communicated to all employees *and* enforced (Cheeseman, 2009).

Proximate (Legal) Cause

Actual cause includes all antecedents leading to a given result. **Proximate (legal) cause** is that to which liability attaches. It results from an action or inaction that directly leads to damage to property, or to the injury or death of another person. Proximate cause action or inaction is *foreseeable,* and the damage, injury, or death would not have occurred if the individual had not committed the action or inaction leading to the foreseeable result (*West's Encyclopedia of American Law,* 2008c). Situations involving high-speed police-vehicle pursuits, domestic abuse, and persons with mental illness all provide examples of situations that lay a foundation for proximate cause and liability for the results of such activities (or inactivity) if injury to others is foreseeable.

Actual cause → Proximate (legal) cause = Liability

High-Speed Chases   Proximate cause can occur when (for example) police officers engage in a high-speed vehicle pursuit of a suspect and the pursuit results in injury to the officer, to the driver being chased, or to an innocent third party. When this happens, the police officer who gave chase, as well as the agency employing that officer, may be considered liable for any injuries. The issue of proximate cause may be argued if the officer and the pursuit supervisor are not reasonably sure that the person being chased and/or innocent bystanders are not in imminent danger due to the police actively pursuing a vehicle. If injury is foreseeable, proximate cause exists.

High-speed pursuit is an area of considerable liability for any officer or agency. Some suspects have filed lawsuits against an officer after having been

Actual cause: all antecedents leading to a given result.

Proximate (legal) cause: that to which liability attaches; results from an action or inaction that directly leads to damage to property, or to the injury or death of another person.

High-speed vehicle pursuits can lead to collisions that result in injuries, deaths, and considerable liability for the driver-officer and the agency.

injured during a chase, charging that the officer was negligent in continuing the chase. In many jurisdictions, an agency's supervisors must monitor trends in police-vehicle chases and approve all such chases. Supervisors may order an officer to stop a high-speed pursuit if the chase poses a danger to innocent bystanders, other drivers, and any of the involved parties, including the officer and the suspect. As a general rule, it is best to discontinue the pursuit when public safety becomes an issue (foreseeable that person being pursued, officers, or other people could be killed or injured) or environmental conditions (e.g., rain, ice) dictate that the pursuit should be terminated.

Domestic Abuse   Domestic abuse presents another example of proximate cause. Suppose that an officer has responded to several calls for help from a woman whose husband has battered her. If this same woman calls for help again, claiming that the man is threatening her, the officer has a duty to protect her from this threat because he knows the history of the situation. If the officer fails to act on the threat and the woman is assaulted once again, the officer may be deemed negligent.

Mental Illness   As a final example of proximate cause, consider an officer who encounters a person with mental illness who is threatening self-harm or harm to others. Failing to take action regarding this individual—for instance, not restraining the person—may be considered negligence if the individual causes harm to self or others after the officer leaves the area. A citizen could sue the officer for negligence if the citizen successfully argues that the officer should have known (foreseen) the risks in not controlling the person.

What Police Agencies Can Do

How can police officers and their superiors minimize (mitigate) their agency's exposure to liability lawsuits? The following practices can help:

- *Employ officers with higher education.* Evidence suggests that police agencies employing officers with higher education are subjected to fewer complaints and, by extension, have fewer lawsuits filed against them (Bohm & Haley, 2005; Goldstein, 1990).

- *Demonstrate ethical leadership.* For instance, lead by engaging in morally correct behavior.

- *Demonstrate effective communication skills.* To illustrate, ensure that communications are clear, concise, and understood by the receiver.

- *Know the law.* Gain familiarity with state and federal laws regarding the topics examined in this chapter.

- *Stick to the code.* Adhere to professional codes of ethics and conduct for the police profession. (See Chapter 1 for a detailed presentation of ethics and conduct codes for police.)

- *Conduct in-service legal training.* Offer training programs that explain the law and how it works and that give officers opportunities to role-play the correct attitude and language to use in specific situations. For officers against whom minor complaints have been made, use remedial training and counseling to prevent major complaints. For officers who have been the recipients of major complaints, take appropriate action; for example, assign them to desk duty for a specified period of time while providing them with remedial training and/or counseling.

- *Document behavior and measures taken.* Regularly observe, evaluate, and document officers' performance as well as actions taken to address problematic behavior. When an agency can prove that it has made reasonable efforts to improve a police officer's knowledge, skills, and abilities, it will be less vulnerable to lawsuits (Cheeseman, 2009; Hunter & Barker, 2011; Mann & Roberts, 2006; Ortmeier, 2009; Ross, 2006).

summary

- **National Employment Laws.** The U.S. government has enacted numerous laws intended to foster fairness and safety in the workplace. All organizations are subject to these laws, which have the common theme of protecting employees against discrimination and other forms of harm. Affirmative action is not a law; it is an approach that some organizations use to ensure fairness in hiring and employment and that has stirred some controversy. Some police agencies are striving to hire a diverse workforce to reflect the diversity in the communities they serve.

- **Unionization.** Unions have developed over several centuries. Unionization of police experienced a setback with the Boston Police Strike of 1919, which resulted in mandates prohibiting police officers from going on strike. Police have unions today as well as other representative organizations (such as the Fraternal Order of Police) that lobby for their interests. There are numerous labor laws affecting unions. Such laws stipulate matters including unfair labor practices and management rights. While individuals gain certain advantages by joining a union, the relationships between union leaders, union members, and management can be complex and tense, especially during labor negotiations. To negotiate a labor contract, unionized workers engage in collective bargaining with managers. Grievances filed by unionized employees must also go through a specific process.

- **Contract Law.** In addition to labor contracts, a police agency may forge other types of contracts; for example, to lease or purchase a facility or equipment. Contracts can be expressed or implied and must meet specific criteria to be considered valid.

- **Administrative Law.** Administrative law is public law promulgated by administrative agencies at the federal, state, and local levels. Police agencies are affected by administrative law at all three levels.

- **Property Law.** Laws governing property (whether it is tangle or intangible, personal or real) are relevant to police agencies not only because their responsibilities include protecting citizens' property but also because agencies may own or lease property themselves.

- **Tort Law.** A tort is a private wrong committed against a person or a person's property. Torts may be unintentional or intentional (including libel and slander). Police may be held civilly liable for unintentional torts, including invasion of privacy, false arrest, and use of excessive force, as well as intentional torts in the form of libel or slander.

- **Privacy Law.** Privacy law involves confidential information—anything written or spoken that is intended only for the eyes and/or ears of the receiver. Police agencies have policies or rules regarding disclosure of information that is considered confidential. Disclosing such information about crime investigations is particularly egregious, as it can put individuals in danger and compromise current and future investigations.

- **Liability Management.** Civil lawsuits are on the rise and are expensive. To reduce their vulnerability to such lawsuits, police managers and officers should familiarize themselves with all laws related to employment, unionization, contracts, administrative rules and regulations, torts, property, and privacy. They should also understand the differences between three types of liability: direct, strict, and vicarious. Areas of liability of particular importance for police agencies include negligence, sexual harassment, and proximate cause. Police officers and their superiors can minimize their agency's (and their own) exposure to liability lawsuits through practices such as employing officers with higher education, demonstrating ethical leadership and effective communication skills, adhering to codes of ethics and conduct established for the police profession, conducting in-service legal training, and documenting problematic behavior and measures taken.

key terms

actual cause

administrative law

affirmative action

binding arbitration

breach of contract

collective agreement

collective bargaining

confidential information

contract

direct liability

good faith

grievance

negligence

negotiable management rights

nonnegotiable management rights

proximate (legal) cause

sexual harassment

strict liability

tort

unfair labor practices

vicarious (indirect) liability

1. Employment law is a critical and complicated area. Three laws that have affected police agencies significantly are the Civil Rights Act of 1964, the Age Discrimination Act, and the Americans with Disabilities Act. Describe how these laws affect a police agency and why the agency must address the implications of the laws.

2. Police agencies must constantly struggle to ensure that their workforces represent the population of the community they serve. Describe how affirmative action or similar approaches or policies can help or hinder an agency striving for this representation. Can an agency build a diverse workforce without affirmative action practices or policies? Why or why not?

3. Unionization has been and is still a controversial area for police agencies throughout the United States. What advantages and disadvantages does unionization afford—for employees and for management?

4. Unions and other representative organizations, along with management, must abide by laws regarding unfair labor practices and management rights. What are the consequences for a police agency of failing to address unfair labor practice?

5. Police officers may feel the need to have adequate representation when addressing conditions of employment. What conditions might exist where a labor organization or a police union may benefit a police officer or group of officers?

6. A police manager may be faced with a grievance brought by a line officer. What is a grievance, and how does the grievance process work?

7. What other contracts might a police agency forge, in addition to labor contracts negotiated through the collective bargaining process? How would you know that a contract had been breached, and what would you do to resolve the breach?

8. What is administrative law, and how does such law affect police agencies?

9. What are two major reasons that police managers and officers should understand property law?

10. What is a tort? For what kinds of torts might a police officer or agency be held liable?

11. What is the most effective way in which police can avoid violating laws related to privacy?

12. Why is it important for police agencies to be familiar with the many categories of law presented in this chapter?

13. What are the three types of liability? Cite examples of how a police officer or agency can be vulnerable to each type.

14. How might police officers and managers best protect themselves and their agency from liability?

WHAT WOULD YOU DO?

When Is an Investigator Not an Investigator?

In a midsize police agency, 33 officers brought a lawsuit against the agency. In the lawsuit, they asserted that they should receive the *investigator* title and back pay because, according to state law, a person should receive the designation after 18 months of temporary assignment to investigator duties. Many of these officers had been performing the duties for more than 18 months; in some cases, for years. In response to the filing of the lawsuit, the agency demoted or "temporarily reassigned" six "genuine" investigators. The reason? If the judge ruled in favor of the 33 officers, the agency would be overstaffed with investigators and its budget would be severely strained.

Although the police union did not support the lawsuit, the union president publicly chastised the police agency for promoting the six demoted investigators in the first place. The union president told the press, "It's the worst mismanagement I have ever seen." Throughout this time, police and union officials tried to resolve the matter without resorting to the courts. But their efforts failed.

The officers who sued lost, and the six demoted investigators were reinstated. However, the toll on morale among officers has yet to be determined. If the officers decide to appeal the decision, the matter could prove even more divisive for the agency.

1. In what ways might the union have helped prevent this situation from arising in the first place?

2. In what ways could the agency's managers have helped prevent the lawsuit?

3. What might the 33 officers have done differently to have their concerns met, rather than resorting to a lawsuit?

4. Did this scenario involve any unfair labor practices? Why or why not?

5. What steps would you advise this agency to take to avoid being subjected to another similar lawsuit in the future?

◀ An entrance to a police building should be well maintained.

Procurement and Facilities Management

After completing this chapter, readers should be able to:

- distinguish purchasing, leasing, and outsourcing as methods for procurement of supplies, equipment, facilities, or services.

- compare the benefits and challenges or purchasing, leasing, and outsourcing.

- explain how the competitive bidding process functions.

- compare and contrast service contracts and warranties.

- describe the steps a police agency takes to forge agreements with outsourcing providers.

- identify the information that should be contained in an outsourcing contract.

- list the various duties of a facilities manager and some of the qualifications for the job.
- describe the steps required to build or renovate a police facility.
- analyze why site surveys of police facilities are valuable, even when a new project or renovation is not being performed.
- discuss how a site survey is conducted.
- explain the steps a police agency can take to acquire new technology and ensure that it is installed and used correctly.

Introduction

The police would have a hard time doing their job without the equipment, tools, supplies, services, and physical facilities that many officers take for granted—everything from patrol cars, radios, evidence preservation kits, weapons, and fleet-maintenance services to the squad rooms, detention cells, firing ranges, and information technology (IT) systems so crucial to their work.

To ensure that essential equipment, supplies, services, and facilities are available for police personnel to do their work, an agency must take a disciplined approach to procurement (acquisition) of needed resources and services as well as management of all facilities used by the agency. In this chapter, we take a close look at these two crucial responsibilities. We examine several approaches to procurement of equipment, supplies, and services—purchasing, leasing, and outsourcing—and consider key tasks related to these procurement processes, such as obtaining competitive bids and developing contracts. We then turn to facilities management, with emphasis on the skills, experience, and personal attributes that distinguish exceptional facilities managers; suggestions for how to plan and execute construction or renovation of a police facility; and ideas for updating facilities with needed law enforcement technologies.

Although procurement and facilities management may seem to take a back seat to other more visible police functions, these two activities help lay a solid foundation from which officers can carry out their mission and serve their community well.

PROCUREMENT

For a police agency, as with any organization, procurement is the obtaining of needed equipment, supplies, and services. Procurement can be done through purchasing, leasing, or outsourcing. Regardless of the approach used, agency leaders must know how to select the right supplier, negotiate terms of the deal, ensure quality of the goods or services obtained, and manage the agency's relationship with suppliers. We explore these topics next.

Purchasing

Purchasing: an organization's procurement of goods and services in the correct amounts, from the most appropriate source, for the best possible price.

In the context of organizations, **purchasing** refers to the procurement of goods and services in the correct amounts, from the most appropriate source, for the best possible price. Once the good or service is purchased, the buyer owns it. Police agencies use the purchasing process to:

- Obtain needed goods, services, and other supplies at the best price
- Obtain the materials, equipment, supplies, and facilities that are appropriate for what the agency does
- Procure the correct quantities, and avoid underbuying or overbuying
- Arrange for necessary technical services or service agreements on purchased equipment
- Ensure that materials purchased are delivered in a timely manner
- Avoid becoming overly dependent on too few suppliers, so goods and services will be available at all times
- Dispose of unneeded items through trade-in, salvage, sale, or transfer to another agency (Moak & Hillhouse, 2009)

Purchasing by a public entity, such as a police agency, differs markedly from purchasing by a corporation because the money used comes from the public that the agency serves, mostly in the form of tax revenues. Not surprisingly, most citizens feel that their police agency has an obligation to maximize use of their tax dollars. By developing specific policies and procedures for making purchases, a police agency can help reassure community members that purchasing is being handled ethically, correctly, and consistently—with an eye toward getting the most value in return for tax dollars (Colorado Municipal League, 1996).

Developing a Purchasing Process   Every police agency should have a manual detailing policies and procedures governing the purchasing process. While the thought of developing a process and writing an entire manual on this subject may seem daunting to some, they can look to any government purchasing manual as a model and modify the manual's contents to suit their agency's particular circumstances. Ideally, the individual who writes the agency's purchasing manual should be the purchasing agent, supervisor, or manager.

Most agencies have guidelines for purchasing items based on their dollar value. Typically, these guidelines provide a range of values for the type of purchasing request needed and the person/group who must approve the purchase. To illustrate, for an item with a dollar value of $0 to $999, a manager or other designee may have the authority to approve a single price and vendor quote before the agency can buy the item. In contrast, a purchase of $50,000 or more might require formal competitive bids from a specific number of suppliers. Moreover, the city council will likely want to examine the bids and select what it sees as the best, most cost-effective supplier. In some cases, only one supplier of a product or service may exist. When this situation occurs, the provider is considered a *sole source*.

Organizing the Purchasing Function   The purchasing responsibility in large police agencies is usually handled in a separate department or division within the agency. In smaller agencies or those that are downsizing, purchasing might be coordinated

Police equestrian unit center. Mounted police officers are used for crowd control and in ceremonies, and they can enhance police–community relations.

and centralized in a department that serves the purchasing needs of other local government agencies in addition to police, such as the fire service and environmental services in the same jurisdiction. In very small police agencies, purchasing might be the part-time responsibility of one administrator who has other responsibilities as well. However purchasing is accomplished, it demands a certain expertise.

The purchasing agent need not be a police officer, although the person does need in-depth knowledge of police equipment and supplies (including how they are used and how much they cost). For example, the agent must be familiar with fire-arms and other weapons, including less-than-lethal items used to subdue suspects (such as chemical agents and police batons). In large agencies that possess a canine or mounted equestrian unit, the purchasing agent should have at least a working knowledge of how dogs or horses are selected, trained, purchased, housed, and maintained for use by a police agency.

The person in charge of purchasing (variously known as the purchasing agent, director, or manager) should have a thorough knowledge of not only equipment and supplies but also the leading vendors of these items, as well as their pricing arrangements. Vendors must typically undergo a process, including a credit check, to be approved to supply to government agencies. Vendor representatives often meet with purchasing individuals to establish good working relationships and add a personal touch to the supply business.

Understanding Ethical Challenges in Purchasing   There is also an ethical element to the purchasing process. Specifically, agents who have a friendship with the vendor of a service or product may be tempted to purchase more than their organization needs. Others have deferred some supplies for their own personal use or have resold purchased goods for personal profit. When purchasing agents have access to their organization's credit cards, the temptation to steal in these ways may prove irresistible. Some purchasing agents have even falsified documents to hide the fact that they made certain purchases specifically to resell the goods for personal profit. Others have used their agency's gasoline (fuel) credit cards to fill the tanks in their own personal vehicles. By clearly communicating the police agency's codes of ethics and behavior, and promptly addressing violations of the codes, agency managers can help discourage unethical actions related to purchasing.

Leasing

In the past, there was only one way for an agency to obtain equipment or facilities: purchase them outright. This meant the agency needed enough cash on hand to purchase the necessary items or to arrange a line of credit through a financing source (e.g., municipal comptroller or bank) for more significant purchases, including cars and computers. But today, government agencies have an additional option that has long been available to citizens and businesses who wish to have expensive equipment without providing cash upfront: leasing.

A **lease** enables an individual or organization to obtain or secure the use of items or property in exchange for payments made at agreed-upon intervals. There

Lease:
a procurement arrangement that enables an individual or organization to obtain or secure the use of items or property in exchange for payments made at agreed-upon intervals.

Spotlight on Police Vehicles

While police agencies make the same use of photocopiers and computers as do corporations, their use of police vehicles differs dramatically from that of other types of organizations. In some agencies, unmarked police vehicles are basically the same as cars driven by ordinary citizens. However, many police agencies use uniquely built vehicles that possess special heavy-duty suspension, brakes, and high-performance engines. Patrol cars may be driven by numerous officers, and in many cases, used 24 hours a day, 7 days a week. Police vehicles experience unpredictable types of demand, ranging from long periods at idle to excessive speeds and sharp braking—all of which strain a vehicle's engine, brakes, suspension, and other systems. Many police agencies prefer rear-wheel-drive vehicles because they tend to perform better (and longer) in hilly or curved areas than do their front-wheel-drive counterparts. An agency may also select white vehicles because they generally have a higher resale value at auction after service use than other-colored vehicles.

Maintenance of an agency's police-car fleet may be performed by two different entities: experts within the government or police agency, or outside providers. For instance, a large police organization may have a vehicle-maintenance division headed by its own manager and staffed by full-time mechanics. For any additional vehicle-related concerns that cannot be managed by in-house personnel (including warranty service and collision repair), the agency may contract with local reputable car dealers and repair specialists. In some jurisdictions, a police agency's fleet is maintained entirely by an outside provider (outsourced).

The Michigan State Police evaluated eight 2010 model year police vehicles in six categories. The results of the agency's evaluation can be viewed at www.michigan.gov/msp/0,1607,7-123--16274--,00.html.

Fleet of police motorcycles.

are two parties involved in the lease: the lessor, who owns (and continues to own) the items or property, and the lessee, who pays for the use of the property (Brigham & Ehrhardt, 2005). Leased equipment is often accompanied by a better service contract than equipment that is purchased and can usually be replaced without cost to the lessee if the item fails to function owing to a manufacturing or other defect. However, misuse of leased equipment by the lessee usually negates the maintenance or replacement portion of the contract. Photocopiers and fax machines, cellular phones, computer equipment, buildings, vehicles, facility security systems, and virtually any other item can be leased.

In response to increased budgetary constraints on police agencies, many suppliers of equipment used by such agencies have instituted a leasing system through which the agency can use the equipment while paying a monthly fee. Often, the lease payments can be credited toward the agency's eventual ownership of the equipment. This process is referred to as a *lease-purchase* agreement. Moreover, agencies can upgrade to newer, more technologically advanced equipment for only a slight increase in their monthly lease payments.

Outsourcing

When it comes to police equipment, supplies, and facilities, purchasing or leasing are common approaches to procurement. To obtain needed products or services, more and more agencies are using another approach: outsourcing. (See the box titled "Spotlight on Police Vehicles.") But what is outsourcing, exactly? And why has it become increasingly popular? In simplest terms, **outsourcing** is a process by which a company or government entity contracts with another company or government entity to provide products or services that were formerly provided or performed by the original entity.

Outsourcing:
a process by which a company or government entity contracts with another company or government entity to provide products or services that were formerly provided or performed by the original entity.

Advantages and Disadvantages of Outsourcing   The most obvious force driving outsourcing is that it can save money for a police agency, if the vendor can provide equivalent service and is located in a place where general labor costs are low. Besides saving money, outsourcing enables leaders and managers to focus on the real work of the agency—including formulating strategies for better service and increasing public safety in the community. A disadvantage of outsourcing is that, because employees of an outside organization are carrying out some of the police agency's business processes, the agency has less direct communication with and control over the employees performing the services. This can lead to service quality concerns and discontent between the agency and the service provider. Further, the contract service industry is often extremely competitive, leading to a depression in wage rates paid and high attrition (turnover that can reach 300 percent per year) of employees (Ortmeier, 1999; Thompson, 2010).

Moreover, in recent years, the term *outsourcing* has taken on negative connotations for many workers. Numerous American corporations, in an effort to cut manufacturing and other costs, have outsourced manufacturing processes, customer call centers, and other business activities and processes to providers based in foreign countries, where labor and other costs are often less than those in the United States. In doing so, these companies have reduced the number of jobs available for U.S. workers on American soil. Outsourcing has thus become a sensitive and in some respects a highly politicized subject. A police agency that decides to use outsourcing may face rumblings of protest from its own workforce (especially unionized workers) as well as from members of the community it serves. Further, it may not be legally possible to outsource all police functions to a private company because policing is a public function of government. As part of establishing an outsourcing arrangement, an agency would do well to anticipate such reactions and develop strategies for managing them.

Only time will reveal whether outsourcing is a temporary or permanent phenomenon, but budgetary constraints will continue to force businesses and public agencies alike to trim funding wherever they can. Eliminating or supplanting whole functions by outsourcing presents a viable means of reducing costs.

Selecting Processes and Activities to Outsource   Outsourcing has become more common not only in big corporations but also for cities and towns. For example, rather than maintain a janitorial staff, some companies are hiring janitorial service providers for facility upkeep and maintenance. Many businesses that had their own fleet of delivery trucks now hire trucking companies to make their deliveries. Many private organizations are also contracting with security companies to provide security officers, investigative services, first response to crisis situations, and data protection.

What processes and activities do police agencies typically decide to outsource? Many agencies are outsourcing some of their ancillary or supplementary functions. For instance, they may outsource police-vehicle maintenance or information technology services (such as computer maintenance) to a service provider that performs such work for the entire city, county, or state where the police agency is based. Agencies may also outsource blood, drug, and weapon analysis; emergency communication (9-1-1 phone service); or training academy services to a centralized regional or statewide academy that presents training for numerous agencies. Finally, an agency may outsource services that are too costly for it (or a government

A 9-1-1 emergency communications center.

outsourcing provider) to support financially. Such services might include information system technology maintenance and upgrade; environmental system review; and upgrading of existing, renovated, or new facilities.

Obviously, the main duties of police—such as patrol, investigation, arrest, gathering and maintenance of evidence, and testifying in court—cannot be outsourced from the sworn body of the agency's police officers. However, many agencies have elected to outsource such needs as building and fleet maintenance, and correctional facility staffing, food, and health services. As demonstrated with the advent of 9-1-1 emergency communication services, agencies that once managed emergency phone and dispatching services internally now have them routed through a 9-1-1 communications center managed by a county, state, or other government entity. This can save police agencies significant money. Agencies can use the savings to invest in other critical resources and activities, such as the hiring of additional sworn officers, purchasing of updated equipment, or crime prevention initiatives.

When an Entire Police Department Is Outsourced   Unfortunately, while many individual police duties cannot be outsourced, there is a growing trend toward outsourcing entire police departments. Many municipal mayors, town boards, and city council members have placed their budgets under a microscope and identified the police department as the costliest item in the budget. Their solution? Outsource policing services to the county sheriff's department or another regional or state police agency responsible for countywide public safety.

The movement away from village and town police departments has caused significant strife for many citizens in areas considering this change. To outsource a local police department, town or village leaders must dismantle their police agency, sell off its equipment and other appurtenances, and lay off or place its sworn officers with the sheriff's department or other agency. The sheriff or regional agency must also change patrol routes to encompass the community that is giving up its department. Usually, the town or village and the county will share the cost of policing over a specified period of time, often saving the jurisdictions as much as thousands to millions of dollars annually (Bair, 2008; Rogers, 2009).

County Sheriff's departments often outsource their services to municipalities.

Advocates of this change believe that a sheriff's department can be just as effective at protecting life and property as the local police agency. Taxes will stabilize, they maintain, as the government entity (for instance, the municipality) saves money by dispensing with a separate police department. Opponents argue that the sheriff's department, even with the infusion of town or village police officers into its ranks, cannot possibly cover the jurisdiction and the county as effectively or be as sensitive and responsive to local needs as a local police department can.

Reactions to Local Police Department Outsourcing   Jurisdictions have reacted differently to the notion of outsourcing local police departments. For example:

- In Pewaukee, Wisconsin, a county judge refused to block police outsourcing (Behm, 2009).

- In Lakeland, Florida, residents voted to retain their local police force rather than outsource the function to the county sheriff's office (Bair, 2008).

- Since 1998, the Mackinac Center for Public Policy in Michigan has advocated privatizing public safety services for citizens and their property, by outsourcing non-law enforcement services (such as parking regulation, communications, and animal control) to private corporations (*Privatizing the Long Arm of the Law*, 1998).

- In 2006, the citizens of Walbridge, Ohio, voted to keep their police department rather than outsource police functions to Lake Township (Rogers, 2009).

In Los Angeles County in California, two towns experienced outsourcing in entirely different ways. Westlake Village used the LA County Sheriff's Department for police services for a savings of $2,082,435 for the years 2009 to 2010. Sierra Madre, whose residents wanted to outsource police services but whose police force was skeptical about the benefits of this initiative, expected to spend $3.4 million for police services over the years 2009 to 2010. The citizens involved were sharply divided as to whether the police are paid too little or too much (*Sierra Madre Divided over Possible Police Outsourcing*, 2009).

Possibly the only form of outsourcing acceptable to most police officers is the use of volunteers or reserve police officers or deputies. Still, police unions are often reluctant to approve the use of volunteers or reserve police officers or deputies. A very clear distinction must be made between strictly police duties and those that can be performed by volunteers, and volunteer programs have been working well in many jurisdictions. Volunteers and their uses are covered extensively in Chapter 6.

Obtaining Competitive Bids

Whether a police agency is purchasing, leasing, or outsourcing goods or services, items or services above a certain dollar value often must be obtained through a competitive bidding system. Before requesting competitive bids from potential vendors, an agency establishes criteria that it will use to judge all vendor-submitted bids. It then uses these criteria to select the supplier that offers the best price and quality for the goods or services the agency needs. Agencies use competitive bidding for both the purchase and leasing of expensive property or services (Ortmeier & Meese, 2010; Overton & Bockelman, 1993), as well as the outsourcing of specific processes or activities to a third party. The competitive-bid process is especially effective for construction or renovation projects that require a significant outlay of public funds. Through a **competitive bid,** qualified vendors submit their best estimate of what a specific item, service, or combination of both will cost an agency. The lowest bidder generally wins the contract, unless it can be shown that a higher bid better meets the bid specifications (deliverables) established by the agency's request for bids.

Competitive bid: a vendor's best estimate of what a specific item, service, or combination of both will cost an organization seeking to purchase, lease, or outsource the item, service, or combination of both.

Before seeking competitive bids, however, an agency must define an appropriate range of bidding amounts. That is, managers need to review the potential costs of the items required in light of the quantity of items needed, quality, longevity, anticipated discounts based on quantity purchased, service-related issues, and the possibility that personnel will need training to use the items once they are procured. After considering these matters, the agency determines the bid ranges by analyzing the cost of one item either as a single unit (for example, one police vehicle) or a bulk quantity (10 vehicles). The bid range is set based on the total costs of an item, the quantity of items needed, inflation costs, and the timing of the procurement (yearly, quarterly, or monthly).

For instance, police vehicles are usually replaced every three years or when a vehicle reaches 80,000 to 100,000 miles. Based on the number of vehicles an agency deploys, the agency anticipates the number of items (police vehicles) it will need to purchase and establishes a bidding range after researching current police vehicle costs. Ideally, one of the agency's budget analysts or a comparable government employee takes responsibility for this task. The budget analyst usually has access to current government contracts that can be used to compare costs for similar equipment and services. As a rule, the agency does not reveal its preliminary bidding ranges to the vendors who will be submitting bids.

The agency puts out a request for bids by advertising for proposals (bids) based on materiel or services specifications, and by giving vendors a deadline by which to respond. Once the agency has received all bids, the procurement officer or team reviews them with an eye toward the apparent quality of services or equipment being offered, the terms of service or purchase, and the proposed costs. The person or team in charge of hiring the vendor reviews all bids, may phone the vendors to clear up any questions, and makes a final determination. In some cases, depending on the dollar amount involved, a supervisor, the mayor, or the city council may give final approval to the selected bid.

Like all government contracts, those signed with a police agency can be lucrative. Vendors and suppliers often hope to work for other government entities once they have established a relationship with a police jurisdiction. Therefore, agency leaders must exercise caution to ensure that the bids submitted by vendors are realistic and that the performance goals (deliverables) are not inflated. Budget, purchasing, and agency personnel must verify that inferior products, materials, and/or workers are not used on a job to cut a vendor's expenses.

Understanding Service Contracts and Warranties

When you buy a car or a major appliance such as a washing machine or refrigerator, you may elect to purchase a service contract along with the product. When a police agency is leasing or purchasing big-ticket items like a fleet of police cars or a new, agency-wide computer system, it will also likely be offered a service contract as part of the purchase.

Service contract: an agreement by which a seller agrees to provide repair or maintenance services for the specified purchased equipment for a certain time period.

A **service contract** is similar to the warranty you may have on your car: Through the contract, the seller agrees to provide repair or maintenance services for the specified equipment for a certain time period. Unlike a warranty, the fee for a service contract is not included in the purchase price of the equipment; the buyer purchases it separately. Police agency administrators should closely examine the terms of every service contact to determine what it covers—and what it does not cover. Repair or routine maintenance of an item not specified in the service contract will need to be performed by another party.

Most service contracts specify that the contract does not cover repairs resulting from the police agency's failure to maintain the product properly or the agency personnel's misuse of the product. Contracts may also include a clause that renders the agreement void if the agency does not contact the service contract company when a problem arises with the equipment in question.

Service contracts also have some similarities to insurance policies. Many come with a deductible, or an initial amount that the agency must pay before the

Service contracts may be established with outside vendors to repair vital equipment such as computers.

contract provider will cover repairs. A contract may specify where repairs can be made; for example, at a designated local service center. If an agency takes the equipment to another source for repair, the contract will not cover the cost of repair.

A major drawback to a service contract is that it is often issued through a service company that may not be affiliated with the manufacturer of the item being covered. Should the service company go out of business, a police agency will have little recourse in activating the service contract. Therefore, before entering into a service contract, agency managers should ensure that the service company is reputable and financially solvent. They can do so by contacting the local or state Better Business Bureau or a consumer protection office. They can also speak with several of the company's customers to gauge the firm's service quality and reliability before making a commitment.

Warranties can exist alongside service contracts. A **warranty** on a product is basically an insurance policy that comes with the product. It implies a promise by the manufacturer that it will repair any defects or replace the product if a major malfunction occurs. Like service contracts, warranties exclude certain things, such as repairs needed as a result of misuse or abuse. In some cases, certain parts of equipment may be excluded from the warranty. Thus agency personnel should know what those exclusions are before purchasing the item. Usually, organizations purchase service contracts immediately before the warranty on a piece of equipment is about to expire.

To summarize these important concepts, a service contract is similar to a warranty in that it provides for specified services. A warranty is usually included in the price of the product whereas a service contract costs extra. A warranty is a promise that the product will perform as specified if the buyer uses the product or service according to specific terms and conditions of operation (Ellis-Christensen, 2003; *Facts for Consumers: Service Contracts*, 2009).

Warranty: a promise by the manufacturer that it will repair any defects or replace the product if a major malfunction occurs.

Forging Agreements with Outsourcing Providers

Contracts with outsourcing service providers can be more complex than agreements made with organizations from which a police agency is purchasing or leasing equipment or other goods. If a police agency is considering using outsourcing to manage needed services, it should follow a comprehensive process to set up and manage the deal.

Setting the Stage   The following steps can help an agency establish an effective agreement with a services provider:

1. Plan strategically for outsourcing functions and services. For example, if an agency is considering outsourcing its canine (K9) service, managers should assess the costs of the current service as to officer wages and benefits, dog purchase and care, equipment needs, training, and calls for K9 service. They should also conduct research to determine whether there is an existing K9 service to which the agency may have access (for instance, at a sheriff's or state police agency).

2. Determine which providers can best manage the outsourced services and what specific tasks they must perform.

3. Identify the services to be outsourced—including physical location where the work will be performed, times it will be performed, anticipated performance on each task, and cost of the service.

4. Decide what roles the agency and the outsourcing company will fulfill.

5. Anticipate and mitigate any workforce morale problems that may arise from the decision to outsource a particular process or activity. For instance,

Almost anything can be outsourced, including K9 services.

discuss with agency management and personnel why outsourcing is being considered. Brainstorm possible negative effects of the outsourcing with respect to service delivery, personnel, or agency image, then seek consensus on solutions for mitigating those effects. By including agency personnel in these discussions and problem-solving sessions, you stand a better chance of winning their buy-in for the outsourcing decision, even if some individuals do not agree with the decision. If one or more people actively resist the outsourcing decision, the supervisor, manager, or facilitator may need to speak privately with them to alleviate their concerns; for example, by assuring them they will not lose their jobs and that their contributions are still valued (*Outsourcing—What Is Outsourcing?*, 2003).

Covering All the Bases   An outsourcing contract is best developed with the assistance of legal counsel. The police agency's counsel will draft the contract and recommend approval of the contract to the respective governing body (such as the mayor, city manager, city council, or county supervisors). The outsourcing contract should include the following information:

- *Work to be completed:* The contract spells out the amount and quality of the work to be completed, including training and performance standards. It may include a clause stipulating that if the agency wants the outsourcing provider to take on additional work not currently defined in the contract, both parties must agree on the new work (which is usually indicated in an addendum to the original contract).

- *Fees to be charged:* The contract defines the wage rates for contractor employees, contingency fees (such as wage adjustments based on labor-market fluctuations and inflation reviews), costs of any required materials, and any additional expenses the police agency must bear. It may also include a payment schedule (including the payment periods, invoicing schedule, and when the first payment is due) and a notice of the contractee's (agency's) right to have an independent party audit the contractor's operations and records.

- *Wage rates:* If a premium wage rate (a rate above the prevailing wage) is specified, the agency should audit the contractor to ensure that the premium rate is paid.

- *Adjustment to compensation clause:* The agency (client) is allowed to reduce fees charged (compensation) if the contractor fails to meet obligations expressed in the contract.

- *Liability of parties:* The contract lays out the limits of liability for the outsourcing provider and the agency regarding provider negligence, gross misconduct, or intentional damage to the agency's property or to its image within the community. An indemnity (hold-harmless) clause should be included, holding the agency harmless for any wrongful act of a contractor's employees.

- *Screening of provider employees:* Owing to the sensitive nature of police agency information, processes, and the ability to access secure areas, the contract should specify that the agency has a right to perform thorough background checks on the outsourcing provider's personnel and to reject personnel whose background checks unearth information of concern to the agency.

- *Provider insurance coverage:* The contract stipulates that the provider agrees to secure and produce proof of adequate insurance coverage for its employees and the work to be completed. Some contractors are underinsured and/or underfinanced, and they may not have the necessary financial resources to withstand a lawsuit.

- *Proprietary or confidential information:* Both parties agree that all information gathered regarding each other's business actions or task completion shall remain confidential unless both parties agree otherwise.

- *Information and significant work output:* The contract describes the significant work products and information the outsourcing provider will produce and when it will be produced (for example, monthly, quarterly, or yearly). It delineates the final work product (deliverables) desired and specifies who will own any materials generated over the course of the contract after the relationship is terminated.

- *Letter(s) of authorization:* Since an outside contractor is authorized to act on behalf of the client (agency), letters of authorization should express the contractor's limits of authority.

- *Audit rights:* The agency should reserve the right to audit the contractor's operations to prevent unscrupulous activities and ensure adherence to performance standards.

- *Length of contract:* The contract specifies the duration of the outsourcing arrangement, including start-up and ending dates, termination, and defaulting rights for each party (Ortmeier, 1999; Ortmeier & Meese, 2010; *Sample Business Contracts, Outsourcing Service Agreement,* 2010).

FACILITIES MANAGEMENT

Facilities constitute a major category of assets a police agency needs to function. Thus, facilities merit a focused examination in this chapter. Police facilities generally include the following:

- *Precinct (substation, district) buildings* that provide office space and lockers for police officers, interview and interrogation rooms, temporary secure detention areas, administrative office space, meeting and conference rooms, and volunteer accommodations

- *Private office areas* for specialized activities such as training; professional responsibility/standards (internal affairs) investigations; and special crime units, including gang intelligence and drug enforcement

- *Properties or buildings* where marked and unmarked cars are kept

- *A county or city facility* where pretrial and adjudicated persons are accommodated (in large cities, the county or city jail may be under the direction of the jurisdiction's or state's department of corrections)

Understanding the Facilities Manager Role

In most police jurisdictions, the acquisition, management, and upkeep of police facilities is the responsibility of one or more persons dedicated exclusively to this work. These persons may work in a separate unit or department of the police agency. Alternatively, they may report to and take some direction from a facilities

A county or city jail typically houses pretrial detainees and those serving short-term sentences of less than one year.

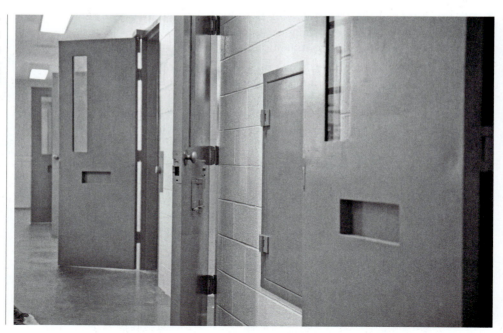

Police office areas should be clean, neat, and well equipped.

management division that is part of the broader government entity overseeing the agency. Small agencies may delegate responsibility for facilities to one person who is employed by the agency while using service providers to carry out actual work such as cleaning or repair of buildings used by the agency.

Monitoring the Condition of Agency Sites   A basic role of a **facilities manager** is to ensure that all police property is maintained according to state and city building codes and safety standards, including those put forth by the Occupational Safety and Health Administration (OSHA). To fulfill this role, the manager must constantly monitor the condition of all police property. Often, workers at each location will report ongoing conditions or problems with the facility, such as nonfunctioning drains or toilets, broken locks on detention cells, or water leaks.

While such reports are helpful, the facilities manager should still regularly visit the agency's properties to review their condition. In some agencies, the manager or a staff member will then prepare a report describing the condition of each property, including overall site condition, a detailed assessment of the building's condition, estimated costs for repair or maintenance of a property, available upgrades for equipment such as computers or office furniture, an inventory of all current equipment housed at the site, and photographs of the site's exterior and interior (City of Tacoma, 2009).

Maintaining Agency Sites   Reviewing and documenting site conditions is just one aspect of a police facilities manager's role. The manager must also ensure that all police properties are carefully maintained so they can be used around the clock.

Facilities manager: an individual whose basic role is to ensure that all police property is maintained according to state and city building codes and safety standards, including those put forth by the Occupational Safety and Health Administration (OSHA).

Leadership on the job

Reorganization of a Police Agency

To enhance police–community relations and promote community policing and problem-solving concepts and practices, a police agency decentralized its facilities—setting up seven community-based offices across the jurisdiction served. But as the agency's facilities-related costs rose, managers decided to consolidate the offices into two large district offices. The agency relocated its four west-side district locations to a single leased office building that also housed private corporations. It moved its three east-side district offices to a government-owned location that needed renovation to accommodate the police personnel who came with the move. Adequate private and police-vehicle parking, administrative office space, locker rooms, and communication enhancements were provided for each of the two new locations. The command personnel at each centralized new location made arrangements for telephone services, computer setup and appropriate linkages, and customer service areas within the facility.

After completing consolidation into the two new sites, the agency made numerous personnel changes within the management ranks and investigative duties to establish a greater sense of leadership accountability and responsibility. For example, before the reorganization, the investigators had been responsible to the precinct captain, with police sergeants and lieutenants acting as liaisons or facilitators of investigators or investigative actions. Accountability for police investigator performance was not consistent among the seven police captains. After the reorganization, a Field Investigations Section (FIS) was established and commanded by a police captain. The new FIS command structure included 2 investigative lieutenants, 6 investigative sergeants, 35 investigators, 6 field crime coordinators, and a centralized crime coordination unit. The FIS became responsible for the investigation of most of the agency's major investigations,

crime coordination, investigation assignments, and performance reviews of all investigators assigned to the section. The accountability for field investigations became the responsibility of 1 police captain rather than 7. The new FIS proved a valuable model of investigative responsibility, accountability, and crime information analysis and dissemination throughout the agency.

Still, reactions to the reorganization were mixed. Community members expressed a feeling of being disconnected from their police agency after the change, perhaps because there were far fewer police offices than before, and the two new offices were located farther away from their neighborhoods. However, the agency's managers found that the change led to an improvement in response time to calls-for-service, owing to better coordination of on-duty officers, and that the centralization of police facilities saved the community money.

1. What steps should an agency take to prepare its workers and citizens/customers for a major reorganization of agency services so the needs of the agency and the community are reasonably met?

2. If you were a police facilities manager, how would you prepare for leasing a facility to accommodate additional personnel and equipment from adjoining police facilities? How would you prepare to renovate an existing facility to accommodate additional police personnel and equipment from adjoining facilities?

3. What advantages and disadvantages of the reorganization of police facilities were cited in the story? What (if any) additional advantages and disadvantages can you think of that might come with such a reorganization?

After all, a police agency operates 24 hours a day, 7 days a week. Something as seemingly minor as a flooded restroom or a broken lock on a firing-range door can spawn extreme inconvenience (at best) or put officers' safety at risk (at worst).

If a particular maintenance or repair project is beyond the expertise of the facilities management team, the supervisor may decide to outsource the project, including requesting bids from service providers or using previously approved providers. Obviously, there is no need to ask for bids to repair one broken lock or leaky faucet. However, the facilities manager should take responsibility for interacting with and overseeing the work of any project that is outsourced, including communicating with the site supervisor to monitor progress and address any problems that arise.

Excelling at Facilities Management To be a facilities manager with a police agency, one does not need to become a sworn police officer, although an officer with appropriate experience may be assigned to this position. More important, the individual who assumes these responsibilities must be familiar with building safety, construction, and the maintenance of police facilities. A facilities manager should possess supervisory and management competencies including the skills and abilities necessary to schedule maintenance, understand outside contractor agreements, read blueprints, and be knowledgeable about the working systems that make up a public facility. Last, the facilities manager must be capable of supervising, evaluating, and training employees who will perform maintenance tasks, repairs, and other such work.

Some agencies may require their facilities managers to possess specific academic credentials. These may include a bachelor's degree in public administration or a related academic field, along with applicable experience, or an associate degree in business administration with experience in building maintenance and construction. Many agencies prefer applicants with experience in the construction and building trades, especially as a construction supervisor or with crew experience (City of Scottsdale, 2007; City of West Palm Beach, 2001).

Effective facilities managers also need strong interpersonal skills, as they continually interact with a wide array of individuals—including administrative personnel, police officers, police supervisors, outside contractors, employees, and other agency staff members. A savvy facilities manager will be aware of the political dynamics behind proposals and projects and, without pandering to those who have a pet project under way, ensure that the project is completed properly and in a timely fashion.

Building or Renovating a Police Facility

Sometimes a police agency must design and construct a new facility or renovate an existing one. When this situation arises, following a disciplined process and conducting a site survey can help agency leaders end up with a facility that meets all constituents' needs.

Planning a New or Renovated Facility An agency may decide to construct a new facility or renovate an existing one when the need arises and financial resources permit. To ensure that the resulting structure suits the agency's needs, managers should apply the following process:

1. Conduct a site survey (discussed in more detail later in this chapter).
   The survey includes interviewing agency personnel, building experts, and
   appropriate community members for input concerning the facility. For

example, obtain interviewees' thoughts about how the facility would fulfill a clearly identifiable need. (Is an existing facility dysfunctional, or do long-term maintenance or repair costs for the facility far exceed the cost of new construction?) Simultaneously, conduct a space needs analysis and determine what facility options are available, including renovation of an existing facility or the building of a new one.

2. If the agency is building a new facility, contract for the services of an architect or other building professional to create blueprints to specifications. If the agency is renovating an existing facility, document all problems with the current facility, drawing on feedback from agency personnel and building experts.

3. Assemble a team comprising police personnel and construction professionals to prepare preliminary plans and to estimate costs. Contact appropriate individuals in the government and the jurisdiction, and ask for their input, to begin winning political support and, ultimately, financial support for the project.

4. Obtain the funding for the new or renovation project and identify a site for construction (if a new facility).

5. Working with the professionals hired to complete the project, construct or renovate the facility. As the work progresses, envision where occasional and full-time occupants will reside. For an existing facility that is being renovated, determine where people will work (an alternative site) while their usual area is being renovated. For a new facility, the occupancy will probably be planned in stages for patrol officers, secretarial and administrative staff, and volunteers (International Association of Chiefs of Police, 2008).

Gaining the Proper Approvals   When an agency wants to make a major change to its facilities, the change must generally meet the approval of police administrators, town or government administrators, and the city or town council or other governing body/person of the jurisdiction. Agency managers should strive to arrange funding for the project during the planning stage. If and when they solicit bids from local contractors, they should emphasize strict adherence to the approved facility plans and budget. Proposed plans must be submitted and approved with agreed-upon necessary changes or modifications documented. Once the plans and the contractor

A police building under construction in Fairfax, Virginia.

have been approved by all responsible parties, work may begin. After renovation or construction begins, modifications to plans can be very costly.

Conducting Site Surveys

A **site survey** is another key element of facilities maintenance. Through site surveys, personnel assess existing facilities to determine whether they need any equipment or materials upgrades, such as improved computer systems or a new roof or exterior siding. A site survey can also shed light on whether the facility meets building code requirements. An agency may also use site surveys to review progress on facilities construction or renovation projects.

To be useful, any site survey must begin with clearly stated goals (for example, "We want a centrally located police building that will serve as precinct housing for 50 police officers, open 24 hours a day, 7 days a week"). Agency personnel must gather data (such as the number of lockers needed for male and female officers, meeting room space, and so forth), through site inspection and interviews with appropriate personnel. They must then assess the data collected (for instance, "Will the new building provide easy access and accommodation for police officers and community residents?"). Finally, they must prepare a final inclusive report completed with any recommended actions, and deliver the report to the chief of police or delegated representative of the government entity (*Survey Design*, 2009). The site survey should also include graphic illustrations of the facility in question.

The facilities manager must conduct a walk-through assessment of the site and determine who will be affected by the proposed project and how the new upgrades, renovation, or construction will affect agency personnel's workflow. The manager documents all findings for inspection, review, possible alteration, and finalization and delivers the findings report to the project coordinator and the person responsible for constructing or upgrading the facility (Geier, 2002). Generally, the facilities

Site survey: assessment of existing facilities to determine whether they need any equipment or materials upgrades, such as improved computer systems or a new roof or siding.

Police officers should be provided with a personal space for storage of gear, personal clothing, and uniforms.

manager is responsible for overseeing progress on building construction, renovation, or minor upgrades. The mayor, town supervisor, or city council members may also want to evaluate the site periodically.

The facilities manager should also take responsibility for interacting with building inspectors, guiding them on tours of facility construction and renovation, and responding to inspectors' questions and concerns. The manager may be required to verbally report to a superior with the building inspector's findings and document the findings with a determination of how to address any issues or inadequacies identified. Both the facilities manager's superior and the building inspector must be satisfied that the project is progressing in a timely fashion and will adhere to all applicable laws and codes. The city or town council may also want periodic updates on any renovations or new construction for which they voted and set aside funds.

While renovation, construction, or upgrading is under way, the facilities manager should survey the site regularly to ensure that the effort is progressing satisfactorily and that the workers and crew leaders know that their efforts and activities are being monitored. When performing such surveys, the manager must be knowledgeable about the work that is being performed and know whether the work is progressing according to approved plans and processes. As just one example, the manager should know that drywall board in a new building cannot be installed until the building inspector has approved electrical wiring and other utility structure installations.

Likewise, the facilities manager should have a thorough knowledge of materials and labor costs in the building industry, to ensure that the jurisdiction is not being overcharged or billed for add-on adjustments for these items. A working knowledge paired with practical expertise gained through some form of construction experience is an invaluable asset to the supervisor when conducting site reviews and interacting with construction personnel.

Regular inspections of buildings should take place.

Updating Technology in a Police Facility

Most managers today understand that their organization's facilities must have up-to-date, reliable technology to serve their customers and achieve their mission. In a perfect world, organizations buy and install new technology as soon as this need is identified, and promptly train employees to use the new systems. However, in a

---

ETHICS IN ACTION

Lead Poisoning versus Firearms Training

The department of health for a county conducted an audit of a police agency's indoor firing range facility and discovered that the level of lead particulate at the range exceeded maximum standards. Medical tests for the range's instructors revealed that lead levels in their blood were above acceptable limits. However, under pressure to certify and recertify recruit and in-service police officers, the range continued to operate with the same instructors.

The department of health also tested the range's air quality, and the results strongly suggested that the facility's ventilation system needed repair. Still, training continued at the range, in part because the agency lacked an alternative training site and funding to build another indoor range or to make the needed heating, ventilation, and air conditioning (HVAC) upgrades.

The officer responsible for the required police training and maintenance of the range asked the department of health to conduct another, more detailed inspection to assess air quality. The indoor range failed the test, indicating that the level of lead particulate in the air being breathed by affected personnel exceeded safety standards for trainers on the range as well as police officer trainees. The officer then tried to persuade managers at the police agency and the building/engineering department of the government entity to shut down the range and to authorize the needed repairs for the existing range or build a new range that met the required air quality safety standards. When his requests fell on deaf ears, the officer asked the department of health to shut down the range and issue appropriate health violation summons. The officer received a summons from the department of health citing the code violations, the range was formally closed and locked down, and firearms' training was suspended.

Eventually, a new indoor range was constructed, and the old range was closed and dismantled. Officers and trainers were no longer exposed to lead poisoning and poor air quality.

1. What other courses of action could the facilities manager in this story have taken to foster remediation of the range facility's problems?

2. Was it ethical for the manager to involve the department of health as a way to stimulate a renovation of the range facility? Why or why not?

3. Does the happy ending in this story justify the means the manager used to produce that end, given the apparent inaction of the government entity toward the range employees' health? Explain your reasoning.

police agency struggling with rising labor costs and budgetary constraints, finding ways to make technological upgrades or replacements may require some creative thinking.

Police administrators might cite needed funds for technology in a proposed budget, but those funds may not win approval by decision makers for the final budget. Depending on the challenges facing the agency, funds earmarked for technology updates may be diverted to another need that the agency's constituents deem more urgent. The hoped-for funding could be eliminated altogether to accommodate budget constraints or political agendas. To achieve their technology goals, agencies may need to seek other sources of funding. Grants can sometimes provide a solution to this challenge. (See the box "Acquiring New Technology: A Three-Phase Process.")

Acquiring New Technology: A Three-Phase Process

A police agency does not need to embark on a lengthy process when acquiring new software that will be installed on just a few computers. However, it should use a disciplined process to acquire any technology that will call for extensive training and that will be used by a large number of people across the entire agency. This process comprises three phases:

Phase 1: Lay a Solid Foundation

- Assemble a team to lead the effort, conduct or review the needs analysis, and develop a budget for the project.
- Develop a strategic plan indicating the project goals and objectives, a mission statement, and a project timeline with significant objectives highlighted. Analyze the viability of the technology being considered, with an eye toward costs, usability, and compatibility with the agency's current technology and that of partner agencies.
- Choose an articulate project leader to spearhead the effort. Inform staff as to the nature of the project. Continually solicit stakeholder support.

Phase 2: Select a Vendor

- Identify standards for the technology the agency is interested in, and define installation and service needs, on-site assistance, and staff training required.
- List potential vendors and the metrics on which vendors' quality and performance will be evaluated. Develop a Request for Proposal (RFP) to be published or sent to the listed vendors. When all proposals are received, review them and choose an acceptable vendor. If an acceptable vendor is not found, revisit the vendor list and project criteria, and readvertise the RFP.
- With the selected vendor, prepare a contract including project goals, objectives and tasks, project timetable, liability clauses, anticipated project contingencies, enhancements and unanticipated costs, anticipated vendor staff dedicated to the project, and audit rights. Clearly describe agency staff members' and vendor representatives' responsibilities (as discussed earlier in this chapter).

- Develop a process for acquiring hardware, software, and related equipment. Inform the vendor as to government payment processes, necessary documentation, and timelines.

Phase 3: Prepare for Installation and Training

- Design and implement an evaluation protocol for installed technology. Devise a timetable for training employees who will be using the new technology.

- Consider phasing in the technology so operations can proceed normally while segments of personnel receive training.

- Prepare the warranty and maintenance agreement with agency-government entity legal counsel and the vendor. Arrange for acceptance and installation of equipment. Once installation is confirmed, initiate staff training.

Sources: Bryson & Alston, 2005; Kotter, 1996; Stolting, Barrett, & Kurz, 2008.

Identifying Potential Grant Providers   Grants can constitute alternative sources of funding for technology upgrades that are necessary but that cannot be included in an ever-shrinking budget that depends heavily on tax revenues. (See Chapter 5 for more detailed information on grants.) Agency managers should familiarize themselves with how different grant providers operate and in what types of resources they specialize. For instance, new body armor for officers might be funded by a different grant provider than computers in patrol cars and software for tracking drug investigations. Private foundations and corporations may constitute additional sources of funding for needed technology (Labbe, 2008).

Writing Grant Applications   A police agency's facilities manager may not be required to write the actual grant application; in many agencies, people in the budget division perform this specialized task. Alternatively, an agency may contract a freelance grant writer for the project. However, the agency or contracted grant writers may not have time to research grants specific to facilities' technology needs. In such cases, the facilities manager should provide the grant writer with all pertinent information concerning the grant. If grant writers are not available to write a specific application, managers may consider asking volunteers experienced in attaining grants to handle the writing.

Sharing Grant Money   Agencies seeking grant money for technology upgrades may also partner with community and other affected groups to share funding. Grant funding entities typically encourage and look favorably upon such partnerships. Consider a community group dedicated to controlling or eradicating gang activity in its neighborhood. This group might be willing to partner with the local police department to obtain a grant for the purchase of hardware and software that monitor gang activity. The acquisition may generate valuable information such as profiles of major players and the locations of their operations, and investigations may lead to arrests and successful prosecutions. The police department and community group can work together to use the insights gained from the technology to develop effective solutions to gang problems plaguing the neighborhood.

To learn more about which grant providers fund which types of needs, visit the website for the Bureau of Justice Assistance (www.ojp.usdoj.gov/bja; www.usdoj.gov) or www.grants.gov.

Demonstrating Community Involvement   A police agency may provide a more compelling argument for the grantor to approve funding if the application demonstrates community involvement on the part of the agency. For example, in the grant application, agency managers could point out that the computer equipment and software that they wish to acquire will help the agency collaborate with citizens to identify and solve problems plaguing the community. This approach has another benefit as well: the accurate public perception that police personnel are genuinely interested in solving problems in the community the agency serves.

Emphasizing Dedication to Homeland Security   Currently, U.S. government grants are rich sources of funding for technology especially, because many members of Congress are acutely aware of the lack of current technology in their constituent jurisdictions. If a police agency can show that a technological improvement will help it better carry out its homeland security duties, it may stand a better chance of winning the grant.

summary

- **Procurement.** Procurement is the obtaining of equipment, supplies, and services needed by a police agency. Procurement can be done through three means: purchasing, leasing, or outsourcing.
- **Purchasing.** Purchasing is the procurement of goods or services from a supplier. The police agency that makes the purchase owns the good or service once the purchase is complete. Police agencies need a disciplined process for making purchases and a purchasing agent, director, or manager to coordinate the process. Purchasing presents some ethical challenges for agents tempted to steal.
- **Leasing.** Leasing is the procurement of equipment or property in exchange for payments made at agreed-upon intervals. The police agency does not own the items, though it may have the option to eventually purchase and thus own the items through lease-purchase agreement.
- **Outsourcing.** Outsourcing is a process by which a police agency contracts with another organization to provide products or services formerly provided by the agency's employees. Outsourcing can help an agency save money, but it also is a politically sensitive decision. Many agencies outsource ancillary or supplementary functions, such as police-vehicle maintenance. In some jurisdictions, entire police departments have been outsourced, a development that has stirred controversy.
- **Obtaining Competitive Bids.** Whether purchasing, leasing, or outsourcing, a police agency must obtain competitive bids from suppliers of the items or services it wants to procure, including deciding on bidding ranges.
- **Understanding Service Contracts and Warranties.** Equipment procured by a police agency often comes with a service contract, an agreement by which the seller provides repair or maintenance services for the equipment for a certain time period. A warranty—a promise by the manufacturer to repair any defects or replace the product if a major malfunction occurs—may exist alongside a service contract for equipment.
- **Forging Agreements with Outsourcing Providers.** To forge an agreement with an outsourcing provider, a police agency must set the stage (for example, by

planning strategically for outsourcing, identifying providers who could best manage the outsourced services, identifying specific services to be outsourced, deciding what roles the agency and provider will fulfill, and anticipating and mitigating workforce morale problems that may arise with outsourcing). The agency must also ensure that the outsourcing contract contains all relevant information, including work to be completed, fees to be charged, wage rates, adjustments to compensation, liability of parties, and so forth.

- **Facilities Management.** A police agency's facilities may consist of precinct (substation, district) buildings, private office areas, properties or buildings housing vehicles, and a county or city facility where pretrial and adjudicated persons are accommodated.

- **Understanding the Facilities Manager Role.** A police agency's facilities manager ensures that all police property is maintained according to state and city building codes and safety standards. This manager monitors the condition of agency sites and takes responsibility for maintenance of the sites. The manager should possess specific knowledge and skills, such as familiarity with building safety and construction; the ability to supervise, evaluate, and train employees who perform repairs, construction, and other such work; and strong interpersonal skills.

- **Building or Renovating a Police Facility.** Whether constructing or renovating a police facility, an agency must use a disciplined planning process that includes conducting site surveys, estimating costs, obtaining funding, and gaining the proper approvals.

- **Conducting Site Surveys.** Through site surveys, a police agency assesses its existing facilities to determine whether they need upgrading. To conduct an effective site survey, agency personnel must clearly state the goals of the facility in question, gather and assess data on the facility, and prepare a report containing recommendations.

- **Updating Technology in a Police Facility.** To procure technology that will require extensive training and that will be used by many people across an agency, managers must use a three-phase process that includes conducting or reviewing a needs analysis and clarifying the project's goals, selecting a vendor, and preparing for installation and training. Police agencies often face difficulty obtaining funds for technology upgrades. They can sometimes obtain funding through grant providers.

competitive bid

facilities manager

lease

outsourcing

purchasing

service contract

site survey

warranty

key terms

1. A police agency must purchase numerous pieces of equipment and technology on a constant basis. Describe the purchasing process and how it applies to a government entity.

2. The leasing of equipment or facilities has become a popular trend owing to budget constraints. Describe the leasing process and assess when a police agency should use leasing as opposed to purchasing to procure equipment, services, and facilities.

3. When might a police agency decide to outsource a process or function? What are the benefits of outsourcing? What challenges does it present?

4. Owing to financial constraints in the public sector, many cities and towns are outsourcing their entire policing function to other agencies or private companies. What are the positive and negative aspects of outsourcing a police agency? Can all public policing activities be outsourced to private companies? Explain.

5. Most government agencies must use a competitive bidding process to procure equipment, facilities, supplies, or services. What does this process accomplish?

6. Compare and contrast warranties and service contracts. Can they exist together?

7. Must a facilities manager be a sworn police officer? Why or why not? What are the duties and responsibilities of a facilities manager?

8. Site surveys are important for renovation and construction of current or new buildings. Why are site surveys necessary, and how are they conducted?

9. In what respects might a police agency have difficulty obtaining the funding needed for technology upgrades? Where might the agency obtain funding if expected budgeted funds are no longer available?

10. What steps should a police agency take to procure, install, and use new technology?

WHAT WOULD YOU DO?

The Best Laid Plans . . .

The difficulty that faces police agency managers who wish to upgrade or improve their computer capabilities is probably best illustrated by the failure of the Supervision Management and Recidivist Tracking (SMART) system in Seattle over the six years from its inception to its demise.

SMART had its origins in a collaboration between Redmond, Washington, police and local corrections officers, who together created a paper-based system to better track ex-convicts. Prison officials notified the Redmond police when a convict was being released, and the police visited these convicts to let them know they were being watched. If the police suspected a parole violation, the officer prepared a note card with information about the encounter and sent it to the individual's parole officer. The program was soon replicated in other local jurisdictions.

In 1995, this paper-based program attracted the attention of supervisors of the Homicide Investigation Tracking System (HITS). The HITS program was designed by a former detective who investigated several serial murder cases in Washington State. The system—which uses databases and investigative personnel to analyze crime data and patterns—was designed to track information about murders, rapes, and other major crimes. HITS program managers presented the idea of combining the Redmond and HITS programs to representatives of the Washington State Legislature to secure state funding to computerize the Redmond and HITS programs to create SMART.

The state legislature budgeted $850,000 to start the program and subsequently another $869,000 to maintain it, directing the funds through the state's attorney general's office. Over the six years from approval of funding to abandonment of the project, the position of project director changed several times due to retirement, resignations, and loss of software designers to corporations that offered higher salaries. Members of the SMART project have maintained that members of the attorney general's office associated with the project were removed from the project through elimination of their jobs or requests for them to resign. The removals were stimulated by their inquiring about the funding and suggesting that the funds were spent in other areas of government. Advocates of the program who are disheartened by these developments allege mishandling of funds by the attorney general's office and demand an accounting. The attorney general's office expressed concern that developers had difficulties with the complexities of the SMART project and that there was a general ambivalence and lack of cooperation within a broad spectrum of law enforcement.

According to the attorney general's office, the funding shortfall that hampered SMART's development stemmed from salary and rent increases and the loss of general fund financing. At the same time, spokespersons for the office claimed that it would not be possible to track where all of the SMART funding dollars went. The attorney general's office has claimed that SMART is ready to go into operation, and that it would be running if the state had not suffered a budgetary shortfall in the previous year.

Even if SMART is ready to go, it cannot do so until funding is restored. In the meantime, Washington police are developing a similar program with the State Corrections Department. Yet as some sources stated, it will never be as effective as SMART would have been (Kamb & Galloway, 2004; Morgan, 2002).

1. Do you believe that the HITS and SMART programs (or either program on its own) are worthy of funding? Explain your reasoning.

2. Drawing on what you have learned about police agencies and politics, and about the difficulties police agencies face in upgrading technology, describe what you would have recommended regarding the appropriation and management of the SMART program funding. In your view, could any of the funding concerns have been prevented? If so, which ones? How?

3. Budget shortfalls and rechanneling of funding for current and proposed projects are realities of government. How would you attempt to regain or secure new funding for SMART? What leadership strategies would you recommend?

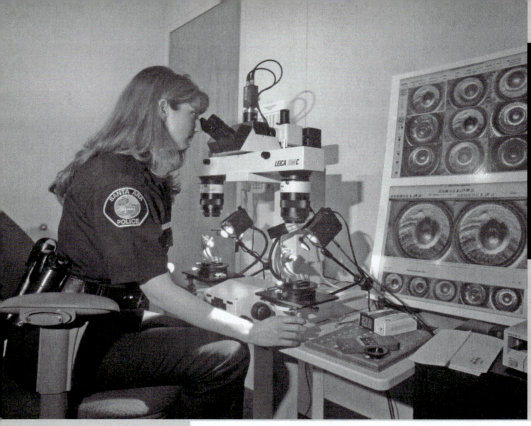

◀ A comparison microscope in use in Santa Ana, California. The microscope is being used to compare ballistic evidence.

The Future of Police Administration

After completing this chapter, readers should be able to:

- explain why ethical leadership and professionalism in policing will become more crucial than ever in the future.

- analyze how counterterrorism and homeland security efforts are evolving and how police can support these efforts in the coming years.

- appraise the budgeting challenges police agencies may expect to encounter and evaluate strategies for surmounting those challenges.

- discuss emerging trends in how police agencies are assessing and evaluating their own performance as well as that of individual officers.

- evaluate the strategies that police agencies will need to adopt to build an effective workforce and to develop employees' knowledge, skills, and abilities.

- explain how constructive engagement and constructive confrontation will enable police to communicate effectively with a broad range of constituents.
- describe three ways in which police leaders can broaden their thinking and practice to surmount the new challenges facing their organizations.
- discuss how police leaders can better drive needed change in their organizations.
- compare three change-leadership models.
- construct an argument for how police unions can best combat negative public perceptions and become more effective in the future.
- illustrate new ways in which police jurisdictions are managing their facilities to reduce costs and improve customer service, and compare the advantages and disadvantages of each approach.
- discuss the benefits and challenges of new technologies developed to fight street crime, identify important forms of cybercrime, and examine the trade-offs between protection and privacy presented by cybercrime.

Introduction

No one can predict what the future will hold for individuals, organizations, nation-states, or the world. Why then do we insist on trying? Every day, we strive to make predictions about the weather, the stock market, the economy, the outcome of sporting events—the list goes on.

Many predictions do not come to pass, but some do. One of the most notable accurate futurists was the French apothecary Nostradamus (1503–1566), who made a series of predictions that, his supporters claim, foretold the reigns of Napoleon and Hitler, and even the September 11, 2001, terrorist attacks. Another futurist, the French philosopher, mathematician, and political scientist Marquis de Condorcet (1743–1794), foretold that in the New World there would someday be social insurance and equality between men and women. British scholar and clergyman Thomas Malthus (1766–1834) predicted (seemingly accurately) that the global population would increase to the point where the food supply would fail. And the Russian-American sociologist Pitirim Sorokin (1889–1968) insisted that the world would grow more secular and immoral in its orientation (California Commission on Peace Officer Standards and Training, 1976).

These seers all foretold large-scale, sweeping developments in human history. But what about the future of police administration? To be sure, police administration is a much more sharply focused subject than, say, global population changes or the reigns of dictators. Nevertheless, we believe that it merits a little fortune-telling; that is, some thought and discussion about what police administration may look like in the future. The shapes that police administration take in the coming years, decades, and even centuries will play a pivotal role in how police interact with the communities they serve and how police perform their jobs. And these things, in turn, can powerfully mold entire societies.

For that reason, we devote this chapter to speculation about the future of police administration. Of course, we will not be gazing into a crystal ball to "see" this future. Rather, we will rely on a legitimate area of study that uses past and present performance, expert opinion, and statistics to describe changes that may occur in the near future and those that are harder to describe, many years ahead. This study is called futures research, or **futuristics**.

Futuristics: an area of study that uses past and present performance, expert opinion, and statistics to describe changes that may occur in the near and distant future.

In seeking to envision the future of police administration, we focus our efforts on several key themes we have traced throughout this book. This chapter thus serves as both a review of the book's chapters as well as a bridge between what you learned in those chapters and how you might use that knowledge to build a successful and safe career in policing. With these goals in mind, we first examine emerging developments in the areas of police ethics, leadership, professionalism, and principles of policing—overarching themes that inform every chapter in this book. In particular, we look at how public trust in police is at risk and how police must respond.

We then shine a spotlight on two of the challenges you read about in Chapter 3: counterterrorism and homeland security. We delve into how terrorists become radicalized and organize themselves, and how new developments in these areas are redefining the role of police and presenting fresh challenges.

Next we examine the question of how tomorrow's police administrators will manage the budgeting process (covered in Chapter 5) to fulfill the mandate to do even more—with even less. We look at trends in outsourcing, consider their implications for police, and explore strategies for creatively addressing budgeting constraints.

The chapter then turns to emerging developments in organizational and individual performance assessment and evaluation (discussed in chapters 7 and 12). In particular, *we reinforce the notion that police managers must help every officer, regardless of rank, become an ethical leader,* and we offer additional recommendations for doing so.

Tomorrow's police administrator will not be able to foster stellar performance at the organizational and individual level without the right hiring and training practices (examined in Chapters 8 and 10). Accordingly, these form the focus of the next section in the chapter.

Further tracking the sequence of themes covered in this book, we then address the question of how police in the coming years can master techniques known as constructive engagement and constructive confrontation to communicate effectively with a widening array of constituents. (You read about communication in Chapter 9.)

The chapter next moves to the subject of police leadership, which was covered extensively in Chapter 11. We propose several ways in which police leaders of the future will need to expand their boundaries in terms of how they work and how they think. And because driving needed change is a vital aspect of leadership, we devote a section to this subject as well. We wish to reinforce the need for all police officers to be self-contained leadership agents. Further, true leadership does not exist without courageous ethical behavior to accompany it.

The final three sections of the chapter focus on what police agencies in the future might expect to encounter in the areas of unionization (discussed in Chapter 13), facilities management (covered in Chapter 14), and technology and crime fighting (also introduced in Chapter 14).

ETHICS AND PROFESSIONALISM: WILL POLICE BE TRUSTED?

We have treated ethics and professionalism as major themes throughout this book for good reason: One glance at today's news headlines, and it seems that unethical behavior is on the rise in every aspect of our lives—business, education, politics, even religion. One cannot scan a newspaper, listen to the radio, or view television without being exposed to yet another scandal or fresh example of malfeasance by people who should know better. Experts attribute the increase in unethical behavior to everything from human beings' genetic wiring to misguided parenting to a lack of spiritual anchoring. Ethical failures such as greed, intolerance of diversity, and inappropriate use of authority or personal power are continually highlighted by the media, who appear to delight in exposing scandals "for the greater good" (Ritchie, 2007).

Unethical behavior on the part of police, along with lurid headlines about police misconduct in the press, has already eroded trust in the police. To prevent further erosion, police executives must send a crystal-clear message about the importance of adhering to ethical standards, as well as take action against unethical behavior promptly.

The Question of Trust

Unethical behavior erodes our trust in the major institutions that define our lives and breeds cynicism and bitterness within us. When it comes to policing, this vicious cycle can have uniquely destructive consequences. Think about it: If citizens believe that even one police officer in their jurisdiction lacks integrity, they may come to distrust the entire agency. At best, they will become less willing to support police services with their tax dollars; at worst, mistrust of police can spawn civil unrest and even vigilantism.

And yet, some police agencies are considering taking steps that risk giving the impression of moral bankruptcy. For instance, to cast its recruitment net wider, an agency might relax its hiring standards—accepting job applications from individuals who were previously rejected because of a history of questionable behaviors. (Note, however, that some agencies may accept applicants with previous drug use, if the use was minor and if it happened when the candidate was a juvenile.) To secure enough candidates, agencies should not discount an applicant's history but instead should view it through a lens that considers the totality of the circumstances. Can the applicant be trusted or will the candidate dishonor the office?

Can people who break the law or who have engaged in questionable behavior become effective, ethical police officers? Can ethical behavior and leadership skills be learned? These questions have stirred intense debate. As police agencies gain experience in hiring such individuals, only time will reveal how questionable pre-service behavior affects a police officer's performance on the job. Until then, we cannot know whether such behavior indicates an orientation to unethical practices while the person is working as a police officer (Schafer, 2007b; Shusta et al., 2011).

Captured on Video

With increased video recording of incidents involving police officers, ethical and unethical behavior on the part of police has moved to the forefront of citizens' minds. And most people today possess cell phones with video-recording capability. Ethics training for recruits must include some reference to this phenomenon. However, misconduct prevention and prompt disciplinary action after an unethical incident will go much further toward restoring the public's trust in police officers.

Remember: Each time a police officer performs an unethical act and people learn about it, the public's trust in the police diminishes. Unfortunately, one unethical act can lead citizens to believe that all officers behave in the same way, thus tarnishing the reputations of blameless officers in the agency. Moreover, it is very difficult to rebuild trust once you have done something to violate it. Even if you offer a series of behaviors or statements to communicate your honest desire to

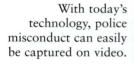

With today's technology, police misconduct can easily be captured on video.

"make things right," the individuals whose trust you violated may never be able to trust you again.

To avoid this scenario, police agencies must ascribe to and publish codes of ethics and conduct for all employees. Besides formal ethics training during the recruit stage and regular refresher sessions thereafter, agencies should begin using roll-call sessions, case studies, and ethical-behavior modeling to reinforce the message about what behavior is acceptable and what is not. Officers must also start demanding ethical behavior from one another and addressing questionable behavior swiftly. Line officers are in the perfect position to detect the possibility of unethical behavior and to step in before it occurs. If every officer expresses the intent to hold other officers accountable for their actions, while also modeling the correct behaviors, police agencies will stand a good chance of restoring trust among the public. This is part of being a courageous self-contained ethical leadership agent—one who earns the respect of others and can respect oneself.

THE CHALLENGES OF COUNTERTERRORISM AND HOMELAND SECURITY: WHAT ROLE WILL POLICE PLAY?

In Chapter 3, you read about a range of challenges facing police agencies today. Counterterrorism and homeland security represent particularly daunting challenges that will force police agencies to adapt in the future and to clarify their role. For this reason, we closely examine these themes in the pages that follow.

Counterterrorism

Historically, many people believed that terrorists were more interested in capturing media and other attention rather than in killing large numbers of people. Now we know better. And we have learned that small groups who are motivated by political, ideological, or religious zeal and who can blend in with the general population wreak the most havoc.

The question of what shape terrorism will take in the future has generated intense debate. Some experts suggest that the greatest threat of terrorism will come from a reconstituted al-Qaeda sheltered in places like Pakistan. Others contend that the worst threat will emanate from radicalized individuals who form terrorist groups in the United States or Europe. In the coming years, police agencies will need to focus their resources on both sources of terrorism: radicalization within a community and radicalization directed from foreign countries. With the former, police must invest in intelligence gathering and sharing through community outreach and interagency communication. With terrorism directed from abroad, intelligence sharing becomes even more critical. Regardless of the source, police will need to understand how terrorists are radicalized and how they organize themselves.

The Radicalization Process Radicalization occurs when individuals (recruits) align their ideology with that of a group and commit themselves to achieving the group's goals through violence. If radicals are recruited, organized, and trained in centralized clandestine facilities, police agencies might best track foreign-born or domestic radicals through intelligence fusion centers or similar interagency task forces. Alternatively, if terror groups organize within local communities, the police

Counterterrorism: procedures adopted by the military, police, and governments to assist in preventing, reacting to, and investigating acts or suspected acts of terrorism. (NSW, 2007)

Radicalization: the process by which individuals align their ideology with that of a group and commit themselves to achieving the group's goals through violence.

should focus on sources of radicalization within these communities. Such sources may range from correctional facilities and social, political, or religious radical websites to conferences attended by political or religious radicals (Martin, 2008; Picarelli, 2009; Shane & Mekhennet, 2010).

A 2007 National Institute of Justice study revealed that radicalization of correctional clients is occurring in prisons mostly through personal relationships among inmates. The radicalization process for inmates begins with a political or religious conversion through extremist teachings, ultimately leading some inmates to commit violent acts once they have been released from prison (Hamm, 2007).

Outreach programs, such as those developed through community policing, help police build links to community members who can identify radicals within the community. Citizens tend to respond more favorably to outreach efforts of state, county, and local police agencies rather than those at the federal level, affirming the critical role of local police in combating terrorism. Counterradicalization strategies designed to prevent radicalization in the first place are as important—perhaps even more so—than strategies aimed at reacting once a terrorist act has occurred.

A particularly disturbing development in the rise of terrorism against Americans is the radicalization of U.S. citizens who go on to commit terrorist acts within this country. These include Timothy McVeigh, a U.S. Army veteran who detonated a bomb that destroyed the Alfred P. Murrah building in Oklahoma City in 1995. McVeigh sympathized with the militia movement and wanted to inspire a revolt against what he saw as a tyrannical federal government. A more recent example is the November 5, 2009, Fort Hood shooting allegedly committed by Nidal Malik Hasan, a U.S. Army major serving as a psychiatrist. An American-born Muslim of Palestinian descent, Hasan had shown tendencies toward radical Islam since 2005. Even more recently, Faisal Shazad, a Pakistan-born naturalized U.S. citizen, reputedly made a failed attempt to detonate a car bomb in New York City's Times Square

Times Square is seen blocked off as NYPD bomb squad units respond to a suspicious package on May 7, 2010. The attempted bombing was attributed to Faisal Shazad.

Fighters participate in military training in this undated still frame from a recruitment video for Osama bin Laden's extremist al-Qaeda network.

in May 2010. As difficult as it is for anyone to accept that U.S. citizens would wish to inflict terror or harm on fellow Americans, police will need to face this harsh fact to contribute to the fight against terror.

Organization of Terrorist Groups   Research also indicates that terrorist groups may organize in different ways. In some cases, leadership and training terrorist cells remain in safe-haven (host) countries, drawing information and assistance from support cells in target countries. Attack cells enter and exit the target country quickly, with the assistance of the already embedded support cell. Other terrorist organizations are small groups that provide their own support and training without leaving the country.

Clearly, terrorism is an increasingly complex, ever-changing phenomenon. To combat it, police agencies must adopt flexible strategies and tactics in the future as sources of terrorism shift and as terrorists' own strategies and tactics change shape (Oliver, 2007; Picarelli, 2009).

Homeland Security   The U.S. government has launched numerous initiatives intended to enhance homeland defense, including the Civilian Biodefense Research Programs (U.S. Department of Health and Human Services) and the National Biological Warfare Defense Analysis Center (U.S. Department of Defense). Other programs and entities, such as the Federal Emergency Management Agency (FEMA), a small division of the U.S. Department of Homeland Security (DHS), focus less on specific terrorist activities and more on emergency management in a broad sense.

To be most effective, such efforts will need to adopt an all-hazards approach rather than focusing only on counterterrorism or only on emergency management. In addition, anyone managing a homeland security program would do well to leverage support and contributions from police organizations at all levels—national, state, and municipal.

The Need for an All-Hazards Approach DHS should be more than a counterterrorism agency as it moves into the future. The department must take an *all-hazards* approach—defining its mission as addressing any situation (such as the radicalization of recruits or an immediate threat) that endangers U.S. citizens. The department must develop mitigation and recovery programs for natural and technological disasters as well as terrorist incidents. It must also train and leverage local, nongovernmental organizations, businesses, and volunteers in emergency management. State and local response to threats must be honed, and first responders—police, firefighters, emergency medical technicians—must receive training in handling disasters (Waugh, 2005).

The Role of Local Police in Homeland Security The toughest challenge in using local police to support homeland security efforts is coordinating the 17,000 to 20,000 police agencies that exist across the United States. The local police, not federal authorities, are the first responders to an emergency. As local police are used in the counterterrorism effort, many proponents of this strategy suggest that police become more vigilant in their communities, are trained in counterterrorism tactics, learn how to investigate more effectively, and share information and insights with the military (Maguire & King, 2004).

On the surface this idea has merit, but it fails to take into account how local governments operate and how diverse they are. The primary mission of the police—to protect and serve—will not change. Therefore, local police agencies probably will never function in the same manner as federal investigative agencies like the Federal Bureau of Investigation (FBI) (Thacher, 2005). After all, FBI personnel are not police officers. Thus some federal-level agencies may resist drawing on local resources. However, local police bring unique strengths to the counterterrorism table. These include deep presence in the communities they serve, the ability to respond swiftly to crises, and access to information that could prove vital for identifying and stopping terrorists. Indeed, local police count among the nation's first lines of defense against terrorism. They are well-positioned to notice suspicious persons, suspicious activities, and actions that contradict community norms. In addition, private security services—the largest protective resource in the United States—now outnumber the police three to one. Therefore, the eyes and ears of private security personnel should be tapped as well. But to take advantage of these strengths, police agency administrators must assume leadership roles and establish and nurture lines of communication between and among local, county, state, and federal agencies, as well as private businesses.

Trade-Offs in Police Priorities As police have come under increasing pressure to contribute to counterterrorism efforts, their budgets have continued to shrink. Police are thus being asked to take on more responsibilities without receiving more resources. When this happens in any organization, people in the organization—as well as those it serves—must make trade-offs in what services the organization will provide. In the case of policing, U.S. citizens will have to decide which responsibilities they want their local police to focus on. Would citizens rather see most of their tax dollars go toward ordinary quality-of-life issues such as enforcing building codes and reducing trespassing, or would they rather that police focus on protecting the community against terrorist attacks? Police cannot do everything, and the citizens who fund police activities through taxes must decide what the trade-offs will be.

Leadership on the job
Line Officers Can Make a Difference

Two days before Christmas one year, a police officer in a southern U.S. city responded to a tip about a possible bomb in a crowded mall. Although bomb threat tips were fairly common in that city and almost always proved a misunderstanding or empty threat, the officer reported it to a commanding officer, following a rule the officer learned in a recent training exercise to treat every threat as real. In this case, the officer's commitment to following this rule paid big dividends: The Special Investigative Division located and arrested a young man who was preparing to enter a restaurant and detonate a bomb.

The perpetrator was not a foreign national or a member of any extremist group, but an Army infantry tank specialist recently returned from Iraq. Police found he was making improvised explosive devices (IEDs) similar to those he had encountered in Iraq,

and he intended to sell them to gang members and other criminals.

The training that the officer received was geared to making front-line police the predominant gatherers of important intelligence. Developers of such training assume that officers are the best suited to recognize unusual situations on their beats that could represent terrorist activity or a new criminal threat.

1. This responding officer made several critical decisions regarding the investigation of the bomb threat. What were those decisions, and how did they lead to the averting of a tragic situation?

2. What lessons might other local police agencies and the communities they serve draw from this event in their efforts to prevent terrorist acts?

Indeed, many resources devoted to community policing and problem solving were diverted to counterterrorism after the terrorist attacks of September 11, 2001.

Of course, gauging the likelihood of a terrorist attack can help community members clarify their local police force's priorities. Major ports of entry like New York City and San Francisco will always be viewed as vulnerable, whereas it is difficult for most of us to imagine terrorists targeting places that offer few advantages to terrorists, like Butte, Montana, or Circleville, Ohio.

Decisions about how to deploy local police for antiterrorist activities will likely depend on the level of threat facing the jurisdiction. While DHS officials have pledged to cover the additional costs associated with such deployment, there is always the possibility that such assistance will fall through or that the government will issue additional mandates without commensurate financial support (the unfunded mandate). If this should happen, some police jurisdictions will have to decide what portion of their resources will go to "conventional" crime control and what portion will be spent on homeland security (Mastrofski, 2006).

Terrorism as a Global Threat   Terrorism will continue to present a threat not just to the United States but to the rest of the world as well. Evidence suggests that justice systems around the world are changing to address this reality, and are drawing inspiration from one another. For instance, a court management system developed in Europe has attracted interest in South Africa. And it is widely suspected that American television programming that portrays trials by jury helped to introduce this innovation in Russia (Ritter, 2006). Across the globe, national leaders are debating how to incarcerate and adjudicate those suspected of terrorist activities.

In this atmosphere of globalization, free and democratic societies everywhere will need to collaborate more than ever to fight terrorism. If they can manage this feat, all criminals, including terrorists, may find themselves with nowhere in the world to hide.

BUDGETING: CAN POLICE DO EVEN MORE—WITH EVEN LESS?

In Chapter 5 of this book, you learned about budgeting in a police agency. All signs point to the strong possibility that budgeting will become increasingly difficult for police organizations. Ordinary citizens may be unaware of the cost-reduction efforts being made at their local police agencies, but police officers are fully aware. Speculation and rumors of hiring and salary freezes as well as administrative layoffs are running rampant among police forces everywhere. Even worse, some agencies face dismantling, with only a portion of laid-off officers being offered employment by the consolidating, contracted, or adjacent agency. Budget constraints appear to affect everyone.

What does this mean for the years ahead? For the immediate future, most police agencies will have to do the same job of providing public safety with severely limited resources. It is not unreasonable to assume that this trend will continue for some time. Therefore, police agencies may face some difficult decisions each year budgets are constrained.

Outsourcing of Police Services

In recent years, outsourcing of some police services has emerged as citizens balk at rising taxes. Some city police agencies are being dissolved in favor of agreements with county and state police agencies to take over the policing of municipalities. In some communities, such outsourcing can generate savings that run into the millions of dollars. But what will those millions really cost in terms of citizen safety and the personal nature of police–community relations?

Critics of police outsourcing argue that consolidating local police services with a larger police entity will compromise citizens' safety. They fear that police will be unable to respond quickly to calls for service, will not know who community members are, and will be less sensitive to the people they serve, thus providing criminals with more and better opportunities to victimize citizens. This may lead citizens and business owners to hire private security firms to make up for the loss of police presence. People may also move to gated communities where residents pay for private security to keep out unauthorized persons. Thus, the wealthy may be afforded better protection than the poor. An interesting question remains: Can the government relegate public safety to a private firm?

The Question of Police Purpose

Although many people argue that services like policing, emergency medical assistance, and firefighting cannot easily be replaced, in some areas of the country, such replacement is happening anyway. This trend is forcing endangered agencies to prove their worth to taxpayers tired of funding costly government services.

A private security officer checks cars entering a gated community in Palm Desert, California.

Meanwhile, all government agencies—including police departments—are facing competition not only from other government entities but also from private industry. In some jurisdictions, functions such as parking enforcement, security, and even crime investigation are being performed by outside service providers instead of the local police department. In the future, people may increasingly depend on private organizations for such services, primarily because of constrained public police resources. That raises some provocative questions: What do the police actually do? What *should* they do? What is their mission? Their business?

Pros and Cons of Citizen Involvement

On a positive note, public budget constraints may lead citizens to take more responsibility for their own safety by installing house and auto alarms, and by staying alert to crime and disorder in their communities. Neighborhood Watch programs may flourish and function appropriately, and every law-abiding citizen will serve as the eyes and ears of the police.

Yet, the absence of a visible police presence may result in more citizens arming themselves. Neighborhood Watch groups may become more aggressive, challenging strangers and brandishing weapons to scare them away. Moreover, the presence of private security and gated communities may widen the gap between people who can afford to pay for such amenities and those who must rely on the public police for their safety. This is a recipe for unrest similar to what happened in the 1960s, when riots revealed a widening gap between the rich and the poor.

The Need for Creative Budget Strategies

Large cities like New York, Los Angeles, San Francisco, and Chicago will probably not dissolve or replace their police agencies. But they will need to change the way they approach budgeting. Police leaders must recognize that economic downturns and citizen resistance to paying higher taxes will continue to present tough challenges for government and police administrators everywhere. Balancing a police budget during lean economic times demands more than just tactics such as hiring freezes, delays in procuring needed equipment, and postponement of capital investments. The police administrator of the future must demonstrate leadership skills and develop a comprehensive budget strategy that includes immediate measures for reducing spending as well as proposals for expanding funding opportunities. If you find yourself in this difficult position, the following guidelines can help:

- Commit to operating responsibly and frugally as a police agency during lean *and* flush times.
- Expect the unexpected and craft contingency plans for unforeseen problems.
- Do not rest after solving a budget problem. Monitor your budgeting process, and incorporate lessons learned from each budgeting cycle into the next cycle (Rabin et al., 1996; Robbins & Judge, 2008).

Can Police Think Like Business Leaders?

The police administrator of the future must think like a businessperson to apply business principles to planning, budgeting, and other administrative activities. Therefore, those who aspire to managerial positions within a police agency should prepare themselves for this demanding task. In particular, there is a strong trend toward applying ethical leadership and economic and fiscal management principles to police administration. This trend will continue, thanks to a growing emphasis on relationship building and fiscal management. Deployment of human and material resources must be efficient *and* effective. To strike this balance, more police agencies will be looking for employees with strong business and financial management skills (Allen & Sawhney, 2010; Schulte, 1996).

And just as corporations provide shareholders with an annual report that explains how the business used its financial resources and what outcomes it achieved, police agencies will need to provide citizens with an annual master plan and budget report conveying similar information. Citizens are demanding more police transparency and accountability. An understandable report outlining the police agency's vision, mission, goals, and objectives—and explaining where dollars are spent, and why—can go a long way toward saving local police agencies from downsizing or extinction. Private businesses and units within public and private companies must constantly justify their spending; public entities such as police agencies will be held to the same standards.

ASSESSMENT AND EVALUATION: WILL POLICE GRADE THEMSELVES ON THE RIGHT CURVE?

To excel in the coming years, police agencies will also need to take new approaches to organizational and individual performance assessment and evaluation (discussed in Chapters 7 and 12, respectively). Next, we explore such approaches in the context of the future.

Measuring Performance at the Organizational Level

When police agencies assess and evaluate their own organizational performance, too often the effort becomes an exercise in celebrating positive results while minimizing any troubling news. This approach does not support continuous improvement in any organization. Even more disturbing, some police agencies do not bother to assess any aspect of their operations unless someone with political importance outside the agency—a city council member, county supervisor, the mayor—requests it.

As time passes, these approaches will no longer be tenable. Citizens are increasingly insisting on more police accountability. To demonstrate that accountability, police agencies must take a disciplined approach to assessing and evaluating their own performance. They will have to show through their assessments and evaluations that they are making efficient and effective use of their resources, and that they deserve to exist and receive taxpayer dollars.

Agency personnel must also view community members as partners—inviting them to offer suggestions for improvement, and being willing to implement the best and most appropriate of citizens' ideas. Once again, the police could take a page from the book of business. How do corporations elicit and use customer complaints and ideas? At the very least, they acknowledge them. And they try implementing suggestions for improvement that seem most feasible and valuable. Police agencies must pay more than lip service to what citizens want and need.

As you read in Chapter 7, police agencies should consider the accreditation process as a useful guide to organizational assessment and evaluation—and thus continual improvement. Accreditation, be it at the state or national level or through an independent organization, helps a police agency ensure that it is meeting appropriate and acceptable organizational and personnel standards, and that can earn an agency an A+ in citizens' eyes.

Representatives of an accrediting body will visit a police agency for evaluation and assessment.

Measuring Performance at the Individual Level

Police agencies must also take a more rigorous approach toward performance assessment and evaluation at the individual level. When deciding whether to promote an officer, managers and supervisors would do well to take feedback from coworkers and community members into account. For example, if feedback shows that a particular officer is especially customer focused, this should count among the criteria for promotion, just as courage in the line of duty counts. Further, individuals seeking promotion should be required to assess themselves, identifying their own strengths and weaknesses.

In making promotion decisions, managers and supervisors should also consider how well their subordinates demonstrate the ethical leadership skills we have discussed throughout this book—including Level 5 leadership (Collins, 2001) and servant leadership (Greenleaf, 1991). As we have written, it is important that all police officers—no matter what their rank—become self-contained ethical leadership agents. Managers and supervisors can ask themselves how well the officers reporting to them leave their ego behind and proceed with confidence and courage to do the right thing at the right time for the community, the agency, and their colleagues (Tichy & Bennis, 2007).

HIRING AND TRAINING: HOW WILL POLICE BUILD AN EFFECTIVE WORKFORCE?

Hiring and training (examined in Chapters 8 and 10, respectively) will almost certainly continue to pose challenges for police agencies in the future. To surmount those challenges, police administrators must develop fresh strategies to attract talent and offer creative solutions to any characteristics of policing that discourage people from entering the profession.

Hiring

Many police agencies experience difficulty recruiting new officers. At first glance, the problem appears to stem from the widespread perception that policing is not a "real" profession. This belief was aided by the notoriously low wages paid for police work and the lack of applicants with diverse background or college educations. Over the years, the pay has improved considerably. However, at the same time, police work has acquired a reputation for being a thankless job characterized by impossible levels of stress and danger. Thus, people with a college education may find other occupations more attractive and challenging.

To draw qualified and desirable candidates, police agency recruiters have begun resorting to incentives like signing bonuses and advertising campaigns similar to the U.S. Army's "Be all that you can be." They may need to step up such efforts in the future to overcome recruitment challenges.

Numerous police agencies currently offer their own extensive, job-specific training to recruits. Therefore, in recruiting applicants with college educations, agencies may choose to select college graduates with degrees in subjects other than criminal justice, such as liberal arts and science. Candidates who are bilingual, trilingual, or willing to master several languages in addition to their first language will prove even more attractive in the future as American society continues to grow more diverse.

Police agencies use job fairs to recruit police officer candidates.

Training

In addition to adopting new hiring strategies, police agencies must develop fresh approaches to training. Besides providing standard training for new recruits, which includes weapons proficiency, knowledge of the law, and physical fitness, future training must accomplish the following:

- Address societal and cultural changes. For example, younger generations have been raised with technology, multitasking, and extensive external stimuli. They thus learn differently than older generations.
- Focus on the actual types of problem-based situations officers encounter most on the job.
- Offer classes in change management, customer relations, ethics, leadership, and intensive cultural orientation.
- Discuss the use of new policing technologies and devices that may play a crucial role in the future (such as DNA-sample collection tools and nonconfrontational, less-than-lethal weaponry), as well as proficiency with the Internet as a superior investigative tool.

Cross-training and virtual academies offer additional—and less expensive—avenues for building recruits' skills.

Cross-Training   With police agencies under close scrutiny for financial accountability, *cross-training*—training in different types of tasks and job specifications—will probably become the norm rather than the exception in the years ahead. Administrators are finding it expedient to use personnel in creative ways to get the job done, without having to employ additional people. Cross-training exposes employees to knowledge about the workings of the agency and such specialized tasks as investigations, and it positions the agency to deploy individuals where they are needed most.

The ability to shift personnel seamlessly between and among job tasks not only saves money, but it also promotes **knowledge management** in a learning organization—that is, the retention of knowledge most important to the police agency. The premise is that if only a few individuals possess specific knowledge of a process or task (such as how to store crime scene evidence or how to extract a report from the agency's IT system), that knowledge could be lost if those individuals leave the agency. Theoretically, cross-training ensures that expertise and knowledge remain in-house. Moreover, if a person who possesses knowledge of an important process is unavailable, another individual can temporarily step in and perform the tasks proficiently.

How might cross-training work in a police agency? An apt example is the assignment of any investigator to a number of diverse cases that normally would have been handled by a specialized investigator, such as controlled substances, sex crimes, arson, burglary, or homicide. A side benefit of this development could be increased cooperation and collaboration among previously specialized personnel, and closure of cases in a more timely manner as more people have access to and information about the investigative process (Bandics, 1997; Haberfeld, 2002). The synergistic effect of people working together often helps a police agency develop more powerful solutions to problems.

Virtual Academies   Another interesting training development is the advent of *virtual academy* classes, whereby recruits and senior officers take courses online. This approach allows flexibility for learners, who can take a course any time rather than having to attend classes in person during prescribed hours. No live instructor

Knowledge management: the retention of knowledge most important to an organization.

Virtual academy class, "FBI—Operation Knockout: LA Gang Investigation, May 21, 2009". Training and information presentation through the use of the Internet emphasizing interagency cooperation among federal, state and local police agencies. http://www.fbi.gov/news/videos/operation-knockout/?searchterm=None

is necessary, and officers in locations remote from the normal training site are no longer required to travel long distances to receive the training. Some classes that have been taught in this manner include hazardous materials handling, weapons of mass destruction, and incident command (Boninfante, 2004). We expect the use of virtual academies to increase in the future, especially as virtual reality and simulators become more sophisticated.

COMMUNICATION: WILL A WIDER ARRAY OF CONSTITUENTS REQUIRE BROADER SKILLS?

Administrators as well as line officers in police agencies will continue to face the question of how best to communicate with an ever-widening array of increasingly demanding constituents. (Communication is discussed in detail in Chapter 9.) Some of these constituents, such as the general public and members of communities served by police, have begun calling for more transparency and communication from the police. They want clear, understandable information about what the police are doing, not police jargon or law enforcement directives.

But communicating with the public in a nonenforcement manner is a challenge for many police personnel. Police officers of all ranks, as visible leaders in the communities they serve, will need to master the art of using plain language when conversing with the public. Moreover, they must always perform their duties in a civil manner and demonstrate positive interaction through their verbal and nonverbal behaviors; for instance, by acting as human beings rather than *robocops*.

Within a police agency, effective communication is just as crucial. Managers and officers must know how to interact constructively not only in one-on-one exchanges but also in small groups, before angry crowds or citizens at a community gathering, and in meetings with colleagues and superiors. Effective communication hinges on the application of useful practices, which you learned about in Chapter 9.

Constructive Engagement

In addition to the practices presented in Chapter 9, police personnel can use **constructive engagement**—a coaching and mentoring rapport that encourages a genuinely warm relationship between individuals—to strengthen their communication with others. How do you know when someone is practicing constructive engagement? The person may compliment others and show a genuine interest in them; demonstrate attentive, noncritical listening; share thoughts and ideas; and gather informally with people other than their peers, staff, or police officers. Merely by saying hello and making eye contact with another person can help anyone engage constructively and forge strong working relationships and trust with others (Davis & Wildman, 2009). We are not suggesting that police officers become full-time counselors or social workers (although they function as both), but that officers act as human beings.

Constructive engagement: a coaching and mentoring rapport that encourages a genuinely warm relationship between individuals.

Constructive Confrontation

Effective communication also includes practicing *constructive confrontation*— challenging one another's ideas in a nonthreatening manner and supporting the final outcome even if you do not agree with it. Constructive confrontation encourages openness and discourages personal attacks, emotional outbursts, and bullying. Learning how and when to disagree productively can help all members of a police agency uncover fresh perspectives on problems and generate fruitful ideas for solving them. By actively participating in constructive confrontation, people commit to implementing the solutions they have generated together (Sutton, 2007).

ETHICS IN ACTION

The Challenge of Prioritization

An elderly woman is arrested for neglecting her yard. (An overgrown yard lowers property values in the neighborhood, making it harder for homeowners to sell their homes.)

Parents are ticketed and fined because their children are riding their bicycles without helmets or knee and elbow pads. (Children have suffered serious head and limb injuries when unprotected.)

Boisterous new high school graduates are arrested for disturbing the peace during a graduation party. (Noise ordinances protect the serenity of suburban neighborhoods.)

Every law that is passed is designed to correct undesirable behavior, with penalties ranging from fines to jail time. However, with so many new laws on the books at the federal, state, and municipal level, police officers may have difficulty prioritizing enforcement of the laws in the future. Should officers stop helmetless bicyclists to write citations for that illegal activity, or let the riders go so they can write more speeding tickets, since speeding is arguably more dangerous? The sad reality is that officers can be in only one place at a time. They have to ignore some minor violations of the law so they can address more serious offenses. Some municipalities recognize this and have hired people specifically to write tickets for parking meter violations, so police can focus on other tasks that require more of their specialized skills.

But the ethics of policing call for officers to uphold *all* laws, whether they seem frivolous or not. And citizens expect officers to uphold the law without favoritism and the justice system to punish violators, most often in an effort to correct behavior. Yet some government policies encourage police to enforce laws according to their spirit rather than according to their letter. In other words, most people do want all the laws enforced all the time.

1. Police officers come under pressure from political leaders and citizens to make trade-offs in the laws they enforce. If you came under such pressure as a police officer, how would you resolve this ethical dilemma?

2. What ethical standards should a police officer use to determine which statutes to enforce at any given time? In answering this question, consider the issues of criticality and timeliness of response.

3. Should all laws be enforced all of the time? Why or why not?

POLICE LEADERSHIP: CAN BOUNDARIES EXPAND?

Excellence in ethical police leadership—discussed in Chapter 11—will become increasingly important in the future, as police agencies grapple with ever more daunting challenges. For example, many agencies are having more and more difficulty attracting qualified job candidates, as interest in policing as a career dwindles along with budgets. Meanwhile, criminals are proving frustratingly innovative in their schemes (especially in cybercrime), sometimes leaving police struggling to catch up. These and other challenges will likely only intensify in the future.

To tackle their toughest difficulties, police must expand their boundaries in terms of how they work and how they think. Specifically, the police must embrace the virtual world, broaden their notions of management, and challenge the status quo.

Embracing the Virtual World

The Internet is here to stay, and like most technologies, it is a double-edged sword. On the one hand, it promises to enable police to do their jobs more effectively and efficiently. On the other hand, it also opened up a whole new category of crime. To seize the advantages offered by the Internet as well as grapple with the problems, police agency administrators must become more *net-centric,* or Internet savvy. The Internet offers not just information about current criminals and their activities but a gateway to data, and possibly even evidence, about future criminals.

For instance, there have already been numerous examples of one person selling an old computer to another, and the new owner finds pictures of nude images of

Virtual reality allows exploration of many areas such as computer crime and employment opportunities.

children left on the computer's hard drive. By understanding how evidence of crimes including child pornography can come in seemingly innocuous objects like computers, police will stand a much better chance of staying one step ahead of criminals.

To become net-centric, police executives must embrace the virtual world in addition to the physical world. By doing so, they can become nimble enough to anticipate and vanquish problems that arise in the dynamic environment of cyberspace, in addition to those arising in the physical environment (Lewin, 2010; Schafer, 2007a). For instance, the police must know how to process virtual as well as physical crime scenes.

The virtual world can also help police master the art of toleration. Indeed, interesting developments are taking place with the use of **virtual reality,** a computer simulation of a real or imaginary system that enables a user to perform operations on the simulated system and illustrates the effects in real time. Police recruits will soon be able to use virtual reality to experience life as a person of a different age, race, gender, or cultural orientation. The program relies on a social psychology premise that negative stereotyping decreases when an individual gains intensive experience as a member of a different group. In testing of such simulation, participants showed a significant reduction in elder stereotyping when they were placed in the avatars (virtual persons) of elderly people (Yee & Bailenson, 2006).

Virtual reality: a computer simulation of a real or imaginary system that enables a user to perform operations on the simulated system and shows the effects in real time.

Broadening Notions of Management

To effect real and lasting change, police executives must surrender the previously predominant idea of management as a rigid and tall hierarchical structure for one that is more flat, fluid, and learn to cooperate with many levels of the command structure and workforce. For instance, instead of issuing directives, they can encourage the personnel who are closest to particular problems to develop solutions to those problems. Because many police agencies have committed to augmenting traditional policing with some form of the community policing strategy, executives will also need to view the horizon that lies beyond their agency. That is, when they make decisions, they would do well to take into account the potential impact on the community the agency serves. To illustrate, a decision to close parks early to reduce vandalism might force young people to play in the streets instead of in safer areas.

Continuing resource constraints have further changed traditional ideas about police management. In particular, officers in the future will receive fewer direct orders and less direct supervision than ever before, because resources are shrinking and officers are being held more responsible and accountable. They will have to be allowed to use their discretionary power to make choices and take action in the course of their ordinary workday. For police administrators, this means releasing control and trusting subordinates to make the correct decisions. However, an agency's chief executive will still be ultimately accountable for what officers do; thus, ultimate responsibility rests with the agency's chief executive.

Policing strategies (as you recall from Chapter 2) have continued to evolve—and will keep doing so. For example, most citizens have become accustomed to working more closely with their local police agency to share information and solve problems. This trend will likely persist. Citizens in jurisdictions where the police agency does not reach out to the community or acknowledge citizen feedback will probably protest this isolation. But just as police have learned to partner with citizens and outside organizations to effect change, they must also learn to view their subordinates and others in the organization as full partners. This requires a shift in mindset: Managers and supervisors must come to appreciate subordinates as inherently valuable individuals who can offer insight, wisdom, and fresh perspectives. To build such partnerships and extract value from them, police administrators must get to know their subordinates as individuals, each with their own interests, skills, and ability to contribute (International Association of Chiefs of Police, 1999; Schulte, 1996; Stevens, 2011; Stohr & Collins, 2009).

Challenging the Status Quo

As another way to expand boundaries, police managers must reach beyond the assumption that the *status quo* is the ideal state. Thankfully, today's line-level police officers and managers are more willing to examine prevailing practices' strengths and weaknesses. For example, unplanned random patrol may catch would-be criminal offenders off guard because of its unpredictability, but this approach does not help police target potentially high-crime areas.

Yet, it can still be difficult for police to accept that tried-and-true ways of doing things may no longer be the best ways. By asking tough questions, trying new practices, and challenging ingrained ideas, police managers and officers can begin reshaping the policing profession in constructive ways (Schafer, 2007a).

Embracing the virtual world, broadening ideas about management, and challenging the status quo—none of this is easy. In the box titled "Recommendations for Current and Future Police Executives," the International Association of Chiefs of Police (IACP) offers additional guidance, drawn from a conference on leadership held in 1999 in which police executives were counseled and encouraged to develop and improve their leadership team, their organization, and the community their agency served. The recommendations are reinforced through the IACP's *Leadership in Police Organizations (LPO)* program (Rosser, 2010).

Recommendations for Current and Future Police Executives

1. Be enthusiastic and positive about the job, and commit yourself to the leadership position that you occupy.

2. Embrace and comprehend your agency's vision for yourself, your agency, and the community you serve, and clearly and passionately communicate the agency's goals and objectives to inspire all involved parties to accomplish them.

3. Seek out individuals, organizations, and associations to establish community partnerships, and develop those relationships so you achieve goals and have reliable support in times of crisis.

4. Maintain two priorities simultaneously: crime control/victim services and customer satisfaction. While customer satisfaction should never overshadow the crime control/victim services mission, understand that the two reinforce one another; they are not alternative strategies.

(continued)

5. Make succession planning at all leadership levels a goal. Career development, knowledge of strategic leadership practices, and mentoring for new and current leaders should be an agency's personnel development model.

6. Reward and promote superior day-to-day performance at all levels of your organization. Encourage innovation and "thinking outside the box" in addressing current and future policing strategies. Promote and reward creative discussion and experimentation for groups (formal and informal) and individuals within your agency.

7. Enlist others' help when you encounter challenges, including consultants, other government and community resources, and gifted and capable individuals within your agency. Making decisions unilaterally will only alienate subordinates and peers, whereas work teams will foster collaboration.

8. Encourage agency members to personally embrace their own innovative ideas and achievements. Always acknowledge such contributions when speaking with others. Praising agency team members will empower your colleagues and subordinates, leading to better morale and more acceptance of new ideas and change.

9. Aggressively seek out and hire qualified people from diverse backgrounds. A diverse applicant pool may bring in adequate numbers of qualified individuals from underrepresented populations. Proactive and continuous recruitment efforts are necessary to achieve an appropriately diverse workforce. Value diversity as a more complete way to understand and address agency problems. Seek to improve diversity (in race, religion, gender, age, and lifestyle) in your entire agency and its subsections.

10. Be aware that forces of change are at work continuously. Stay abreast of internal trends (such as in your agency's workforce). Cross-train employees and regularly deploy them to tasks where they are most needed. You will help address employee concerns before they can become overblown. Also be aware of external shifts (for example in politics and the community), so you can proactively shape their impact on your agency.

Source: International Association of Chiefs of Police, 1999.

CHANGE LEADERSHIP: WHAT MODEL SHOULD POLICE USE?

Driving needed change in a police agency is a vital aspect of leadership. It will become more crucial than ever in the future because we live in a world of accelerating change. For this reason, we devote the following pages to a discussion of how police may master the art of change leadership in the coming years. Technological advances, shifts in social mores, increased globalization—these and other changes seem to be unfolding at an ever-faster pace. To surmount the problems and seize the opportunities that such shifts will bring in the future, police agencies themselves will have to change.

But altering how work is done in a police agency is difficult (just as it is in any organization), and those seeking to effect change can expect to meet with resistance. Most people in an organization would rather defend current ways of doing things (the status quo) than open themselves to exploring other ways of operating— whether the proposed change is a simple modification to a business process or a large-scale transformation of a unit or division.

To lead change effectively, police administrators must craft and communicate a compelling vision of the benefits that a proposed change can bring. They must also take a disciplined approach to executing the change—by selecting and applying a change-leadership model.

Crafting and Communicating a Compelling Vision

To combat resistance to change, police leaders must develop a *meaningful vision* of a better future available to the agency if people can bring themselves to make needed changes. Leaders should then communicate the vision in clear and compelling terms, so all employees and other stakeholders yearn to become part of the change effort. To develop a vision, leaders must diagnose the problem or opportunity that the pro- posed change is intended to address. Problems and opportunities can be technical, political, and/or cultural.

For example, officers at a police agency may determine that advances in com- puter technology present both a problem (criminals have easier access to victims' personal information) and an opportunity (police have readier access to information about cybercrime patterns). To address this problem and opportunity, the officers craft a compelling vision in which the agency has adopted the new technology and all employees have mastered using it. In this vision, thanks to widespread mastery of the technology, the agency has succeeded in reducing crime.

Administrators at another police agency may decide to focus on risk manage- ment and liability mitigation as an opportunity that requires change. The vision they present to agency personnel centers on leveraging new technologies. For example, managers propose adopting patrol-car dashboard cameras that document officers' interactions with drivers who are pulled over, street cameras that record drivers running traffic lights or gang members possessing and brandishing guns, and video records that capture every detail of an interrogation. This use of technology, the leaders explain, can help protect officers and the agency from unwarranted lawsuits (Ortmeier & Meese, 2010; Tichy, 1977).

Selecting a Change-Leadership Model

Even with a clear and compelling vision, many people find change difficult—whether it takes the form of new reward systems, job designs, or teamwork protocols. All changes require people to demonstrate new behaviors, attitudes, and practices on the job (Gee, 2005). Moreover, there will always be tension between changing some ways of operating in an organization while maintaining other approaches. For example, the challenges of dwindling budgets, increasing homeland security requirements, community involvement, and crime suppression all demand that police take new approaches to their work while also maintaining the traditional calls-for-service model of customer service. This tension between having to change some things while keeping other things the same makes leading change even more difficult. Only a true leader can manage it (Kotter, 1996).

Because of this conflict between change and continuity, police managers can expect at least some resistance to proposed new ways of doing things even when employees have embraced the vision and understand the need for change. Selecting and implementing a disciplined change-leadership model can help administrators guide agency employees through this conflict. Effective leaders have several change-leadership models to choose from. In the pages that follow, we examine three such models—the Lewin basic change model, the Weisbord six-box model, and the Kotter strategic change model—each developed by a highly regarded expert.

The Lewin Basic Change Model   The Lewin basic change model proposes three stages of change:

1. *Unfreeze.* Change leaders break down old habits in an attempt to create a sense of urgency, modify cultural norms, and develop a vision of the better future that change could bring. Leaders assess the problem or opportunity that requires change and prescribe a change strategy.

2. *Change.* Leaders persuade people to begin using the proposed new processes and provide any needed training. Role models, mentors, and benchmarking help facilitate the change process. Some observers describe this phase as an intervention, which requires intensive collaboration and cooperation among all players in the organization.

3. *Refreeze.* Leaders help employees integrate the new behaviors and attitudes into their everyday work lives, evaluate the effectiveness of the change process, and drive further change if needed to improve the organization's performance (Lewin, 1951).

The Weisbord Six-Box Model   The Weisbord six-box model starts with diagnosis of a problem or opportunity facing the organization. Based on the diagnosis, a change leader or group decides what formal changes need to be made (for example, in the organization's policies and procedures) and what informal changes are required (that is, how people carry out their work). To effect formal and informal changes, change leaders must balance six interrelated "boxes":

- *Purpose:* goal clarity and goal achievement
- *Structure:* elements of organizational architecture including role definition, physical layout of offices, and reporting relationships
- *Relationships:* cooperation and conflict management
- *Rewards:* incentives to reinforce growth, responsibility, and achievement
- *Leadership:* efforts to keep the six boxes in balance
- *Helpful mechanisms:* coordinating technologies such as policies, procedures, budgeting processes, and measurement protocols (Weisbord, 1978).

The Kotter Strategic Change Model   The Kotter strategic change model rests on the premise that successful transformations are very difficult, and that managers and employees alike can be easily sidetracked away from the effort. Kotter (1996) advocates an eight-step model of change leadership:

1. Establish a sense of urgency.
2. Create a guiding coalition to lead change.
3. Develop a vision and a change strategy.
4. Communicate the change vision.
5. Empower employees for broad-based action.
6. Generate short-term wins.
7. Consolidate change and produce more change.
8. Anchor new approaches in the organization's culture.

Complementary Models   The three models of change leadership discussed can be seen as complementary. When used together, they can help police administrators navigate the rough terrain of change in their agency. The Lewin model explains the process in simple, understandable language and procedure. The Weisbord model assists with the diagnosis of the problem or future challenges in a clear and reasonable manner. The Kotter model suggests a comprehensive, sequential approach to defining the problem and bringing the needed change to fruition.

POLICE UNIONS: WILL THEY SURVIVE?

In Chapter 13, you read about a variety of legal issues important to police work—including employment law and the role of unions. In policing and other professions, unions are encountering serious difficulties, so we take the following pages to explore the potential implications for police.

Unions under Fire

Some experts contend that labor unions have served their purpose and are no longer useful in today's world. Others assert that unions must be preserved because they might be among the only entities left that protect ordinary workers' rights. It is no secret that labor unions as a group are under fire. The automobile industry, the steel industry, and other widely unionized sectors have experienced massive layoffs. As jobs disappear and formerly strong corporations close their doors, there appears to be no more room for workers to negotiate with management. The outlook for many government and other public-employee unions, including police unions, is no less grim. Yet, budget constraints affect every segment of policing, from administrative workers to sworn officers, and the unions seem powerless to effect change in any meaningful way when budgets tighten.

Potential New Paths for Unions

Some observers believe that police unions can survive *if* they adapt to the changing circumstances that surround employment in this country. They should continue

Police unions can encourage continuous professional education and training of police officers.

to serve as strong advocates and negotiators for workers, striving to ensure that employees receive adequate wages and benefits in return for their skills, time, and commitment. But unions must also transform themselves from demanding, unsatisfied ideologues to open, attentive, problem-oriented, responsive, and flexible partners with management and the community at large. Unions can no longer be the insular organizations of the past; instead, they should become connecting and collaborative associations of the future. Union leaders must acknowledge the currently negative perceptions of labor organizations harbored by many members of the public and reengineer their image and brand.

Unions must also recognize that continuing education and new learning are the keys to jobs of the future, and all union members must have the opportunity for education appropriate to those jobs. During contract negotiations, union leaders and members can express their willingness to advance their own training, education, and professionalism by paying (in full or in part) for college tuition or course fees. Unions can also provide educational opportunities for their members in the form of workshops, training exercises, and various other continuing-education mechanisms (Dator, 1999; Hunter & Barker, 2011).

FACILITIES MANAGEMENT: WHAT WILL IT LOOK LIKE IN THE FUTURE?

In Chapter 14, you learned about procurement and facilities management in police organizations. Many people rarely think about the facilities where they work—at least until something changes or malfunctions. Consider the panic you experience when the pipes burst in your home or the roof starts leaking—then magnify that sensation to reflect the distress experienced at the organizational level in a police agency when such failures occur.

To ensure the seamless operation of a police agency, someone—an individual or a team—must take responsibility for facilities management. The police leader of the future must know how to plan for and manage this important organizational concern, rather than merely panicking when a crisis occurs.

Consolidation of Police Facilities

Many jurisdictions have begun restructuring their police facilities in a variety of ways to meet the conflicting needs of saving money and better serving the community. For instance, some jurisdictions are consolidating their police facilities to cut expenses. Instead of having several neighborhood precincts, divisions, districts, or substations, police agencies may concentrate these structures in one or two sections covering geographic areas such as the west precinct and east precinct, or the north division and south division.

While this scheme may yield cost savings, it also has a major drawback: It leaves some neighborhoods with no local police station in their immediate community—which can be disconcerting to citizens and alienate the police from the public. Established police substations have become the hub of some neighborhoods, particularly in densely populated parts of a city, where people view the police facility as a haven amid a dangerous area. Citizens are more willing to take problems to *local* police officers as opposed to making a trip to a centralized location where they may not know any of the officers. In managing their facilities, police agencies must make painful trade-offs between citizens' safety and cost reductions.

Subdivision of Police Facilities

Whereas some jurisdictions are consolidating organizational structures, other large jurisdictions are being subdivided for the purpose of improving service to the community. The resulting smaller divisions are operating as mini-police departments, each of which takes care of local concerns. Some police agencies have even begun using mobile facilities such as trailers to locate resources where they are most needed and to ensure that police personnel have ready access to specific locations within the community the agency serves.

Use of Donated Space

Another trend regarding facilities is an increase in police use of donated space in storefronts in downtown office locations, suburban shopping malls, and major food stores. This approach lowers costs, but police may unrealistically assume they are increasing their visibility in the community and providing access to local neighborhood citizens. But nothing works better than outreach that engages people where they work and live. Therefore, the police should not simply sit in a storefront office and wait for people to come to them. Additionally, most of these small adjunct locations do not have the support of computer technology, administrative personnel, or access to incident reports that citizens generally expect from the police.

Mobile police communications units, community policing offices, and command posts are used in many jurisdictions.

TECHNOLOGY AND CRIME FIGHTING: WHERE ARE WE HEADED?

Like facilities management, technology upgrading and maintenance are essential functions in any police agency. To fight crime, police need access to the best technology—whether it is a new surveillance device or high-speed Internet access and, hopefully, a computer for every desk. For this reason, we devote the following pages to a close examination of technological advances, including how police may use them to fight street crime and how new technologies are reshaping the face of crime.

Technology and Street Crime

Advances in technologies designed to combat street crime have stirred enthusiasm and interest within the policing profession and promise to give police important advantages in the future. Notable examples include surveillance kites, gunshot detection sensors, and the use of virtual reality in police lineups. While these and other technologies hold much promise, they also raise provocative questions about the role of police and the protection of citizens' privacy.

Surveillance Kites   In California, a new high-tech kite may soon take the place of police helicopters. The SkySeer is only three feet long and, when not in use, collapses into a small bag. Any officer may possess and deploy the kite within minutes. The camera in the SkySeer sends images to the officer's laptop computer. The kite flies at a speed of up to 30 miles an hour, and officers can track its position using a Global Positioning System (GPS).

A SkySeer unmanned aerial vehicle (kite) is demonstrated by members of the Los Angeles Sheriff's Department.

One of the biggest advantages of the SkySeer is that it can go where helicopters cannot, such as near trees, utility lines, and buildings. Moreover, it is silent and practically invisible. One police manager envisions using the device to find missing children or lost hikers, to track fleeing criminals or suspects, or to provide visual details of a fire zone. Touted as the wave of the future in law enforcement surveillance, the device costs about $30,000, considerably less than the $3 to $5 million that police agencies pay for helicopters (Staff, *New Scientist Tech,* 2006). Technology adapted from military-type drones may also be used to replace some civilian police aircraft.

Gunshot Detection Sensors   Another crime fighting device that is quickly coming into its own is the gunshot detection sensor. Generally, within one second after a firearm is discharged, microphones in the sensor detect the event, a camera zooms in on the location, and authorities can view the situation on a computer screen and deploy officers as needed. These sensors have been used to detect gunfire from homicide suspects almost instantly (Lisaius, 2009).

Virtual Reality   Virtual reality will be used someday to conduct police lineups. In a computer simulation, police can reconstruct the conditions under which a witness saw a suspect, including time of day or night, the scene, and other details that might aid in eyewitness accuracy. Testing has demonstrated that accuracy improves when the virtual scene containing the suspect replicates the actual conditions during the incident (Bailenson, Davies, Blascovich, Beall, McCall, & Guadagno, 2008).

The Age of the "Robocop"?   Although technological devices are excellent tools, the police officer will never be replaced. Whatever else policing might be, it is an intensely people-oriented profession that thrives on the human, personal approach. Technology proponents might fully expect a robot police officer to make its debut in the future, as in the 1987 film *Robocop,* where an injured police officer is fitted with robotics that turn him into a crime fighting machine. However, such a

Robocop (1987).

device-creature cannot replace the eyes, ears, cognitive, communication, emotional, and human relations qualities and skills of a proficient human line officer who is functioning as a self-contained ethical leadership agent.

The Question of Privacy

Advances in street-crime technology are forcing cities to strike a balance between public safety and citizen privacy, as surveillance cameras become more common and audio sensors pinpoint the exact location of sounds like gunshots. Jay Stanley of the American Civil Liberties Union (ACLU) maintains that technology use by police is "trashing" the "reasonable expectation of privacy" guaranteed by the Fourth Amendment of the Constitution. For example, just how much privacy do citizens have if their activities are being recorded by police cameras situated on telephone poles and other structures located in public places (Stanley, 2010)?

However, police officers who have experience using such technologies might disagree with this assessment. Cities including Newark, New Jersey, and Baltimore, Maryland, have invested significant time and money in state-of-the-art surveillance technology to make their downtown areas safer so they might attract more tourists and businesses. In Newark, a balance between the individual right to privacy and police use of cameras as an investigative tool has been addressed. Police cameras are not allowed to peer into private homes, and all video files are destroyed after 30 days (Ante, 2008).

The Rise of Cybercrime

Cybercrime:
criminal misconduct
perpetrated through
information
technology.

No one can predict the exact types and levels of crime that will prevail in the future, but experts suggest that many future crimes will center on computers and digital communications technology. Although street crime will never completely disappear, computers enable **cybercrime**—criminal misconduct perpetrated through information technology. Cybercrime takes many different forms and provides a virtual venue for conventional crimes such as the exploitation of children, fraud, and attacks on home computers (Schafer, 2007a). In addition, it is crossing state and national borders, and will do so even more in the coming years. All these trends will force citizens to make trade-offs between protection from cybercrime—and protection of their privacy.

Exploitation of Children   The sophistication of virtual reality raises another question: Are thoughts or behavior that would be criminal in the real world because for concern when they occur in the virtual world (Schafer, 2007a)? The answer is yes if online fantasies lead people to harm living, breathing human beings. And the spillover from virtual-world fantasies to real-world crime has already begun. Some pedophiles, for example, trawl the Internet for victims. They pose as harmless young people, befriending children through social networking sites and other virtual channels. Once they have gained a youngster's trust, some pedophiles have proposed face-to-face meetings where they have abducted, raped, and even killed their victims.

Bud Levin, professor of psychology and administration of justice at Blue Ridge Community College, theorizes that any law enforcement officer can go online at any time and, within a few minutes, open a new felony case involving child exploitation. In 2003, the number of children under age 9 in the United States was about 38 million. Levin estimates that by 2030, there will be about 46 million children who are under the age of 9, meaning about a 21 percent increase in available victims for online pedophiles if those children use the Internet. Internet crime committed against children may manifest itself as postings of unsolicited sexual content and various types of online annoying and intimidating behavior. Although the tracking of online incidents against youth is in its infancy, many experts believe that online incidents against youth are rarely reported to police (Cyber Crime Statistics, 2010; U.S. Department of Justice, Office of Juvenile Justice and Delinquency Prevention, 2009).

Women and girls display posters and tee shirts with information about a missing friend at a rally against crime in Austin, Texas.

Fraud Most experts believe that online fraud—especially against seniors—will become a major category of cybercrime in the future. For example, cybercriminals known as phishers use spam, malicious websites, e-mail messages, and instant messages to trick unsuspecting individuals into divulging sensitive information, such as their bank and credit card account numbers. According to the FBI, seniors are particularly susceptible to fraud for several reasons. For one thing, many elderly people have saved up a "nest egg"—a retirement account, a valuable piece of property—which makes a tempting target for cybercriminals. In addition, seniors tend to be trusting, and they are less likely to report a fraud than younger people are because they do not know how the reporting process works (Dickson, 2008).

In the year 2000, there were 35 million people in the United States who were 65 or older. As the baby boom generation ages, this segment of the population will grow more rapidly than any other. Approximately 7,000 boomers retire each day. By 2030, this group will number about 70 million, presenting fresh victims for cybercriminals specializing in fraud (Levin, 2003). Fraud against the elderly through the Internet may include fraudulent bank notices, enhanced telemarketing with follow-up Internet dialogue for investments, vacations, charities, and get-rich schemes (Montaldo, 2010). Gathering valid statistical data regarding the number of Internet crimes committed against elderly individuals is difficult because some victims are reluctant to report that they have been subjected to these types of scams. However, with respect to online fraud, the Internet Crime Complaint Center (2010) reported that the number of complaints has exploded from approximately 17,000 in the year 2000, to approximately 340,000 in 2009. Annual dollar loss grew from approximately $18 million in 2001 to about $.5 billion in 2009 (Cyber Crime Statistics, 2010).

Attacks on Home Computers Cybercriminals are multiplying rapidly, and evidence suggests that attacks on home computers will increase in the coming years. The net-centric home today contains many vulnerable devices, such as home

A phishing e-mail attempting to trick unsuspecting individuals into divulging personal information.

security systems, IP phones, and the storage of financial forms such as those generated by personal-income-tax software programs. This represents a rich environment for cybercriminals to target and exploit.

Online threats to vulnerable consumers take many forms, including e-mail cons (phishing); viruses, worms, and other infections; spyware; and botnets. All of these are unlawful invasions, and they affect numerous home and business computers. Criminals use the large number of computers to send huge volumes of messages to overwhelm and cripple the targeted computers. In a home user study conducted by the National Cyber Security Alliance, Symantec, & Zogby International (2009), about one-quarter of the respondents felt that their home computer systems were secure from Internet infections. However, between 30 and 40 percent of respondents stated they store bank and tax information on their computers, with over 50 percent indicating that they have never learned how to secure their home computer systems. Although consumers appear to have a peripheral awareness of computer security threats, computer attacks from perpetrators occur over 70 percent of the time through e-mail intrusions and approximately 35 percent via websites (Cyber Crime Statistics, 2010).

Cross-Border Cybercrime   Today's criminals are more mobile than ever, and, with the right technology, they can invade someone else's private life without doing so physically. This means that many crimes, including identity theft, are now affecting people beyond the jurisdiction where the criminal is located. A person living in one state can steal from others residing in another state or country thousands of miles away.

This situation will make law enforcement cooperation across jurisdictional lines crucial in the future. Those in policing must learn to set aside old prejudices against working with other law enforcement entities. If police refuse to cooperate locally, regionally, nationally, and globally, criminals will operate without much fear of apprehension and punishment. However, if agencies at all levels of law enforcement and in all locations collaborate more effectively today, they will open the door to law enforcement cooperation on an international scale (International Association of Chiefs of Police, 1999).

Levin highlights several specific areas of concern when it comes to cross-border cybercrime. Many U.S. software developers are increasingly outsourcing development of their products to other nations. This will create vulnerabilities for U.S. computer users because of the difficulty of prosecuting someone who is located in another country but commits a crime against a U.S. citizen. Investigators must possess and demonstrate different knowledge and skills to combat this kind of crime—including broad-based knowledge of other nations and their cultures, as well as the ability to communicate easily with people in other countries. Effective communication is a skill learned and practiced by the self-contained ethical leadership agent.

Trade-Offs between Protection and Privacy   No matter how tech-savvy police and justice systems become, cybercriminals are not all that different from conventional criminals. Police will not be able to crush cybercrime any more than they have been able to crush gang-related crimes and, unfortunately, the more cybercriminals police prosecute, the more clogged the justice system will become. The wheels of justice will turn even more slowly as prosecutors, defense attorneys, and judges struggle to increase their knowledge of this kind of crime.

One of the biggest obstacles to fighting cybercrime will be the average person's resistance to investigative practices. Just as the use of surveillance technologies has raised questions about citizens' privacy, the notion that police should combat cybercrime through access to people's computers has many citizens asking where the line between protection and privacy should go. The ongoing conflict between security and U.S. citizens' right to privacy will not be an easy one to resolve. And unfortunately, it enables cybercriminals to flourish. It fragments the fight against cybercriminals because citizens are not yet ready to give up some privacy in return for some protection. Just as some people have objected to the idea that police cameras may be watching them as they go about their daily routines, they will likely also resist having officers gain ready access to their computers.

However, all is not lost. If experts are correct in their forecasts, cybercrime units will play a critical role in tomorrow's police agency. Why? Cybercrimes cross all department divisions: sex crimes, fraud, identity theft, stalking, and intellectual property crime, to name just a few. Divisional lines must blur if a police agency hopes to tackle cybercrime with any effectiveness. Cybercrimes also cross jurisdictional lines, further complicating the challenge. But while cybercriminals will eventually become no more remarkable than pickpockets as police gain proficiency in prosecuting them, they will continue to hone their sophistication—and police will need to keep pace (Levin, 2003).

summary

- **Ethics and Professionalism: Will Police Be Trusted?** Unethical behavior on the part of police has eroded the public's trust. To prevent further erosion in the future and to rebuild trust, police executives must ensure that all personnel understand and adhere to ethical standards. A lowering of hiring standards may make it more challenging to retain or restore the public's trust. The increased ease with which police misconduct can be captured on video by citizens has made the issue of ethics and professionalism more urgent than ever. As reinforced throughout this book, true leadership does not exist without courageous ethical behavior to accompany it.

- **The Challenges of Counterterrorism and Homeland Security: What Role Will Police Play?** Police will need to help combat terrorism regardless of its source (foreign or domestic). Understanding how individuals become radicalized and how terrorist groups organize themselves will help, as will leveraging police officers' connections with and deep knowledge of local communities. To adopt an all-hazards approach, those leading homeland security efforts will face a challenge in coordinating local police agencies across the nation. Meanwhile, fulfilling mandates to contribute to homeland security efforts will force citizens and police to make trade-offs in police services.

- **Budgeting: Can Police Do Even More—with Even Less?** As outsourcing of police services increases, the public may begin asking what the purpose of police should be. Ever-tighter budget constraints may prompt police to involve citizens more in ensuring their own safety—a trend that presents benefits and costs. To combat budget constraints, police will need to formulate creative strategies and think like businesspeople.

- **Assessment and Evaluation: Will Police Grade Themselves on the Right Curve?** To excel in the coming years, police must adopt new approaches to organizational and individual performance assessment and evaluation. These include demonstrating greater accountability to citizens, drawing on the public's suggestions for performance improvement, and demanding ethical leadership skills from every officer, regardless of rank.

- **Hiring and Training: How Will Police Build an Effective Workforce?** Police must work harder to recruit a diverse and well-educated workforce, as well as taking advantage of promising new approaches to training, such as cross-training and virtual academies.

- **Communication: Will a Wider Array of Constituents Require Broader Skills?** To communicate effectively with an ever-expanding range of constituents, police will need to strengthen their communication skills, including mastering the art of constructive engagement and constructive confrontation.

- **Police Leadership: Can Boundaries Expand?** Police leaders of the future must expand their boundaries in terms of how they think and work—including embracing the virtual world, broadening their notions of how management should operate, and challenging current practices within their agency. Every officer and civilian employee of an agency should function as a courageous self-contained ethical leadership agent.

- **Change Leadership: What Model Should Police Use?** Driving needed change is a vital aspect of leadership in a police agency and will become more critical in the future as the pace of change accelerates. Police administrators can lead change effectively by crafting and communicating a compelling vision of how a proposed change will benefit the agency and community, and by blending complementary change-leadership models, including the Lewin basic change model, the Weisbord six-box model, and the Kotter strategic change model.

- **Police Unions: Will They Survive?** The question of whether labor unions have served their purpose has stirred debate. Meanwhile, unions as a group have come under fire, as heavily unionized industries experience massive layoffs. Police unions can survive if they adapt to the changing circumstances surrounding employment in the United States. In particular, they must partner more constructively with management and the community at large, as well as support educational opportunities for members.

- **Facilities Management: What Will It Look Like in the Future?** Trends in police facilities management—including consolidation of facilities, subdivision of facilities, and use of donated space—will present both advantages and disadvantages for police and the communities they serve in the future. To meet the conflicting needs of reducing expenses and improving community service, police administrators will need to understand the pros and cons of these trends and make intelligent trade-offs.

- **Technology and Crime Fighting: Where Are We Headed?** Technological advances such as surveillance kites, gunshot detection sensors, and virtual reality promise to strengthen police officers' ability to fight street crime. However, some of these technologies have raised questions about whether citizens' privacy is being put at risk. Meanwhile, advances in information technology have spawned the rise of cybercrime, which can take many forms including exploitation of children, fraud (especially against elderly citizens), and attacks on home computers. As cybercrime begins crossing more and more state, regional, and national borders, police will need to collaborate with law enforcement organizations across jurisdictions and geographical boundaries to combat this form of crime. Moreover, efforts to fight cybercrime through information technology will force citizens to decide where the line between cyberprotection and cyberprivacy should be located.

key terms

constructive engagement
counterterrorism
cybercrime
futuristics
knowledge management
radicalization
virtual reality

discussion questions

1. Are ethical standards for police officers changing? If so, how? How might future standards jeopardize police agencies' efforts to hire ethical police officers? What is the link between ethics and leadership?

2. What unique strengths do local police possess that enable them to play a valuable role in counterterrorism and homeland security efforts? In what respects might local police combat radicalization of terrorists in their area? If police are channeling more resources into counterterrorism and homeland security, what might this mean for other services they provide their local communities?

3. What are the advantages and disadvantages presented by outsourcing of police services? If you were responsible for preparing this year's budget for a police agency, how would you deal with the challenge of providing better services with fewer resources?

4. What innovative approaches might a police agency use to assess and evaluate its own overall performance as an organization? If you were a police supervisor deciding whether to promote an officer who is under your command, what criteria would you consider in making your decision?

5. What strategies do you think would best enable a police agency to hire a diverse workforce and bring more officers onboard who have a higher level of education? What innovative training approaches would you suggest to help a police agency reduce costs and provide better community service?

6. In what respects have you demonstrated constructive engagement and constructive confrontation with others? How might you strengthen these communication skills?

7. What is a courageous self-contained ethical leadership agent? In your view, which of the Recommendations for Current and Future Police Executives provided by the International Association of Chiefs of Police will be *most* relevant for tomorrow's police administrator? Explain the rationale behind your choices.

8. Identify a change (for example, shifting demographics, technological advances, trends in crime) that you believe will have especially important ramifications for policing in the future. What opportunities does the change objective present to the agency and the community? What challenges does it present? Assuming you are the agency manager, describe the change initiative you are proposing, the anticipated opportunities you are attempting to seize, and the threats or challenges you are attempting to mitigate. What actions would you take to ensure that the change initiative you have proposed is successfully executed in your agency?

9. In your view, do police labor unions still have a valuable role to play? Why or why not?

10. Of the trends in police facilities management discussed in this chapter, which strike you as most promising? Most troubling? Why?

11. Where do you stand on the question of whether new technologies for fighting street crime violate citizens' privacy? Where do you stand on the question of whether such technologies will someday make police officers obsolete? Explain the reasoning behind your responses to both of these questions.

12. Imagine that you have just been promoted to head the cybercrime division in a police agency. What forms of cybercrime do you think would be most important to combat? Why? What strategies and tactics would you suggest for fighting these forms of cybercrime?

WHAT WOULD YOU DO?

"It's for Your Own Good": The Proliferation of Safety Laws

For some time now, federal, state, and municipal legislatures have proposed and passed laws making certain actions illegal because they harm the public good. For instance, every state now requires people to wear safety belts while driving or riding in an automobile and to position infant and children's car seats in a specific configuration to ensure safety. Thanks to the rising number of accidents in which people have been talking on a cell phone or texting on a handheld device while driving, lawmakers in many states have also made these behaviors illegal.

Those who write and pass the laws would no doubt defend these laws as necessary for citizens' health and well-being. Detractors argue that such laws are bringing us closer to a police state. Citizens over age 50 might well point out that they survived childhood without ever wearing a bicycle helmet, knee pads, or elbow pads.

(continued)

Consider the trends in passage of federal, state, and municipal laws designed to safeguard various aspects of the public good:

2007

- *California:* Lawmakers ban sales of carbonated soft drinks on school campuses during school hours and put new limits on the sugar and fat content in school lunches.
- *South Dakota:* Legislature requires repeat drunk drivers to check in at jails twice daily for blood-alcohol testing.
- *Georgia and Mississippi:* Hospitals and clinics serving women who seek to abort their fetuses must show women an ultrasound of the fetus and force the women to listen to the heartbeat of the fetus before proceeding with the abortion.

2008

- *Canton, Ohio:* Residents who neglect their lawns, allowing high grass and weeds to grow unabated, face a fine of up to $250 and up to 30 days in jail. This law was later amended to include the removal of dead trees and the pruning of branches that might prove hazardous to people on sidewalks and streets.

2009

- *Illinois:* First-time Driving Under the Influence (DUI) offenders must install an *ignition interlock device* in their cars. If they want to drive the car, they must exhale into the device so their blood-alcohol content (BAC) can be tested. If the device detects alcohol in the person's breath, the vehicle cannot be started.

2010

- *Texas:* Teenagers who use a tanning salon must be accompanied by an adult.
- *Ohio:* Anyone driving a vehicle without headlights illuminated during a snowfall may be fined as much as $150.
- *California:* Media members may incur civil penalties up to $50,000 if they buy or sell unlawfully obtained photos and/or videos.

1. What are the benefits of the so-called public-good laws at the federal, state, and municipal levels?

2. In your view, what disadvantages do public-good laws pose for police? For citizens?

3. If you were a police chief with concerns about a proliferation of public-good legislation, how would you communicate your concerns to lawmakers and citizens? How would you develop a case for limiting or expanding such laws?

Adams, T. F. (2007). *Police field operations* (7th ed.). Upper Saddle River, NJ: Pearson Prentice Hall.

Adler, N. J. (2007). *International dimensions of organizational behavior* (5th ed.). Cincinnati, OH: Cengage.

Adler, R. B., & Proctor, R. F. (2011). *Looking out/looking in* (13th ed.). Belmont, CA: Thomson Wadsworth.

Aitchison, W. (2004). *The rights of law enforcement officers* (5th ed.). Portland, OR: Labor Relations Information Systems in reference to *Hillsdale PBA v. Borough of Hillsdale,* 644A 2d 564 (N.J. 1994).

Alderfer, C. P. (1972). *Existence, relatedness and growth: Human needs in organizational settings.* New York: Free Press.

All About Performance. (2005). *Assessment centers.* Retrieved May 7, 2008, from http://www.allaboutperformance.biz/assessment.html

Allen, J. M., & Sawhney, R. (2010). *Administration and management in criminal justice: A service quality approach.* Thousand Oaks, CA: Sage.

AME Info. (2007). *Ernst & Young's Middle East human capital practices survey 2006–2007 reveals shortfall in leadership and succession planning in private sector organizations.* Retrieved May 2, 2008, from http://www.ameinfo.com/119281.html

American Heritage Dictionary—Dictionary of Business Terms. (2009). Indirect liability. Retrieved March 2, 2010, from http://www.yourdictionary.com/business/indirect-liability

American Heritage Dictionary of the English Language (4th ed). (2005a). Chain of command. Retrieved August 25, 2009, from http://www.ask.com/web?q=dictionary%3A+chain+of+command&content=ahdict%7C650

American Heritage Dictionary of the English Language (4th ed.). (2005b). Discipline. Retrieved May 7, 2008, from http://www.ask.com/web?qrsc=2417&o=0&1=dir&q=dictionary%3Adiscipline

American Heritage Dictionary of the English Language (4th ed.). (2005c). Incentive. Retrieved May 29, 2009, from http://www.ask.com/web?q=dictionary:incentives&qsrc=8&content=ahdict\128420

American Society for Quality. (2008). *Quality assurance and quality control.* Retrieved October 20, 2008, from http://www.asq.org/learn-about-quality/quality-assurance-quality-control/overview/overview.html

Amnesty International USA. (2009). *Racial profiling.* Retrieved October 20, 2009, from http://www.AmnestyUSA.org

Anderson, T. D. (2006). *Every officer is a leader: Coaching leadership, learning and performance in justice, public safety, and security organizations.* Victoria, British Columbia, Canada: Trafford.

Anderson, T. D., & King, D. (1996a). *Managerial leadership training needs assessment in justice and public safety.* New Westminster, British Columbia, Canada: Justice Institute of British Columbia.

Anderson, T. D., & King, D. (1996b). *Police supervisory leadership training needs assessment.* New Westminster, British Columbia, Canada: Justice Institute of British Columbia.

Angelfire.com. (2009). *Intuition.* Retrieved February 22, 2009, from http://www.angelfire.com/hi/TheSeer/intuition.html

Ante, S. E. (2008, August 25). Newark and the future of crime fighting. *Bloomberg Business Week.* Retrieved January 26, 2010, from http://businessweek.com/print/technology/content/aug2008/tc20080822_240216.htm

Atkinson, P. Political correctness. (2009). Retrieved November 10, 2009, from http://www.ourcivilization.com/pc.htm

Aveni, T. J. (1999). Shift work and officer survival. *S&W Academy Newsletter,* No. 31. Retrieved December 18, 2009, from http://www.theppsc.org/Staff_Views/Avenue/Shift-Survival.htm

Ayton-Shenker, D. (1995). *The challenge of human rights and cultural diversity.* Retrieved January 29, 2010, from http://www.un.org/rights/idpil627e.htm

Bailenson, J. N., Davies, A., Blascovich, J., Beall, A. C., McCall, C., & Guadagno, R. E. (2008). The effects of witness viewpoint distance, angle, and choice on eyewitness accuracy in police lineups conducted in immersive virtual environments. *Presence, 17,* 242–255.

Bair, B. (2008, May). Police outsourcing plan rejected. *The Ledger.* Retrieved January 4, 2010, from http://www.theledger.com

Baker, A. (2006, January 30). Police command shake-up elevates counterterrorism. *New York Times,* pp. A1–A3.

Baker, T. E. (2006). *Effective police leadership: Moving beyond management* (2nd ed.). Flushing, NY: Looseleaf Law Publications.

Baker, T. E. (2009). *Intelligence-led policing: Leadership, strategies & tactics.* Flushing, NY: Looseleaf Law Publications.

Bandics, G. R. (1997, June). Cross-training: A step toward the future—police training. *The FBI Law Enforcement Bulletin.* Retrieved April 30, 2010, from http://findarticles.com/p/articles/mi_m2194/i5_n6_v66/ai_202130731

Barron's Educational Services Inc. (2007). *Chain of command.* Retrieved August 25, 2009, from http://www.allbusiness.com/glossaries.chain-command/4960860-1.html

Bass, B. M. (1981). *Stogdill's handbook of leadership: A survey of theory and research.* New York: Free Press.

Bass, B. M. (1990). *Handbook of leadership.* New York: Free Press.

Beauchamp, T. L., Bowie, N. E., & Arnold, D. (2009). *Ethical theory and business* (8th ed). Englewood Cliffs, NJ: Prentice Hall.

Behm, D. (2009, October). *Judge won't block police outsourcing; Pewaukee considers sheriff deal Monday. Milwaukee Journal Sentinel (Wisconsin).* Retrieved January 4, 2010, from http://www.Allbusiness.com/government/government-bodies-offices-regional/13354345-1.htm

Bennett, W. J. (1993). *The book of virtues.* New York: Simon & Schuster.

Bennett, W. W., & Hess, K. M. (2007). *Management and supervision in law enforcement* (5th ed.). Belmont, CA: Thomson Wadsworth.

Bennis, W. G. (1961, January). Revisionist theory of leadership. *Harvard Business Review, 31*(1), 26–36, 146–150.

Bennis, W. G. (1993). Managing the dream: Leadership in the 21st century. In W. E. Rosenbach & R. L. Taylor (Eds.), *Contemporary issues in leadership* (3rd ed., pp. 213–218). Boulder, CO: Westview Press.

Bernard, L. L. (1926). *An introduction to social psychology.* New York: Holt.

Bernstein, N. (15, April 2009). Study says police misuse immigration inquiry rule. *New York Times.* Retrieved July 13, 2009, from http://www.NYTimes.com/2009/04/150NYregion/15immigration.html

Bernstein, N. M. (2010). *Norris-Laguardia Act (1932).* Retrieved February 21, 2010, from http://www.enotes.com/major-acts-congress/norris-laguardia-act

Blake, R. R., & Mouton, J. S. (1965). A 9.9 approach for increasing organizational productivity. In E. H. Schein & W. G. Bennis (Eds.), *Personal and organizational change through group methods* (pp. 169–183). New York: Wiley.

Blanchard, K., & Johnson, S. (1982). *The one-minute manager.* New York: William Morrow.

Bohm, R. M., & Haley, K. N. (2005). *Introduction to criminal justice* (4th ed.). New York: McGraw-Hill.

Boninfante, L. (2004, December 9). *Virtual academy at public safety training center: County unveils new virtual academy.* Retrieved April 30, 2010, from http://www.co.cape-may.nj.us/Cit-e-Access/news/archnews.cfm?NID=3246&TID=5&jump2=0

Book, E., & Schneider, R. (2010, January). Crime prevention through environmental design: CPTED 40 years later. *Police Chief, 77*(1), 34–36.

Bossidy, L., & Charan, R. (2002). *Execution: The discipline of getting things done.* New York: Crown Random House.

Bostrom, M. D. (2005). *The influence of higher education on police officer work habits.* Retrieved March 16, 2009, from http://policechiefmagazine.org/magazine/index.cfm?fuseaction=display_arch&article_id=722&issue

Bostrom, R. P., Anson, R., & Clawson, V. K. (1993). Group facilitation and group support systems. In L. M. Jessup & J. S. Valacich (Eds.), *Gmul! Support systems: New perspectives* (pp. 146–168). New York: Macmillan.

Braga, A. A. (2008). Police enforcement strategies to prevent crime in hot spot areas. *Crime Prevention Research Review No. 2.* Washington, DC: U.S. Department of Justice, Office of Community Oriented Policing Services.

Brassard, M., & Ritter, D. (1995). *The memory jogger II: A pocket guide of tools for continuous improvement & effective planning.* Methuen, MA: Goal/QPC.

Brigham, E. F., & Ehrhardt, M. C. (2003). *Financial management: Theory and practice* (11th ed.). Mason, OH: Thomson South-Western.

Brigham, E. F., & Ehrhardt, M. C. (2005). *Financial management: Theory and practice* (12th ed.). Mason, OH: Thomson South-Western.

Bryant, S. (2010). *Chicago pd comes up with foolproof plan to hire more minorities and keep the federal government off their back?* Retrieved February 27, 2010, from http://pafop38.com/2010/01/07/chicago-pd-comes-up-with-fool-proof-plan-to-hire-more-minorities

Bryson, J. M. (2004). *Strategic planning for public and non-profit organizations: A guide to strengthening and sustaining organizational achievement.* San Francisco: Jossey-Bass.

Bryson, J. M., & Alston, F. K. (2005). *Creating and implementing your strategic plan: A workbook for public and nonprofit organizations* (2nd ed.). Hoboken, NJ: Wiley.

Buckingham, M., & Clifton, D. O. (2001). *Now, discover your strengths.* New York: Free Press/Simon & Schuster.

Burke, K. (2009). *Meet and confer ordinance.* Retrieved March 10, 2010, from http://www.flagstaff.az.gov/DocumentView.aspx?DID=10208

Burns, J. M. (1978). *Leadership.* New York: Harper & Row.

Burress, G. W., Giblin, M. J., & Schafer, J. A. (2010, February). Threatened globally, acting locally: Modeling law enforcement homeland security practices. *Justice Quarterly, 27*(1), 77–101.

Business Dictionary. (2007). Customer. Retrieved July 22, 2008, from http://www.businessdictionary.com/definition/customer.html

Cahn, S. (1995). *Stephen Cahn on the history of affirmative action.* Retrieved February 21, 2010, from http://aad.english.ucsb.edu/docs/Cahn.html

California Commission on Peace Officer Standards and Training. (1976). *The impact of social trends on crime and criminal justice.* Cincinnati, OH: Anderson and Davis.

California Emergency Management Agency. (2007). *Be smart. Be responsible. Be prepared. Get ready.* Retrieved February 12, 2010, from http:/www.oes.ca.gov

California Commission on Peace Officer Standards and Training. (2009). *Regular peace officer basic course.* Sacramento, CA: Commission on Peace Officer Standards and Training.

California State Department of Justice, Office of the Attorney General. (1996). *Community oriented policing and problem solving: Definitions and principles.* Sacramento, CA: Commission on Peace Officer Standards and Training.

Casto, M. L. (2009). *Growth and leadership: What is intuition and how do I use it?* Retrieved February 22, 2009, from http://www.businessknowhow.com/manage/intuition.htm

Centers for Disease Control and Prevention. (2006). Helicobacter pylori and peptic ulcer disease: Have a stressful job? Retrieved August 5, 2009, from http://www.cdc.gov/ulcer/myth.htm

Champion, D. H., Sr., & Hooper, M. K. (2003). *Introduction to American policing.* New York: McGraw-Hill.

Champoux, J. E. (2000). *Organizational behavior: Using film to visualize principles and practices.* Cincinnati, OH: Thomson South-Western.

Charisma. (n.d.). Retrieved July 4, 2010, from http://cbae.nmsu.edu/~dboje/teaching/338/charisma.htm

Cheeseman, H. R. (2009). *Business law* (7th ed.). Upper Saddle River, NJ: Pearson Prentice Hall.

Citizens Information Board. (1999). *Managing volunteers: A good practice guide.* Retrieved July 16, 2008, from http://www.citiznsinformationboard.ie/publications/voluntary_sector/managing_volunteers/index.html

City of Los Angeles. (2003). *Training the 21st century police officer.* Santa Monica, CA: RAND Public Safety and Justice.

City of Scottsdale. (2007, December). *Arizona police facilities manager.* Retrieved January 25, 2010, from http://www.scottsdaleaz.gov/assets/documents/jobs/job_desc/2089_1.PDF

City of Tacoma. (2009, September 25). *Condition assessment of city owned buildings: Police department facilities.* Meng Analysis. Retrieved January 22, 2010, from http://cms.cityoftacoma.org/CRO/TacomaPoliceDepartment.pdf

City of West Palm Beach. (2001, October). *Class description police facilities supervisor.* Retrieved September 16, 2009, from http://www.wpb.org

Clark, K. E., & Clark, M. B. (1996). *Choosing to lead* (2nd ed.). Greensboro, NC: Center for Creative Leadership.

Clarke, R. V. (2002). *Burglary of retail establishments: Problem-oriented guides for police series no. 15.* Washington, DC: U.S. Department of Justice, Office of Community Oriented Policing Services.

Coffey, A. (1990). *Law enforcement: A human relations approach.* Englewood Cliffs, NJ: Prentice Hall.

Coleman, P. (2007). *New ideas for solving police chief recruitment crisis.* Retrieved October 20, 2009, from http:www.cacities.org

Collins, J. (2001). *Good to great: Why some companies make leaps and others don't.* New York: Harper Business.

Collins, J. (2002). *Library discussion guide.* Retrieved March 1, 2005, from http://www.jimcollins.com/lib/discussion.html

Collins, J. (2005). *Good to great and the social sectors.* Boulder, CO: Author.

Colorado Municipal League. (1996). *Purchasing and bidding: Purchasing procedures, policies, and manuals; municipal purchasing.* Retrieved August 12, 2010, from http://www.mrsc.org/Subjects/PubWorks/pb/purchasing.aspx

Columbia Electronic Encyclopedia (6th ed.). (2007a). *Landrum-Griffin Act.* Retrieved February 21, 2010, from http://www.infoplease.com/ce6/bus/A0820769.html

Columbia Electronic Encyclopedia (6th ed.). (2007b). *Taft-Hartley Labor Act.* Retrieved February 21, 2010, from http://www.infoplease.com/ce6/bus/A0847620.html

Commission on Accreditation for Law Enforcement Agencies. (2008). *Accreditationworks!* Retrieved June 25, 2010, from http://www.calea.org

Concepts of leadership. (2010). Retrieved July 4, 2010, from http://NWlink.com/~donclark/leader/leadcon.htm

Cooke, J. (2003, February). Changing management's ways. *Training,* pp. 14–15.

Cordner, G. W., & Scarborough, K. E. (2007). *Police administration* (6th ed.). New Providence, NJ: Matthew Bender.

Couper, D. C., & Lobitz, S. H. (1991). *Quality policing: The Madison experience.* Washington, DC: Police Executive Research Forum.

Covey, S. R. (1991). *Principle-centered leadership.* New York: Free Press.

CPTED Watch. (2008). *CPTED crime prevention.* Retrieved December 15, 2008, from http://www.cpted-watch.com

Crank, J. P. (2004). *Understanding police culture* (2nd ed.). Cincinnati, OH: Anderson.

Cronkhite, C. (1995, October–November). An eclectic approach to policing: Applying past principles to community policing. *CJ (Criminal Justice) in the Americas, 8*(5), 9–11.

Crowder, W. S. (1998). *Law enforcement accreditation: Has it professionalized American law enforcement?* Unpublished doctoral dissertation. Ann Arbor, MI: University Microfilms Dissertation Services.

Cyber Crime Statistics. (2010). *Computer forensics recruiter.com.* Retrieved June 1, 2010, from http://www/computer-forensics-recruiter.com-home-cyber_crime_statistics.html

Dabney, D. (2010, February). Observations regarding key operational realities in a CompStat model of policing. *Justice Quarterly, 27*(1), 28–51.

Dator, J. (1999). *Bright future for unions?* Retrieved May 5, 2010, from http://www.hawaii.edu/dator/unions/brightfut.html

Davis, J. J. (1994). *Stress Management Program Development for the Rochester, New York Police Department.* Rochester Police Department, Rochester, NY.

Davis, J. J. (2006). *Leadership survival techniques in the police organization.* Unpublished master's thesis, Roberts Wesleyan College, Rochester, NY.

Davis, J. J., & Colaprete, F. A. (2005). *Achieving organizational excellence in policing: Model research and development.* Academy of Criminal Justice Sciences Panel Presentation, Chicago, IL.

Davis, J. J., Givens, D., Perez, A., Bialaszewski, M., & Williams, K. (2004). *Achieving organizational excellence.* Unpublished professional research study, St. John Fisher College, Rochester, NY.

Davis, J. J., & Prawel, G. J. (2008). *Transformational leadership in criminal justice/public safety: Transitioning from good management to great leadership.* Cincinnati, OH: Academy of Criminal Justice Sciences.

Davis, J. J., & Wildman, L. R. (2007). *Personal and organizational effectiveness training.* Rochester, NY: Authors.

Davis, J. J., & Wildman, L. (2009). *Constructive engagement.* Rochester, New York: Self-Published Instructional Guides.

Decision-making-confidence.com. (2008). *What is intuition?* Retrieved February 22, 2009, from http://www.decision-making-confidence.com/what-is-intuition.html

de Janasz, S. C., Dowd, K. O., & Schneider, B. Z. (2006). *Interpersonal skills in organizations* (2nd ed.). New York: McGraw-Hill Irwin.

deKoning, G. M. J. (2005). *Building your "bench strength": Part 1. How the best organizations select and develop tomorrow's leaders.* Retrieved June 28, 2010, from http://govleaders.org/gallup_bench_strength1.htm

Delattre, E. (1989). *Character and cops: Ethics in policing.* Lanham, MD: University Press of America.

Delattre, E. J., & Behan, C. J. (2003). Practical ideals for managing in the new millennium. In W. A. Geller and D. W. Stephens (Eds.),

Local government police management (4th ed., pp. 500–614). Washington, DC: International City/County Management Association.

del Carmen, R. V. (1989). Civil liabilities of police supervisors. *American Journal of Police, 8*(1), 107–136.

Delderfield, E. R. (1978). *Kings and queens of England.* New York: Weathervane Books.

DeLord, R. G., & Sanders, J. (2006). *Navigating the dangerous waters in the real world of police labor-management relations: Practical and principled solutions for implementing change, making reforms, and handling crisis for police managers and police union leaders.* U.S. Department of Justice. Retrieved March 5, 2010, from http://www.cops.usdoj.gov/files/RIC/Publications/e07063417.pdf

Derrick, K. S. (2009). *Management vs. supervisors vs. leadership.* Retrieved February 22, 2010, from http://www.slideshare.net

Dickson, E. (2008). *FBI reports scams against senior citizens are growing.* Retrieved August 13, 2010, from http://www.bloggernews.net/115117

Dossett, J. C. (2004). *Budgets and financial management in special libraries.* Retrieved April 9, 2008, from http://www.libsci.sc.edu

Downton, J. V. (1973). *Rebel leadership: Commitment and charisma in the revolutionary process.* New York: Free Press.

Durant, W. (1966). *The life of Greece.* New York: Simon and Schuster.

Dwyer, K. P. (2008). *How to win at office politics.* BNET Crash Course. Retrieved August 12, 2009, from http://www.bnet.com/2403-13070_23-93243.html

Eastman Kodak Company. (1995). *Total quality management: Quality coordinator's guide.* Rochester, NY: Author.

Ellis-Christensen, T. (2003). *What is a warranty?* Retrieved January 22, 2009, from http://wisegeek.com/what-is-a-warranty.htm

eNotes. (2010). *The Landrum-Griffin Act targets union corruption.* Retrieved February 21, 2010, from http://www.enotes.com

Esserman, D. (2005, Winter). Community policing in Providence: Combating crime and fear. *Communities and Banking,* pp. 20–23. Retrieved July 3, 2010, from http://www.bos.frb.org/commdev/c&b/2005/winter.Esserman.pdf

Estey, J. G. (2005, April). Communication critical to law enforcement. *Police Chief, 72*(3), 6.

Eterno, J. A., & Silverman, E. B. (2010). *Unveiling Compstat.* Retrieved March 4, 2010, from http://unveilingnypdcompstat.blogstoto.com

Etheridge, J. (2008). *Oswego police patrol officers join union. Metropolitan Alliance of Police to bargain collectively for department's 40 officers.* Retrieved March 8, 2010, from http://www.ledgersentinel.com

Examination announcement Montgomery County consortium of communities examination—police officer. Retrieved August 13, 2009, from http://abingtonpd.org

Facts for consumers: Service contracts. (2009, April 24). Federal Trade Commission. Retrieved January 22, 2010, from http://www.ftc.gov

Faherty, C. (2007). *NYPD diversity-hire leader returns to oversee training.* Retrieved February 27, 2010, from http://www.NYSun.com/New-York/nypd-diversity-hire-leader-returns-to-oversee/60586

Farrow, J. (2003). Citizen oversight of law enforcement: Challenge and opportunity. *Police Chief, 70*(10), 22–29.

Federal response to Hurricane Katrina: Lessons learned. (2006, February 23). Retrieved February 9, 2010, from www.au.af.mil/au/awc/awcgate/whitehouse/katrina/katrina-lesns-chaps.pdf

Fiedler, F. E. (1967). *A theory of leadership effectiveness.* New York: McGraw-Hill.

Fishel, J., Gabbidon, S. L., & Hummer, D. (2007). A quantitative analysis of wrongful death lawsuits involving police officers in the United States. *Police Quarterly, 10,* 455. Retrieved February 6, 2010, from http://pqx.sagepub.com

Fournies, F. F. (2007). *Why employees don't do what they're supposed to and what you can do about it* (2nd ed.). New York: McGraw-Hill.

Freedom of Information Act/Privacy Act Team. (2010). *What is the privacy act?* USDA Forest Service. Retrieved March 13, 2010, from http://www.fs.fed.us/im/foia/pa.htm

Friedmann, R. R. (2006). *University perspective: The policing profession in 2050.* Retrieved March 16, 2009, from http://policechiefmagazine.org/magazine/index.cfm?fuseaction=display_arch&article_id=958&issue_id=82006

Fridell, L. A. (2004). *By the numbers: A guide for analyzing race data from vehicle stops.* Retrieved from http://policeforum.org/library.asp?MENU=229

Frost, P. J. (2003). *Emotions in the workplace and the important role of toxin handlers.* London, Ontario, Canada: Ivey Publishing, IVEY Management Services.

Gaines, L. K., & Miller, R. L. (2005). *Criminal justice in action* (3rd ed.). Belmont, CA: Wadsworth/Thomson Learning.

Gaines, L. K., Worrall, J. L., Southerland, M. D., & Angell, J. E. (2003). *Police administration* (2nd ed.). New York: McGraw-Hill.

Garner, G. W. (2005, June). Putting on an effective news conference. *Law and Order,* pp. 28–34.

Garrison, R. H., Noreen, E. W., & Brewer, P. C. (2006). *Managerial accounting* (11th ed.) New York: McGraw-Hill Irwin.

Gary, C. (2003, December). How to . . . cope with the press. *Police,* pp. 24–29.

Gau, J. M., & Brunson, R. K. (2010, April). Procedural justice and order maintenance policing: A study of inner-city young men's perceptions of police legitimacy. *Justice Quarterly, 27*(2), 255–279.

Gee, R. (2005). *Managing change.* Second Avenue Tools. Organizational Management, MSM510. Rochester, NY: Roberts Wesleyan College.

Geier, J. (2002). *RF site survey steps.* Retrieved January 25, 2010, from http://www.wi-fiplanet.com/tutorials/article.php/1116311

George, S., & Weimerskirch, W. (1998). *Total quality management: Strategies and techniques proven at today's most successful companies* (2nd ed.). New York: Wiley.

Githens, S. (1991). *Men and women in conversation: An analysis of gender styles in language.* Retrieved July 24, 2009, from http://www9.georgetown.edu/faculty/bassr/githens/tannen.htm

Goldstein, H. (1977). *Policing in a free society.* Cambridge, MA: Ballinger.

Goldstein, H. (1990). *Problem-oriented policing.* New York: McGraw-Hill.

Goldstein, H. (2001, December 7). Address. Speech presented to the annual International Problem-Oriented Policing Conference, San Diego, CA.

Goleman, D., Boyatzis, R., & McKee, A. (2002). *Primal leadership: Realizing the power of emotional intelligence.* Boston: Harvard Business School Press.

Gorham, R. (2010). *Leadership motivation: Three pillars for success.* Retrieved March 2, 2010, from http://www.leadership-tools.com/leadership-motivation.html

Governor's Office of Emergency Services. (2007). *Standardized emergency management system (SEMS) guidelines.* Retrieved December 17, 2008, from http://www.oes.ca.gov/Operational/OESHome.nsf/PDF/SEMS%20Guidelines/$file/1INTRO_1.pdf

Graen, G. B., & Uhl-Bien, M. (1995, Spring). Relationship-based approach to leadership: Development of leader-exchange (LMX) theory of leadership over 25 years: Applying a multi-level multi-domain perspective. *Leadership Quarterly, 6*(2), 219–247.

Gravenkemper, S. (2008). *Leadership development: A new business imperative.* Retrieved May 2, 2008, from http://www.plantemoran.com/perspectives/articles/Pages/leadership-development-a-new-imperative.aspx

Graziano, L., Schuck, A., & Martin, C. (2010, February). Police misconduct, media coverage, and public perceptions of racial profiling: An experiment. *Justice Quarterly, 27*(1), 52–76.

Greenhouse, S. (2010). *Most US union members are working for the government, data shows.* Retrieved March 9, 2010, from http://www.NYTimes.com/2010/01/23/business/23labor.html

Greenleaf, R. K. (1991). *The servant as leader.* Westfield, IN: Robert K. Greenleaf Center.

Greenwood, P. W. (1979). *The Rand Criminal Investigation study: Its findings and impacts to date.* Santa Monica, CA: Rand Corporation.

Greer, C. R., & Plunkett, W. R. (2007). *Supervisory management* (11th ed.). Upper Saddle River, NJ: Pearson Prentice Hall.

Gross, A. (2009, July 11). Ex-cons now help diffuse gang violence. Kansas City program a success, police say. Fox4kc.com Associated Press. Retrieved August 30, 2010, from http://www.fox4kc.com/wdaf-story-aim4peace-071109,0,1328799.story

Guffey, J. E. (2005). *Report writing fundamentals for police and correctional officers.* Upper Saddle River, NJ: Pearson Prentice Hall.

Guild, K. (1998). *New York State Taylor law: Negotiating to avoid strikes in the public sector.* Retrieved March 9, 2010, from http://govenment.cce.cornell.edu/doc/reports/labor-management/ny_civil_service_law.asp

Gulf Coast Community Foundation. (2007a). *Because it matters at work, too.* Retrieved March 26, 2008, from http://www.becauseitmatters.net/workplace.cfm

Gulf Coast Community Foundation. (2007b). *10 keys to civility.* Retrieved March 26, 2008, from http://www.becauseitmatters.net/10keys.cfm

Haar, R. N. (2005, December). Factors affecting the decision of police recruits to "drop out" of police work. *Police Quarterly, 8*(4), 431–453.

Haberfeld, M. R. (2002). *Critical issues in police training.* Upper Saddle River, NJ: Prentice Hall.

Haberfeld, M. R. (2006). *Police leadership.* Upper Saddle River, NJ: Pearson Prentice Hall.

Hamm, M. S. (2007, December). *Terrorist recruitment in American correctional institution: An exploratory study of non-traditional faith groups.* Washington, DC: U.S. Department of Justice, National Institute of Justice.

Hammond, A., Slobody, Z., Tonkin, P., Stephens, R., Teasdale, B., Grey, S. F., et al. (2008). Do adolescents perceive police officers as credible instructors of substance abuse programs? *Health Education Research, 23,* 682–696.

Hartt, C. (1999). *Sticks, stones and broken careers: Verbal abuse in the workplace.* Retrieved March 26, 2008, from http://www.verbalabuse.com/page3/page3/page6.html

Harvey, L. R. (2000). *Federal, state and local fiscal partnership.* Retrieved November 24, 2008, from http://www.aec.msu.edu

Hastings, T. F., & Rickard, T. (1976). *Managing investigations in Rochester, New York.* NCJRS. Retrieved from http://www.NCJRS.gov

Hellriegel, D., Jackson, S. E., & Slocum, J. W. (2008). *Management: A competency-based approach* (11th ed.). Cincinnati, OH: South-Western Cengage Learning.

Hellriegel, D., Jackson, S. E., & Slocum, J. W., Jr. (2005). *Management: A competency-based approach* (10th ed.). Mason, OH: Thomson/South-Western.

Hellriegel, D., & Slocum, J. W. (2009). *Organizational behavior* (12th ed.). Cincinnati, OH: South-Western Cengage Learning.

Hemphill, J. K. (1949). *Situational factors in leadership.* Columbus: Ohio State University, Bureau of Education Research.

Heniff, B., Jr. (2003). *The federal fiscal year.* Retrieved May 27, 2009, from http://www.rules.house.gov/Archives/98-325.pdf

Henry, V. E. (2002). *The COMPSTAT paradigm: Management accountability in policing, business, and the public sector.* Flushing, NY: Looseleaf Law Publications.

Herbert, S. (1998). Police subculture reconsidered. *Criminology, 36,* 343–369.

Hersey, P. (2008). *Management of organizational behavior: Leading human resources* (9th ed.). Upper Saddle River, NJ: Pearson Education.

Hersey, P., & Blanchard, K. H. (1982). *Management of organizational behavior: Utilizing human resources.* Englewood Cliffs, NJ: Prentice Hall.

Herzberg, F., Mausner, B., & Snyderman, B. B. (1959). *The motivation to work.* New York: Wiley.

Hitt, W. D. (1988). *The leader-manager: Guidelines for action.* Columbus, OH: Battelle Press.

Ho, T. (2005). Do racial minority applicants have a better chance to be recruited in predominantly white neighborhoods? An empirical study. *Police Quarterly, 8*(4), 454–475.

Hodge, B. J., & Anthony, W. P. (1979). *Organizational theory: An environmental approach.* Boston: Allyn & Bacon.

Hosang, D. (2006). *The economics of the new brutality.* Retrieved June 1, 2009, from http://www.black-collegian.com/african/archives/brutality1299.shtml

House, R. J. (1971). A path-goal theory of leadership effectiveness. *Administrative Science Quarterly, 16*(3), 321–328.

House, R. J. (1996). Path-goal theory of leadership: Lessons, legacy, and a reformulated theory. *Leadership Quarterly, 7*(3), 323–352.

Hughes, F., & Andre, L. B. (2007). *Problem officer variables and early-warning systems.* Retrieved June 21, 2010, from http://policechiefmagazine.org

Human Capital Advisor. (2005). *Getting the right people on the bus: Assessment solutions for five critical business stages.* Retrieved May 2, 2008, from http://www.plantemoran.com

Hunter, D. H., & Barker, T. (2011). *Police-community relations and the administration of justice* (8th ed.). Upper Saddle River, NJ: Pearson Prentice Hall.

Iannone, N. F. (1987). *Supervision of police personnel* (4th ed.). Englewood Cliffs, NJ: Prentice Hall.

Inciardi, J. A. (2005). *Criminal justice* (7th ed.). New York: McGraw-Hill.

Inn, A. (2000). *A consultant's casebook.* Retrieved May 7, 2008, from http://internatlconsult.tripod.com/AssessmentCenters/Problems%20with%20Assessment.htm

International Association of Chiefs of Police. (1999). *Police leadership in the 21st century: Achieving & sustaining executive success.* Retrieved March 31, 2010, from http://www.theiacp.org/PoliceServices/ExecutiveServices/ProfessionalAssistance/Ethics/ReportsResources/PoliceLeadershipinthe21stcentury/tabid/190/Default.aspx

International Association of Chiefs of Police. (2005). Leadership styles. *Leadership in Police Organizations Training Bulletins 1 and 2.* Washington, DC: Author.

International Association of Chiefs of Police. (2008). *Police chiefs desk reference: A guide for newly appointed police leaders* (2nd ed.). New York: McGraw-Hill.

International Association of Chiefs of Police. (2010a). *Law enforcement code of ethics.* Washington, DC: Author.

International Association of Chiefs of Police. (2010b). *Police officer code of conduct.* Washington, DC: Author.

Internet Crime Complaint Center. (2010). *2009 Internet crime report.* Retrieved June 1, 2010, from http://www.ic3.gov

Ivers, T. (2008). *Union squabbles more about power struggles.* Retrieved March 8, 2010, from http://www.newsherald.com/articles/police-4442-officers-union.html

Johnson, B. R. (2010, February). DHS Office of Intelligence and Analysis: Supporting the front lines of homeland security. *Police Chief, 77*(2), 28–30, 32.

Johnson, C. E. (2004). *Meeting the ethical challenges of leadership: Casting light or shadow* (2nd ed.). Thousand Oaks, CA: Sage.

Johnson, J. W. (2003, February). Get the most from your guard force. *Security Management, 47*(2), 73–74, 76, 79–80.

Jones-Brown, D. D., & Terry, K. J. (2004). *Policing and minority communities: Bridging the gap.* Upper Saddle River, NJ: Pearson Prentice Hall.

Jurkanin, T. J., Hoover, L. T., Dowling, J. L., & Aymad, J. (2001). *Enduring, surviving, and thriving as a law enforcement executive.* Springfield, IL: Charles C Thomas.

Justice dept. settles lawsuit regarding Delaware police hiring practices. (n.d.). Retrieved February 23, 2010, from http://www.minorityjobs.net

Kamb, L., & Galloway, A. (2004, May 26). Gregoire faces questions over shelved database. *Seattle Post-Intelligencer.* Retrieved January 4, 2010, from http://www.seattlepi.com/Local/175016_smart26.html

Kaplan, R. S., & Norton, D. P. (2001). *The strategy focused organization: How balanced scorecard companies thrive in the new business environment.* Boston: Harvard Business School Press.

Karnow, C. E. A. (n.d.). *Indirect liability on the Internet and the loss of control.* Retrieved March 2, 2010, from http://www.isoc.org/inet99/proceedings/3e/3e/_2.htm

Kearney, R. (2009). *Labor relations in the public sector* (4th ed.). Boca Raton, FL: CRC Press.

Kearns, P. (2005). *HR strategy: Business focused, individually centered.* Burlington, MA: Elsevier Butterworth-Heinemann.

Kelling, G. L. (1999, October). *"Broken windows" and police discretion: Research report.* Washington, DC: U.S. Department of Justice, Office of Justice Programs, National Institute of Justice.

Kelling, G. L., & Sousa, W. H., Jr. (2001). *Do police matter? An analysis of the impact of New York City's police reforms.* Retrieved April 18, 2009, from http://manhattan-institute.org/huml/cr_22.htm

Kerlikowske, R. G. (2004). The end of community policing: Remembering lessons learned. *FBI Law Enforcement Bulletin.*

Kleinig, J. (1996). *The ethics of policing.* New York: Cambridge University Press.

Koerner, C. (2010). *Police field interview incident report form.* Clyde, New York, Police Department.

Korn, P. A., & Hastings, T. F. (1980). *Rochester Police Department Rules & Regulations.* City of Rochester, New York.

Kotter, J. P. (1990). *A force for change.* New York: Free Press.

Kotter, J. P. (1996). *Leading change.* Boston: Harvard Business School Press.

Labbe, C. (2008). Introduction to funding resources. In International Association of Chiefs of Police, *Police chiefs desk reference: A guide for newly appointed police leaders* (2nd ed.). New York: McGraw-Hill.

Lad, K. (2010). *Characteristics of a role model.* Retrieved July 4, 2010, from http://www.buzzle.com/articles/characteristics-of-a-role-model.html

Lamm Weisel, D. (2002). *Graffiti: Problem-oriented guides for police series no. 9.* Washington, DC: U.S. Department of Justice, Office of Community Oriented Policing Services.

LaPla, L., & Gravenkemper, S. (2007). The four myths of succession planning: Developing your organization's future leaders. *Universal Advisor No. 3.* Retrieved May 2, 2008, from http://www.plantemoran.com

Lawrence, P. R., & Lorsch, J. W. (1967). *Organization and environment: Managing differentiation and integration* (pp. 213–218). Boston: Division of Research, Graduate School of Business Administration, Harvard University.

Lawyers.com. (2010). *Criminal law: Witnesses FAQs.* Retrieved March 16, 2010, from http://criminal.lawyers.com/Criminal-Law–Witnesses-FAQ.html

Leadership development around the states. (2009, May). *Police Chief, 76*(5), 34–37.

Lectric Law Library. (2009). *Fiscal year.* Retrieved May 6, 2009, from http://www.lectlaw.com/def/f043.htm

Lee, W. L. M. (1901). *A history of police in England.* London: Methuen (Oxford University Press).

Lentz, S. A., & Chaires, R. H. (2007, January/ February). Invention of Peel's principles: A study of policing textbook history. *Journal of Criminal Justice, 35*(1), 69–79.

Leonard, V. A., & More, H. W. (2000). *Police organization and management* (9th ed.). New York: Foundation Press.

Levin, B. (2003). *Cyber criminals and victims: The social context.* Proceedings of Confronting the Future Challenges of Cybercriminal Behavior, FBI Academy, Quantico, Virginia. Retrieved March 16, 2010, from http://policefuturists.org/newsletter/webarticles/cybercriminals.htm

Lewin, K. (1951). *Field theory in social science.* New York: Harper.

Lewin, T. (2010, March 21). Rethinking sex offender laws for youths showing off online. *New York Times,* pp. A1, A14.

Lewis, P. V. (1975). *Organizational communication: The essence of effective management.* Columbus, OH: Grid.

Lindsey, D., & Kelly, S. (2004, July). Issue in small town policing: Understanding stress. *FBI Law Enforcement Bulletin, 73*(7), 1–7.

Lisaius, S. (2009, November 9). *Shot sensors: The future of crime-fighting?* KOLD News 13 [Television news broadcast]. Retrieved April 30, 2010, from http://www.kold.com/Global/story.asp?s=11410620&clienttype=printable

Londoño, E. (2006). *For county police force, diversity is elusive. Numerous obstacles hinder minority hiring.* Retrieved February 23, 2010, from http://www.washingtonpost.com

Lord, V. B., & Peak, K. J. (2005). *Women in law enforcement careers: A guide for preparing and succeeding.* Upper Saddle River, NJ: Pearson Prentice Hall.

Lutz, C. (2010). *The three pillars of leadership.* Retrieved March 2, 2010, from http://ezinearticles.com/?experts=charles_lutz

Maguire, E., & King, W. (2004). Trends in the policing industry. *Annals of American Academy of Political and Social Sciences, 593,* 15–41.

Mann, R. A., & Roberts, B. S. (2006). *Smith & Robertson's business law* (13th ed.). Belmont, CA: Cengage.

Manning, P. K., & Van Maanen, J. (1978). *Policing: A view from the streets.* Santa Monica, CA: Goodyear.

Marcus, L. J., Dorn, B. C., & Henderson, J. H. (2006, February). Meta-leadership and national emergency preparedness: A model to build government connectivity. *Biosecurity and Bioterrorism: Biodefense Strategy, Practice, and Science, 4*(2), 128.

Marshall, J. (1999). *Zero tolerance policing.* Retrieved July 23, 2010, from http://www.ocsar.sa.gov.au/docs/information_bulletins/IB9.pdf

Martin, G. (2008). *Essentials of terrorism: Concepts and controversies.* Los Angeles: Sage.

Maslow, A. H. (1970). *Motivation and personality.* New York: Harper & Row.

Mastrofski, S. D. (2006). *Police organization and management issues for the next decade.* Proceedings at the National Institute of Justice Policing Research Workshop: Planning for the Future, Washington, DC.

Mathis, R. L., & Jackson, J. H. (2005). *Human resource management essential perspectives* (3rd ed.). Mason, OH: Thomson South-Western.

McClelland, D. C. (1971). *Motivational trends in society.* Morristown, NJ: General Learning Press.

McDermott, M. M. (2009). Greece inquiry putting pieces together. *Democrat and Chronicle,* p. A1.

McGregor, D. (1960). *The human side of enterprise.* New York: McGraw-Hill.

McNamara, C. (2008). *Organizational culture.* Retrieved August 25, 2009, from http://managementhelp.org/org_thry/culture/culture.htm

Meese, E., III. (1993, January). Community policing and the police officer. *National Institute of Justice, No. 15.* Washington, DC: National Institute of Justice.

Meese, E., III, & Kurz, A. T. (1993, December). Community policing and the investigator. *Journal of Contemporary Criminal Justice, 9,* 289–302.

Meese, E., III, & Ortmeier, P. J. (2004). *Leadership, ethics, and policing: Challenges for the 21st century.* Upper Saddle River, NJ: Pearson Prentice Hall

Merriam-Webster's Dictionary and Thesaurus. (2006). Springfield, MA: Merriam-Webster.

Michaels, A. C. (1999). *Vicarious liability—vicarious liability and strict liability distinguished, why vicarious liability is disfavored, vicarious liability for accomplices and co-conspirators—conclusion.* Retrieved March 2, 2010, from http://law.jrank.org/pages/2255/Vicarious-Liability.html

Michelson, R. (1999). *The California criminal justice system to accompany introduction to criminal justice.* New York: Glencoe/McGraw-Hill.

Michelson, R., & Maher, P. T. (1993). *Preparing for promotion: A guide to law enforcement assessment centers.* Blue Lake, CA: Innovative Systems.

Moak, L. L., & Hillhouse, A. M. (2009). *Purchasing and bidding: Purchasing procedures, policies, and manuals.* Retrieved September 25, 2009, from http://www.mrsc.org/Subjects/PubWorks/pb/purchasing.aspx

Montaldo, C. (2010). *Frauds and scams used against the elderly: Frauds vary widely in the means used to commit them.* Retrieved June 1, 2010, from http://crime.about.com/od/elderabuse/a/frauds.htm

Monteith, D. (2007). *Leadership rises to the top through trust and purpose.* Retrieved May 16, 2008, from http://www.leadership-development.com/html/magazine2.php?page_id=5&sub_id=79

Montgomery, D. (2008). *The engine of change. Reading, PA, has proven it's deft at switching tracks. As residents head to the polls, the question is: Where is next.* Retrieved February 23, 2010, from http://www.washingtonpost.com/wp-dyn/content/article/2008/04/21/AR20080442103112.html

Moore, C. (2004, May). If there must be gossip, use it for good. *Law Enforcement Technology,* p. 110.

Morgan, T. (2002). HITS/SMART Washington State's crime-fighting tool. *FBI Law Enforcement Bulletin, 71*(2), 1–10. Retrieved April 26, 2010, from http://www.fbi.gov/publications/leb/2002/dec2002/dec02/eb.htm

Morreale, S. A. (2002). *Analysis of perceived leader behaviors in law enforcement.* DPA dissertation, Nova Southeastern University,

Morrell, A. (2010, May 17). Brockport officers' cut in salary fails to please critics. *Democrat and Chronicle,* pp. B3, B4.

Mumola, C. J. (2007). *Arrest-related deaths in the United States.* Bureau of Justice Statistics Special Report. Retrieved February 12, 2010, from http://www.bjs.ojp.usdoj.gov/content/pub/pdf/ardus05.pdf

Municipality of Anchorage. (2005). *Appropriation from the U.S. Department of Justice, Office of Justice programs for a Bureau of Justice assistance grant award 2005-VT-BX-1166 ($629,911).* City of Anchorage, Alaska, No. AR 2005-266.

National Advisory Commission on Civil Disorders. (1968). *Kerner commission.* Washington, DC: U.S. Government Printing Office.

National Advisory Commission on Criminal Justice Standards and Goals. (1973). *Police.* Washington, DC: U.S. Government Printing Office.

National Advisory Commission on the Causes and Prevention of Violence. (1969). *Law and order reconsidered.* Washington, DC: U.S. Government Printing Office.

National Commission on Law Observance and Enforcement. (1931). *Wickersham Commission.* Retrieved March 17, 2010, from http://legal-dictionary.thefreedictionary.com/National+Commission

National Cyber Security Alliance, Symantec, & Zogby International. (2009). *2009 NCSA/Symantec home user study.* Retrieved June 1, 2010, from http://www.staysafeonline.org/content/2009-cyber-security-study

National Institute of Standards and Technology. (2001). *Baldrige: Recognizing role model practices of world class organizations.* Retrieved July 4, 2010, from http://www.quality.nist.gov/PDF_files/Issue_Sheet_Model.pdf

National Law Enforcement Officers Memorial Fund. (2010). *Officer deaths by year.* Retrieved February 21, 2010, from http:www.nleomf.org/facts/officer-fatalities-data/year.html

National P.O.L.I.C.E. Suicide Foundation. (2010). *Police suicide reporting.* Retrieved February 21, 2010, from http://www.psf.org/reporting.html

Neumeier, M. (2006). *The brand gap: How to bridge the distance between business strategy and design. A whiteboard overview.* Berkeley, CA: New Riders/Pearson Education.

Niederhoffer, A., & Blumberg, A. S. (1976). *The ambivalent force: Perspectives on the police* (2nd ed.). Waltham, MA: Ginn.

Northouse, P. G. (2007). *Leadership: Theory and practice* (4th ed.). Thousand Oaks, CA: Sage.

Northouse, P. G. (2009). *Introduction to leadership concepts and practice.* Thousand Oaks, CA: Sage.

Nowicki, D. F. (2003). *Human resource management and development in local government police management* (4th ed.; W. Geller & D. W. Stephens, Eds.). Washington, DC: International City/County Management Association.

NSW. (2007). *Counter terrorism arrangements in NSW.* Retrieved August 13, 2010, from http://www.secure.nsw.gov.au/Resources-and-links/Frequently-asked-questions/Counter-Terrorism-Arrangements-FAQ/Counter-terrorism-arrangements-in-NSW.aspx

NYPD working to improve its diversity. (2010). Retrieved February 27, 2010, from http://wcbstv.com/local/nypd.diversity.nationalities.2.1403513.html

O'Hara, P. (2005). *Why law enforcement organizations fail: Mapping the organizational fault lines in policing.* Durham, NC: Carolina Academic Press.

Oliver, W. M. (2007). *Homeland security for policing.* Upper Saddle River, NJ: Pearson Prentice Hall.

Oliver, W. M. (2008). *Community-oriented policing: A systematic approach to policing* (4th ed.). Upper Saddle River, NJ: Pearson Prentice Hall.

One team, one mission, securing our homeland. (2008). Retrieved September 15, 2009, from http://www.dhs.gov/xlibrary/assets/DHS_StratPlan_FINAL_spread.pdf

Orrick, W. D. (2008). A best practices guide for maneuvering successfully in the political environment. In International Association of Chiefs of Police, *Police chiefs desk reference: A guide for newly appointed police leaders* (2nd ed., pp. 172–183). New York: McGraw-Hill.

Ortmeier, P. J. (1995, July/August). Educating law enforcement officers for community policing. *Police and Security News, 11*(4), 46–47.

Ortmeier, P. J. (1996). *Community policing leadership: A Delphi study to identify essential competencies.* Ann Arbor, MI: University Microfilms International (Bell & Howell Information and Learning).

Ortmeier, P. J. (1997, October). Leadership for community policing: Identifying essential officer competencies. *Police Chief, 64*(10), 88–91, 93, 95.

Ortmeier, P. J. (1999). *Public safety and security administration.* Boston: Butterworth-Heinemann.

Ortmeier, P. J. (2002). *Policing the community: A guide for patrol operations.* Upper Saddle River, NJ: Prentice Hall.

Ortmeier, P. J. (2006). *Introduction to law enforcement and criminal justice* (2nd ed.). Upper Saddle River, NJ: Prentice Hall.

Ortmeier, P. J. (2009). *Introduction to security: Operations and management* (3rd ed.). Upper Saddle River, NJ: Pearson Prentice Hall.

Ortmeier, P. J., & Meese, E., III. (2010). *Leadership, ethics, and policing: Challenges for the 21st century* (2nd ed.). Upper Saddle River, NJ: Pearson Prentice Hall.

Ottenheimer, H. J. (2007). *The anthropology of language: Introduction to linguistic anthropology.* Belmont, CA: Thomson Wadsworth.

Ouchi, W. G. (1981). *Theory Z: How American business can meet the Japanese challenge.* Reading, MA: Addison-Wesley.

Our documents. (2010). *National Labor Relations Act (1935), 2010.* Retrieved February 21, 2010, from http://www.ourdocuments.gov/doc.php?flash=false&doc=67

Outsourcing—What is outsourcing? (2003). SourcingMag.com. Retrieved January 25, 2010, from http://www.sourcingmag.com/content/what_is_outsourcing.asp

Overton, J. P., & Bockelman, A. (1993, November 1). *What is the importance of competitive bidding?* Mackinac Center. Retrieved January 22, 2010, from http://www.mackinac.org/825

Parr, L. A. (1999). *Police report writing essentials.* Placerville, CA: Custom.

Parrish, G. (2006, May 1). *Why May Day?* TomPaine.commonsense. Retrieved May 17, 2010, from http://www.tompaine.com/articles/2006/05/01/why_may_day.php

Parrish, P. (2003). Media relations instructor at the FBI Academy: Personal conversation.

Payton, G. T., & Amaral, M. (2004). *Patrol operations and enforcement tactics* (11th ed.). San Jose, CA: Criminal Justice Services.

Peak, K. J. (2007). *Justice administration: Police, courts, and corrections management* (5th ed.). Upper Saddle River, NJ: Pearson Prentice Hall.

Peak, K. J., Gaines, L. K., & Glensor, R. W. (2010). *Police supervision and management: In an era of community policing* (3rd ed.). Upper Saddle River, NJ: Pearson Education.

Pelfrey, W. V. (2004, September). The inchoate nature of community policing: Differences between community policing and traditional police officers. *Justice Quarterly, 21*(3), 579–601.

Picarelli, J. T. (2009, November). The future of terrorism. *National Institute of Justice Journal, No. 264.* Washington, DC: National Institute of Justice.

Police Executive Research Forum. (2004). *By the numbers: A guide for analyzing race data from vehicle stops.* Available: http://www.policeforum.org/library.asp?MENU=229

Police facilities planning guidelines. (2008). In International Association of Chiefs of Police, *Police chiefs desk reference: A guide for newly appointed police leaders* (2nd ed.). New York: McGraw-Hill.

Police officer incentives: Hiring ban uses. (2009). Retrieved May 28, 2009, from http://banning.ca.us

Polisar, J. M. (2004). *The IACP center for police leadership.* Retrieved May 12, 2008, from http://policechiefmagazine.org/magazine/index.cfm?fuseaction=display&article_id=260&issue_id=42004

Pollard, C. (1998). *Zero tolerance: Short-term fix, long-term liability?* Retrieved July 3, 2010, from http://www.civitas.org.uk/pdf/cw35.pdf

Pollock, J. M. (2007). *Ethical dilemmas and decisions in criminal justice* (5th ed.). Belmont, CA: West/Wadsworth.

President's Commission on Campus Unrest. (1970). *Scranton commission.* Washington, DC: U.S. Government Printing Office.

President's Commission on Law Enforcement and the Administration of Justice. (1967). *Task force report: Police.* Washington, DC: U.S. Government Printing Office.

Pressed for applicants, NYPD waives two-year college standard. (2000, October 31). *Law Enforcement News, 26*(542), 1, 10. Retrieved June 23, 2010, from http://www.lib.jjay.cuny.edu/len/2000/10.31

Privatizing the long arm of the law. (1998, November 16). Mackinac Center for Public Policy. Retrieved January 4, 2010, from http://www.mackinac.org/796

Quick, J. C., Quick, J. D., Nelson, D. L., & Hurrell, J. J., Jr. (2003). *Preventive stress management in organizations.* Washington, DC: American Psychological Association.

Quimby, M. (2009). Organizational politics: Using your power for good. *Systems Thinker, 20,* 7–9.

Rabin, J., Hildreth, W. B., & Miller, G. J. (1996). *Budgeting formulation and execution.* Athens: University of Georgia, Carl Vinson Institute of Government.

Reed, G. E. (2004, July–August). Toxic leadership. *Military Review, 84*(4), 67–71.

Ritchie, D. L. (2007, April 20). Speech titled *The Future of Ethics* presented at the Peterson Lectures by the International Baccalaureate Organization.

Ritter, N. (2009). CeaseFire: A public health approach to reduce shootings and killings. *National Institute of Justice Journal No. 264.* Retrieved August 31, 2010, from http://www.ojp.usdoj.gov/nij/pubs-sum/228386.htm

Ritter, N. M. (2006). Preparing for the future: Criminal justice in 2040. *National Institute of Justice Journal No. 255.* Retrieved January 9, 2010, from http://www.ojp.usdoj.gov/nij/journals/255/2040_print.html

Robbins, S. P., & Judge, T. A. (2008). *Essentials of organizational behavior* (9th ed.). Upper Saddle River, NJ: Prentice Hall.

Rochester Police Department. (1981). *Rules and regulations.* City of Rochester, New York.

Rochester Police Department. (1996). *Rochester police department general order: Grand jury referral form, grand jury clearances, G.O. 409.* City of Rochester, New York.

Rochester Police Department. (2001). *Serious personal incidents, G.O. 280.* City of Rochester, New York.

Rogers, D. (2009, March 5). Wallbridge refuses to outsource its police. *BG Sentinel-Tribune.* Retrieved January 5, 2010, from http://www.foxToledo.com

Rosenthal, R. (2003, October/November/December). Training in media. *ILEETA Digest,* p. 3.

Rosenthal, R. (2005, July/August/September). Yes, you do need a p.i.o. *ILEETA Digest,* pp. 6–7.

Ross, D. L. (2006). *Civil liability in criminal justice* (4th ed.). Albany, NY: LexisNexis/Anderson.

Rosser, C. (2010, May). Developing leaders through leadership in police organizations (LPOs). *Police Chief, 78*(5), 38–41, 44.

Rubin, I. S. (2006). *The politics of public budgeting: Getting and spending* (5th ed.). Washington, DC: CQ Press.

Rutledge, D. (2000). *California criminal procedure* (4th ed.). Incline Village, NV: Copperhouse.

Sample business contracts, outsourcing services agreement. (2010). Retrieved January 26, 2010, from http://contracts.onecle.com/navisite/clearblue.outsource.2003.01.01.shtml

Say, R. (2007). *12 rules for self-management.* Retrieved December 17, 2008, from http://www.sayleadershipcoaching.com/slc/12RulesforSelfManagement.html

Schafer, J. A. (2007a). *Exploring the future of crime, communities, & policing.* Carbondale: Southern Illinois University Carbondale.

Schafer, J. A. (2007b). The future of police image and ethics. *Police Chief, 74,* 6. Retrieved January 26, 2010, from http://policechiefmagazine.org/magazine/index.cfm?fuseaction=print_display&article_id

Scheider, M. (2008, March). The role of traditional policing in community policing. *Community Policing Dispatch, 1*(3), 1–3.

Schulte, R. (1996). *Which challenges will police managers have to meet in the future?* Retrieved December 29, 2008, from http://www.ncjrs.gov/policing/which9.htm

Schultz, P. D. (2008). *Lengthening tenure by following proven principles.* Retrieved October 20, 2009, from http://policechiefmagazine.org

Scott, M. S. (2001). *Street prostitution: Problem-oriented guides for police series no. 2.* Washington, DC: U.S. Department of Justice, Office of Community Oriented Policing Services.

Scuro, J. E., Jr. (2004). Supreme Court redefines affirmative action. *Law and Order,* pp. 24–26.

Section 11.45. Contract grievance procedure. (2008, February). Retrieved March 10, 2010, from http://www.das.hre.iowa.gov/html_documents/ms_manual/11-45.htm

Seo, M., Putnam, L. L., & Bartunck, J. M. (2003). Dualities and tensions of planned organizational change. In M. S. Poole & A. V. deVen (Eds.), *Handbook of organizational change* (pp. 73–107). Thousand Oaks, CA: Sage. Retrieved May 5, 2010, from http://siteresources.worldbank.org/EXTGOVACC/Resources/ChangeManagementweb.pdf

Shahani, A., & Green, J. (2009). *Local democracy on ice: Why state and local governments have no business in federal immigration law enforcement.* Retrieved June 28, 2010, from http://www.justicestrategies.org/sites/default/files/JS-Democracy-On-Ice.pdf

Shane, J. M. (2007). *What every chief executive should know: Using data to measure police performance.* Flushing, NY: Looseleaf Law Publications.

Shane, S., & Mekhennet, S. (2010, May 9). From condemning terror to preaching jihad. *New York Times,* pp. A1, A14, A15.

Sharp, B. (2009, July 12). RPD fails to attract diversity in recruits. *Democrat and Chronicle,* pp. A1, A6.

Sherman, L. (2010, April 21). *Less prison, more police, less crime: How criminology can save the states from bankruptcy.* Speech presented at U.S. Office of Justice Programs, Washington, DC.

Sherman, L. W., Gottfredson, D., MacKenzie, D., Eck, J., Reuter, P., & Bushway, S. (1996). *Preventing crime: What works, what doesn't, what's promising.* Retrieved December 15, 2008, from http://www.ncjrs.gov/works

Shusta, R. M., Levine, D. R., Wong, H. Z., Olson, A. T., & Harris, P. R. (2011). *Multicultural law enforcement: Strategies for peacekeeping in a diverse society* (5th ed.). Upper Saddle River, NJ: Pearson Prentice Hall.

Sierra Madre divided over possible police outsourcing. (2009, July 28). *Arcadia Weekly.* Retrieved January 5, 2010, from http://arcadiaweekly.com/latest-news/sierra-madre-divided-over-possible-police-outsourcing

Silverman, E. B. (2001). *NYPD Battles crime: Innovative strategies in policing.* Boston: Northeastern University Press.

Skogan, W. G. (2005). Evaluating community policing in Chicago. In K. R. Kerley (Ed.), *Policing and program evaluation* (pp. 27–41). Upper Saddle River, NJ: Pearson Prentice Hall.

Skogan, W. G., Hartnett, S. M., DuBois, J., Comey, J. T., Kaiser, M., & Loving, J. H. (1999). *On the beat: Police and community problem solving.* Boulder, CO: Westview Press.

Souryal, S. S. (2003). *Ethics in criminal justice: In search of the truth* (3rd ed.). Cincinnati, OH: Anderson.

Spelman, W., & Eck, J. E. (1987, January). Problem-oriented policing. *National Institute of Justice: Research in Brief,* 2–3. Washington, DC: National Institute of Justice.

Staff, *Associated Press.* (2009, April 7). 911 operator didn't tell Pittsburgh police about guns. Retrieved June 29, 2010, from http://www.cnsnews.com/news/print/46234

Staff, *New Scientist Tech.* (2006). The sky-drone: Is the eye in the sky the future of crime-fighting? Retrieved April 30, 2010, from http://sixwise.com/newsletters/06/07/05/the_sky-drone_is_this_eye_in_the_sky_the_future_of_crime-fighting.htm

Stanley, J. (2010, May 28). Reviving the Fourth Amendment and American privacy. *ACLU Blog of Rights.* Retrieved June 3, 2010, from http://www.aclu.org/blog/author/Jay-Stanley%2C-Speech%2C-Privacy-and-Technology-Pr

Stech, E. L. (2001). Psychodynamic approach. In P. G. Northouse, *Leadership: Theory and practice* (2nd ed., pp. 189–213). Thousand Oaks, CA: Sage.

Stevens, D. J. (2011). *Media and criminal justice: The CSI effect.* Boston: Jones & Bartlett.

Stillman, R. J. (2005). *Public administration: Concepts and cases* (8th ed.). New York: Houghton Mifflin.

Stogdill, R. M. (1948). Personal factors associated with leadership: A survey of the literature. *Journal of Psychology, 25,* 35–71.

Stogdill, R. M. (1959). *Individual behavior and group achievement: A theory, the experimental evidence.* New York: Oxford University Press.

Stohr, M. K., & Collins, P. A. (2009). *Criminal justice management: Theory and practice in justice centered organizations.* New York: Oxford University Press.

Stojkovic, S., Kalinich, D., & Klofas, J. (2008). *Criminal justice organizations: Administration and management* (4th ed.). Belmont, CA: Cengage Learning.

Stolting, S., Barrett, S. M., & Kurz, D. (2008). *The best practice guide for acquisition of new technology.* In International Association of Chiefs of Police, *Police chiefs desk reference: A guide for newly appointed police leaders* (2nd ed.). New York: McGraw-Hill.

Stress and the police. (2007). Retrieved June 29, 2010, from http://stresshealthsolutions.com/stress&police.htm

Succession Planning 101. (2007). *What is succession planning?* Retrieved from May 2, 2008, from http://www.successionplanning101.com

Sunnyvale. (2008). *Operating budget: Comparison of traditional line item budget and performance based budget.* Retrieved April 12, 2008, from http://sunnyvale.ca.gov/NR/rdonlyres/1DAPCOE5-B621-4CFO-B5ED-98DE14671E21/0/0708roperatingbudgetguide.pdg

Survey design. (2009) Creative Research Systems. Retrieved January 25, 2010, from http://www.surveysystem.com/sdesign.htm

Sutton, R. (2006). *Ethical survival: Officers must prepare for not only physical danger but ethical danger as well.* Retrieved July 30, 2009, from http://www.policeone.com/.../129744-Ethical-Survival-Officers-must-prepare-for-not-only-physical-danger-but-ethical-danger-as-well

Sutton, R. I. (2007). *The no asshole rule: Building a civilized workplace and surviving one that isn't.* New York: Warner Business Books.

Swanson, C. R., Territo, L., & Taylor, R. W. (2008). *Police administration: Structures, processes, and behavior* (7th ed.). Upper Saddle River, NJ: Pearson Education.

Sward, S., Wallace, B., & Fernandez, E. (2006, February 8). The use of force discipline's obstacles: Few complaints against police upheld—even fewer bring serious discipline. *San Francisco Chronicle,* p. A1.

Taft, P. J., Jr. (1986). *Fighting fear: The Baltimore County C.O.P.E. project.* Washington, DC: Police Executive Research Forum.

Tannen, D. (1990). *You just don't understand: Women and men in conversation.* New York: Ballantine Books.

Taser International Inc. (2008). *Law enforcement overview.* Retrieved February 22, 2009, from http://www.taser.com/Pages?lw_overview.aspx

Texas Municipal League. (2009). *Cities use meet and confer authority to their advantage.* Retrieved March 10, 2010, from http://www.tml.org/leg_updates/legis_update100908d_meet.html

Thacher, D. (2005). The local role in homeland security. *Law and Society Review, 39,* 635–676.

Thompson, T. (2010, January 10). *What is outsourcing?* Retrieved January 25, 2010, from http://www.wisegeek.com/what-is-oursourcing.htm

Tichy, N. (1997, April). Bob Knowling's change manual. *Fast Company,* pp. 76–82.

Tichy, N. M. (1977). *Organizational design for primary healthcare.* Praeger.

Tichy, N. M., & Bennis, W. G. (2007). *Judgment: How winning leaders make great calls.* New York: Penguin Group.

Toolingu. (2008). *What is the definition of continuous improvement?* Retrieved August 20, 2008, from http://www.toolingu.com/definition-900130-12156-continuous-improvement.html

Townsend, R. (1970). *Up the organization.* Greenwich, CT: Fawcett.

Toxic bosses and toxic handlers. (2004). Retrieved July 1, 2009, from http://trainingconference.co.uk/skills/personal_development/toxic.htm

Travis, L. F., III, & Langworthy, R. H. (2008). *Policing in America: A balance of forces* (4th ed.). Upper Saddle River, NJ: Pearson Prentice Hall.

Tytel, M. (2007). *Develop a civil work environment.* Retrieved March 28, 2008, from http://www.businesseeek.com/smallbiz/tips/archives/2007/11/develop_a_civil.html

United University Professions. (2006). *Know your contract—frequently asked questions.* Retrieved March 10, 2010, from http://www.uuphost.org/purchase/contact_faqs.html

U.S. Census Bureau. (1999). *Dynamic diversity: Projected changes in U.S. race and ethnic composition 1995 to 2050.* Retrieved February 12, 2010, from http://www.mbda.gov/documents/unpubtext.pdf

U.S. Department of Homeland Security. (2006). *Communications and information management.* Retrieved February 10, 2010, from http://www.fema.gov/emergency/nims/CommunicationsInfoMngmnt.shtm

U.S. Department of Homeland Security, Office of Management and Budget. (2007). *National strategy for homeland security.* Retrieved February 10, 2010 from http://www.whitehouse.gov/infocus/homeland

U.S. Department of Homeland Security, SAFECOM Program. (2004). *Welcome to SAFECOM.* Retrieved July 24, 2009, from http://www.safecomprogram.gov/SAFECOM

U.S. Department of Justice Juvenile Accountability Block Grant. (2008). *Juvenile accountability block grant.* Retrieved November 25, 2008, from http://www.in/gov/cji/2660.htm

U.S. Department of Justice, Office of Community Oriented Policing Services. (2007). *What is community policing?* Retrieved July 3, 2010, from http://www.cops.usdoj.gov/Default.asp?Item=36

U.S. Department of Justice, Office of Community Oriented Policing Services. (2008). *Resource Information Center.* Retrieved from http://www.cops.usdoj.gov/ric/resourceSearch.aspx

U.S. Department of Justice, Office of Justice Programs, Bureau of Justice Statistics. (2006). *State and local law enforcement training academies, 2006.* Retrieved March 16, 2009, from http://www.ojp.usdoj.gov/bjs/abstract/slleta06.htm

U.S. Department of Justice, Office of Justice Programs, Bureau of Justice Statistics. (2009). *State and local law enforcement training academies, 2006, revised 02/09.* NCJ222987. Retrieved March 16, 2009, from http://www.ojp.usdoj.gov/bjs/abstract/slleta.06.htm

U.S. Department of Justice, Office of Justice Programs, National Institute of Justice. (2007). *Public safety communications and interoperability.* Washington, DC: Author.

U.S. Department of Justice, Office of Juvenile Justice and Delinquency Prevention. (2009). *Statistical briefing book: Juveniles as victims.* Retrieved June 1, 2010, from http://ojjdp.ncjrs.gov/ojstatbb/victims/overview.html

U.S. Department of Labor. (2010a). *Affirmative action.* Retrieved February 21, 2010, from http://dol.gov/dol/topic/hiring/affirmativeact.htm

U.S. Department of Labor. (2010b). *Employee polygraph protection act (EPPA).* Retrieved February 20, 2010, from http://www.dol.gov/compliance/laws/comp-eppa.htm

U.S. Department of Labor. (2010c). *Equal employment opportunity age discrimination.* Retrieved February 20, 2010, from http://dol.gov/dol/topic/discrimination/agedisc.htm

U.S. Department of Labor. (2010d). *Fair Labor Standards Act (FLSA).* Retrieved February 21, 2010, from http://www.dol.gov/compliance/laws/comp-flsa.htm

U.S. Department of Labor. (2010e). *Uniformed Services Employment and Reemployment Rights Act of 1994 (USERRA 38 U.S.C. 4301-4335).* Retrieved February 20, 2010, from http://www.dol.gov/vets/programs/userra/userra_fs.htm

U.S. Department of Labor. (2010f). *Worker Adjustment and Retraining Notification Act (WARN).* Retrieved February 20, 2010, from http://www.dol.gov/compliance/laws/comp-warn.htm

U.S. Department of Labor, Bureau of Labor Statistics. (2010, January). *Union members summary.* Retrieved March 9, 2010, from http://www.bld.gov/news.release/union2.nro.htm

U.S. Department of Labor, Employment Relations Service. (2009a, October). *Collective bargaining.* Retrieved March 9, 2010, from http://www.ers.dol.govt.nz/bargaining

U.S. Department of Labor, Employment Relations Service. (2009b, December). *Good faith in collective bargaining.* Retrieved March 9, 2010, from http://www.erc.dol.govt.nz/bargaining/good_faith.html

U.S. Department of Labor, Occupational Safety and Health Administration. (2010). Retrieved February 20, 2010, from http://www.osha.gov/pls/oshaweb/owasrch_search_form?p_doc_type=STANDARD&p_toc_level=o&p_keyvalue=

U.S. Department of the Treasury, Internal Revenue Service. (2010). *Enforcement strategy—criminal investigation.* Retrieved June 29, 2010, from http://www.irs.gov/compliance/enforcement/article/0..id=107522.00.htm

U.S. Government Accountability Office. (2007). *Department of Homeland Security: Progress report on implementation of mission and management functions.* Retrieved from http//www.gao.gov/docsearch/abstract.php?rptno=GAO-07-1081T

U.S. Government Printing Office. (2008). *U.S. Code Browse Title 5—Government organization and employees.* Retrieved March 8, 2010, from http://frwegate.access.gpo.gov/cgi-bin/usc.cgi?ACTION=Browse&title=5usc&PDFS=YES

U.S. House of Representatives Committee on the Judiciary, the Republicans. (2009). *54 members of Congress to Obama: We support 287(g) program.* Retrieved December 17, 2009, from http://republicans.judiciary.house.gov/News/Read.aspx?ID=255

U.S. Immigration and Customs Enforcement. (2009). *Delegation of immigration authority section 287(g) Immigration and Nationality Act: The ICE 287(g) program: A law enforcement partnership.* Retrieved December 18, 2009, from http://www.ice.gov/pi/news/factsheets/section287_g.htm

U.S. Office of Personnel Management. (2010). *Family and medical leave entitlement.* Retrieved February 20, 2010, from http://www.opm.gov/ocal/leave/HTML/fmlafac2esp

U.S. police officer compensation survey. (2004). Retrieved May 28, 2009, from http://www.theblueline.com.salaryl.html

Vaknin, S. (2006). *What is intuition?* Retrieved February 22, 2009, from http://www.globalpolitican.com/21917-sociology

Vaughn. R. G. (2003). *Civil Service Reform Act (1978).* Retrieved February 20, 2010, from http://www.enotes.com/major-acts-congress/civil-service-reform-act

Veale, S. (2009, July 7). "Johns" will face tougher sentences. *Democrat and Chronicle.* Retrieved July 3, 2010, from http://pqash.pqarchive.com/democratand chronicle/access/1779551801.htm

Vikesland, G. (1998). *The Family and Medical Leave Act: Balancing work and family.* Retrieved February 20, 2010, from http://employer-employee.com/fmla.html

Vinzant, J. C., & Crothers, L. (1998). *Street-level leadership: Discretion and legitimacy in front-line public service.* Washington, DC: Georgetown University Press.

Violanti, J.M. (2002). *Dying from the job: The mortality risk for police officers.* Retrieved October 21, 2010, from http://www.cophealth.com/articles/articles_dying_a.html

Vodicka, A. T. (1994). Educational requirements for police recruits. *Law and Order, 42,* 91–94.

Vollmer, A. (1936). *The police in modern society.* Los Angeles: University of California.

Volunteers in Police Service. (2008). *About VIPS: Origin of the volunteers in police service (VIPS) program.* Retrieved July 18, 2008, from http://www.policevolunteers.org/about/

Vroom, V. H. (1964). *Work and motivation.* New York: Wiley.

Vroom, V. H. (2000, Spring). Leadership and the decision-making process. *Organizational Dynamics,* 82–94.

Walker, S. (2001). *Police accountability: The role of civilian oversight.* Belmont, CA: Wadsworth/Thomson Learning.

Walker, S., Alpert, G. P., & Kenney, D. J. (2001, July). *Early warning systems: Responding to the problem police officer.* Research in brief. Washington, DC: U.S. Department of Justice, National Institute of Justice.

Walker, S., Spohn, C., & Delone, M. (2004). *The color of justice: Race.* Belmont, CA: Wadsworth/Cengage Learning.

Wallace, H., & Roberson, C. (2009). *Written and interpersonal communication: Methods for law enforcement* (4th ed.). Upper Saddle River, NJ: Pearson Prentice Hall.

Waugh, W. L., Jr. (2005). *2005 higher education conference: The future of homeland security and emergency management.* Emmitsburg, MD: Emergency Management Institute.

Weisbord, M. R. (1978). *Organizational diagnosis: A workbook of theory and practice.* Cambridge, MA: Perseus Books.

Welsh, W. N., & Harris, P. W. (2004). *Criminal justice policy & planning* (2nd ed.). Cincinnati, OH: Anderson.

West's Encyclopedia of American Law (2nd ed.). (2008a). Binding arbitration. Retrieved March 2, 2010, from http://legal-dictionary.thefreedictionary.com/p/Binding%20arbitration

West's Encyclopedia of American Law (2nd ed.). (2008b). Negligence. Retrieved March 11, 2010, from http://legal-dictionary.thefreedictionary.com/negligence

West's Encyclopedia of American Law (2nd ed.). (2008c). Proximate cause. Retrieved March 10, 2010, from http://legal-dictionary.thefreedictionary.com/proximate+cause

West's Encyclopedia of American Law (2010). Forfeiture. Retrieved June 29, 2010, from http://www.answers.com/topic/forfeiture

Whisenand, P. M., & Ferguson, R. F. (2005). *The managing of police organizations* (6th ed.). Upper Saddle River, NJ: Pearson Prentice Hall.

Whisenand, P. M., & Rush, G. E. (2007). *Supervising police personnel: The fifteen responsibilities* (6th ed.). Upper Saddle River, NJ: Pearson Prentice Hall.

Wideman, M. (2001). *Project management issues and considerations (Isaacons).* Retrieved October 20, 2008, from http://www.maxwideman.com/issacons1/iac1190/img002.gif

Wildman, L., & Morschauser, P. (2007). *Police mental health training program, officer's guide.* Albany, NY: NYS Office of Mental Health.

Wilson, J. Q., & Kelling, G. L. (1989, February). Making neighborhoods safe. *The Atlantic Monthly,* 46–52.

Wilson, O. W. (1952). *Police planning.* Springfield, IL: Charles C Thomas.

Wilson, O. W. (1963). *Police administration.* New York: McGraw-Hill.

Wood, M. B. (2005). *The marketing plan handbook* (2nd ed.). Upper Saddle River, NJ: Pearson Prentice Hall.

Wuestewald, T. (2006). *Shared leadership: An assessment of participative management in a police organization.* Retrieved August 2, 2010, from http://www.ou.edu/cas/psc/pa/Shared%20Leadership.pdf

Yee, N., & Bailenson, J. N. (2006). *Walk a mile in digital shoes: The impact of embodied perspective—talking on the reduction of negative stereotyping in immersive virtual environments.* Proceedings of Presence 2006: The 9th Annual International Workshop on Presence, Cleveland, OH.

Young, T., & Ortmeier, P. J. (2011). *Crime scene investigation: The forensic technician's field manual.* Upper Saddle River, NJ: Pearson Prentice Hall.

Zalman, M. (2011). *Criminal procedure: Constitution and society* (6th ed.). Upper Saddle River, NJ: Pearson Prentice Hall.

A

Activity-based budget a budget that defines and analyzes all the activities consuming an organization's financial resources. (118)

Actual cause all antecedents leading to a given result. (360)

Administrative law public law promulgated by administrative agencies at the federal, state, and local levels. (350)

Affirmative action the means by which employers ensure that applicants and persons seeking advancement in their respective agencies or companies are not discriminated against or denied employment or promotion based on race, creed, color, or national origin. (332)

Agency politics political machinations, ambitions, and personal agendas that shape interpersonal dynamics within a police agency. (319)

Alternative courses of action possible action plans for meeting identified needs or mitigating identified risks. (101)

Assessment the completion of an appraisal with respect to an object or an activity. (163)

Assessment center process a series of activities designed to measure an applicant's or officer's knowledge, skills, and abilities (KSAs) as well as personal attributes and behavioral characteristics related to work-specific scenarios. (200)

Audit an evaluation of a process, system, or project. (129)

August Vollmer chief of police in Berkeley, California, from 1902 to 1932; considered a founder of modern policing. (10)

Authority a legitimate right bestowed by an organization on an individual to direct activities or persons. (277)

B

Background investigation (BI) a step in the pre-employment screening process in which a police agency verifies a candidate's qualifications including criminal and credit histories, educational and employment histories, and claims about matters such as moral character, work habits, and stress tolerance. (198)

Balanced scorecard a performance-management framework based on the assumption that to improve performance, organizations must execute the strategy they have defined for generating desired results. (169)

Balanced-based budget a budget based on an estimate of future revenues. (118)

Barriers to effective communication mind-sets or cultural orientations that stand between a communication receiver and giver, preventing one from understanding the other. (215)

Basic preservice training academy-based training that introduces recruits to police work, provides an overview of the justice system, and includes classes on specific skills and knowledge areas related to police work. (245)

Behavior theory theory that identifies the behaviors distinguishing leaders who achieve desired results. (266)

Behavioral standards (standards of conduct) standards of conduct as defined by the police agency. The standards are particularly valuable and advantageous to the agency's culture and structure. (145)

Bias-based policing intentional or nonintentional practices that incorporate prejudicial judgments based on gender, race, ethnicity, and other differences that are inappropriately applied. (65)

Binding arbitration a negotiation process through which the involved parties agree to adhere to an arbitrator's decision and award. (345)

Block grant general-purpose award designed to help meet unfunded services or objectives. Not as expenditure restrictive as closed-end or categorical grants. (124)

Brand image an instinctive response from individuals toward an agency or a service. (193)

Breach of contract failure of any party to a contract to comply with the terms and conditions spelled out in the contract. (350)

Budget categories categories in a budget representing types of expenses. (121)

Budget a plan expressed in financial terms. (110)

C

Capital budget a budget that shows projects and expenses designed to yield benefits well into the future. (119)

Career plan a document describing a police officer's personal career vision; a timetable for action; and detailed descriptions of any training, education, and career steps necessary to complete the plan. (252)

Categorical grant spending is not as restrictive as for closed-end grant. Expenditures are allowed within a category of programs or services. (124)

Chain of command the notion that authority and decision making should flow down from higher to lower levels in a police agency. Official discussions typically flow up or down through the chain of command. (136)

Citizen review board   an independent group comprising local citizens appointed by the mayor or other politicians that investigates complaints, decides whether a complaint is justified based on the evidence at hand, and offers recommendations. (310)

Civil work environment   a workplace characterized by positive interactions, optimism, and the dismissal of cynicism and pessimistic beliefs. (205)

Closed-end grant   limits fund expenditures to narrowly defined products or services and typically includes highly detailed compliance requirements. (123)

Collective agreement   a labor contract that covers two or more employees who are union members. (343)

Collective bargaining   a series of steps through which certified unions and employers arrive at collective agreements. (343)

Communication   a process involving the exchange of information between a sender and a receiver. (211)

Community mapping   process of visually displaying specific locations, addresses, or areas of noted concern. (99)

Community policing   an alternative strategy to traditional policing that emphasizes close interaction between police and the neighborhoods they serve. (32)

Competency-based compensation   payment for competencies acquired and exhibited by members of the organization. (204)

Competitive bid   a vendor's best estimate of what a specific item, service, or combination of both will cost an organization seeking to purchase, lease, or outsource the item, service, or combination of both. (375)

CompStat   a policing approach involving the generation of as much real-time data as possible about crimes and the frequent evaluation of the data to develop strategies to reduce crime as quickly and effectively as possible. (96)

Confidential information   anything written or spoken that is intended only for the eyes and/or ears of the receiver. (354)

Constructive engagement   a coaching and mentoring rapport that encourages a genuinely warm relationship between individuals. (411)

Contingency plan   a plan activated during serious emergencies, critical events, or disasters that affect the agency and demand immediate and/or prolonged response. (92)

Contingency theory   theory that attempts to match leaders to specific types of situations. (268)

Continuous evaluation   the process by which an organization, on an ongoing basis, measures actual performance outcomes against intended outcomes to identify and close gaps. (164)

Continuous improvement   a process through which an organization repeatedly assesses the effectiveness of the policies and procedures it has established for achieving key objectives. (163)

Contract   legally binding, voluntary promise between two or more people. (349)

Cost–benefit analysis   an analysis through which an organization compares the cost of a program or initiative to the benefit it provides (or may provide) to the organization and/or its constituents. (126)

Counterterrorism   procedures adopted by the military, police, and governments to assist in preventing, reacting to, and investigating acts or suspected acts of terrorism. (NSW, 2007) (399)

Crime analysis   analytical process used to define current and predict future quality-of-life concerns, crime patterns, or trends. (99)

Crime Prevention Through Environmental Design (CPTED)   the process of deciding how to construct or modify the physical environment to deter or discourage criminal activity. (94)

Cross-cultural communication   a process that occurs anytime a person of one culture sends a message to, or receives a message from, a person of another culture. (227)

Cross-gender communication   a process that occurs anytime a person of one gender sends a message to, or receives a message from, a person of another gender. (228)

Cybercrime   criminal misconduct perpetrated through information technology. (424)

D

Deployment of human resources   the process of placing the right person in the right job or on the right tasks or projects, according to a candidate's strengths, weaknesses, knowledge, skills, and abilities (KSAs)—as well as interests. (256)

Direct compensation   compensation that includes base pay (hourly wages or salaried) plus overtime pay for hourly employees. (203)

Direct liability   liability that is embodied in the person who commits the act in question. (358)

Directed change   a carefully planned, strategic process designed to improve every area of a police agency. (148)

Discipline   actions taken to correct problematic behavior. (313)

Diversity   differences among people with respect to wealth, age, gender, culture, lifestyle, race, ethnicity, and sexual orientation. (193)

E

Early warning system   a set of practices enabling a police agency to identify and address problematic behaviors before they can reach disastrous levels. (313)

Education   the learning of concepts and development of problem-solving and critical thinking skills through a school, college, or university experience. (243)

Effectiveness   the degree to which objectives are achieved and the extent to which targeted problems are resolved. (166)

Efficiency   a comparison of what is actually produced or performed with what can be achieved with the same consumption of resources (money, time, and labor). Efficiency is an important factor in determination of productivity. (166)

Entitlement-oriented compensation   automatic pay increases for employees, along with increases in benefits. (203)

ERG theory   Clay Alderfer's framework proposing that human beings need elements for physical survival, relatedness, and personal growth. (281)

Ethical leadership   ethical behavior on display. (16)

Ethics   the philosophical study of conduct that adheres to certain principles of morality. (12)

Evaluation   an examination or deliberation to decide the quality, value, criticalness, scope, or necessity of a service or activity; a summary of an assessment's findings and assignment of a value to the performance assessed. (163)

Expectancy theory   Victor Vroom's framework holding that people will be motivated to deliver their best on the job if they believe that a specific level of performance will lead to an outcome that they value highly. (282)

F

Facilitation   a communication skill through which police personnel develop solutions to problems. (235)

Facilities manager   an individual whose basic role is to ensure that all police property is maintained according to state and city building codes and safety standards, including those put forth by the Occupational Safety and Health Administration (OSHA). (381)

Feedback   a special kind of communication through which a sender gives specific information (a response) to a receiver. (237)

Field training officer (FTO)   a knowledgeable, seasoned, and competent officer trained in adult education and evaluation procedures, who supervises recruits' on-the-job (field) training. (248)

Field training program   training that focuses on the knowledge, skills, and abilities (KSAs) required of a police officer on the job. (248)

Financial audit   an examination of randomly selected accounting transactions in an organization with the goal of checking for accuracy, completeness, and timeliness. (130)

Fraud examination   an examination of each accounting transaction in an organization in search of any discrepancy. (130)

Futuristics   an area of study that uses past and present performance, expert opinion, and statistics to describe changes that may occur in the near and distant future. (396)

G

General orders   a police agency's documented policies and procedures. (298)

Goals   long-range achievements desired by an organization. (91)

Good faith   bargaining behaviors required by the Employee Relations Act of 2000. (344)

Grievance   an employee claim that a policy or contract provision has been misapplied, interpreted incorrectly, or violated, thereby causing injury, loss, or inconvenience to the employee. (347)

H

Hierarchy of needs model   Abraham Maslow's framework proposing five needs that human beings attempt to meet in a specific sequence. (280)

Homeland security   public and private policies, procedures, tactics, strategies, equipment, facilities, and personnel designed or utilized to defend the homeland against domestic- or foreign-initiated threats or hazards (for example, terrorism, natural or human-caused disasters, and pandemics). (76)

I

Immoral political power   manipulation of others for personal gain. (320)

In-service continuous professional training (CPT)   training designed to enable police practitioners to maintain and periodically update their skills. (249)

Incremental change   a police agency's gradual adoption of new ways of operating designed to improve community service over time. (148)

Indirect compensation   compensation that includes items such as medical and life insurance, paid time off, pensions, flexible schedules, education incentives, and a take-home police vehicle. (203)

Intelligence-led policing   a strategy that integrates problem-oriented policing and zero-tolerance policing through continuous analysis of information about problems and development of action plans to resolve problems. (43)

Interaction–expectation theory   theory proposing that leadership is the act of initiating a structure that group members support. (267)

Interagency politics   political dynamics taking place in the interactions between a police agency and other public safety organizations in the same jurisdiction. (59)

Intergovernment politics   political dynamics taking place in interactions between a police agency and other governmental agencies serving or affecting the same jurisdiction. (61)

Intra-agency politics   political dynamics taking place within a police organization. (58)

K

Knowledge management   the retention of knowledge most important to an organization. (410)

L

Law Enforcement Code of Ethics and Law Enforcement Code of Conduct   codes developed by the International Association of Chiefs of Police (IACP) in its early years. (13)

Leader–follower exchange theory   theory that examines the nature and quality of the relationships between leaders and followers. (269)

Leadership   the art and science of ethically using communication, activities, and behaviors to influence, motivate (not manipulate), or mobilize others to action. (16)

Leadership skill   an ability that can be measured objectively. (271)

Learned needs theory   David McClelland's framework suggesting that human beings have three key needs: affiliation, achievement, and power. (282)

Lease   a procurement arrangement that enables an individual or organization to obtain or secure the use of items or property in exchange for payments made at agreed-upon intervals. (370)

Level 5 leadership   Jim Collins's concept proposing that leaders channel their ambition toward building a better organization rather than promoting themselves and their personal agendas. (289)

Line-item budget   a budget in which each item is described and assigned a place (line), with a corresponding dollar value. (116)

M

Maintenance of effort   the annual cost necessary to maintain a police agency's existing level of service for the fiscal operating year. (129)

Managerial grid   Robert Blake and Jane Mouton's model identifying five leadership styles that vary in concern for people and concern for productivity. (284)

Meta-leadership   overarching leadership framework designed to link organizational units or organizations; attempts to transcend usual organizational confines. (268)

Mission   a short-range task or assignment an organization wishes to achieve. (90)

Moral political power   attempts to influence and motivate others with an eye toward achieving organizational goals rather than satisfying one's own interests. (320)

Morale   the state of the spirits of a person or group as exhibited by confidence, cheerfulness, discipline, and willingness to perform assigned tasks. (306)

Motivation–hygiene theory   theory proposing which factors increase satisfaction and dissatisfaction among employees in an organization. (267)

N

National Incident Management System (NIMS)   a nationwide program by which public safety agencies develop policies and processes for collectively preventing and managing emergencies. (77)

Needs assessment   the process an organization uses to determine whether a need (or problem) exists that could be addressed by a particular course of action. (98)

Negligence   failure to exercise the degree of care that an ordinary, reasonable, and prudent person would demonstrate under the same circumstances. (358)

Negotiable management rights   areas wherein nothing in Title 5 precludes an agency or a labor organization from negotiating the numbers, types, and grades (ranks) of employees or positions assigned to any organizational subdivision, work project, or tour of duty; the technology, methods, and means of performing work; or the procedures an agency uses to exercise authority. (339)

Nondirected change   an informal process of altering the way tasks are accomplished, affecting only those individuals who will implement the change. (149)

Nonnegotiable management rights   what the management of a government agency may do without having to negotiate with a labor organization. (339)

Nonverbal communication   the use of voluntary and involuntary body movements and, in some cases, clothing, hairstyle, physical attractiveness, and speaking style, to communicate a message. (221)

O

O. W. Wilson   August Vollmer's protégé; introduced a merit system for promotions and other innovations influential in modern policing. (10)

Objectives   short-term accomplishments that lead to achievement of a particular goal. (91)

Operating budget   a short-term budget that accounts for the agency's current operating expenses as distinct from major financial transactions or permanent capital improvements. (119)

Operational plan   a plan delineating functional activities and agency change processes. Drives an entire agency or units within an agency. (92)

Organizational culture   shaped by the thoughts, speech, actions, values, and beliefs held by people in the organization. (141)

Organizational learning   a social process in which individuals interact with one another to exchange information that enables them to make well-informed decisions. (151)

Organizational structure   refers to the configuration of relationships within an organization. (136)

Outsourcing   a process by which a company or government entity contracts with another company or government entity to provide products or services that were formerly provided or performed by the original entity. (371)

P

Path–goal motivational leadership model   R. J. House's framework suggesting that followers will be motivated to give their best if they believe that they are capable of performing the tasks assigned, that their efforts will produce certain results, and that the rewards for completing tasks are worthwhile. (288)

Path–goal theory   theory suggesting that a leader's role is to enhance followers' performance by motivating them and by rewarding achievement of goals. (268)

Performance appraisal   assessment of an individual's job performance in an organization. (300)

Performance-based budget   a budget that links measurable activities to established strategic objectives. (116)

Personal–situational theory   theory proposing that a mix of personal characteristics interact with specific conditions in an individual's environment to produce leadership. (267)

Persuasion   the ability to influence outcomes, using methods other than the issuance of direct orders. (236)

Planning   a process, formulation, or design used to achieve an intended result. (87)

Police administration the process, art, and science of the management, supervision, and ethical leadership of a police agency. (3)

Police misconduct inappropriate behaviors (often including use of excessive force, theft, and other destructive behaviors) and conduct prohibited by a police agency. (69)

Police–community partnerships collaborations between officers and community citizens to address citizens' concerns. (260)

Policies the basic principles directing and limiting a police agency's actions in pursuit of long-term goals. (298)

Policing strategy an approach to delivering police services based on specific assumptions about matters such as how police and community residents should interact, what causes crime to worsen, and how technology might be leveraged. (29)

Political correctness often used to refer to the avoidance of saying or doing something that risks offending a particular individual's or group's sensibilities. (62)

Power the ability of an individual to influence others; shape an organization's direction and priorities; and influence situations, affairs, and objects. (277)

Pre-employment screening process a sequence of steps designed to help a police agency compare job applicants and select the most promising candidates. Elements of the process include an employment application/questionnaire, aptitude test, physical abilities test, and other assessments. (196)

Principles of policing principles regarding the mission and acceptable behavior of police, attributed to Sir Robert Peel. (6)

Problem-oriented policing the tactical implementation of community policing. (36)

Procedures the sequence of activities or courses of action that must be followed in a police agency to correctly perform tasks. (298)

Profession an occupation or discipline that requires its members to adhere to prescribed standards of behavior and competence and that has characteristics including common goals and principles, a common language, a system for licensing or credentialing members, and an association that promotes the profession's standards and interest. (17)

Program budget a budget that presents programs and services separately in categories. (116)

Project management the process of planning and guiding an initiative from inception to completion. (129)

Proximate (legal) cause that to which liability attaches; results from an action or inaction that directly leads to damage to property, or to the injury or death of another person. (360)

Psychodynamic approach an approach suggesting that leaders are more effective if they have insight into the psychological makeup of themselves and their followers. (270)

Purchasing an organization's procurement of goods and services in the correct amounts, from the most appropriate source, for the best possible price. (368)

Q

Quality assurance ensuring that service actions comply with agency directives and that they support the agency's mission. (172)

Quality control verifying that an activity is completed correctly (efficiently and effectively) the first time. (171)

R

Radical change new ways of operation stemming from a specific innovation that transforms the way a police agency delivers customer service. (147)

Radicalization the process by which individuals align their ideology with that of a group and commit themselves to achieving the group's goals through violence. (399)

Repeat-use plan a plan that may be replicated for similar events or tactical situations. (92)

Return on investment (ROI) the benefits that result from an activity. (127)

Rewards-based compensation also known as merit pay; compensation that enhances the earnings of top performers and places value on people rather than job categories. (203)

Risk assessment the process an organization uses to determine whether a known or foreseeable threat exists, how likely it is that the threat will materialize, and how severe the consequences would be if it did materialize. (99)

Role model a person who exhibits values, attitudes, and behaviors considered desirable in a particular organization. (276)

S

Self-contained ethical leadership agent an individual with the knowledge, skills, and abilities to motivate others to deliver their best performance and who can garner their trust, respect, and admiration. (4)

Self-management the process of monitoring and controlling one's emotions and remaining flexible and balanced in the face of disappointment or frustration. (105)

Servant leadership Robert K. Greenleaf's approach to leadership emphasizing sensitivity, awareness, and empathy toward followers. (289)

Service contract an agreement by which a seller agrees to provide repair or maintenance services for the specified purchased equipment for a certain time period. (376)

Sexual harassment touching, intimidation, lewd remarks, and other conduct or communication of a sexual nature that is offensive to a prudent and reasonable person. (359)

Single-use plan a plan for a one-time event or special circumstance. (92)

Sir Robert Peel the nineteenth-century British home secretary influential in passing the Metropolitan Police Act, which established the world's first recognizable local police department. (5)

Site survey assessment of existing facilities to determine whether they need any equipment or materials upgrades, such as improved computer systems or a new roof or siding. (385)

Situational leadership model   Paul Hersey and Ken Blanchard's model suggesting four leadership styles   delegating, supportive, selling, and telling. (285)

Situational theory   theory proposing that different situations demand different styles of leadership. (268)

Span of control   the idea that each manager in a police agency should supervise only a reasonable number of individuals or units. (136)

Special populations   populations that include people with hearing or visual impairments, developmental disabilities, mental illnesses or substance-abuse problems, and those who present an immediate danger to themselves or others. (228)

Standardized Emergency Management System (SEMS)   a set of guidelines that aims to ensure that state-level agencies' emergency management system comply with NIMS guidelines. (79)

Strategic plans   long-term courses of action intended to apply to the entire police organization. (93)

Strategic policing   an approach that seeks to integrate proven private- and public-sector management techniques with public policing strategy. (45)

Stress management   a blend of prevention, training, and intervention programs that a police agency puts in place to mitigate dangerous levels of stress among officers. (315)

Strict liability   liability for damages, injury, or loss regardless of the person's culpability (blame or fault). (358)

Succession management   preparation of individuals in a police agency who are interested in leadership for higher-level management and supervisory positions as well as specialized assignments. (302)

Succession planning   activities intended to ensure that adequate qualified personnel are available to replace those who vacate positions through promotion, transfer, retirement, termination, or agency expansion; the identification of high-potential employees in a police agency and the provision of training, coaching, and developmental opportunities needed to enable them to move into influential or specialized positions. (256 & 302)

T

Tactical plan   a plan for special events, unique or extraordinary circumstances, or intra-agency or interagency operational needs. (92)

Task force   a temporary working group assembled to address a specific problem or manage a particular event requiring specialized expertise. (260)

Team   a group of people who receive specialized training and use that training to address a specific incident. (259)

Team policing and neighborhood policing   examples of how community policing may be implemented to address problems on a small scale. (39)

Theory X   Douglas McGregor's model describing command-and-control management style in an organization. (283)

Theory Y   Douglas McGregor's description of a motivational management style in organizations. (283)

Theory Z   William Ouchi's adaptation of Theory Y emphasizing a leadership style that advocates trusting followers and enabling them to feel they are part of the organization. (284)

Tort   a private wrong committed against a person or a person's property. (352)

Total quality leadership   the commitment and behavior needed to carry out and integrate TQM practices throughout a police agency. (173)

Total quality management (TQM)   a performance-management framework that can help a police agency take a disciplined approach to quality control and assurance. (171)

Toxic management   a situation in which a manager exhibits poor judgment and negative behaviors, has no skill at building rapport and positive relationships, and cannot cultivate an environment of mutual respect. (291)

Traditional budget   a budget that reflects a simple percentage increase in funding over the most recent budget. (115)

Traditional policing   an authoritarian, paramilitary strategy developed to mitigate corruption in the police service. (29)

Training   knowledge and skill development and on-the-job preparation. (243)

Trait theory   theory that seeks to identify the individual traits distinguishing leaders from followers. (266)

Transactional theory   process in which the leader and follower make simple exchanges or transactions (e.g., money for work completed). (269)

Transformational theory   theory that proposes a process through which leaders engage others and create a connection that enhances motivation and morality in themselves as well as followers. (269)

U

Unfair labor practices   actions taken by unions or employers that violate the U.S. National Labor Relations Act (NLRA). (337)

Unity of command   the concept that each individual working in the agency should report to only one supervisor and that each unit or situation should be under the control of a single individual. (136)

V

Value-added contribution (VAC)   additional value (beyond basic requirements) that an activity contributes to a program or service. (127)

Values   fundamental beliefs, principles, or standards that an individual or members of an organization regard as desirable or worthwhile. (89)

Variable compensation   compensation that is tied to personal, team, or organizational performance and that may include bonuses and incentives for special assignments as well as shift differential. (203)

Vicarious (indirect) liability   legal responsibility for the actions or damages that have resulted from someone else's negligence. (358)

Virtual reality   a computer simulation of a real or imaginary system that enables a user to perform operations on the simulated system and shows the effects in real time. (414)

Vision   the image an organization or individual has in mind for a desired future state. (90)

Volunteerism   the process by which community members donate their time and effort to a police agency's operations. (138)

Vroom–Jago Time–Drive Leadership Model   Victor Vroom's model postulating that time constraints drive a leader's decision-making process. (286)

W

Warranty   a promise by the manufacturer that it will repair any defects or replace the product if a major malfunction occurs. (377)

Z

Zero-based budget   a budget in which all available revenue is allocated to expense categories. (117)

Zero-tolerance policing   a strategy based on the assumption that full enforcement of the laws will ultimately decrease crime and disorder. (40)

Chapter 1

Page 2: © Spencer Grant/PhotoEdit; **5:** © Hulton Archive/Getty Images; **8:** © Bettmann/Corbis; **9:** (top) © Popperfoto/Getty Images, (bottom) © Bettmann/Corbis; **10:** © Bettmann/Corbis; **13:** © Stockbyte/Getty Images; **17:** © Ann Johansson/Corbis; **18:** © Susan Watts/NY Daily News Archive via Getty Images; **20:** © Stan Honda/AFP/Getty Images; **23:** © Chris Hondros/Getty Images.

Chapter 2

Page 28: © Spencer Grant/Alamy; **30:** © North Wind Picture Archives/Alamy; **31:** © Brand X Pictures; **33:** © Peter Casolino/Alamy; **38:** © Brand X Pictures; **39:** © S. Meltzer/PhotoLink/Getty Images; **41:** © The McGraw-Hill Companies, Inc./John Flournoy, photographer; **42:** © Robert Maass/Corbis; **43:** © Joel Gordon; **45:** © Jim West/Alamy; **46:** © David McNew/Getty Images.

Chapter 3

Page 51: © Glow Images/Getty Images; **56:** © Scott Olson/Getty Images; **59:** © The McGraw-Hill Companies, Inc./Rick Brady, photographer; **60:** © Jeff Greenberg/PhotoEdit; **61:** © David R. Frazier Photolibrary, Inc.; **64:** © Lars A. Niki; **66:** © Gilles Mingasson/Getty Images; **67:** © epa/Corbis; **69:** © Mikael Karlsson/Arresting Images; **73:** © Thinkstock/PunchStock; **76:** © David Allocca/Timepix/Time Life Pictures/Getty Images.

Chapter 4

Page 86: © Jeff Zelevansky/Getty Images; **88:** © Douglas Graham/Roll Call/Getty Images; **89:** © Lorenzo Ciniglio/Sygma/Corbis; **93:** © Mikael Karlsson; **95:** © imagebroker/Alamy; **97:** © Robert Nickelsberg/Getty Images; **98:** © Mike Powell/Stone/Getty Images; **100:** © Scott J. Ferrell/Congressional Quarterly/Getty Images; **101:** © Spencer Platt/Getty Images; **103:** © Skip Nall/Getty Images; **105:** © Ryan McVay/Getty Images.

Chapter 5

Page 109: © Nick Scalera/Express-Times/Landov; **111:** © Reed Kaestner/Corbis; **112:** © Michal Czerwonka/Getty Images; **113:** © Michael Newman/PhotoEdit; **115:** © Mario Tama/Getty Images; **117:** © Gene Blevins/LA DailyNews/Corbis; **119:** © Peter Cavanagh/Alamy; **120:** © Ricky Carioti/Washington Post/Getty Images; **123:** © Dennis MacDonald/Alamy; **124:** © Mikael Karlsson/Arresting Images; **126:** © Stephen Chernin/Getty Images.

Chapter 6

Page 134: © Jeff Greenberg/Alamy; **137:** © Chip Somodevilla/Getty Images; **139:** AP Photo/Prescott Courier, Jo. L. Keener; **140:** © Bill Clark/Roll Call/Getty Images; **142:** © Tom Williams/Roll Call/Getty Images; **143:** © Timothy A. Clary/AFP/Getty Images; **144:** AP Photo/Mary Altaffer; **145:** AP Photo/John Bazemore;

Chapter 12

Page 296: © Spencer Grant/Alamy; **299:** © David McNew/Getty Images; **303:** AP Photo/Al Goldis; **304:** © Spencer Grant/Alamy; **305:** © Bob Daemmrich/The Image Works; **307:** AP Photo/The Plain Dealer, Roadell Hickman; **308:** AP Photo/The Guymon Daily Herald, Shawn Yorks; **310:** © John Moore/Getty Images; **312:** © Mikael Karlsson/Alamy; **314:** © Irwin Thompson/Dallas Morning News/Corbis; **317:** © Michael Newman/PhotoEdit; **318:** © Marvin Joseph/The Washington Post/ Getty Images; **319:** AP Photo/Reed Saxon.

Chapter 13

Page 326: © Ron Chapple/Taxi/Getty Images; **329:** © Fotosearch/Stringer/Getty Images; **331:** © liquidlibrary/PictureQuest; **333:** © Darrin Klimek/Getty Images; **335:** © Lebrecht Music and Arts Photo Library/Alamy; **336:** © Bettmann/Corbis; **340:** AP Photo; **343:** © Keith Brofsky/Getty Images; **345:** © Tom Carter/Alamy; **348:** © Polka Dot Images/Jupiterimages; **349:** © Stockbyte/Getty Images; **351:** © George Frey/Bloomberg via Getty Images; **352:** © The McGraw-Hill Companies, Inc./Gary He, photographer; **353:** © Photodisc/PunchStock; **356:** © Benjamin Lowy/Corbis; **357:** © Brand X Pictures; **360:** © Steve Allen/Getty Images.

Chapter 14

Page 366: © Owaki/Kulla/Corbis; **369:** © Chris Maddaloni/Roll Call/Getty Images; **371:** © Gabriel Bouys/AFP/Getty Images; **373:** © Syracuse Newspaper/John Berry/ The Image Works; **374:** © The Washington Post/Getty Images; **376:** © Spencer Grant/PhotoEdit; **378:** © Mandel Ngan/AFP/Getty Images; **380:** © Alfredo Sosa/ The Christian Science Monitor via Getty Images; **381:** © Richard A. Lipski/The Washington Post/Getty Images; **384:** © Tracy A. Woodward/The Washington Post/Getty Images; **385:** © Shepard Sherbell/Corbis Saba; **386:** © Kayte Deioma/ PhotoEdit.

Chapter 15

Page 394: © Spencer Grant/PhotoEdit; **398:** © Brian Bates/Getty Images; **400:** © Shannon Stapleton/Reuters/Corbis; **401:** © Al Rai Al Aam/Feature Story News/ Getty Images; **405:** © David Butow/Corbis Saba; **407:** © Michael Newman/ PhotoEdit; **409:** © Mark Wilson/Getty Images; **420:** © Ted Soqui/Corbis; **422:** © Erik S. Lesser/epa/Corbis; **423:** © Robyn Beck/AFP/Getty Images; **424:** © Orion Pictures Corporation/Photofest; **425:** © Bob Daemmrich/PhotoEdit.